INTRODUCTION
TO THE
OLD TESTAMENT

Originally published in French under the title INTRODUCTION A LA BIBLE, Vol. I : *Ancien Testament* (Desclée & Co., Tournai, Belgium), the present English edition is based on the latest French edition.   Moreover, the bibliography has been updated and adapted for the English-speaking reader.

Nihil obstat — Donald A. Panella, M.A., S.T.L., S.S.L., Censor Deputatus

Imprimatur — Terence J. Cooke, D.D., Archbishop of New York
         New York, New York — June 25, 1968

The nihil obstat and imprimatur are official declarations that a book or pamphlet is free of doctrinal or moral error.   No implication is contained therein that those who have granted the nihil obstat and imprimatur agree with the contents, opinions or statements expressed.

Library of Congress Catalog Card Number : 68-25351

Printed in Belgium

A. Robert — A. Feuillet

INTRODUCTION TO THE OLD TESTAMENT

translated from the second French edition by

Msgr. Patrick W. Skehan — Fidelis Buck, S.J.
Lasalle P. Caron — Juniper Cummings, O.F.M.Conv.
Bro. Aloysius FitzGerald — Robert L. MacFayden
Roland E. Murphy, O.CARM. — Peter Nickels, O.F.M.Conv.
Patrick Stevens — Marcian Strange, O.S.B.

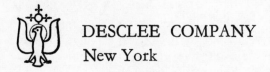

DESCLEE COMPANY
New York

CONTRIBUTORS

Paul AUVRAY, *Cong. Or.*

André BARUCQ, *S.D.B., Professor at the Catholic Faculties of Lyon.*

Eugène CAVAIGNAC, *Professor at the Catholic Institute of Paris.*

Henri CAZELLES, *P.S.S., Professor at the Catholic Institute of Paris.*

Jean DELORME, *Professor at the Major Seminary of Annecy.*

André GELIN (†), *P.S.S., Late Professor at the Catholic Faculties of Lyon.*

Pierre GRELOT, *Professor at the Catholic Institute of Paris.*

André LEFÈVRE, *S.J., Professor at the Jesuit Scholasticate of Chantilly.*

Msgr. Henri LUSSEAU, *Dean of the Faculty of Theology at Angers.*

FOREWORD
TO THE SECOND FRENCH EDITION

There are several ways of speaking about the Bible and aiding our contemporaries to grasp the meaning of God's word.

Let no one mistake the purpose and character of the present work. It is not a manual in the classic sense, of which certain passages are to be memorized, and which offers precise and definite answers to every question. It is rather what many, especially professors, requested of the late A. Robert : a general presentation of the currents of contemporary exegesis written in the spirit of Catholic doctrine.

This is a critical Introduction according to the guidelines of Pope Pius XII, which treats those " many things which call for a fresh investigation, and which stimulate not a little the practical zest of the present-day interpreter " (enc. *Divino Afflante Spiritu*, EB 555). It is precisely these questions that our contemporaries are insisting on more and more.

The authors did not intend to write a textbook for use in schools of theology, but rather a book to complement the teaching of such schools, a book that introduces to a scientific study of the Bible those who already have a solid theological and cultural foundation. The authors wished to offer, first to professors, but also to the clergy and educated laity, a presentation of current research and possible solutions. Thus the professor will be helped to put his own teaching on a more informed and solid scientific basis. His students can acquire a more precise understanding of the Scriptures in the light of the Church's teaching through acquaintance with modern critical discussions.

The authors have striven to offer, more in a literary than scholarly manner, reasonable solutions which are based on the facts, but which naturally include, to a greater or less degree, hypotheses and doubtful matters. They have deliberately left to professors the choice of the best pedagogical method and the best manual for initiating students to the Bible message. A Catholic commentary will of course be of help in putting them in direct contact with the sacred text.

The editors express deep gratitude to all who have worked on this project, and to those who by their personal advice have made it possible to complete this second edition, in particular to His Eminence August Cardinal Bea and the Very Reverend A. Miller, as well as many professors of the Pontifical Biblical Institute and other Roman Pontifical Faculties.

PREFACE

It is commonplace to speak of the progress of the biblical sciences; everyone who has been in contact with Bible studies the last fifty years can testify to the fact. This progress has been conditioned by scrupulously studied textual and archeological discoveries, which have furnished researchers with sometimes unexpected and unhoped for facts. Precise studies concerning the holy books have appeared—studies which are truly scientific and for the most part free of the systematically rationalistic and aprioristic tendencies which marred the products of earlier exegetical schools. Need it be added that, for its own good, this progress was occasionally slowed down when it risked losing its way? But at the same time it was always guided and sustained by the decisions of ecclesiastical authority especially since Leo XIII to Pius XII, whose encyclical *Divino Afflante Spiritu* laid down for this moderating and directing action its right role, and happily synthesized its import in the face of a new and broader scientific horizon.

This development of biblical studies has had its repercussions in the body of the faithful, especially among the more educated, whose desire to return to sources has led them more and more to read and meditate the Bible. To help these readers, various popular works have appeared. Numerous too have been the editions of the sacred text. One of the most recent, the Jerusalem Bible, is a credit to our Catholic exegetes.

Something else, however, was needed : a book which would provide the clergy and the intellectually prepared laity an introduction to the scientific study of the Bible, that would give them a completely orthodox and loyal orientation, using the latest publications, and taking into account the most recent discoveries, those of Qumran, for instance. What was needed was a sound synthesis of this vastly diffused research, even if one or the other of its conclusions should not be the last word, or if one or the other detail should need further refinement. What was especially needed was a book that would point out the theological content of the sacred books, their contribution to the divine work of revelation; a book which would help to discover in every part of them or even in every fragment, their eternal religious value, through the inevitable contingencies of writings which are human but at the same time divine, written at times and in places so different from our own. This is what our generation is looking for.

We have had Bible manuals for more than fifty years now; it would be useless to contest their value and usefulness. It has been over twenty-five years since the appearance of *Initiation Biblique;* it was later reedited. But must these works not be carried forward, developed, and adapted to more recent research? The present state of the science must be presented and directions indicated; otherwise Catholic biblical science will risk atrophy and a halt in its development. Then will our generation, which seeks exactitude and serious confrontation as well as fidelity to the tradition of the Church, be attracted to biblical studies? If we refuse, it means sending the best minds to similar non-Catholic works which are never without danger for those not prepared for them.

It is this need that the authors of this *Introduction* have proposed to fill. The authors have put their competence, which is vouched for by specialists in their fields whose doctrinal integrity cannot be doubted, their experience and application into the composition of this book. They offer it to those who desire to make a serious study of the written word of God. They offer it especially to priests and informed students of theological faculties and seminaries. We want to thank them sincerely.

This book may astonish, at first sight, readers unaccustomed to using the standard introductions to Sacred Scripture which exist in different languages, but to using types of " compendia, " which summarize, more or less well, the results of biblical studies, and place them in easy terms to be assimilated by any and everybody. Perhaps also some readers who have not followed the development of biblical research will be surprised to see to what lengths the authors go to distinguish in the inspired books the documents used, to analyze the doctrinal currents of different parts of the Old and even the New Testament. A patient and attentive reading will show that there is in this nothing contrary to our faith. Did not God, before He spoke to men through His Son, speak " at various times and in various different ways " through the Prophets (in the biblical sense of that word), and did not some of the authors of the New Testament indicate their sources?

We are obviously not dealing with a book that professors can put into the hands of their students and tell them " *Tolle et lege.* " They cannot give them a résumé of it which they can demand to see reproduced in reviews and exams. But that is precisely the point : whether that is what a critical exposition of the solutions provided by contemporary exegetical science ought to be. It ought rather to aid them after they have acquired the knowledge required of all priests. It will also facilitate the work of the teacher : he can find here the doctrine that he can bring down to the level of his students, and he can send his students to it, especially the more gifted ones, after having instructed them in the fundamentals of a science which must have about it nothing of the over-simple or primary in the bad sense of those words, but which must take into account the complexity of the problems and the nuances that present research demands,—otherwise it is irrelevant.

Each author endeavored to stress that which seemed personally to him most apt to lead to the word of God, without writing a commentary. Each one wanted to leave room for the initiative and originality of the professor. Neither a book nor a professor can say everything. In some matters the teacher refers to the book, in another he summarizes it, in others he supplies for it. The book gives the facts, the lines of research, the state of the question; the professor contributes his living contact with the Scriptures. Book and professor do not contradict nor exclude each other, but they help each other mutually in the " *traditio Sacrae Scripturae* " which should constitute a course of exegesis. That is certainly the hope of the authors, and I dare to believe, basing myself on my past experience, the intention of those whom the Church has called to the honor and the responsibility of being instructors of the clergy in the science of the written word of God contained in the Scriptures.

✝ Jean Julien Weber
Bishop of Strasbourg

TABLE OF CONTENTS

Section II.   The Other Hagiographers
by Msgr. H. Lusseau, Dean of the Faculty of Theology at Angers

NOTICE

This English translation of *Introduction à la Bible*, I : *Ancien Testament* does not include the General Introduction which in the French edition appeared before the study of the Old Testament proper. Since this introduction applies to both Testaments, it was thought more advisable to publish it in a separate volume.

The maps, particularly useful for the study of the history of the Ancient Near East (pp. 7-64) have been gathered, for ease in consulting, in a separate fascicule which will be found in the back of the book.

The bibliographies are admittedly incomplete. Consultation by the reader of the works listed there will make it possible to complete them. At the beginning of each part and each section the principal works dealing with the matter are given. The bibliography at the head of each chapter merely completes those lists. Important monographs on particular points are included in the footnotes.

The asterisk * indicates the *Imprimatur* or the Catholic character of the book, periodical, etc. submitted to ecclesiastical censorship. The raised figure indicates the edition.

LIST OF ABBREVIATIONS

1) Books of the Bible :

Abd	Abdias	Lam	Lamentations
Acts	Acts of the Apostles	Lk	Gospel of St. Luke
Ag	Aggeus	Lv	Leviticus
Am	Amos		
Ap	Apocalypse	Mal	Malachias
		1 Mc	1st Book of Machabees
Bar	Baruch	2 Mc	2nd Book of Machabees
		Mi	Micheas
Col	Epistle to the Colossians	Mk	Gospel of St. Mark
1 Cor	1st Epistle to the Corinthians	Mt	Gospel of St. Matthew
2 Cor	2nd Epistle to the Corinthians		
Ct	Canticle of Canticles	Na	Nahum
		Neh	Nehemias
Dn	Daniel	Nm	Numbers
Dt	Deuteronomy		
		Os	Osee
Eccl	Ecclesiastes		
Eph	Epistle to the Ephesians	1 Par	1st Book of Paralipomenon
Esd	Esdras	2 Par	2nd Book of Paralipomenon
Est	Esther	Phil	Epistle to the Philippians
Ex	Exodus	Phlm	Epistle to Philemon
Ez	Ezechiel	Prv	Proverbs
		Ps	Psalms
Gal	Epistle to the Galatians	1 Pt	1st Epistle of St. Peter
Gn	Genesis	2 Pt	2nd Epistle of St. Peter
Hb	Habacuc	Rom	Epistle to the Romans
Heb	Epistle to the Hebrews	Ru	Ruth
Is	Isaias	Sir	Ecclesiasticus
		1 Sm	1st Book of Samuel
Jas	Epistle of James	2 Sm	2nd Book of Samuel
Jb	Job	So	Sophonias
Jdt	Judith		
Jer	Jeremias	Tb	Tobias
Jgs	Judges	1 Thes	1st Epistle to the Thessalonians
Jl	Joel		
Jn	Gospel of St. John	2 Thes	2nd Epistle to the Thessalonians
1 Jn	1st Epistle of St. John		
2 Jn	2nd Epistle of St. John	Ti	Epistle to Titus
Jon	Jonas	1 Tm	1st Epistle to Timothy
Jos	Josue	2 Tm	2nd Epistle to Timothy
Jude	Jude		
		Wis	Wisdom
3 Kgs	1st Book of Kings		
4 Kgs	2nd Book of Kings	Za	Zacharias

MT means Massoretic Text, LXX indicates the Greek translation of the Old Testament called the Septuagint.

2) Dictionaries, collections and reviews :

AAS *Acta Apostolicae Sedis* (Vatican City).

AASOR *Annual of American Schools of Oriental Research.*

ANEP The Ancient Near East in Pictures relating to the Old Testament (PRITCHARD) Princeton Univ., 1954).

ANET Ancien Near Eastern Texts relating to the Old Testament ² (PRITCHARD) (Princeton Univ., 1955).

AOAT Altorientalische Texte und Bilder zum Alten Testament², 2 Vols. (H. GRESSMANN) (Berlin-Leipzig, 1927).

APOT R. H. CHARLES, *Apocrypha and Pseudepigrapha of the Old Testament* (Oxford, 1913).

BA *Biblical Archaeologist* (Baltimore).

BASOR *Bulletin of the American School of Oriental Research* (New Haven).

Bi *Biblica** (Rome).

BiTod *The Bible Today* (Collegeville, Minn.)

BJRL *Bulletin of John Ryland's Library* (Manchester).

BO *Bibliotheca Orientalis* (Leyden).

BZ *Biblische Zeitschrift** (Freibourg im Breisgau).

CBQ *Catholic Biblical Quarterly** (Washington).

CSEL *Corpus Scriptorum Ecclesiasticorum Latinorum* (Vienna, 1866 ff.).

DAFC *Dictionnaire Apologétique de la Foi Catholique** (Paris, 1911-1922).

DBV *Dictionnaire de la Bible** (F. VIGOUROUX) (Paris, 1895-1912).

Denzinger or DB *Enchiridion symbolorum** (Freiburg im Breisgau : Herder).

DTC *Dictionnaire de Théologie Catholique** (Paris).

EB *Enchiridion Biblicum** (Rome, 1955).

ERE *Encyclopaedia of Religion and Ethics* (J. HASTINGS) (Edinburgh).

EsBi *Estudios Biblicos** (Madrid).

ETL *Ephemerides Theologicae Lovanienses** (Louvain).

HE *Histoire Ecclésiastique d'Eusèbe de Césarée.*

IB *Interpreter's Bible* (New York, 1952 ff.).

IDB *Interpreter's Dictionnary of the Bible* (New York, 1962).

JBL *Journal of Biblical Literature* (Philadelphia).

JBR *Journal of Bible and Religion.*

JNES *Journal of Near Eastern Studies* (Chicago).

JTS *Journal of Theological Studies* (London-Oxford).

NRT *Nouvelle Revue Théologique** (Louvain).

NT *Novum Testamentum* (Leyden).

NTS *New Testament Studies* (Cambridge).

OGIS *Orientis Graeci Inscriptiones Selectae* (DITTENBERGER) (Leipzig, 1903-1905).

OTMS *Old Testament and Modern Study*, ed. H. Rowley (Oxford, 1951).

PG *Patrologia Graeca* (J. B. MIGNE) (Paris).

PL *Patrologia Latina* (J. B. MIGNE) (Paris).

PO *Patrologia Orientalis* (R. GRAFFIN) (Paris).

RB *Revue Biblique** (Paris).

REJ *Revue des Études Juives* (Paris).

REP   *Real-Encyclopädie der klassischen Altertumswissenschaft* (PAULY-WISSOWA) (Stuttgart).

RGG   *Die Religion in Geschichte und Gegenwart*[2] (Tübingen, 1927-1932).

RHE   *Revue d'Histoire Ecclésiastique** (Louvain).

RHPR   *Revue d'Histoire et de Philosophie Religieuse* (Strasbourg).

RHR   *Revue de l'Histoire des Religions* (Paris).

RSPT   *Revue des Sciences Philosophiques et Théologiques** (Le Saulchoir).

RSR   *Recherches de Sciences Religieuses** (Paris).

RTP   *Revue de Théologie et de Philosophie* (Lausanne).

Scr   *Scripture** (Edinburgh).

SDB   *Supplément au Dictionnaire de la Bible** (L. PIROT, A. ROBERT, H. CAZELLES) (Paris, 1928 ff.).

STh   *Summa Theologica of Saint Thomas Aquinas.*

TD   *Theology Digest* (St. Marys, Kansas).

TLZ   *Theologische Literaturzeitung* (Berlin).

TS   *Theological Studies** (Woodstock, Md.).

TWNT   *Theologische Worterbuch zum Neuen Testament* (G. KITTEL) (Stuttgart).

TZ   *Theologische Zeitschrift* (Basel).

VC   *Verbum Caro* (Lausanne).

VD   *Verbum Domini** (Rome).

VT   *Vetus Testamentum* (Leyden).

ZAW   *Zeitschrift für die Alttestamentliche Wissenschaft* (Giessen-Berlin).

ZKT   *Zeitschrift für Katholische Theologie** (Innsbruck).

ZNW   *Zeitschrift für die Neutestamentliche Wissenschaft* (Giessen-Berlin).

ZTK   *Zeitschrift für Theologie und Kirche* (Tübingen).

For the abbreviations of the large commentaries, see p. 1f.

General Bibliography of the Old Testament

I.   Introductions to the Old Testament

A.   Catholic

A. MILLER—A. METZINGER, *Introductio specialis in Vetus Testamentum*[5]* (Rome, 1946).

SIMÓN-PRADO, *Praelectiones biblicae*[5]* (Rome-Turin, 1946).

J. RENIÉ, *Manuel d'Écriture Sainte*[6]* (Paris-Lyon, 1949).

A. ROBERT—A. TRICOT, *Guide to the Bible*, 2 Vols. (New York : Desclée, 1955 ff.).

P. ELLIS, *Men and Message of the Old Testament** (Collegeville : Liturgical Press, 1962).

B.   Non-Catholic

S. DRIVER, *Introduction to the Literature of the Old Testament*[3] (Edinburgh, 1909).

J. HEMPEL, *Althebräische Literatur und ihr hellenistisch-jüdisches Nachleben* (Potsdam, 1930).

L. GAUTIER, *Introduction à l'Ancien Testament*[3] (Lausanne, 1939) ([1]1905).

A. WEISER, *Einleitung in das alte Testament*[2] (Stuttgart, 1949) ([1]1939).

H. ROWLEY, *Growth of the Old Testament* (New York : Harper, 1950).

A. LODS, *Histoire de la littérature hébraïque et juive* (Paris, 1950).

H. ROWLEY, *The Old Testament and Modern Study* (Oxford, 1951).

R. H. PFEIFFER, *Introduction to the Old Testament*[2] (New York : Harper, 1952).

A. BENTZEN, *Introduction to the Old Testament*[2] (Copenhagen, 1952) ([1]1948-1949).

O. EISSFELDT, *Einleitung in das alte Testament*[2] (Tübingen, 1956) ([1]1934); Eng. trans. *The Old Testament, An Introduction* (New York : Harper, 1965).

B. ANDERSON, *Understanding the Old Testament* (Englewood Cliffs : Prentice Hall, 1957).

N. GOTTWALD, *A Light to the Nations. An Introduction to the Old Testament* (New York : Harper, 1959).

A. WEISER, *Introduction to the Old Testament* (New York : Association, 1961).

II.   General commentaries

L. PIROT—A. CLAMER, *La sainte Bible** (Paris) = *BPC.*

La Sainte Bible,* translated into French under the direction of L'ÉCOLE BIBLIQUE DE JÉRUSALEM (Paris) = *BJ.*

A. VACCARI, *La Sacra Bibbia** (Florence) = *SB*.
Das Alte Testament, Echterbibel* (Wurtzburg) = *EBi*.
Handkommentar zum Alten Testament (Göttingen) = *HKAT*.
Die Heilige Schrift des Alten Testaments* (Bonn) = *HSAT*.
E. SELLIN, *Kommentar zum Alten Testament* (Leipzig) = *KAT*.
A Catholic Commentary on Holy Scripture* (London) = *CCHS*.
International Critical Commentary, missing Exodus, Leviticus, Isaias 28 ff., Jeremias, Lamentations, Canticle of Canticles and all Deuteronomy (Edinburgh) = *ICC*.
Cambridge Bible for Schools and Colleges (Cambridge) = *CBSC*.
La Biblia* (Monastery of Montserrat) = *BM*.
G. A. BUTTRICK, *et al.* (eds.), *The Interpreter's Bible* (New York : Abingdon, 1952 ff.).
N. J. MCELENEY, ed., *Pamphlet Bible Series** (New York : Paulist, 1959 ff.).
G. E. WRIGHT, *et al.* eds., *The Old Testament Library* (Philadelphia : Westminster, 1961 ff.).
M. BLACK—H. ROWLEY, eds. *Peake's Commentary on the Bible* (New York : Nelson, 1963).
W. F. ALBRIGHT—D. N. FREEDMAN, eds., *The Anchor Bible* (Garden City : Doubleday, 1964 ff.).
Old Testament Reading Guide* (Collegeville : Liturgical Press, 1965 ff.).

N.B. The other general commentaries are either too old or too incomplete.
See also the bibliography given in reviews such as *Biblica* (Rome), *Catholic Biblical Quarterly* (Washington, D. C.), *Internationale Zeitschriftenanschau für Bibelwissenanschaft und Grenzgebiete* (Düsseldorf).

PRELIMINARIES

THE HISTORICAL FRAMEWORK OF THE BIBLE

by E. Cavaignac and P. Grelot

a) *Histories of the Near East*

Collection " L'Évolution de l'humanité, " directed by H. BERR : VI, *Des clans aux empires* (A. MORET—G. DAVY); VII, *Le Nil et la civilisation égyptienne* (A. MORET); VIII, *La Mésopotamie* (L. DELAPORTE); VIIIbis, *Les Hittites* (L. DELAPORTE); IX, *La civilisation égéenne* (G. GLOTZ); XXIV, *L'Iran antique et la civilisation iranienne* (Cl. HUART and L. DELAPORTE). The latest editions of these works have been updated according to most recent discoveries.

Collection " Clio " : I, *Les peuples de l'Orient méditerranéen* : 1, *Le Proche Orient asiatique* (L. DELAPORTE), 2, *L'Égypte* (E. DRIOTON and J. VANDIER). These works contain the most detailed bibliographies.

E. CAVAIGNAC, *Histoire du monde* : II, *Le monde méditerranéen jusqu'au IVe siècle* (Paris, 1929).

A. MORET, *Histoire de l'Orient* : I : *IVe et IIIe millénaires;* II : *IIe et Ier millénaires* (in *L'Histoire générale de* G. GLOTZ) (Paris, 1929-1936).

E. A. SPEISER, *Mesopotamian Origins* (Philadelphia : Univ. of Penn., 1930).

L. HOMO, *Histoire de l'Ancien Orient* (Paris, 1943).

E. CAVAIGNAC, *Histoire générale de l'Antiquité* (Publications of the University of Strasbourg, 1946).

H. FRANKFORT, *et al., The Intellectual Adventure of Ancient Man* (Chicago : Univ. of Chicago, 1946); *Kingship and the Gods* (Chicago : Univ. of Chicago, 1948).

Collection " Peuples et civilisations " directed by L. HALPHEN and P. SAGNAC : I, *Les premières civilisations* (collected works) (Paris, 1950).

H. FRANKFORT, *The Birth of Civilization in the Near East* (Lafayette : Indiana University, 1951).

V. G. CHILDE, *New Light on the Most Ancient East* (New York : Praeger 1953).

W. F. ALBRIGHT, *From the Stone Age to Christianity*[2] (Garden City : Doubleday, 1957).

b) *Histories of Israel*

E. SCHÜRER, *Geschichte der jüdischen Volkes im Zeitalter Jesu Christi*[4], 3 Vols. (1909); Eng. trans. *History of the Jewish People in the Time of Jesus* (New York : Schocken, 1961 ff.)

G. KITTEL, *Geschichte des Volkes Israël*[6] (Gotha-Stuttgart, 1922-1929).

L. DESNOYERS, *Histoire du peuple hébreu des Juges à la Captivité* (Paris, 1922-1930).

W. O. E. OESTERLEY—T. H. ROBINSON, *A History of Israel* (Oxford, 1932).

R. DE VAUX, " Israël, " *SDB*, IV (Paris, 1947-1948), cols. 729-777.

P. HEINISCH, *History of the Old Testament** (Collegeville : Liturgical Press, 1952).

J. MUILENBURG, " The History of the Religion of Israel, " *IB*, I, pp. 292-348.

H. ROWLEY, " Israel, History of, " *IDB*, II, pp. 750-765.

A. ALT, *Kleine Schriften zur Geschichte des Volkes Israel* (Munich, 1953).

P. LEMAIRE—D. BALDI, *Atlante biblico** (Turin, 1954).

M. NOTH, *Geschichte Israels²* (Göttingen, 1954).

L. H. GROLLENBERG, *Atlas de la Bible** (Paris-Brussels, 1955).

G. RICCIOTTI, *The History of Israel** (Milwaukee : Bruce, 1955).

S. W. BARON, *Histoire d'Israël, vie sociale et religieuse*, 2 Vols. (Paris, 1956-1957).

J. BRIGHT, *A History of Israel* (Philadelphia : Westminster, 1959).

A. GELIN, *Religion of Israel** (London : Burns and Oates, 1959).

M. NOTH, *The History of Israël** (New York : Harper, 1960, rev. ed.).

R. DE VAUX, *Ancient Israel** (New York : McGraw-Hill, 1961).

W. F. ALBRIGHT, *The Biblical Period from Abraham to Ezra* (New York : Harper, 1963, rev. ed.).

c) *Collections of texts and inscriptions from the Ancient Orient : ANET, AOAT.*

J. B. PRITCHARD, ed., *Ancient Near Eastern Texts Relating to the Old Testament* (Princeton : Princeton Univ., 1950); *The Ancient Near East in Pictures* (Princeton : Princeton Univ., 1954).

D. W. THOMAS, ed., *Documents from Old Testament Times* (New York : Harper, 1961).

CHAPTER I

THE ANCIENT NEAR EAST BEFORE THE ISRAELITES

BIBLIOGRAPHY

See the bibliography cited on p. 5.

E. A. SPEISER, " Ethnic Movements in the Near East in the Second Millennium B. C., " *BASOR*, 13 (1933), pp. 13-54.

R. A. BOWMAN, " Arameans, Aramaic, and the Bible, " *JNES*, 7 (1948), pp. 65-90.

H. FRANKFORT, *Ancient Egyptian Religion* (New York : Columbia Univ., 1948).

A. DUPONT-SOMMER, *Les Araméens* (L'Ancien Orient illustré, 2) (Paris, 1949).

E. CAVAIGNAC, *Les Hittites* (L'Ancien Orient illustré, 3) (Paris, 1950).

E. DHORME, *Les Amorrhéens*, (Paris, 1951), pp. 81-165, with bibliography, pp. 759-762.

E. A. SPEISER, " The Sumerian Problem Reviewed, " *HUCA*, 23 (1950-1951), pp. 399-455.

J. A. WILSON, *The Burden of Egypt* (Chicago : Univ. of Chicago, 1951); " Egypt, " *IDB*, II, pp. 39-66.

L. CERNY, *Ancient Egyptian Religion* (London : Hutchinson, 1952).

O. R. GURNEY, *The Hittites* (Baltimore : Penguin, 1952).

K. KENYON, *Digging up Jericho* (New York : Praeger, 1957).

G. STEINDORFF and K. C. STEELE, *When Egypt Ruled the East*[2] (Chicago : Univ. of Chicago, 1957).

The Mediterranean basin, linking as it does the lands of Western and Central Europe on one side with the high Iranian plateau on the other, is one of the most clearly bounded geographical and historical areas. Its southern border is the vast deserts (Sahara, Arabia), that of the northeast the farreaching steppes (Russia and Siberia), while rugged mountain ranges of Central Asia mark its eastern limits. Although the Asian and African lands of its eastern reaches have long been known as the " Levant, " modern usage now favors the term " Near East. " It is the history then of this specific area, the natural framework and setting of all Jewish history until the rise of Christianity, that we are about to retrace, emphasizing especially those instances where historical facts and biblical narrative are one.

§ 1. Egypt and Mesopotamia

Egypt and Lower Mesopotamia supply us with the most ancient documents which we can date approximately because of the almost uninterrupted succession of royal records in these countries. In Lower Mesopotamia, the tombs of the sacred city of Ur and the pyramids of the Pharaos of Egypt's Third and Fourth Dynasties take us back to the first half of the third millennium, between B.C. 2500 and 3000. In Egypt, the kings who built the great pyramids flourished around B.C. 2700. Then, after a time of upheavals and strife, a new and brilliant epoch dawned under the Twelfth Dynasty, between B.C. 2000 and 1800. And even at these remote dates Egyptian documents cast occasional light upon Ethiopia, Palestine and Phoenicia, Cyprus and even Crete and the lands of the Aegean coastline; these last already are the cradle of a remarkably advanced civilization which today is virtually unknown to us.

In Mesopotamia the first well-known kings sprang from Sumerian stock, the oldest ethnic group in the land. The first important dynasty of Semites at Akkad was founded by Sargon I about the year 2300. Later, after a period of domination by the Goutis, an eastern mountain people, a second Sumerian dynasty ruled at Ur around the year 2000. Then the Amorite Semites gained control under their great king Hammurabi and the first Babylonian dynasty (*ca.* 1700). Mesopotamian documents make it possible for us to classify and assign rough dates to those from Elam, Assyria, Upper Mesopotamia, Northern Syria and Eastern Asia Minor. And so it is as events fall into place that ancient history begins to take recognizable form.

During the following centuries, Egypt experienced the occupation of much of her territory by the Hyksos, Semitic invaders from Asia (1700-1600). In 1580, however, the princes of Thebes drove the Hyksos out of Egypt into Palestine, thus founding a new national empire and opening an era of Egyptian conquest in Asia.

In Mesopotamian history the outstanding event is the capture of Babylon around the year 1580 by the Hittites of Asia Minor, which brought about the collapse of the first Babylonian dynasty. A large part of the country now came under the domination of the Cassites (or Cosseans), an Eastern mountain people. The Hittites were never again to extend their rule so far from their homeland. The Hurrites, from the north, settled in Northern Mesopotamia and founded the kingdom of Mitanni. Thence forward the Mitanni barred the road to further Hittite expansion and proceeded to establish itself in Syria where it remained the main power until the Egyptian invasions.

The excavations at Mari, a city of the Upper Euphrates and an important trading center at the start of the second millennium, have now shown us how rare indeed were contacts of any kind between the Sumero-Akkadian territories and those of the Egyptian sphere of influence. The most painstaking search through thousands of tablets scarcely yields a single mention of Egypt. Thus, over the first 1,500 years of written history—one third of recorded time!—these two great centers of civilization were hardly aware of each other's existence. [1]

§ 2. The Egyptian Empire and the Hittites

The situation changes completely when the Pharaos of the Eighteenth Dynasty invade Asia.

Thutmose III (*ca.* 1500-1450) subjugated all the Syrian rulers and defeated the king of Mitanni, receiving gifts from all whom this potentate harassed : kings of Babylon and Assyria, kings from as far as the Zagros Mountains, the Hittites of Asia Minor and even from Minoan Crete. Egypt was plainly embarked upon a policy of maximum expansion. But her power declined during the next century. No doubt, Amenophis III (*ca.* 1406-1370) and Amenophis IV (*ca.* 1370-1352) still maintained intense diplomatic activity, for their archives found at Tell-el-Amarna contain letters from Burnaburiash the Cassite king of Babylon, Assur-uballit, king of Assyria and from Suppiluliuma the Hittite, whose own records tell us that he defeated the Egyptians in Syria. During the 14th century the Egyptians fell back before the advances of the Hittite kings.

These kings had their capital (Hattusas) at Boghaz-Koy, at the bend in the Halys River and their archives have verified the information supplied us by Egyptian and Assyro-Babylonian records. Thus, for example, we have come to know of the treaty between Hattusil and Ramesis II (*ca.* 1271), for a copy of it was found at Boghaz-Koy. And also, throughout the 14th and 13th centuries, Hittite and Assyrian kings each tell us of the battles they waged for the possession of Mitanni. Finally, the texts of Boghaz-Koy help put some life into the documents of Mycenae and the Aegean coast, complete mysteries until only yesterday, for the Hittite kings were in frequent contact with the Achaeans of those districts.

It was around the year B.C. 1200 that these two centers of civilization were subjected to parallel attacks by roving tribes from the northwest.

---

[1] On the peoples of the desert cf. J. R. KUPPER, *Les nomades en Mésopotamie au temps des rois de Mari* (Paris, 1957).

The People of the Sea made several retreats into Africa and Ramesis III stopped on Egypt's borders an invasion which had pillaged the Syrian coasts (*ca.* 1180). The tiny Philistine principalities were the result of this thrust. During this same period, the Boghaz-Koy kingdom collapsed under the attacks of barbarians, Phrygian tribes from Thrace, who appeared near the Upper Euphrates and Tigris Rivers near Assyria around 1165. And so, without great risk of error we are able to catch a glimpse of the twofold migration that carried the Dorians to the shores formerly inhabited by the Achaeans, down to the Peloponesus and then on to Crete and southwestern Asia Minor.

From the 16th to the 12th century, then, the eastern sector of the Mediterranean basin formed an historical and geographical unity whose diverse peoples were in constant and active political and cultural contact.

§ 3. First Expansion of the Assyrian Empire

After the end of the Egyptian hegemony in Syria, the first extensive source of information we have about the Mediterranean world is the Assyrian king Teglath-pilessar I (*ca.* 1100) who campaigned in the Zagros Mountains and Armenia, crossed the Euphrates and pressed on to the Mediterranean shores. His chief adversaries were the Aramean Semites who were beginning their climb to power in Mesopotamia and northern Syria. For several centuries their presence had been be felt along the borders of the Syrian desert. Their invasion is of great importance to biblical history, if indeed the Hebrew patriarchs (Dt 26, 5) were part of it, as is generally believed. After this period of initial expansion, Assyria kept outposts along the Euphrates until the year 1000 when she began a lengthy decline.

This, then, is the international history of the Near East traced in bold outline down to the 12th century B.C. And with this overall view behind us, we shall now be able to concentrate at length upon Syria and Palestine.

CHAPTER II

SYRIA AND PALESTINE
UNTIL THE 8th CENTURY B.C.

BIBLIOGRAPHY

See the bibliography cited on pp. 5 and 7.

N. GLUECK, *The Other Side of the Jordan* (New Haven : American Schools of Oriental Research, 1940).

W. F. ALBRIGHT, " The Role of the Canaanites in the History of Civilization, " *Studies in the History of Culture* (New York : Banta, 1942).

S. COHEN, " Edom, " *IDB*, II, pp. 24-26.

R. DE VAUX, " Les patriarches hébreux et les découvertes modernes, "*
RB (1946), pp. 321-348; (1948), pp. 321-347; (1949), pp. 5-36.

H. H. ROWLEY, *From Joseph to Josuah* (London, 1950), cf. *RB* (1951), p. 279.

T. J. MEEK, *Hebrew Origins* (New York : Harper, 1950).

A. PARROT, *Ninive et l'Ancien Testament* (*Cahiers d'Archéologie biblique*, 3) (Paris-Neuchatel, 1953).

J. BOTTÉRO, *Le problème des Habiru* (Paris, 1954).

A. PARROT, *Samarie, capitale du royaume d'Israël* (Paris-Neuchatel, 1955).

R. DUSSAUD, *La pénétration des Arabes en Syrie avant l'Islam* (Paris, 1955).

S. MOSCATI, *I Predecessori d'Israele* (Rome, 1956).

W. F. ALBRIGHT, *The Archaeology of Palestine* (Baltimore : Penguin, 1956).

G. E. WRIGHT and D. N. FREEDMAN, eds., *Biblical Archaeologist Reader, I and II* (New York : Doubleday, 1961 and 1965).

K. KENYON, " Archaeology of Palestine—I, " *Peake's Commentary on the Bible* (New York : Nelson, 1963), pp. 42-49.

J. GRAY, *The Canaanites* (New York : Praeger, 1965).

G. M. LANDES, " Ammon, " *IDB*, I, pp. 24-26.

J. C. GREENFIELD, " Philistines, " *IDB*, III, pp. 791-795.

E. D. GROHMAN, " Moab, " *IDB*, III, pp. 409-419.

A. S. KAPELRUD, " Phoenicia, " *IDB*, III, pp. 800-805; " Ugarit, " *IDB*, IV, pp. 724-732.

§ 1. Syria and the Land of Chanaan

The Syro-Palestinian coast together with its hinterland is a vast crossroad where many currents of international exchanges intermingle. One,

through the port towns and cities strung out from Ugarit all the way
to Tyre, stretches from Mesopotamia as far as the Mediterranean shores
(Ionia, continental Greece, Crete, Egypt, North Africa, Southern Italy
and Spain).   The other connects Egypt with the banks of the Euphrates
and Asia Minor by means of a network of land routes running from the
coast to the Syro-Arabian steppe.   And so it is that this narrow corridor
between the sea and the desert has been invaded and settled by the most
diverse peoples down through the ages.

In the third millennium Semitic invaders established or developed
along the coast a chain of ports which traded with Egypt at even that
early date.   Later, the Greeks knew this race of daring seafarers as
Phoenicians *(Phoinikes)* but in the Bible, the cuneiform texts and
Egyptian records they are called Chanaanites *(Kena 'ani, Kinahni,
Kinahhi)* and their country Chanaan.   Both terms, it would seem'
referred originally to the purple dye made and traded along the Syrian
coast and only later were they transferred first to the coastal region, then
to its interior (the land of Chanaan = the land of purple dye) and finally
to the people themselves (Moscati).   In ancient Mesopotamia, however,
the term " Land of Amurru " (Land of the West) was more frequently
used and, thus, the peoples living in Syria came to be called Amorites.
In Egypt present-day Palestine was called Haru since the Horites
inhabited its southern mountains, as we know from the Bible (Gn 36,
20-30).   Because archeology has been unable to discover any traces of
urban civilization among the Horites, some historians view them as a
branch of Semitic nomads (Dussaud) while others consider them to have
been a tribe of cave dwellers.   But their name closely resembles that of
the Hurrites of northern Mesopotamia and it is not unlikely that some
Hurrite clans settled in Palestine during the Hyksos invasions as, indeed,
did some of those Indo-European peoples whose descendants developed
the warlike aristocracy of Mitanni.   Some of the El-Amarna tablets
contain Indo-European names *(Shuwardata)* while others bear witness
to the cult of the Hurrite goddess Hepa *(Abdu? - Hepa*, king of Jerusalem)
in Chanaan.   From these facts, then, we can picture ancient Palestine
as the melting-pot of highly diverse ethnic groups which were eventually
united by a common agricultural civilization and city-state organization
although its borders remained the homeland of nomadic, and hence,
unstable peoples.

It is understandable, then, that after Egypt's political decline in the
14th century Chanaan experienced a time of extreme anarchy : rivalries
between city-states, constant attacks by roving bands of pillagers *(Hapiru*
and *Sutu)* and the weakness of the central government borne out in the

correspondence of the petty local rulers with their distant overlord (Tell-el-Amarna period). Egypt's national renaissance under Seti I and especially Ramesis II (*ca.* 1292-1226) re-established Egyptian authority throughout the land. Nevertheless, Semitic tribes resulting from the Amorite and Aramean invasions managed, at last, to establish themselves in Palestine, Transjordan and the southern steppes in those areas not controlled by the autochthonous cities, thus giving birth to the kingdoms of Edom, Moab and the Ammonites, all closely related to the Israelites and more quick than they to adapt themselves to a civilization at once autochthonous, urban and agricultural (cf. Gn 26, 34-35; 36; Nm 22 and 25). This, then, was the land of Chanaan when the Israelites firmly established themselves there after the Exodus.

§ 2. The Problem of the Hebrew Patriarchs

We would like to be able to place precisely the Hebrew patriarchs within this general framework. [1] However, the traditions contained in the Bible present the historian with many an intricate problem. Since the literary genres of these traditions are so far removed from our own it is not always easy to isolate their historical content. And even the chronology is obscure. Thus, Exodus 1, 11 would have us place the end of the oppression of the Hebrews in the land of Goshen in the 13th century, during the reign of either Ramesis II or Menephtah, and archeology favors this date as do the majority of modern historians. But, if we take Exodus 1, 3 and 6, 16-20 literally, the history of Joseph was scarcely two generations earlier, during the reign of Amenophis IV (1370) (Rowley) and, therefore, the period of oppression would run parallel with the national revival under Seti I (1312-1292). But we are faced with a span of some four centuries between the descent into Egypt and Abraham's wanderings in the Negev (Gn 12—13) if, according to many archeologists, we must place the descent in the 19th century. [2]

Therefore, most historians place the descent into Egypt during the Hyksos period (17th century), but between then and the time of the Exodus there also stretches a gap of four centuries and of their history we are told nothing. It is evident, no matter which set of dates we

---

[1] D. DIRINGER, "The Origins of the Hebrew People," *Mélanges Furlani* (Rome, 1957), pp. 301-313.
[2] R. DE VAUX, *RB* (1948), p. 336. — N. GLUECK, *BA* (1955), pp. 2-9. — A. RASCO, "Migratio Abrahae circa 1650*," *VD*, 35, pp. 143-154.

choose, that the traditions in Genesis 12 ff. are recorded in brief and sketchy outline. Nevertheless, their underlying unity and theme in regard to the historical Israel are boldly highlighted by those biblical authors who collected and recorded them. All the traditions of the tribes are melted and fused, thus presenting the history of a single family, as it were, for four generations. And although everybody agrees that this is an abridgement, it is difficult to be more specific or precise.

We are only able to trace a few general lines throughout this chain of events which must have been rather complex. Abraham's migration is not just another element in a process of secular history whose other elements we have learnt from various sources : it is a religious event. The camp grounds of the patriarch's household are quite clearly stated. Starting at Aram Naharaim,[3] they traveled over the Syrian steppe, the grazing ground of sleep and goatherds, as far as the mountains of central Palestine and the Negev. This, then, was Abraham's itinerary. Under Isaac's leadership, however, they remained more or less settled in the south while during Jacob's life they returned briefly to nomadic ways before settling permanently in southern Palestine. All the traditions of central Palestine and Transjordan are especially linked with Jacob's name as are the dealings with the Arameans (Laban)and the quarrels with the ancient Edomites (Esau). Finally, in the story of Joseph we find the " children of Jacob " settling in one of Egypt's border provinces. Unfortunately, it is nearly impossible to exceed this brief outline with any certainty since those popular traditions which are our only source of information are difficult to interpret according to exacting scientific criteria.

Occasionally one wonders if the biblical traditions do not combine two distinct tribal memories in the Exodus narrative[4]. The first of these, and the least apparent in the text itself, would have to do with Egypt's oppression of the tribes of south Palestine. Indeed, one of the Exodus routes leads the fleeing Hebrews along the same coastal path the Hyksos used from Egypt directly to the oasis of Cades. But it must be admitted that there are only hints and traces of this and that they are difficult to unravel and interpret. The other tribal memories, ever so much clearer, deal with the oppression of the people who had, for some time at least, been living along Egypt's eastern borders and with their subsequent departure along the Horeb road under Moses' leadership. But be that

---

[3] R. T. O'CALLAGHAN, *Aram Naharaïm** (Rome, 1947).

[4] Cf. H. CAZELLES, " Les localisations de l'Exode et la critique littéraire*, " *RB*, 62 (1955), pp. 360-364.

as it may, what we must remember is that Israel's real political history, which was to develop and take form in succeeding centuries, has its beginnings in that event we call the Exodus. As for its exact date, we prefer the first half of the 13th century (between 1290 and 1250 B.C.) although some would place it during the reign of Menephtah (1226-1218).

§ 3. Israelites and Philistines

Egyptian power suffered a rapid decline after Ramesis II, but his successor, Menephtah, took great pride in having stamped out revolts along his western border as well as in Chanaan. On his triumphal stele he lists Israel among the vanquished and here the word refers to a people rather than a territory. [5] This would probably be the beginning of the reconquest, as the sack of Lachish to the south (before 1220) and Hasor in Galilee (cf. Jos 10, 31-32 and 11, 10), which occurred at this time, bear out. However, the conquest itself presents us with difficult problems. There are certain details of the traditions that could suggest a double invasion route, from the east and from the south. [6] In any event, the conquest is quite differently recounted in Josue 1—11 and Judges 1, 1-21. Briefly then, if in fact certain Hebrew clans, although affiliated with the Israelite confederation at the time of the Judges, did not go down into Egypt (as for example the Galilean tribes) or perhaps left Egypt before the 13th century (and this question arises in the case of the southern tribes), it is quite possible that side by side with the military operations of Josue's time there was a certain historical continuity in Chanaan spanning the days of the patriarchs and the time of the Judges. But this matter is far from clear.

---

[5] *From the end of the stele of Menephtah :*
The princes prostrated themselves crying out " Peace! "
    No head is now raised from among the Nine-Bows (vassal lands).
Tehenu (Libya) is ravaged and Hatti has been pacified.
    Chanaan is pillaged together with all that is evil (?).
Ascalon has been deported, Gezer has been captured;
    Yanoam has been made a wilderness.
Israel has been devastated ; this people no longer exists.
    Haru is become as a widow before Egypt.
All these lands are now at peace;
    Whosoever caused trouble has been enslaved by the king of Upper and Lower Egypt......,
Menephtah, the beloved of Amon, the son of Ra....
  [6] A. ALLGEIER, *Biblische Zeitgeschichte**, pp. 90-92.

Nevertheless, we do know that the confederation of tribes which eventually made up the Israel of history were grouped around that particular people of the Exodus. And this new force whose steady inroad gradually brought the land of Chanaan under its control carved out its desired living space as much by peaceful occupation of under-populated areas as by treaties with the native city-states or outright war with no quarter granted. There followed what we might call a " civilization crisis " which modern archeology has discovered, and a political anarchy vividly recorded in the Book of Judges. There were also new population shifts, especially in the south. Indeed, the tribes came to allow elements of highly diverse ethnic origin into their league : allied cities such as Gabaon (Jos 9; cf. 2 Sm 21, 2) and Calebite, Kenites clans, etc. who were linked to Juda (Jgs 1, 12—16, 20; cf. Nm 11, 29-32; 1 Par 2). Studying the genealogical lists we also find a high proportion of indigenous blood in Juda (1 Par 2, 3; cf. Gn 38). We should also consider the incorporation into this same tribe of Horite elements from Mount Seir (1 Par 3, 50 ff.) whose eponymn is joined to Aaron (Ex 17, 10; 24, 14), the ancestor of Jerusalem's clergy. These are not useless details for they demonstrate that national unity was the result of a long and complex process. And this was but one of the many problems besetting the time of the Judges. Devoid of all central power and authority we see the tribes defending themselves as best they could against the encroachments of Chanaanite kinglets (Jgs 4—5) and petty neighboring kingdoms (Jgs 3 and 10—11) or the raids of pillaging Arabs who subjected them to extortion and destroyed their crops (Jgs 6—8). There were times, too, when the tribes descended to internecine struggles (Jgs 19—21). By and large however, they were expansion-bent and in the case of Gideon's son we even find them trying out the Chanaanite notions of royalty (Jgs 9).

However, a chain of indigenous strongholds stood firm against Israel's invasion for many years. Most importantly, the Israelites were unable to reach the sea since the coastal territory from Egypt's borders right up to Carmel's headland had been settled since the beginning of the 12th century by the Philistines and their kinsmen (Kereti and Zakkala), all of whom sought to expand inland. These long-time masters of the caravan route linking Egypt and Asia gradually forced the Israelites back towards the mountains during the 11th century and after a war of skirmishes (Jgs 14—16) they set out to control all important routes and especially those in Galilee where they were heavily concentrated. The Israelites forces were crushed at Apheq (*ca.* 1050) [7] and after this disaster

---

[7] Concerning chronological uncertainties, cf. pp. 194 ff.

all of the central territory up to the Jordan fell under the domination of the Philistines who seized the iron monopoly in order to forestall any attempts at revolt (1 Sm 4—6).

But now, forced by the needs of the time, the Israelites overcame their leanings towards anarchy and chose a king. Saul, of the tribe of Benjamin, distinguished himself in a punitive expedition against the Ammonites (1 Sm 11). He was anointed by Samuel the " seer " (*ca.* 1030) and thereupon launched the war for independence (1 Sm 13—14) which was quickly met by a powerful Philistine counter-attack. The Philistines together with their allies, the lords of the Chanaanite strongholds on the Plain of Esdralon, won the decisive victory of Gilboa where both Saul and his son Jonathan perished (*ca.* 1010). His surviving troops regrouped across the Jordan where Abner proclaimed Ishbaal, another of Saul's sons, king of Israel (1 Sm 28 and 31; 2 Sm 1—2).

§ 4. The Israelite Empire

Within a few years, however, the situation will be less grim thanks to David. One of Saul's officers, he fell from favor and became the leader of a roving band in the hire of the Philistine prince of Gath. With the death of King Saul, David was free to return to Juda, of which tribe he was a member, and its leaders proclaimed him king at Hebron upon his return (2 Sm 2, 1-4). Some few years later, after the murders of Abner and Ishbaal, the leaders of the northern tribes offered him the crown of their peoples (2 Sm 5, 1-5). It was at this time that the struggle to free their territory began in earnest and David's military ability together with the superior numbers of his troops quickly brought Israel to a position of definite advantage against its enemies (2 Sm 5, 17-24; 21, 15-22; 23, 8-39). After their defeat the Philistine principalities were allowed to remain autonomous, although they did become tributaries to the king of Israel and were obliged to fill the ranks of his personal guard with warriors of proven skill. Determined to establish his authority, David now struck his most masterful blow. The fortress-city of Jerusalem, then held by the Jebusites, enjoyed a reputation of impregnability due in large part to its situation high up the central mountain range. But David conquered it and Jerusalem, set roughly at the center of the land, became not only the capital of the united kingdom of Juda and Israel (2 Sm 5, 6-10) but the religious center of the land as well (2 Sm 6). This occurred just after the year 1000 B.C. and the territory of this former city-state was to remain the personal apanage of David's dynasty until the year 586.

King David was not yet satisfied and he profited from the simultaneous decline of the great powers (Egypt, Assyria, the Hittite kingdom) to carve out an empire in Syria.   The remaining Chanaanite cities were brought under his rule and their citizens no longer distinguished themselves from the people of Israel.   Edom and Ammon became part of the empire.   Moab paid him tribute.   Finally, David intervened in the quarrels between the petty Aramean states, conquered Hadad-Ezer, king of Zobah, and brought the kingdom of Hamath under his protection (2 Sm 8, 1-14; 10—11; 12, 26-31; 3 Kgs 11, 15-17).   Israel's sphere of influence now reached from Egypt to the Euphrates.   The Phoenician ports along the coast escaped her control but David established friendly relations with Hiram, king of Tyre (2 Sm 5, 11-12).   As he turned his kingdom into a great power David also undertook its internal organization (2 Sm 8, 16-18; 20, 23-26).   The history of his succession does reveal one weak point, however : the latent opposition of the north (Israel), centering around the " house of Joseph, " against the south (Juda) ran the risk of crystalizing around the personal quarrels of his sons and rival clan supporters.

Solomon came to the throne surrounded by plots and intrigues (3 Kgs 1—2).   Thanks to his father's victories and political acumen he never had to defend his frontiers and was able to concentrate on other tasks : the creation of a unifying administration which would break tribal power and be patterned after the great empires (3 Kgs 4, 1—5, 8); large public works which added an elegant palace and sumptuous temple to the capital city (5, 12—7, 51; 9, 15-24); a brisk horse trade with Cilicia and Egypt for which sprawling stables were built, recently discovered by modern excavation (10, 26-29); the establishment of a copper foundry at Ezion-geber on the Gulf of Aqaba.   Tyre also enjoyed a time of prosperity during this period.   King Hiram ruled over part of Cyprus and his ships sailed as far as Spain (Tartessos, the biblical Tarshish). It was he who supplied Solomon with the cedar wood needed for the Jerusalem Temple and with able technicians, architects and metalworkers as well.   It was also to Hiram that Solomon turned when he set about building a merchant fleet on the Red Sea to trade with Ophir (9, 26-28).

But brilliant exterior notwithstanding, the internal structure was a network of cracks and fissures.   King Solomon lacked his father's courage and his policies created many malcontents especially among the northern tribes (1 Kgs 11, 26-40).   Long reduced to inaction, the army had lost its taste for war and during Solomon's own lifetime a son of the king of Edom whom David had dethroned managed to regain his father's crown.

But this was not all for Rezin established an Aramean kingdom at Damascus which was soon to become Israel's rival (3 Kgs 11, 14-25). Fortunately, however, Solomon was at peace with Egypt which was then far from powerful and Assyria was still in a period of decline. The Hittites of the second era (known mainly through Assyrian texts) were busy building handsome monuments and were not yet dangerous from a military point of view. But with Solomon's death this delicate balance of power was to crumble and topple as any house of cards.

§ 5. Israelites, Phoenicians, Arameans

With the accession of Roboam (*ca.* 931) the united kingdom split in two. In the south, the domain of Jerusalem remained joined to the tribe of Juda and a small part of the holdings of the tribe of Benjamin. In the north, Jeroboam I ruled over the most heavily populated and strongest area with Galilee and Transjordan forming part of the kingdom of Israel. Juda, however, was seriously weakened by a series of events about the year 928. After the downfall of the Ramesids, Egypt was under the condominium of the pharaos of Tanis and the high priests of Thebes but around the middle of the 10th century the leaders of the Libyan mercenaries seized power and founded the Bubastite dynasty which brought about a fleeting resurgence of Egypt's military power. King Sheshonq (Sesac) invaded Palestine, exacted a ransom from Jerusalem and marched across Israel. For the present, at least, Israel and Juda were in a permanent state of war. Egypt's triumph proved short-lived for she was unable to regain her Asian empire. And so, since no power was able to establish its rule after David's empire fell apart, the entire Syro-Palestinian zone experienced a period of near anarchy.

Because of the succession of palace revolutions racking Israel up to the accession of Omri (885), Edom, the Ammonites and the Philistine principalities were now able to regain their respective independence. Moab, too, under the strong leadership of its king Mesha [8] was at last

---

[8] *The Stele of Mesha* found in 1868 at Diban, Transjordan, is now in the Louvre:

"I am Mesha the Dibonite, son of Kamosh-[kan], king of Moab. My father reigned over Moab for 30 years and I reigned after my father. I raised up this high-place for Kamosh-of-Qorha..., for he saved me from among the kings and brought me to triumph over my adversaries. Omri, king of Israel, oppressed Moab during many long days, for Kamosh was angry with his people. When his son succeeded him he, too, said to himself, 'I shall oppress Moab.' It was of my years

able to throw off Israel's yoke (*ca.* 850). This weakening favored not
only the Phoenicians but the Arameans above all. Along the coast, the
kingdom of Tyre, after some minor troubles, found a capable ruler in
Ithobaal (*ca.* 890-860) and the Phoenician ports, the continent's natural
middlemen with the Mediterranean trade, worked a strong attraction
over the population of the interior through their brilliant civilization.
During this time, Israel became vividly aware of pressure along its
northern borders from the Arameans of Damascus whose aid had been
sought by the kings of Juda around the year 900. And so, Omri, who
had graced his kingdom with the new capital of Samaria and sealed his
alliance with Tyre by marrying his son Achab with Ithobaal's daughter
Jezabel, began to dream of a new policy. Achab (874-853) realized this
by allying himself with Juda and marrying his daughter Athalia to
Joram, the son of Josaphat (*ca.* 865). The time was ripe : Ben-Hadad II,
king of Damascus, assuming the role of Hadad-Ezer, had already formed
a coalition of the dynasties of central Syria and those of the Hittites in
north Syria in order to besiege Achab in Samaria. With some difficulty,
however, Achab broke out of Samaria and established his capital at
Apheq (3 Kgs 20) only to be killed three years later at Ramoth in Galaad
over which Aram and Israel were squabbling. Meanwhile, a new peril

------

that he spoke (thus); but I triumphed over him and his house, and Israel has perished
forever. Omri held all the land of Madaba and Israel lived there in his time and
for half of his son's days, nearly 40 years. But Kamosh lived there in my time.
I built Baal-Meon and its reservoir and I also built Qiriataïn. The people of Gad
have always lived in the land of Attaroth and it was the king of Israel who built
Attaroth for himself. But I fought against that city; I captured it and slaughtered
all its people to sate and gorge the desires of Kamosh and Moab. I carried off its
chieftain, Ariel, and dragged him before Kamosh at Qerioth and I established there
the people of Sharon and Maharith. And Kamosh said to me : ' Go! Take Nebo
from Israel. ' I came by night and fought against the city from dawn to midday
and I conquered and slaughtered all, 7,000 people, young men, women, girls and
slaves, for I had vowed them as *herem* to Ashtar-Kamosh. I carried off the (vessels?)
of Yahweh and cast them before Kamosh. Israel's king had built Yahas and dwelt
there when he fought against me but Kamosh chased him before me. I chose
200 of Moab's best warriors and sent them against Yahas and conquered it to make
it a part of (the district of) Dibon. At Qorha I built the garden (?) walls and the
walls of the citadel. I built its gates and towers. I built the house of the king and
the double reservoir for water in the heart of the city. There was not one cistern
in all of Qorha and I said to its people, ' Build yourselves cisterns, one for each
house. ' And I dug trenches (?) for Qorha with the captives of Israel. I built
Aroer and the roadway in (the valley of the) Arnon. I built Beth-Bamoth for it
had been destroyed. I built Bezer, for it lay in ruins, with 50 men of Dibon for
all Dibon obeyed (me).... "

threatening all the rival states of Syria and Palestine loomed over the horizon : Assyria had come to life. [9]

§ 6. Assyrian Intervention

After loosing their holdings along the Euphrates (*ca.* 1000) the Assyrian kings underwent a time of throubles which would have been much worse had not Babylon suffered a decline at the same time. Around 900, though, Assyria began a vigorous campaign to overcome the encroaching Arameans along the vast bend of the Euphrates. Assurnazirpal (883-860) achieved this goal at the cost of incredible savagery, crossed the Euphrates and for the first time since Theglathphalasar I, Assyrian troops camped along the shores of the Mediterranean. Salmanasar III (859-824) enlarged this new program of conquest and marched against the king of Damascus whose influence was then widespread throughout Syria. At Qarqar in 853 he attacked the army of the coalition of Aramean kingdoms to whose aid (according to Assyrian documents) Achab had sent 2,000 chariots and 10,000 troops and the Pharao Osorkon an unspecified number of soldiers. Despite the great bluster and swagger of the Assyrians, however, the outcome of the battle seems to have been indecisive and, in any event, the king of Damascus was not defeated.

In 843 (4 Kgs 1, 7-15), a palace conspiracy brought Hazael to the throne of Damascus and the war between Aram and Israel began anew. Events moved rapidly. Jehu, general of Israel's army, toppled the dynasty of Omri (841). Salmanasar III, returning from battles in Babylonia, Media and eastern Asia Minor, reappeared in Syria with a powerful army and besieged Hazael in Damascus. Jehu sent him tribute. [10] Nevertheless, Hazael managed to maintain his position and,

---

[9] R. H. PFEIFFER, " Assyria and Israel, " *Mélanges Furlani* (Rome, 1957), pp. 145-154.

[10] *Annals of Salmanasar III* :

" In the eighteenth year of my reign I crossed the Euphrates for the sixth time. Hazael of Damascus placed his confidence in his large army; he summoned his troops in great numbers and made his stronghold at Mount Senir, a mountain that looks out over Lebanon. I fought against him and brought him to defeat and killed by the sword 16,000 of his best warriors. I captured 1,121 chariots and 470 horses along with his camp. He fled to save his life but I pursued him and besieged him in Damascus, his royal city. I cut down his orchards outside the city and went away. I marched as far as the mountain of Hauran destroying, demolishing, burning countless towns along the way and seized vast booty. I marched as far as the mountains of Ba'li-Ra'si along the seashore and there I raised a stele with my kingly image. At this time I received tribute from the peoples of Tyre and Sidon and from Jehu, the son of Omri. "

while the priests of Juda put an end to Athalia's usurpation (841-835), Aram gained the upper hand and Jehu saw part of his territory captured (4 Kgs 10, 32-33). It was not until the reign of Joas (798-783), Jehu's grandson, that Israel would recover these cities (4 Kgs 13, 22-25). Meanwhile, Samaria was suffering the horrors of a prolonged siege (4 Kgs 6, 8—7, 17).

The death of Salmanasar III in 824 split Assyria into factions quarreling over the succession and then she was faced with revolt in Babylonia where the Chaldeans were coming to power over older ethnic groups. At the beginning of the reign of Adad-Nirari III (809-782), the queen-regent Samuramath (known to the Greeks as Semiramis) was bothered by the incursions of the Medes against the eastern borders of the kingdom and it was her son who finally succeeded in re-establishing the Assyrian hegemony in Syria. It was he who boasted of capturing Damascus and carrying off 2,300 talents of silver and 20 talents of gold. He extended his power as far as Tyre and Sidon, Bît-Humri (Israel), Edom and Philistia. Damascus was sufficiently shaken and weakened that Joas of Israel was able to regain his lost territories (4 Kgs 13, 25) and from this time on Aram ceased to be a threat to Israel. Throughout this period of power Assyria supported Israel indirectly through its attacks against the rival kingdom, but since they were never in direct contact there is no trace of Assyrian intervention in the Bible.

§ 7. The Assyrian Setback

Although Adad-Nirari remained active throughout his life a new power, the Urartu (cf. Gn 8, 4 : Mount Ararat), arose on the shores of Lake Van, spread throughout Armenia and brought pressure to bear on Assyria. Now, after 784 Assyria underwent a rapid succession of kings under whom all royal power was exercised by the mayor of the palace while the nobles and high officials gained some political independence. Furthermore, the many wars of the 9th century, which in one instant alone had required the mobilization of some 120,000 troops, had effected a certain demographic decline. While the kings of Assur remained the masters of northern Mesopotamia, Babylon had cast off their rule and Lower Mesopotamia came to be numbered among the several Aramean or Chaldean principalities. In the north, the Urartu replaced Assyria along the borders of Media and in Asia Minor while in northern Syria the kings resisted Assyria's attempts to re-establish her now weakened prestige. Sarduris (acceded *ca.* 760), the last Urartu king, was sufficiently powerful to create a coalition of Syrian dynasties.

The eclipse of Assyria greatly benefited Syria now freed from pillage and enforced tribute at last and the excavations at Carchemish and elsewhere yield evidence of largescale restoration during this period. It must be said, however, that Damascus never regained its former power. But the Phoenicians and Israelites enjoyed a stretch of prosperity. Tyre, during the forty-seven year reign of Pygmalion (*ca.* 821-774), enjoyed an inward flow of silver from Tarshish and the chain of outposts connecting it with this distant colony was further enhanced by the foundation of Carthage (*Qart-Hadasht* = New City). In Israel the long reign of Jeroboam II (783-743) almost recalled that of Solomon and once again the king extended his sphere of influence from Hamath to the Gulf of Aqaba (4 Kgs 14, 25). In Juda his contemporary Azarias (or Ozias) (781-740?) tried to reestablish the Red Sea trade with the kingdom of Saba and the fabulous Ophir. This was a time of economic prosperity and general well-being but as Amos, the first prophet whose words have been preserved for us, tells us it was also a time of moral and religious carelessness. With the reappearance of Assyrian power the prophet's warnings will acquire terrible reality.

CHAPTER III

FROM ASSYRIAN TO BABYLONIAN HEGEMONY

BIBLIOGRAPHY

See the bibliography cited on pp. 5 and 11 (A. PARROT).

R. DE VAUX, " Les ostraka de Lâchis*, " *RB* (1939), pp. 163-180.

M. RUTTEN, *Babylone* (Paris, 1948).

E. DHORME, " La fin de l'empire assyrien, " *Recueil E. Dhorme* (Paris, 1951), pp. 305-323.

S. H. HOOKE, *Babylonian and Assyrian Religion* (London : Hutchinson, 1953).

A. PARROT, *Nineveh and the Old Testament* (London : SCM, 1956); *Babylon and the Old Testament* (London : SCM, 1957).

E. VOGT, " Nova chronica babylonica de pugna apud Karkemish et expugnatione Jerusalem*, " *Bi* (1956), pp. 389-397; " Die neubabylonische Chronik über die Schlacht bei Karkemisch und die Einnahme von Jerusalem*, " *Suppl. VT*, IV (Congress volume), pp. 67-96.

A. L. OPPENHEIM, " Assyria and Babylonia, " *IDB*, I, pp. 262-304.

§ 1. Assyria's Renaissance

I. THEGLATHPHALASAR III AND SALMANASAR V

It is with Adad-Nirari's youngest son, Theglathphalasar III (745-727), that Assyria re-enters the mainstream of history. As early as 743 he won so tremendous a victory over King Sarduris and his vassals on the banks of the Upper Euphrates that he was able to boast of having dispatched 72,950 of the opposing forces! He went on to crush all centers of resistance in northern Syria, capturing Arpad in 739, Calneh in 738 (cf. Am 6, 2) and establishing his authority even in Palestine. The kings of Tyre and Israel both paid him large tributes (738) in order to remain in peace. Meanwhile, in Samaria a series of revolutions had dethroned Jehu's dynasty in favor of Manahem (743) who, feeling his position rather uncertain, sent 1,000 talents of silver to the Assyrian king in 738 (4 Kgs 15, 19-20). Monahem raised this tribute money by levying a poll tax of 50 shekels on every householder able to pay (and since this amounts to 72,000 persons, we have a rather clear picture of the density of the Syrian population at the time).

Theglathphalasar spent the following years forcing the Urartu to stay within their borders and re-establishing Assyrian rule over the Medes and the eastern reaches of Asia Minor. Events in Syria then drew his attentions for Peqah, Manahem's second successor in Israel (737-732), and Rezin of Damascus were forming a new coalition with Tyre and Gaza. Unable to bring Ozias' grandson, Achaz of Juda, into their league they planned to bring about his downfall. Achaz, however, spurned the advice of the prophet Isaias (Is 7) at this critical moment and sought the aid of the ruler of Assur whom he acknowledged as his overlord (4 Kgs 16). Achaz received the help he asked for, Damascus was captured (732), 8,000 of its inhabitants were deported and an Assyrian governor was installed. Northern Israel was ravaged, the maritime province (Dor) was annexed together with Galilee and Transjordan (4 Kgs 15, 29) and the Assyrian annals speak of a first deportation. Peqah was murdered by an Assyrian henchman who then ruled in his stead. This was Osee, the last king of Israel (732-724). Thus, Theglathphalasar reached Egypt's frontiers and as far as the oasis of Teima in the Arabian desert. Returning to Mesopotamia, he defeated Babylon (729), annexed its territory and ruled over it under the name of Phul (cf. 4 Kgs 15, 19). And then while still at the height of his power he died in 727.

The reign of Salmanasar V (727-722) would be little known indeed had not the kingdom of Israel met total destruction as a direct result of contemporary Egyptian intrigue. During this last quarter of the 8th century, Egypt was struggling to end a period of internal anarchy. The Libyan military leaders had long opposed the legitimate dynasty and had even made the insignia of the pharaos their own. At Napata in Ethiopia, however, there was a monarchy dating from the Ramessid downfall and following the cult of Theban Amon whose kings were determined to make Thebes their legitimate capital. King Piankhi realized this goal (*ca.* 725) when a group of northern princes grew fearful of the ambitions of the ruler of Saïs and begged Piankhi to come to their aid. Piankhi then conquered Egypt and set up his brother, Shabaka, as its ruler. To the various petty kings of Syria Egypt now looked like a military power strong enough to withstand and block the might of Assyria and, working on this assumption, the king of Israel allowed his nation to enter into the conspiracy. Thereupon, Salmanasar proceeded to blockade Samaria and resolved to destroy it. The city held out for three years and when it finally surrendered (Dec. 722/Jan. 721) Salmanasar had just died and Sargon II was left with the task of disposing of the conquered nation. Sargon annexed the entire country, set up an Assyrian governor, deported 27,290 of the inhabitants including all the leaders, replacing them with colonists from Mesopotamia and Media (4 Kgs 17, 3-6.24). [1] There are traces of the Israelite deportation found in 17 contracts, dating from 650 to 608, discovered near Nisibis at Kannu. Throughout all these events, however, Juda remained quite neutral and this wise policy gained the kingdom another 150 years of existence and survival.

Although we would very much like to know precisely who was king at Jerusalem at this time the chronology of Juda's kings is, unfortunately, terribly jumbled. [2] The mass of information given us in the Second Book of Kings, the Second Book of Chronicles and other texts is really impossible to coordinate for either the scribes based their calculations on imprecise sources or else the numbers and dates have been carelessly transcribed and poorly preserved. The one point of true importance is the date of Ezechias' accession to the throne. Some authorities, following 4 Kgs 18, 1, favor the year 726 while others, following 4 Kgs 18, 16, prefer 716 (as does the *Jerusalem Bible*). Another source, 2 Par 29, 3, places his religious reform during the first year of his reign. But is this date really trustworthy? Briefly then, in 722/1 the king of Juda was either Ezechias or Achaz and, according to which hypothesis is favored, the Judean religious reform was already accomplished or not yet begun.

II. The reign of Sargon II (722-705)

The empire which Sargon, Salmanasar's brother, inherited borders on all sides lands of civilized peoples upon whose respective destinies he would work considerable influence, for this was a worldwide empire according to the then prevailing notion. Sargon was immediately embroiled in a war in Babylonia against the old Elamite monarchy which was trying for a revival after a lengthy decline. At the same time he also had to face Egypt's Ethiopian rulers in Palestine (cf. Is 18). Sargon met and vanquished their forces at Gaza whose king, Hannon, he deported (720)

---

[1] *Sargon's Annals :* " At the begin[ning of my reign... I besieged and captured the city of the Sama]ritans... I carried off as prisoners [27,290 inhabitants and seized] from them 50 chariots for my royal army... [I] rebuilt [the city] better than it had been and I [established] there people from the nations I had vanquished. I set one of my officers as governor over them and imposed upon them the tribute and taxes common among Assyrians " (lines 10-17). " I besieged and conquered Samaria. As booty I carried off 27,290 inhabitants. I seized a contingent of 50 chariots and allowed them to keep the rest according to their social standing. I set up one of my officers over them and imposed upon them the tribute exacted by the former king " (lines 23-24).

[2] For a detailed treatment of this problem, see pp. 241 ff.

because of his alliance with Egypt. Victorious on both fronts, Sargon directed his attentions to the north. King Rusâ had inspired Urartu with new life and was stirring up Media and Asia Minor even while in this latter region the Phrygian king Mitâ (Midas) was advancing towards Cappadocia (Tabal) and Cilicia. Sargon, then, captured Carchemish (717), the last of the Hittite states among the Aramean kingdoms. Next he attacked Rusâ and defeated him during a campaign of which a detailed account is still extant (8th campaign : 714). As of this date Urartu ceases to be a great power. The Medes and the Persians, both still nomadic peoples in the northwestern reaches of Iran, were now subjugated and Tabal was reconquered from the Phrygians (whom the Assyrians called "Mushki"). And now from across the Caucasus Mountains came the Cimmerians to trouble all Asia Minor for more than the next hundred years.

In 711 Sargon's leading general captured Ashdod in Philistia in order to forestall once more the intrigues of Egypt (Is 20). But another danger came to light in Babylonia where an adventurer, Marduk-apla-iddin (known in the Bible as Merodach Baladan), supported by Aramean and Chaldean freebooters had seized the empire's second capital and had proclaimed himself king. Despite Elamite support the Assyrian troops were able to drive him from Babylon. It was to Juda's good fortune that Ezechias paid no heed to the ambassadors sent by the usurper to draw him into the fight (4 Kgs 20, 12-19). Egypt, too, remained neutral for at the time Shabaka was busy smashing the revolt of Bocchoris, prince of Saïs. Palestine and Syria were now calm and at peace. Tyre, isolated on its island, remained independent but Sargon did receive tribute from the Greek kings of Cyprus. Each year his campaigns carried him to different frontiers of the empire : Commagene, Chaldea and Tabal, while deep in the heartlands of Assyria he caused the fortress-city of Dur-Sharrukin ("Sargon City," the present Khorsabad) to be built. He died in 705, " killed by a soldier " probably far from his capital.

§ 2. Sennacherib (704-681) and Assarhaddon (681-668)

Sennacherib's accession was greeted by an almost total revolt and his first campaign took him to Chaldea where Merodach Baladan had reappeared. Then he ravaged the Zagros Mountains in order to subdue the Cassites; the Medes also paid him tribute. In Palestine a new coalition was forming secretly, backed by Egypt; and despite the many efforts of Isaias, King Ezechias gave it his support (Is 30, 1-7; 31, 1-3).

Sennacherib's first action was to bring the Phoenician ports under his control. Tyre, protected both by its island position and its fleet, remained unconquerable although it lost its mainland territories. Sidon, whose king was an Assyrian vassal, rose to become the leading Phoenician city once again.

The campaign against Juda took place in 701/700. Ezechias hastily fortified his capital against the approach of the enemy, mending the walls and towers, restoring the Millo, filling the reservoirs with water and building under the hill of Ophel an aqueduct which modern excavation has brought to light and whose inscription is well known (Is 22, 8-14; 2 Par 32, 2-5. 30).[3] The king of Assur first defeated the Egyptian relief force at Elteqeh (Philistia) and then proceeded to capture Juda's strongholds one by one. His next move was to blockade Ezechias in Jerusalem "like a bird in a cage." The Assyrian annals[4] and the Bible both agree that Ezechias paid a heavy tribute (4 Kgs 18, 13-16). Sennacherib

---

[3] *The Shiloh Inscription* : " ...the breakthrough. The breakthrough was effected in the following way. While (the miners dug) with picks, one group towards the other, and while they still had three cubits' digging to go they could hear the voices of the others as they talked together for there was a breach in the rock on the right as well as on the left side. And on the day of the breakthrough the miners met each other, striking pick against pick. And the waters flowed through from their source down to the tank some 200 cubits. And the height of the rock above the miners' heads was about 100 cubits. "

[4] *Sennacherib's Campaign* : " As for Ezechias, king of Juda, he did not submit himself to my yoke. I besieged 46 of his strongholds, surrounded by walls, as well as the neighboring small towns beyond number and I seized them with scaling ladders and platforms, battering rams and footsoldiers, tunnelling beneath the walls, collapsing sections of walls and all other kinds of sappers' work. I drove out 200,150 (2,150 perhaps?) inhabitants, both young and old, men and women, horses, mules and asses, camels, oxen and small cattle beyond number and counted all as my booty. He himself I enclosed within Jerusalem, his royal capital, like a bird in a cage. I completely surrounded him and whoever came out of the city gates I made pay for his crime. His cities which I had plundered I took from him and gave to Mitinti, king of Ashdod, Padi, king of Eqron and to Sillibel, king of Gaza, and I took away his territory but increased the tribute and taxes due to my majesty each year above the former amount. And as for him, Ezechias, the splendor of my majesty utterly crushed him. The standing army and the irregulars he had with him to defend Jerusalem, his royal residence, abandoned him. He then sent to me at Ninive, my lordly city, not only 30 talents of gold and 800 talents of silver but precious stones, antimony, *daggassu* stones, large pieces of lapis-lazuli, ivory (encrusted) couches, ivory (encrusted) chairs, elephant hides, elephant tusks, ebony..., precious treasure of every kind, his very daughters, concubines, male and female musicians. And to present this tribute and perform the act of obedience he sent his personal ambassadors. "

allowed himself to be appeased for he was satisfied with sacking the kingdom and annexing part of its lands. Ezechias acknowledged himself a vassal and would henceforth rule over only the ancient city-state of Jerusalem and a tiny parcel of Judean countryside. The Bible, however, has preserved the lively account of Sennacherib's defeat before Jerusalem (4 Kgs 18, 17—19, 34; Is 36—37), as Isaias the prophet had foretold (cf. Is 29, 1-8) : a scourge struck the Assyrian army (4 Kgs 19, 35) and this is confirmed by Herodotus who speaks of an " invasion of rats "; [5] Egypt, too, re-entered the battle (4 Kgs 19, 8-9). These events are usually attributed to the siege of 701, but some historians claim to find herein the traces of a later campaign between 689 and 686. [6] The question remains unsettled.

In 701, Sennacherib was called to Chaldea by events of greater gravity. Even after the flight of Merodach Baladan, who took refuge in the swamps along the Persian Gulf, the country grew restive and the Elamites intervened openly. The Assyrian king probably suffered some reversals there which he glossed over in his annals but he finally conquered Babylon (689). This time he sacked the city and even refused to pass himself off as the national king of this capital as his predecessors had done. Now he was free to begin the embellishment of Ninive for the hundreds of thousands of captives from Chaldea, Syria, Palestine and other areas would supply the labor required by his plans. Thus, war, Assyria's national industry, made it possible to realize gigantic works of art for the glory of the king and the national god. Surely an unusual alliance of refined civilization and inhuman cruelty!

Sennacherib perished at the hands of an assassin in 681 (4 Kgs 19, 37) and Assarhaddon, his chosen heir, had to win his throne at the price of fearsome battles. From Media to the far reaches of Asia Minor where the Cimmerians had destroyed the Phrygian monarchy, the whole of the

---

[5] " Sennacherib, king of the Arabs and Assyrians, sent a large army against Egypt but the Egyptian soldiers did not want to defend their country. At this catastrophe, the priest of Hephaistos entered the temple of his god and began to bewail the evils so soon to befall them all. And as he wept with grief he fell asleep and the god appeared in a dream assuring him that he would suffer no harm marching out against the army of the Arabs. Trusting his dream, he took with him those Egyptians who agreed to follow him and prepared for battle in the territory of Pelusium. . . . Arrived there, he found that during the night rats from the fields and surrounding countryside had infested the enemy camp, gnawing and destroying their quivers and bows and even the straps of their bucklers so that at daybreak the invaders could only flee without arms and they fell in great number " (Herodotus, Book II, 143).

[6] W. F. ALBRIGHT, *BASOR*, 130 (April, 1953), pp. 8-11.

north was restive and unsettled. The Cimmerians (*Gimirri* in Assyrian, *Gomer* in the Bible, *Saka* in Persian texts) seem to have been an offshoot of the Scythians, barbarians from the Russo-Siberian steppe living along the eastern shores of the Caspian Sea. Assarhaddon routed and chased them into Cappadocia (678) and in Chaldea he was obliged to launch continuing attacks to subdue the turbulent and skirmishing tribes. The king's main objective, however, lay in the west. Beguiled, as had been Tyre, by the promises of Egypt's king Taharqa (Tirhaqa), Sidon was sacked in 676 and now even the king of Tyre, blockaded on his island, was reduced to submission. Phoenicia, now weakened and exhausted, began to lose control over her colonies in the western Mediterranean to the profit of the Greeks who now started to settle in Italy and Sicily. At long last Assarhaddon clashed directly with Egypt. An early campaign turned aside into Arabia (673) and after operations against the hordes of Medes and Scythians he returned to the main conflict in 671. Now Taharqa was vanquished, Memphis put to the torch and the royal family deported. The conqueror split up the country and set up the local princes as vassal kings to govern it. Egypt would owe her renaissance to the princes of Saïs, by far the most enterprising of the new kings.

§ 3. Assurbanipal (668-*ca.* 630)

Assarhaddon had chosen his son Assurbanipal to succeed him and had made his other son, Shamash-shum-ukin, the viceroy of Babylon. Assurbanipal began his reign by putting an end to the troubles the change in rule had occasioned in Egypt : Taharqa had returned and, after his death, his son claimed to rule from Thebes. The Assyrian army sacked Thebes (664) and this time the Ethiopian dynasty was definitively ended. But Psammeticus, prince of Saïs, was not about to delay furthering his own interests by uniting the country through the elimination of the other petty kings with the aid of Greek or Carian mercenaries. In 653 he recaptured Thebes and by carefully abstaining from meddling in Syrian affairs managed not to provoke his overlord's anger and so began to determine his own and Egypt's future.

Throughout this entire period the real troublespot still was the northwest where the Cimmerians continued to keep Asia Minor in turmoil. Only the Lydian monarchy was powerful enough to resist their onslaught. Around the year 660, the Lydian king Gyges sent his greetings to the court of Ninive and asked its help against their common enemy. As it happened, Gyges was none too faithful to his commitments and so when in 652 the Cimmerians pillaged Sardis, his capital, and the sanctuary at Ephesus which was venerated equally by barbarians and Ionian Greeks, Assurbanipal saw it all as a punishment from the gods. Ardys, Gyges' successor, admitted his errors and when the Cimmerians attempted another attack on Cilicia they met a terrible defeat.

Assurbanipal was now able to deal with Elam. The general discord pervading the Elamite royal family allowed him to win an early victory and place an Assyrophile prince upon the throne at Susa (665). But the situation was jeopardized by the revolt of Shamash-shum-ukin in 652 who held out in Babylon for four years. When he finally capitulated in 648 the city was sacked once again but not as severely as under Sennacherib in 689 and the inhabitants of Akkad and the Aramean / Chaldean tribes were bound to a heavy annual tribute. As for the Elamites still persisting in their resistence, Assurbanipal now determined to eliminate them forever. And so Susa was captured and sacked (649) and the ancient monarchy came to its end. The Elamite plain was now under Assyrian control. But up in the hill-country (Anshan) the Persians, who ever since the time of Sargon had been slowly spreading south, now managed to establish themselves and before long the area would bear their name. Among the petty kings who owed homage to Assurbanipal there now appeared one Cyrus, an ancestor of Cyrus the Great.

Away on the other side of the empire the Arab tribes were growing restive but a punitive expedition crushed their resistance and their captured sheikhs were " put in cages. " Damascus was now bursting with booty. The same treatment was meted out to the lands of Syria and Palestine that had helped in the rebellion (between 640 and 638). Returning from his campaigns, Assurbanipal forced the kings of Elam and Arabia to pull his triumphal chariot in homage to his god. We should note here that this mixture of pride, cruelty and religious fervor was very characteristic of Assyrian culture. Indeed, Assurbanipal was far from barbarian : he dedicated part of his efforts to the beautification of his capital and to promoting its intellectual activity. Above all, he founded the famous library of Kuyundik, to which we owe so many priceless documents from several periods, for as the heir of a thousand-year old civilization, this well educated and highly cultivated king wished to gather its many works together. And therefore there is a touch of pleasant opulence in the memory left by this ruler whose captains and warriors carried war to so many fields of battle : he was the prototype of Sardanapalus of the Greeks.

Set in the middle of this vast empire, the king of Juda was hardly more than a very minor vassal among the dozens of others—Syrians,

Phoenicians, Cypriots—who sent their contingents to the Egyptian war. Assyria's influence weighed heavily over Jerusalem during Manasses' long reign (687-642) and the cults of the conqueror were found even within the confines of Solomon's Temple. The tides of history rock and toss the people of the Bible on every level of human existence.

§ 4. The End of the Assyrian Empire

Throughout Assurbanipal's last years the threats and dangers in the northeast and east grew steadily worse. After Sargon, the Medes became accustomed to a settled life and by this time had a royal dynasty whose capital, Ecbatana, claimed to rival Ninive and Babylon. Now, after his Arabian campaigns, the Assyrian king was content to keep a close guard on his frontiers and to organize the administration of his domains so that he might devote himself to his great love of the arts and belles-lettres in peace. Such a policy of centralized power was bound to have repercussions throughout the empire.

In Egypt, Psammetichus I (663-609) turned it to his personal advantage and became practically independent. Between 640 and 630 and for reasons still unknown to us, the Scythians began to move from the Caspian Sea towards the west. According to Herodotus (I, 104-106), they defeated the Cimmerians of Asia Minor and together with uprooted Anatolian and Armenian peoples poured over northern Mesopotamia and Syria and pushed on towards Egypt where Psammetichus held them off with gifts. With the death of Assurbanipal around 630, Assyrian authority was losing ground everywhere. In Juda, King Josias (640-609) began a policy of national independence [7]; the Assyrian cults were driven out and the king little by little recovered the districts annexed by Sennacherib. Finally, he undertook to restore Israel's ancient unity to his benefit by annexing a large part of the Assyrian province of Samaria and even a few Philistine holdings. When he achieved the religious reform of his kingdom in 622, he proceeded to impose it by law over his recent conquests.

In short, the Assyrian Empire had scarcely reached its high point when it began to fall apart. In 623, according to Herodotus (and now confirmed by the Babylonian Chronicle), the Median king Phraortes dared attack Ninive. A Chaldean, Nabopolassar, set himself up as king of Babylon and ruled for twenty years (626-605). Some few years later, he allied himself with Cyaxares, the new king of the Medes who had built up his army along Assyrian lines and together they put an end to Ninive's

---

[7] P. BUIS, *Josias** (Paris, 1958).

power. After Assur (614), the capital was seized in 612 by the two allies and the city disappeared so completely that its site was unknown until the 19th century! The last Assyrian king took refuge in Harran and the town fell in 610. Egypt now grew troubled for she was intent upon preserving the balance of power in Asia. In 616, Egypt allied herself with Assyria and when in 609 the Assyrian king wanted to recapture Harran, Pharao Nechao rushed to his aid. To do so he had to cross Juda where Josias, ever mindful of his policy of independence, tried to bar the way. Nechao defeated and killed him at Megiddo (Summer, 609; cf. 4 Kgs 23, 29-30). The Egyptians and Assyrians were unable to recapture Harran and had to retreat. Assyria and her king disappear from history. The Medes and the Babylonians now determined the fate of the land as they divided the spoils : Cyaxares took Urartu and northern Mesopotamia; Nabopolassar claimed Central Assyria, Elam and suzerain's rights over Syria and Palestine.

§ 5. Nabuchodonosor (605-562)

Nechao would not admit defeat. His troops remained in Syria where they so threatened the burgeoning Babylonian Empire that all Syria fell under Egyptian control. Juda's king Joakim (609-598) was Nechao's puppet (4 Kgs 23, 31-35) and the same obtained in the neighboring countries. Upon his accession, however, Nabuchodonosor defeated the Egyptian forces at Carchemish on the Euphrates, the Assyrians' last refuge (Jer 46, 2-12). The Egyptians made their way back to the Nile valley, but Babylon would have to reconquer the entire Syro-Palestinian territory were she to follow after them.

Nabuchodonosor laid his plans accordingly. At Jerusalem, King Joakim was unwisely pursuing a nationalistic policy bitterly criticized by Jeremias the prophet (Jer 25) and the Babylonian troops, after a brief clash with the Egyptian army (601), besieged his capital (597). His son, Joachin (Jechonias), who had recently ascended the throne, had the good sense to surrender. [8] Nabuchodonosor pillaged the city and the Temple

---

[8] *Babylonian Chronicle. The Reign of Nabuchodonosor* (598-597) : " In the seventh year, in the month of Kislev, the king of Akkad assembled his troops; he marched towards the land of Hatti and made camp over against the city of Juda. On the second day of the month of Adar, he took the city and made the king his prisoner. He set up a king of his choice, claimed heavy tribute and sent him off to Babylon. " (D. J. WISEMAN, *Chronicles of Chaldean Kings*, pp. 72-73). For the chronology see H. TADMOR, " Chronology of the Last Kings of Juda, " *JNES* (1956), pp. 226-230; E. VOGT, *Bi** (1957), pp. 229-232. Others side with W. F. ALBRIGHT (*BASOR*, 143, 32) and prefer the date 587.

and the king went into exile with his immediate family and 10,000 Judeans, nobles, officials and qualified artisans.

There was calm for several years but from the accession of Psammetichus II (594-588) in Egypt yet another conspiracy was forming with Jerusalem as its center (Jer 27—28). Matters grew worse under Apries (Hophra : 588-568) who led the revolt of Tyre and Juda. Sedecias, a vassal of the king of Babylon, broke his oath of allegiance and took up arms against him. Besieged now for a second time, Jerusalem held out for one year, waiting in vain for Egyptian relief. Apart from the biblical texts, the ostraca of Lachish, discovered in 1938, have shed some further light on the last stages of the Israelite resistance. [9] At last Jerusalem surrendered and was delivered to pillage and the torch. Forced to watch the massacre of his family, the king was blinded and deported. The other officials went into exile and only the peasants of the countryside were left behind. Nabuchodonosor appointed a Jewish governor, Godolias, who was killed by fanatics within a short time. And now through fear of the Chaldeans, many Jews went into Egypt taking the old prophet Jeremias with them (4 Kgs 24, 18—25, 26; Jer 37, 3—43, 7). Juda was now completely sundered. Jerusalem's territory was made part of the province of Samaria, administered by a foreign governor and ruled by the aristocracy formerly introduced by the Assyrians. By a stroke of luck the situation created forty years earlier by Josias had repeated itself to the benefit of the Samaritans.

After making Juda toe the line, Nabuchodonosor brought about the downfall of Tyre in 574 (Ez 27—28), accepting however the national dynasty as his vassal. Egypt was foremost in his thoughts. Hophra had just suffered a crushing defeat from the Greeks of Cyrene and this was quickly followed by a military coup which dethroned him and raised Amasis, of Libyan origin, to the throne (568-525). There is no doubt that Nabuchodonosor tried to intervene at this time but it seems that he refrained from any serious involvement. The enterprising Amasis, however, set out to conquer Cyprus. Nevertheless, this Babylonian king who throughout the Bible appears as a mighty warrior makes little mention of his military exploits in the many documents he has left us. In his eyes, his greatest claim to glory lay in the restoration of Babylon which had suffered terribly in the sacks of 689 and 648. Nabuchodonosor made it the most brilliant city of the East. This claim to glory, however, never appears in Greek histories : Herodotus, who visited Babylon after

---

[9] Plate IV, p. 263.

her downfall, skips over Nabuchodonosor and replaces him with a queen—Nitocris (sic!).

Besides, Babylon's empire possessed neither the vast territories nor the prestige of Ninive. It was also shorter-lived and after Nabuchodonosor only two kings sat briefly on its throne. These were the years that saw Joachin regain his freedom and a rank of honor at the court of Babylon (4 Kgs 25, 27-30). The last king, Nabonidus (556-549), neglected the affairs of state and was preoccupied with religious matters. In his desire to establish throughout the realm the cult of the god Sin, whose priestess his mother was, he alienated the Babylonian priests of Bel-Marduk, the national god, and so prepared the swift collapse of his monarchy. Babylon was soon to open her gates to Cyrus and welcome him as her liberator.

CHAPTER IV

THE PERSIAN EMPIRE

BIBLIOGRAPHY

See the bibliography cited on p. 5.

A. COWLEY, *Aramaic Papyri of the Fifth Century BC* (Oxford, 1923).

A. VINCENT, *La religion des Juifs d'Eléphantine** (Paris, 1937).

J. DUCHESNE-GUILLEMIN, *Zoroastre* (Paris, 1948).

A. T. OLMSTEAD, *History of the Persian Empire* (Chicago, 1948).

E. G. KRAELING, *The Brooklyn Museum Aramaic Papyri* (New Haven, 1953).

R. GHIRSHAM, *Iran* (Baltimore : Penguin, 1954).

G. R. DRIVER, *Aramaic Documents of the Fifth Century* (Oxford, 1953).

M. J. DRESDEN, " Persia, " *IDB*, III, pp. 739-747.

§ 1. Medes and Persians

We must go back a little earlier to examine the development of the kingdom of Media, through which the Iranians enter into world history. After the fall of Ninive, while Nabuchodonosor was consolidating his power over Syria, Cyaxares was gaining control over Armenia (Urartu) and the Scythians remaining in Cappadocia (*ca.* 600). On the river Halys, however, he came into conflict with the Lydians who had taken advantage of the defeat inflicted on the Cimmerians by the Scythians and conquered the western part of Asia Minor. Alyattes, their king, led a long war against the Medes, which was ended by a solar eclipse that terrified the two armies (probably the eclipse of May 28, 584, which was predicted by Thales of Miletus). Peace followed and there began an era of active trade relations between Iran and Asia Minor from Ecbatana to Sardis; the commercial center was Ptera, near the place where the old capital of the Hittite imperialists was flourishing.

Thus the Greeks can tell us of the Western policy of the Medean kings who conducted their affairs in the vicinity of Miletus, the principal city of Ionia, and in the vicinity of Sinope, its colony on the Black Sea. They do not tell us, however, the extent of their power eastward. Their rule was acknowledged by the Achaemenid kings of Anshan who, for their part, had gathered the tribes of Persia under their sway. It is likely that the Empire of the Medes also included Hyrcania, where there was probably established already a young branch of the Achemenid family, that of Hystaspes, father of the future Darius. At any rate, a caravan route had long connected Media with the Iranians from Bactria, and from there with Indians and the steppes of central Asia. The Medes, then, knew of the elephant and the two-humped camel.

It would be very good if we could establish precisely the exact connection between the Medes of the 6th century and the religious reformer Zoroaster whom we know through the ancient hymns of the Gathes. All that we can say for certain in the actual state of the problem is that " Zoroaster must have lived somewhere in Iran between the 10th and the 5th centuries B.C. Only the province of Fars, seat of Achaemenid power, is excluded because of a difference in dialect. There remains, however, a choice between Media and Eastern Iran. " [1] Eastern Iran is preferred by many historians. As for the date, they usually retain that proposed by the Parsian tradition (258 years before Alexander), inasmuch as the Greek witnesses make Zoroaster a contempary of Pythagoras (who was born around 572). Reviewing this difficult problem a few years ago, J. Duchesne-Guillemin thinks he can admit this : Zoroaster would have lived in the 6th century in an outer province of eastern Iran, controlled at the time by Chorasma and to the north of Margiane and Sogdiane. [2] Consequently it would be impossible that at the moment when the Median Empire was on the rise, the old Iranian religion in the hands of the Magi caste had already been influenced by the prophet.

Around 559, Cyrus, the Achaemenid king of Anshan, thought himself strong enough to revolt against the king of Media, Astyages. The latter died around 550 and Cyrus united the Medes and the Persians. He easily rallied the aristocracy of Media and the Magi, it seems. The Iranian Empire went on being able to consolidate itself for some decades.

Cresus, the king of Lydia, sensed the impending danger. Anticipating the moves of Cyrus, he challenged him by concluding an alliance with Babylon and Egypt. Cyrus crossed the Halys River frontier, showed himself the superior in two battles, took Sardis after a siege of 14 days, and captured Cresus (546). Leaving to his generals the task of completing his conquest by capturing the Greek coastal cities, he turned quickly toward Babylonia. Already master of the Orient from Cilicia to the Persian Gulf, he encircled the Chaldean Empire governed by the incapable Nabonidus.

---

[1] J. Duchesne-Guillemin, *Zoroastre*, p. 12.
[2] J. Duchesne-Guillemin, *Ormazd et Ahriman* (Paris, 1953), pp. 6-10.

§ 2. Creation of the Persian Empire : Cyrus (551-530) and Cambyses (530-522)

As early as 546, Cyrus crossed the Tigris near Arbela and Nabonidus remained inactive. In 539, he launched a terrible campaign against Babylon. Gubaru, the Babylonian governor of Gutium, went over to his side. He entered the capital without striking a blow and respected the lives of the Babylonians, their property and their temples. The priests of Marduk and the people immediately considered him as the rightful king of the country. Even though Baltassar, son of Nabonidus and heir to the throne was killed in the palace, Nabonidus himself was spared. This gentle policy was also the most clever one. The business world was not troubled by the fall of the national dynasty, and the western part of Syria accepted its new master without the slightest resistance. Tolerant in religious matters Cyrus won all the people over by officially protecting in each part of his empire the religion which was proper to it : thus, in Babylonia he abrogated the unfortunate reforms of Nabonidus. Shrewdly he set himself up as the legitimate heir of the Assyrian Empire, as the restorer of the law violated by Babylonian extortions, and as the liberator of the oppressed people. [3]

From the very first year of his reign in Babylonia (538) Cyrus returned to the Jews the spoils stolen long ago from the Temple of Jerusalem and he authorized them to restore their sanctuary (Esd 1; 6, 1-5). A first caravan which left towards Juda was under the direction of Sassabasar, a prince of the house of David (cf. Is 52, 12). Yet we notice that from the administrative point of view Jerusalem still lived under the sword

---

[3] *Babylonian Chronicle of Cyrus.*

" I am Cyrus, king of the universe, great king, mighty king, king of Babylon, king of Sumer and Akkad, king of the world quarters; son of Cambyses, great king, king of Anshan... seed of royalty from of old, whose rule Bel and Nabu love, over whose sovereignty they rejoice in their heart. When I made my gracious entry into Babylon, with rejoicing and pleasure I took up my lordly residence in the royal palace. Marduk, the great lord, turned the noble race of the Babylonians toward me, and I gave daily care to his worship. My numerous troops marched peacefully into Babylon. In all Sumer and Akkad I permitted no unfriendly treatment. The dishonoring yoke was removed from them. Their fallen dwellings I restored; I cleared out the ruins.... "

Chronicle of Nabonidus.

" He proclaimed peace to the inhabitants of Babylon. He ordered his soldiers to keep off the approach to the temple. He slaughtered a lamb for the offering. The incense for the god's offering he increased... he prostrated himself before the gods.... " (A. T. OLMSTEAD, *History of the Persian Empire*, Un. of Chicago Press, 1958, pp. 51 ff.).

of Samaria. This is why the undertaking of reconstructing the Jewish Temple immediately ran into some considerable obstacles : the Samaritan aristocracy was little concerned with being replaced by the Jewish leaders who were returning to their country after fifty years of absence.

This small local affair evidently was overlooked by the conqueror. At this time, he entered into a friendly relationship with Amasis, the king of Egypt. He also had to assure his rear side so he could devote himself to other tasks. In the east, he had to stabilize his frontiers and to defend them against the still nomadic Iranian tribes. He pushed on as far as Bactriane and probably up to Pendjab. It was in the midst of these struggles that he died while fighting on the shore of the Aral Sea.

At his accession, Cambyses thus inherited an immense empire, much more vast than that of Assyria two centuries earlier; also more diverse, for he brought together people of all races and of all languages. The old dream of the former Mesopotamian conquerors took hold of their successors : to conquer Africa. Besides Cyprus, the king of Egypt Amasis dominated some advanced posts on the Phoenician side. He could have been tempted to cause disturbances in Syria. Cambyses forestalled the event, entered into Egypt and in one battle made himself master of the country (525). The last Saite Pharao, Psammetichus III, had only ascended to the throne to perish. At first, Cambyses was no less tolerant than his father. He needed peace in Egypt to push his expedition further. But his attempts against Ethiopia, the Libyan oasis and the Phoenician colony of Carthage failed piteously. His reversals disturbed his mind. He succumbed to many acts of vexation against the Egyptians. The temples especially were pillaged and destroyed.

One of them, however, was able to escape from this sacrilegious madness. On the far-off island of Elephantine, in the upper Nile, a military colony of Jewish origin, which had been installed there by the Pharaos perhaps a century before, possessed a local sanctuary dedicated to its God Yaho. [4] Its religion perhaps represented an illegitimate Judaism of little importance to the king; the fact is that towards those soldiers whose loyalty to him could not be suspect, Cambyses took no annoying steps. Thus, he made them Persian supporters who would watch not only the southern frontier, but even, if the occasion presented itself, the Egyptians themselves.

While Cambyses lingered in Egypt, an uprising broke forth in the midst of Iran. The magian, *Gaumata*, a Mede, posed as Bardiya (the Smerdis of the Greeks), another son of Cyrus whom Cambyses had had

---

[4] Cf. p. 45, note 9.

killed. He found some supporters and dupes in the eastern provinces.
Cambyses hastened back to fight him. It was then, while crossing Syria
(in the autumn of 522), that he died under rather mysterious circumstances.

§ 3. Darius I (522-486) and Xerxes (486-465)

I. THE REIGN OF DARIUS

However, Gaumata did not succeed. The Persian aristocracy overthrew
him shortly after with the help of the army. The ringleader of the coup
was Darius, a son of Hystaspes, representing the younger branch of the
Achaemenids. Since Cambyses left no sons, he was proclaimed king.
But, first he had to crush the revolts, for the whole empire was restless.
In Media, an imposter who assumed the name Phaortes, posed as a descendant of the former kings. In eastern Iran, where a feudal regime had
existed for centuries, some local dynasties appeared. Darius left the job
of putting down these local rebellions to his generals; he devoted himself
to the struggle against Phaortes, who was overcome early in the year 520.
One faction of the Median aristocracy, moreover, remained loyal, and
the Magi, despite a momentary disfavor, were not deprived of their
official position. Outside of Iran, the western provinces had not been
restless, except Babylonia, which had been harshly punished (in January
of 521). Once the peace was restored, Darius was able to have engraved
on the Behistun Rock, in Persian, Elamite and Babylonian, an account
of the civil war; copies of this gigantic "communiqué," diffused
throughout the empire, carried far and wide the dread of the king; a copy
of it in Aramaic has been found in the archives of the Elephantine Jews.

These tragedies were felt in Juda. It seems that one new caravan
of repatriates arrived there about 520 under the leadership of the royal
prince Zorobabel and the high priest Josue. In all, there would have
been some 50,000 Jews who would have arrived thus far, taking advantage
for a few years of the edict of Cyrus and aided by the subsidies of the
government and their wealthier compatriots (Esd 2, 68-69; Za 6, 9-15).
In Jerusalem certain circles dreamed perhaps of a restoration of the
Davidic line; but the triumph of Darius quickly dashed these false hopes.
Still, under the direction of Zorobabel and Josue, and with the support
of the prophets Aggeus and Zacharias, the Temple of Jerusalem was
finally rebuilt. The Samaritans intrigued in vain in the central
government : a decree of Darius confirmed the edict of 538 so much so
that the building was able to be dedicated in 515 (Esd 5—6). There is

no further mention of Zorobabel. Undoubtedly he had been given only a temporary mission, for, from the administrative point of view, Juda still depended on Samaria. The only authority which the Persian governors allowed the high priest was in the religious and ethnic order : from this twofold point of view he was the head of all the dispersed Jews, who still formed some numerous and strong colonies in Babylon.

With Darius, the Persian Empire reached its climax. Some magnificent palaces were built in Susa and Persepolis. The Persians remained the privileged class, exempt from taxation but subject to military service—furnishing the guard of 10,000 " immortals. " The rest of the empire was divided into twenty satrapies, and the East came to know a steady administration which the Egyptians and Assyrians had never given. Thus Juda became part of the 5th satrapy, which included the land west of the Habur River, Syria, Phoenicia, Palestine and Cyprus. The tributes of the satrapies, fixed once and for all, soon produced considerable reserves in the royal treasury. Darius was personally interested in the prosperity of the provinces. In Egypt, where he traveled in 517, he developed the sea trade with India; at his behest, Skylax explored the course of the Indus River. From Sardis to Susa, he built the " royal road " which allowed rapid communication from one end of his domain to the other. To protect the northern provinces from the invasions of nomads, he led a very long expedition into southern Russia : for two centuries the civilized East will no longer hear of the Scythians. Following this expedition, he added to the empire in Europe Thrace and the kingdom of Macedonia.

His prestige radiated as far as the western Greeks and to Carthage. We know the repercussion of this : the war between Persia and Greece. In 499, the Greeks of Cyprus and of Ionia revolted. The rebellion was crushed and Miletus captured (494); but beyond the Ionian colonies, Darius intended to smash the strength of the European Greeks which supported them. The first expedition failed at Marathon (490).

II. The reign of Xerxes

When Xerxes reached the throne (485), the usual disorders of royal succession broke out at various points of the empire.

As early as the end of the preceding reign, Egypt had fallen into dissidence : Xerxes ravaged the Nile Delta (484). In Babylon, an autochthon had himself proclaimed king : Xerxes besieged the city and sacked it. It never did recover from this disaster. Herodotus, a few decades later, will only contemplate its fallen, splendor (I, 178-200). Finally, the king tried two successful efforts against Greece.

The first, although supported by considerable land and sea forces, failed at Salamis and at Platea (479). We know what echo it caused in "The Persians" of Aeschylus, a tragedy staged in 472. The second failed again on the Eurymedon (469).

These events, of foremost importance in Greek history, only superficially attacked the integrity of the Persian Empire : for two generations, the Hellenes of Ionia and of the Hellespont refused to pay tribute but even Cyprus will remain subjected.

The colossal administrative machine oiled by Darius was revealed as both strong and flexible in the experience. It is necessary to point out a curious detail on this subject : the language usually used in the chancery documents and for the official correspondence of the Great King was Aramaic (cf. Esd 4). We see there an inherited tradition of the Babylonian administration. The language of international commerce, then of diplomacy (4 Kgs 18, 26), Aramaic thus experienced widespread use, thanks to Achaemenids! It is used from Upper Egypt to India. It is not surprising, given these conditions, that in Judea it gradually gained on Hebrew. As for the alphabet which serves for writing Aramaic, it will soon be adapted to the Iranian language then spread as far as India and central Asia.

III. RELIGIOUS POLICY

A word should be said here about the religious policy of Darius and of his successors. We have already spoken of Zoroaster. At the end of the 6th century and the beginning of the 5th, did the prophet's influence make itself felt in Western Iran? A good number of historians have admitted it, others have been more reticent. The reform of Zoroaster oscillating between monotheism and dualism, radically transformed the structures of the ancient Iranian religion; to the single principle of Good and Order, the God Ahura-Mazda (Ormazd, " the Wise Lord "), it opposed the Evil principle in the person of Ahura-Manyu (Ahriman, " the Evil Spirit "); the ancient divinities, at the same time as personified metaphysical entities like " Good-Thought " etc., divided into opposite pairs, were debased to the subordinate order of auxiliaries of Ahura-Mazda or of demons.

But, if the texts emanating from Cyrus or from Cambyses do not shed any light on the problem, it is certain that Darius exalted in his inscriptions Ahura-Mazda, his god (without excluding however other Iranian divinities).

More clearly still, Xerxes showed fanaticism with regard to the *daivas* : he prided himself on having destroyed a sanctuary consecrated to some demonical beings and forbidden their adoration. [5] Contrary to these observations, it has been emphasized for a long time that the religion of the first Achaemenids, to say nothing of some distinct traces of polytheism, does not make any allusion to a Zoroastrian dualism. [6] Even in the attitude of Xerxes, Duchesne-Guillemin refuses to see it as a result of the influence of Zoroaster. The latter would only have reached Western Iran through the Magi under Artaxerxes I. Again at this period the thought of the prophet would have already undergone a serious transformation because of the offensive return of old divinities reintroduced into his system, whose dualist framework became hardened and strengthened. [7] At any rate, it is impossible to explain the respective attitudes of the Achaemenids kings and of Judaism by the affinity between the reform of Zoroaster and the religion of Yahweh. At most the Jews were able to perceive something special in the cult of Ahura-Mazda, so unlike the nature-religions of Chanaan or Mesopotamia. This is perhaps why, in the Jewish document of Elephantine a Persian official is qualified as a " mazdean " (*mazdayazna* : adorer of Mazda). So also, the Persians were able to find a certain similarity between Ahura-Mazda and the " God of Heaven, " a formal title given to Yahweh in the official documents (Esd 7, 21 and the Elephantine papyrus).

§ 4. Artaxerxes I (464-424) and Darius II (424-404)

Xerxes having died in a palace tragedy, Artaxerxes I (called Long-hand) overcame his brother Hystaspes without too much difficulty. It would be during the seventh year of his reign, according to certain historians, that the mission of Esdras to Jerusalem [8] took place; but we probably should give a later date. In 460 Egypt, which bore foreign bondage rather

---

[5] *Xerxes' inscription at Persepolis.*

" When I became king, there was among these countries, which are inscribed above, one which was in commotion. Afterwards Ahuramazda bore me aid; by the favor of Ahuramazda I smote that country and put it down in its place. And among these countries there was (a place) where previously false gods were worshipped. Afterwards, by the favor of Ahuramazda, I destroyed that sanctuary of the demons, and I made this proclamation, ' The demons shall not be worshipped! ' Where previously the demons were worshipped, there I worshipped Ahuramazda and Arta reverently. " (KENT, *Old Persian Grammar*, p. 151).

[6] Cf. E. DHORME, " La religion des Achéménides, " *RB* (1913); Recueil E. DHORME, pp. 619-641.

[7] J. DUCHESNE-GUILLEMIN, Ormazd et Ahriman, pp. 24-25, 27-28, 57 f.

[8] R. DE VAUX, " Israël, " *SDB*, cols. 765-766. Cf. *below*, pp. 487 f.

badly, rose in arms. Athens sent there a fleet as a reinforcement. Only six years later the Persians restored their authority. A local dynasty, moreover, remained in force in the Delta until 449; this is when Athens dealt with the Great King.

Should one perhaps relate to these events the attempt of the Jews to rebuild the fortified walls of their former capital? Still, the fact remains that, due to the complaint of the Samaritans, the central administration gave orders to stop the work (Esd 4, 7-23; Neh 1, 3). One judges by that how much attention it paid to all the endeavors at local independence. Jerusalem belonged to the prefecture of Samaria : this was a state which would not change. In the long run, there were, moreover, established some peaceful relationships between the two rival cities; intermarriages were frequent, even in the family of the Jewish high priest (Neh 13, 28). It seems that the Samaritans had the right of access to the Temple rebuilt by the repatriates under the rule of Darius. Under these circumstances Nehemias, an official of the royal palace of Susa, obtained an official mission from Artaxerxes (445). Not only was he able to rebuild the walls of Jerusalem thanks to the personal esteem he enjoyed in the eyes of the King, but also he fulfilled the office of *peha* which allowed him to reorganize the district and to reform it religiously according to an uncompromising Yahwism. From now on Judea wasa prefecture distinct from Samaria. Certain historians place the 37th year of Artaxerxes as the date of the mission of Esdras (428) (A. Gelin, W. Albright), but this date is perhaps still too early.

Darius II, having become king after a new domestic tragedy (424), causes Persia to return into the history of the Grecian world. Athens recognizes the " period of Pericles " as the Golden Age. Sophocles and Euripides were in the full maturity of their genius between 460 and 420. The Parthenon is being built (447-438). Thucydides was born in 471, Socrates around 470 and Plato around 428. But the Peloponnesian war (431-404) was going to dangerously weaken continental Greece. The disaster suffered by the Athenians at Syracuse in Sicily, which the Spartans supported (413), allowed Darius to require tribute from the Greek cities of Asia Minor, because Sparta joined forces with the Great King and Athens could no longer defend the colonies which traditionally looked up to her : Cyrus, the son of Darius, was sent to Sardis with full powers in 407.

Things did not go so well in Egypt. This is known from two sources. On the one hand, the military colony of Elephantine connected more closely with official Judaism since the first years of the rule, suffered in 411 a repercussion from a local rebellion during which the temple was destroyed; it wrote to the *peha* of Judea Bagohi to obtain the right to rebuild it. ⁹

---

⁹ *The petition from Elephantine.*

" To our Lord Bagoas, governor of Judah, your servants Yedoniah and his colleagues, the priests who are in the fortress of Elephantine. May the God of Heaven seek after the welfare of our Lord exceedingly at all times and give you favor before King Darius and the nobles a thousand times more than now. May you be happy and healthy at all times. Now, your servant Yedoniah and his colleagues depose as follows : In the month of Tammuz in the 14th year of King Darius, when Arsames departed and went to the king, the priests of the god Khnub, who is in the fortress of Elephantine, conspired with Vidaranag, who was commander-in-chief here, to wipe out the temple of the god Yaho from the fortress of Elephantine. So that wretch Vidaranag sent to his son Nefayan, who was in command of the garrison of the fortress of Syene, this order, ' The temple of the god Yaho in the fortress of Yeb is to be destroyed. ' Nefayan thereupon led the Egyptians with the other troops. Coming with their weapons to the fortress of Elephantine, they entered that temple and razed it to the ground. The stone pillars that were there they smashed. Five ' great ' gateways built with hewn blocks of stone which were in that temple they demolished, but their doors are *standing*, and the hinges of those doors are of bronze; and *their* roof of cedarwood, all of it, with the... and whatever else was there, everything they burnt with fire. As for the basins of gold and silver and other articles that were in that temple, they carried all of them off and made them their own. — Now, our forefathers built this temple in the fortress of Elephantine back in the days of the kingdom of Egypt, and when Cambyses came to Egypt he found it built. They knocked down all the temples of the gods of Egypt, but no one did any damage to this temple. But when this happened, we and our wives and our children wore sack cloth, and fasted, and prayed to Yaho the Lord of Heaven, who has let us see our desire upon that Vidaranag. The shegs took the fetter out of his feet, and any property he had gained was lost; and any men who have sought to do evil to this temple have all been killed and we have seen our desire upon them. — We have also sent a letter before now, when this evil was done to us, (to) our lord and to the high priest Johanan and his colleagues the priests in Jerusalem and to Astones the brother of Anain and the nobles of the Jews. Never a letter have they sent to us. Also, from the month of Tammuz, year 14 of King Darius, to this day, we have been wearing sackcloth and fasting, making our wives as widows, not anointing ourselves with oil or drinking wine. Also, from then to now, in the year 17 of King Darius, no meal-offering, in(cen)se, nor burnt offering have been offered in this temple. Now your servant Yedoniah, and his colleagues, and the Jews, the citizens of Elephantine, all say thus : If it please our Lord, take thought of this temple to rebuild it, since they do not let us rebuild it. Look to your well-wishers and friends here in Egypt. Let a letter be sent from you to them concerning the temple of the god Yaho to build it in the fortress of Elephantine as it was built before; and the meal-offering, incense, and burnt offering will be offered in your name, and we shall pray for you at all times, we and our wives, and our children and the Jews who are here, all of them, if you do thus so that that temple is rebuilt. And you shall have a merit before Yaho the God of Heaven more than a man who offers to him burnt offering and sacrifices worth a thousand talents of silver and (because of) gold. Because of this we have

On the other hand, the same revolt is mentioned in the correspondence exchanged between Arsham the satrap of Egypt and his intendant. [10] In fact it is likely that the dynast Amyrteus started to agitate in the Nile Delta; he is going to take advantage of the change of hands to reestablish the independence of Egypt.

§ 5. The Last Persian Kings (404-333)

Cyrus thought he was to accede to the throne, thanks to the support of Queen Parysatis. But when he came back to Babylon in 404, he found his father dead and his brother an already self-proclaimed king. There followed a war of succession at the end of which Cyrus was conquered and killed at Cunaxa (401). The retreat of the Greek mercenaries who were in his service has been immortalized by Xenophon in his *Anabasis*. Artaxerxes II could thus accede to the throne (404-359). But in Northern Egypt, as early as 404, Amyrteus substituted his authority to that of the Persians. His influence gained progressively more ground : a Jewish contract from Elephantine dates from the fourth year of Artaxerxes, another from the fifth year of Amyrteus; between these two, Upper Egypt was subjected to the king of the Delta. At the accession of Nepherites (398), the schism between Persia and Egypt was already a *fait accompli*.

It is not difficult to understand that in such circumstances the Persian king wished to solidly organize Palestine, an area bordering on Egypt : this buffer state would be able to protect him against possible invasions. The mission of Esdras, " during the seventh year of Artaxerxes " (398) becomes fully intelligible when it is placed into this framework. Its purpose, then, does not seem to be a purely religious and administrative matter : the king wanted to settle the Judeo-Samaritan dispute and strongly unite all the " worshippers of the God of heaven "

---

written to inform you. We have also set the whole matter forth in a letter in our name to Delaiah and Shelemiah, the sons of Sanfallat the governor of Samaria. Also, Arsames knew nothing of all that was done to us. On the 20th of Marheshwan, year 17 of King Darius.

Answer to this petition :

Memorandum of what Bagoas and Delaiah said to me : Let this be an instruction to you in Egypt to say before Arsames about the house of offering of the God of Heaven which had been in existence in the fortress of Elephantine since ancient times, before Cambyses, and was destroyed by that wretch Vidaranag in the year 14 of King Darius to rebuild it on this site as it was before, and the meal-offering and incense to be made on that altar as it used to be. (ANET, 1955, p. 492.)

[10] Cf. DRIVER, *Aramaic Documents* (Oxford, 1954); cf. H. CAZELLES, *Syria* (1955), pp. 76-87.

who were dispersed throughout the empire. This is not a disinterested function : by granting a special status determined by the " Law of the God of heaven " (Esd 7, 21) to all the members of this community united around its high-priest and its Temple, Artaxerxes tried to gain their favor. It is possible therefore to envisage a temporary Judeo-Samaritan union having as its charter the Pentateuch, definitively fixed by the authority of Esdras. [11] Because of a lack of certitude on this controverted question, this is at least a plausible explanation.

The first problems of the reign do not however come from Egypt but from Asia Minor. The peace of Antalcides (387) allowed Artaxerxes to reaffirm his authority over the Greek colonies and oblige them to pay tribute. It is curious to note that at this time the military value of the Greeks is recognized everywhere but not always in the service of their own country : mercenaries of Greek origin are to be found in the Persian and Egyptian armies! But Egypt and Persia do battle more than once : two expeditions launched by Artaxerxes in 390 and 373 fail one after the other. About 360, Egypt takes up the offensive which comes to a halt after a palace revolution.

When Artaxerxes III Ochos (359-337) comes to the throne, the kingdom is in rather difficult straits. The satraps of Syria and of Asia Minor are in open revolt, more or less supported by Athens, Macedonia and Egypt. After having defeated the satraps (with some difficulty), the king turned against Egypt in 351; but he failed. It would be useful to know what was happening in Judea at this time; but the sources are almost silent. They allude vaguely to a deportation of Jews into Hyrcania, which could have taken place at the time of the expedition to Egypt : it is very probable that the revolt of the satraps occasioned some unrest in Palestine. It is even likely that in these critical times the fragile Judeo-Samaritan union may have undergone certain rifts. For, twenty-five years later the break seems complete. However, in 343 Artaxerxes finally crushed the Nile Delta. The Pharao Nectanebo II fled into Upper Egypt where he disappeared. From 341 to 333, Egypt becomes once again a Persian province. But at the horizon, there is rising a new power which is underestimated by the Great King : Philip of Macedonia, conqueror of Thebes and Athens at Cheronea (338), is working toward (the unity of continental Greece for his own advantage.

In 337, the eunuch Bagoas poisons Artaxerxes; two years later, he assassinated his son Oarses and placed on the throne Darius III Codoman (335-331). Then came Alexander.

---

[11] See p. 163.

CHAPTER V

THE GREEKS AND THE ORIENT

BIBLIOGRAPHY

See the bibliography cited on p. 5.

P. JOUGUET, L'impérialisme macédonien et l'hellénisation de l'Orient (Paris, 1927), coll. " L'évolution de l'humanité, " XV.

W. W. TARN, Hellenistic Civilisation (London, 1927).

M. J. LAGRANGE, Le Judaïsme avant Jésus-Christ* (Paris, 1931).

W. W. TARN, Alexander the Great and the Unity of Mankind (London, 1933).

E. BIKERMAN, Der Gott der Makkabäer (Berlin, 1937); Institutions des Séleucides (Paris, 1938).

R. COHEN, La Grèce et l'hellénisation du monde antique² (col. " Clio, " II), with detailed bibliography (1939).

M. I. ROSTOVTZEFF, Social and Economic History of the Hellenistic World (New York : Oxford, 1941).

G. GLOTZ, Histoire grecque, IV, Alexandre et l'hellénisation du monde antique² (1945).

W. W. TARN, Alexander the Great, I and II (London, 1948-1950).

J. B. BURY, A History of Greece to the Death of Alexander³ (1951).

F. M. ABEL, Histoire de la Palestine*, I (Paris, 1952).

W. W. TARN, Hellenistic Civilization⁵ (London, 1952).

P. CLOCHÉ, Alexandre le Grand (Paris, 1954).

C. H. GORDON, Before the Bible (1962).

§ 1. The Conquests of Alexander

After his victory at Cheronea, Philip of Macedonia had put an end to the anarchical state of affairs in Greece. He availed himself of this situation in order to initiate a retaliatory war against Persia. Very soon afterwards, however, he was assassinated. His twenty-year old son, Alexander, assumed leadership. His destruction of Thebes served as a serious warning to turmoil-ridden Greece. He then marched into Asia. The battle of the Granicus (B.C. 334) secured Asia Minor for him, while Syria and Egypt fell under his control at the battle of Issus (B.C. 333). Although King Darius III Codoman was cut off from the aid which Greece could have provided, he nevertheless gambled once again with the fortunes of

war at Gaugameles (B.C. 331) and was beaten. Without lifting a sword
Alexander seized the chief cities of Persia, while Darius, the last survivor
of the royal ancestral line, was assassinated by his military commanders
(330). Meanwhile, Palestine had become a part of the conqueror's lands.
His successive triumphs in Tyre and Gaza opened up a path for him into
Egypt, where Memphis accorded him a liberator's reception. The Jewish
historian Josephus relates that while en route Alexander was supposed
to have gone to view the Temple at Jerusalem. (The Jewish Temple was
a curious oddity to the Greeks because the worship of idols was not
included in its rites.) Josephus also records Alexander's supposed
suppression of a Samaritan revolution directed against the Macedonian
garrison which he had stationed in the country. What validity is to be
attributed to this tradition is difficult to ascertain. On the other hand,
many historians date the construction of the schismatic temple which
the Samaritans erected on Mount Garizim from this period. (But whether
its origin dates from this period or an even earlier period is open to
question.)

Once he became master of the chief cities of Persia, Alexander
undertook an extensive visitation of the eastern provinces of the empire.
He demonstrated to the nomads of the Scythian steppe that the frontiers
of the civilized world were well guarded; he pushed on as far as Bactriana
and did not hesitate to approach mysterious India. Having defeated
King Porus (326), he would have proceeded still further, had not the low
morale of his army forced him to turn back. He slowly made his way
back to Babylon, where envoys from the entire known world, even the
Far West, were waiting for him. He died in Babylonia in June, 323, at
the age of thirty-three, exhausted by so many journeys and excesses
which the Asian climate did not allow.

§ 2. The Dismembered Empire of Alexander

Alexander left no heir except his mentally retarded brother, and a son
soon to be born. His generals, the *diadochi*, divided the satrapies among
themselves and designated Perdiccas as administrator of the empire.
Soon afterwards, the satrap of Egypt, Ptolemy, took up arms against
him, and Perdiccas died in combat (321). A lull follows until the death
of Antipater, an old general of Philip and Alexander, who lorded over
everyone (319). After he vanished ambitions were aroused. Cassander,
his son, busily destroyed the royal family of Macedonia in order to clear
the road to the throne for himself. In Asia, Antigone took it upon
himself to overthrow Eumene, who still alone defended the cause of

legitimacy. He pursued him into the interior of Iran and, when Eumene had succumbed (316), his preeminence was recognized by all the satraps from the Indus to the Mediterranean : only the satrap of Babylon, Seleucus, escaped and fled to Egypt. But neither Ptolemy, Cassander, nor Lysimachus, who was the governor of Thrace, were disposed to bow before Antigone. In the war that followed, Antigone saw his son, Demetrius Poliorcetes, beaten at Gaza by Ptolemy. Nevertheless, in the peace of 311, he remained master of Asia : Seleucus, having returned to Babylon, remained there with great difficulty.

Antigone broke the peace by sending his son to entice Greece to revolt against Cassander (307). He himself led an expedition against Egypt, which failed. Then he found it necessary to defend Asia Minor against Lysimachus, who had crossed the straits. In the meantime, Seleucus marshaled all the Iranian satrapies under his command. The return of Seleucus and his alliance with Lysimachus forced Antigone to show his hand : he succumbed at Ipsus (301). The dismemberment of the empire was realized : Seleucus got Asia from the Taurus to the Indus; Ptolemy, Egypt; Lysimachus, Thrace and Asia Minor; and Cassander, Macedonia.

Demetrius retained some ports along the whole coast of the eastern Mediterranean with a fleet which assured him the supremacy of the waters. After the death of Cassander, he was for a while ruler of Macedonia (294-287). But, while Lysimachus was taking it away from him, Seleucus made him a prisoner and allowed his son Antigone Gonatas little more than Corinth and what was left of his fleet. The last episode in this war of the Diadochi was the struggle between Lysimachus and Seleucus, both eighty years old. Lysimachus died at Kouropedion (281), and a few months later Seleucus was assassinated.

In the troubled years that followed, the Gauls along the Danube made inroads into Macedonia, Thrace and even into Asia Minor. Antigone Gonatas found in this situation an opportunity to distinguish himself. In 277 he was recognized as king of Macedonia. Nevertheless, he was not solidly established until Pyrrhus, the adventurer-king of Epirus, after having vainly sought his fortune in the West had perished trying to wrest control of Greece from him (272). Alexander's empire thus remained partitioned among three dynasties : the Antigonids in Macedonia, the Lagids in Egypt, and the Seleucids in Asia. Is there any need to recall that, about this same time, there came to the throne of western India King Açoka, who in 262 was converted to Buddhism? The tradition of Çakya Mouni in the Far East pursued a progressive conquest even more spectacular than that of Judaism.

Like all Egyptian rulers, Ptolemy I had from the beginning the desire to add Syria, or at least Palestine to his domain. As early as 320 he had seized Jerusalem and carried away several thousand Jews to Alexandria. After the battle of Gaza, he had tried hard to rally the Jews to his side but, as long as Antigone was alive, only token allegiance was given. On the eve of the battle of Ipsus, he was finally able to fulfill his dream of annexing southern Syria. Seleucus thought that this Asiatic country was part of his own booty : only the undertakings of Demetrius Poliorcetes, who in 297 pillaged Samaria, prevented the conflict between the two generals from becoming acute. It is not known whether a formal agreement was reached between the two. What is certain is that Ptolemy Philadelphus (284-247), at the beginning of his reign, was master of southern Syria as far as Damascus inclusively. Judea would remain in the hands of the Ptolemies for a century.

Among the Greeks, it is the subjects and guests of Ptolemies who were the first to be interested in the Jews, their institutions and their sacred books. Hecateus of Abdera (about 300) already knew them quite well, but he only had a few precise notions about the Torah. The Jewish theocracy appeared to him to be derived directly from Moses and Aaron; the royal period and the prophets were not known. This state of mind will continue a long time with pagan historians, even with Trogue-Pompei in the first century B.C. On the other hand, the Jews, uprooted and transported to Greek cities founded by Alexander and his successors, where they sometimes enjoyed citizenship, began to speak Greek rather than Aramaic, which in the fourth century had succeeded in invading Judea as it had Samaria. That is why the sacred books were little by little translated for their use, first the Torah, then the Prophets and the Psalms. These translations were used when they gathered to pray in the synagogues. Such is the origin of the version called the " Septuagint "; eventually viewed with suspicion by the priests and doctors of Jerusalem, it will nevertheless be the Bible of the Alexandrian Jews and of the new-born Christian Church.

§ 3. The Ptolemies and Palestine

The East was then for all practical purposes divided among three great powers, and the life of the smaller states depended on the alliances or conflicts of these three. In general, the Ptolemies, who were masters not only of Egypt and Palestine, but of Cyrene, of Cyprus, of many ports in Phoenicia and in Asia Minor, and even, in the beginning, in the Cyclades, were in opposition to the Seleucids and the dynasty of Antigonis. But between these latter two dynasties there was no friction after the Gauls founded states in Thrace and in Asia Minor (the Galatians). Their relations then became harmonious.

Here is a brief summary of the relations of the Ptolemies with their contemporaries.

1. The bone of contention between Egypt and Syria was southern Syria. In about 274 a first war broke out. King Antiochus Soter conquered Damascus. Ptolemy was afterwards occupied with a war in Greece against Antigonus Gonatas (266-263), and Antiochus with his fight against the Gauls and the rising monarchy of Pergamum.

2. A second " war of Syria " brought Ptolemy II and Antiochus Theos into conflict. We know nothing of this war except that a treaty was made about 253, and that Antiochus then married the Egyptian princess Berenice. Elsewhere, the power of the Ptolemies waned in the Cyclades where Antigonus Gonatas supplanted them.

3. The simultaneous deaths of Ptolemy Philadelphos and Antiochus Theos (247-246) occasioned dramatic events : Laodice, the repudiated wife of Antiochus had Berenice and her children murdered. Ptolemy III Evergete (247-221) was determined to avenge his sister. He entered Antioch, the enemies' capital, and seemed for a time to have supplanted the Seleucids. He consolidated his conquests, but was finally halted by Seleucus II, the son of Laodice. A peace treaty was concluded in 241. Ptolemy left Seleucus to confront his younger brother, the eastern Iranians of Bactria and Parthia. At the same time, the kings of Macedonia were in conflict with the little Greek states supported by Egyptian politics. Because of these concurrent circumstances, the fortunate Euergetes could lapse into a peaceful indolence for the rest of his reign, which perhaps marks the high point of Alexandrian civilization.

4. His son Ptolemy Philopator (223-203) was immediately challenged by Antiochus III the Great (223-187). But he was victorious at Raphia (217) and maintained all of his predominance in Asia, while Antiochus was forced to reestablish his authority in Iran, and Philip of Macedonia imprudently became involved in the struggle between Rome and Carthage.

5. When Ptolemy V Epiphanus (203-181), a young child, came to the throne of Egypt, Antiochus and Philip considered the time ripe for stripping Egypt of its foreign possessions. This time Antiochus was the victor. At the battle of Paneas (200), he assured himself of the predominance of Palestine. He subsequently made a pact with Ptolemy and gave him his daughter in marriage, but he retained what he had won in the war. The taxes gathered from the conquered lands were to be divided between their two treasuries.

If it is true that content people do not have a history, then Judea must have been content under the dominance of the Ptolemies. There were certainly Egyptian taxes, of which the papyri of Zenon give us some idea. But the high priests of the 3rd century made a strong impression on the author of Ecclesiasticus, Jesus the son of Sira, who lived peacefully right at the end of this period (about 200-180). This is the age in which Palestine became Hellenized. All around the Jewish centers of population, the villages and their inhabitants assumed Greek names; Greek customs and art were adopted (the tombs of Maresa); Greek myths were localized in the region. Among the Jews themselves, a part of the landed or merchant aristocracy, such as the Tobiad family, which rivaled in influence the dynasty of the high priests, the Onias, was open to Hellenization.

The Jews of the Diaspora of this period had as their principal center of activity Egypt and its dependencies : Alexandria, Cyrene, Cyprus. But they were not absent from the Seleucid Empire : their important and ancient colony of Babylonia was near the new eastern capital, Seleucia. Others lived in Media and Iran, and it is difficult to discern exactly the origin of all these groups and the date of their establishment. Finally the Seleucids had invited them to Antioch and to their other possessions to the south and west of Asia Minor. All of these communities generally enjoyed favorable treatment, and they merited it. The regulations drawn up under the Persian kings continued to apply to them. In Judea, which remained their national home, they were ill prepared for the new regime, which was to be instituted at Jerusalem under the domination of the Seleucids.

§ 4. Rome Appears in the East : Antiochus Epiphanes

Then the Romans appeared on the scene in the Orient, after completing the conquest of peninsular Italy in 272 and finishing in 201 the struggle to wrest the hegemony of the barbarian West from Carthage. As soon as Hannibal was vanquished, they sought to punish Philip of Macedonia, who had imprudently aided him. They defeated him at Cynocephale (197). Previously they had treated carefully their ally Antiochus, but the role that they assumed as protector of the small Greek cities, even in Asia Minor, caused them to break with him. Antiochus was defeated at Magnesia (190), and he had to surrender his possessions in Asia Minor, which were divided between the King of Pergamum and the Republic of Rhodes. The remote protectorate of Rome began to be instituted in the Orient.

The situation evolved with the accession of Perseus in Macedonia (179-178) and Antiochus IV Epiphanes in Syria (176-175). The former disturbed the Romans by his negotiations with the Greeks, and especially with the barbarians of the Danube who could furnish him a road to Italy; Rome declared war on him. Antiochus, who had usurped the Syrian throne, avoided provoking Rome, but he thought that he could profit from the war in Macedonia to oust the young king of Egypt, Ptolemy IV Philometor (181-145), or at least make him his vassal. Perseus was defeated at Pydna (168) and the Macedonian monarchy disappeared. As for Antiochus, an insolent gesture of the ambassador Popilius Laenas was sufficient to make him decide to evacuate Egypt. An " agony of terror " then spread throughout the Orient.

Repulsed from Egypt, Antiochus took revenge on the Jews of Judea. The loss of Asia Minor greatly diminished the resources of the Seleucid empire. Antiochus the Great had already perished in an attempt to despoil the shrines of Susiana; then his son Seleucus IV tried to dip his hand into the Jerusalem Temple treasure (2 Mc 3). Antiochus went further : he took advantage of his right to approve the Jewish high priest to make the position a mercenary one, and the Temple seemed to him a tempting prize within his reach.

Meanwhile Hellenization, which was already advanced among the Jews of the Diaspora, was making progress in Judea itself, a small province surrounded for years by Greek cities, whose citizens felt the influence of the schools of philosophy. In a city like Gadara, there was even an Epicurian colony from which came the philosopher Philodem, a contemporary of Cicero. Also certain Greek customs were beginning to be introduced into the country, monogamous marriage, for example. A considerable part of the merchant or lettered class, and even some members of the priestly caste, supported the movement. Antiochus thought he could take advantage of them to try to introduce religious syncretism, which seemed normal enough to the Greeks, as to all the polytheistic peoples of antiquity. Moreover, he aimed to put an end to the particularism of the Jews, who were entrenched behind their regulations and their Law. But he was to stumble on that unforeseen obstacle.

CHAPTER VI

THE ROMAN HEGEMONY

BIBLIOGRAPHY

See the general bibliography on pp. 5 and 48 (E. SCHÜRER, M. J. LA-GRANGE, F. M. ABEL).

J. JUSTER, *Les juifs dans l'empire romain* (Paris, 1914).
A. PIGANIOL, *Histoire de Rome* (Paris, 1939), coll. " Clio, " III.
R. H. BARROW, *The Romans* (1953).
H. J. ROSE, *Religion in Greece and Rome* (New York : Harper, 1959).

§ 1. The Wars of Jewish Liberation

I. JUDAS MACHABEE

From the year 168 the fate of the East depended to a great extent upon the attitude of mind of the Roman senatorial government. This latter, however, was not without problems in the West. After a period of peace, it saw the Spanish wars spring up again in 153. With the destruction of Carthage and Corinth (146), Punic Africa and Greece were subject to it, but because of resistance from the Lusitanians and from Numantia, the Spanish wars lasted until 133. Nevertheless, in 144-143 Aemilius Scipio carried out a triumphal tour of the East.

This was because the Romans followed the destinies of the Seleucid monarchy with a suspicious eye. By its distance, its vast area and the powerful character of its kings, this was the only Eastern power which was capable of overshadowing them. The Jewish resistance to the political undertaking of Hellenization by Antiochus Epiphanes thus served their purposes at just the right moment. In fact the Jews took up arms in 166. The war of independence, conducted shortly by Judas Machabee, ended as early as 164 with the liberation of Jerusalem, while Antiochus was dying in Susiana.

His succession gave the signal for the internal struggles between the two branches of the Seleucid dynasty : his son, Antiochus Eupator, a child, was killed by his first cousin, Demetrius Soter, whom Antiochus had sent to Rome as a hostage and who had just escaped (162). Overthrown in turn by Alexander Balas, the self-styled son of Epiphanes,

Demetrius Soter vanished from the scene; but Alexander fell out with the king of Egypt, Ptolemy VI, who supported him from the very start. Then Demetrius II Nicator, the son of Soter, also rose up against him and Alexander perished in the battle of the Oinoparas (early in 145). It is at the same time that Ptolemy VI himself disappeared and left the throne of Egypt to his deplorable brother, Physcon. Naturally there was immediately a general, Trypho, who placed the son left by Balas, Antiochus Theos, in opposition to Demetrius II. But at this hour Demetrius' attention was directed toward serious events then taking place in Iran.

The Greek kings of Bactriana were the first to avail themselves of the weakening of the Seleucid monarchy after the battle of Magnesia (190). They stretched into eastern Iran and next thrust their ambitions towards India where, about 150, King Menander brilliantly reigned over the Pundjab. These distant kings were still able to be regarded as the vassals of the Seleucids without ridicule; but for the Parthians it was something else. These came down from the steppes in the North around 247 in order to settle at the southeast corner of the Caspian Sea. In spite of the merely political Hellenization of their Arsacid kings they were full-blooded Iranians. From 171 they were governed by the great Mithridates I. Benefitting from the dissensions which arose in the domain of the Bactro-Indian kings and from the quarrels of the Seleucids, Mithridates conquered all of Iran little by little. Having arrived at the Tigris, he dared to place his capital at Ctesiphon, across from the large Greek city of Seleucia. Next he crossed the river. Starting in 141 Babylonian documents were dated according to the era of the Arsacids.

One can well understand that the war of independence in Judea benefited from these events. After the taking of Jerusalem and the purification of the Temple (Dec. 165), the fortress at Acre alone was left in the hands of the Syrian troops. The death of Antiochus Epiphanes led up to some measures of appeasement, but Demetrius Soter tried afterwards to reaffirm his authority over the region by supporting a certain Alcimus, a descendant of the Aaronic line, who aspired to the high priesthood. Judas Machabee did not disarm. He formed an alliance with the Romans who promised a wholly platonic support to this dissenter whose resistance served them (1 Mc 8). The war was rekindled and Judas perished in combat in 160.

II. THE ORIGIN OF THE ASMONEAN DYNASTY

Jonathan (160-142), the brother of Judas, assumed the leadership of the resistance. Soon after, the question of the high priesthood would allow him to affirm his authority. After the death of Alcimus, the office was left vacant. Onias IV, last descendant of the Sadoqite line, which had been eliminated by Antiochus Epiphanes, sought refuge in Egypt. There he built an illegal temple in Leontopolis that will subsist until the 1st century of our era. Then Jonathan playing on the dissensions before the different aspirants to the throne of Syria, found himself nominated high priest by Alexander Balas in October 152, then " strategist and *meridarche* " in 150. His power was great enough so that Demetrius II strove to make of him an ally and proposed to the Jews a charter of exemption (145). Led into a trap, and put to death by Trypho (142), Jonathan had nonetheless made of his people a political force which from now on must be taken into account.

That is why Simon Machabee (142-134) was recognized by Demetrius as " high priest and ethnarch " of the Jews (1 Mc 13, 35-42; 15, 1-9). He used this to seize the citadel of Jerusalem, which was still occupied by the Syrian troops. Furthermore, he renewed the alliance with Rome and obtained from the consul Lucius Metellus (142) a letter of recommendation for all the rulers and cities " friends and allies of the Roman people. " However, Demetrius II Nicator went off to be defeated by the Parthians. As a prisoner he was well treated by Mithridates I who gave him his daughter Rodogune in marriage and kept him in reserve to serve his Syrian policy (139). Having hurried because of the news of the disaster, the brother of Demetrius, Antiochus Sidetes, had firmly grasped the reins of the government. In 137, he slaughtered Trypho, but he was not disposed to lose the tribute of Judea that the Jews had stopped paying for a long time : 300 talents less each year in his royal treasury! Now the circumstances were propitious : Simon had just been assassinated (Feb. 134) and his son John (Hyrcanus) succeeded him with great difficulty. Thus Antiochus came to attack Hyrcanus in Jerusalem. But finally an agreement was reached : Hyrcanus was recognized as " high priest, strategist and ethnarch, " a tribute-paying vassal. The religious intransigence of the Jews won out. But the clemency of Antiochus was probably due to the fact that the support of Rome weighed on his decision : he did not want " to hassle with the Republic. " In fact, his principal objective was to take revenge on the Parthians. He succeeded in levying an army in Syria that was composed, it is said, of 120,000 men; Hyrcanus brought his contingent. Antiochus, at the head, penetrated to the plateau of Media, but King Phraates, successor to Mithridates, surprised the Syrian army in temporary encampment and destroyed it (129). This was the time when Attalus, the king of Pergamum, left his states to Rome.

The victorious Parthians extended their frontier to the Euphrates. Since Antiochus Sidetes had perished in combat, they let Demetrius Nicator be installed in Syria again. But since the latter committed the blunder of hassling with Egypt, Ptolemy Physcon (145-116) confronted him with an opponent, Alexander Zebinas. The Seleucid monarchy thus ended its decline in deplorable quarrels. John Hyrcanus took advantage of this to regain complete independence; thus it is that he governed the land until his death (104), without however assuming the title of king.

The history of Judea was important enough during this period to attract the attention of the secular historians. Polybius whose history extends to 145 has not left a single fragment relative to the Jewish insurrections. But his successor, Posidonius, speaks at length of the capture of Jerusalem by Antiochus Sidetes and this is for him the opportunity to vent for the first time what we know as anti-Semitism.

§ 2. Seleucid and Jewish Quarrels

I. The weakening of Syria and Egypt

At the period we are now in, Rome is in full course of expansion. The reforms of the Gracchi (133-121) open the era of civil troubles without stopping the development of imperialism. After the Pergamum kingdom (129), it is the time for Narbonnaise Gaul to be annexed (124-118). After that the Roman armies reduced Jugurtha in Numidia (106) and Marius stopped the invasion of the Cimbres that could have been formidable without his victories of Aix (102) and Verceil (101). Let us add to this picture two large-scale insurrections of slaves in Sicily (134-132 and 102-99). But good luck had it that Rome had no serious preoccupations in the East at the same time. The colony of Delos, the business center between the provinces of Greece and of Asia Minor, was prosperous. A single dark spot : the development of piracy. To remedy this the Romans occupied in 102 that part of Cilicia that the Seleucids had abandoned, and in 100 they sent out a circular to try to get the friendly kings, and allies interested in the suppression of the plague of piracy. But not all these were in a situation to answer this appeal.

In Egypt, the disastrous reign of Physcon ended in 116. This is when Cyrenaica broke off from Egypt : it will soon become in turn a Roman province. Ptolemy Latyres, who kept the remainder of the monarchy, saw his brother Ptolemy Alexander rise up against him : he had to be content with Cyprus and left Egypt to Alexander until the latter's death (88). He then returned to Alexandria; but when he disappeared, the throne went to a Lagid of doubtful birth, Ptolemy Auletes.

In Syria, the situation is even worse. The defeat of the usurper Zebinas left the throne to the son of Demetrius Nicator, Antiochus Grypos. But from 114 onwards, his brother, Antiochus of Cyzikos, fought him for it. The bitter battle that they fought against one another resulted in the impoverishment and dislocation of the empire. After their disappearance (96-95), their very numerous sons perpetuated the tradition. These internal wars were mixed with anachronistic attempts to liberate Mesopotamia from the Parthians, who were ruled by the great king Mithridates II (121-87).

II. THE JEWISH STATE

All these quarrels among the Lagids and the Seleucids, due to inter-marriages, caused disturbances from one monarchy to another, and often caused their repercussions to be felt in Judea. Nevertheless, thanks to them, the Jewish State became a kind of power for the first time since David and Solomon.

John Hyrcanus (134-104) was compared to David by his contemporaries who attributed to him the gift of prophecy. By means of favorable circumstances, he extended his domain. He conquered the ancient territory of Moab and Samaria where he destroyed the temple of Garizim. Annexing Idumea, he forced the inhabitants of that place to become Jews by means of circumcision. Likewise Galilee, whose population was until that time rather heterogeneous, became a solidly Jewish land. However, under this prosperous exterior, some positive quarrels began again to be secretly manifested in the interior of the kingdom. A party of diehard Sadoqites had never accepted the reign of the Asmoneans : it is perhaps this party which after many wanderings will be located at Qumran, involved in an almost borderline Judaism. Under Hyrcanus, another party, at first an ally, went over to the opposition : the Pharisees, a party of legalists and lay doctors. The Asmonean dynasty thus had for its main support the apparently opportunistic Sadducees. At the death of Hyrcanus his son Aristobulus (104-103) dared to take the title of king. The Jewish State then extended itself as far as the mountains of Iturea.

Alexander Janneus (103-76) developed further the policy of annexations, especially at the expense of the Hellenistic cities of Philistia and Transjordania. This high priest preferred army life to liturgical service; he hired an army of mercenaries where foreigners abounded, especially the Thracians, and the Greek historians presented his wars of conquest as pure acts of pillaging. He also forced the conquered peoples to be circumcised which, along with the prohibition of pork and the observance of the Sabbath even for the armies in the field, was for the Greeks a theme of malevolent pleasantry. Nevertheless, at the end of his reign, the Jewish State was probably the most consistent of the Syrian States, with the exception of the Nabatean Arabs who blocked the caravan route and strove to occupy the important center of Damascus. But in the interior of the kingdom, Alexander had to face a growing opposition, especially from the Pharisees. His worldly life, his debaucheries, his exactions were indisposing his subjects more and more. However, he drowned in a blood bath all attempts at revolt : a strained situation which augured no good for the future.

Alexander realized this. That is why, on his death-bed, he counseled his widow Alexandra to overthrow the domestic policy of the country and to govern it by depending upon the Pharisees. This is what she did, by choosing for high priest her son Hyrcanus II, still a minor. But Aristobulus, her other son, evicted from every position, soon rallied to the Sadducees. The Jewish State will perish because of this dissent, for after the death of Alexandra (67), the royalty and the pontificate will be disputed between the two brothers who had depended upon rival parties. And Rome will put its sword in the balance .... In the meantime, the reign of Alexander will have witnessed an important change in national organization. The Sanhedrin, the council of the high priest, was until that time essentially priestly and aristocratic. Because of this, the lay scribes and doctors of the Law will be in the majority there and their " traditions " added to the Torah will acquire legal status. In this way, Pharisaism will gain the upper hand over Sadduceeism, more archaic but also less zealous and more accommodating.

III. THE RISE OF ROME

Rome had been led into the East by the undertakings of the king of the Hellespont, Mithridates Eupator (120-63), against Bithynia and Cappadocia; inasmuch as Tigranes, king of Armenia since 95, had united with Mithridates. In 92, the pro-praetor of Cilicia, Sulla, had had to force the two kings to return to their own states while, at the Euphrates, he made contact with the ambassador of the Parthian king who considered Tigranes as a rebellious vassal. When the revolt of the Italians (90) had detained the majority of the Roman forces in Italy, Mithridates of Pontus judged himself strong enough to stand up against Rome. He flooded Asia Minorand Greece with his troops. The victories of Sulla and the Peace of Dardanos (85) forced him to return to his hereditary realm and Sulla, having become dictator (82-79) and inimical to all enlargement of the empire, compelled his lieutenants to respect the truce. During this time, Tigranes increased his domains at the expense of the Parthian monarchy whose king, Sinatrices, had to seek refuge with the Saces of Arachosia. He took possession of Mesopotamia and there built his capital, Tigranocerta, liquidated the last of the Seleucids (83) and became king of Syria. Next, to the South he drove even as far as Ptolemais, and the Jews were fearful for a moment lest he call for their submission.

In 75, Mithridates took up arms again. This time Lucullus overcame him and pursued him even into his own kingdom from which he drove him. Taking refuge with Tigranes, Mithridates drew him into the war. Lucullus was again victor at Tigranocerta (69) and at Artaxata (68). Once, he drove even further. But the new king of the Parthians, Phraates, considered the conquests of Tigranes in Mesopotamia as a theft and decided not to abandon the country either to him or to the Romans. On the other hand, the unruliness of his troops compelled Lucullus to draw back as far as Asia Minor. It was at this moment that Pompey entered the scene. He had just distinguished himself in Spain by killing Sertorius and then in Italy by ending the slave rebellion led by Spartacus. He cleared the Mediterranean of pirates and Rome designated him to replace Lucullus (66). Through him, the Jews of the motherland will enter into direct contact with Rome.

§ 3. The Jews in the Roman Empire

At this time, it is necessary to reconsider an important document which we have already mentioned : the letter of Lucius Metellus (consul in 142) to the high priest Simon (1 Mc 15, 16-24). This letter contains a list of twenty-four names of sovereigns or of free states to whom a copy was sent. Evidently the Romans became acquainted through the ambassadors of Simon with the places in which important colonies of Jews and proselytes to Judaism were to be found. Thus we have a complete view of the *Diaspora*.

The name of Ptolemy (Physcon) is natural. We are already aware of the colony at Alexandria and the sanctuary at Leontopolis. Indeed, around 100, the Jews of Egypt supplied Ptolemy with two generals for his armies. Cyrene and Cyprus, Egyptian possessions, are mentioned apart by reason of the importance of their ghettos. Moreover, it is known that the second book of Machabees, in the final analysis, is the work of a Jew from Cyrene.

The name of Demetrius (Nicator) is also natural. There were then Jews at Antioch and elsewhere in the states of Syria. The city which is mentioned apart is Aradus, seen to be acting as a sovereign state at precisely this period.

The name of Arsaces is strange. It was the common name of all the Parthian kings (Mithridates I, in 142). It is accounted for in that the Jews never forgot the very important colony of Babylon nor the other colonies of Iran (such as Rhagae in Media : cf. Tb 4, 1), in the process of passing into the power of the Parthians. But at the same time it is noticed that the Romans did not look with an evil eye upon this far-off kingdom which was pressing hard upon the Seleucids. They were not able to foresee what a dangerous neighbor the Arsacids would be for them one day.

The name of Ariarathes proves that there were Jews in Cappadocia. That of Attalia, king of Pergamum, recalls the existence of ghettos in Eastern Asia Minor (Pergamum and Apamea).

On the coast of the sea of Cyprus, the Greek cities of Side and Phasaelis can be made out. The Pamphylians were named apart, as well as the Lysians who formed an important federation.

Next comes Rhodes, the great seat of Greek commerce. At Cos the Jewish colony must have been large, for it served as the deposit bank for the monies which the Jews of Asia Minor had contributed toward the Temple at Jerusalem. In the area, Cnidus, Halicarnassus and Gortyna in Crete are named. Along the coasts of Ionia and the Hellespont one discovers only the names of the Carians, the small town of Myndos, the great island of Samos and Lampsacus.

Delos could not be left out. This was already the Roman commercial center in the East. Besides, excavations have revealed the presence of a synagogue used during the second and first centuries before Christ. In Greece Sicyones appears : Corinth had just been destroyed and it can be supposed that the Jewish colony of this important commercial center emigrated there. Why Sparta? Elsewhere, there are indications of the strange relations between Jerusalem and the city of Lycurgus. These relations go back to King Arius who served as *condottiere* to Ptolemy Philadelphus (around 276) and had a Greek village in Palestine named after him. The name of Sparta in the Roman document must be explained by these friendly relations (cf. 1 Mc 14, 20-23) because the presence of a Jewish colony at Sparta would be surprising.

In this time, there has not yet been found any trace of the presence of Jews at Pozzuoli, the port of arrival for the Orientals into Italy, nor at Rome itself.

The Romans knew the Jews still better from the moment the kingdom of Pergamum became a Roman province (129). The governors were then called upon more than once to play the role of arbiters between the Greek cities and the Jewish colonists. The Jews tended to seek citizenship while maintaining their special status, and this provoked conflicts, in regard to the observance of the Sabbath, for example. In the documents which we possess we see the Roman magistrate regularly declare himself in favor of the Jews. It is true that these documents come from a brief made up by Nicholas of Damascus, the friend of King Herod (B.C. 37-4), in preparation for a defense of the Jews. Thus, it is highly tendentious and Nicholas could have omitted the less favorable documents. Those which he did show us are sufficient to prove that there was no systematic ill will on the part of the Romans towards the Jews, quite the contrary.

As for Mithridates, it is only known that in the course of his first expedition into Asia Minor (88), he confiscated the 8,000 (?) talents deposited by the Jews at Cos. It is thus not very probable that the Jews would have been hostile to the Romans in their wars against Mithridates. Until the period at which we have arrived, moreover, they never had any reason to be. In the fragments of the *Sybilline Oracles* which bear the Jewish stamp and which circulated at about this time in the East, one sees no trace of Romanophobia. But this frame of mind is going to change after the passing of Pompey.

§ 4. The Taking of Jerusalem by Pompey

Called urgently into Asia, Pompey began by forcing Mithridates (of Pontus) to take refuge in his Crimean states where he died. Next, he compelled Tigranes to surrender. He himself then went into Syria, turned aside the last Seleucid claimants and made the country a Roman province.

But while he was residing at Damascus, he was asked by the Jews to arbitrate a quarrel between Hyrcanus II, whom the Pharisees supported, and Aristobulus who was backed by the Sadducees. Engaged in an expedition against the Nabateans, Pompey hesitated, though leaning toward Hyrcanus. Aristobulus did not submit and tried to resist. Pompey finally made him a prisoner : his partisans entrenched first in Jerusalem and then in the Temple. The daily service in the besieged Temple continued for three months. Finally the Temple fell; there was the massacre of the priests, killed near the altar, then defiling of the Holy of Holies by Pompey and the conditions for peace which he imposed threw the Jews back into the opposition to Rome, even though Hyrcanus,

Pompey's candidate, certainly enjoyed the sympathy of the majority. This was in 63 when Cicero was consul.

Installed by Pompey, Hyrcanus thus remained ethnarch and high priest, but he had to accept an onerous treaty which imposed a tribute on the country, cut this off from the coastal cities and those of Transjordania and made him a tool of the Roman governor of Syria. After the triumphal hopes at the beginning of the century, it was subjugation once again.

The great majority of Jews were now subjects of the Roman Empire. Only the ghettos of Babylonia and Iran remained in Parthian territory, since the two empires had tacitly recognized the Euphrates as their common frontier. Nevertheless, the Eastern *Diaspora* continued to play an important role in Judaism. For example, it was in contact with the Magi who had regained under the Arsacids nearly the same status which was theirs under the Achaemenids. As for Palestine, a kind of more or less autonomous province, it was in wholly new conditions. These are examined in our *Introduction to the New Testament*.

PART I

THE TORAH (PENTATEUCH)

by H. Cazelles

Introductions, translations, commentaries, pp. 1 f.

A. T. CHAPMAN, " An Introduction to the Pentateuch, " *CBSC* (Cambridge, 1911).

J. COPPENS, *L'histoire critique des livres de l'Ancien Testament*[3]* (Paris-Bruges, 1942) (Eng. trans. : *The Old Testament and the Critics*, Paterson, N. J., 1942).

S. H. HOOKE, *In the Beginning* (Oxford : Clarendon, 1947).

H. ROWLEY, *The Biblical Doctrine of Election* (London, 1950).

J. VAN DER PLOEG, " Studies in Hebrew Law, " *CBQ*, 12 (1950), pp. 248-249, 416-427; 13 (1951), pp. 28-43, 164-171, 296-307.

R. DE VAUX, *La Genèse, Introduction Générale au Pentateuque** (Paris, 1951).

J. RYLAARSDAM, " The Book of Exodus, " *IB* (1952).

C. A. SIMPSON, " The Book of Genesis, " *IB* (1952).

A. CLAMER, *La Genèse, le Pentateuque, Introduction Générale** (Paris, 1953).

J. MARSH, " The Book of Numbers, " *IB* (1953).

N. MICKLEM, " The Book of Leviticus, " *IB* (1953).

G. E. WRIGHT, " The Book of Deuteronomy, " *IB* (1953); " Recent European Study of the Pentateuch, " *JBR*, 18 (1950), pp. 216-229.

I. LEWY, *The Growth of the Pentateuch* (1955).

G. E. MENDENHALL, *Law and Covenant in the Ancient Near East* (Philadelphia : Biblical Colloquium, 1955).

P. KAHLE, " Untersuchungen zur Geschichte des Pentateuchtextes, " *Opera Minora* (Leyden, 1956), pp. 3-38.

J. L. MCKENZIE, *The Two-Edged Sword** (Milwaukee, 1956), pp. 72-131.

B. VAWTER, *A Path Through Genesis** (New York, 1956).

E. VOEGLIN, *Israel and Revelation* (Baton Rouge : Louisiana State Univ., 1956).

R. MURPHY, " Moses and the Pentateuch, " *CBQ*, 21 (1959), pp. 165-178.

C. R. NORTH, " Pentateuchal Criticism, " *OTMS*, pp. 48-83.

H. CASSUTO, *The Documentary Hypothesis and the Composition of the Pentateuch* (1961).

G. VON RAD, *Genesis, A Commentary* (Philadelphia : Westminster, 1961).

M. NOTH, *Exodus, A Commentary* (Philadelphia : Westminster, 1962); *Leviticus, A Commentary* (Philadelphia : Westminster, 1962).

D. J. MCCARTHY, *Treaty and Covenant** (Rome : Pontifical Biblical Institute, 1963).

H. GUNKEL, *The Legends of Genesis* (New York : Schocken, 1964).

H. RENCKENS, *Israel's Concept of the Beginning** (New York : Herder and Herder, 1964).

E. A. SPEISER, *Genesis* (Garden City, N.Y. : Doubleday, 1964).

J. DE FRAINE, *The Bible and the Origin of Man** (New York : Desclée, 1961); *Adam and the Family of Man** (New York : Alba, 1965).

I. THE FIVE BOOKS

The Old Testament begins with a collection of five books which the Greeks entitled Pentateuch (*penta* = " five, " *teuche* = " instrument, " hence " sheath, " for a papyrus scroll, [1] and finally, " books "). The Jews spoke of the Torah, or Law, and each of the books was a " fifth " of the Law, indicated merely by the first words : 1) *Bereshit*, 2) *We'elleh shemot*, 3) *Wayyiqra*, 4) *Wayyedabber* or *Bammidbar*, 5) *'Elleh haddebarim*. It is the Greeks who gave the titles that express something of the content, and the moderns, following the Latin, have merely adopted the Greek term. The first book, *Genesis*, describes the origins of the world, the human race, and the people of God. The second, *Exodus*, treats of the journey from Egypt. *Leviticus* contains the ritual ceremonies. It is followed by *Numbers*, which owes its name to the census lists found in it. Finally, *Deuteronomy* presents a " second " *(deuteros)* law, because at first sight the laws given by Moses in the fields of Moab seem to complement the legislation given at Sinai; such was the interpretation of Dt 17, 18 by the Greek translator. [2]

These books have a certain inner unity — the thread of events extending from the creation of the world to the death of Moses. Even some dates correspond in various books, showing a chronological scheme (Ex 40, 17 and Nm 1, 1). Since the Book of Josue seems to continue the description of events after the death of Moses (which is explicitly mentioned in 1, 1), it may be asked whether it should not be included with the preceding books, so that one should speak of a Hexateuch rather than a Pentateuch. Many critics favor this view, which was already held in the 17th century (Bonfrère, Spinoza). On the other hand, some recent critics (Nyberg, Noth) want to exclude Deuteronomy on the grounds that it forms an introduction to the large historical work that goes from Moses to the Exile (the so-called Deuteronomic history); then we would have a Tetrateuch. Both these views take their orientation from certain literary aspects of the whole, rather than from the considerable legal material which older tradition considered so important.

II. OBJECT

These books have been considered as the Law of Israel because they contain most of the biblical legislation. The only other laws are in a few verses of Josue (20, 4-6, an application of Nm 35, 9 ff.), and the plan

---

[1] So already in the letter of Aristeas to Philocratus (310) in the 3rd or 2nd century B.C.

[2] The text refers properly to a copy of the Law.

laid down in Ezechiel 40—48. As the Law of the people chosen by the true God, the Pentateuch was recognized as binding and hence *canonical* by both Jews and Samaritans. When the grandson of Ben Sira wrote the prologue to his translation of Ecclesiasticus towards 130 B.C., he made a distinction between the *Torah*, the *Prophets*, and the other *Writings*. The so-called Septuagint translation comprised strictly the Pentateuch alone. [3] The same division is found in the New Testament : St. Matthew and St. Luke distinguish between the *Law* and the *Prophets* (Mt 5, 17; Lk 16, 16). The Law is what was given to Moses (Lk 24, 44), as St. John also recognizes (1, 17.45; 7, 19, etc.). Finally, post-biblical Judaism also recognizes the unique position of the five books of the Torah.

As the Law of the Chosen People, these books were set apart, and their exceptional religious value duly acknowledged. Because a law determines the structure, the social habits, of a people, the Torah is the basis of Israel's life. The principal purpose of the Pentateuch is thus to provide us with the constitution of the people of God; but at the same time it situates this people among its neighbors and reveals the manner in which God chose them.

We are going to stress the new problems which call for a new terminology — the " serious problems " of which the encyclical *Divino Afflante* (§ 41) speaks. Then, by way of conclusion, we will present the main doctrinal points of the Pentateuch, which had already been emphasized in the writings of the Fathers of the Church, such as the creation of the world by the one God, freedom from the power of sin, the call to the Promised Land, etc.

---

[3] Cf. the letter of Aristeas; P. KAHLE, *The Cairo Geniza* (London, 1947), p. 157; H. B. SWETE, *Introduction to the Old Testament in Greek* (Cambridge, 1914), p. 23.

CHAPTER I

THE PENTATEUCH
FROM A LITERARY POINT OF VIEW

BIBLIOGRAPHY

See the introductions cited on p. 1 and p. 67 (R. DE VAUX,
A. CLAMER, O. EISSFELDT, A. BENTZEN...).

E. MANGENOT, *L'Authenticité mosaïque du Pentateuque** (Paris, 1907).

J. BREWER, *The Literature of the Old Testament in its Historical
Development* (New York : Columbia, 1933).

D. B. MCDONALD, *The Hebrew Literary Genius* (1933).

M. J. LAGRANGE, " L'Authenticité mosaïque de la Genèse et la théorie
des documents* " *RB* (1938), pp. 163-183.

W. O. E. OESTERLEY, *Ancient Hebrew Poems* (1938).

J. CHAINE, *La Genèse** (Paris, 1948).

L. MORALDI, " In Principio, " *Secoli sul Mundo** (Turin, 1955), pp. 23-42.

J. L. MCKENZIE, " Literary Characteristics of Gen. 2-3, "* *TS*, 15
(1954), pp. 541-572; " Myth and the Old Testament, " *CBQ*, 21 (1959),
pp. 265-282.

B. CHILDS, *Myth and Reality in the Old Testament* (London : SCM, 1960).

S. MOWINCKEL, " Literature, " *IDB*, III, pp. 139-143.

Because the Pentateuch is primarily the *Law* of Israel, it would be a
mistake to approach it as though it were first a *History*. One is dissuaded
from such an approach by the uneven and episodic character of the
narrative, by the many omissions that are in surprising contrast to the
repetitions. But if the Pentateuch is primarily a Law, we must also
recognize that this law is presented in a very special manner. The
legislation is persistently interrupted by historical narratives, and does
not reach any appreciable size until the middle of the Book of Exodus
(chap. 20). The narratives dealing with prehistory, the Patriarchs and
Moses are a sort of introduction to the Mosaic law. There is nothing
like this in the modern or ancient oriental codes. At the most the modern
codes may be preceded by the motives on which the legislation is based.
Among the various ancient codes discovered since 1901, [1] there is a varied
pattern. The articles of law are simply stated without preamble or

[1] J. LEROY, *Introduction à l'étude des anciens codes orientaux** (Paris, 1944).

conclusion in the Assyrian laws (18th-15th centuries B.C.), in the nearly
contemporary Hittite laws, and in the Neo-Babylonian laws of the
6th century B.C. But the law of Eshnunna is preceded by a short
statement which gives its date (18th century); the code of Lipit-Ishtar
(about the 19th century) has a prologue; the code of Hammurabi (18th-
17th centuries) has both a prologue and epilogue. [2]

The epilogue to the code of Hammurabi contains blessings and curses
that are analogous to those at the end of Deuteronomy (chaps. 28 and 29;
cf. 27 and 33). The prologues of the codes of Lipit-Ishtar and Hammurabi
record how these men were chosen by the god, and some of their great
deeds are mentioned. But the Pentateuch is not satisfied with anything
like this; the historical background is constantly cutting across the
legislation. The *mixture of historical narrative and legal material* is its
most characteristic feature, and it calls attention to the vast designs
of Providence in which the gift of the Law to Israel plays but a small
part : God did far more than choose Moses as a lawgiver — He chose
a people whom He is constantly pursuing. The laws, then, fit into a
historical framework that cannot be systematized; rather, this framework
is Providence as the various traditions of the people remembered it, the
signature God appended to the Law by which He would govern and
vivify His people (Dt 7, 12 ff.).

This mixture of history and law is not the only characteristic of the
literary structure of the Pentateuch. A more detailed analysis which
penetrates beneath the obvious fivefold division reveals another plan,
much more real, which clearly portrays the profound meaning of the
whole; but before such a synthesis is reached, we must analyze the work
further.

§ 1. Lack of Continuity in the Narrative

Even when a narrative is not interrupted by a legal clause, it may lack
a harmonious continuity of events such as we find, for example, in the
story of the succession to the throne of David (2 Sm 13—20). One story
may succeed another without any connecting link, or, on the other hand,
a story may begin abruptly without the introduction or context that
would render it intelligible to the reader. For example, the creation
story is finished at Gn 2, 4a, only to have the creation of heaven and
earth repeat itself. In 2, 4b the reader finds himself back at a time

---

[2] See the texts in *ANET* and *AOAT*; G. R. DRIVER and S. C. MILES, *The
Babylonian Laws*, 2 Vols. (Oxford, 1952-1955); *The Assyrian Laws* (Oxford, 1955).

when the earth is empty and uncultivated; for a second time, but from a different point of view, he learns of the creation of man, animals, and the fruits of the earth. Passing on to 4, 26, we learn that Adam had a son, Seth, and that mankind then began to call upon the name of Yahweh. But suddenly, in 5, 1, the story of Adam is taken up again *ab ovo*, the birth of Seth is mentioned a second time a few verses later, and the name of Yahweh does not occur until 5, 29.

There are still more examples. In 7, 7 we learn that Noe entered the ark with his children and the animals, and the flood began; but in 7, 10 the narrative is interrupted by another mention of the flood's beginning, and the text continues with Noe and his sons entering the ark, as if this had not been stated before. Chapter 20 begins, " Abraham journeyed from there..., " but the preceding verses do not even mention Abraham. In Ex 19, 25 it is said that " Moses went down to the people and said to them.... " But the next verse, instead of giving us his words, begins *ex abrupto :* " Then God spoke all these words. " This verse introduces the Decalogue, but without any continuity with the immediate context.

§ 2. Interruptions and Logical Units

It would be a mistake, however, to think that the Pentateuch is just a series of disconnected episodes. Although the course of the narrative may suddenly disappear, it will reappear later on without any real break between the last verse that seemed to be left hanging and the verse that begins a new section. Thus Gn 26, 35 records that the Hittite wives of Esau were a source of bitterness to Isaac and Rebecca; in chapter 27 there is no further mention of this : Isaac does not hold it against Esau and Rebecca does not use it to justify her trickery. But finally in 27, 46 the theme of the Hittite wives reappears and introduces another version to explain why Jacob journeyed to Haran.

The same literary phenomenon can be seen in the story of the flood. One version mentions the wickedness of mankind, but " Noe found favor with the Lord " (Gn 6, 8). This version stops and a new " story of Noe " begins in verse 9, which mentions again the corruption of mankind and the divine command to build the ark. But the first version takes up again at 7, 1, with a new command to Noe to enter the ark with seven pairs of clean animals and one pair of unclean. It continues (after an interruption in v. 6) in vv. 7-10 with Noe carrying out the order of God. To it also belongs the note in v. 12 about the forty-day

duration, but it is not until v. 16 that the same version picks up again
with Noe's entry in the ark and the shutting of the door. As the waters
increase, the ark is borne up (v. 17), and all creatures outside the ark
die (vv. 22-23). The story takes up again in 8, 2b-3a with the end
of the rain and the recession of the waters (one should notice that 7, 18-21
and 8, 3b-5 are doublets that encumber the narrative). At the end
of forty days, Noe releases the raven and then the dove (8, 6-12). If we
skip 8, 13a and 8, 14-19, we obtain the right sequence again : the earth
is dry and Noe offers a sacrifice in thanksgiving.

This unevenness is found also in other books. Ex 4, 19 is the logical
sequel to 2, 23a concerning the death of Pharao. In fact, Ex 2, 23b
and the following verses do not mesh with 23a, any more than 4, 1-18
(the vision at Horeb) prepares for the new oracle of Yahweh in 4, 19.
The commands given by God are carried out in Ex 28—39, but there
is an interruption in 39, 32 ff. without any warning to the reader, and
the divine commands take up again in Lv 8, 1. Moses' dealings with
Dathan and Abiram and his appeal to Yahweh in Numbers 16, 12-15
have their logical sequel in vv. 25 ff. (not in vv. 16-24 which describe
the revolt of Core). In Dt 31, 16-22 there is question of a song that
is witness against Israel, and this connects well with vv. 8 and 14, but
not with vv. 9 ff., which prepare for v. 26, where it is now the Law that
is witness against Israel.

If literary criticism is done sensitively, it allows us to restore a neat
sequence, finished and well articulated, in contrast to the present state
of the text which does not satisfy all the demands of art and psychology.
Later we shall see that the present state of the text has a profound
justification, but with its unevenness it is much less intelligible than
what literary criticism achieves : clarity, as can be seen in such stories
as the flood versions (one of which we have just analyzed).

In addition to this, criticism also allows us to group together stories
that belong in the same sequence or schema. We have already noted
the story that begins, " This is the story (Hebrew : *toledot* i.e., generation)
of Noe " (Gn 6, 9). We have a similar reference to generation for the
creation of heaven and earth (Gn 2, 4a), for Adam (5, 1), Noe (6, 9),
Sem (11, 10), Thare (11, 27), Ismael (25, 12), Isaac (25, 19), Esau (36, 1),
Jacob (37, 2), Aaron and Moses (Nm 3, 1). We have here a historical
framework in terms of generations, which presents in abbreviated form
the development of mankind.

But the stories can be unified, even without a formal framework,
by the *thread* of events, or by the evolution of the life of a hero. Thus
we have a complete cycle of the life of Abraham : his wanderings (chap. 12),

his parting from Lot (chap. 13), the Covenant with God (chap. 15), the birth of Ishmael (chap. 16), Abraham's intercession in Lot's favor and the promise of Isaac's birth, (chaps. 18—19). When the infant is born (21, 1 ff.), Abraham does not hold him back from God (22, 14-18); before he dies, he sends his servant to look for a wife in his family home (chap. 24). Sometimes a central *theme*, instead of a person, gives unity to the stories. The events of Genesis chaps. 2—4 are grouped around the theme of sin : sin which appears at the beginning of human history and which evolves as mankind evolves. The same idea reappears in one of the flood versions (chaps. 6—9) and is further developed in the story of Noe's children (9, 18-29) and the tower of Babel (11, 1-9). All this is by way of an introduction to the salvation to be wrought through Abraham and his seed. Thus careful study allows us to pick up the guidelines which reveal coherent units at various points.

§ 3. Repetitions and Doublets

This unevenness, along with the units that appear, gives rise to repetitions. Certain repetitions can be explained by the Semitic parallelism in which two lines, whose parts correspond to each other, express but one idea. But usually this is not the case; rather, the same event is told with details and expressions which do not correspond in the two versions. These repetitions, in narrative or in law, are called *doublets*. Thus there are two stories of creation (Gn 1, 1—2, 4a; 2, 4b ff.); two genealogies of Adam's descendants (chaps. 4—5); this is all the more striking in that the majority of the names are found in both lists. This kind of repetition allows one to separate the two stories of the flood (note that Noe enters the ark twice, 7, 7.13). Twice Abraham sends Agar away (Gn 16 and 21); twice the vocation of Moses is described (Ex 3 and 6). The miracle of the quail and the manna (Ex 16) is described again in Nm 11, as if it had not been told before. Sometimes the same theme is treated three times : the abduction of the wife of a patriarch. In Gn 12, 20 and 26 she is taken by a prince and then returned after God intervenes; this happens to both Abraham and Isaac, though there are some differences in the details.

The doublets are even more obvious in the legal narratives. The Decalogue is given twice (Ex 20 and Dt 5), as is also the law for slaves (Ex 21 and Dt 15); murder is treated three times (Ex 21, Dt 19, Nm 35); the list of feasts, five times (Ex 23, 14 ff.; 34, 18 ff.; Dt 16, 1 ff.; Lv 23, 4 ff.; Nm 28 and 29), and there is evidence of at least five rulings on the tithes

(Lv 27, 30 ff.; Nm 28, 21 ff.; Nm 28, 26-32; Dt 14 and 26). More examples could be found in the legislation concerning the Passover, loans, the Sabbath, etc. Sometimes the laws are almost identical, but ordinarily each has its own point of view and supposes its own economic, social and religious conditions. Thus, the law of the sabbatical year applies only to agricultural products in Ex 23, 10 ff., but in Dt 15, 1 ff. it is referred also to the relaxation of debts.

§ 4. Vocabulary and Style

These stories, cycles, and parallel laws are further characterized by different styles and vocabulary. This fact was pointed out first of all with respect to the divine name. It is noteworthy that in one of the versions of Agar's expulsion, God is called Yahweh (Gn 16), but in the other, Elohim (21, 9 ff.). In the Joseph story one group of texts uses the term Yahweh (39, 3.23) and the other, Elohim (40 and 41); the same holds also for the versions of the flood. Finally, the first creation story speaks of Elohim, and the other, of both Yahweh-Elohim and then Elohim alone (cf. chap. 4, the story of Cain and Abel, which follows upon the creation narrative). Hence it is customary to speak of the Elohist and the Yahwist.

Of itself this criterion of the divine names would not suffice to establish literary strata within the Pentateuch. [3] First of all, the manuscript tradition is not completely certain, and the LXX translators seem to have worked with a text in which the names were treated differently. But neither can one deny that redactors tended to harmonize the names by their grouping of the texts. Finally, beginning with Exodus 3, in which God reveals His name Yahweh, all the narratives tend to use this name. But the fact remains that we have here a sign of an unusual vocabulary.

And this is merely one sign among many. The desert mountain where God revealed Himself — identified simply as Sinai (Ex 3, 12) — is called Horeb in Deuteronomy and in such texts as Ex 3, 1; 17, 6; 33, 6, but in another group of texts, Sinai. Moses' father-in-law is called Raguel in Ex 2, 18, but Jethro in Ex 3, 1; 18, 1. There is also a corresponding variation in the use of ordinary words. Thus, there is a group of Elohist texts with a very special vocabulary proper to itself : *mishkan* indicates the sanctuary tent; *miqdash* the sanctuary itself; *qorban*, the sacrifices; *'edah*, the congregation of Israel. With one or two exceptions, only

---

[3] A. BEA, *De Pentateucho*＊ (Rome, 1933).

here mention is made of " holocausts, " " anointing, " or " purification " — all cultic terms; hence these texts have been attributed to the " priestly writings. " Other examples can be mentioned, such as the word for maid-servant, which is *'amah* in one group of texts, but *shiphehah* in another. A word that has a general meaning in certain chapters can have a precise, even technical, meaning in others : *minhah,* which has often the general meaning of " gift, present " is used in the priestly writings to indicate a special category of gifts, the vegetable offerings for God.

Deuteronomy also has its own special vocabulary, certain favorite phrases. There is frequent mention of " holding fast to " God, who is called " Yahweh, your Elohim, " or simply, " your Elohim. " Certain expressions occur on almost every page : " Do what is right in the sight of the Lord "; " purge the evil from the midst of "; " observe the commandments, " etc. But it is the style, more than the vocabulary, which stamps Deuteronomy with an original literary flavor : an oratorical style, majestic and, for a language that lacks subordinating particles, remarkably full.

On the other hand, the style of the priestly writings is dry and precise. Not only are technical terms and numbers preferred, but there is a tendency to schematize and make use of short refrains : " God saw that it was good "; " and there was evening and morning. " All the genealogies of Genesis 5 are built on the same schema : " X lived so many years and he begot Y. After the birth of Y, X lived so many years and begot sons and daughters. The whole lifetime of X was so many years; then he died. " The articles of the law are regularly introduced by : " God spoke to Moses, saying " or " God spoke to Moses and Aaron, saying. "

But a third type of narrative is noteworthy for its lack of monotony and stiffness. This would be exemplified in the Abraham cycle referred to above; here words are evocative and dialogues frequent — words and deeds are used to paint a picture. Each scene is a unit, thanks to the development within it, but without any use of refrains or stereotyped formulas. The two scenes in Gn 18—19 bear this out. In one, Abraham and Sara play host to the three unknown men, and at the end the birth of Isaac is proclaimed. In the other, Sodom plays host to the angels, and here the memory of Lot is not unsullied, owing to the origins of the Ammonites and Moabites from him. These two scenes are, as it were, two sides of a dyptich, bound together by the great prayer of Abraham (18, 23 ff.). Here we reach the heart of the author's method of composition, his finesse, his depth. He can suggest the presence of God just as well as he can jab at Israel's neighbors.

These narratives are formed from scenes that follow upon one another, but with some unity between each of them. In all one finds Yahwist and Elohist writings, but the interruptions, doublets and other signs enable us to distinguish two strata. Despite a similarity in vocabulary and manner of presentation, each one has its own peculiar literary texture. The Yahwist stands out more than the Elohist, because of its fresh and vivid manner. The differences between the two are more basic than merely questions of form. The Elohist is more moral, less psychological, portraying the action of God in a more spiritual and less anthropomorphic manner. Thus, it is by dreams that God reveals Himself; this is an echo of a mentality quite different from the Yahwistic. We have already indicated the literary characteristics of the Deuteronomic and the priestly writings; these too have their own peculiar outlook and theology.

Thus there are four strands distinguished in the Pentateuch : Yahwist (J), Elohist (E), Deuteronomist (D) and Priestly (P). Obviously this distinction of sources is not to be proved by clear and indisputable arguments; the many different solutions proposed by the experts testify to this. Literary criticism is not a mechanical thing, and it derives but little support from word lists. Rather, it calls for a wide knowledge of the times, the milieu and religious data. But however vague our knowledge, we know that we are not dealing with a literary deformity or a shapeless mass, and we realize that there still remains room for discussion.

How many questions have to be answered before we truly understand the Pentateuch!

Are these four strands to be taken as four primitive documents which were collected and worked together into our present Pentateuch? Are there more strands, or less? For what reason and under what circumstances was the present text, with all its unevenness and discontinuity and editorial patching, put together? It was and remains the task of criticism to offer an explanation for the various literary characteristics we have just pointed out. So we shall now turn to a history of criticism and a description of the current theories.

CHAPTER II

THE WORK OF HIGHER CRITICISM

BIBLIOGRAPHY

J. E. CARPENTER — G. HARFORD-BALLERSBY, *The Hexateuch According to the Revised Version* (London, 1900).

M. J. LAGRANGE, *Historical Criticism and the Old Testament** (London, 1906).

C. R. NORTH, " Pentateuchal Criticism, " *OTMS*, pp. 48-83.

J. TOUZARD, " Moïse et Josué, " *Dictionnaire Apologétique de la Foi Catholique*, III (Paris, 1921), cols. 695-860 (censor's text, 1926 ed., col. 860).

C. A. SIMPSON, *Pentateuchal Criticism* (London : Oxford, 1924).

J. PEDERSEN, *Israel : Its Life and Culture* (London : Oxford, 1940).

E. ROBERTSON, " The Pentateuchal Problem : Some New Aspects, " *BJRL*, 29 (1945), pp. 121-142.

J. BONSIRVEN — G. BARDY — M. JUGIE — C. SPICQ — A. ROBERT, " Histoire de l'Interprétation, " *SDB*, IV (1946), cols. 561-637.

H. HÖPFL, " Critique Biblique, " *SDB*, II (1946), cols. 175-240.

A. LODS, *Histoire de la littérature hébraïque et juive* (Paris, 1950), pp. 83-185 with bibliography.

S. R. DRIVER, *Introduction to the Literature of the Old Testament* (New York : Meridian, 1956).

D. N. FREEDMAN, " Pentateuch, " *IDB*, III, pp. 711-727.

H. J. KRAUS, *Geschichte der Historisch-Kritischen Erforschung des Alten Testaments* (Neukirchen, 1956) (a good knowledge of Protestant works).

§ 1. From Christian Antiquity to the Eighteenth Century

While the Fathers employed the Scriptures for spiritual and moral ends, they were also aware of what truly critical work meant : the text had to be established, and its meaning determined by reason. Tertullian, an ardent polemicist, sought to show against Marcion what was the true meaning of Jacob's vision by the use of several biblical texts (Gn 28; cf. *Adv. Marc.* 3, 24). When Eusebius of Caesarea wrote about the creation story and the Mosaic law in his *Praeparatio evangelica*, he

compared the biblical text with the Phoenician cosmogonies. Finally,
Jerome, a Hebrew scholar, put philology to serious use in order to arrive
at the literal sense *(Liber hebraicarum quaestionum in Genesim)*. [1] The
foundations of biblical criticism were already laid by the Fathers. But
in their time there was not enough knowledge of the history or the
philology of the Semites to enable them to build on this foundation.
Moreover, the problems they met were of a different kind. Like Christ
Himself, who made no effort to master the history of Old Testament
literature, the Church simply took over from the Synagogue the Bible
and the traditional story of how it came to be. And this was quite
explicit : according to Josephus *(Againt Apion* 1, 39) Moses wrote the
five books of the Pentateuch with the events it contains and the Prophets
wrote the later history; but Moses himself wrote about his own death
(Antiquities IV, 8, 48; cf. Philo, *Vita Mosis* II, 51)! Any deviation
from this point of view could only be considered as infidelity to tradition. [2]
There was just no real foundation for carrying out literary and historical
criticism, and spiritual and theological exegesis prevailed. The Fathers
will give very diverse explanations of the first chapters of Genesis, but
none of them will have any difficulty in admitting the universality of the
Deluge.

In the Middle Ages Christians were no longer arguing against pagans
and their depreciation of Jewish traditions. But they were no better
equipped than the Fathers to practice what we would call scientific
criticism. By virtue of the dictum, " *Nihil est in divina Scriptura quod
non pertinet ad Ecclesiam,* " the main preoccupation was to search out
biblical allusions to the Church, thanks to allegorism. But the twelfth
century turned more to reason, and so to a more literal explanation,
as exemplified by Pseudo-Thomas in his exegesis of the temptation in
Paradise. All this did not take place without some blunders. But the
need for philology as a basis of discussion made itself felt, and certain
scholars, as Andrew of Saint Victor, learned Hebrew. Obviously better
trained than Andrew were the Jews, such as Ibn Ezra or David Kimchi,
or the converted Jew, Jude Hermann. Saadia, in the Egypt of the
tenth century, and Rashi, who died at Troyes in 1105, knew how to
appreciate words and analyze texts. Ibn Ezra of Toledo, in his
commentary on the Pentateuch (1152-1153) seems to have been the
first to catch a glimpse of the problems of Pentateuchal literary criticism.

[1] MIGNE, *PL* 23, pp. 936-1010.

[2] However, the position of the Fathers was nuanced; St. Jerome wrote : *sive
Moysen dicere volueris auctorem Pentateuchi, sive Ezram ejusdem instauratorem
operis, non recuso.* " Cf. MIGNE, *PL* 23, p. 190.

To him we owe the enigmatic words : " You will have the real meaning only when you understand : the secret of the twelve, Moses wrote the Law; then the Chanaanites were in the Land; provision will be made on the mountain of the Lord; His bed was a bed of iron. " For Spinoza and Adolphe Lods these words point up some essential difficulties urged against the traditional Mosaic authorship. Thus, the Pentateuch was too big to be written on the twelve stones of Dt 27, 2-7 (cf. Jos 8, 35); Moses could not have spoken about the Chanaanites in the past tense, since they were still in Palestine in the period of the Judges, long after his death. The mountain of the Lord (Gn 22, 14) seems to refer to the Jerusalem Temple which was not built until the time of Solomon. The tradition about the iron bed of Og, king of Bashan, could hardly originate with Moses who was his contemporary. Tostatus, bishop of Avila in the 15th century, admits that this last passage, like the story of Moses' death, could not have been written by Moses. The movement of biblical criticism had begun.

From the point of view of Pentateuchal criticism, the 16th and 17th centuries witnessed great confusion : dogmatism, radical criticism (like that of Carlstadt), wild hypotheses — it was hard to find the right approach to the problem. In a posthumous work, Masius, a Belgian Catholic, was of the opinion that the five books were to be attributed to Esdras, or someone like him, who would have substituted new names for the old ones. Cornelius a Lapide, S.J. (1637) restricted the role of Moses to notes that would have been compiled and completed by Josue. His confrères, B. Pereira (1589) and J. Bonfrère (1625), admitted that the Pentateuch had been subjected to revision and interpolations.

Gradually a more objective approach evolved; a distinction was made between literary criticism and Mosaic authenticity. T. Hobbes (1651) sought indications of the dating within the work itself. I. de la Peyrère (1655) thought that the lacunae, transpositions, disorders and detailed divergences ruled out one man as the author of the Pentateuch. In 1670 Spinoza stressed the doublets, and ascribed to Moses only what was expressly attributed to him. The Oratorian, R. Simon (1678), arguing from the repetitions, the logical and chronological discontinuity and the stylistic variations, concluded that the work was made up of several sources older than Moses, or else of later annals. J. Leclerc, the Protestant theologian (1685), approached the problem from the point of view of the historical background presupposed by individual sections; since both Samaritans and Jews accepted the Pentateuch, it must have been written before the schism (4th century?). Voltaire had some interesting suggestions (e.g., the date of Deuteronomy), and he

recognized the contribution the prophetic books made to the study
of the Pentateuch, but he was naturally inclined to very negative views.
He failed to recognize clear associations between the Law and the
Prophets, and he made some errors which even a friendly critic
(P. Sackmann) termed " comical. "

§ 2.   Literary Criticism from Astruc to Wellhausen

After all this groping, the objective bases for history began to appear
in the 18th century.   The best scholars now turned from hasty syntheses
to " the thankless task of editing text, deciphering documents, scraping
stones and cleaning coins " (P. Hazard).   By the end of the century
Semitic epigraphy would begin.   Inspired by historical methodology,
the Protestant Witter (1711) and the Catholic (a convert from Protes-
tantism) Astruc (1753) were occupied with the less sensational elements
in the Pentateuchal text : examining the words themselves in an effort
to resolve literary and historical problems.   The former compared the
creation and paradise narratives and pointed out the differences in the
style and in the divine names, and the repetitions.   Astruc continued
the study of the use of the divine names throughout Genesis and the
first chapters of Exodus.   He showed that the variation in the divine
names was to be explained by the hypothesis of parallel stories; thus
the documentary hypothesis was born.   Eichhorn gave it a wide
circulation, and made his own contribution, determining the literary
characteristic of each of the flood narratives, and working his study
through the Book of Leviticus.   Astruc and Eichhorn (1781) admitted
some other sources (e.g., Gn 14) besides the Yahwist and Elohist
documents.   Ilgen was the first (1798) to distinguish two sources within
the Elohist; thus there was the Yahwist (J), a first Elohist (E^1, later
to be called P) and a second Elohist (E^2, later to be called E).   At the
time Ilgen's observation received no support, and this first form of the
documentary hypothesis was to be supplanted by other theories.

All these authors had to recognize certain independent sources,
as well as basic differences within the chief documents.   Thus their
successors were unwilling to admit the existence of large units, and
Geddes (1792), Vater (1802-1805) and de Wette (1805-1807) advocated
a new approach : the *fragment hypothesis*, according to which the
Pentateuch was a compilation of various pieces.   But in 1840 de Wette
went over to the *hypothesis of complements*, advocated by Kelle (1812)
and especially by Ewald (1823).   The latter had been impressed by the

basic unity that had been recognized in the Pentateuch. In his *Komposition der Genesis* he sought to harmonize this unity in diversity : a basic source *(Grundschrift)* (identified as the Elohist) would have been *complemented* by the addition of texts different both in form and extent. But neither Ewald nor de Wette (1806) supported Ilgen's distinction between the two Elohists, and their basic source itself lacked unity. Besides, the striking unity of the Yahwist writing was reduced, in their hypothesis, to mere complements which were added to bring older texts up to date.

Although H. Hupfeld in 1853 still retained the idea of the basic source, he actually reintroduced the *documentary* theory. He wrote several articles on the sources of Genesis and the manner in which they were put together. The basic source was for him the first Elohist (later to be called the priestly code); it was the oldest, and it held together the different parts of the Pentateuch, from the creation narrative to the settlement of the Hebrews in Chanaan. Then came an independent work, the Yahwist, which covered the same period, but in a very different style. Mixed in with the Yahwist was a second Elohist, not very well preserved, but much closer to the Yahwist in language and ideas than to the first Elohist. Genesis is the combination of the first Elohist with this Yahwist-Elohist mixture.

The whole Pentateuch was accounted for, once Deuteronomy was added. From 1854 on, Riehm adopted this view, utilizing the arguments of de Wette on the relationship of Deuteronomy to the reform of Josias (4 Kgs 22—23). T. Nöldeke added the book of Josue and then there was the Hexateuch! From the point of view of literary criticism, the documentary theory seemed firmly entrenched. There were *four documents* in the Pentateuch or Hexateuch : the three indicated in Genesis by Ilgen and Hupfeld, and Deuteronomy.

But the dating of these documents remained a problem. De Wette had proposed a date for Deuteronomy, but what was to be done with the other sources? Was Hupfeld right in dating the basic source before the Yahwist and the Elohist? In 1835 a new factor appeared which was to influence greatly Pentateuchal criticism. In a study of the laws and feasts George pointed out that the priestly and ritual legislation reflected a spirit different from that of Israelite antiquity. It was then that Vatke published his *Biblical Theology*, in which the religious history of Israel was conceived in terms of the Hegelian philosophy. In the first period of Judges and the early kings (thesis) the religion of Israel was primitive and naturalist. In the second period, the end of the monarchy, the idealism of the prophets produced a higher, truly spiritual,

religion (antithesis).   Finally, during and after the Exile, we have the
third period (synthesis) when law and religion were legalized.

Studies on the Pentateuchal legislation followed.   Some authors,
among whom Kuenen stands out, showed that some of the priestly
laws were later than Deuteronomy.   At the end of 1865 K. H. Graf
published a work on the historical books of the Old Testament in which
he admitted the four sources of Hupfeld.   Not all of his detailed and
complex conclusions were to be adopted.   But he made a new contribution
as regards the relative age of the sources.   Influenced by George, Vatke
and Reuss (his teacher) he reversed the chronological order that was
commonly held.   Until then the P document had been considered the
oldest and most basic; Graf put it at the end, during or after the Exile.
This important part of the legislation, instead of being the beginning
of the religion of Israel, was the final product.   He also distinguished
between several layers in the priestly laws (*Priestercodex*, hence the
abbreviation P).   The law of holiness (Lv 17—26) was attributed to
Ezechiel, but Leviticus in general, along with other priestly laws, seemed
not to have been in effect before the Exile.   A good part of it was to be
attributed to Esdras (5th century before Christ).

In 1869 A. Kuenen, perhaps the most influential critic of his time,
professed adherence to the Grafian chronology and made it the basis
for the first history of Israel and her religion.   He even developed the
hypothesis further.   Graf was inclined to distinguish the narrative
elements (as the older portion) from the legislative part in the priestly
code.   He gave this up after correspondence with Kuenen and in 1869
he proposed the following scheme for the manner in which the Pentateuch
was written.   The oldest documents are the Yahwist and Elohist (E² of
Hupfeld).   These were followed by Deuteronomy a little before the reform
of Josias (622).   During the Exile a redactor combined these three
documents.   The priestly code was composed after the Exile and
promulgated by Esdras.   It served as the structure of the Pentateuch
when it was combined with the other three writings.   Such is the system
which the works of J. Wellhausen were to popularize with both clarity
and strong arguments.   In its main points it had already been accepted
by Kuenen and A. Kayser.

§ 3.   The Wellhausen Theory

Born in 1844, J. Wellhausen was a student of Ewald; he taught on the
Protestant faculty of theology at Greifswald until 1882, when he became

professor of oriental languages in the faculty of philosophy. Before he died in 1918 he taught at Halle, Marburg and Göttingen, where he finally retired.

His special interest was the history of Israel *(Prolegomena zur Geschichte Israels, Israelitische und judische Geschichte)*. He frankly admitted that his interpretation of this history was deeply influenced by the Hegelian concepts of Vatke. At the beginning Israel's was a naturist religion; then the prophets introduced ethical monotheism. [3] During and after the Exile the Law reached its full development. This approach was argued in his *Prolegomena* on the basis of the distinction of sources. The chronological succession of the sources was established in terms of a history of Israelite cult which in turn was a reconstruction based on data that were partly valid. But he worked this chronological succession into Vatke's interpretation of the sweep of Israelite history. Moreover, his interpretation of both texts and events was based on pagan Arabic parallels. Wellhausen shared the 19th century ignorance of the ancient world, and was guilty of not making certain necessary distinctions (e.g., between the age of the documents and the institutions they describe). With his data he arrived at a history of Israelite religion and Pentateuchal sources that was simple, rectilinear, compact and truly impressive. But despite its simple, clear appearance, the Wellhausen system was in reality very complex; he put together facts and *a priori* assumptions in such a way that one must, at every point, distinguish between what is still valid, and what is false.

We will limit ourselves here to the key items in his literary criticism. His article *Israel* in the *Encyclopaedia Britannica* won over to him the Anglo-Saxon world; but the best resumé of his views is to be found in the article, *Hexateuch*, in the *Encyclopaedia Biblica* (1901).

I. BASES OF WELLHAUSEN'S THEORY

The various strata in the Pentateuch are to be compared one with the other, especially as regards the laws which they contain. The laws relative to the place of sacrifices can be taken as an example. The oldest legislation is in JE, for Ex 20, 24-26 foresees several altars. As the patriarchal narratives of JE show, there was not in the beginning one altar in one place. Whenever Yahweh communicated with His servant, an altar was erected; at that time steles *(massebôt)* were still in favor and Jacob set one up (Gn 28, 18). On the other hand, Deuteronomy (chap. 12) situates the cult in one place alone with great emphasis and

---

[3] Cf. *Prolegomena...* (1894), pp. 72-75.

even in a certain polemical tone. This development in the law is to be connected with the measures taken by King Josias against the local sanctuary (4 Kgs 23). Still further development is to be found in the priestly code. The polemical tone is lacking; the unity of the sanctuary is simply presupposed, and only one sanctuary is allowed to have been in existence since the Sinai desert : the Tabernacle.

The legislation concerning the priesthood developed in a manner parallel to that concerning the sanctuary. In the beginning, each sanctuary had its own priesthood. While the Deuteronomic legislation suppressed the sanctuaries, it considered all the levites as priests and thus preserved for them all the right of sacrifice at Jerusalem (Dt 18, 6-8). When this did not happen (4 Kgs 23, 9), Ezechiel (chap. 44) explained the statute about the levites as a punishment for having ministered at the high places. The priestly code no longer regarded the statute as a degradation, but pushed the distinction between priests and levites (as well as the Tabernacle itself, and its liturgy) back to the Mosaic period (Nm 1, 1—4, 18). Only in these texts is there mention of a high priest who alone disposes of the Urim and Thummim (which belong to *all* levites in Dt 33, 8), who is clothed in royal garments and anointed as if he were a king; but the high priest did not become the real head of the Israelite theocracy until after the Exile.

There are similar changes in the tithes and sacred privileges. Before the Exile there are merely offerings made during the great feasts, and the tithes are only a royal tax in 1 Sm 8, 15. But the priestly code makes them a tax payable to the priesthood. The tribute of one-third of a sicle per capita is not mentioned before Nehemias (2 Esd 10, 32). Likewise, the nature of the feasts changes : the feast of the new moon is eliminated, and the daily sacrifices, such as the *Tamid* (Nm 28, 3-8), take on a completely new importance.

Turning to the historical narratives, J. Wellhausen showed that the comparison of their various strata confirmed the conclusions he had achieved with the legal texts. " In JE the general plan of the whole is still very loose; each story in particular is the important thing, and they all have a vital unity. They always have a relation to a given place and we can often detect the motive which inspired their formation. " On the other hand, the priestly code is not interested in the details of the stories; passions and life disappear in a framework, a genealogical schema. The text is no longer based on popular traditions; it is a synthesis worked out from written sources. It systematizes history in terms of its own religious ideas and its own general culture. Between these two approaches (JE and P) stands the Deuteronomic genre.

It should be pointed out that the arguments of Wellhausen are not as strong for the narratives as they are for the laws. Without sufficient proof, he considered the lists and details in the priestly code as inventions; the Pentateuch was basically legend and not history. The scholars who came after him saw themselves forced to modify these views considerably. They also recognized, within JE, a difference between the Joseph cycle and that dealing with the three patriarchs.

Wellhausen finished the explanation of his theory with a reply to objections and a correction of certain erroneous interpretations. It could not be said that the priestly code invented the Israelite liturgy. " Moses could have been the founder of the Torah even if the Pentateuchal legislation had been codified nearly a thousand years later " — the Torah being understood as originally not a written law but the oral reply given by a priest in the sanctuary. [4] The ancient Jews looked upon their " civil constitution as a miracle "; the theocracy was the State. But with the Exile, the liturgy became the bond which permeated the theocracy, or better, the hierocracy. It was then that a new form was given to the old customs and statutes. The Israelite community was reorganized on the basis of liturgy and priesthood, and at the end of this long process came the priestly code and the present Pentateuch.

Such are the main points of Wellhausen's theory, which was to be perfected by the literary studies of the critical school. It is the basis of the Introductions by H. Cornill and C. Steuernagel in Germany, S. R. Driver in England, L. Gautier in France, and of the commentaries such as Nowack's *Handkommentar zum Alten Testament*, Marti's *Kurzer Handkommentar zum Alten Testament*, the *Cambridge Bible for Schools and Colleges*, the *International Critical Commentary*, the *Bible du Centenaire*. It also inspired *The Sacred Books of the Old Testament*, the so-called Polychrome Bible, of P. Haupt, in which the Hebrew text was printed on a color background which varied according to the alleged document or redaction of the Pentateuch (cf. the reproduction in *SDB*, III, 1408). Thus, Wellhausen's theory achieved considerable success. In his works Wellhausen described *an evolution rather than writing himself as an evolutionist*, but the end result of his studies seemed to correspond perfectly to the evolution characteristic of the age; he worked the history of Israel into the general scheme of the evolution of mankind without having any recourse to the supernatural. The Wellhausen school continued the literary analysis, distinguishing several

---

[4] In his *Prolegomena* Wellhausen is more precise; he admits that Moses made use of ancient liturgical customs for the Yahwist cult, and that he sometimes gave practical legal decisions at Cades.

strata in each document (J^1, J^2, J^3; E^1 and E^2; D^1 and D^2, etc.). Despite some differences in details, they presented the evolutionary schema we shall now describe.

II. DESCRIPTION OF THE THEORY

1. — There was first a period in which the traditions were developed — perhaps the age of Moses, or at least the period of the Judges. They were attached to sanctuaries, formed by particular rites or historical memories of the tribes. Finally in the time of the united monarchy (David and Solomon), they took shape and found written expression especially in the poetical works like the Book of Yashar (Jos 10, 12), and the Book of the Wars of Yahweh (Nm 12, 14 ff.). After the schism these traditions continued to circulate in both the North and South, thus receiving a certain local coloring while remaining faithful to the general idea of the special Providence through which Yahweh's plans for Israel were realized, despite all the obstacles.

2. — The Yahwist tradition was formed in the South. An author (or a school — there is no unanimity on this point) who worked in the second half of the 9th century (J^2) reworked an ancient source (J^1, which contained the old traditions about Cain and all the material which does not presuppose the Flood). Later this was completed by a J^3. One of the principal arguments advanced for dating the group of Yahwist passages is Gn 27, 40. Isaac proclaims to Esau that he will serve his brother, but adds that he will also shake off his yoke. This is interpreted as an allusion to the liberation of Edom from Juda, which occurred under Joram (about 853-841; cf. 4 Kgs 8, 20-22). But one may ask if this verse is not an addition (as many think) or an allusion to the revolt of Adad in Edom at the time of Solomon (3 Kgs 11, 21 ff.).

3. — Some authors, as Kittel and Riehm, think that the Elohist is to be dated before the Yahwist, but this is not the general view of the school. Following Wellhausen, most critics emphasize the prophetic elements in the Elohist narratives; this influence, as well as the evolution of religion, accounts for the higher moral and spiritual concept of Israel's God in these texts. Now the Balaam oracles (Nm 23), in which Moab appears as a State settled north of the Arnon — a condition that seems to reflect the beginning of the 8th century — belong to the oldest portion of E. This portion would have been incorporated into the Elohist document properly so-called (E^2) which is to be dated after the victories of Jeroboam II (towards 770) but before the fall of Samaria, because it presupposes that Moab has been eliminated from the land north of

the Arnon (Nm 21, 13b). The optimistic vein of the document would fit the victorious reign of Jeroboam. Finally, the document makes more use of the written law than the Yahwist (cf. Os 8, 12) and includes the code of the covenant (of doubtful date, Ex 20, 24—23, 19).

4. — After the fall of Samaria a redactor (RJE, sometimes called the " Jehovist "), would have united the two documents, giving a certain priority to J in the Pentateuch, and introducing certain harmonizations. Thus, in order to harmonize the two accounts of Hagar's expulsion, the redactor mentions her return to Abraham after the first flight (Gn 16, 9). The work was finished before 622, the date of the publication of Deuteronomy.

5. — For the Wellhausen school, Deuteronomy is the Law found under Josias in 622 when the Temple was being remodeled (4 Kgs 22). " *Is fecit cui prodest* "; because this book proclaims Jerusalem is the only sanctuary, it is the work of the Jerusalem clergy, and the " discovery " is, many think, a " pious deceit. " Although Deuteronomic literature is marked by unity of style and thought, the Wellhausen school postulates several redactions in Deuteronomy. Wellhausen paid little attention to this, but Steuernagel took an extreme view, relying particularly on the passages in which Moses speaks to a plural audience, and those in which he addresses an individual. The original Deuteronomy discovered in the reign of Josias (D¹) would have received a number of successive additions in a rather short space of time : D2b, discourses redacted in the second person plural (e.g., 9, 9—11, 28); D2a, likewise addressed to several (including the first introduction, 1, 5—4, 2); D2c, redacted in the second person singular, including most of the second introduction (6, 4—9, 7) and laws relative to kindness and to war. Finally, a redactor (Rd) put this work into the framework of JE which was then slightly modified. Some think that at this time the code of the covenant was displaced and revised.

6. — For Wellhausen and his school, Ezechiel in exile laid the foundation of the work which the priest redactors of the priestly code were to build on. But this work, which canonized ritual, was not realized at once; it is the result of a compilation of documents. The oldest of them (called since Klostermann the *Law of Holiness*, Lv 17, 26) bears a relationship to Deuteronomy, but it should be said at once that the alleged age of this document the is one of weak points of the theory. S. Driver, already, thought that the law of holiness was older than Ezechiel and could be dated from the end of the monarchy. But the *relative* age of the different

strata of the priestly writing (or better, priestly writings) seems to have been correctly established by the school of literary criticism.

The first codification done by the priests, then, is the *Law of Holiness* (Ph). Like the code of the covenant and Deuteronomy, it begins with an ordinance concerning sacrifices and finishes, like Deuteronomy, with blessings and cursings (Lv 26). Then comes a text that is as much narrative as legislative, called " the basic writing " (from the German *Grund*-basis, and given the siglum Pg). This is a schematic narrative which begins with creation (Gn 1, 1—2, 4a) and continues with genealogies *(toledôt)* through the whole history of the patriarchs. While it gives brief résumés of the lives of these men, it highlights some scenes which introduce a religious law (Noe and prohibition of blood, Abraham and circumcision), or right (burial of Sara). It lingers over the Egyptian plagues which are a preparation for the establishment of the liturgy of the Tabernacle by Moses (Ex 25—30; 35—40).

From Sinai on, it is more difficult to detect the basic writing, since it has received additions and supplements (given the siglum Ps). Some of these are easy to detect, such as the *Law concerning Sacrifices* (Lv 1—7), which interrupts the sequence between Exodus 40 and Leviticus 8. The *Law of Purity* (Lv 11—15) is likewise an addition. In Numbers a mass of supplementary laws slows the course of the narrative but the basic writing continues to the death of Moses and the establishment of the Israelites in Chanaan. Wellhausen and his school fixed the redaction of the basic writing after the Exile and were inclined to attribute it (against Budde and Cornill) to Esdras, who would have also promulgated it when he came to Jerusalem in 444. They also admitted that a great part of the additional laws arose after the coming of this envoy of the Persian king. Towards 400 a priestly redactor would have united the earlier documents with P. By the time of Alexander, towards 330, the Pentateuch was considered as canonical; no additions were permitted after that date.

§ 4. Influence of the Wellhausen Theory

Although we speak of the " Wellhausen Theory, " we have see that when Wellhausen began to write, the distinction between the various documents was already taken for granted; Graf had fixed their chronology and Vatke had indicated the direction of the religious development. Wellhausen emphasized the religious and liturgical institutions and refined the distinction between the sources, but after him the work also continued. Nevertheless, it was he who really made the synthesis accessible to the general public, thanks to his clarity. The question remained whether or not certain elements should be separated : the historical and religious data, and the religious philosophy which informed them. He constructed a theory about the development of Israelite religion which the future was going to prove false, but he had certainly made some valid points. The evolution of Israel's history had to be refined by portraying the human elements which, from the beginning, had been impregnated with the supernatural.

This powerful synthesis gave a clear view of the development of Israelite law and of the composition of the Pentateuch; it seemed to satisfy the demands of textual analysis. It conquered the world of the universities and won the adherence of most. In our own day still, the theory forms the basis of the Introductions to the Old Testament, such as those of R. Pfeiffer (Harper's, second edition, 1953), and of histories of Hebrew literature, such as those of A. Lods (Paris, 1950) and C. Kuhl (Bern, 1953). Even authors who favor different analyses, such as O. Eissfeldt (Tübingen, 1956[2]) or A. Bentzen (Copenhagen, 1952[2]) still hold to the general lines. Eissfeldt admits of an older stratum than J, which presupposes a society still without a priesthood (hence the siglum L = laity), and which corresponds in part to the old J[1]. Bentzen is a moderate of the Scandinavian school which tends to play down the role of literary criticism and is most opposed to Wellhausen. In fact there has always been some opposition and the theory has never completely triumphed.

I. WEAKNESSES OF THE THEORY

We have already found it necessary to indicate some weaknesses in the theory. Above all, there were three great defects which were to produce controversies and also further the development of exegesis :

1. The rejection of the supernatural order. Most men read the Bible as a religious book, not as a learned work. The Wellhausen theory seemed to say that they would find here a merely human witness to man and his evolution, not a divine record.

The theory carried with it certain value judgments which depreciated the Law and particularly the priestly writing. This appeared to be no more than the end-term of an evolution, a decadent work, narrowly legalist and contemptuous of true history. Thus, instead of being a continuous divine revelation, the development of Israel was just another setback in the history of man. To man's search for salvation a negative reply was given by the theory; it gave the lie both to those who had found in the Bible a message of hope, as well as to the biblical writers themselves who proclaimed salvation through Israel. The theory could well appear as destructive of tradition and faith.

But certain intelligent and deeply religious minds could ask if the documentary theory might not be separated from the Wellhausen theory. The critical works constituted legitimate research and in the end they could throw light on religion itself. Whatever be the determinisms and the evolution of Israel, the action of the God of Abraham, of Isaac, and Jacob could stand out more clearly and in a manner that would satisfy man's spirit and reason.

2. The second weakness was due to a defective knowledge of the ancient East. The epigraphical discoveries in Syria-Palestine and the interpretation of the great cuneiform and hieroglyphic literatures was just beginning. And the literary critics could hardly study the Bible as an independent product of the Hebrew people. But according to the theory, the prophets were the dominating figures of the literary and religious development of Israel, and the Law was merely the communal codification of the moral and theological insights achieved by the prophets.

Archeological discoveries were going to bring widespread changes to this picture. Egyptian inscriptions and Assyrian annals helped define Israel's position in the changing Near East. Its history was seen to be highly conditioned by the neighboring civilizations. From now on the essential problem was no longer the independent development of Israel! Rather, it was the manner in which she found it necessary, in virtue of her own nature, at every period to assimilate or to reject the ambient cultures.

As far as the Law in particular was concerned, there were to be new discoveries of a whole series of legislations in the Near East, much older than the prophetic movement, that were related to Israel's law. These were new data which Wellhausen obviously never knew. The law was now seen to be in existence before the prophetic movement, and the documentary theory was simply unable of itself to explain the origins of law. Even before archeology revealed these documents certain minds were able to see that the method of literary criticism, however valid in its own right, was extending itself too far in trying to explain the whole evolution of Israel. Here again, it was necessary to distinguish between the Wellhausen theory and documentary theory.

3. A third defect was revealed by later discoveries, but it could have been foreseen already from the beginning. Despite the importance

they attached to vocabulary and textual analysis, the literary critics were superficial in their treatment of the various literary forms within the Pentateuch. They were well equipped to prove the literary relationship of one passage to another, but much less so to define the nature of these texts. It was all very well to point out traces of Deuteronomic or priestly redaction on the basis of Deuteronomic phraseology or the stages of the priestly code — but what of the passages themselves? These were classified as narratives or laws, without any appreciation that there are many types of both. The emerging science of ethnology was beginning to elaborate many concepts which the critics were unaware of, and they lacked also any historical or legal texts of the ancient East (except for the Greeks) that would serve for comparison.

There were more serious problems. Once a late date had been assigned to the editing of the *documents*, it was hard to recognize any real historicity in these narratives since they had been written so long after the events they described. For Wellhausen and his school, these were legends. There was no attempt to analyze the events themselves or the social conditions that marked their origins and development until they were finally written down. The critics simply considered these narratives as free (but not disinterested) *creations* of more or less gifted men. Likewise, the laws were conceived as decrees of a more or less secondary authority rather than as the expression of a search to determine the common good. This resulted in a general suspicion toward all the texts of the Pentateuch, which could only give ground to certain reactions.

II. OPPOSITION TO THE THEORY

Through Reuss and Renan the critical works of the German school reached France and the ranks of the educated people. At first the reaction was like that of Bossuet to the studies of Richard Simon : biblical criticism seemed to threaten tradition. This first reaction, then, was of a religious nature; faith in Christ risked being destroyed by criticism. But this religious reaction was always accompanied by an effort to reason the problem out, especially among Catholics who were more concerned than Protestants to establish harmony between faith and reason. This does not mean that the solutions proposed were good ones, and the Catholic Church was never in fact bound to any of them.

An attempt was made to prove, by critical arguments, the Mosaic authorship of the Pentateuch, the traditional view of both Christians and Jews. P. Cornely and Vigouroux especially took this position in their *Manual* and *Introduction*. In 1907 E. Mangenot systematized this approach : " Moses not only has the major role in most of the Pentateuch, but is also the author and editor of the first five books of the Bible which carry his name " (*L'Authenticité mosaïque du Pentateuque**, p. 203).

Mangenot began by acknowledging that " the Pentateuch does not explicitly purport to be the work of Moses " (p. 206). Certain texts (Ex 17, 14; 24, 4; 34, 27; Nm 33, 1 ff.) bear witness to a partial literary activity of Moses. They do not mean to deny that he is the author of the whole; it is just that he wrote these at a special order from God. Finally, Deuteronomy 31, 24-26 records the command that Moses should put the law in writing. This refers to the book itself, not just to the previous chapters, since Dt 1, 5 indicates that the great lawgiver promulgated the previous laws, without necessarily putting them in writing.

The other books of the Old Testament confirm this point of view, Mangenot thinks. The Book of Josue several times makes mention of a law written by Moses (Jos 1, 7 ff., etc.). Although there is no indication of the literary activity of Moses in Judges or Samuel, the Books of Kings (3 Kgs 2, 3; 4 Kgs 14, 6), Esdras-Nehemias, and Chronicles testify to it. The preexilic prophets speak often of the " law of God " and many exegetes have seen here a clear reference to the existence of the Pentateuch. E. Mangenot allows that such a conclusion does not necessarily follow; some of the laws alluded to can be found in the Pentateuch, but one must wait until Malachias before there is a real reference to the " law of Moses. " On the basis of this evidence, one " cannot conclude with absolute certainty that the Mosaic authorship of the Pentateuch is expressly affirmed in the Old Testament, but it is explicitly indicated in the books of Esdras-Nehemias and Paralipomenon. "

The evidence of the New Testament would seem to be even stronger. In about twenty-five cases there is a clear assumption on the part of the Jews, the apostles and Christ Himself that Moses wrote the Pentateuch. Christ speaks of the Book of Moses (Mk 12, 26), the Law of Moses (Lk 24, 44), the things that Moses ordered (Mt 8, 4 par.) and permitted (Mt 19, 8). The most impressive passage is Jn 5, 45-47, where Christ says that Moses has written of Him. The language of the apostles is similar to this (Lk 2, 22; Acts 3, 22; Rom 10, 5, etc.). E. Mangenot also appealed to " the constant belief of the Jewish people " (cf. Philo, Josephus and the Talmud), to the " constant tradition of the Church (perhaps Tertullian, but certainly Origen, St. Cyril of Alexandria, St. Gregory of Nyssa...). "

Finally, he tried to marshal intrinsic evidence based on the very contents of the Pentateuch. The Pentateuch, he claimed (and others with him), was written by an author who was very well acquainted with Egypt, and an Egypt that was not that of the first millennium, but the second, and hence before David or Solomon. This is a united Egypt; there is no Ethiopian rule, as at the time of Ezechias. The names of the towns are those of the 19th Dynasty (Ramses), and not later, for there is no mention of Migdol (this is not certain, cf. Ex 14, 2) or of Taphnes; it is a mistake to try to correlate with the 22nd Dynasty names like Putiphar or Sapheneth-phanee. The Egyptian army did not yet include foreign mercenaries (but it may be asked if the texts had to mention these). Moreover, the Pentateuch presupposes its being composed when the Israelites lived in the desert and did not occupy the land of Chanaan. The Egyptian oppression appears to be recent, the wandering in the desert merely a transition; hence the legislation anticipates what will be the future, " giving laws suitable for the sedentary and farm life which the Israelites were going to live in the Land promised to their fathers.... The law about the kingship is merely directed to a distant future. " Finally it was argued that the Pentateuch had been written in a special language that had the flavor of antiquity (the orthography *hw'* being used for *hy'*, the feminine personal pronoun).

However, the critics would not admit the special character of this language; on the contrary, they distinguished several layers of language in the Pentateuch, some archaic, others recent. Authors like E. Mangenot then had to refute arguments drawn from literary criticism. The anachronisms are glosses, they said; the doublets are in fact two different events. The views of the critics are at odds with each other, and hence uncertain; it is often impossible to distinguish the Yahwist from the Elohist. Therefore the method and the particular arguments of literary criticism are questionable. With regard to the principle of cultic centralization, it can be admitted that the law of Deuteronomy refers to the future even though it is due to Moses; Yahweh did not have to choose one place until the Jerusalem Temple was built (other critics have other interpretations). As for the cultic laws, an effort was made to find preexilic traces of the priestly code on sacrifices : " the ancient feasts are mentioned in the historical books, when this is justified by circumstances. " In short, there is nothing impossible about Moses organizing the public worship at Sinai. Finally, philological arguments are subjective : " all the narratives of such and such nature are put in one category, and the others in another... but it is necessary to take into account the differences in content and in literary form. "

III. SOLUTIONS ATTEMPTED

Not all were convinced by these arguments. Many were of the opinion that the late texts of Chronicles and of the New Testament should be interpreted in the light of the opinions of those times; hence there was here no solid argument for the Mosaic authorship. A. Van Hoonacker, [5] in particular, proved that the author of Deuteronomy indicated that he was not Moses. Between 1895 and 1901 Fr. de Hummelauer published his commentaries on the Pentateuch in the *Cursus Scripturae Sacrae*. He had his own theory, quite different from Wellhausen's, where Deuteronomy (authored by Samuel) and several laws were judged to be later than Moses. He admitted a Pentateuch of Moses, considerably modified through the years, which was finished by the time of Esdras. He also admitted the existence of different sources, in particular the Yahwist and Elohist.

At the Fribourg Catholic Congress (1897), both von Hügel, who had modernist tendencies, and Fr. Lagrange, who had just worked out a truly Thomistic theory of inspiration, were in agreement : the validity of the work of the literary school demanded a broader point of view. In the memoir presented to the congress, Fr. Lagrange did not insist on dates, but rather on the methods of composition current in the ancient East, and on the evolution of law. He remarked that there was no essential connection between the Bible, or tradition or the historical worth of the Pentateuch, and the Mosaic authorship. He perfected and presented these ideas in conferences published as " *La Méthode historique.* " He admitted the distinction between the four documents and the late date of the priestly writing (p. 181), but he showed that the true problem lay elsewhere : " Deuteronomy, Fr. von Hummelauer says, was not written by Moses — nor, *a fortiori*, was the priestly code, say the critics —. Can the code of the covenant or at least the Decalogue be ascribed to him? We think that much more is to be ascribed to him. The Torah is a collection of laws about sacrifices, priesthood, the distinctions between clean and unclean, vows, uncleannesses.... Is all that supposed to be later than Moses if he is not the author of the Torah? A hundred times better to claim that all that was one or two thousand years before him. All these customs, some universal among the Semites, some characteristic of Semitic nomads — these Moses knew and for them he received divine approval. " [6]

---

[5] *De compositione litteraria et de origine mosaica Hexateuchi*. This was edited and published by J. Coppens (Brussels, 1949).

[6] *RB* (1901), p. 615.

Similarly, Father Prat admitted that the Law had received additions, not only while Moses was alive, but after his death. It was necessary to distinguish " between the author of the Law and the author of the Pentateuch.... Thus we do not believe that the Pentateuch makes itself out to be the work of Moses. " [7] Fr. Durand wrote : " All the texts which demonstrably cannot have been written by Moses are to be attributed to someone else. The traditional view which ascribed the Pentateuch en bloc to Moses is still to be kept; it remains true, but not in the strict sense in which it has been understood.... " [8] Finally, Fr. Brucker (*L'Église et la critique biblique,** 1908, p. 145), and following him, Msgr. J. Nikel and others, without abandoning the Mosaic authorship, admitted the existence of four documents which would have been joined together only after the Exile.

But precisely on this point of Mosaic authorship, Fr. Brucker had some reservations about the view of Fr. Lagrange after the Fribourg congress, and he proposed returning to the idea of Richard Simon about the secretaries of Moses; in this way he sought to satisfy both the demands of literary criticism and the traditional Jewish view. But the opposition of Fr. Mechineau [9] and Fr. Delattre (*Autour de la question biblique**, 1904) went deeper than this. The former considered the question of authorship as based on the irrefutable authority of tradition, and hence not of secondary importance; the position of Fr. Lagrange was " a dangerous concession. " The latter judged that Lagrange's point of view reduced the Bible to " the appearance of history, " and this was without any basis in the Fathers.

IV. Intervention of the Church's Magisterium

Confusion kept growing. When critical exegetes like Loisy and von Hügel were turning towards modernism, the unrest increased. Questions of philosophy and theology were confused with those of criticism; only very alert minds were sensitive to distinctions. In order to protect the faith of the faithful in this troubled time the magisterium had to take precautionary measures. As J. Coppens was to write later, " We must picture the anguish of the Church when the plague of Modernism was at its height. Philological and historical exegesis were literally besieged, with no time for the mustering of forces. Caught unaware, the Church had at its disposal neither seasoned troops nor a complete plan of defense.

---

[7] *Études* (1898), p. 48.

[8] *Études* (1902), p. 351.

[9] *Études* (1898), pp. 189-311.

To cap the climax, confusion was rampant in the ranks of Catholic exegesis itself and the Church could not trust all her defenders. What was to be done in such a situation? The Church could only call back her soldiers and draw them up in strong retreat positions in simple formation which offered no opportunity for ambush or encirclement. If we are allowed to continue the comparison, we may say that the responses of the Commission represent the defense measures adopted during the Modernist crisis by the ecclesiastical high command. " [10]

The Biblical Commission, created by Pope Leo XIII in 1902, had to meet these difficulties. Guided by the magisterium of the Church it had to defend faith and morals. In this crisis the defense had to be made in terms of higher criticism. The solutions it proposed were those of the conservative school, whose arguments still appeared valid to the majority of Catholic exegetes. However, its decrees also allowed room for further research and for the discovery of new arguments that would allow the questions to be raised again. This is shown by the two replies which touch indirectly on the Pentateuch : February 13, 1905, on implicit citations; June 23, on narratives which only appear to be historical (both signed by Fr. Fleming). One should keep in mind these principles, and the common teaching, when one reads the reply of June 27, 1906 (signed by Fathers Vigouroux and Janssens) on the Mosaic authorship of the Pentateuch.

Here are the texts of the decrees : [11]

1. *Authenticity* — Whether the arguments amassed by critics to impugn the Mosaic authenticity of the sacred books designated by the name Pentateuch are of sufficient weight, notwithstanding the very many evidences to the contrary contained in both Testaments taken collectively, the persistent agreement of the Jewish people, and constant tradition of the Church, and internal arguments derived from the text itself, to justify the statement that these books have not Moses for their author but have been compiled from sources for the most part posterior to the time of Moses.

Answer : In the negative.

2. *Writer* — Whether the Mosaic authenticity of the Pentateuch necessarily postulates such a redaction of the whole work as to render it absolutely imperative to maintain that Moses wrote with his own

---

[10] J. COPPENS, *The Old Testament and the Critics* (Paterson, N.J., 1942), pp. 156 f.; cf. R. P. CLOSEN, *Bi* (1940), p. 332.

[11] *AAS*, 39 (1906), p. 377; Eng. trans. from *Rome and the Study of Scripture* (St. Meinrad, Indiana : Grail, 1958).

hand or dictated to amanuenses all and everything contained in it; or whether it is possible to admit the hypothesis of those who think that he entrusted the composition of the work itself, conceived by himself under the influence of divine inspiration, to some other person or persons, but in such a manner that they rendered faithfully his own thoughts, wrote nothing contrary to his will, and omitted nothing; and that the work thus produced, approved by Moses as the principal and inspired author, was made public under his name.

Answer : In the negative to the first part, in the affirmative to the second part.

3. *Sources* — Whether it may be granted, without prejudice to the Mosaic authenticity of the Pentateuch, that Moses employed sources in the production of his work, i.e., written documents or oral traditions, from which, to suit his special purpose and under the influence of divine inspiration, he selected some things and inserted them in his work, either literally or in substance, summarized or amplified.

Answer : In the affirmative.

4. *Changes and textual corruptions* — Whether, granted the substantial Mosaic authenticity and the integrity of the Pentateuch, it may be admitted that in the long course of centuries some modifications have been introduced into the work, such as additions after the death of Moses, either appended by an inspired author or inserted into the text as glosses and explanations; certains words and forms translated from the ancient language to more recent language, and finally, faulty readings to be ascribed to the error of amanuenses, concerning which it is lawful to investigate and judge according to the laws of criticism.

Answer : In the affirmative, subject to the judgment of the Church.

To translate these replies is already to interpret them. But the interpretation also involves a question of principle of which we are today more aware than in 1906. We now see clearly that " these decrees represent opinions which are not connected with the truths of faith and morals, either directly or indirectly. It is obvious that the exegete *(Forscher)* can of course pursue his research with complete liberty, and evaluate the results, although always with due regard for the authority of the Church's teaching *(allerdings immer mit Vorbehalt der kirchlichen Lehrautorität).* " [12] In fact these replies were then usually taken as a rejection, pure and simple, of the view that finds four documents

---

[12] A. MILLER, *Benediktinische Monatsschrift** (1955), p. 49; cf. A. KLEINHANS, " De nova Enchiridii Biblici editione, " *Antonianum**, 30 (1955), pp. 63-65; E. VOGT, " De decretis Commissionis biblicae distinguendis, " *Bi* (1955), pp. 564 ff.

in the Pentateuch, all of them after the time of Moses; as for the changes acknowledged as later than Moses, they would have been merely additions or differences in vocabulary. Among Catholics, such an interpretation was held by E. Mangenot and Dom Höpfl and many later manuals. The critics understood these decrees in the same way. Von Hügel and C. A. Briggs (*The Biblical Commission and the Pentateuch*, 1907) again brought up the conclusions of literary analysis, the comparison of the Pentateuch with the prophetical writings, and they boldly stated that not only four different writers, but four different dates, had to be admitted. Hence Catholic exegetes, anxious to have the question studied further, often found themselves in an unpleasant position which was not made easier for them by certain scholars (Houtin). The attempts of J. Touzard (*Moïse et Josué*, Paris, 1921) and of Schmidtke (*Die Einwanderung Israels in Kanaan*, Bratislava, 1933) were not acceptable to ecclesiastical authority.

This had its reasons for upholding the *status quo*. The critical problem was just one aspect of the knowledge of the biblical revelation. Critical studies were being warmly encouraged by civil authority, and it seemed that the work proper to the Church should bear on other points. While the remarkable development in the sciences shed such new and full light on the biblical texts, the Christian message was in danger of being wiped out. And yet, according to the Bible itself, salvation comes only through Christ, of whom the Law and the Prophets bear witness. So the Roman authorities asked their exegetes to apply themselves to the study of the continuity of the Mosaic revelation down through the history of Israel, and the continuity of Christianity in the history of the Church. They had recourse to both the *École Biblique* of Jerusalem, which they supported, and to the Pontifical Biblical Institute at Rome, which was founded in 1909. With the 1943 encyclical *Divino Afflante Spiritu*, [13] the Church found it necessary to put an end to the misunderstandings, and to integrate into the traditional teaching the valuable results of modern criticism which had been tested and perfected by the archeological and exegetical work of the past fifty years.

The reaction of religious minds to the defects of literary criticism was not confined to the Catholic Church. The General Assembly of the Free Church of Scotland issued a judgment against W. Robertson Smith and his *Lectures on the Religion of the Semites;* the General Assembly of American Presbyterians passed public judgment on the Reverend

---

[13] And also the letter of the Biblical Commission to Cardinal Suhard; see pp. 125 f.

C. A. Briggs.   Given the state of our knowledge at the beginning of the
century, the conclusions of the Wellhausen school could appear quite
uncertain, even in the field of literary criticism.

Some, like M. Löhr, Harold Wiener and Dahse, disputed the claims
of literary criticism.   The Genesis commentaries of B. Jacob and
U. Cassuto were not based on the distinction between the sources.   The
strongest attack came from P. Volz and W. Rudolph who denied the
unity and independent existence of the Elohist document (*Der Elohist
als Erzähler*, 1933; *Der Elohist von Exodus bis Josua*, 1938).   The
Scandinavian school (Nyberg and Engnell) made little of literary criticism
itself.   Although certain studies (Noth) questioned successfully the
existence of documents outside the Pentateuch, the *literary* analysis
of Wellhausen and his school was not really shaken as far as the Torah
was concerned.   O. Eissfeldt (*Die Komposition von Exodus I-XII*, 1939)
raised serious objections to the work of Volz and Rudolph.   In other
fields new efforts were going to be made which would considerably enrich
our knowledge of the Torah : the archeology of the Ancient Near East,
the history of literary forms, and the history of religion.

CHAPTER III

THE PENTATEUCH
AND NEAR EASTERN ARCHEOLOGY,
FROM 1890 TO 1914

BIBLIOGRAPHY

Introduction p. 67.

W. F. ALBRIGHT, *The Archeology of Palestine and the Bible* (New York, 1935); Fr. trans. *L'Archéologie de la Palestine* (Paris, 1955).

L. HENNEQUIN, " Fouilles et champs de fouilles en Palestine et en Phénicie, " *SDB*, III (1936), cols. 318-524.

H. ROWLEY, *From Joseph to Joshua* (New York : Oxford, 1950).

A. BARROIS, *Manuel d'Archéologie Biblique*, 2 Vols. (Paris, 1939 and 1953).

C. GORDON, *Introduction to Old Testament Times* (New York : Ventor, 1953).

N. GLUECK, " The Age of Abraham in the Negeb, " *BA*, 18 (1955), pp. 2-9.

G. E. WRIGHT, *Biblical Archeology* (Philadelphia : Westminster, 1957); (ed.), *The Bible and the Ancient Near East* (Garden City, N.Y. : Doubleday, 1961); with D. N. FREEDMAN (eds.), *Biblical Archaeologist Reader, I and II* (Garden City, N.Y. : Doubleday, 1961 and 1965).

§ 1. Discoveries

In 1799 an expedition to Egypt, accompanied by many scholars, initiated a truly scientific study of pre-Hellenic antiquity. In 1822 Champollion deciphered the hieroglyphics and the texts began to speak. But the problem of the Pentateuch was not solved merely because Champollion was able to read the name of Ramses! First of all, many generations were required before Egyptology became a science, with a grammar, a dictionary, a chronology, a history of art, a political and religious history. With the greatest interest biblical scholars followed the development, as well as, one should admit, the fumblings of the new science.

It was obvious that the hieroglyphics would be scrutinized most diligently as regards the Exodus, but here least of all were answers forthcoming. For one reason, Lower Egypt had been better preserved and more easily explored than the Suez region, and also such an event was not the type of thing to merit mention in the records of the pharaos. The views of Schleiden (1858) and Brugsch (1876) which had the Hebrews leaving by the north route of the isthmus, were opposed to those of Naville and Lepsius who had them leaving by the south. Apart from this delicate problem, however, the Egyptian texts and monuments documented many other points in important fashion : the customs, crafts and dress of antiquity. Dictionaries (like the *Dictionnaire de la Bible* of Vigouroux) made wide use of these pictures. In 1875 a scholar like Abbé V. Ancessi, well acquainted with the works of Brugsch, Mariette and de Rougé, sought to describe the Israelite liturgical dress and the sacrificial rite (that of the doves) " according to the Egyptian paintings and monuments. " For the purposes of apologetics Vigouroux relied on the same evidence in his " *La Bible et les découvertes modernes.* " But a detailed comparison between Egypt and Israel was not successful, and at the turn of the century the honeymoon was over. A. Gardiner, who was to perform the most outstanding work for our exact knowledge of Egyptian language and grammar, criticized certain premature parallelisms. Fr. Prat claimed to be impressed more with the differences between Egypt and the Bible than with the similarities. This negative reaction was climaxed by a rather noncommittal book by E. Peet : *Egypt and the Old Testament* (1924). Finally, Yahuda's studies on the relationship between the language of the Pentateuch and Egyptian (1933) were very severely criticized.

With the decipherment of cuneiform, another source of information had just appeared, and it offered remarkable parallels. Somewhat later than Egypt, Mesopotamia had entered into the light of history. Beginning with the 18th century Europeans traveled through the area and in 1786 the Michaux " caillou, " provided with an inscription of several lines, had been brought back to Paris by that botanist. In 1802 Grotefend was working on the inscriptions recorded by Niebuhr, and he definitively identified two vowels in the old Persian and established the consonant of ten syllabic signs. Then he succeeded in identifying in Babylonian the signs indicating " Nabuchodonosor. " At that time, Botta, and then Layard discovered Ninive (Kuyunyik) and Khorsabad. In 1850 the library of Ashurbanipal came to light. De Saulcy had been able to read 96 lines from Khorsabad, but the system appeared so complicated that the scholarly world hesitated to follow the Assyriologists. It surrendered only in 1857 when the Asiatic Society of London offered to several scholars a text of 800 lines. The translations sent by Rawlinson,

Hincks, Fox Talbot and Oppert were unsealed and published in four columns; the agreement in the results obtained by each scholar following his own method proved that the texts had been mastered.

Assyrian (and Babylonian) turned out to be a Semitic language related to Hebrew. But with these modest beginnings Hebrew was more helpful in identifying the Assyrian roots than Assyrian was for the interpretation of the Pentateuch! Nevertheless, some exciting texts came to light very quickly. In the tablets found by Rassam in 1852 George Smith discovered fragments of a work about the creation of the world. In 1873 and 1874 he found more of these at Ninive, and in 1876 he published at London his *Chaldean Account of Genesis*. The Babylonian Flood was found in the mouth of Uta-Napishtim, the Babylonian Noe, in the eleventh tablet of the *Gilgamesh* epic. The same epic told how the plant of life, which was to bring immortality to Gilgamesh, king of Uruk, had been stolen from him by a serpent. A little later, in 1906, Hilprecht found a list of ten antediluvian patriarchs who were fabulously long-lived, much longer than the ten biblical patriarchs between Adam and Noe (even Methuselah). A cultic tablet from Sippar afforded some interesting parallels to the levitic ritual, and the traditions about the birth of Sargon the elder were oddly similar to those about Moses. Finally, in addition to the texts and the seal impressions, the land itself yielded the stepped towers, called *ziggurats*, which were a remarkable illustration of the Tower of Babel.

These discoveries could not fail to leave a deep impression upon biblical scholars and historians. In France the men most influenced were E. Ledrain, who went on to teach Assyrian and Aramean at the Ecole du Louvre, F. Lenormant and A. Loisy. In the *Revue des Religions* for 1891-1892 the latter published an article on the " Mythes chaldéens de la création et du déluge " (a study he was to take up again later); but already in 1880 F. Lenormant had published his *Origines de l'histoire*. He wrote that the Israelite version of the beginnings of the world was " similar, in all fundamental points, to the teaching of the sacred books from the banks of the Euphrates and Tigris " (p. XVIII).... " It is the same story... and yet... the meaning is quite different.... Polytheism has been carefully eliminated to make place for an unyielding monotheism. That which naturalistic notions expressed with singular vulgarity became the clothing for moral truths of the highest and most spiritual order. As for me, I see here without any hesitation the result of a supernatural intervention of divine Providence " (p. XX).

§ 2.   First Reactions of the Holy See

Lenormant's book was condemned in 1887. It was not in line with that school which was trying to establish harmony between science and faith by a " concordism " between the data of science and the biblical record of the beginnings of the world. Also, the faithful were too little prepared for their faith not to be somewhat upset by these new ideas, and F. Lenormant doubtless did not insist strongly enough on certain key facts (like original sin), important for the understanding of man. These last points are recalled in the reply of the Biblical Commission on June 30, 1909, concerning the *historical character of the first three chapters of Genesis*. These decrees which follow [1] are to be interpreted according to the same norms mentioned for these quoted above. They do not give an exegesis of the chapters, but they indicate a certain number of facts " which bear on fundamental teachings of the Christian religion. "

1. *False exegesis* — Whether the various exegetical systems, which have been elaborated and defended by the aid of a science falsely so-called, for the purpose of excluding the literal historical sense of the first three chapters of Genesis, are based upon solid arguments.

Answer : In the negative.

2. *Historical character of the three chapters* — Whether we may, in spite of the character and historic form of the book of Genesis, of the close connection of the first three chapters with one another and with those which follow, of the manifold testimony of the Scriptures both of the Old and the New Testament, of the almost unanimous opinion of the Fathers, and of the traditional view which — transmitted also by the Jewish people — has always been held by the Church, teach that the three aforesaid chapters do not contain the narrative of things which actually happened, a narrative which corresponds to objective reality and historic truth; and whether we may teach that these chapters contain fables derived from mythologies and cosmologies belonging to older nations, but purified of all polytheistic error and accommodated to monotheistic teaching by the sacred author or that they contain allegories and symbols destitute of any foundation in objective reality but presented under the garb of history for the purpose of inculcating religious and philosophical truth; or, finally, that they contain legends

---

[1] *AAS*, 1 (1909), pp. 567-569; Eng. trans. from *Rome and the Study of Scripture* [6] (St. Meinrad, Indiana : Grail, 1958).

partly historical and partly fictitious, freely handled for the instruction and edification of souls.

Answer : In the negative to each part.

3. *Historical character of certain parts* — Whether, in particular, we may call in question the literal and historical meaning where there is question of facts narrated in these chapters which touch the fundamental teachings of the Christian religion, as for example, the creation of all things which was accomplished by God at the beginning of time, the special creation of man, the formation of the first woman from man, the unity of the human race, the original happiness of our first parents in a state of justice, integrity, and immortality, the divine command laid upon man to prove his obedience, the transgression of that divine command at the instigation of the devil under the form of a serpent, the fall of our first parents from their primitive state of innocence, and the promise of a future Redeemer.

Answer : In the negative.

4. *Interpretation* — Whether, in interpreting those passages of these chapters which the Fathers and Doctors have interpreted in divers ways without leaving us anything definite or certain, anyone may, subject to the decision of the Church and following the analogy of faith, follow and defend that opinion at which he has prudently arrived.

Answer : In the affirmative.

5. *Literal sense* — Whether all and each of the parts, namely, the single words and phrases, in these chapters must always and of necessity be interpreted in a proper literal sense, so that it is never lawful to deviate from it, even when expressions are manifestly used figuratively, that is metaphorically or anthropomorphically, and when reason forbids us to hold, or necessity impels us to depart from, the proper literal sense.

Answer : In the negative.

6. *Allegory and prophecy* — Whether, granting always the literal and historical sense, the allegorical and prophetical interpretation of certain passages of these chapters — an interpretation justified by the example of the Fathers and the Church — may be prudently and usefully applied.

Answer : In the affirmative.

7. *Scientific expression* — Whether, since it was not the intention of the sacred author, when writing the first chapter of Genesis, to teach us in a scientific manner the innermost nature of visible things, and to present the complete order of creation but rather to furnish his people

with a popular account, such as the common parlance of that age allowed, one, namely, adapted to the senses and to man's intelligence, we are strictly and always bound, when interpreting these chapters to seek for scientific exactitude of expression.

Answer : In the negative.

8. *Yom* — Whether the word *Yom* (day), which is used in the first chapter of Genesis to describe and distinguish the six days, may be taken either in its strict sense as the natural day, or in a less strict sense as signifying a certain space of time; and whether free discussion of this question is permitted to interpreters.

Answer : In the affirmative.

These decrees have often been interpreted as demanding a *material* historicity for the narrative, namely, the material reality of the serpent who tempts Eve.   In reality, however, they merely recall what has often been repeated since : the *historical* character of the Old Testament revelation, which is the message of a God who has intervened in human history.   But they do not spell out how these events actually took place. The points they mention must be *inferred* from the text, rather than *read* there, and the Commission insisted on these because they are backed up by other sources of revelation.   The Commission also admits the use of literary devices and also metaphor in certain expressions.   But more progress in the knowledge of the Ancient East was necessary before reaching greater precision as to the meaning of the words, images and methods of composition.

§ 3. New Advances in Oriental Studies

Without waiting for the settlement of the controversies over concordism and modernism, Assyriology had pushed on.   In 1872 E. Schrader published the first edition of his " Cuneiform Texts and the Old Testament, " a rich source of data that was to be increased even more in later editions.   The third edition appeared just before a discovery that was of major importance.   In December 1901, the Morgan expedition uncovered at Susa the first pieces of a Babylonian legal text that had been captured as a trophy by the ancient Elamites.   In record time Father Scheil translated and published the entire code promulgated by King Hammurabi at the beginning of the second millennium, several centuries before Moses.   The undeniable similarities in form and content led some to claim that the Hebrew Pentateuch, in both its laws and narratives, was merely an offshoot of the great Mesopotamian literature.

This discovery occurred at the height of the controversy started by the Assyriologist Friedrich Delitzsch on January 13, 1902, with a conference delivered before the Emperor William II : " Babylon and the Bible. " Delitzsch not only insisted on the importance of the knowledge of cuneiform for a correct understanding of the Bible, but he opposed the " great illusion " or " deceit " *(Täuschung)* which attributed to the Hebrew people what rightfully belonged to the Babylonians : monotheism, religious values, a high moral integrity. Thus Delitzsch became the protagonist of *Panbabylonianism.* The controversy raged, and the adversaries, like A. Jeremias, were able to show Delitzsch that he knew cuneiform better than he understood the Bible.

Not all were touched by the new fever; certain scholars wanted to measure carefully the cultural factors which influenced Israel and they returned to the study of Israel's relations with Egypt (A. Alt). Others, like Evans, dug on Crete and discovered the palace of Minos at Cnossos. The influence of the Cretan civilization on Syria-Palestine seemed unquestionable, especially during the Mycenean age (1400-1200); but since it was impossible for many years to decipher the Cretan scripts there was no way of determining the influence of this great source or civilization on the geographical center of the Ancient Near East that was Syria-Palestine.

§ 4. Palestinian Archeology

How far had Palestinian archeology itself come? It had begun several decades later than that of Greece, Egypt and Mesopotamia, and it was going to prove much less attractive. First of all one should mention the travelers who extended the sphere of activity of the ancient pilgrims. Long before A. Musil, Rowlands and then Palmer took note of the site of Ain Qades (Cades-Barnea). Then came a French consul, also a remarkable epigraphist, Clermont-Ganneau, who discovered the Siloe inscription and the stele of King Mesha of Moab. The so-called Tell-el-Amarna letters merit special mention. They came from Egypt (1887), but circulated secretly, in need of Assyriologists to decipher their cuneiform script; the study of these texts showed that they had been written, for the most part, in Chanaan during the fourteenth century B.C.

At this time archeologists had already opened the soil of Palestine, under the leadership of Flinders Petrie who came, appropriately, from

Egypt. Since 1887 Warren had investigated Jerusalem, but under adverse circumstances; then there was the methodical exploration of eastern Jordan from 1871 to 1877 under the auspices of the Palestine Exploration Fund. But real archeology began with Flinders Petrie in 1890 in the hilly area of Tell-el-Hesy. Bliss continued this work before Dickie arrived to dig at Jerusalem. Father H. Vincent came to Jerusalem in 1891 and was to attend the whole development of Palestinian archeology. In 1907 he was able to make his first synthesis in *Chanaan*. Archeological digs were in full swing, and had already produced considerable results. In the plain of Esdrelon E. Sellin worked at Taanak which yielded cuneiform texts (1902-3) and Schumacher at Megiddo (1903-4). Macalister completed his work at Gezer and this gave the first glimpse of the ceramic development, the important criterion for dating. Reisner was on the point of beginning his researches with Lyon at Samaria (1908-10), Sellin and Watzinger at Jericho, Mackenzie at Beth-Shemesh. Others deserving mention are Thiersch at Maresa (Tell-el-Sandahanna) and Tell-es-Safi, Bliss and Macalister at Tell-Zakariya, all in the southwest.

The paucity of texts made it difficult to apply archeology to the biblical narrative, especially to the Pentateuch. But they showed that Israel and Palestine were to be fitted into the total picture of the Near East. They also provided the Chanaanite background to which Israel reacted, assimilating the culture but rejecting the religion. The fortifications which had scared the Hebrews (Nm 13, 25 ff.) were now something very real. Henceforth one would be able to illustrate burial customs, temples, sacred pillars *(massebôt)*, foundation sacrifices and child sacrifices.

The history of Palestine was thus revealed in all its complexity. The land was poor, and yet the neighbor of rich countries which influenced and even afflicted it. It was a land with many contacts : from certain points of view, very close to northern Syria where the investigations of M. Pognon (who deciphered in 1885 two inscriptions of Nabuchodonosor from the Wadi Brissa) and Princeton University unearthed some texts; here also the German work at Zinjirli and the English digs at Carchemish (Jerablus) brought to life the Aramean cities of the first millennium : Israel was truly the wandering Aramean of Dt 26, 5, who parted at Harran from the rest of his brethren. At the same time, the land has kept its original character of the desert which surrounds it on the East and South. Even without the climax of the years 1920-1939, Palestinian archeology was showing its worth, refining its methods, gradually attaining precision in its means of dating. It already permitted the conclusion that the text of the Pentateuch was not an abstract product, but was to be worked into a very living context, for it called forth a world that truly existed. One could already foresee that the Pentateuchal laws betrayed the life of a society which had to grow and protect itself in a land where many geographical and historical factors were acting upon it. Sometimes biblical scholars were tempted to overestimate the value of archeology and ask it to settle literary questions in which it has no voice; nonetheless it provided a whole series of facts that constituted a new approach, differing from, while correcting, some of the conclusions of literary criticism.

CHAPTER IV

THE SCHOOL OF FORMGESCHICHTE
(FORM CRITICISM)

BIBLIOGRAPHY

Introduction p. 67.

F. M. BRAUN, " Formgeschichte (école de la), " *SDB*, III (1936), cols. 312-317.

H. W. ROBINSON, " The Forms of Oral Tradition, " *Record and Revelation*, ed. H. W. ROBINSON (Oxford : Clarendon, 1938).

H. RINGGREN, " Oral and Written Transmission in the Old Testament, " *Studia Theologica*, 3 (1950-1951), pp. 34-54.

H. F. HAHN, *Old Testament in Modern Research* (Philadelphia, 1954), pp. 119-156.

E. NIELSEN, *Oral Tradition* (London : SCM, 1954).

A. ROBERT — H. CAZELLES, *Bulletin du Comité des Études de la Compagnie de St. Sulpice**, 7 (Paris, 1954), pp. 19-43.

E. MALY, " Gen 12, 10-20, 20, 1-18, 26, 7-11, and the Pentateuchal Question, " *CBQ*, 18 (1956), pp. 255-266.

J. BARR, " Tradition and Expectation in Ancient Israel, " *Scottish Journal of Theology*, 10 (1957), pp. 24-34.

K. STENDAHL, " Implications of Form Criticism and Tradition Criticism for Biblical Interpretation, " *JBL*, 77 (1958), pp. 33-38.

I. ENGNELL, " Methodological Aspects of Old Testament Study, " *VT*, 7 (1960), pp. 13-30.

J. DE VRIES, " The Hexateuchal Criticism of Abraham Kuenen, " *JBL*, 82 (1963), pp. 31-57.

§ 1. A New Orientation

Since 1895 the knowledge of the ancient literatures of the Near East had progressed far enough for a new method to be proposed for the study of the Pentateuch. H. Gunkel, *Privatdozent* at Halle, dedicated to Eichhorn the book that he wrote on Creation and Chaos *(Schöpfung und Chaos in Urzeit und Endzeit)*. The first half of the book treated Genesis 1, and the second half, Apocalypse 12. He adopted the distinction

between J, E, D and P, as it had been established by Wellhausen and
Holzinger. For him the priestly story of creation was relatively late;
but it would be an error, he thought, to see here a mere construction,
a free and independent creation of the priestly writer. This writer was
dependent upon the past, upon a literary history, and the elements
he used came from the distant past. Certain of them (the Sabbath)
went back to the origins of Israel; others were to be found in the
Babylonian cosmogony, such as chaos and the creation of the stars.
But the Babylonian influence on the priestly writing did not date from
the Exile; it is much older — before the arrival of the Hebrews the
Babylonian myths had reached Chanaan. The Hebrews found them when
they came and made use of them as they pleased. There is no reason,
Gunkel wrote, for denying that ancient Israel had the idea of the creation
(p. 163).

Moreover, he went on to say, one must understand precisely the
meaning of " influence " and " borrowings. " Whatever myths are
used in the imagery of the author of Gn 1, he wrote something quite
different. " The difference between the Babylonian story of creation
and that of Gn 1 is very great; one could hardly conceive a greater.
On the one hand, a poetry savage and grotesque, monstrous and
barbarous; on the other, the majestic and sublime serenity of a full
and normally sober prose. Gods appear there during the course of
events — but here God remains the same from beginning to end. A god
conquers a monster during a heated battle and makes the world out
of its body — God speaks and things are made. The least bit of the
poetry of myth has disappeared. And let us not regret this, for the gap
has been filled with thoughts of a higher religion. The theologian
therefore should treat the myth of Marduk with a certain religious
sensitivity; it is a dishonor to one's parents to judge one's ancestors
unfavorably. We have no less right to evaluate Gn 1 in a manner
different from the ancient myths. Even if our concepts of natural
history are very remote from those supposed by Gn 1, even if the Jewish
and supernatural concept of God supposed by Gn 1 does not strike our
religious sense as the highest, the fact remains that we can find in Gn 1
the God in whom we believe, while the other cosmogonies are for us
merely interesting antiquities " (p. 118). Throughout the Bible (especially
in the Prophets and Psalms) Gunkel studied the different literary forms
in which the themes of the creation narrative appeared : the primordial
ocean, the dragon, light and darkness, down to the final synthesis in
Gn 1. Thus he sketched a history of a literary form from beginning
to end.

§ 2. The Principles of this School

One can already see in Gunkel's work the principles of the Protestant School which will include such remarkable exegetes as H. Gressmann, and, more recently, G. von Rad.

1. This School concentrated its efforts on the history of literary forms and their place in social life. Critical study emphasized not so much the word or verse, as the literary unit, the structure and meaning of a passage. In a given literary piece one sees not so much the author's own idea, but rather what this tells about the social conditions, the collective psychology or the historical development. Hence one looks for the life-setting, the *Sitz im Leben*, which allows us to fix a text as a reaction of man in a certain situation, and at the same time to follow the general lines of the development of a literary genre through its complicated history. This approach conceived of the development in a manner still somewhat linear, but less so than the Wellhausen approach. For example, the " literary form " in the creation story is followed from the Babylonian stage through all its Phoenician, Chanaanite and Israelite representatives down to Jewish apocalyptic and the Apocalypse of St. John.

2. Therefore the School had constant recourse to the comparative method. This did not mean simply reducing Israel and its literature to other literatures, but rather, searching for objective points of comparison. Thanks to these one will be able to identify with certainty the literary forms utilized by the Israelite writers; one will then study how the events and the changes in milieu have influenced the evolution of the form. The most fertile field for comparison is certainly the cuneiform literature, but Gunkel did not neglect Egypt. The School will come to utilize also all the forms of primitive literatures that might throw light on the beginnings of Israelite literature; it will pay serious attention to the Nordic *sagas*, the old tribal stories of Germany, Iceland and Scandinavia, echoes of a dim history in which one can find a parallel to the tribal histories now recorded in Genesis. The *saga* is neither a myth nor pure legend; it is something more complex, in which history has its role. But one must still admit that explaining Genesis by the Eddas is sometimes explaining *obscurum per obscurius*.

3. The School is neither non-religious nor unbelieving. It is influenced by the atmosphere of intellectual skepticism in which it was born, although its stance leads it to acknowledge the value of the Old Testament. The Bible is no longer for these men the arbitrary construction of Israelite nationalism or of an educated class that became a priestly class; it is not an independent and freak development in which each

writer outstrips his predecessor. It is the expression of a profound sociological fact; the Bible finds its roots in the world and the biblical process
begins again. However, the transcendent character of the message does
not always appear clearly in the forests of legends and parallel stories.
Without denying the supernatural as a matter of principle, the School
is hardly able to affirm it, since it would need other means for this.

Gunkel himself was not prejudiced against religious feeling and
theological work. In two articles of 1904 and 1906 which later appeared
in *Reden und Aufsätze* he indicated this clearly : " The one for whom
religion is merely an interesting pathological phenomenon cannot
understand its history. We ask of a biblical exegete that he be able
to understand the religious content of a book; we are convinced that
he cannot do so unless a certain chord is struck within him. A training
which, even in theology, would try to cut itself off from religion, would
proclaim its own death-sentence, because it would have lost the meaning
of religion. Certainly, the faith of the Old Testament is not purely and
simply the same as ours. We consider ourselves close to the Prophets
and Psalmists in religion, but not simply the same. The exegete must
see this clearly and convey it to his readers. He must find the just
means between a false assimilation of the Old Testament to Christianity,
and a no less false depreciation of the Old Testament. " From this
principle, Gunkel goes on to discuss the various stages in research. He
begins by demanding textual criticism, and then the study of political
history, archeology and literary criticism. And he asks that the student
go further : " One must first of all distinguish the *Gattungen* (literary
forms) of Hebrew literature. This task is all the more important because
the ancient world knew of many *Gattungen* that we no longer have, and
which therefore are not as readily accessible to the modern reader.
Hence one must define the characteristics of the *Gattungen*. The final
goal is to establish the inner history which these *Gattungen* traversed;
this will be a literary history that will allow us to evaluate the originality
of each biblical author. " But it will not suffice to construct a history
of style or esthetics in the Bible. Exegetical work is perfected in
theological research : " biblical exegesis is theological exegesis " (p. 24).
The rest of his remarks are doubtless equivocal; he condemns dogmatic
exegesis in the name of historical exegesis and fails to note that dogma
contains eternal truths taught by a God who reveals himself in the
contingent facts of history. But it is none the less true that the School
of Gunkel looks for religion in exegesis. [1]

---

[1] Some would perhaps object most of all to certain expressions in " Sagen und
Legenden, " *RGG*[2] (Tübingen, 1931), pp. 49-60.

§ 3. The Results

The school of Form Criticism produced some important works, such as Gunkel's *Genesis*. In order to aid this type of study H. Gressmann published in two volumes texts and pictures of the Ancient East which could be used for biblical exegesis. Legal texts were included, but the school was more interested in the study of types of popular narrative, namely, folklore and stories (cf. H. Gunkel, *Das Märchen im A. T.*, 1917). In the broad summary of biblical exegesis found in the *Schriften des A. T.* (Göttingen), there were only two pages on the origin of the laws in the Pentateuch, a half-page on Deuteronomy, one page for the priestly writings, as against thirty-six for the various kinds of *sagas!* This was a regrettable lack which might easily give a false view of the Pentateuch which is above all a Torah, a Law. Moreover, the authors of " *Schriften...* ", while excellent in their analysis of literary forms and psychology, did not give full attention to the historical background of the narratives. Sometimes it was treated, but in a confused manner. Gunkel judged these narratives as having been written in view of universal types of folklore rather than in view of the contingent facts of tribal history and their sociological structures. Others, like M. Noth and A. Alt, were eventually to do more research on their life-setting in tribal origins and history, and the pertinent geographical data.

But the School had a tremendous, and one may say fortunate, influence in making the texts live. The study of literary forms owes much to it. O. Eissfeldt in his " *Einleitung in Das Alte Testament,* " stands very clearly on the side of literary criticism, but he prefixes a study of basic literary forms which he entitled : " preliterary stage " *(die vorliterarische Stufe) :* sayings, sermons (discourse of Deuteronomy), prayers (e.g., those of Abraham in Genesis), documents (e.g., the treaty between Jacob and Laban), letters (Nm 21, Moses to the king of Edom), ritual civil laws, poetic narratives, stories and *sagas* (defined as stories which instead of being sheerly imaginary are connected with some historical or geographical fact), legends, historical narratives (Eissfeldt cites hardly any from the Pentateuch), autobiographies (something of this genre, so widespread in Egypt, may be found in the poems of Balaam), oracles, blessings and curses. These would be some of the primitive pieces, used and recast by the biblical writers who are responsible for the " documents " of the Pentateuch.

More recently, certain scholars like J. Hempel in his *Althebräische Literatur* broke new ground by situating each literary genre in the development of the history of Israel. The Yahwist is studied at an older period while Deuteronomy does not appear until after Micheas. The author gives much space to law and ritual — proof that the new studies have given a keener understanding of the Pentateuch and have led some back to traditional positions which would recognize especially a law and ritual contained in these books. One of the recent works from the Form Criticism School is the study of G. van Rad on the historical problem of the form of the Hexateuch (*Das Formgeschichtliche Problem des Hexateuchs*, 1938). At the beginning of the development of the Pentateuchal texts he sees a kind of " Historical Credo, " a confession of faith concerning the intervention of God in Israel's history. Traces are to be found in Dt 26, 5, " My father was a wandering Aramean... " and 6, 20-24, " When your son asks you... you shall say...we were once slaves of Pharao in Egypt.... " This primitive *Credo*, von Rad thinks, developed into the narratives about the Sinai traditions and these narratives in turn became the norm for later worship, being read on the occasion of national feasts. The commandments were introduced, then exhortations, and finally traditions about the conquest and division of Chanaan. All these cultic elements received their first written form thanks to the genius of the Yahwist. He joined the Sinai traditions with the Conquest traditions — " the Law and the Gospel. " And he added the stories about the patriarchs which proclaim in advance the covenant and the conquest. Finally, he prefaced the whole with the primitive history (Gn 1—11), " the etiology of all the etiologies of Israel, " through which the history of Israel, itself composed of narratives and laws which expressed its life and structure, received a universal meaning, a value for all peoples. In virtue of the primitive Credo to which he adhered, the Yahwist constructed a history of salvation out of all the traditions. For von Rad then, it is the Yahwist who gave the Pentateuch its form; the addition of E, D and P did not change the fundamental literary form.

One cannot be sure that all these views are valid. 1. One cannot be sure that the basic element is the historical Credo. The formulas occur only in Deuteronomy, and the Pentateuch makes itself out more as teaching, a Law, than as a confession. It is preferable to see the beginning of the Pentateuch in the teachings which were accompanied by narratives explaining the religious importance of the oracle or the sanctuary where the oracle was given. 2. One cannot be sure that the basic content of E is not older than that of J. Even if we admit that the literary dress of E is later than that of J, it is possible that its historical and legal content goes back to an earlier age — von Rad himself admits the " archaic " character of the Elohist. From the point of view of the Law and the Decalogue, the Elohist could very well be more basic, and could have given the Pentateuch its character. But the study of von Rad, like those of the school of Form Criticism, well illustrates how the understanding of the Pentateuch is to be sought in the knowledge of Israel's faith, and in the desire of Israel's faithful to be loyal to the divine Providence that had been revealed to earlier generations.

Thus we can see the advantages and the limitations of this School. Of course there remain many questionable hypotheses in these works. While they have shown how a certain feeling for religious life is to be found in the Pentateuch, they have not shown how its historicity can be securely established, nor the primary role that Moses played. [2] When the method was applied to the New Testament the defects and presuppositions appeared more clearly and the consequences of the theology of a man like Bultmann, for example, have produced among Catholics even greater reservations about the method. [3] The Greco-Roman milieu is much better known, and whereas the New Testament was written in less than a century, the redaction of the Old Testament covers more than a millenary. For these reasons, the method of Form Criticism cannot be applied to both in the same way.

---

[2] This can be seen in H. GRESSMANN, *Moses und seine Zeit* (Göttingen, 1913).

[3] See ROBERT-FEUILLET, *Introduction to the New Testament* (New York : Desclée, 1965), pp. 288 ff.

CHAPTER V

THE PRESENT STATUS
OF PENTATEUCH STUDIES

BIBLIOGRAPHY

See the bibliography cited on p. 67.

T. JACOBSEN, *The Sumerian King List* (Chicago : Univ. of Chicago, 1939).

S. N. KRAMER, *Sumerian Mythology* (1944).

M. NOTH, *Ueberlieferungsgeschichte des Pentateuchs* (Stuttgart, 1948); *Ueberlieferungsgeschichtliche Studien* (Halle, 1943), pp. 180-217.

R. DE VAUX, " Les Patriarches hébreux et les découvertes modernes, " *RB* (1946), pp. 321-348; (1948), pp. 321-347; (1949), pp. 5-36; " A Propos du Second Centenaire d'Astruc, Réflexions sur l'État Actuel de la Critique du Pentateuque, " *Supplement to Vetus Testamentum*, I (Leiden, 1953).

R. A. DYSON, " A Propos a New Study of Genesis, " *Biblica* (1954), pp. 225 ff.

A. PARROT, *The Flood and Noah's Ark* (London : SCM, 1955).

M. POPE, *El in the Ugaritic Texts* (Leiden : Brill, 1955).

G. R. DRIVER, *Canaanite Myths and Legends* (Edinburgh, 1956); and J. MILES, *The Babylonian Laws, I and II* (1952 and 1955); *The Assyrian Laws* (1935).

J. ALBERTSON, " Genesis I and the Babylonian Creation Myth, " *Thought* 37 (1962), pp. 226-244.

A. HEIDEL, *The Babylonian Genesis* (Chicago : Univ. of Chicago, 1963); *The Gilgamesh Epic and Old Testament Parallels*[2] (Chicago : Univ. of Chicago, 1954).

S. H. HOOKE, *Babylonian and Assyrian Religion* (Tulsa : Univ. of Oklahoma, 1963).

§ 1. The Contributions of Recent Palestinian Archeology

Palestinian archeology pursued a brilliant course after 1918. The British had the Mandate and they published the Quarterly Statement of the Palestine Exploration Fund. The American School of Oriental Research had been founded and was now to be directed by W. F. Albright. The Zionists built the Hebrew University. Archeologists agreed on the ceramic chronology proposed by P. Vincent : Eneolithic (or Chalcolithic, fourth millennium), Ancient Bronze (about 3000-2000), Middle Bronze (2000-1600), Late Bronze (1600-1200), Iron Age, and then the Persian, Hellenistic and Roman periods. The actual excavations increased, the most important being those of Beisan, Jericho, Megiddo, Beth-Shemesh, Tell-en-Nasbeh, Sichem and especially Lachish (Tell ed-Duweir, interrupted by the assassination of Starckey). Under the leadership of R. Dussaud and C. Virolleaud the French Mandate organized excavations in Syria and Lebanon. The most important discoveries for ancient Hebrew and Proto-Hebrew took place at Byblos (Dunand), at Mari (Parrot) and especially at Ras Shamra-Ugarit (Schaeffer) in Syria in 1929. The Nuzi excavations in Iraq also deserve mention. Interrupted by the Second World War, archeological activities began again after 1945, but at a slower pace. The Qumran discoveries (1947) near the Dead Sea yielded many interesting items for the textual criticism of the Torah.

The mass of newly discovered data produced considerable modifications in the approach to and study of the Pentateuch. Any kind of synthesis now appeared much more difficult and several abandoned any such attempt. None received unanimous approval, although the great majority of authors, even if they refused to admit the Wellhausen synthesis, spoke of the J, E, D and P narratives. The studies of these recent years have yielded precise information concerning the destructions that took place in Chanaan at the beginning of the Iron Age, and these can be correlated with the Israelite invasion. They also presented a much clearer picture of Chanaan, its cities, its sanctuaries (Beisan, Megiddo), its ritual, its culture, especially its political structure, thanks to the so-called " execration " texts. These were found in Egypt and published by Sethe in 1926 and Posener in 1940, and contain allusions to the princes and states of Chanaan. The exploration of Transjordan (beginning with 1932) by N. Glueck tended to prove that when the Hebrew tribes entered, that country had been only recently settled. But more important than the precise data, the meaning of which might be disputed, were the new approaches to the understanding of the Pentateuchal narratives which the recent studies suggested.

§ 2. New Methods of Approach

1. The discovery of Phoenician texts at Byblos (11th-9th centuries), Ugaritic texts at Ras-Shamra (14th century), and Amorite texts at

Mari (18th-17th centuries) contributed to a better knowledge of Semitic languages and opened up the way to the ancient orthography and the archaic structure of Hebrew. As regards poetic texts, such as the oracles of Balaam, many such studies were to be expected. They provided scholars with the means to gradually determine the Chanaanite character and substructure of the literature of the Israelites (who themselves used to speak the language of Chanaan : Is 19, 18), and also the influence from North Semitic Aramean and South Semitic Arabic. Like the vocabulary, Hebrew grammar evolved, and many apparent anomalies are such only when they are explained by the grammar of a certain period. Instead of correcting these texts, one can conclude to certain important dialectical variations and even to the place of origin. But this long and patient work must also be carried out with great prudence.

2. The knowledge of literary styles has made great progress since the first works of the school of Form Criticism. Exodus 35—40 had always given cause for surprise because it repeats in detail what God had ordered in 25—31 concerning the desert sanctuary. But the literal repetition of order and its execution is also to be found now in the Ugaritic text of King Keret. The Ugaritic story of Aqhat finds an echo in some of the traits of Gn 18, where in a very impressive scene God visits Abraham, partakes of a meal prepared by Sara, and gives her the promise of a son. Certain Aramean covenant texts, such as the Sfiré-Sujin stele, end in blessings and cursings; they throw light on Pentateuchal narratives, like Deuteronomy, which record the covenant of Israel with God, and also end in blessings and curses. Finally we have not only the Gilgamesh epic and the Etana text for comparisons with the first chapters of Genesis, but a whole series of tablets published by S. N. Kramer since 1944. They are difficult to interpret because the Sumerian language is only gradually being understood (thanks to Falkenstein, Jestin, Lambert), but it is none the less clear that they will tell us of the manner in which the ancient viewed the origins of life, the condition of man, and the elements of worship. As in the Egyptian Pyramid texts, we find here plays on words, contrived, but by the same token meaningful, which help us understand certain etymologies given in Genesis (e.g., Babel connected with *balal*=mix, Gn 11, 9).

3. The striking parallels between Egyptian texts and the Joseph story have long been pointed out. Although the Patriarchs and the events of Genesis have never received direct archeological confirmation, the relations between these Patriarchs and the surrounding world have been remarkably illustrated, in particular by Fr. de Vaux, H. H. Rowley and C. H. Gordon. The name of Abram has been found both in

Mesopotamia and in Ugarit, that of Jacob in Upper Mesopotamia and in Egypt, that of Israel in Ugarit (name of person) and in Egypt (tribal name in stele of Menephtah). The paintings in the tombs of Beni-Hasan in Egypt (19th century) give us an idea of the way in which Asiatic shepherds used to request asylum; the texts of Mari (about 18th century) throw light on the wandering of the relatives of Abraham in the Middle Euphrates region (the much discussed tribe of the *Bne Yamina* — Benjaminites? — are mentioned here). In Gn 14, mention is made of Abraham the Hebrew, and the Israelites are often called Hebrews by Egyptians and Philistines; now the texts about the Habiru or Apiru are more abundant. The term seems to indicate a nomadic group, now peaceable, now dangerous, somewhat on the margin of the contemporary civilization, but their identification remains a moot question. [1] The social milieu, the legal and social customs of the Patriarchs, have been paralleled especially at Nuzi in the plains to the east of the Tigris. For example, a certain Gilimninu must give a woman to her husband, if her sterility continues, just as Sara gave Hagar to Abraham (Gn 21). The family idols go to the one who inherits — and it was in order to gain the inheritance that Rachel stole the *teraphim* of her father Laban (Gn 31). The legal texts are not limited to merely the Hammurabi code. Hrozny deciphered two series of Hittite laws in 1922 and Fr. Scheil worked out the contemporary Assyrian laws. The Neo-Babylonian laws date from the first millennium, but very recently there have been published laws that antedate Hammurabi himself : those of Eshnunna and of Lipit Ishtar (about the 19th century). And to these can be added large collections of contracts, decrees and economic documents. The Ras-Shamra contracts published in 1955 [2] betrayed the influence of Mesopotamian law on the Syrian coast. And the Hittite treaties have enriched our knowledge of the forms of covenant treaties (Mendenhall).

4. This information about the biblical text was to be completed by knowledge about biblical customs. Many texts in Genesis and the legal narratives deal with ancient customs of the Israelite tribes which reflect an area before their contact with civilizations that knew how to write. Here ethnological methods are to be employed. Fr. Jaussen *(Coutumes des Arabes au pays de Moab*)* and A. Musil *(Arabia Petraea, Arabia deserta,* etc.) had already collected much information (e.g., the theft of a lamb is punished with a fourfold restitution, among both the Bedouins and the Israelites, Ex 22, 37). Von Oppenheim presented

---

[1] Cf. J. BOTTÉRO, *Le problème des Habiru* (Paris, 1954).

[2] J. NOUGAYROL, *Palais d'Ugarit,* III; *textes diplomatiques* in *Palais d'Ugarit,* IV.

a general tableau in his *Die Beduinen*. The most interesting conclusions dealt with the structure of the family and marriage, the spring feasts like the Passover (J. Henninger), tribal organization and fictional genealogies, and blood vengeance as criminal punishment. There are also interesting data concerning the wanderings of tribes (transhumance), and gradual change through semi-nomadic state to sedentary way of life (Ashkenazi, Couroyer). [3]

5. But the discoveries and studies of the Ancient East have contributed most of all to our knowledge of cult and ritual texts. These liturgies included not only such rites as the sacred repast, invocations and prayers, but also the reading of texts which commemorated the works of the gods, and the foundation of temples. Thus there was recited on the New Year Feast in Babylon the seven tablets of creation (cf. Thureau-Dangin, *Rituels accadiens*); at Ras Shamra there was a series of tablets which commemorate the granting of a temple to Baal by the god El. The history of the Near East also proves that many of the ceremonial gestures eventually took on a new meaning and were interpreted in terms of the lives and natures of the gods themselves (e.g., the *Dramatische Texte* dealing with royal succession in Egypt, published by K. Sethe). The next step was to forge stronger links between the texts (often called myths) and ritual (cf. Hooke, *Myth and Ritual*). Hence there was a temptation to regard the historical narratives of the Pentateuch as legends from Israelite sanctuaries which were read during the celebration of various feasts; these texts were supposed to recall a particular event which portrayed the divine Providence over Israel, or to explain a given rite whose meaning was lost in terms of Yahwism. Certain scholars (J. Pedersen) thought that the Exodus narratives should be considered as the heart of the whole Pentateuch; they were the liturgical text used on the Passover Feast, and which then underwent a development. This is not enough to explain our present Pentateuch; but it is certain that the Israelites gradually associated the feasts of Azymes, Pentecost and Tabernacles, which had been seasonal agricultural feasts of the Chanaanites, with the actions of divine Providence in their own history. At least the works of this school have led to the Pentateuch being interpreted in terms of liturgy and not just in terms of literary development.

6. Hence less importance came to be given to the *written* form of the texts than to the *oral* tradition which preceded their definitive

---

[3] " Histoire d'une tribu semi-nomade de Palestine, " *RB* (1951), pp. 75-91. On the sedentariness of the Israelite tribes, see R. DUSSAUD, *La pénétration des Arabes en Syrie avant l'Islam* (Paris, 1955), pp. 163-203.

redaction. I. Engnell, in particular, became the defender of the " traditio-historical " interpretation, and went so far as to deny that the traditions were given a written redaction until the postexilic period, maintaining all the while that this late date in no way contradicted the antiquity of the traditions themselves. Just as the oracles of the prophets were kept and completed by their disciples, so the Pentateuchal traditions would have been kept and adapted in traditionist circles. His skepticism about the literary criteria of the Wellhausen school is far from being shared by most critics. But many important studies of oral tradition, its trustworthiness and formation, have resulted; research has been carried on in the light of the biblical, Arabic, and Iranian data (Widengren, Nyberg, Mowinckel, Nielsen). [4]

§ 3. New Solutions

All these avenues of research proved to be fruitful, and also made each scholar nuance his own position; hence they cannot be grouped together without some artificiality. Nevertheless we will present the principal solutions that are offered at present to the problem of the origin and development of the Pentateuch.

1. The first group remains loyal to the so-called traditional thesis about the unity of the Pentateuch and its Mosaic authorship. Emphasis is placed on the defects of the Wellhausen theory and the difficulties met in dividing the verses among the four documents. Hence this school provides no solution to the irregularities pointed out by literary analysis. [5]

2. But certain scholars try to meet the critical demands. Some, like P. Heinisch, tend to a renewal of the complementary hypothesis, in that they admit many additions to the Mosaic law. Others have recourse rather to the hypothesis of fragments, which have been compiled by an editor. Thus E. Robertson recognized in Deuteronomy the nucleus of the Pentateuch around which grew an " apparently confused collection " (*The O.T. Problem*, p. 158) of literature which came from various sanctuaries.

3. P. Volz is closer to the theory of documents. He keeps J as a sort of basic document, E would be only a new edition, and P contains supplementary legislation, whereas D keeps its individuality. Rudolph keeps J, D and P, and sees in E " a development of the material which was already in existence " (*Der " Elohist " von Exodus bis Josua*, p. 262).

---

[4] Cf. J. VAN DER PLOEG, *RB* (1947), pp. 5-41.
[5] U. Cassuto would be included in this group.

4. Others eliminate Deuteronomy from the Pentateuch, and thus form a Tetrateuch. Engnell and Noth, both Protestants, have quite different approaches. Engnell denies the existence of documents and sees in Genesis a collection of cycles of traditions; Exodus to Numbers would be another collection of traditions which were redacted at a late period by the priestly writer. Noth connects Deuteronomy with the large historical work that goes from Josue through the Books of Kings; but for the rest of the Pentateuch he retains J, E, P, regarding J and E as being derived from a common basic source, G.

5. Most scholars retain the distinction of the J, E, D, P narratives. But some regard literary criticism as being too rigid, and prefer to speak less of " documents " than of " strata " (Bentzen) or of " traditions " (de Vaux, J. Prado). These strata or traditions are the result of schools, not of an individual, but some (Robert, de Vaux) recognize a true literary personality in some places, especially in J.

6. The date proposed for J is usually pushed back by certain scholars (von Rad), but the classical late dates proposed by the Wellhausen school are still defended by many (Pfeiffer, Hölscher). The literary analysis of the documents themselves still finds many supporters. The strongest arguments have been advanced for the J documents, because certain narratives in the primitive history seem to be unaware of the deluge, and Gn 12, 10 ff. seems to be a doublet of Gn 26, 7 ff. Morgenstern speaks of a K (Kenite) source; O. Eissfeldt of an L (Lay) source; others of an Edomite (S : Seir) source, but the texts being as they are, it is difficult to find any consistency in this source which more or less corresponds to the old J[1] of the literary critics. At least there is a tendency to separate the question of the date of the redaction of the four documents from that of the sources used in them.

§ 4. Directives of the Church

In view of such a wide variety of opinions, the Holy See has given certain directives for the correct orientation of the faithful. [6]

1. The encyclical *Divino Afflante* of September 30, 1943, does not speak directly about the Pentateuch, but it insists on the fact that " ...not a few things, especially in matters pertaining to history, were scarcely at all or not fully explained by the commentators of past ages, since they lacked almost all the information, which was needed for their

---

[6] A. BEA, " L'enciclica ' Pascendi ' e gli studi biblici, " *Bi*, 39 (1958), pp. 121-138.

clearer exposition. " To be able to understand those ancient texts " ...the interpreter must, as it were, go back wholly in spirit to those remote centuries of the East and with the aid of history, archeology, ethnology and other sciences, accurately determine what modes of writing, so to speak, the authors of that ancient period would be likely to use, and in fact did use. For the ancient peoples of the East, in order to express their ideas, did not always employ those forms or kinds of speech, which we use today; but rather those used by the men of their times and countries. What those were exactly the commentator cannot determine in advance, as it were, but only after a careful examination of the ancient literature of the East.... Nevertheless no one will be surprised, if all difficulties are not yet solved and overcome; but that even today serious problems greatly exercise the minds of Catholic exegetes. " This is " the true liberty of the children of God, which adheres faithfully to the teaching of the Church and accepts and uses gratefully the contributions of profane science.... "

2. The reply of the Secretary of the Biblical Commission to His Eminence Cardinal Suhard, archbishop of Paris, is dated January 16, 1948. It says that the previous decrees of the Biblical Commission " are in no way opposed to further and truly scientific examination of these problems in accordance with the results obtained during these last forty years. " The Commission did not judge it appropriate to promulgate new decrees, but it did offer more precise judgments concerning two questions, the composition of the Pentateuch, and the literary forms of the first eleven chapters of Genesis :

" In what concerns the composition of the Pentateuch, in the above-named decree of June 27, 1906, the Biblical Commission already recognized that it may be affirmed that Moses " in order to compose his work, made use of written documents or oral traditions, " and also that modifications and additions have been made after the time of Moses (*Ench. Bibl.*, 183-184). There is no one today who doubts the existence of these sources or refuses to admit a progressive development of the Mosaic laws due to social and religious conditions of later times, a development which is also manifest in the historical narratives. Even, however, within the field of non-Catholic commentators, very divergent opinions are professed today concerning the nature and number of these documents, their denomination and date. There are, indeed, not a few authors in different countries who, for purely critical and historical reasons and with no apologetic intention, resolutely set aside the theories most in vogue until now, and who look for the elucidation of certain redactional peculiarities of the Pentateuch, not so much in the diversity of the supposed documents as in the special psychology, the peculiar processes of thought and expression, better known today, of the early Oriental peoples, or again in the different literary style demanded by the diversity of subject matter. Therefore we invite Catholic scholars to study these problems, without prepossession, in the light of sound criticism and of the findings of other sciences connected with the subject matter. Such study will doubtless establish the great part and profound influence Moses exercised both as author and as lawgiver.

" The question of the literary forms of the first eleven chapters of Genesis is far more obscure and complex. These literary forms correspond to none of our classical categories and cannot be judged in the light of Greco-Latin or modern literary styles. One can, therefore, neither deny or affirm their historicity, taken as a whole, without unduly attributing to them the canons of a literary style within which it is impossible to classify them. If one agrees not to recognize in these chapters history in the classical and modern sense, one must, however, admit that the actual scientific data do not allow of giving all the problems they set a *positive* solution. The first duty here incumbent upon scientific exegesis consists above all in the attentive study of all the literary, scientific, historical, cultural and religious problems connected with these chapters; one should then examine closely the literary processes of the early Oriental peoples, their psychology, their way of expressing themselves and their very notion of historical truth; in a word, one should collate without prejudice all the subject matter of the paleontological and historical, epigraphic and literary sciences. Only thus can we hope to look more clearly into the true nature of certain narratives in the first chapters of Genesis. To declare *a priori* that their narratives contain no history in the modern sense of the term would easily convey the idea that they contain no history whatever, whereas they relate in simple and figurative language, adapted to the understanding of a less developed people, the fundamental truths presupposed for the economy of salvation, as well as the popular description of the origin of the human race and of the Chosen People. "

3. The encyclical *Humani Generis* *, of August 12, 1950, returned to these chapters of Genesis — not that it gave a direct and precise exegesis of these texts, but as regards the problems of evolution, polygenism, and the data of primitive history, it recalled certains truths known by Faith which can help to a real understanding of the text.

" The teaching of the Church leaves the doctrine of evolution an

---

* English translation courtesy of Catholic Truth Society, London.

open question, as long as it confines its speculations to the development, from other living matter already in existence, of the human body. (That souls are immediately created by God is a view which the Catholic faith imposes on us.) In the present state of scientific and theological opinion, this question may be legitimately canvassed by research, and by discussion between those who are expert in both subjects. At the same time, the reasons for and against either view must be weighed and adjudged with all seriousness, fairness, and restraint; and there must be a readiness on all sides to accept the arbitrament of the Church, as being entrusted by Christ with the task of interpreting the Scriptures aright, and the duty of safeguarding the doctrines of the faith. There are some who take rash advantage of this liberty of debate, by treating the subject as if the whole matter were closed — as if the discoveries hitherto made, and the arguments based on them, were sufficiently certain to prove, beyond doubt, the development of the human body from other living matter already in existence. They forget, too, that there are certain references to the subject in the sources of divine revelation, which call for the greatest caution and prudence in discussing it.

"There are other conjectures, about polygenism (as it is called), which leave the faithful no such freedom of debate. Christians cannot lend their support to a theory which involves the existence, after Adam's time, of some earthly race of men, truly so called, who were not descended ultimately from him, or else supposes that Adam was the name given to some group of our primordial ancestors. It does not appear how such views can be reconciled with the doctrine of original sin, as this is guaranteed to us by Scripture and tradition, and proposed to us by the Church. Original sin is the result of a sin committed, in actual historical fact, by an individual man named Adam, and it is a quality native to all of us, only because it has been handed down by descent from him.

"As with biology and anthropology, so with history; there are some who make bold to overstep the warning landmarks which the Church has laid down. One especially regrettable tendency is to interpret the historical books of the Old Testament with overmuch freedom. In vain do the exponents of this method appeal, for their defense, to the letter recently received by the Archbishop of Paris from the Pontifical Commission on Biblical Studies. It was clearly laid down in that letter that the first eleven chapters of Genesis, although it is not right to judge them by modern standards of historical composition, such as would be applied to the great classical authors, or to the learned of our own day, do nevertheless come under the heading of history; in what exact sense, it is for the further labors of the exegete to determine. These chapters have a *naïf*, symbolical way of talking, well suited to the understanding of a primitive people. But they do disclose to us certain important truths, upon which the attainment of our eternal salvation depends, and they do also give a popularly-written description of how the human race, and the Chosen People in particular, came to be. It may be true that these old writers of sacred history drew some of their material from the stories current among the people of their day. So much may be granted; but it must be remembered on the other side that they did so under the impulse of divine inspiration, which preserved them from all error in selecting and assessing the material they used.

" These excerpts from current stories, which are found in the sacred books, must not be put on a level with mere myths, or with legend in general. Myths arise from the untrammeled exercise of the imagination; whereas in our sacred books, even in the Old Testament, a love of truth and a cult of simplicity shine out, in such a way as to put these writers on a demonstrably different level from their profane contemporaries. "

In view of our exposition of the state of the question (including both the directives of the Church and the present critical positions), it may be said that the historical and literary cadre which the " documentary " hypothesis offers is the least inadequate for an explanation of the religious message of the Pentateuch. The five books are contained in the J, E, D, P layers, but also in their synthesis. One should never forget that the word " document " has a special meaning here : each document is itself made up of sources and finds a basis in Moses; moreover, the joining of the documents was neither mechanical nor arbitrary, but was the result of a providential and intelligent action. Finally, we may look forward to more investigation and refinement of these views. Father Dyson, reviewing Von Rad's *Genesis* commentary, wrote : " The progress made since Wellhausen's attempt to solve the Pentateuchal problem is immense. It is true that the four ' classical documents ' J, E, D, P are still there, but with what a difference in the conception of them! " [7]

---

[7] *Bi*, 35 (1954), p. 227. See also G. DUNCKER in *Angelicum*, 36 (1959), p. 57 " ...*quatenus postea a catholicis auctoribus critice recognita, correcta, adaptata, ista deinde apparuit in* ' Bible de Jerusalem ' *et theoria documentorum* ' Bible Pirot-Clamer. ' *Mosaica authentia Pentateuchi, prout in istis editionibus exponitur, haud* ' *difficulter conciliatur cum traditione et documentis ecclesiasticis, quae Moysen auctorem litterarium Pentateuchi, saltem in sensu latiore faciunt,* ' *si Epistula ad Card. Suhard bene intelligitur. "

NOTES ON THE CONTENT AND THEOLOGY OF THE PENTATEUCH

BIBLIOGRAPHY

See the bibliography cited, p. 67.

S. DRIVER, *Introduction to the Literature of the Old Testament*[8] (Edinburgh, 1909), pp. 1-159.

E. JACOB, *La Tradition historique en Israël* (Montpellier, 1946).

A. BENTZEN, *Introduction to the Old Testament*, II (Copenhagen, 1952), pp. 9-81.

H. CAZELLES, " Loi Israélite, " *SDB*, V, cols. 498-530 (with bibliography up to 1953).

G. E. WRIGHT, *God Who Acts* (London : SCM, 1952); *The Old Testament Against Its Environment* (London : SCM, 1957).

L. KÖHLER, *Old Testament Theology* (Philadelphia : Westminster, 1957).

E. JACOB, *Theology of the Old Testament* (New York : Harper, 1958).

T. VRIEZEN, *An Outline of Old Testament Theology* (London : Blackwell, 1958).

W. EICHRODT, *Theology of the Old Testament*, I (Philadelphia : Westminster, 1961).

G. VON RAD, *Old Testament Theology*, I and II (New York : Harper, 1962 and 1966).

A. ROBERT, " Historique (genre), "[*] *SDB*, IV, cols. 9-12.

Sound exegesis demands that the texts be understood in the light of the age and the milieux in which they were composed; only then can they deliver the message of the author, their literal sense. But for the Pentateuch one may not forget that they have been re-used in several successive syntheses. In line with the procedure studied by I. Guidi [1] and His Eminence Cardinal Tisserant, [2] the Semitic writer is inclined to respect the basic text he is using, while at the same time he gives it a new meaning with corrections that are sometimes very small. The exegete must try, even if he does not always succeed, to give due emphasis

---

[1] " L'historiographie chez les Sémites, " *RB* (1906), pp. 509 ff.

[2] " Fragments syriaques du Livre des Jubilés, " *RB* (1921, pp. 55-86; 206-232).

to this development in the meaning of the texts, which is an expression of the continuity of tradition and its enrichment through the years. [3]

After a few notes concerning the oldest texts and traditions, this chapter will then study the development of the Mosaic tradition in the literary collections that were formed and preserved in the final redaction. Although the results of the school of literary criticism are not admitted by all, we will give an exposition of the theology which is found in the J, E, D, P texts. At the present time it seems to be the method best adapted for explaining the thought of the Pentateuch and the progress of Revelation as willed and achieved by God by means of the men whom His Spirit chose and directed. For our part, we are inclined to recognize here " documents, " literary units. Should one only see these as " traditions, " nevertheless each one has its own proper mentality and theology. The union itself of these strata was controlled by certain religious beliefs. It should not be forgotten that almost all the points to be raised are subject to difference of opinion.

§ 1. The Ancient Traditions

I. THE BEGINNINGS

No one doubts that the Pentateuch has preserved many traditions and customs that reach back to the origins of Israel. [4] It is much more difficult to determine what had already received written form at this time and then preserved that form in the present Pentateuch. There are a few examples of these small literary units which are generally accepted. What are they? 1) The clearest seem to be found in certain very old rhythmic songs that are easy to memorize, such as the song of Lamech (Gn 4, 23 f.) which reflects the savage vengeance of the desert, the song of the well (Nm 21, 18), another nomadic piece that was perhaps originally a war cry like Hesebon's curse of Moab (Nm 21, 27-30). 2) The blessings and curses (Gn 9, 25 ff.; 27, 28 ff. 39 ff.) which echo a very human and ancient religious feeling. Some of these have been grouped together to serve as a nucleus for the blessings of Jacob (Gn 49), Moses (Dt 33), Balaam (Nm 23 and 24) and the cursings of Sichem (Dt 27). 3) In the blessings of Jacob and of Moses there are also to be found a certain number of very old sayings about a person or a tribe (see also

---

[3] E. P. ARBEZ, " Some Parallels from Arabic Literature to Problems of the O.T., " *CBQ*, 8 (1946), pp. 58-71.

[4] See pp. 562 ff.

Gn 21, 7; 25, 22 ff.). Akin to the saying is the juridical formula, typified in the extremely ancient formulation of the talion (perhaps this has a cultic origin; see A. Alt). 4) The saying can also refer to an important event in tribal life (Gn 49, 5-7 concerning Simeon and Levi), and grow quite naturally into poetry with symbol and parallelism *(ibid.)*, or into small prose narratives. As A. Lods has noted, the ancient stories are brief, very sober in descriptive detail, centered on an action which they carry to the finish; they illustrate the help given by God to men in trouble — all this in simple psychological fashion. Their antiquity is recognized by the fact that they betray often a mentality and preoccupations which are no longer those of the authors of the documents in which they have been inserted. Thus the struggle of Jacob with the angel (Gn 32, 25-33), which highlights the character of Jacob, both his weakness and his dignity as one chosen by God. Likewise, the story of the circumcision of the son of Moses (Ex 4, 24-26) which explains the meaning of the rite in an archaizing manner. Others deal with the problems of sedentariness and with the relations of the Israelites with the lords of the land who do not believe in Yahweh, such as the incident at the Bersheba well (Gn 26, 23-31).

Towards the middle of the second millennium the Semites had invented an alphabet that was used at Sinai (Proto-Sinaitic inscriptions), in the south of Chanaan (Lachish ewer), near the Dead Sea (the inscribed arrow [-heads?] found near Bethlehem) and Galilee (Hazor jar). Hence some parts of the Pentateuch could have been put down in writing fairly soon, and collections could have been formed at an early period : thus the Madianite-Kenite traditions, which considered Cain as the eponymous ancestor, would have been known by the Israelites in the desert. Thus, for example, one might unite in one group (S, L, K or J[1]) the rather mutilated narratives about Seth (Gn 4, 25; Nm 24, 17); these are perhaps the *Sutu* [5] nomads known from Egyptian and Assyrian texts; Cain would be the Cainites that were expelled from their " nest " (Gn 4, 12; cf. 4, 22 : Tubal-Cain, and Nm 24, 21 ff.), and perhaps the fearful giants of Chanaan (Gn 6, 1-4) as they would have been seen by a nomad (cf. Nm 13, 33).

II. THE ROLE OF MOSES

The role of Moses in the Pentateuch as *Law* must have been considerable, otherwise the documents would not have been associated with him;

---

[5] R. KUPPER, *Les nomades en Mésopotamie au temps des rois de Mari* (Paris, 1957).

but it is difficult to spell this out. The studies of A. Alt have shown
(*Die Ursprünge des israelitischen Rechts*, 1934) the specifically Israelite
portion of biblical law, namely, " apodictic law. " The " casuistic " formulae (e.g., Ex 21, 28-37), in which the case is put in conditional form (" If
some one does this or that... ") are to be found in all the eastern law
codes. On the other hand, all those which are expressed in different
(especially imperative) formulae (" Thou shalt do this and not that)
are characteristic of Israel, and seem to convey customs that predate
the conquest. These form the essence of the *Decalogue*, especially the
second part which demands that the Israelite respect his neighbor, his
life and goods. The age of the Decalogue has been much discussed;
those who favor a linear development of Israel's religion think that these
moral commands, expressed in pithy form, must belong to a relatively
late age in Israel's history (8th century). In fact, additions had to
be made to the Decalogue and we have two different editions in the
Pentateuch (Ex 20, 2-17; Dt 5, 6-17). But one can point to the similar
prescriptions which are to be found in the Egyptian Book of the Dead
(16th-14th centuries), although these reflect a different religious spirit
(" I have not killed, I have not stolen, I have not committed injustice,
I have not harmed the bread of the gods... "). These imperative
formulae seem to meet 1) the personal religion of the God of Abraham
(who is active already on this earth, and not just after death, like Osiris);
2) a morality that is elevated and concerned with the individual, such
as is to be found in the Egyptian wisdom literature of the second
millennium; 3) the historical situation of Israel when it has not yet
settled in Chanaan and lives definitely outside the contemporary
civilization, following the rugged demands of the desert and the ancient
practices like the Sabbath rest. In this imperative the heart of the
divine command was expressed in Israel — whatever be the order given
to Adam not to touch the tree (Gn 2, 17) or the commands contained
in the *Book of the Covenant* (Ex 20, 22—23, 14) which provide the framework and religious meaning for the Genesis story.

Although this is not the general opinion, very strong reasons favor
the Mosaic authorship of this first legal compilation that is called the
code of the covenant. We have here an ancient legislation which does
not demand centralization of the sanctuary (20, 24), ignores the kingdom,
and knows only of a very loose tribal unity. It addresses itself to a
society that is only beginning to settle down, in which agriculture is
important, but can be dispensed with every seventh year (23, 11), and
in which cattle constitutes the most precious treasure. This collection
already includes the casuistic laws, and adds some ancient prohibitions

(participial formulae), the law of the talion and some religious laws that aim to keep Israel faithful in the face of the Chanaanite sanctuaries (doubtless those of Transjordan, like Baal-Phegor; cf. Nm 25). This might very well be the last legacy of Moses in Transjordan after the tribes of Ruben, Gad and Manasses had settled down. This would be enough to establish the great influence of Moses as author and lawgiver : later laws will preserve this mixture of style and key legislation that are to be found in these texts.

It is an even more delicate task to reveal the role of Moses in the *narratives*. The E document, which contains the Decalogue and the Book of the Covenant, comes from the northern tribes which had the principal role, with Josue, " the servant of Moses " (Nm 12, 28) in the conquest. It has faithfully preserved the moral and spiritual characteristics of Mosaism and it includes the ancient traditions about Jacob's residence in Transjordan (Gn 29—33) and the departure from Egypt (Ex 3—15) that may go back to Moses. But one can not yet clearly distinguish this first layer from the later redaction which we shall study further on. [6]

III. COLLECTIONS OF POEMS

The Bible itself tells us that there were other ancient collections, especially of poetry : the " Book of the wars of Yahweh " (Nm 21, 14) and the Book of *Jashar* (Jos 10, 13), and extracts from these have been preserved in the canonical books. It is difficult to determine the content of the book mentioned in Ex 17, 14. But with the period of the Judges writing develops in Israel, not only in the form of lists (Jgs 8, 14), but in the form of apologues and stories. The sanctuary traditions come to be fixed, and rituals are written down. The studies of M. Noth have been able to specify the particular places that gave rise to real cycles. In the reign of David and Solomon the court becomes the scene of an intense literary activity, due partially to the creation of a scribal class which the kingdom itself needs.

§ 2. The Yahwist

Although there is no universal agreement among exegetes about the verses that are to be attributed to the Yahwist tradition, von Hügel in 1897 could write " there is unanimous consent on all the main points, and often even for the details. " The Yahwist narrative contains unified scenes that are bound together by a continuous thread. The work is

---

[6] Cf. *Moïse, l'homme de l'Alliance** (Cahiers Sioniens, VIII, 2-4; Paris, 1955).

a synthesis, in form and content, which draws together tribal and sanctuary traditions.   This it does for the sake of a religious teaching that is already formed, and in an original manner that reflects a real literary personality.   We have seen that the Yahwist has his own vocabulary, but even more characteristic is his style.   He prefers the concrete and the picturesque, and excels in character portraits.   He is a psychologist interested in the secrets of man's heart, and also a story-teller who is to be admired for his liveliness, clarity and finished style, a painter who with a few strokes draws a scene that often comes alive by means of a dialogue.   This style is not without some relation to Egyptian wisdom literature, but it draws its lifeblood from the race and the soil, and its feeling for what is human is not to be compared with the contemporary decadent works in Egypt.

His theology is also profoundly original, and is expressed in a very concrete way; there are no technical terms, but well-balanced symbols and scenes.   Behind the apparent naïveté of the Genesis stories is a philosophy that is sure of itself and discreetly expressed, such as the presence of God which often appears only faintly — but in the end the stories that appear to be " profane " find their explanation only in a teaching about Providence.   The work of the Yahwist is not the work of a " primitive. "   He wrote in a world in which the most profound classical works of Egypt and Babylonia were circulating.

I.   THE SUPERNATURAL WORLD OF THE YAHWIST [7]

One should not ask of the Yahwist clear formulae about such natural truths as monotheism, God's omnipotence or omniscience.   He knows of these truths and lives by them, but it is not his task to formulate them.   The purpose of his writing is to deal with truths of another order.   He has to express in human language, that can be understood by contemporaries who are not metaphysicians, the very mysteries of God and His action on human life.   In order to understand him one must adopt the point of view of his age and appreciate the religious problems that faced him.

In his age there is no problem about the existence of God.   The real task is : Where is this God and where can He be found?   Man is conscious of being the toy of powerful forces that affect his life and attract him; whom is he to follow?   The forces of nature, the political

---

[7] Cf. J. L. McKENZIE, " The Hebrew Attitude towards Mythological Poly-theism, " *CBQ*, 14 (1952), pp. 323-335; " God and Nature in the Old Testament, " *CBQ*, 14 (1952), pp. 18-39; 124-145.

realities, or the God of Israel's tradition? Again, everyone of his age admitted that man lived in daily contact with the god(s). Supernatural powers can be invoked, and their response obtained. But one can still remain ignorant of just who is the supreme deity, the only one who is truly God and whose power is above all others. He is the one who truly upholds and protects life. Will it be nature, politics, conscience or tradition that will reveal Him to mankind?

The contemporaries of the Yahwist will also freely admit that God is the author of life; fecundity is the sign of the divine presence and power. They would not have the difficulties we feel in saying that man is a son of God. The Egyptian pharao was considered to be the particular offspring of God; but in a more general way, that needs to be specified, Meri-Ka-Re (an Egyptian sage of about 2000 B.C.) said that man was the image of God. Among the philosophical and religious uncertainties of the time, the problem was : What is the divine element in man that makes him resemble God? Just how is God a father?

Those who read the Yahwist will not ask if human society is directed by God. This is an admitted fact; the Assyrian king after a campaign makes a report to the sovereign deity. But in the midst of all the nations and kingdoms often in conflict, who was *the* king, *the* leader, who was truly *the* representative of the master of the world where the nations had to live?

Finally, it is easy to admit that the cause of man's suffering is his sin against God. But it is harder to tell if this god is capricious or not, and more difficult still, to know what is the sin to be avoided, or even if it can be avoided.

The Yahwist thinks and writes in terms of this supernatural view of the world and the problems entailed by man's relationship to God. He does not write for readers who need to be taught the first principles of morality and theodicy; he writes for a restless generation that should understand from its own national life *where the truly supernatural lies, and where lies the temptation to yield to the false supernatural*. The problems of his age are not ours. His contemporaries granted the existence of the supernatural which ours call into question; but ideas about the unity of the universe, natural laws, universal morality which are very familiar to people of the twentieth century, were foreign to them. And perhaps the best manner of approaching this age is to entertain the notion of mystery which Christianity envisions. According to the Christian idea, God is not alone, but communicates His life; there is a presence of God in history and in the visible world (the mystery

of the Incarnation); God does not abandon sinful man (the Redemption)
but constantly helps him, instead of being merely the supreme Law
of a well-ordered universe.

II. The religious optimism of the Yahwist

The Yahwist looks at man without any illusions and his narrative may
even give scandal by its portrayal of human weakness. He is preoccupied
with the influence of woman in the destiny of man : she is not only
a seducer (Gn 3, 6) but also the mother who gives life and begets a child
with the help of God (Gn 4, 1). He is intrigued by the problem of fertility,
the dispensing of life. Even while he recognizes the powers of evil and
human misery at work, he is an optimist. He has enough trust in nature
and its laws to know that a new deluge will never come again. He shows
life on the move : Jacob's sons, blessed in their descendants; Israel,
delivered from slavery; the tribes, established in a land flowing with
milk and honey.

This is a religious optimism, based uniquely on the knowledge of
Yahweh, His plans, His power. Yahweh wants to live with man, and
in order to describe this living presence of God in the world, the Yahwist
does not fear to use the boldest anthropomorphism : Yahweh visits
Adam and Eve in the cool of the day; He makes garments of skin for
them; He Himself closes the entrance to the ark. This is all the more
noteworthy, since the Yahwist does show an interest in secondary causes :
physical (the wind from the east which Yahweh uses for the miracle
of crossing the Red Sea), psychological (ambition, envy, love). His
God is transcendant, and His unequaled majesty is portrayed in a most
harsh manner : Adam and Eve attain a superhuman knowledge and can
partake of the tree of life — but they are expelled from paradise; mankind
seems to reach heaven with its tower — but still they are scattered.
Most of all, Yahweh is close to man and speaks with him; He takes
dinner with him : Abraham, Moses, or the elders. The Law of Yahweh
is a command which is addressed directly and authoritatively to man's
conscience; but for the Yahwist this command has an essentially
liturgical flavor : the expulsion from the earthly Paradise is presented
as a food taboo; the paschal law implies azymes, and the only legal
code given by the Yahwist is the " ritual Decalogue " in which the
three seasonal Chanaanite feasts become pilgrimages to the sanctuary
of Israel's God, analogous to that of the old Passover. What Yahweh
demands is faith, courage, trust in the traditions and the life of the
nation.

III. NATIONALISM AND " MESSIANISM "

Yahweh is the God of the nation. As God of the universe, He was worshiped by Enos, son of Seth, since before the Flood. When He revealed Himself to Abraham and his descendants, delivering them from a foreign yoke and giving them the Law through Moses, He then became *their* God. Hence the optimism of the Yahwist; it is a national, but not a nationalistic optimism : all the families of the world can find a blessing in Abraham. The tribe of Juda, while it holds the scepter, includes the son of Shua the Chanaanite woman; Hobab, son of Raguel the Madianite, has a share in the promises; it is a " mixed ancestry " that leaves Egypt with Moses. But the future belongs to Israel because only Yahweh its God has power over the earth and He gives it to whom He pleases.

Here we touch on the second of the fundamental problems in the Yahwist tradition (the first being that of fidelity to the God of the commandments, despite the attraction of Egyptian wisdom or fertility cults) : How is the power that comes from God to be passed on? [8] The contemporaries of Israel never disputed the fact that in a nation the human leader governs in the name of the national God. But the Yahwist disputes the idea that the heir must be the first-born, as nature seems to suggest. The prayer of Abel is heard over that of Cain; Isaac wins out over Ishmael, Jacob over Esau, Juda over his three older brothers, and it is he who saves his brothers with his speech to Joseph. Moreover, it has often been pointed out that it is the J document in the Pentateuch which contains the Messianic prophecies [9] : the *protoevangelium* in Gn 3, 15, which proclaims deliverance through the seed of the woman; the prophecy of Jacob about Juda and the mysterious *Shilo* (" him to whom the rule belongs " : Gn 49, 10 explained by Ez 21, 32); the prophecies of Balaam about a hero greater than Agag (Nm 24, 7 according to the Greek text) and about the star coming from Jacob (Nm 24, 17). These enable us to see a relationship between J and 2 Sm 7, in which Nathan announces the eternal support of God for the dynasty of David of Juda. [10]

IV. THE YAHWIST, A JUDEAN WRITER

The Yahwist is certainly from the south because he utilizes and synthesizes particularly the old traditions that had gathered around

---

[8] This is an essential theme in the mythological texts of Ras Shamra; cf. C. VIROLLEAUD, *Légendes de Babylone et de Canaan* (Paris, 1949), pp. 67, 71, 98.

[9] G. L. GUYOT, " Messianism in the Book of Genesis, " *CBQ*, 13 (1951), pp. 415-421.

[10] H. SCHULTZE, " *Die Grossreichsidee Davids, wie sie sich im Werk des Jahwisten spiegelt,* " *TLZ* (1957), p. 752.

the southern sanctuaries. But he does not carry on any polemics against the north; indeed he records Abraham's travels to the sanctuaries of this area (Gn 12). His problem is not the dynasty as such, but the heir within the dynasty. Finally, he does not oppose the north to the south because he presupposes that they are united. It is clear that Gn 27, 40 about the liberation of Edom, does not offer a good argument for the 9th century date of the Yahwist. The redaction would be much more intelligible in the reign of Solomon, among those who disliked the king because of his internationalism (which led him to import Egyptian wisdom) and because of his imitating Chanaanite cults (which led him to build a Temple). The Yahwist criticizes the blind confidence in Egyptian wisdom and everything that would mean an abandonment of Yahweh and the commandments transmitted through Moses. But he hallows the legitimacy of David's heir and sees the heart of Yahwism in the three annual pilgrimages to the national sanctuary which housed the ark of Yahweh's presence (Ex 34). The Israelites have settled down, the feasts are agricultural, the future should be happy and fruitful for Israel, if it listens to Yahweh and remains faithful to the statutes of the God of the Fathers and of Moses.

We must now see how he expressed this theology in his synthesis of the national traditions; for in his work everything is made concrete and the doctrinal points often appear by means of a story in a quite unexpected way.

V. PRIMITIVE HISTORY

The beginnings [11]

These chapters serve as an introduction to the call of Abraham and the divine blessing which the people of the earth are to receive through him (Gn 12, 3). Mankind is unhappy, it is subjected to a curse which it has merited — this is the religious meaning of man's present condition. In order to express this in a tableau, the Yahwist has recourse to traditions of various kinds (while leaving his own imprint upon them) : Mesopotamia, southern Palestine.   Hence there are some disparities in the text : P. Humbert *(Études sur le récit du paradis et de la chute dans la Genèse)* admits of two sources in chapters 2—3; others claim there are more. For a detailed exegesis of these chapters one can consult the *Genèse* of A. Clamer and *Origines, Genèse I-III* of C. Hauret, as well as the interesting viewpoints of G. von Rad *(Das erste Buch Moses)*. We may note that A. Lods recognized a later addition in the flood story.

---

[11] A. BEA, " Il problema del Pentateucho e della storia primordiale, " *CC*, 2 (1948), pp. 116-127.

Gn 2, 4b—3, 26 forms a complete unit. After a beginning of the same stripe as the Babylonian cosmogonies, man is presented as the center of creation. He is made of up of a double element : he is of the earth, *adam* taken from *adamah*; but he receives from God the breath that makes him a living being. All round him vegetation appears; it is to him that the animals come and he names them; it is for him that woman was created, the only possible companion he can have, " bone of his bone and flesh of his flesh, " that is to say, having the same nature as his (Jgs 9, 2). But man finds temptation in this world. The tempter, under the form of a serpent, turns back against him his union with the woman to entice him to disobey the divine command. The nature of this disobedience is still disputed [12] because the Yahwist expresses himself in sibylline style, but the " knowledge of good and evil " certainly has some relationship to wisdom, the practical knowledge of human happiness. The Yahwist does not deny that man by his action acquired a higher knowledge, but he acquired it sinfully; also, he finds weakness instead of happiness, and brings a curse upon himself. Man has separated himself from the God of life; therefore he cannot avoid death. The present state of man, subject to suffering and death, is not God's doing, but man's, since the sin of his first parent. That is why this state affects every man coming into this world, even before he is personally guilty (original sin). But ultimately man was not conquered and enslaved by the forces of evil. The Yahwist attaches to motherhood a hope that is based on God himself (Gn 3, 15). [13] It is quite possible that he saw in the saving motherhood of Eve the prototype of the royal maternity (cf. Is 7, 14; Mi 5, 2, and the persistent mention of queen-mothers in the Books of Kings) and hence of Messianic motherhood. This text can then take its place in Marian theology in conformity with Christian tradition. [14] The tree of life (cf. Prv 3, 18 and 11, 30) was prohibited to Adam; the domain of God was henceforth guarded by the Cherubim and the lightning (a zigzag sword, 3, 22-24). The Yahwist uses well-known religious symbols here in order to express his theology.

From the beginnings to Abraham

The following chapters are intimately connected with what precedes. The development of life, although willed by God since Eve begets her

---

[12] A. M. DUBARLE, " Le péché originel dans la Genèse, " *RB* (1957), pp. 5-34; L. F. HARTMAN, " Sin in Paradise, " *CBQ*, 20 (1958), pp. 26-40.

[13] H. CAZELLES, " L'exégèse contemporaine de Gn. 3, 15, " *La Nouvelle Ève*, III (1957).

[14] B. RIGAUX, " La femme et son lignage dans Genèse III, 14-15, "* *RB* (1954), pp. 321-348.

first-born (4, 1) [15] " with " God, results in murders and their punishment
(4, 3-16). Here the author uses the sociological data of his time in order
to describe the state of mankind. One cannot be sure about the origin
of the name of the first man *Adam* (associated with *Adama*, meaning
earth), which could be due to the name of the eponymous ancestor of
Edom, the elder brother of Israel whence certain southern tribes
originated, and also about the name of Eve *(hawwa)* which may be
associated with the *hawwôt Yair* (Nm 32, 41; Dt 3, 14; Jgs 10, 4),
settlements that produced both farmers and shepherds *(hawwôt* can
also mean " serpent "). But it is certain that Cain *(Qayin)* stands
for the eponymous ancestor of the Kenites, a nomad southern tribe
whose fate was more or less tied to Israel before the conquest. Perhaps
Seth represents the *Sutu* of the cuneiform texts *(Shasu* in the Egyptian
sources?) who were nomads from the boundaries of Egypt and Chanaan.
Several of the proper names mentioned in chapter 4 may also be identified.
By means of these definite memories the Yahwist sketches the
development of mankind : the foundation of cities, the beginning of the
arts; yet both are deeply rent with unhappiness. It is not just temptation
that is to be found in the world, but sin " which crouches at the gate "
(Gn 4, 7). Enos, son of Seth, calls upon Yahweh the true God (4, 25 ff.).
But after the sons of Elohim had married the daughters of men, the God
of life limited the human life span (6, 1-3); then, after the giants were
born, He recognized man's perversity and determined to destroy him
(6, 4-7). In these obscure traditions, however they be interpreted, is
reflected man's continual departure from divine life. His days are
limited to 120 years, then comes the universal punishment of the Flood
(7, 1-2.4-5.7.10.12.16b-17.22 ff.; 8, 2b-3a.6-12.13b.20-22).

The Yahwist had indicated, by his interpretation of the name
of Eve (3, 20), that God had not meant to allow the human race to be
extinguished because of original sin. In the person of Seth, he had
indicated that the life of God would prevail over the murders of man
(4, 25). Noe, the hero of the flood, " who shall bring comfort to his
father from his work in the accursed ground " (5, 29), is assured that
sin will not rule out natural law (8, 22) : God will accept the sacrifice
of him whom He pardons, and due to him, will preserve the rhythm
of the seasons which make nature fruitful. The human race continues
to propagate itself (9, 19 ff.), but it is a weak human race, such as the
drunken Noe, father of a wicked Cham. At this point the Yahwist
makes use of a southern Judean narrative which divides the human
race in three branches : Semites, Chamites (here, the Chanaanites) and the

---
[15] C. HAURET, *RSR*, 32 (1958), pp. 358-367.

descendants of Japhet (the name of Iapetos, son of the earth and father of Prometheus, appears in Homer and Hesiod; here it reminds one of the " peoples of the Sea "). As always, the Yahwist synthesizes, and appeals to another tradition that is based on sociological notes similar to those of chapter 4. These are given over to Noe the farmer (9, 20-27), Nimrod the hunter (10, 9), the Chanaanites and their home (10, 19), and finally to the descendants of Eber (10, 25 ff.), to whom Abraham is related through Pheleg. The episode of the Tower of Babel (11, 1-9) betrays a thoroughly Mesopotamian color with its allusion to bitumen and a stepped tower called Ziggurat. [16] Thus the author shows that the great empires could not reach the level of the divine; they pretend to unify men by merely human resources which are as vain as the pretention of Adam to have the knowledge of good and evil by his own power. It is through Abraham, whose progenitors are described in 11, 28 ff., that the nations of the earth are unified and blessed, thanks to Abraham's faith in Yahweh (12, 1-3).

VI. PATRIARCHAL HISTORY

Abraham and Isaac

The Yahwist pursues his theological synthesis by using the patriarchal traditions. Unlike Adam, Abram obeys the divine order, as Noe did. His journey gives religious meaning to the holy places of the north, Sichem and Bethel (12, 6-9), but his memory is fixed in the south, at Mamre (the holy place near Hebron). For the Yahwist, Abraham is the typical patriarch, with his virtues, his power and fruitfulness. He comes as a stranger into the midst of powerful princes who even wish to take his wife from him (12, 10-20), but thanks to the help of God he is prosperous. He yields the best part to his relatives, like Lot (13, 1-13, in part), but he intercedes in their behalf before God (18). The promises of God are in view of his descendants, not himself; for the Yahwist, the whole life of Abram (called Abraham after his taking up residence at Mamre) is orientated towards his posterity, just as the hope of the monarchy is later turned towards the heir of the throne. This posterity is greater than that of Lot (13, 14-17); it will count Ishmael and Midian in addition to Israel. Abram (like Adam) is gifted with a supernatural sleep *(tardemah)* which brings to him not an Eve, the mother of the living, but a posterity that inherits the promises he received. After a time of subjection they will possess the land (chap. 15, in part). But the true heir will not be the first-born. Ishmael's birth is due to an earthy

---

[16] A. PARROT, *Ziggurats et Tour de Babel* (Paris, 1949).

custom, but Isaac is born as a result of the divine promise given during a sacred repast which the patriarch offers to the mysterious visitors (18, 1-15; 21, 2, in contrast to Lot's posterity which has been contaminated by Sodom, chap. 19). [17]

The Yahwist narrative then turns to Bersabee (21, 33 ff.). Here the Isaac cycle begins and the memories of the second patriarch are associated with this place. The Yahwist records the sacrifice of Isaac (Gn 22, 14-18) when the *Angel of Yahweh* (that is, the messenger who carries out the will of the transcendant God on earth) recalls the promises which were made previously; but most of the story comes from the Elohist. In line with his general interests, the Yahwist gives a long chapter to Isaac's marriage with one of his Aramean relatives (chap. 24). He emphasizes the providential action of God in this marriage (v. 27). The role of Rebecca the Aramean will be important in the transfer of the promise from the elder Esau to the younger Jacob. She it is who receives the oracle of Yahweh (23, 21-25) and carries it out through a ruse for which she assumes the responsibility (chap. 27).

Jacob and his sons

The Yahwist united the Abraham and Isaac cycles (there are doublets in both; compare chap. 26 with the parallel events in Abraham's life), and thereby intended to indicate the basic unity of the worship of the Elohim of Abraham with the worship of *El 'Olam* (the God worshiped in antiquity rather than " God of eternity ") who was worshiped at Bersabee, and in the Negeb. The Jacob cycle, which emphasizes above all the north and the relationship with the Arameans, permits him to show the identity of this God (who is the author of living water, and with whom the sacred repast under the tree at Mamre is celebrated), with the God of the northern sanctuaries. He is the God present at the Bethel sanctuary where Jacob receives the promises of Abraham and of Isaac (28, 10-22 in part). The basic unit of the patriarchal age is not due simply to a genealogy; it is guaranteed by the worship of the same God (" the God of the Fathers ") and by the fact that later generations share in the same divine promises that are to be fulfilled in the history of Israel.

Similarly, the marriages of Jacob are key events since they associate him with the twelve tribes, although these come from different mothers (chaps. 29-30 in part). It is the presence of Jacob that brings to Laban, his father-in-law, the blessing of Yahweh (30, 30). By his own cleverness

---

[17] For Abraham, cf. *Abraham, père des croyants* by His Eminence Cardinal TISSERANT, R. DE VAUX, J. STARCKY... (Cahiers Sioniens, V, 2; Paris, 1951).

he makes himself rich (30, 37-43), and Yahweh protects him by keeping him at a distance from both the Arameans of Laban (chap. 31 in part) and the Edomites of Esau (32 in part). The Yahwist, always concerned with the role of woman in human and also divine affairs, recalls two unhappy incidents, the rape of Dina (34 in part) and of Bilha (35, 21 ff.). Then there is the incest of Juda (38); this group of stories portrays the sons of Jacob in a somewhat doubtful light. In the present form of the narrative it is difficult to distinguish the role of the ancestors (being eponymous ancestors of the tribes that are named after them) from the role of the tribe that has inherited the character of the ancestors. The writer does not make saints out of them, but he emphasizes that they are favored with a divine heritage.

Important parts of the Joseph cycle are the work of the Yahwist. Both in form and content this story recalls the rule, the customs and literary traditions of Egypt, but the Yahwist takes this occasion to dwell on other aspects of his theology. Joseph is not the heir, he is a wise minister; the heir is Juda; it is he who assumes in the Yahwist narrative the great role of protecting his brother (37, 26 ff.) and his family (43, 8 ff.; 44, 18 ff.). He begets a family in Chanaan (chap. 38) while the Ishmaelites take Joseph captive into Egypt; it is he who keeps the scepter until the coming of the mysterious *Shiloh* (49, 10). Joseph, the victim of his brothers' jealousy which the Yahwist denounces (37, 2 ff.) and of the jealousy of Putiphar's wife whose advances are rejected (chap. 39), succeeds by his cleverness, as Jacob did : a divining cup (44, 5), the ruse to save only his brother Benjamin (chap. 44), the acquisition of land for the Pharao by means of the famine (47, 13-26). There is a strong Egyptian flavor in the Joseph story, but the Yahwist distrusts Egyptian wisdom (as in Gn 3), despite the political successes. The present success, which ends with the Israelites being installed in Gessen, is itself ambivalent, since it ends with oppression. What is more important is the blessing of the dying patriarch. Joseph succeeds cleverly in obtaining a double portion in the blessing of his two sons, Ephraim and Manasses, but he cannot change as he pleases the desire of Jacob to confer on Ephraim the rights of the elder. The " blessings " of Jacob (Gn 49) map out the role of each tribe : Joseph will have the better part, he will be the *nazir* of his brothers; but the kingship will go to Juda because the faults of the three eldest have made them unfit. Finally, the Yahwist lingers (chap. 50 in part) over the death of Jacob instead of that of Joseph; although he shows great sympathy for him and recognizes his greatness, the Yahwist does not consider Joseph his prime interest.

VII. MOSES

For the Yahwist Moses is the last of the patriarchs, but he also represents
something else. Moses is associated with Cades, just as Abraham with
Hebron, Isaac with Bersabee, Jacob with Bethel and the Jordan. It has
long been noted that in J it is to Cades that the Israelites come after
passing through the " Reed Sea. " From here Moses went to the holy
mountain, and it is here that the Kenites, into whom he married, lived.
As always, the Yahwist stresses the marriage of Moses (Ex 2), just as
he has habitually emphasized the role of women in the infancy of his
hero. Moses owes the circumcision of his son (4, 24-26) to the intervention
of his Madianite wife, and he will invite his brother-in-law to follow
him (or rather, to precede her) into Chanaan (Nm 10, 29-32). The problem
of descendants, fecundity and fertility rites is always in the mind of the
Yahwist, but he rejects the naturist interpretation of the Chanaanites.
Circumcision (4, 24-26) is for him a substitution and salvation rite, just
like the Passover (to which he attaches the legislation) and the seasonal
feasts that he associates with the Passover rite (Ex 34).

The God who reveals Himself to Moses when he is living among
the Kenites is the God of Sinai, the God of the burning bush *(seneh)*,
identical with the " God of the Fathers. " He is not a mere nature
divinity who produces vegetation in the desert, but a *God of fire*, such
as He appeared to Abraham (Gn 15, 17). This God is the master of nature
not only in the desert, but in the land of Egypt. For the Yahwist seven
of the plagues are typically Egyptian phenomena : the red Nile, the
frogs, the gnats, the pestilence among the cattle, the hail and the locusts.
Yahweh is the master of these for they take place at His command.
He is also the God who has chosen Israel as His first-born and will save
him at the price of the first-born of Egypt (Ex 4, 22-26); this substitution
is understandable, since Yahweh, God of the desert nomads, guarantees
fruitfulness to the tribes with their annual spring offering of the animal
first-born (substituted for human first-born, 13, 11-16; 34, 19-20).
Through Moses Yahweh reveals Himself as He who really *exists*, saves
His people, and makes of the Passover a national feast of liberation;
God of the *burning* bush and the East *wind* which dries the sea (Ex 14),
He gives *water* to His people at the Massah-Meriba fountain at Cades
(17, 1-7 in part). As God of war, He brings victory over the Amalecites
(17, 8-16). As God of the holy mountain, He wants pilgrims to visit
Him and partake in the sacred repast (24, 1-2, 9-11, with Driver), and
it is here that Israel receives from Him commandments in the form
of a ritual Decalogue (34 in part). Union with God is further assured
by the national Israelite pilgrimage at the seasonal feasts, and the Yahwist

is careful to eliminate the naturistic and Chanaanite character from these feasts (34, 18, 22-23).

Thus for the Yahwist the central personality and creator of Israel's religion is neither patriarch nor king nor clever minister; it is Moses, who communicates to the people the will of Yahweh, His *words*. Moses does not save them by his own power, nor in virtue of his birth, marriage or wisdom; he brings about deliverance through the divine revelation which he receives at the holy place and then transmits to the people when they come to Yahweh in pilgrimage.

VIII. THE FUTURE

Moses himself proves unfaithful to the Word, and he will die outside the Promised Land. As the result of a vow Israel enters Chanaan with the capture of Horma (Nm 21, 1-3), and then another seer, the foreigner Balaam (protected by his ass, as Eve had been seduced by the serpent, Nm 22 in part) is the one to proclaim the occupation, prosperity and kingship of Israel! This seems to occur in the Cades area, because the political horizon is that of southern Judea : Amalec and its king Agag, Seir, Seth (Sutu?) and the Kenites (Nm 24). Hope is still centered in the monarchy, in the heir of the dynasty : " A star shall come from Jacob, a scepter from Israel. " The monarchy is foreseen to go beyond Israel and include the peoples (Gn 49, 10) : " Edom will be his possession. " The God of the Yahwist is the God of the universe who will exercise government over the peoples by means of Juda. But at the same time He is the God of nature, of the fountains and storm and wants to bring prosperity to His people in a new paradise (Nm 24 : 6) through a descendant of Eve (Gn 4, 1) who will not necessarily be a first-born but who can take over the rights of the first-born as Seth did in the case of Cain.

This theology of the Yahwist can already be called Messianic, and it takes on considerable depth if we attribute to him (or to his school, at least) the passages in Judges and Samuel which describe the preparations and establishment of the Davidic monarchy. Gedeon (and Abimelech), Jephte, Samson and Saul lay the foundations of Israel's monarchy which Samson establishes and dedicates in the person of David. After David the heir is not the first-born, but Solomon. Of old, God had promised His fruitfulness to the patriarchs; now He promises to the house of David His eternal assistance (2 Sm 7). The kinship between the Yahwist and the great story of the succession to David has often been pointed out [18] : the same artful narrative, the same psychology,

---

[18] J. HEMPEL, *Althebräische Literatur...*, pp. 108 ff., 116 ff.

and often the same vocabulary (" good and evil "). The same problem
is also present : Why is Solomon, although he is not the first-born, the
true heir of the divine promises? There is the same literary approach
(a connected chain of events) and the same theology of divine Providence,
all powerful in contrast to human wisdom (2 Sm 17, 14) but honoring
the physical and psychological causes at work. Thus the author portrays
Solomon as the heir of David and the promises made to him, just as Jacob
was the heir of Abraham and Isaac. The choice of the patriarchs throws
light on the choice of Solomon in the intrigue of women, births and
jealousies. The ark of the covenant, Yahweh's throne, remains henceforth
at Sion and it is to this national sanctuary that an Israelite must come
in order to find his God, in obedience to the Mosaic code of Ex 34. The
faith and hope of Israel are thus sharply sketched; one knows where to
find the presence of the true God and his oracle. The desire to share
in the creative urge of divine life — a desire deeply rooted in the mentality
of the ancient East — is not contradicted, but it can be achieved only
by fidelity to the God of the Fathers, Yahweh, who gave His Law through
Moses on Sinai and who will guarantee the triumph of His people in the
person of a leader who comes from Juda. Such is Israel's hope in the
tenth century.

§ 3. The Elohist

I. THE INTERESTS OF THE ELOHIST

Although the data in J and E are very often identical, the latter presents
another aspect of God and His action. The Elohist narratives have
not the lively picturesque manner of the Yahwist; there is less dramatic
vigor, less of the warmth of nationalism, but they are simpler, smoother,
and even more disciplined. Their archaizing manner has often been
noted. Narratives and legal codes are associated with the national
heritage without much interest in the conquest of the world. The writer
is less interested in the problem of fruitfulness and the development
of life, than in that of preserving the inheritance promised to the Fathers
and conquered by Josue, Moses' disciple. Although some dispute it,
the Elohist seems to have written a continuous narrative, with its focus
on the northern tribes. In the Joseph story, Ruben, the eldest brother,
takes the place that the Yahwist had assigned to Juda. It is the Elohist
texts that mention the Arameans who bordered on Israel; the inhabitants
of Palestine are Amorites rather than Chanaanites. In the stories that
deal with the South, the Elohist seems to be but a pale reflection of the

Yahwist from whom he derives the traditions concerning Abraham, Hagar and Bersabee.

What the Elohist loses in dynamic quality he gains in moral depth. His understanding of sin is more refined than that of the Yahwist. He rejects the notion that Abraham could have lied to Abimelech, and specifies that Sara was the patriarch's half-sister (Gn 20, 12). He knows the way in which Jacob increased his flocks, but in his presentation there is no deceit : it is God who protects Jacob by keeping Laban from harming him (Gn 31, 4-13).

Revelation and Law have for him a moral rather than ritual character. God's gift is to make His people know more clearly what faults should be avoided. The foundations of the Law, as expressed in the Decalogue, deal with duties towards God and neighbor. These duties are then specified in the Code of the Covenant, in which respect for one's neighbor and his goods is guaranteed by statutes and precepts *(mishpatim* and *debarim)* to which God has given His sanction. The Elohist, like the Yahwist, knows that all life and well-being come from God, but he does not describe this union of God and man in terms of fatherhood nor fertility rites. For him it is a question of wills that are united in a covenant which the two parties must honor. This aspect is not unknown to the Yahwist, but the latter writes at an age when the vitality of Israel seemed able to absorb everything, to assimilate both Chanaan and the nations. The necessary limitations appear more sharply in the Elohist : man needs to take more care in order to remain united with God!

Indeed, man can totally fall away, even so far as to put Yahweh on a level with the common Baal. Hence the Elohist insists on the spirituality of God. The true God is the God of conscience and commandments; above all, one may not make statues or images! One no longer *sees* God at a sanctuary (as the Yahwist writes, Ex 24, 10); rather, one must remember that there is no approach to God through human eyes : " No one can see God and live " (Ex 33, 20; cf. 20, 19). Hence anthropomorphisms tend to disappear : God appears to Abraham, Abimelech, Jacob and Joseph in dreams. It is not that God is distant from man, but man must realize he must become more spiritual if he is not to be distant from God.

A similar distrust of Chanaan and its naturistic ideas is to be found in the prophets : Amos, and especially Osee. In the Elohist redaction one can catch the echo of the prophetic movement that is just beginning. There are frequent allusions to the cult, and if there are no reprimands, there is the fear of possible deviations. He allows the Passover and the substitution sacrifices, such as that of Abraham (Gn 22, 1-13), but he criticizes Aaron and the reveling in the case of the golden calf (Ex 32 in part), and the meals of Qibrot-Aa-Taawah (Nm 11, 18). Levi receives the blessing of God, but Levi's offerings are not so much animal and vegetable sacrifices as incense and the smoke of holocausts, and his essential function is to make known the will of God through the Urim and Thummim (Dt 33, 8-10).

The Elohist is thus orientated towards the tradition of Moses and the desert, and has retained traditions and customs that are very old, even archaic. In a similar way the Rechabites archaized during the period of the prophets (Jer 35, 1-11; 4 Kgs 10, 15). All things considered, his redaction betrays an age later than that of the Yahwist. Like the prophets he brings out the necessity of sorrow and forgiveness (Ex 33). It is not so much the knowledge of the Messianic mystery that he prepares for, as the mystery of redemption sketched in the old historical traditions of Israel.

II. THE PATRIARCHAL PERIOD

This story, centered on *covenant* and not on *blessing*, does not begin with creation, but with the Abrahamic covenant (Gn 15, in part). The heirs of the patriarch are already in opposition to the Arameans of Damascus (15, 2), and they will possess the land (15, 16) when the wickedness of the Amorites has reached its height (note here the moral consideration). Abimelech is saved because he is morally sound (chap. 20) and God comes to the aid of Hagar whom Abraham, with great reluctance, had been forced to send away (21, 6-21). If Abraham takes up residence in the south, it is due to a covenant with Abimelech (21, 22-32); in his faithfulness he refuses nothing to God, even his son and the inheritance (22, 1-13).

Without delaying on the history of Isaac, the Elohist passes on quickly to Jacob. The story about the pottage of lentils is probably due to him : Esau does not appear simply as one who is disinherited, but as a glutton who has no appreciation of the divine gift of inheritance rights; this lends more of a justifying tone to the choice of Jacob (25, 29-34). In any case he is aware of Jacob's trip to Bethel, which is not the place of Yahweh's presence (v. 16 is from J), but " the gate of heaven " where angels ascend and descend in order to unite God and men. Here a sort of covenant is concluded under the form of a vow : if God protects him, Jacob will come to pay the tithe at Bethel (28, 11 f.; 20 ff.). God will protect him against Laban who has treated him unjustly (31, 36-42). With Jacob's flight a frontier agreement is made between the Arameans and Israelites, to which God is the witness (31, 43-54 in part). Jacob stays at Mahanaim and at Penuel, and manages by peaceful means to keep Esau at a distance (chaps. 32—33 in part). He is unable to stay in Sichem because of the treacherous conduct of Simeon and Levi which he himself reprimands (34, 30). Faithful to the God who has protected him, and who granted him a privileged vision at Penuel without harm (32, 31) Jacob returns to fulfill his vow at Bethel after burying the strange gods under the terebinth at Sichem (35, 1-8.14; cf. Jos 24, 14-23).

It is not surprising that the Elohist presents many details of the story of Joseph, the ancestor of the two powerful northern tribes of Ephraim and Manasses. Joseph is close to God because of the dreams he receives which presage his future greatness. This makes the sons of Bilha and Zilpha jealous and, despite the efforts of Ruben, they sell him to the Madianites (in the Yahwist narrative it is to the Ishmaelites) not far from Dothain. From God he has the power to interpret dreams (41, 16) and to foresee the future of the butler and baker (chap. 40) and even of the Pharao (chap. 41) who acknowledges that Joseph possesses the spirit of God (41, 38). From this point of view, Joseph takes on the stature of a prophet. But the spirit of God also brings him ability to rule, and he provides Egypt with a prosperity unrivaled in the whole world (41, 53-57). When his brothers come to him, he charges them with spying, demands to see Benjamin and keeps Simeon as a hostage; now they have to acknowledge that they have been justly punished (chap. 42 in part). Ruben is generous, but Joseph more so : he brings his father to Egypt. After a vision from God (46, 1-4), Jacob arrives; he expresses his last wishes to Joseph and gives a special blessing to Joseph's two sons (chap. 48 in part). When Joseph is at the point of death he pardons his brothers and speaks of their return to Chanaan. He reveals to them the religious significance of their history : " Can I take God's place? You intended evil against me, but God intended it for good, to do as he has done today, namely, to save the lives of many people (50, 19b-20). Here is a theology that shows God grappling with evil and adapting it to His own good purposes.

III. MOSES

This theology is even more prominent in the story of Moses. If the patriarchs had lived and settled in Chanaan by a series of pacts and covenants, Moses is going to found the people of Israel by the covenant par excellence. The Hebrews are in a sorry state, subjected to hard labor. But they are not wiped out, thanks to the Egyptian midwives

who " fear God " and let the Hebrew males live. The child Moses also
survives. But he fails to find understanding among his own, and has
to flee to Madian. When he generously protects the daughters of Raguel
(Ex 2), he is rewarded by Madianite hospitality. At Horeb he receives
the revelation of the name of Yahweh — no longer the God of Jacob
who refused to divulge His name at the Jabbok (Gn 32, 30) — " He
who is " (Ex 3, 13-15). Moses is given a specific commission : to lead
out his people on a three-day march (Ex 5, 3) to the mountain (3, 12)
where they are to offer sacrifices. As foreseen by God, Pharao refuses
to let them go and afflicts them the more (chap. 5 in part). But Yahweh
employs His own weapons : the plagues of Egypt. The five plagues
preserved in the Elohist narrative (water changed into blood, hail, frogs,
darkness, death of first-born) are all related to the feast of spring : the
early growth of vegetation (9, 25a.31 f.) and animal sacrifice. The
people leave on good terms with the Egyptians (11, 1-3; 12, 35 f.; E is
not anti-Egyptian), and Moses, carrying the staff that is the sign of his
divine authority, leads them to Horeb by a southern route instead of
by the way of the Philistines (13, 17-19). There he takes up again with
the Madianites, with Jethro who gives him advice concerning the
organization of the people (chap. 18). The climax is on the holy mountain
where Moses receives the Decalogue (20, 1-17), the ten commandments
that are the stipulations of the covenant between Yahweh and His
people (24, 3-8). The unfaithfulness of the people and the compliance
of Aaron bring on the breaking of the covenant and the tablets of the
Law (chap. 32). This polemic against the golden calf, which sullies
the Aaronic priesthood, is very similar to the preaching of the prophets
(Os 8, 5 f.; 10, 5). The Israelites must do penance, removing their
jewelry. Moses sets up outside the camp the Tent where Yahweh appears
in a cloud and transmits to him His oracles (Ex 33, 7-11). It is here
that Yahweh shows Himself to be a " merciful and gracious God, slow
to anger and rich in kindness and fidelity, continuing His kindness
for a thousand generations, and forgiving wickedness and crime and sin;
yet not declaring the guilty guiltless, but punishing children and grand-
children to the third and fourth generation for their fathers' wickedness "
(34, 6 f.). Any wrongdoing can be forgiven, but sooner or later it must
be expiated.

In the midst of this stiff-necked people (Ex 32, 9) Moses appears
as a superhuman being (34, 29-35, doubtless belonging to E), incomparably
greater than Aaron or Mariam (Nm 12, 1-16) because he sees God face
to face and his own face is radiant from conversing with God. He is
the prophet par excellence, because he has the Spirit, which he

communicates to the elders (Nm 11, 10-30 in part). From this time on Josue, Moses' assistant at the Tent, begins to take on importance (Ex 33, 11b). At Cades he proves his faithfulness to Yahweh by voting for immediate conquest of Chanaan which he had reconnoitered (Nm 13—14 in part). The infidelity of the people is the reason for an unsuccessful invasion from the south (Nm 14, 39-45) : ever the same problem of a rebellious group, unwilling to listen to the voice of a prophet! The Israelites pass through Edom (20, 14-21) and take possession of Transjordan (21, 10-20) where they are in conflict with Moab. The Moabite king summons Balaam from Phathur on the Euphrates. This diviner, a worshiper of Yahweh, has to bless Jacob against whom " there is no sorcery nor omen " (Nm 22—23). The Elohist then describes the settlement of Israel in Transjordan (chap. 32) and on this occasion no doubt, in the primitive redaction of the text, Moses gave the people the code of the covenant as his last will. The later addition of the Book of Deuteronomy causes the code to be displaced to Ex 20, 24—23, 15. Moses' final act is to summon Josue to his tent and give him instructions about the conquest (Dt 31, 1-3.14a.15.23); then he blesses the tribes (Dt 33). From the point of view of the Elohist (which is reflected also in the inscriptions of this period), the blessings correspond to the curses pronounced at Sichem (Dt 27), where again the Elohist highlights the moral demands of the religion of Israel.

IV. THE ELOHIST AND THE STORY OF THE CONQUEST

It is possible that the Benjaminite stories of the Book of Josue were originally a continuation of the Pentateuch. The narrative seems in effect to be orientated towards the conquest and the gathering at Sichem. There are the same fundamental ideas of Elohist theology (concerning sin, penance and pardon) in the Books of Jos, Jgs and Sm (e.g., Jos 24; 1 Sm 12). Some critics think that these latter narratives come from an ancient work which dealt with the conquest and the other saving actions of Yahweh. Then an author of the prophetic tradition would have completed and adapted this material, adding interpretations of the patriarchal and Mosaic times in which certain Yahwist narratives were given a reinterpretation. Other hypotheses are also possible. But the entire Elohist narrative was finished at the latest in the first half of the 8th century B.C., some time before the fall of Samaria.

§ 4. Deuteronomy

I. THE YAHWIST AND ELOHIST COMBINED

When the Assyrians annexed the Northern Kingdom, the Israelites who wanted to remain faithful to Yahweh returned to Jerusalem where He was still honored as sovereign God. King Ezechias was then encouraging a national and religious renewal. The " documentary " hypothesis allows us to propose a plausible explanation for this renewal which centered about the Davidic dynasty. In order to indicate the reunion of North and South in their common faith in the God of Israel, the two historical traditions which extolled Yahweh's action on behalf of His people were united in one work (called the " Jehovist " by some critics). This combination intended to preserve as much as possible the texts in which the beliefs peculiar to both the North and South were expressed; in fact they were so well preserved that critical analysis of the present day allows us, not without some difficulty, to locate the lacunae which sometimes occur. However, the redactor was mindful that the whole should cohere; the Joseph story is particularly well done, with its staging and epilogue. In the other narratives the redactor preferred the Yahwist except where the religious meaning of certain rites was to be explained, such as the substitution of animal for human sacrifice (Gn 22). He kept the dynamism and the national and monarchical hope of the Yahwist, while he incorporated the moral and spiritual ideals of the Elohist.

II. FROM THE ELOHIST TO DEUTERONOMY

Parallel to this work of preserving and combining, another activity was going on : the redaction of Deuteronomy, a more creative work, even if also traditional. We have long recognized that in this book the Jerusalem clergy emphasized centralization of worship in its own interest, and here it was following Josias' condemnation of the high places. More profound studies (those of Welch, Alt and von Rad among others) [19] tend now to associate Deuteronomy with the Northern Kingdom. The Jerusalem clergy do not seem to have looked with favor on a work that gave equal rights at a central sanctuary to all levites. Deuteronomy is in the line of the Elohist narrative. For both, the holy mountain is Horeb, not Sinai. Aside from a few variations, it is the same moral

---

[19] G. VON RAD, *Das Gottesvolk im Deuteronomium* (Stuttgart, 1929); *Deutero-nomium-Studien* (Göttingen, 1948); A. ALT, *Die Heimat des Deuteronomiums* (Munich, 1953).

Decalogue that is revealed. D and E are more concerned about national welfare whereas J is concerned with Israel's role in the world. Like the Elohist work, Dt ends with blessings and curses as the sanctions for the fidelity or infidelity of the Chosen People. The God of Deuteronomy is ever Elohim, who punishes and also shows mercy (5, 10; 7, 12); He covenanted with Israel and gave her the commandments but she has already shown herself unfaithful (9, 8 ff.). It is through this Elohist heritage that Moses plays a substantial role in the composition of Deuteronomy.

Yet Deuteronomy is quite different from the Elohist narratives both in form and in basic character. It is not a narrative that enshrines laws; it is a code (chaps. 12—26) which is preceded (1—11) and concluded (27—30) by discourses. There is also history, even in the code (23, 5 f.), but it begins with Horeb; the patriarchs are not mentioned as the receivers of the divine promises. Moses alone, in all his greatness, dominates Israel's history. The Law given through him is kept beside the Ark of the covenant (31, 26), in the place which Yahweh has chosen out of all " as the dwelling place for His name. " Every seven years it will be read to the people. The sanctuaries which were formerly honored because of their association with the patriarchs are now rejected; all the tribes must celebrate the feasts in one place alone (12, 5). Doubtless there is to be found here a trace of some old sanctuary about which the tribes had gathered; but now, in fact, the Ark is at Jerusalem. With the fall of the Northern Kingdom, the true Israelite would recognize as valid only the sanctuary of David, and this attitude remained even after Nabuchodonosor captured Jerusalem (Jer 41, 5).

III. THE SPIRIT OF DEUTERONOMY

Chanaan is the guilty one : she is responsible for the high places and the perversion of Israel; she is a snare for Israel's faith. Deuteronomy has a real theology of the " people of God. " " Yahweh your God " or " thy God " constantly occurs when Israel is addressed (4, 24...). This people has been selected, " chosen, " (7, 6) by a special act of God; they form a unit, a *qahal* (5, 19) and all the Israelites are brothers (15, 7...). This choice of God has been free (9, 5...) like the gift of this land which not they, but others, had tilled (6, 10 ff.). The choice and the gift can be explained only in terms of Yahweh's love (7, 8), a passionate, jealous love (6, 15). Israel must keep herself for Yahweh; she must love Him " with all your heart, and with all your soul, and with all your strength " (6, 4 ff.). Hence she may contract no political alliance or intermarriage with Chanaanites. Yahweh alone is God, alone worthy of love and loyalty. He proved this in the desert where he " disciplines you even as a man disciplines his son " (8, 5). Israel will retain possession of her " good land flowing with milk and honey " (6, 3) only if she keeps His commandments. The people and the country have their own institutions : Israel is a state, with its kings, priests, prophets, tribunals (17—18); it has its own religious customs and feasts; but all this is subordinate to the Law of Yahweh and to His Decalogue. Certain acts are forbidden because they are " abominations " to Yahweh (12, 31...). The book tells Israel to " heed the voice of the Lord " (13, 19...) and " to purge the evil from your midst " (13, 6...).

These " statutes, commandments and decrees " (26, 17) which " Yahweh has prescribed, " and which constitute a " Torah, " are not viewed as a simple command. Just as the relationship between Yahweh and His people is described in terms of favor and affection, so the divine commands are likewise regarded as something very close and intimate to man : " This command which I enjoin on you today is not too mysterious and remote for you. It is not up in the sky, that you should say, ' Who will go up in the sky to get it for us, and tell us of it, that we may carry it out? ' Nor is it across the sea, that you should say, ' Who will cross the sea to get it for us and tell us of it, that we may carry it out? ' No, it is something very near to you, already in your mouths and in your hearts; you have only to carry it out " (30, 11-14). Deuteronomy, perhaps influenced by the wisdom movement, tries thus to reach man's heart and to convince him. These discourses try to open the *heart* of man, that is to say, to touch the understanding and will in the most personal way (6, 5). Less than ever could the God of Israel tolerate any image or statue of Himself (4, 15 ff.); He is a father who has given His vivifying Word to Israel, a Word that can bring her happiness and long life. She gives herself up to this Word : " The hidden things belong to Yahweh; but the things that have been revealed belong to us and to our children forever, that we may carry out the words of this Law " (29, 28). A theology of the people of God, a theology of the life-giving Word — this is also a theology of the Revelation which is being given, and of the miracle which confirms it.

IV. PURPOSE AND DATE OF THE BOOK

This profoundly human book, which urges care for the captive, the alien, the widow and orphan, for debtors and levites (14, 27.29) is totally without an apocalyptic thrust. Some would see in it a definite program, but this is rather a pensive, disturbed mood, a thinking back over an unhappy experience. Israel appreciates the gift of God and fears to lose it. The inspired authors make a new effort to reach the leaders, that shows the influence of the culture inspired by international wisdom : " For thus will you give evidence of your wisdom and intelligence to the nations, who will hear of all these statutes and say, ' This great nation is truly a wise and intelligent people. ' For what great nation is there that has gods so close to it as the Lord, our God, is to us whenever we call upon Him? " (4, 6).

Some scholars date Deuteronomy in the reign of Ezechias who caused Proverbs to be gathered together (Prv 25, 1). Because it did not win the favor of the Jerusalem clergy, it was ignored until Josias saw that he might be able to win over the provinces of the North by appealing to a Law that emanated from there. In the judgment of others the work was composed during the reign of Manasses — or in the reign of Josias himself. At any rate we need hardly say that the book is certainly rooted in an old tradition that derives directly from the northern areas where the prophets of the 8th and 9th centuries preached and where the Elohist traditions came into being. But critical scholars are unanimously agreed that neither the code nor the discourses come from the same source. Steuernagel distinguished a whole series of D (D^1 D^{2}a D^{2}b) on the basis that certain passages were in the singular and others in the plural. This criterion is difficult to cope with. There are some reasons in favor of a double edition. The first, before or during the time of Josias, would begin at chap. 5 and end with the blessings and curses of chap. 29; the second would date from the Exile, which is presupposed by the canticle of Moses (chap. 32) and by chaps. 1—4 where, against the background of the Exile, events subsequent to the following chapters are narrated (4, 28-31).

The book wielded considerable influence; its theology inspired the redaction of the historical books (Josue to Kings). The reforms of Nehemias were based on the law code, and the Books of Chronicles are in this tradition. It is hard to determine just when Deuteronomy was added to the " Jehovist " narrative. It is usually admitted that this joint (which led to the displacement of the code of the covenant) occurred before the combination of J-E-D with the priestly writings, which we shall now discuss.

§ 5.   Priestly Writings

BIBLIOGRAPHY

R. ABBA, " Priests and Levites, " *IDB*, III, pp. 876-889.

G. B. GRAY, *Sacrifice in the Old Testament* (London, 1925).

G. VON RAD, *Die Priesterschrift im Hexateuch* (Stuttgart, 1934).

W. O. E. OESTERLEY, *Sacrifices in Ancient Israel* (London, 1939).

J. PEDERSEN, " The Priest, " *Israel, Its Life and Culture*, III-IV (London, 1940), pp. 150-197.

E. ROBERTSON, " The Priestly Code : The Legislation of the Old Testament and Graf-Wellhausen, " *BJRL*, 26 (1942), pp. 369-392; " The Riddle of the Torah, " *BJRL*, 27 (1943), pp. 359-383.

T. GASTER, *Passover. Its History and Traditions* (London, 1949).

H. ROWLEY, *The Meaning of Sacrifice in the Old Testament* (Manchester 1950).

A. KUSHKE, " Die Lagevorstellung der Priesterlicher Erzählung, " *ZAW* (1951), pp. 75-105.

A. VAN DER VOORT, " Gen 1, 1—2, 4a et le Psaume CIV, " *RB* (1951), pp. 321-346.

G. AUZOU, *Connaissance du Lévitique** (Paris, 1953).

A. C. WELCH, *Post-Exilic Judaism* (London, 1935); *Priest and Prophet in Old Israel*[2] (London : Oxford, 1953).

J. HEMPEL, " Priestercodex, " PAULY-WISSOWA, *Realencyclopedie der Class, Alt. Wiss.*, XXII, 2, cols. 1943-1967 (Stuttgart, 1954).

M. HARAN, " The Priestly Tradition in the Pentateuch, " *JBL*, 81 (1962), pp. 14-24.

G. VON RAD, *Old Testament Theology*, I (New York : Harper, 1962), pp. 132-180.

I.   THE LAW OF HOLINESS

The Jerusalem clergy, which descended through Sadok from Aaron, the priest who died near Cades in the southern desert (Nm 20, 22-29), never really accepted Deuteronomy (cf. 4 Kgs 23, 9 and Dt 18, 8). Insensible to this northern trend [20], and more or less influenced by the humanist and lighter spirit of the wisdom movement, it found its inspiration rather in the traditional theology of the transcendence of Yahweh, the inaccessible, the " holy " God, whose herald Isaias had made himself.   For them it was less a question of making the Word

---

[20] Concerning the northern traditions in the OT, see A. VACCARI, *VD* (1937), p. 372.

of God close to men, than of lifting man up to God by faithful observance of the traditions : " Be holy, for I, the Lord, your God, am holy " (Lv 19, 2). If God is totally other, man can still live with Him and share in His holiness through the liturgy, the law and the statutes.

According to the documentary hypothesis it is to be admitted that some of the Jerusalem customs were gathered together and inspired by this theology. Parallel to Deuteronomy, the *Law of Holiness* (Lv 17—26, with some later additions) was put together. It begins, like the Deuteronomic code, with the law concerning the sanctuary, followed by various prescriptions concerning morality, marriage (chap. 20), priests (chap. 21), sacrifices (chap. 22), feasts (chap. 23). Like Deuteronomy, it finishes with blessings and curses (chap. 26). Holiness has to permeate the whole life of an individual; apart from any historical consideration, it is presented as an absolute requirement, already in the desert period. The community of Israel, the *qahal* of Deuteronomy, is a more or less liturgical community, *('edah)*, in which one loves his neighbor as himself (19, 18), but with hardly any sign of joy or generosity. The *'edah* is a hierarchy : the high priest (21, 10), priests, perhaps levites, and finally the Israelites *(beney Israel)*. The code itself contains very old customs and one perceives in this work a defense-reflex on the part of the descendants of Aaron. Since Ezechiel, the prophet-priest captured and exiled in Babylon, relies upon this Law or on similar customs, it is very possible that a first redaction took place during the reign of Josias.

II. THE PRIESTLY HISTORY

After the fall of Jerusalem in 587, the important group of Judean captives that were transferred to Babylon realized that they were faced with completely new religious problems. It was no longer a question of regulating life and individual differences in the land of Chanaan nor of continuing or reforming the civil or monarchical institutions so as to maintain in Israel the religion of Yahweh which Moses had established. Now in a foreign land there had to be a new organization of life for the old community that had been scattered among the nations and incorporated in a worldwide but pagan empire whose religious worship was both impressive and attractive. The same blood, the same traditions, a clergy that taught with authority — these were the only foundation that could keep alive the religious life of captive Israel, an Israel that was no longer a state, but was not yet a Church. This was the time for the redaction of what Père Lagrange has called a *précis :* the priestly history (Pg of the critical school). This synthesis gives a universal validity to the religious institutions of Israel by putting them into the framework of general history which is thus ruled by a theology of the divine presence and its demands. The style is dry, the vocabulary exact and technical, like that of a catechism; the narratives will above all illustrate spiritual teachings; the genealogies and years will make possible a distinction of several areas of thought. Finally, the background of all this will be faith in the Law of Yahweh and hope in a return to the Holy Land.

The work begins with a great tableau of the universe, [21] " heavens and earth, " in which man has the first place because he is the only creature made *in the image of God*. Like God, he has dominion and a share in creativity; like Him, he rests on the seventh day; like Him, after having labored in this world, he is called to an eternal Sabbath, without morning or evening (Gn 1—2, 4a). The life that has been received from God is transmitted faithfully from generation to generation by the patriarchs before the Flood (chap. 5.) Although the earth is corrupt in the sight of God (6, 11) because of the sons and daughters that have been born, some of this line is good : Enoch goes to God without dying; his descendant, Noe, also walks with God and he is a just man (6, 9). He escapes the Flood, thanks to the ark, a sort of sanctuary whose dimensions are determined by God, as those of the tabernacle of Moses will later be specified. Along with Noe, a pair of all the kinds of animals are saved. When the liturgical cycle of a year has been completed, God blesses Noe and makes the *first covenant* with all living beings. Its only stipulation deals with respect for life and the blood; its sign is the rainbow (9, 1-17). The priestly writer then gives a table of nations, grouped in genealogical relationship (Gn 10), which portrays the fundamental unity in the various human groups — unity of blood and destiny. There follows the generation from Sem to Abraham (11, 10 ff.).

God's *choice* of Abraham is made known to him in a vision. God selects a *people* to whom He will give a *land*; it is the *second covenant*, and its new sign is not in the heavens but in the flesh : circumcision (chap. 17). Nahor, Abraham's brother, receives no such sign or promise for his descendants (22, 20-24). The first pledge of the future : Abraham purchases from the Hittites the cave at Machpela where he buries Sara and where he himself will be buried (25, 7-10) — without owing anything to the inhabitants of the land (chap. 23). The priestly writer had insisted on the fact that Abraham had lived in the land of the Chaldeans, like the Judean exiles; he called it Ur of the Chaldeans, a deliberate

---

[21] On the patristic interpretations, cf. F. VIGOUROUX, *La cosmogonie mosaïque, d'après les Pères de l'Église* (Paris, 1889).

anachronism, since there were no Chaldeans at Ur in Abraham's time. He mentions Isaac very briefly (25, 11), and gives more attention to Ishmael (25, 12-18) and Esau (25, 19-21; 26, 34-35; 27, 46—28, 9). But this is only to emphasize that both are outside the holy line : they come to terms with the Chanaanites, while Jacob leaves for Phaddan-Aram in order to avoid marrying any Chanaanite. He marries there (29, 24.29) and returns to his father with twelve children (31, 18b; 33, 18a; 35, 9-13. 15.23-29) and settles down not far from Esau (chap. 36; 37, 1.2a). Joseph receives a brief mention (41, 46); it is only the story of the settlement of Jacob's family in Egypt which interests the author (46, 6-27; 47, 5.6a.7-11.27b.28; 48, 3-6); finally, there is the burial of the patriarch at Machpela (49, 29-33; 50, 12 f.).

Exodus 1, 1-5 and 2, 23-25 gives the list of descendants born as slaves in a foreign land, an omen of the later exile. Among the sons of Levi are Moses and his brother Aaron (6, 13-25). Yahweh, who up to this time had been known as El-Shadday, commissions them to save His people (6, 2-12). A typical indication of the priestly writer : it is Aaron who will speak and who will wield the miraculous staff (6, 26—7, 13). We witness the struggle between the wondrous signs of Yahweh and the prodigies worked by the Egyptian magicians (there were many such in Babylon also!). The plagues in the priestly version are peculiar in that they are the work of both Moses and Aaron together. The five plagues of P correspond to those of J (the southern tradition), but there are two missing as well as two slight changes : for the flies of J is substituted the dust that is changed into gnats, and for the pestilence among the animals is substituted the soot that causes boils. The plague of the first-born introduces the paschal legislation in which the *sacrifice of the paschal lamb* has more importance than the unleavened bread. The Israelites depart from Egypt in a solemn procession in marching order (12, 40 f.) and cross the sea between two walls of water (14, 22). In the desert the wondrous signs are still the work of both Moses and Aaron (Ex 16, 6 f.) and the Sabbath is observed.

At Sinai (19, 1.2a) there is a new revelation and the *third covenant*, which follows upon that of Noe and Abraham. This is marked by the cult and the sanctuary through the intermediary of Moses (24, 15-18a; chaps. 25—31) who is also the builder (chaps. 35—40). The favored ones are Aaron and his descendants, assisted by other levites (Lv 8—10). Unlike the other tribes, the levites do not take part in the census (Nm 1—4 in part). The sign of this covenant is the presence of the cloud (Nm 9, 15 f.); when it ascends, the Israelites start out, but the trumpets of Aaron are to give the signal (10, 1-13). In the desert of

Pharan, Moses and Aaron cannot convince the people to go on
(13, 3-17. 26; 14, 1-9.26 f.). A revolt led by Core is aimed against the
liturgical privileges of Aaron (16, 1—17, 15 in part), but Aaron's staff
blossoms as proof of his intercessory power (17, 16-28). Along with
Moses, he can even produce water for the Israelites in the desert of Sin
(20, 1-11). Here he dies and his son Eleazar succeeds him (20, 22-29).
The " children of Israel " then arrive in Moab (22, 1). Eleazar and
his son Phineas have to protect them from the seduction of the worship
of Baal-Phogor (25, 1-18) and a second census takes place (chap. 26).
The victory over the Madianites occasion the proclamation of the rules
of holy war (chap. 31), because the wandering in the desert is over
(chap. 33); they are on the eve of the conquest and division of the Holy
Land (chap. 34) and the assignment of the cities of refuge (Dt 4, 41-43).
Moses ascends Mount Nebo (Dt 32, 48-52) and dies there (chap. 34 in part).

This schematic outline of the priestly history is followed by the
victories of Josue and the partition of Chanaan among the tribes. The
work is permeated from start to finish with the hope of the Promised
Land. There are traces of priestly editing in the Book of Judges
(chaps 19—21) and the Books of Samuel (1 Sm 2, 27-36; 2 Sm 20, 23-26,
in which the priesthood attributed to the sons of David in 2 Sm 8, 18
is taken away from them since they do not descend from Levi).

Thus the priestly history can be described as the fruit of a theological
reflection upon the ancient liturgical customs preserved by the Aaronic
priesthood of Jerusalem. Fidelity to these customs is the sole guarantee
of a life of union with God, which the all-powerful love of God is going
to accomplish in Chanaan for the descendants of Abraham. There is
a covenant between God and all mankind which has been saved in Noe,
assuring mankind of life on earth if the life of creatures is respected.
There is a covenant of choice with the descendants of Abraham,
guaranteeing them a future in the Promised Land if they observe the
Sabbath and circumcision. Finally there is a more intimate covenant
with the Aaronic priesthood which makes the priests the table-guests
of God and the necessary dispensers of divine favors, for worship is the
outward sign of divine love. Since the monarchy has passed way, it is
Aaron who will, in the perspective of the priestly writer, carry out its
functions. Israel in exile will find the strength to be faithful to the
national and religious traditions in the institution of this priesthood,
" a kingdom of priests and a holy nation " (Ex 19, 6). [22]

---

[22] The meaning is disputed. In the Bible, *mamleket* (kingdom) is always
connected with the name of the ruling power, and not that of the group ruled (with
one doubtful exception).

III. The law of sacrifices and the law of purity

In 538 Cyrus made it possible for the Jews to return to Jerusalem. Gradually they banded together and they returned home in waves. The worship was restored, and the Temple rebuilt (515). The Books of Zacharias (c. 3) and of Aggeus (1, 12; 2, 2.4) tell us of the important role played by the priesthood and by the high priest Josue in this period of restoration. They clearly relied on the tradition laid down by Ezechiel and the priestly writings. But these basic texts had to be completed by the demands created by a new-born liturgical life. So some codes were drawn up : the law of sacrifices (Lv 1—7) and the law of ritual purity (Lv 11—16).

The prescriptions concerning the *Sacrifices* (Lv 1—7) are an expression of the theology which brought them together. The communion sacrifice (sacred banquet) is relegated to second place. The highest sacrifice is the holocaust, a total offering to God of an animal who has received an imposition of hands. The holocaust is an expiatory sacrifice *(kipper)*, like the sin offering *(hattat)* and the guilt offering *(asham)* which includes an admission of sin, a confession. The sacrifice has now turned into an expiation for the faults committed against the covenant, and the sacred " meal " *(ishsheh)* is now interpreted as a meal " consumed " in honor of the divinity. However, the sacramental aspect remains; this is not merely a sacrifice to appease a jealous divinity. The principle of Lv 17, 11 still obtains : " it is the blood, as the seat of life, that makes atonement. " One cannot consume the blood (this would be magic), but none the less it is the blood which gives life. Apart from the offering to the divinity and what belongs to the priest (Lv 3, 3; 7, 8 f.) the faithful consume the sacrificial victims, *shelamim* (Lv 7, 15) and the priests may partake of the most sacred which belongs to God (Lv 21, 22).

The *Law of Ritual Purity* (Lv 11—15) also has its theology, in that it indicates the necessary conditions for sharing in the life of the holy community, life with God who dwells in his Tabernacle *(mishkan)*. While Leviticus retains a number of archaic and ancient taboos, it is only for the sake of a theological understanding of God, whose transcendence is not to be sullied by contact with what is human and impure. The real purification of the holy people is secured by the rite of the great day of Atonement (Lv 16), the only day that the high priest may enter " into the tabernacle, inside the veil and before the propitiatory " *(kapporet)*. While the scapegoat is led out into the desert with the faults of the Israelites, the high priest " having made atonement for himself and his household, as well as for the whole Israelite community " sprinkles the blood on the altar seven times : " Thus he

shall render it clean and holy, purged of the defilements of the Israelites "
(Lv 16, 19).

There is also a code for the redemption of votive offerings (Lv 27).
All these minute specifications are inspired not only by the desire of
preserving the reverence and adoration due to God, but also to protect
the rights of each man according to his means. Not only the laws
concerning the expiation sacrifice, but the law for the purification of
a new mother provides that if she is poor she may give two turtledoves
or two pigeons instead of a lamb (12, 8). These texts reflect the work
of a religious authority that is very conscious of its mission and duty.

IV. THE LAST STAGE IN THE PRIESTLY REDACTION

The " last stage in the priestly redaction " [23] is marked by preoccupations
of a theological order (the community and excommunication), of a
juridical order (adapting the codes so that they agree), as well as by
certain clear literary forms. The age in which this was done was
characterized by serious conflicts between those who had returned and
the surrounding population. The Samaritans and their allies, who
actually were in possession of the land when the exiles returned, considered
themselves loyal Yahwists (4 Kgs 17, 32 f.), without adopting all the
priestly traditions. They had continued to come to the site of the
Temple after the fall of Jerusalem (Jer 41, 5) and they would have taken
part in the restoration (1 Esd 4, 2) while still retaining the " old customs "
(4 Kgs 17, 34) contained in the legislation of the Yahwist, Elohist and
Deuteronomist.

The purpose of Esdras' mission [24] seems to have been to unite
these two Palestinian factions. The Persian court saw a political
advantage in such a union and the principle of their religious policy
was to make ancient traditions into a code of law. We find evidence
of their work in the Egyptian documents, especially the Elephantine
papyri. [25] So we can understand the extensive authority which was

---

[23] Cf. P. GRELOT in *VT* (1956), pp. 174-189.

[24] H. CAZELLES, " La mission d'Esdras, " *VT* (1954), pp. 113-140.

[25] *The Passover papyrus of Elephantine* is a letter of a Jewish official, Hananiah,
informing his Jewish confreres at Elephantine of an order sent by the central
administration to Arsham, the satrap of Egypt; it lays down practical directives
borrowed from the priestly regulations concerning Passover and Azymes :

" [To my brothers] Yadeniah and his companions, Jewish soldiers, your brother
Hananiah. May God [grant] prosperity to my brothers! And now, in this year,
the fifth of King Darius, the king has commanded Arsham... [a gap of one line].
You, then, are to count fourteen [days from the first day of Nisan and] celebrate
[the Passover]. Then from the fifteenth day to the twenty-first day of [Nisan,

given to Esdras (1 Esd 7, 12-26). The entire priestly code with its groups of laws and its additions (such as Nm 9, 6-13 concerning the Passover in the second month) was to be acknowledged as the Law of the State — by Samaria as well as by Jerusalem. Our Pentateuch seems to be the result of this final union of texts, and the preponderant influence of Esdras and the Sadokite clergy can be recognized in the fact that the priestly document served as a framework for the whole. The levites were accorded the diminished status found in Ezechiel (44, 10 f.). They were still counted in the census (Nm 3) just the same as the other tribes, although this was not the original intention (Nm 1, 47). They were also considered as substitutes for the Israelite first-born and directly belonging to God (Nm 8, 16) to whom every first-born belongs; the original priestly tradition merely made them the servants of Aaron (Nm 3, 9). These are the first measures directed towards broadening the " holiness " law which had been considered up to that time as the privilege of the Aaronic priesthood (Nm 16, 5-7) because of their anointing (Ex 30, 30).

V. The Theology of the Temple

The " holiness " of the priesthood was due to the power of offering sacrifice in the Temple. The Torah of Ezechiel had allowed only priests to dwell in the Temple and it was this that enabled them, according to the standards of the priestly mentality, to live a perfect life. They prized it highly (Ps 133). In the course of time this theology of holiness, so intimately associated with the Temple, is going to expand. Chronicles already entrusted the levites, i.e., the faithful, with the more important rights and duties in the Temple building and feasts (2 Par 35, 13). But it will be the role of the New Testament to summon all the faithful to holiness and to perfection.

In the final period of biblical revelation the Temple, where God dwells among men, is no longer just a building or place of worship; it is the very Body of Christ (Jn 2, 21; 4, 21 f.) which has been made present in the eucharistic banquet (Mt 26, 26 and parallel passages; cf. Jn 6, 53 f.). By the grace and the sacrifice of the Messias, a life of

---

you are to celebrate the feast of Unleavened Bread]. Purify yourselves and keep the vigil well. Do not [perform] any work on the fifteenth or the twenty-first day. Nor shall you drink *(shekar)* nor eat anything that has fermented. [Eat the unleavened bread from the fourteenth day of Nisan at] sunset until the twenty-first day of Nisan [at sunset. For seven days] bring [nothing fermented] into your homes, and stay away from it during those days...." (This letter dates from 419 B.C., cf. *VT*, 4 [1954], pp. 349-384).

perfect union with God is made possible, provided only that one lives
with the faith of Abraham and obeys the Law of Moses that has been
brought to perfection by the Son of David.   Christ did not come to
" destroy " but to " perfect " (Mt 5, 17) and St. Paul specifies that he
did not destroy the Law by Faith, but rather he strengthened it
(Rom 3, 31).   While pointing towards the New Law, the final word
of the Pentateuch is found in this liturgical life of the Temple, with its
rhythmic annual cycle, its precise details, its way of excluding either
doubts or objections, even making provision for the poor (Lv 5, 7 f.11 f.;
12, 8).   This was an essentially religious life and its soul is revealed
to us in certain Psalms (26; 84, 133; 134).   But despite the ideal which
inspired it, the Law of Moses could give this life only to a few, in addition
to the many pilgrims.   Israel had expected something different and the
prophets had promised something more.

" Moses, the Author of the Pentateuch "

Whatever be the literary strata which the so-called documentary
hypothesis makes use of, it can be said that all would attribute to Moses
an important role " as author and as legislator. " [26]   This is one of the
reasons that justify the statement that the " substance " [27] of the
Pentateuch goes back to Moses.   It is not easy to define exactly this
substance — a term used by the Biblical Commission in its scholastic
meaning. [28]   At least, as the same Commission has written, " there is
no one today who... refuses to admit a progressive development of the
Mosaic laws due to social and religious conditions of later times, a
development which is also manifest in the historical narratives. "   The
study of the Pentateuch begets a clear impression that without Moses
and his influence the entire work becomes an incomprehensible enigma
from a historical point of view.   And a study of the Fathers will
strengthen this impression.   Like St. Paul they recognized that these
five books contained the gift of the Law and the covenant mediated by
Moses.   In their commentaries, sermons and treatises, they emphasized
the riches of this teaching.   St. Augustine wrote apropos of Gn 1, 1 :
" When such a great number of perfectly correct ideas can be derived
from these words, how foolish it would be to claim rashly that Moses
had only one or another idea in mind " (Confessions, 12, 35).   But the
Fathers also drew on the Pentateuch for various mystical themes, such

---

[26] Whether one recognizes " documents " or " traditions "; cf. pp. 130 f.

[27] Cf. the Letter of the Biblical Commission to Cardinal Suhard; cf. p. 125.

[28] J. COPPENS, The Old Testament and the Critics, p. 147.

as Origen's *Sermons on Exodus* and Gregory of Nyssa's *Life of Moses*. All this shows how difficult it is to make a synthesis of a work so vast and so complex.

However, Judaism felt the need of such a synthesis. This effort to understand itself was carried out from the time of Hillel to Maimonides (died in 1204). The latter arrived at a juridical and philosophical synthesis expressed in thirteen articles of faith (existence and unity of God, reward of the just, etc.). [29] Since then, however, the works of critical scholars have raised other problems concerning the progress of history and the comparison of the revealed Law with pagan laws. One who would seek in the Torah an absolute truth would demand more than Maimonides provided.

Can this search succeed? Some non-Catholic writers of a radically evolutionistic turn doubt it, and they would judge the value of the Torah as merely relative, a stage in the development of history. But this is a surrender. The conscience of modern man, like the old treatise *Mekhilta* (XV, 26), has always recognized an absolute value in the principles of the Decalogue — at the minimum.

A critical and historical study can go much further than this; it can show how in and after the time of Moses God prepared by stages the final " Israel of God " (Gal 6, 16). The literary, historical and social study of the various layers in the Pentateuch gradually reveals to us how God gave His people one institution after another, from the Mosaic covenant to the final realization of the kingdom of God by Christ. He completes the Torah and gives to the kingdom a foundation that is neither pastoral, nor agricultural, nor charismatic, nor " priestly, " but apostolic. The hypotheses of the critics, insofar as they are based on objective and certain criteria, allow us to get a glimpse of a synthesis that leads to a better understanding of all the power of the New Testament. One will come to see how the providential preparation behind the divine adaptation to different kinds of material culture, and to the intellectual and spiritual formation of His Chosen People, brought them to the exact point where the New Testament could be born. Christ, coming to this earth, completed the Law; He did not destroy it (Mt 5, 17; cf. Rom 3, 31).

This development is also true of the Torah itself in which the old has not been simply eliminated by the new. The heirs of Moses built

---

[29] See the commentary on the *Mishnah*, treaty *Sanhedrin*, chap. 10; also his *Mishneh* (the repetition of the Torah).

upon him [30]; they worked in the same spirit that we know is the Spirit of God. From a given point of view, historical criticism can show the opposition between an item in the code of the covenant and an item in the Deuteronomic or " priestly " code. But this was not the point of view of the redactors who put these texts together at the critical times of Israelite history. If they joined J and E, it is because they wanted to deepen the faith and hope of the one by the moral considerations of the other. Deuteronomy did not make void previous tradition; it gave it a new force by offering a very pure notion of the love of God. The " priestly " code gives a sincere soul the possibility of living with God present in His Tabernacle. Surely with the destruction of the Temple, a terrible problem confronted those who believed in God — but the apostles and the Jews who accepted Christianity rightly recognized the Temple par excellence in Christ, the God-Man, and in the Eucharist in which He is truly present.

The Torah is law, history, theodicy, spirituality, and much more besides. But it is not a law that can be applied without discretion to present-day society, since certain laws treat of groups belonging to disparate attitudes and eras. It is not a methodical and continuous history since it permits of unusual lacunae and disturbing repetitions. It is not a philosophical collection of truths about God — were one to attempt a formulation, the end result would not be as expected. A. Neher and believing Jews would see in the spirituality of the Pentateuch a " cosmic fidelity " [31] — a rather equivocal phrase.

For the Christian the Pentateuch is the Revelation which guides and rules the life of a people on earth, a life of hopes and of dangers. This Revelation gives evidence of the presence of an omnipotent Person who governs, even when He is rejected; it is the God of Abraham, of Isaac and of Jacob, the God of the living and not of the dead (Mt 22, 32). The gift of the Torah enabled the Jewish faith to live through the centuries. The one who believes in Christ, the incarnate Word of God, will understand even more vitally the deep meaning of the Pentateuch in its theology of the presence of God and of redemption and of grace. " The Law was given by Moses, grace and truth have come to us through Jesus Christ " (Jn 1, 17).

---

[30] St. Thomas, *Sum. Th.*, II^a-II^{ae}, q. 174, a. 6 : " *Utrum gradus prophetiae varientur secundum temporis processum.* " The answer is in the affirmative, even *sub statu legis.*

[31] *Moise et la vocation juive* (Paris, 1956), p. 150.

PART II

THE FIRST PROPHETICAL BOOKS
by J. Delorme

Introductions, translations, commentaries, pp. 1 f.

A. ROBERT, " Historique (Genre)*, " *SDB*, IV, cols. 7-23.

M. NOTH, *Uberlieferungsgeschichtliche Studien I* (Halle, 1943).

E. JACOB, *La Tradition Historique en Israël* (Montpellier, 1943).

C. R. NORTH, *The Old Testament Interpretation of History* (London, 1946).

O. EISSFELDT, *Geschichtsschreibung im Alten Testament* (Berlin,1948).

G. OESTBORN, *Yahweh's Words and Deeds : A Preliminary Study into the Old Testament Presentation of History* (Uppsala, 1951).

R. DENTAN (ed.), *The Idea of History in the Ancient Near East* (New Haven : Yale Univ., 1955).

J. BRIGHT, *Early Israel in Recent History Writing* (London : SCM, 1956).

J. BARR, " Revelation through History in the Old Testament and in Modern Theology, " *Interpretation* 17 (1963), pp. 192-205.

CURTIS, " A Suggested Interpretation of the Biblical Philosophy of History, " *HUCA*, 34 (1963), pp. 115-123.

O. EISSFELDT, *The Hebrew Kingdom* (New York : Cambridge, 1965).

C. R. NORTH, " History, " *IDB*, II, pp. 607-612.

We are accustomed to distinguish in the Bible between historical and prophetical books. And we are readily inclined to consider the former books as concerned with the past and the latter with the future. Such a schematic consideration, however, does not do justice to reality. The books of the prophets, on the one hand, give considerable importance to the description of the historical setting of their preaching; their prophecies, moreover, begin often with past or contemporary history in order to judge and to explain it. On the other hand, the Books of Josue, Judges, Samuel and Kings, which we call historical, are ranked by the Hebrew Canon of Sacred Scriptures among the Prophets. This classification is partly to be explained by the fact that these books were thought to have been written by prophets (cf. Josephus Flavius, *Against Apion* 1, 8; *Baba Bathra* 14[b] and 15[a]) : the Book of Josue by the man whose name it bears, the Books of Judges and Samuel by Samuel, the Books of Kings by Jeremias. But a more profound explanation can be found in that the Jews sensed a real relationship between these books and the message of the prophets. Their writings formed the object of assiduous meditation, especially after the return from the Exile : whatever of their inspired declarations had been converted into reality by historical happenings offered a guarantee for the eventual fulfilment of all the promises of God. And the great collection of national traditions which recalled the history from the death of Moses to the Exile presented, on the meaning of the past, the duties of the present and of the future, a doctrine quite in harmony with that of the prophets; many a page, besides, showed the prophets at work in the midst of the people of God. It is understandable, therefore, that these books have been joined to the collection of prophetical books under the generic heading of *Nebiîm* (Prophets) which designates the second part of the Hebrew Bible. The Jews, however, distinguish between " the former prophets " (Josue—Kings) and " the latter prophets " (Is, Jer, Ez and the Book of the Twelve) only, it seems, according to the order these books hold in the Canon.

The four " former prophets " constitute a certain unity. They received this unity toward the end of the Monarchy or at the beginning of the Exile, through the hand of redactors who in the light of the Book of Deuteronomy again took up earlier writings. Their intervention can be recognized in moral reflections, even in discourses which they inserted into the narration : this intervention is discreet in Josue and, even more so, in Samuel, but quite evident in Kings. Their aim was to underline the lessons of history : infidelity to the Covenant was always detrimental to the Chosen People. At the time when Israel was dispersed among the nations this was a means of inviting it to an examen of conscience and of reminding it of the way to salvation.

This revision respected the older writings with which it had to deal. Several sources may thus be recognized in the Books of Kings, a considerable work can be traced back to the time of Ezechias as for the Books of Judges and Samuel, and some well-defined units form the basis of Josue. It is possible to go back still further, to the more restricted compositions and particular arrangements of the narratives which were carried out since the beginning of the Monarchy; a description might even be given of the oral traditions which form the foundation of these compositions and arrangements. Our books, therefore, comprise quite distinct elements where we may find the reflections of different historical periods. It is remarkable that at each stage of their formation religious preoccupations assert themselves. History as a literary genre is always illuminated by faith and successive redactions bear witness to the progress of revelation.

Our books, therefore, are historical as far as their object is concerned. They are of great interest for the historian and serve as indispensable sources for him. But the epithet " prophetical " expresses well that which places these books above the works of profane historians, however successfully they may have been composed. These books convert the meditation on the past, sustained by the teaching of the prophets, into a search of light for the present. Or to go deeper yet, they show God, the maker of history, at work. This revelation of a historical God gives to the events their meaning, detaches them from the past and confers on them an orientation towards the future which they prepare and, to a certain extent, already prefigure.

CHAPTER I

THE BOOK OF JOSUE

BIBLIOGRAPHY

Introductions, translations, commentaries, pp. 1 f. and p. 168 (A. GELIN, *BPC**; F. M. ABEL, *BJ**; A. SCHULTZ, *HSAT**...).

A. FERNANDEZ, *Commentarius in Librum Josue** (Paris, 1938).

G. E. WRIGHT, " The Literary and Historical Problem of Joshua 10 and Judges 1, " *JNES*, 5 (1946), pp. 105-114; with F. M. CROSS, " The Boundary and Province Lists of the Kingdom of Judah, " *JBL*, 75 (1956), pp. 202-226.

P. AUVRAY, " Josue, " *SDB*, IV, cols. 1131 ff. (Paris, 1948).

D. BALDI, *Giosué** (Turin, 1952).

B. J. ALFRINK, *Josue** (Roermond, 1952).

J. BRIGHT, " The Book of Joshua, " *IB* (1953).

H. W. HERTZBERG, *Die Bücher Josua, Richter, Ruth* (Göttingen, 1953).

M. NOTH, *Das Buch Josua*² (Tübingen, 1953).

Z. KALLAI-KLEINMANN, " The Town Lists of Judah, Simeon, Benjamin, and Dan, " *VT*, 8 (1958), pp. 135-160.

Y. KAUFMAN, *The Biblical Account of the Conquest of Palestine* (1953); *The Book of Joshua with Commentary and Introduction* (1959).

G. E. MENDENHALL, " The Hebrew Conquest of Palestine, " *BA*, 25 (1962), pp. 66-86.

§ 1. Content and Plan

A simple reading will enable us to recognize quite easily the plan of the book and to uncover the key ideas.

A *prologue* (1) attaches the period which is about to begin to the work of Moses and announces some major themes. God gives the land to His people. But this gift demands vigor and perseverance in their fidelity to the divine law. It also requires the engagement of the whole people.

A first section recalls *the conquest of the Promised Land* by means of some significative narratives and some summary accounts (2—11) :

1. *The entrance into the Land* is lengthily narrated (2—7). First the preparations : spies are sent to Jericho (2); but the narrator is especially

interested in the faith of Rahab who recognizes the true God in the work
He is doing on behalf of His people. The Jordan is crossed (3, 1—5, 12).
This is a religious event : they sanctify themselves, they march in
procession behind the ark of the Covenant, they erect a perpetual memorial
at Galgal, [1] they also remove the reproach of not being circumcised in
order to celebrate solemnly the Passover as they had done in Egypt
before the first " passover. " The capture of Jericho (5, 13—7, 1) appears
as a liturgical as well as a military action. The rites of curse (the circling
of the city and the war cry), the presence of the ark of the priests, the
collapse of the walls : all exalt the divine power. The anathema which
vows the city and its inhabitants to destruction stresses the absolute
right of Yahweh in this conquest which is His work. Thus the violation
of the anathema by Achan cannot but involve disastrous consequences.

2. After a first defeat, the result of Achan's sin, *the capture of Hai*
is a new pledge of the help Yahweh grants whenever His people is faithful
(8, 1-29). The tactics are ingenious, but the narrative also stresses the
divine inspiration of Josue, his curse and the anathema.

3. *The sacrifice and the reading of the Law* on Mount Ebal (8, 30-35)
would not fit well into the context with the preceding narrative if we had
to deal with an account of war. But this narrative manifests very aptly
the message of the book : we assist at the renewal of the Covenant the
reality of which had been revealed to us in the preceding narratives.

4. The enemies of Israel join hands (9, 1-2). By ruse the Gabaonites
trick Josue into concluding an alliance with them and thus escape the
menace of extermination (9, 3-27). Five kings of the south try to punish
the Gabaonites for their defection, but Josue puts them to flight (10, 1-27).
The conquest of the southern towns is then narrated (10, 28-39) and its
lesson brought home (10, 40-43).

5. Now it is the turn of the northern towns which had entered into
an alliance against Israel; they are defeated and vowed to destruction
(11, 1-14).

6. In conclusion it is stated that Josue had remained faithful to the
divine mission entrusted to him through Moses (11, 15-23); finally the
list of the defeated kings is drawn up (12).

A second section describes *the distribution of the Promised Land among
the tribes* (13—21). Ruben, Gad and the half-tribe of Manasse had already
received their portions on the eastern side of the Jordan (13, 8-33). On
the western side, a first distribution by lot in Galgal determines the

---

[1] A. GEORGE, " Les récits de Gilgal en Josué 5, 2-15 "*, *Mémorial Chaine*,
(Lyon, 1950).

territory of Juda and Caleb (14, 6—15), of Ephraim and Manasse (16—17). At Silo, after a survey of the remaining land, the seven other tribes receive their portions (18—19). The cities of asylum (20) and the levitical cities (21, 1-42) are enumerated separately. A remark concerning the fulfilment of the promises (21, 43-45) concludes this section.

Josue now dismisses the Transjordanian tribes. They build an altar on the banks of the Jordan, an action which fills the other tribes with dismay; the explanation of the Transjordanian tribes, however, quickly dispels all apprehensions (22). More important for the purpose of the book are the last recommendations of Josue. In a discourse which is not attached to a particular place Josue summarizes his work and warns against the danger of contamination to which Israel is exposed in the midst of alien nations (23). In a general assembly at Sichem he recalls the work of Yahweh from Abraham until the giving of the land in order to uphold the choice, which the people takes in reply to his call, between Yahweh and the other gods (24, 1-28). A remark concerning the burial of Josue, of Joseph and of the priest Eleazar (24, 29-33) forms the conclusion.

§ 2. The Literary Structure of the Book and its Composition

The present unity of the book allows us to see differences in style and narration which indicate to us multiple sources and various stages of compilation. The exhortatory character of Josue 1 differs markedly from the following accounts. These accounts show considerable overloading and traces of a different tradition which the redactor did not wish to lose (compare 4, 9 with 4, 1-3. 20-24 concerning the memorial stones set up in the midst of the Jordan or at Galgal; 6, 8. 9. 13 with 6, 5. 16. 20^b concerning the use of the horn; 6, 10. 20^a with 6, 5. 20^b as for the signal given by Josue or by a blast of the horn). Several passages give the impression that some material has been recorded within its own context (13, 2-6^a; 14, 6^b-16; 15, 13-19 which represents a tradition different from that of 10, 36-39). Chapter 23, where the same exhortatory style of chapter 1 is found, is similar in certain points to chapter 24 which is more detailed and may be related to the same event as 8, 30-35 (the assembly of Sichem).

These few examples suffice to state the problem : From what sources and in what manner has this book been composed? Literary criticism tried to give an answer. For a long time the system of the four sources which seems to have proved its value as for the Pentateuch has been applied to Josue. Since Wellhausen the term Hexateuch has been used,

and our book has been said to form the necessary conclusion to the
preceding five; an attempt has also been made to find here the
continuation of the Yahvistic (9th cent.) and Elohistic (8th cent.)
documents. These combined documents would have been reworked by
a redactor in order to illustrate the doctrine of Deuteronomy (about 600).
Finally, after the Exile, a priestly redaction would have given the final
form to this work. This theory has been considered as classic for a long
time. And it has been thought possible to perfect it by carrying the
literary analysis to its utmost limits : thus O. Eissfeldt discovers a lay
source older than the Yahvistic (J); the *Bible du Centenaire* distinguishes
between J1 and J2; von Rad subdivides the priestly document.

The study of Josue received a new orientation through the works
of A. Alt and M. Noth who were not only interested in literary criticism
but also in archeology and in the history of the traditions. The
commentary of Noth is used in most of the recent works. He has shown
that there is no Hexateuch. In both form and content the traditions in
Josue differ considerably from those in the Pentateuch. This fact has
been established.

As for the book itself, Noth attaches it to the great Deuteronomistic
history which extends all the way to the Books of Kings. Josue, therefore,
would have received its final shape after the discovery of the Book of
Deuteronomy in 622 (Noth distinguishes two Deuteronomistic redactions,
one concerning 1—12; 21, 43—22, 6; 23, 1-16; and the other which added
13—21, 42 and 24). There is no priestly document; the priestly school
only revised some passages and made some additions like 22, 9-34. The
critics generally accept the hypothesis of the Deuteronomistic redaction
(among Catholics and in various degrees : Gelin, Baldi, Alfrink). There
is less agreement as to its importance. Mowinckel continues to ascribe
a considerable part of 13—21 to the priestly revision. There is also no
agreement as to the exact determination of the elements which the
Deuteronomist is said to have added to the older sources (according to
Noth : 1; 8, 30-35; 12; 21, 43—22, 6; 23; 24, 31, without taking into
account some minor revisions).

The Deuteronomistic redaction used the older writings. Noth speaks
of two documents which in turn had been formed from earlier elements :
an account of the conquest and a description of Palestine. As for the
account of the conquest, a Judean author, about the year 900, grouped
together some Benjamite traditions which had been preserved at the
sanctuary of Galgal (2—9) as well as a few hero tales which at first were
only of local interest (10; 11, 1-19), and ascribed them to Josue. The
description of Palestine would result from the fusion, some time after

Josias, of a document older than the kingdom established by David which outlined the ideal boundaries of the tribes, and of a list of cities of Juda in the time of Josias. This description of Palestine when it was joined with the account of the conquest would have become the division of the land by Josue.

This method has the advantage of ascribing greater antiquity than it was generally done to the documents which are at the basis of Josue. Noth's position, however, has not been unanimously accepted by the experts. Certain reservations must be made with regard to the judgment which Noth, in the name of criticism, pronounced upon the historicity of the accounts (which are said to be mainly etiological tales); it is possible, moreover, to ascribe greater antiquity to the geographical sections and their data, especially to the list of the cities of Juda (15, 21-62) [2] and to that of the levitical cities (21; Albright pushes the age of this list back to the times of David and Solomon). [3] As for the accounts of the first section, they belong to a literary genre which at first was oral : the date when they received their concrete formulation in writing is of less importance than the form, the content and the age of each tradition that has been collected.

With regard to these traditions, we may speak of a first period of oral transmission, then of a second period of partial redactions. It is difficult to reconstruct two series of continuous narratives. In the Benjamite accounts (2—9), at least, we reach probably a combined account which dates already from the beginning of the Monarchy. The present chapter 24, in substance, could be attached to it : the narrative would thus be oriented towards the renewal of the Covenant at Sichem and would uphold the religious teaching concerning the fidelity to Yahweh as a condition of Israel's prosperity. Let it be noted that for A. Weiser this chapter 24 is the very type of a well-defined literary genre : the priestly sermon in which the formula of a confession of faith is commented upon, for example, in Dt 26, 1-11 (cf. the account of Jos 5, 11-12 with the ceremony of the first fruits).

It is impossible to describe the condition of the book at the time when the Deuteronomists began to revise it. They wanted to stress the religious lessons : Yahweh fulfils His promises and guarantees the efficacy of the Covenant as long as Israel remains faithful to its engagements. The Deuteronomistic hand can be recognized in chapter 1;

---

[2] Cf. R. DE VAUX, *RB*, 47 (1938), p. 463.
[3] W. F. ALBRIGHT, " The List of Levitic Cities, " *Ginzberg Jubilee Volume* (New York, 1945).

8, 30-35; 12; 23; and also in other particular revisions. We read now side by side chapter 23, a new composition, and chapter 24 which served as its model and which itself has been reworked. This is perhaps an indication that the Deuteronomistic revision did its work in several stages.

The geographical section must also have been formed in slow stages from documents drawn up at different times between the period of David and that of Josias. Whether it reached its present form through the Deuteronomistic revision or received yet some later additions, it assumes the aspect of an inventory of the inheritance received from God but dissipated by Israel. It also conveys the hope that the inheritance will be restored.

§ 3. The Literary Genre and Purpose

It is not surprising, therefore, to find in Josue passages quite distinct by reason of their literary characteristics. Compare, for example, the account of the capture of Jericho with the elements of the cadastre of the tribes used in the second section, or with the persuasive exhortation of chapters 1 and 23! This diversity constitutes the richness of the book which in its totality cannot simply be assigned to a clearly defined literary genre. It is important, nevertheless, to point out a certain number of traits which are found throughout the book and which must not be overlooked if we wish to appreciate its historical value and religious message. These traits characterize the work as an " epic history " and a " meditated history. "

1. *Epic traits.* It suffices to read the account of the capture of Jericho, of Hai and of the battle at Gabaon in order to perceive the epic grandeur. These victories left a lasting impression in the popular memory. Everything in the account tends to express their importance and, above all, to give glory to Yahweh : emphasis, expanded numbers, the obliteration of the human factors involved in the successes, the insistence on the extraordinary and the marvelous. With regard to Hai, L. H. Vincent speaks of " emphatic formulation, incoherent and exaggerated numbers, stress given to the marvelous, the unlikelihood of which is quite obvious to us but in no way disturbing for the oriental mind. " [4] The book itself, by the way, shows us how to recognize the heroic nature of certain passages : not all the numbers, on the one hand, have been expanded (8, 3. 12) and human tactics [5] play an important part (the

---

[4] L. H. VINCENT, *RB*, 46 (1937), p. 264.
[5] F. M. ABEL, " Les stratagèmes dans le livre de Josué, " *RB*, 56 (1949), pp. 321-339.

spies sent to Jericho, 2; the battle before the city, 24, 11; the ambush at Hai, 8; the overnight march to Gabaon in order to attack in the early morning, 10, 9); on the other hand, an old poem which reports an incantation to the sun and moon is first quoted, then transformed into a narrative. The narrator thus adds to the victory at Gabaon a trait which had to fill his listeners with admiration : the day of victory had been the longest day man has ever seen (10, 12-14). [6]

Another trait of the book is closely related to those typical of the epic style : in order to present the significance of an event, the writers turn to schematization. A picture is thus sketched of Josue leading a united people to the rapid conquest of the entire land and the suppression of all its inhabitants. Within this framework, however, the redactors have loyally preserved traditions and documents which signify the idealized character of this picture. The beginning of the Book of Josue suggests a rather slow and difficult advance, tribes who wage war without any coordination, who fail before important cities, who cannot overcome the inhabitants (compare Jos 12, 21-23; 17, 11-13 with Jgs 1, 27-28; and Jos 12, 14 with Jgs 1, 17; or Jos 19, 28-30 with Jgs 1, 31). We find traces of analogous traditions in Josue. According to 13, 1-6; 17, 12. 16; 16, 10 (compare 10, 33; 12, 12) the conquest has not been complete. Certain groups waged war on their own account (14, 6-15 and 15, 13-19; compare 10, 36-39). We must, therefore, understand the triumphal character of these summaries 10, 28-39 and 10, 40-43 : " All these kings and their lands Josue captured in one single campaign " (v. 42). Josue, the conqueror, draws to himself all the successes won by others, similar in a way to Moses whose patronage covers all Israelite legislation.

2. But these epic traits must not simply be ascribed to a literary art aware of its resources : they are in the service of a religious plan. The recourse to emphasis must exalt the power of Yahweh. He is the master of the enterprise: He takes Chanaan by force in order to give it to His people. In comparison with this statement, the detail of battles and the human means employed are less important to the narrator. Similarly, if he schematizes, he does it in the name of a prophetic vision of history, viewed in its unity. The humble beginnings, from the point of view of God's plan, are already containing the shape of future fulfilments. At the end of the conquest the sacred author contemplates the rest of Israel in the land which God has given her. The distribution among the tribes offers the occasion to describe lovingly and in detail the boundaries and the territories which Israel possesses by right and which she will possess

---

[6] Cf. A. GELIN, p. 69; G. LAMBERT, " Josué à la bataille de Gabaon "*, *NRT*, 76 (1954), pp. 374-391.

at the time of the greatest extension. The conquest brings about the
unanimity of the tribes : does it not contain the promise of their unity?
And if Josue dominates this history, it is in order to bring it back to the
unity of the work of God whose lieutenant he appears.

The Deuteronomistic redactor tries hard to disengage the themes
of meditation which this history suggests : it illustrates the doctrine of
the Covenant.   Yahweh fulfils His promises by giving His land as
inheritance to His people (1, 3. 6. 11; 23, 5. 14; 24, 13; cf. Dt 4, 1; 6, 10;
11, 9. 21...).   The entire account manifests God's fidelity to His word :
" I will be with you " (1, 5. 9. 19; 23, 3. 10; cf. Dt 6, 17-24; 11, 22-25;
31, 6. 8). To this engagement of God, Josue and his people must answer
with theirs : " Be firm and steadfast " (1, 6. 9. 18; see 8, 1; 10, 8. 25;
cf. Dt 31, 6-8. 23).   The engagement involves the fidelity to the divine
law (1, 6-9; 8, 32-35; 11, 15; 23; cf. Dt 5, 32 f.; 31, 9-13).   It demands
first of all " to serve God, for He is our God " (24, 18 and the whole
passage 24, 14-28; 22, 5; cf. Dt 6, 13), that is, in concrete terms, not to
mingle with pagan nations and their gods (23, 6-13; cf. Dt 7, 1-6).   The
insistence on the anathema [7] by extermination proposes to revive the
attachment to the only God of Israel, for the fidelity or infidelity to the
Covenant determines the entire history of fortune and misfortune of the
Chosen People (23, 12-16; cf. Dt 11, 22-32; 31, 16-22).   The conduct of
Josue presents an impressive image of this truth (11, 15-20; cf. 7, 11-12).
And this image illustrates the ideal which Deuteronomy saw in the Mosaic
period : the people of God united under the rule of a leader totally
dedicated to Yahweh and His Law.

The Book of Josue views history thus from a point of view quite
different from that of history in the modern sense and this vision justifies
the literary genre which has been chosen.   " The taking possession of
Chanaan is for the sacred author not simply a profane event, but a
theological happening. " [8]

§ 4. The Historical Value

The literary genre of the book must not lead us to a negative conclusion
with regard to its historical value.   Recent investigations of topographical
and archeological nature, which determine the site of certain localities
mentioned and reveal the Chanaanite civilization as well as the beginnings
of Israelite civilization, oblige us to seriously treat many other textual

[7] F. M. ABEL, " L'anathème de Jéricho et la maison de Rahab, " *RB*, 57 (1950),
pp. 374-391.
[8] R. DE VAUX, *RB*, 61 (1954), p. 261.

data. Besides, the new methods of literary analysis tend to assign greater antiquity to the traditions and documents used. A better knowledge, finally, of the literatures of tradition helps to recognize, in a general way, those historical memories which they exploit. It can be seen, therefore, that critics, even non-Catholics, place greater trust in Josue than had been done twenty or thirty years ago (Albright, Wright, Hertzberg, Bright).

I. ARCHEOLOGY

The historical value of certain accounts of Josue has been put to the test by archeology, but with quite uneven results. The excavations of Tell es-Sultan in 1907-1909, and again in 1930-1935, led to the discovery of Chanaanite Jericho. The experts had no doubt whatsoever that its destruction had to be ascribed to Josue; the only point of discussion was the date (about 1400 for J. Garstang, according to the pottery found in the necropolis; close to 1250 for L. H. Vincent). But new excavations have been undertaken since 1952, under the guidance of Miss Kathleen Kenyon. These excavations show Jericho as the oldest known city that had been fortified (of the Pre-Pottery Neolithic period) and allow us to follow its continuous development until the Middle Bronze Age. But the remains of a city of the Late Bronze Age (1600-1200), the period of Josue whatever date may be adopted, have not been found. Above the ruins of the Middle Bronze Age " layers of débris suggest that there was a gap in occupation, then, close to the surface, foundations of walls subsist and a floor on which a juglet has been found that is probably 14th century in date. " [9] The problem, therefore, remains unsolved. If archeology in this case does not give any support to the biblical account, neither does it weaken the historicity of an Israelite victory at Jericho. As for the remains of the city of that period, if they do not lie buried under another tell, they may have disappeared in one way or another· " It seems that the summit of the tell has been the victim both of erosion and the work of men and there is little chance that further excavations will give decisive evidence as to the date of the capture of Jericho by the Israelites. " [10]

The excavations carried out at Et-Tell, close to Beitin (Bethel) by Mme. Judith Marquet-Krause in 1933-1934 are equally disappointing. There is hardly any doubt that this site has to be identified with Hai. Now, if the city reaches back to the Neolithic period and knew its apogee

---

[9] *RB*, 61 (1954), p. 565.
[10] *Ibid.*

in the third millennium, it had been utterly destroyed about the year 2000 and remained abandoned until 1200. Thus for several critics the account of the capture of Hai is a legend destined to explain, with reference to Josue, a ruin in reality much older than he (*Ha-'Ai* = the ruin). But this legend hardly fits in from every point of view. W. F. Albright thinks that the two cities of Hai and Bethel, very close to each other, may easily have been confused in the popular tradition : the ruin of the first caused the prosperity of the second which definitely has been destroyed in the 13th century, probably by the Israelites. The memory of that historic victory, preserved by a valuable document in Jgs 1, 22-26, has then been attached to that spectacular ruin of Hai so that it gave rise to the account of Josue. [11] L. H. Vincent finds that this solution does not do sufficient justice to the historicity of Jos 7—8. The fortress of Hai, although destroyed, but admirably situated, was still strong enough to serve for the Chanaanites who had gathered as a bastion against the Israelite advance towards the highlands. This would especially explain the mistake of the spies of Josue (7, 3) and also the astonishing presence of the men of Bethel (8, 17). [12]

" In short, as for the two definite places, Jericho and Hai, archeology has raised more problems than it has solved. Is it not so that archeology, rich in precious and indisputable results when it is a question of establishing the general characteristics of a civilization, remains a delicate instrument when we wish to apply it to particular cases, to make it tell us the name of a site, the date of an event, the role of an individual? "[13]

Certainly! In some other places, however, the results of excavations have not been quite as disappointing. It has been established that Lachish (Jos 10, 3. 23. 32) [14] must have fallen under the onslaught of the invaders shortly after 1230, and at the other extremity of Palestine, in Galilee, Hasor (Jos 11, 10) must have been destroyed at about the same time. [15] These concordant results, however, match the indication given on the stele of Menephtah [16] who declares to have been victorious over Israel (the people) in the course of his campaigns in Chanaan. But all taken into account we may retain a date between 1250 and 1230 for the Israelite invasion of Chanaan.

---

[11] *BAZOR*, 56 (1934), p. 11; 58 (1935), p. 15; 60 (1935), pp. 8 ff.

[12] *RB*, 46 (1937), pp. 258 ff.

[13] P. AUVRAY, *SDB*, IV, col. 1138.

[14] W. F. ALBRIGHT, *From the Stone Age to Christianity*, p. 212.

[15] Y. YADIN, " Excavations at Hazor, " *BA*, 19 (1956), pp. 2-11; *Hazor* I (Jerusalem, 1958).

[16] Text, p. 15.

II. LITERARY CRITICISM

Considerations of literary criticism may also intervene in the judgment which we pass upon the historicity of the Book of Josue.

a) Several accounts are concerned with facts whose truth could be established when these accounts were formed : there are twelve stones at the sanctuary of Galgal, [17] the wall of Jericho is overthrown, a heap of stones remains in the valley of Achor " to this day, etc...." Noth considers the accounts of chapters 2—9 as etiological legends destined to explain these facts. But it matters to know whether the interest in facts can create the explanation. " As for accounts transmitted by oral and popular tradition there is often no noticeable difference between a historical or ethnographical legend and an exact tradition, between an etiological legend and a true explanation, between a story and the account of an actual fact. " [18] For there remains a fact that has to be explained : the occupation of Chanaan by the Israelites. A fact of this importance could not remain without memories. But this fact is left without explanation, if every historical value is denied to the accounts of Josue. The judgment in this debate depends on other methods and not only on literary criticism. Literary criticism, nevertheless, inasmuch as it defines the literary genre of a text, can eliminate a certain number of false problems.

b) Thus, for example, from the epic genre of certain passages we cannot conclude that their content is nonhistorical, but we may deduce, indeed, that the narrator did not intend to report history with rigorous fidelity. With regard to Jericho A. Barrois writes : " The details of the siege and of the capture of the city which the sacred author described in a series of marvelous events completely elude our understanding. " [19]

The miracles of Josue have often baffled the interpreters. Some reject them because of a rationalistic prejudice. Others want to have them accepted by reducing them to the size of an extraordinary but natural event : a landslide, as in 1267, is said to have halted the waters of the Jordan; a timely earthquake helped the capture of Jericho; the victory of Gabaon was facilitated by a storm which darkened the sky (Van Hoonacker) or by a hail of meteorites accompanied by an unusual luminosity which prolonged the twilight into the following dawn (Daniel-Rops, Ceuppens).

---

[17] J. MUILENBERG, " The Site of Ancient Gilgal ", *BASOR*, 140 (1955), pp. 11-26.

[18] R. DE VAUX, *RB*, 53 (1946), p. 327.

[19] *RB*, 43 (1934), p. 146.

" Such a solution will be satisfactory which takes into account at the same time the special providence of God towards His people as well as the literary genre of the text. " [20] A young people that finds its strength in its belief in the Covenant undertakes a conquest and obtains results which surpass the means employed and serve as a sign of divine intervention. This people then immortalizes the memory by heroic accounts in which the marvelous is put into the service of faith in order to underline the essential : God's action. These two principles—divine intervention and literary genre—do not always allow a detailed reconstruction of the event which was of little concern to the narrator. But they enable us to dispose of the hypotheses not suggested by the text; and, above all, they allow us to understand the text and to appreciate it in conformity with the intentions of the inspired author.

c) Some have also found encouragement in literary criticism to reduce singularly the role played by Josue in the conquest. M. Noth (and already A. Alt) retains as primitive only the mention of Josue in 17, 14-18 and in 24. But these two texts suppose already that Josue played an essential part in the conquest : he appears as the head of the house of Joseph and as the leading actor of the federation of the tribes at Sichem. His Ephraimite origin could not exclude him from the Benjamite traditions which are at the basis of 2—9 : Benjamin and Ephraim are united by special ties and have preserved the memory of a common occupation of Chanaan under the guidance of Josue. If it remains possible that he attached to himself alien elements (for example 10, 28-43), it will be difficult to explain, apart from his historical role, that accounts of diverse origins have been grouped together under his name.

III. CONCLUSION

The best indication for the historicity is found in the reliable image of the occupation of Chanaan which results from the book. [21] It schematizes and does not relate all. It is possible that Juda and Simeon formed an alliance of their own for the conquest of their territory where they may have rejoined allied groups (Caleb, Kenites) who had come up directly from the south (cf. Jgs 1, 16-17 compared with Nm 21, 3; Jgs 1, 9-15 compared with Jos 15, 13-19). It is also possible that some of the groups united by Josue had never gone down to Egypt or had returned a long time earlier. But the book uses enough ancient data to justify a general reconstruction of the occupation, especially in central Palestine. The

---

[20] A. GELIN, p. 46.
[21] Cf. R. DE VAUX, " Israel "*, *SDB*, IV, cols. 737 f.

various steps can be followed : Jericho, Hai, Bethel open the way to the hill country which was thinly populated and could easily be occupied; the federation of Sichem and the pact with the Gabaonites break the political equilibrium and lead to new battles with the united Chanaanite kings of the south, and then of the north. The general conditions of the conquest can be seen with sufficient clarity : the military inferiority of the Israelites is compensated by their recourse to stratagems, to elements of surprise, to treason, but, above all, by their courage sustained by their faith in the Covenant. And it is not surprising that the fortified cities of the plain were bypassed. At the death of Josue the Israelites are found in three regions separated from each other by powerful Chanaanite cities : Gezer and Jerusalem separate the tribes of the hill country of Juda from Ephraim; Megiddo, Taanach, Beth-Shan separate the tribes in the central region from those of Galilee.

§ 5. The Religious Value and the Spiritual Significance

As we have seen, what was primarily a religious purpose directed the formation of the book. It presents the conquest of Chanaan as an episode of salvation history : the intervention of God reveals His plan for His people. It is by relating the history of Josue to the fulfilment of this plan all along the Old and the New Testament that we may perceive its importance and deep meaning.

1) Yahweh had promised land and posterity to Abraham. He has kept His promise and our book exalts His fidelity. Even in the lists of the conquered kings and of the boundaries love expresses itself, a love which is delighted to describe minutely and to idealize its object : the *land* and the *posterity*, fruits of the *promise*.

At the time of the final redaction, this love also expresses a hope. The posterity is divided into two kingdoms, of which one has fallen already and the other is about to disappear, if it has not yet done so. The land has been invaded by enemies who soon will occupy it completely. Before these contradictions of history, faith puts its trust in the promise by reason of which a new fulfilment is expected. There is a longing for the rest of which the history of Josue offers the image (1, 13. 15; 21, 44; 22, 4; 23, 1; cf. Dt 3, 20; 12, 10; 25, 19; compare Is 14, 3; 28, 12). The cadastre of Israel is preserved as the pledge of a new future. Ezechiel, during the Exile, describes the future distribution of the restored land among the tribes (47—48). To possess or to inherit the land : this is the expression of the hope of Messianic and eschatological salvation (Ez 36, 12; 37, 25; Is 57, 13; 60, 21; 65, 9), the expectation of those who have been tried and who count on God (Ps 25, 13; 37, 3. 9. 11. 22. 29. 34). The New Testament replies : " Blessed are the humble, for they will inherit the land " (Mt 5, 5; see the expression " to inherit the kingdom of God, " Mt 25, 34; 1 Cor 6, 9-10; 15, 50; Gal 5, 21). And the Epistle to the Hebrews invites us to prepare ourselves for the rest of God, of which the rest in Chanaan has only been a figure (4, 8; cf. Ap 14, 13).

2) Since Moses, the *Covenant* defines the relations between Yahweh and His people. The conduct of Josue shows the Covenant in action : God is with Israel whenever Israel obeys His will. This statement is for the Deuteronomistic redactor a way to judge recent history : the fall of Samaria and the misfortunes of Jerusalem find their cause in the infidelity to the Covenant. The most disastrous treason was committed through the worship of other gods, through the adaptation to the ways of other nations.

Now we understand the insistence, which appears so shocking to the modern reader, on the anathema by extermination *(herem)*. The Hebrews conceived God according to the common ideas of their time : war is a religious undertaking and victory comprises the extermination of the conquered in honor of the tutelary deity. That these ideas are found in an inspired book, is a trait of the condescension of God who must adapt the revelation to the progressive possibilities of human intelligence while waiting to reveal Himself through His son, Jesus Christ. " We must not set up the Old Testament as full light, as definitive norm, for it was only the preparation and the dawn of the New Testament. " [22] The hatred against the Chanaanites, moreover, which is expressed in Josue as well as in Dt 20, 16-18, offers something theoretical. The redactor knows that the Hebrews in fact did not exterminate the indigenous population (24, 4. 12), and that they succumbed to the danger of contamination through the worship of the baals. Perhaps he wishes to express his sorrow. He will certainly teach us a lesson : the Chanaanites and their gods represent all the forces that turn the Chosen People away from Yahweh. He sees no future unless the people return to the exclusive service of his God.

This truth retains its value. Every day, according to Ps 95, God invites His people to obedience without which " they will not enter into my rest " (vv. 7-11). And the Epistle to the Hebrews applies this Psalm to the Today of the New Covenant, where the prefigurations of the history of Josue find their fulfilment (4, 1-11; cf. Jos 11, 15. 20; compare Dt 4, 1-5. 25-26; 5, 32-33; 6, 17-19).

---

[22] A. GELIN, p. 20.

3) Thus the image of all the tribes united under the command of Josue assumes the value of a prophetical anticipation. When the book receives its final form, this image is cruelly belied by the facts. It agrees well, on the other hand, with the hope of Jeremias (23, 1-8; 31, 27-28) and of Ezechiel (37, 15-28). God is always working for the unity of His people. But this work demands the participation of all : the Transjordanian tribes are convoked. And the link which joins them all together is assured through the fidelity to the Law : the assembly of Sichem is exemplary.

These lessons receive their full significance through the gathering of the New Israel. The fulfilment illuminates the beginnings. A detail, like the adventure of Rahab, can become the paradigm of the universalistic overture of Messianic salvation (Mt 1, 5) and of the faith which saves by incorporating into the People of God (Jas 2, 25; Heb 11, 21).

The role which fell on Josue illustrates also a constant of God's action. At each stage of the holy history, the plan of God rests upon the shoulders of a man who seems to embody his whole people. Josue incarnates in a certain sense the unity of Israel which God introduces into their inheritance. He lives the ideal of docility which has been proposed to the People of God. His victories manifest the action of God on behalf of the chosen community. His name itself must not be a matter of indifference for the biblical tradition (cf. Nm 13, 16, where Moses changes the name Hoshea, " Liberation, " into Yehoshua, " Yahweh-Liberation "). This name expresses his vocation and his participation in the great work of God which the Bible constantly defines as a liberation. With Josue God gives living space to His people by liberating them from their enemies. Other liberations will follow, and hope will tend yet towards other, more decisive liberations, until God will send another Yeshua, His son Jesus.

CHAPTER II

THE BOOK OF JUDGES

BIBLIOGRAPHY

Introductions, translations, commentaries, p. 1 and p. 168 (R. TAMISIER, BPC*; A. VINCENT, BJ*, F. NOTSCHER, EBi*...).

C. F. KRAFT, " Judges, Book of, " IDB, II, pp. 1013-1023.

M. J. LAGRANGE, " Le Livre Des Juges, " EB (Paris, 1903).

C. F. BURNEY, The Book of Judges (London, 1918).

H. GRESSMANN, " Die Anfange Israels, " Schriften des A.T., fasc. 2 (Göttingen, 1922).

L. DESNOYERS, Histoire du Peuple Hébreu : I, La Période des Juges* (Paris, 1922); " Juges (livres des), " DTC, VIII, cols. 1834-1862 (Paris, 1925).

E. ROBERTSON, " The Period of the Judges, " BJRL, 30 (1946), pp. 91-114.

H. CAZELLES, " Juges (livres des), " SDB, IV (Paris, 1949) cols. 1394-1414.

J. M. MYERS, " The Book of Judges, " IB (1953).

H. W. HERTZBERG, Die Bücher Josua, Richter, Ruth (Göttingen, 1953.)

C. A. SIMPSON, Composition of the Book of Judges (1957).

M. NOTH, " The Background of Judges 17-18, " Israel's Prophetic Heritage, (eds.) B. ANDERSON and W. HARRELSON (New York : Harper, 1962), pp. 68-85.

§ 1. Content of the Book

The title of the book corresponds to its content. The " Judges " are those heroes whose exploits are reported here. We must not think of them as magistrates. Only of Debora is it said that she settled disputes (4, 5). The Hebrew verb " to judge " (shafat) fundamentally signifies " to set a compromised situation right " (to practice justice means to help the right which has been violated to triumph, which in a sense means to bring about deliverance). " The judge, therefore, is the strong man who sets right the situation of Israel, of one or of several tribes, whenever that situation has been compromised by the oppression of neighbors as well as by the infidelity of the nation itself. " [1] " To judge " is the office of the chieftain. At times we may translate it by " to govern " (as in the case, for example, of the *suffetes* of Carthage who differed, however, from the Judges insofar as they enjoyed a stable authority in an organized city).

A historical introduction summarizes the occupation of Chanaan by the tribes (1—2, 5). They act separately, advance slowly, and suffer reverses. This introduction, in its present state, wishes to explain the precarious situation of the Israelites in the times of the Judges.

The accounts of the Judges are put together in 2, 6—16, 31. A doctrinal prologue (2, 6—3, 6) joins them with the conclusion of the book of Josue and suggests to the reader the great lessons which they must illustrate : the Israelites experienced the oppression of their enemies because they abandoned their God in order to turn to the Chanaanite gods; moved by their sighs, Yahweh sent the " Judges " to deliver them; but whenever the Judge had died they relapsed and suffered further crises. Different explanations are given concerning the continued presence of the nations which were threatening the Israelites.

This prologue is followed by the episodic history of certain Judges. Several are mentioned only briefly : they are called " the minor Judges, " Samgar (3, 31), Thola and Jair (10, 1-5), Abesan, Elon and Abdon (12, 8-15). More elaborate accounts are given of the six " major Judges, " accounts destined to exemplify the doctrine of the prologue of which we are reminded in each case : Othoniel (3, 7-11), Aod (3, 12-30), Debora and Barac (4—5), Gedeon and Abimelech (6—9), Jephte (10, 6—12, 7) and Samson (13—16).

Two appendices which describe the anarchy prevailing in Israel at that time conclude the book. The first one tells of the migration of the Danites towards the north and the origin of the sanctuary at Dan (17—18), the second narrates the shocking crime which had been committed at Gabaa and the war of the tribes against the Benjaminites who had refused to punish the guilty (19—21).

§ 2. Literary Analysis

An attentive reading shows the literary diversity of the elements which constitute the book. We can easily perceive the difference especially between the accounts and their doctrinal framework.

---

[1] CAZELLES, col. 1396.

I. THE FRAMEWORK OF THE BOOK

The framework is composed of a kind of theology of history. This theology is stated in the prologue (2, 6—3, 6) and in the introduction to Jephte (10, 6-16). Stereotyped formulae recall it briefly with regard to each of the major Judges. " The people of Israel did what was evil in the sight of Yahweh, " we are told (2, 11; 3, 7. 12; 4, 1; 6, 1; 10, 6; 13, 1), and at times it is said more accurately : " They abandoned Yahweh and served the Baals and the Astharthes " (2, 11. 13; 3, 7; 10, 6). And for that reason it happened : " He delivered them over (or : He sold) to the hands (of such and such an enemy) " (2, 14; 3, 8; 4, 2; 6, 1; 10, 7). Then " the people of Israel cried out to Yahweh " (3, 9. 15; 4, 3; 6, 6; 10, 10); and " Yahweh raised up Judges for them " (2, 16), or " a deliverer " (3, 9. 15). And the account concludes by saying that " (the enemy) was brought under the power of the people of Israel " (3, 30; 4, 23; 8, 28), or that " the land was at rest for so many years " (3, 11. 30; 5, 32; 8, 28).

In this way is stated the religious lesson which the book gathers from the accounts of the Judges : sin brings punishment by foreign oppression; but as for repentance, God answers by sending a deliverer. This teaching confers a certain unity on accounts otherwise quite different in style and mentality. But it seems to be only a later addition. The accounts of the Judges, as a matter of fact, do not always perfectly agree with the framework. Whereas the framework is concerned with the whole of Israel, the accounts focus their attention on one particular hero, his clan or his tribe. And while the framework presents the oppression as punishment, the Canticle of Debora (5), for example, does not reflect any awareness of sin on the part of the allied tribes. The framework brings the mission of the deliverer into relation with conversion, but Gedeon who made a statue does not give the example of a blameless religious life (8, 27), and Samson who marries foreign women was nothing of a religious reformer. We must attribute the doctrinal arrangement, therefore, to the redactors who gathered the traditions or the already well-defined accounts.

II. DETAILED STUDY OF THE ACCOUNTS

If we now pass to the detailed examination of the accounts, we must put aside the notes concerning the " minor Judges, " notes which only mention the name and some topographical or chronological data. It is quite evident that they were added to the accounts of the major Judges (for example 4, 1 continues the story of 3, 30) when an editor wanted to give us a more complete picture by bringing the number of Judges up to twelve (in 10, 6—12, 7, again, the mention of Jephte seems to interrupt the list of the minor Judges). Among the major Judges, *Othoniel* has to be set aside: his mention consists of a series of general formulae which constitute the framework of the book. Just as the framework, so must also Othoniel's account be traced back to a later redaction, anxious to retain a memory, the only one of the whole book which exalts the tribe of Juda. The other accounts, evidently, show traditions, oral or written, already well-defined before there was thought of collecting them. It is worthwhile to analyze them.

As for *Aod* of Benjamin, we have a popular story which reflects the brutality of the ancient times : a daring, crafty left-hander assassinates the king of Moab and appears as the instrument of God's providence in liberating His people (3, 11-30). In order to separate two different traditions said to be present in this story, authors rely on indications all too flimsy to convince anyone of this hypothesis.

The story of *Debora* and *Barac*, on the contrary, decomposes itself into two documents : an account in prose (4) and a poem (5). The critics consider the poem generally as contemporaneous with the events and one of the very first biblical texts ever put down in writing. Still impressed by the danger the Israelite tribes had to face and by the victory won against the united Chanaanite princes, Debora improvises a triumphal ode to the praise of God who has come to the help of His people. The same facts are also told in a prose narrative, the origin of which is independent of the poem (perhaps the fundamental tradition has been enriched, in the course of its transmission, by the mention of Jabin, king of Hasor). The narrative underlines the religious aspect of the event : the prophetess Debora acts as intermediary between Yahweh and Barac, the commander of the army, and reduces the number of the soldiers; all this highlights the divine assistance. It is Barac's lack of faith which causes him to be supplanted by two women, Debora and Jahel, in the beginning and at the end of the battle. This narrative may originate from the prophetical circles of the northern kingdom.

The story of *Gedeon* (6—9) poses more delicate problems. His call and the building of an altar are narrated twice (6, 11-24. 25-32). The account of the campaign against the Madianites (6, 33—8, 3) has its disparities (cf., for example, 6, 35 and 7, 23). The pursuit beyond the Jordan (8, 4-21) is not the sequel of the foregoing narrative, but is taken from another, rather mutilated, account (8, 18-19 : Gedeon avenges a murder that has not been related). Numerous sources, therefore, can be recognized. Critics have tried to group them into two parallel narratives. Gressmann thinks rather of several documents which have been used to fill out the story : a basic account (6, 2-5; 6, 33—8, 3; 8, 24-35) has been enriched by three independent texts (6, 6-10; 6, 11-24; 6, 25-32); from another account have been taken 8, 4-21 and 9. Let us note the anti-monarchical tendency of the story of Abimelech (9) : this may reflect the ideas of the prophetical circles of the northern kingdom. Abimelech has to witness how the fable of the trees in search of a king (9, 7-15) is applied to him. This is one of the earliest specimens of Israelite wisdom.

As for *Jephte* (10, 6—12, 7), we may choose again between two critical hypotheses : a close fusion of two continuous parallel documents, or a collection of several independent traditions joined one to another (Gressmann). Maybe two accounts have been combined, one referring to a campaign against Ammon, the other against Moab. Thus it could be explained that the message of Jephte to the king of the Ammonites (11, 12-28) is really addressed to the king of Moab : Chamos, the god of Moab, is named and not Milcom, the god of the Ammonites; and the cities mentioned, it seems, are Moabite cities (11, 33). But it is less important to dissect a text than to grasp its " manner. " It is here where Gressmann's analysis is of importance. It characterizes well the literary genre of the different accounts and traditions. The negotiation with the enemy king (11, 12-29) wishes to establish the rights of the Israelites to their Transjordanian territories. The account about Jephte's daughter (11, 30-31 and 11, 34-40) is connected with a custom of Transjordan : every year the women observe a period of ritual lamentation. The feud between Jephte and the Ephraimites (12, 1-6) is meant to throw light upon the origins of the Transjordanian tribe, primitively associated with the house of Joseph.

The story of *Samson* (13—16), it seems, has been formed, little by little, in the manner of popular traditions which spring up around a favorite hero and tend to grow in the course of time. A first strand of such a tradition may be seen in 14—15 : Samson is endowed with excep-tional strength; because of his love for a Philistine woman, he is drawn to a series of adventures and quarrels, which at times may have been suggested by the name of the place. Of his religion hardly anything is said, except of his appeal, or rather injunction, to Yahweh (15, 18). The author, however, stresses that Samson's strength is of supernatural origin. Chapter 16 preserves a different kind of tradition : it is the theme of a hero who has a fatal weakness for women; Samson reveals to Dalila the secret of his strength. A later account, which shows a certain similarity with the call of Gedeon, is concerned with the origins of Samson in order to explain by means of the Naziriteship the strength inherent in his hair (13) : the Nazirite, indeed, does not shave his beard nor cut his hair as a sign of his consecration to God. Samson thus appears as one consecrated to God. It is clear that the collection of these traditions differs from the classic portrait of a Judge. Samson does not wage war nor does he liberate his tribe. His adventures, at any rate, illustrate the clashes of the Israelites with the Philistines.

§ 3. The Formation of the Book

It is not easy to say how the various elements, so different from each other, achieved their unity within the present book. We have to take into consideration a period of oral tradition at the beginning. Separate stories of heroes which illustrated such and such a tribe were handed down. Since that period some parts may have received their definitive literary form. This is the case with the Canticle of Debora (5) and the fable of Joatham (9, 7-15).

The work of those who first collected the various traditions has been characterized in different manners by the critics. A classic theory, influenced by the system adopted for the Pentateuch, assumes two parallel collections, one of which is said to have been formed in the southern kingdom in the 9th century (the Yahvistic school) and the other in the northern kingdom in the 8th century (the Elohistic school). This theory is based on the doublets and on the traces of the different traditions we have pointed out. But it is quite difficult to arrange them in continuous and parallel narratives, and even more difficult to attach them to the Yahvistic and Elohistic schools of the Pentateuch. The critique of L. Desnoyers is here quite to the point. The analyses of Gressmann have encouraged the study of the traditions rather than that of documents reconstructed largely on the basis of conjectures. Among these traditions it is possible to distinguish different strands and to attribute them to diverse groups of narrators. The stories of Gedeon and of Jephte have been the object of several recensions. Particular collections have been formed and have enriched each other. Here and there a judgment unfavorable toward the monarchy (Gedeon, Abimelech) is heard : it seems to express the point of view of the prophetical circles of the northern kingdom which we will find again in the antimonarchical account of Saul's accession to power, in the first Book of Samuel. L. Desnoyers and H. Cazelles have tried to indicate the precise outline of the narrative formed in the kingdom of Israel : it is said to present the story of Aod, Barac, Gedeon-Abimelech in order to illustrate a lesson concerning the infidelities of the people and the fidelity of their God.

The critics generally agree that the Book of Judges itself, based on earlier texts and collections, was composed after the fall of Samaria in 722. In its present state, moreover, the book is the result of several editions. A first edition may be ascribed to the time of Ezechias whose court fostered great literary activity. Authors undertook the task of collecting the heritage of the northern kingdom. Many critics declare that at that time the Yahvistic and Elohistic collections were joined. [2] Others, but less exactly, speak of the fusion of narratives originating in the North with those from the South. Cazelles thinks that the partial collection of the North has been completed subsequently by the stories of Othoniel, Jephte, Samson and even Samuel. Accounts dedicated to the latter would later have been separated from the work and joined to the Books of Samuel, as a preface to the establishment of the Davidic monarchy. This latter suggestion (Burney), however, is not accepted by all critics.

The Book of Deuteronomy, discovered under Josias in 622, contributed to inspire a great historical synthesis reaching from Josue to the end of the monarchy in Juda. In order to enter into this ensemble, the Book of Judges underwent a revision. The chronological framework was thus completed. Doctrinal reflections, moreover, put the history into the service of moral instruction. These reflections can easily be discerned in the introductions (2, 6—3, 6 and 10, 6-16) and in the formulae which serve as framework for the narratives. The mention of Othoniel is generally attributed to this revision, as is the fact that the personalities are presented as " Judges, " and not simply as liberators on a particular occasion (3, 15). They are leaders, like governors exercising an authority, which was surely charismatic, but firmly established over all Israel. Into the first part of the book, the Deuteronomistic redactor could have inserted the historical introduction 1—2, 5, following an old document revised in 1, 1-2 and 2, 1-5.

Let us not forget, however, that the redactor takes up an earlier work where the narratives had already to support a doctrine. The redactional framework of the book was already outlined. Thus we can explain the special formulae which conclude the stories of Aod, Debora and Gedeon : " (The enemy) was brought under the power of Israel " (3, 30; 4, 23; 8, 28), and : " The land was at rest for so many years " (3, 30; 5, 31; 8, 28). These three personalities, by the way, are not presented as " Judges " (except Debora in the prose section of her story). The introductions (2, 6—3, 6 and 10, 6-16), moreover, are not entirely

---

[2] Cf. pp. 152 f.

homogeneous. The first introduction, for example, gives different explanations for the delay of the conquest. One explanation is archaic : Yahweh wanted to allow His people to practice the art of war (3, 2). Another explanation is also prior to the Book of Deuteronomy : by leaving Israel in contact with pagan nations Yahweh wanted to prove its fidelity (2, 22; 3, 1. 4). Besides, it was not necessary to wait for the influence of Deuteronomy in order to present the reverses of fortune as punishments (2, 13. 17. 20. 21) or to stress the fidelity of God who raises liberators (2, 16). With regard to a part of its elements, therefore, the doctrinal framework of the book may be older than the Deuteronomic redaction (this fact is recognized by Eissfeldt and Lods who ascribe some elements to the Elohistic edition). In this way the Deuteronomist often clearly defined ideas that had been put forth prior to his days. It was he, however, who probably with all his authority supported the thesis of the book and introduced the scheme of the four successive events : sin, punishment, repentance, deliverance. He presented the history of the Judges as a whole, strictly governed by the principle of divine retribution. By pointing out the consequence of Israel's apostasies and reconciliations he stressed lessons especially opportune in the tragic period of Jerusalem's ruin. He invited his people to make their examen of conscience and recalled to their mind that Yahweh is rich in mercy.

After the Deuteronomistic revision the book suffered yet other modifications. To this latter intervention may be assigned the notes concerning the minor Judges. It is not easy to say at what stage of the formation of our book the appendices 17—18 and 19—21 have been inserted. The first appendix works up ancient traditions (with some differences, compare 17, 4 and 17, 5; 17, 5 and 17, 8-10; 18, 16-17ᵃ and 18, 17ᵇ-18, 30. 31) concerning the far from laudable origins of the sanctuary of Dan which will become one of the principal sanctuaries of the schismatic northern kingdom. The second appendix tells of the almost total destruction of Benjamin by the other tribes, and of its subsequent providential restoration. Here again we have ancient and diverse traditions : there are two accounts of the battle (20, 29-36ᵃ and 20, 36ᵇ-41) and of the repeopling of Benjamin (21, 1-14 and 21, 15-23). But there are indications which show that the text received its present form at the time of the return from Exile : exaggerated numbers, an idealized picture of Israel firmly united, forming a " community, " having " assemblies, " all terms characteristic of the priestly writings. The insertion of the two appendices into the Book of Judges can, therefore, be ascribed to that same postexilic period. They constitute a discreet plea on behalf of the Temple and the priesthood of Jerusalem, and the

example of Benjamin that had been raised up again in spite of its sin
had to inspire the dispirited Israelites with confidence.

Such a complicated literary history must not surprise us. It reflects
the progress of revelation which encouraged men to take up ancient texts
and read them anew. It bears witness to the prophetical character of
the history of the Judges : there God reveals Himself, and each generation
searches for Him with the light that has been given it.

§ 4. The Historical Value

We must not expect to find in the Book of Judges more than a fragmentary
history. Before the introduction of the monarchy the Israelites were not
firmly united. Each group had its own history, and the memories left
by that period were not the same for all. When they were collected, the
purpose was to create a religious rather than a historical synthesis. We
have a series of partial views, arranged according to some theological
teaching.

These memories, on the other hand, were transmitted by means of
different literary genres which borrowed from the treasure of popular
literature such as the anecdote, the tragi-comic detail (the slaying of the
king of Moab by Aod), the fantastic, even the burlesque (the adventures
of Samson). With the historical interest were mingled other intentions :
the glorification of a woman (4), the explanation of a rite (the daughter
of Jephte), edification (the call of Gedeon or of Samson).

Finally, in one point, the book does not try at all to meet the
exigencies of our concept of history : chronology. In this regard, the
data of the book are of diverse origins. Certain numbers may derive
from ancient sources. Most of them, however, are the work of the
redactors who often lay no claim to any mathematical exactitude. Thus
we observe that frequently the number 40 recurs, a conventional number
signifying the duration of one generation, or its double 80 and its half 20.
The sum of the years of the Judges as given by the chronological indications is 410 years; and by adding other numbers given elsewhere we
reach 599 years, a sum which covers the period from Moses to the
construction of the Temple by Solomon. For this same period, the Book
of Kings counts only 480 years (3 Kgs 6, 1), a number that is symbolic :
since the Temple of Jerusalem forms the center of the life of Israel, its
foundation must be in the center of its history and divide into two equal
parts, each of twelve generations, the period extending from the Exodus
from Egypt until the Exile.

The chronology of the times prior to the Monarchy has to be established on other bases. The foundation of the Temple, it seems, has to be placed about the year 968, which would imply a date close to 1030 for Saul's accession to the throne. Palestinian archeology and Egyptian history, on the other hand, recommend the end of the 13th century for the entrance of the Hebrews into Chanaan. [3] In this way we obtain the outside dates of the period of Josue and of the Judges. It remains difficult, however, to reconstruct the sequence of facts between these two dates. The book does not follow a chronological order and, since it collects local traditions, certain Judges may have lived contemporaneously in different regions. Approximately about the year 1125 we may place an important event which marks the halfway point of the period of the Judges : the victory of Thaanach, thanks to which the tribes from the northern and central region were able to join together. [4] This victory is prior to the invasions of the Madianites which were repulsed by Gedeon and prior to the advance of the Philistines beyond their territory (Samson). Their progress and the crushing defeat they will inflict upon the Israelites about the year 1050 at Eben-Ezer will rouse all the tribes who will create a king over themselves in the person of Saul.

The history as narrated by the Book of Judges, although fragmentary, anecdotal and inaccurate in its chronology, offers, nevertheless, several claims to authenticity. The traits of historical realism abound : the guile of Aod, the origins of Jephte, the susceptibility of the tribe of Ephraim, the compromise with the Chanaanite milieu.... The traditions are ancient and the successive redactors respected them. As for Debora, the convergence of a poem and a prose account, which are quite independent of each other and distinct, provide the historian with a solid basis. The author who narrates the failure of Abimelech's kingship recommends himself because of his impartiality and unwillingness to have recourse to the marvelous : the faults of the opponents facing each other are recognized and, if the intervention of Divine Providence manifests itself, it does so in the linking of the facts. Regarding Samson, popular fancy exercised itself on his behalf. But to explain him, by resorting to a solar myth because of his name (*Shimshôn*, derived from *shemesh* = sun), is to forget that similar names occur at Ras-Shamra and that a city of our hero's native country was called Beth-Shemesh, that is " temple of the sun. " His traits as fighter and pillager correspond well to the precarious situation of the Danites, not yet firmly rooted in the land and threatened

---

[3] See pp. 15 f., 179 f.
[4] W. F. ALBRIGHT, *BASOR*, 62 (April 1936), pp. 26 f.

by the Philistines. The notes themselves concerning the minor Judges are not simply artificial : the mention of their burial shows us that their memory was associated with certain known localities.

From the Book of the Judges we may thus derive a reliable picture of their times. It is a period of struggles and difficulties. The Israelites have no political unity. They live under the threat of the Chanaanites, who dispose of formidable strongholds, and of neighbors always ready to engage in bold enterprises : the Transjordanian kingdoms of Ammon and Moab, the marauding Madianites, and the Philistines who only recently had taken possession of the coastal plain south of Jaffa. In the face of danger each group tries to defend itself. A " liberator " rises and assumes the cause of his people. He wields a certain authority, but his mission and the ambit of his activity are limited by the danger which must be overcome. Several groups join together (4—5; 7, 23) and these common enterprises develop the national conscience. The tribe of Ephraim feels offended since it has not been invited (8, 1-3; 12, 1-6); Debora vigorously censures four tribes for not having answered her appeal (5, 15-17). But it is significant that she does not even think of naming the two tribes of the South, Juda and Simeon. This fact already reveals a certain isolationism which contains the germ of the future split into two kingdoms. At times the authority of the Judge tends to establish itself more firmly : Jephte wants to be more than just an occasional captain (11, 6. 8); Gedeon appears as the leader of several cities; he rejects the kingship, but his son Abimelech lays claim to it for his own undoing.

The religion was interested in the enterprises of the Judges. It found itself endangered. The Israelites, after entering Chanaan, mingled with the pagan populations (Abimelech, Samson). When they settled down, they were attracted by the gods of the land, givers of fertility and fecundity. Religion, on the other hand, remained for them the most efficacious factor of unity. It fostered their common conscience, and often spurred them to action when danger threatened. Therefore, valor, ability, physical strength, by which the Judges distinguished themselves, were viewed as the signs of a divine choice, of an intervention of Yahweh on behalf of His people. And the struggle strengthened the belief in the Covenant of which the canticle of Debora is an expressive witness.

§ 5. The Religious Value

The memory of the Judges deserved to be retained in a sacred history. The religious intention had already appeared in the separate accounts transmitted through local traditions. If these accounts express the pride of a clan or a tribe, this is often based upon the certainty of the Covenant. The successive redactors of the book took advantage of these traditions in order to make them serve as exemplary illustration of the regimen of the Covenant. In the history of the misfortunes and successes during the times of the Judges they recognized, through their faith, an illustration of the infidelities and of the conversion of Israel, wherein God reveals Himself.

If Yahweh unites Himself to a people, He does so in order to reveal to them His demands. These may be summed up in faithfulness to Him : to obey His commandments (2, 17; 3, 4), not to forsake Him for other gods (2, 11. 13. 19; 3, 7; 6, 7. 10; 10, 6. 10. 13) which is tantamount to prostitution (2, 17; 8, 27. 33), not to align with worshipers of other gods (2, 2; 3, 6). Since the Israelites are unfaithful, they are turned over to their enemies, and the punishment for sin is expressed in terms of collective temporal retribution. The still incomplete revelation does not allow theology to advance any further. But one permanent truth is already stated : without faithfulness there can be no covenant with God, and sin is the obstacle to His action.

On His part, however, the Covenant is not revoked. He waits only for repentance in order to manifest anew His favors. Against the rather dark background of their times, the victories of the Judges reveal the untiring fidelity of God who never renounces His voluntary grace (cf. Os 11, 8-9; Jer 31, 20). It was expedient that this assurance was given not only to the Israelites in Exile, but also to all the people of God of all times.

The book speaks of liberation. The deliverance from the temporal enemies is a first approximation of that salvation whose true nature the subsequent sacred history was to show. But already now, little by little, we learn that God saves, and the way in which He raises saviors is full of promise. The exploits which distinguish the saviors are explained by the irruption into them of the Spirit of Yahweh (6, 34; 11, 29; 14, 6. 19; 15, 14), a plan, still very rough, of a theology which will be applied to David (1 Sm 16, 13), then to the Messias (Is 11, 2). The Judges belong to their times : the crudeness of their morals bears witness to it (Aod, Jahel, the sacrifice of the daughter of Jephte, Samson). They are also landmarks in a history which leads much further : on the road to final salvation they are presented to us as examples of fidelity to God (Sir 46, 11-12), as witnesses of the faith which leads us toward the realization of the promises (Heb 11, 32).

CHAPTER III

THE BOOKS OF SAMUEL

BIBLIOGRAPHY

Introductions, translations, commentaries, pp. 1 f. and 168 (R. DE VAUX, *BJ*; A. MEDEBIELLE, *BPC*; W. CASPARI, *KAT*....

H. P. SMITH, " The Books of Samuel, " *ICC* (Edinburgh, 1899).

P. DHORME, " Les livres de Samuel, " *EB* (Paris, 1900).

A. SCHULZ, *Die Bücher Samuel** (Münster, 1919).

H. GRESSMANN, *Die älteste Geschichtsschreibung und Prophetie Israels* (Göttingen, 1921).

E. ROBERTSON, " Samuel and Saul, " *BJRL*, 28 (1943), pp. 175-206.

J. SCHILDENBERGER, " Zur Einleitung in die Samuelbücher, " *Misc. Miller* (Rome, 1951), pp. 130-168.

G. B. CAIRD, " The Books of Samuel, " *IB* (1953).

G. BRESSAN, *Samuele** (Turin, 1955).

G. A. WAINWRIGHT, " Some Early Philistine History, " *VT*, 9 (1959), pp. 73-84.

TSEVAT, " Studies in the Book of Samuel, " *HUCA*, 32 (1961), pp. 191-216; 33 (1962), pp. 107-118; 34 (1963), pp. 71-82.

H. W. HERTZBERG, *I and II Samuel, A Commentary* (Philadelphia : Westminster, 1964).

§ 1. Title and Content

The Books of Samuel originally formed one undivided whole. When they were translated into Greek, the translation was written on two scrolls of almost equal length, and this division was carried over into the Hebrew Bible in the 15th century. In the Greek edition, on the other hand, the Books of Samuel were joined to the Book of the Kings, which also had been divided into two volumes, and together formed a unit under the name of *Books of the Kingdoms*. The Vulgate respected this division and named the work eventually *Books of the Kings*; the two books of Samuel according to the Hebrew are called by the Vulgate the first and second book of the Kings. It is worthwhile to remember this since certain modern works retain this designation.

The Hebrew name of the books reflects the late opinion which ascribed the authorship, at least of the major part, to the prophet Samuel; as for the events which followed Samuel's death, the seer Gad and the prophet Nathan were said to have completed his work (*Baba Bathra* 15ᵃ). This opinion based on I Par 29, 29-30, a text which has been poorly interpreted, has to be discarded; thus the title does not even correspond to the content of the book : Samuel plays an important part only in the first fifteen chapters.

According to the personalities which play a prominent part, the work may be divided in the following major sections :

1. *Samuel* (I—7). The vow of his mother who so far had remained without offspring, his birth, and his childhood in the sanctuary of Shiloh show Samuel as one consecrated to God. Soon he becomes Yahweh's confidant and His interpreter before the priest Heli to whom he announces the punishment of his sons (I—4, I). They are killed in a battle against the Philistines, the Ark of the Covenant is taken by the enemy, and Heli dies when he hears about it. But the Ark wreaks so many evils upon its captors that they dispose of it. Eventually the Ark is taken to Kiriath-jearim (4, I—7, I). And Samuel, the liberator of the land, is described as a " judge " (7, 2-17). [1]

2. *Samuel and Saul* (8—15). The people ask for a king and Samuel refuses (8). But a fortunate circumstance leads young Saul into Samuel's presence; instructed from heaven he secretly anoints Saul as king at Galgal (9—10, 16). The one who had been chosen is confirmed by lot before all the people assembled in Maspha (10, 17-25). Saul wages war against the Philistines and Amalekites; but since he failed to obey the command of God and of His prophet, he is rejected (13—15). Henceforth the interest turns toward a new personality, toward David.

3. *David and Saul* (I Sm 16—2 Sm I). David is anointed secretly by Samuel and thus marked with his royal dignity (16, 1-13). He entered into the service of Saul as minstrel and armorbearer (16, 14-23). Special circumstances led him into the camp of the Israelites, demoralized by the challenge of a Philistine giant. A simple shepherd, armed only with his slingshot, he accepts the challenge and kills the giant (17). David wins the friendship of Jonathan, the son of Saul, and the favor of the people; but the jealous king contrives to destroy him. David must flee

---

[1] E. ROBINSON, " Samuel and Saul, " *Bull. J. Rylands Library*, 20 (1944) pp. 175-206.

(18—21). Pursued by Saul he flees into the southern part of the country. Escaping all ambushes, he is magnanimous toward his worst enemy whose life he respects, and gathers a band of men about him. He becomes more powerful, and we hear that even Saul calls him blessed (22—26). In the meantime David takes refuge with the traditional enemy, the Philistines. Under the pretext of serving them as devoted vassal he strives to win the favor of the people of Juda (27). As luck would have it, he was dispensed from giving his support to the Philistine war effort against Israel; and a victorious campaign against the Amalekites allows him to make friends among the people of Juda and to prepare the hour when they will carry him to the throne (28—30). The Philistines, in the meantime, crush the armies of Israel; Saul and Jonathan perish in the battle; David expresses his grief in a dirge vibrant with emotion (31, 1— 2 Sm 1).

4. *David as king* (2 Sm 2—20). In Hebron, the people of Juda anoint David king over Juda, while the son of Saul, Ishbaal, is proclaimed king of Israel. The struggle between the two factions swings soon in favor of David. Abner, Ishbaal's general, goes over to David. After the rather opportune (although condemned by David) assassinations of Abner and Ishbaal, the northern tribes in turn offer the crown to him and he is anointed king over Israel (2—5, 5). The grandeurs of his reign are evoked by the mention of some memorable facts : the capture of Jerusalem; the war against the Philistines; the transfer of the Ark which contributes to consecrate the religious prestige of the new capital; the oracle of Nathan that assures David, on the part of God, of the perpetuity of his dynasty; victorious wars; the interior organization of the kingdom... (5, 6—8).

Then begins a chronicle [2] in which the familial events of the royal house are the object of a continuous, detailed, and tragical narrative. Crimes are committed, provoking a series of crises which threaten David's rule. In the drama which brings about the opposition between the children and their father, there is also the problem of the succession. Meribaal, the last survivor of Saul's family, is set up in David's court (9). The birth of Solomon who eventually will succeed David to the throne follows the king's sinful love for the wife of one of his officers and is connected with the history of a war against the Ammonites which provides David with a convenient occasion for disposing of the embarrassing husband (10—12). The first-born son of David, however, was Amnon,

---

[2] L. Rost, *Die Überlieferung von der Thronnachfolge Davids* (Stuttgart, 1926).

and David loved him. But Amnon, by the rape of his half-sister Tamar, stirs up the hatred of Absalom, brother of Tamar on the mother's side; in the course of a festival Absalom has him killed (13). After three years of exile the assassin is allowed to return to Jerusalem; two years later he is readmitted to the court (14). But Absalom, an ambitious and violent man, enters into intrigue against his father, takes advantage of those subjects who were displeased with him, stages a revolution and forces David to a humiliating flight. This episode is described with stark realism : head veiled, barefoot and weeping, but submitting to the will of God whose grace he does not want to extort by taking along the Ark, the king climbs the slope of the Mount of Olives. He is comforted by demonstrations of fidelity, but he must also accept insults and curses. Shortly afterwards Absalom takes possession of the king's harem and shows that he assumes the succession (15—16). Fortunately David has informers within the capital. After having received information he withdraws to the other side of the Jordan where a battle turns into the defeat of Absalom. Joab kills Absalom in spite of the recommendations of David whose paternal heart is broken. The intervention of Joab, a hard and cold-hearted man, is necessary to stop David's lamentations (17—19, 9ᵃ). Public opinion turns again in favor of David. He gathers those of the tribe of Juda around him and returns to Jerusalem. But the tribes of the north, jealous of Juda who seems to take hold of the king, are drawn by Siba into a revolution which will soon be put down by force (19, 9ᵇ—20).

5. *Supplements* (21—24). Six passages of miscellaneous contents are grouped together at the end of the book. Two accounts have more than a mere resemblance and originally must have followed each other. One reports the execution of the descendants of Saul at the sanctuary of Gibeon at the time of a famine of three years attributed to an infidelity by which Saul had violated the pact with the Gibeonites (21, 1-14).[3] The other is concerned with the construction of an altar on the future site of the Temple after a pestilence of three days brought on by a census, an act by which David encroached upon the prerogatives of Yahweh (24). Two lists enumerate a series of exploits against the Philistines (21, 15-22) and some names of David's heroes (23, 8-39). Between these lists have been inserted two poems attributed to David : a psalm of thanksgiving (22 = Ps 18) and an oracle which makes David a prophet of his dynasty (23, 1-7).

---

[3] H. CAZELLES, " David's Monarchy and the Gibeonite Claim (2 Sm 21, 1-14), " *PEQ*, 87 (1955), pp. 165-175.

§ 2. Literary Analysis

More than once the reader gets the impression that the sequence of the narrative is not very good.   The sustained interest of the chronicle of David's family (2 Sm 9—20) only strengthens this first impression with regard to the rest of the book.   Premature conclusions surprise us. According to 1 Sm 7, 13 " the Philistines did not again enter the territory of Israel throughout all the days of Samuel, " but in 9, 16 and in 13—14 they have established themselves right in the heart of the Israelite territory.   According to 1 Sm 15, 35 " Samuel did not see Saul again until his death, " but in 19, 22-24 they meet again.   After the story of his childhood, Samuel disappears totally from the account concerned with the Ark (1 Sm 4—6).   If we retrace, following the order of the chapters, the wanderings of David on a map, they present a strange pattern.   And certain facts, finally, seem to repeat themselves : the accession of Saul to the throne, the entrance of David into Saul's service, and also his flight are related twice in different forms.   It is worthwhile to have a closer look, for these discrepancies indicate the composite character of the book and allow us to distinguish the different literary units which have been joined there.   In order to describe them, let us begin with the one which singularly attracts our attention : the chronicle of David's family and of the succession.

I. THE CHRONICLE OF THE SUCCESSION (2 Sm 9—20)

We have here a narrative marked by an admirable unity.   We may ask ourselves whether this narrative does not begin earlier.   It is certain, at any rate, that it also includes the first two chapters of 3 Kgs which tell us the last intrigues concerning the succession to the throne.   Two parties oppose each other, the one of Adonias, after the death of Absalom the oldest son of David, and the other of Solomon.   The latter party will win, and rightly so, by taking advantage of the haste with which Adonias tries to vindicate his pretensions : David is displeased and has Solomon anointed.   After his father's death Solomon takes vengeance and gets rid of all his opponents.

The critics, on the whole, see in this chronicle the work of a remarkably well-informed author who wrote at a time still fairly close to the events.   This is, without doubt, the first historical writing of Israel which we find in its original state (abstraction made of some interventions, as the addition of 12, 1-15ᵃ and 14, 25-27, and perhaps a revision of 3 Kgs 2, 1-12).   From a literary point of view, it is simply a masterpiece of the narrative art.

The author depicts for us a series of tableaux which reflect his artful observation and are executed with a startling realism. The events are linked together without the author or a *deus ex machina* intervening to modify the course. The numerous personalities in strong contrast to one another impress us by their very presence. There is Siba, a serviceable person, to whom David gives the possessions of his master; but his eager attention to David is too obsequious to be disinterested (16, 1-4; 19, 18-19). There is his lame master Meribaal, whose embarrassed explanations will never let us know whether he has been calumniated or whether he has been a traitor (19, 26-29). There is that anonymous woman from Tecoa who while telling her invented story causes David to reflect : " We are like water spilt on the ground, which cannot be gathered " (14, 14). She pleads the cause of Absalom, she reverts to her plight, and when the eyes of the king are opened, she uncovers her play with the disarming words : " My Lord has the wisdom of the angel of God " (14, 20).

The narrator masters the art of presenting details true to life so that the very state of the soul is revealed : every commentary would be superfluous. David, resigned after the death of his child, washes and anoints himself, changes his clothes, asks that food be served and eats (12, 20). Absalom in his ambition " got himself a chariot and horses, and fifty men ran before him... and whenever a man came near to him to do obeisance to him, he would put out his hand, took him and embraced him " (15, 1. 5). The characters appear in all their complexity. Joab presents a special mixture of devotion to David and of coldness without pity, of generosity and of unscrupulous interest in his own office. The portrait of David, [4] above all, is drawn by the hand of a master. It is not a flattering portrait, but in all its shades it manifests truth. David is good but shrewd, sensual but repentant, capable of murder but also of forgiveness, a tender, but also weak, father : in him we find a real man. There is also his religious sentiment, all the more impressive since nobody thinks of edifying us. David sees God in the events of his life. He knows how to accept failure, and his faith is capable of freeing itself from traditional practices : he refuses to sorrow for his child (12, 20). He is also ahead of the ideas of his time : the Ark will be of no use to him if God withdraws His benevolence (15, 25). " And a fascinating charm surrounded all this and reached all those who drew close; the writer knew how to spread charm about the figure of his hero. " [5]

We are far from the popular tradition which schematizes and embellishes, as the official annals do, so careful about external and glorious

---

[4] J. STEINMANN, *David, roi d'Israël* (Paris, 1948).

[5] A. LODS, *Histoire de la Littérature hébraïque*, p. 163.

facts. Our author is interested in the individual. In his writing, the events are explained by the characters. He does not judge anyone : the acts suffice. He never draws the lesson : the moral is indicated through the interweaving of the facts; the history of the sin and of its dire consequences speaks for itself. There is no need to use the marvelous in order to indicate God's providence : God appears everywhere present for him who knows how to look. Ancient oriental literature offers nothing comparable. This has known different historical genres, some dry as a repertory (cf. the inscriptions of the Sumero-Accadian *patesis* which commemorate their constructions), some apologetic in their tone (Assyrian annals, works of Egyptian courtscribes, autobiographies of famous personalities written on the walls of their tombs), some rich in imaginative resources (the Egyptian historical novel). [6] But this literature ignores the precise and impartial narration of events brought about by the reactions of individuals on whom attention is concentrated; as far as the historical explanation is concerned, this literature hardly passes beyond the idea of a succession of facts, often due to the whim of the gods. The fact that one of the most ancient literary works of the Israelites is concerned with psychology, is a sign that the Bible, the book of God, is also the book of man.

The critics are not happy that the identity of our ancient chronicler is not known. The name of Abiathar, the priest, has been mentioned; when he was persecuted by Saul, he took refuge with David and followed him in his ascent (1 Sm 22; Duhm, Budde). The chronicler's account, indeed, stops with Solomon, and it was precisely Solomon who exiled Abiathar to Anathoth. But would Abiathar, the partisan of Adonias, have accused his favorite of pride (3 Kgs 1, 5), and would he have vindicated the right of Solomon as for the punishment which was inflicted upon the partisans of his brother (3 Kgs 2)? Other hypotheses have been proposed : Ahimaas, the son of the priest Sadok (L. Rost); Zabud, the son of the prophet Nathan (3 Kgs 4, 5; Vriezen). But the arguments appealed to are rather weak. It is enough to say that the style itself suggests a scribe who knew closely the personalities of whom he speaks. He wrote when Solomon was alive (2 Sm 18, 18 supposes that a certain time had elapsed since the event, but this could also be a gloss). Besides the interest he shows in relating the work of those who founded the national unity, his purpose is to show how the scepter of David passed into the hands of Solomon by a concurrence of circumstances which could not be foreseen, but which reveal a providential intention. The kingship,

---

[6] See pp. 128 f. (French ed.).

indeed, is not seen as a purely political institution : it occupies its place in the development of God's plan concerning Israel.

II. OTHER MATERIALS

The rest of the book offers no other narrative as well knit and as amply developed as the chronicle we have just analyzed. If we compare the chapters dedicated to Saul and then to David prior to his reign (1 Sm 8— 2 Sm 1), they seem to pass from one extreme to the other. Few biblical books offer such an extensive compilation of diverse documents. The importance of the introduction of the monarchy explains that judgments, varied according to the milieu, have been pronounced with regard to it. The tragic destiny of Saul has inspired different traditions, different insofar as they were connected with one or another aspect of his reign. The origin of David, the favorite king of the people, lent itself to narration, and it is not surprising that we have several versions of it. The author of the book respected the particularities of the sources and did not want to sacrifice any of their rich contrasts. This liberalism is no longer found among our historians, but the variety of styles frightened the biblical historians no more than it frightened the builders of the cathedrals.

1. The account dedicated to *Samuel* utilizes various materials. Samuel thus appears under different traits in 1 Sm 1—4, 1ᵃ and in 7, 2-17 : on the one hand, he is the consecrated one, recognized as prophet by all Israel; on the other hand, he is the liberator of the land and the " judge. " The second text, it seems, was not known by the older traditions which mention the seer of Galgal as unknown to Saul (9, 6 ff.) and the Philistine oppression in the very heart of the land (7, 13; 13). The first account must also belong to a relatively recent recension of various traditions, as is often the case with regard to childhood stories of heroes. This account itself has been enlarged by a canticle of the monarchical period (2, 1-10; cf. v. 10) and by a development of the threats pronounced against Heli and his descendants (2, 27-36; cf. 3, 11-14 : in more general terms).

Between these two accounts of Samuel we find the history of the Ark captured by the Philistines; even in defeat the Ark remains formidable (4, 1ᵇ—7, 1). The anecdotal twist and the humor at the expense of the Philistine point to a popular tradition. Its archaic character flows from the primitive concept of the ark and its sanctity, directly harmful to anyone who does not respect it. This account, without doubt, has been borrowed from the traditions handed down by the priests in order to foster the piety of the pilgrims.

2. *The origin of the monarchy* (1 Sm 8—12) is the object of two accounts which are recognized by their favorable or unfavorable attitude towards its introduction. Their connecting links can easily be seen (8, 22ᵇ; 10, 26-27; 11, 12-14). One account (9—10, 16; and 11) " could be entitled : Saul leaves to look for the asses of his father and finds a crown. " [7] The young man does not know Samuel, an obscure " seer, " whom he consults concerning the lost asses and he is consecrated by him, in the end, as king. The Spirit of Yahweh comes over him; God is with him. The victory over the Ammonites is the proof of it and the people proclaim Saul king. The kingship, therefore, is offered by God for the good of His people.

According to the second account (8 and 10, 17-25; and 12), it is the people who want a king " just like the other nations. " Yahweh complains that He has been rejected, and Samuel describes the monarchy as a government which oppresses the people. But nothing is gained : Yahweh and His prophet have to yield. The king is determined by lot at Maspha and Samuel has no choice but to yield to Saul; but before he does so, he insists once more that Yahweh is the only king of Israel and that the fidelity with which He is served measures His help. This account supposes that already a certain experience of monarchy has been had (8, 11-17, it seems, recalls the time of Solomon). It expresses a revindication of Yahweh's primacy, a revindication which in the face of monarchical pretensions resembled that of the prophets of the northern kingdom (cf. Am 7, 10-13; Os 3, 4; 7, 7; 8, 4; 13, 11). It is probably there that we must look for the origin of this account.

3. The accounts dedicated to *Saul* are of no greater homogeneity. In 13, 16—14, 46 he appears as a pious king who consults Yahweh concerning his enterprises and to whom Yahweh answers. He wins a great victory against the Philistines thanks to the fearlessness of his son Jonathan and is preoccupied with how he can keep the dire consequences of the transgression from his army. This account gives evidence of a very primitive concept of sin and its reparation [8]; it could be the continuation of the first version concerning the origin of the monarchy. The rejection of Saul is explained by two accounts which show it to be a religious fault : he disobeyed the prophet who had reserved for himself the right to offer a sacrifice before battle (13, 7ᵇ-15ᵃ), and he failed to act according to the anathema by sparing a conquered king and the best

---

[7] R. DE VAUX, " Israël, "* *SDB*, col. 740.

[8] A. GEORGE, " Fautes contre Yahvé dans les Livres de Samuel, "* *RB*, 53 (1946), pp. 161-184.

of his herd (15). The two accounts are independent, and the first one is inserted artificially into the campaign against the Philistines, for Saul does not figure there as having been rejected.

4. *The entrance of David into the court of Saul* is reported in two different ways. According to 16, 14-23 he is introduced into the service of Saul as a musician in order to soothe him during his mysterious attacks of mental distress; since David, on the other hand, was a man of valor, he became the king's armorbearer. According to 17—18, 5, it was by coincidence that David came into Saul's camp where his brothers were serving; he had never worn any armor and had never performed any other exploits than those of a shepherd. His victory, however, against the giant Goliath brings him to the attention of the king who so far had not even known his name and who now takes him into his service. This last account itself is composite, for according to 17, 32-39 Saul and David talk with each other before the fight, which conflicts with 17, 55-58 where the king does not know the name of David. There existed, therefore, an account of the combat with Goliath which continued the story of David's introduction to Saul's court as a minstrel. The Septuagint retains only this account and omits all passages which would make David a young and unknown shepherd (17, 12-31 and 17, 55—18, 5). Let us also recall that a kind of prologue to the history of David tells us how he had been anointed secretly by Samuel (16, 1-13). No other allusion to it is ever made and David will be anointed officially only much later (2 Sm 2, 4; 5, 3); his brother Eliab, moreover, who must have been present, knows absolutely nothing about it in 17, 28. We have to deal here with a later reflection, which has been inserted into accounts already constituted and intends to stress that the Davidic monarchy is connected with the prophetic movement and with the divine election. Yahweh sees the heart of the young shepherd to whom no one pays attention (maybe in contrast to the handsome shoulders which draw the prophet's attention to Saul, 9, 2).

5. *The rise of David* and his relations with Saul are illustrated by accounts which are too similar to be always based upon different events : the attempt upon David's life (18, 10-11 and 19, 9-10), his success and popularity (18, 12-16 and 18, 28-30), the promise of marriage with one of Saul's daughters (18, 17-19 and 18, 20-27). The Greek translator apparently noticed it, unless he had a different text before him. He omitted 18, 10-11. 17-19. 30 which duplicate the passages he retained. Doublets also abound in the subsequent chapters. Twice Jonathan intervenes with his father on behalf of David : the first time, he is aware of the criminal intentions of Saul (19, 1-7); the second time, he seems

to ignore them (20, 1^b-10. 18-39). The second account gives in
20, 1^b—21, 1 an explanation of David's flight that is different from the
first account in 19, 10^c-17. Twice David, the fugitive, is betrayed by
those he protects (23, 1-13 and 23, 19-28); twice he spares Saul when
he is in his power (24 and 26); twice he takes refuge with Akish, the
Philistine prince of Gath (21, 11-16 and 27). The death of Saul is narrated
twice (31, which forms the continuation of 28, 3-25; and 2 Sm 1, 1-16
which continues 1 Sm 29—30). The second account is followed by a
dirge of David on the death of the heroes, taken from an ancient collection
of poems, the book of *Yashar* (2 Sm 1, 17-27). We cannot escape the
impression that two independent and parallel redactions have been
combined without allowing anything to be lost.

6. With *the reign of David* the account presents greater continuity.
But here also different materials are distinguished. The story of the
twofold anointing as king of Juda, then of Israel, forms a beautiful
unity (2—5, 4). The note concerning the king's sons (3, 2-5) has perhaps
been taken from a document which is continued in 5, 13-16 (1 Par 3, 5-8
joins the two passages). The account of the transfer of the Ark to
Jerusalem (6) is connected with 1 Sm 4—6 and may come from the same
cycle of traditions, although it is written in a different style. The oracle
of Nathan (7) must refer to an old document, which may have been
written over again several times with a view to the development of
Messianic hopes which it already clearly formulated. [9] Its original theme
was this : it is not David who will build a house (a temple) for Yahweh,
but it is Yahweh who will build a house (a posterity) for David; the
throne is assured forever for his posterity. An addition applies to his
first successor, to Solomon (v. 13), an even more far-reaching promise
which carries germ-like the whole Messianic hope. Before we learn how
the scepter finally passed to Solomon, we find a summary of the wars
of David and some information regarding the organization of the
kingdom (8). This genre of summary occurs several times in the course
of the book (1 Sm 7, 13-15; 2 Sm 3, 2-5; 5, 13-16; 20, 23-26) and may
be based on ancient documents or annals.

§ 3. The Formation of the Book

Such a diversity of materials makes the literary history of the book
singularly intricate. Let us put aside some independent compositions

---

[9] VAN DEN BUSSCHE, *Le Texte de la Prophétie de Nathan sur la Dynastie Davidique** (Louvain, 1948).

which found their way into it during the time of its formation : two laments by David (2 Sm 1, 19-27; 3, 33-34), a song from the times of the monarchy (1 Sm 2, 1-10), a psalm which a title connects with David (2 Sm 22), and the oracle which has been preserved among the appendices (2 Sm 23, 1-7). Several notes may go back to archival documents or to more developed annals : a list of the children of David (2 Sm 3, 2-5; 5, 13-16), of the officers of his court (8, 16-18; 20, 23-25), of his heroes (23, 8-39) and of the giants killed by them (21, 15-22); summaries of the campaigns of Saul and of David (1 Sm 14, 47-52; 2 Sm 5, 17-25; 8, 1-14; 21, 15-22). Finally, we also recognized a chronicle, contemporaneous with Solomon at least in 2 Sm 9—20 and 3 Kgs 1—2.

The composition of the book passed through several stages. The abundance of doublets invited the critics to divide them into two series of continuous narratives, and the system adopted with regard to the Pentateuch showed that in the beginning two documents were admitted, which were said to continue the work of the Yahwist and the Elohist, originating from the same school, if not from the same authors (Wellhausen, Budde, Dhorme, Steuernagel). Eissfeldt thought of perfecting the system by attributing a part of the Yahwist to an older source which he called Lay-source (L). Lods, likewise, finds in several chapters the trace of a triple tradition and distinguishes already in J a twofold strand; but the more one advances in the history of David, the more the differences diminish; from the death of Saul onwards the Yahwistic tradition is about the only one used; its historical value is of the first order, for it took as base the memoirs of a direct witness and reproduced them without any change from 2 Sm 9 onwards.

The critics of this system go in different directions. The most vulnerable point seems to be the fact that the documents are brought into a relationship with the Yahwist and the Elohist of the Pentateuch : they do not present the literary and doctrinal characteristics which the Yahwist and Elohist have. Several critics, therefore, still admit two narrative strands as base but give no assurance that they continue J and E. Others go further and express their doubt as to the very existence of these two parallel strands. Gressmann called our attention to the traditions represented by the accounts inasmuch as we consider them *individually*. The distrust with regard to any systematization favors the tendency of multiplying the literary units at the beginning of the book. Rost, however, groups them, as for the main part, into two sources which are no longer used parallelly, but successively : a history of the succession of David, and a history of the persecutions as well as of the victory of David. Weiser thinks of diverse groups of particular traditions : a narrative concerning the wars of Saul and another concerning the Ark, a narrative of the rise of Saul and another of David's rise; a historian joined them and arranged the material in chronological order; his work is said to have been completed by a disciple of the prophets, revised by a Deuteronomistic editor, finally enriched by several additions (especially, the poems). Buber, by analyzing the election of Saul, is of the opinion that a fundamental narrative, which included slightly revised material, finally received additions of two kinds : annalistic materials and complementary details inserted into the narratives. [10]

Vriezen also rejects the analogy with the Pentateuchal documents, but he reacts against the disintegration of the book. [11] Starting from the family chronicle of David which presupposes certain facts and personalities as known by the reader, he maintains that this chronicle began much earlier and told already David's relations with Saul and Jonathan. This chronicle not only attempted to tell how Solomon succeeded David, but also showed the legitimacy of the Davidic dynasty. This history of Saul-Jonathan-David, written by a contemporary of Solomon, would have been reproduced, intermittently from 1 Sm 11 onwards, and continuously from 2 Sm 9 onwards. This history in which Samuel played no part later received various complements : about the year 900 the anti-monarchical version of 1 Sm 7 + 8 + 10, 17 ff; then the history of Heli and the Ark; finally the stories of Samuel, marked by their prophetic spirit, not counting Deuteronomistic revisions. The attempt of Vriezen is interesting. It seems difficult to believe that the chronicle of the succession of David began only with the reception of Meribaal at the court (2 Sm 9) or with the oracle of Nathan (7); and not arbitrarily we may attribute to the chronicle either one of the two tendencies which the analysis discloses in the history of the rise of David and even in that of Saul. May we not also retain certain relationships between this document and the Yahwist, for example : the expression " the good and the evil, " the art of dramatic narration, common sense psychology, interest in the posterity (Abraham and Sara, Isaac and Rebecca, Jacob, Lia and Rachel, Juda and Tamar, David and Michal and Bethsabee) and in the transmission of promises without always taking account of heredity or of birthright (Jacob, David, Solomon)...?

A *general agreement* between the critics in this matter is still far off. It is delicate to decide if these analogies are sufficient to establish a

---

[10] M. BUBER, " Die Erzählung von Sauls Königswahl, " *VT*, 6 (1956), pp. 113-173.

[11] T. C. VRIEZEN, " De Compositie van de Samuël-Boeken, " *Orientalia Neerlandica* (1948), pp. 167-189.

literary continuity. Bentzen continues to distinguish between the court history of David and two groups of stories of a later redaction, meant to serve as an introduction. The second string of stories (including especially the antimonarchical version of the origin of the monarchy) was added to the first one as a complement, destined to correct it and to adapt it to a more theocratic concept of the state. Other items of older material have also been inserted into the book : a history of the Ark (1 Sm 4—6 and 2 Sm 6), a history of David's relations with Ishbaal (2 Sm 2—5 + 8), perhaps details of the relations between Samuel and Saul. R. de Vaux also thinks of several primitive documents : the chronicle of the succession of David (of which the oracle of Nathan would be the preface), two stories of the relations between David and Saul (therefore the frequent doublets in 1 Sm 17—2 Sm 1), a first cycle of stories concerning Samuel. This first cycle of Samuel would already contain a history of the Ark, a favorable account of the introduction of the monarchy, the account of Saul's war against the Philistines. As complement would have been added the childhood of Samuel (1—3), the reprobation of Saul (15), the secret anointing of David (16, 1-13). A more recent composition would represent Samuel as the last of the Judges (7) and give a hostile version of the origin of the monarchy. " It is not excluded that these documents have already been combined about the year 700. " [12]

The critics, in short, recognize a twofold redaction, at least of the strifes of David and of Saul, but not in order to associate them with the different traditions concerning Samuel, nor in order to join one of the two redactions into a continuous narrative with the family chronicle of David. Whatever the theory may be which is proposed concerning the stage of those first redactions, it is generally admitted that they already formed a book prior to the Deuteronomistic revision. This Deuteronomistic revision introduced the book into the great chronicle which retraced Israel's history from the death of Moses until the Exile, by means of some revisions that were far more discreet than in Judges and Kings. These revisions appear in 1 Sm 7, 3. 4. 15; 12, 6-11; perhaps in 2 Sm 7, 13. 22-24, and in the chronological framework of the book (1 Sm 4, 18; 13, 1; 2 Sm 2, 10-11; 5, 4-5; 1 Sm 6, 15 is apparently later). The Deuteronomistic edition separated the account of Solomon's ascension to the throne from the Book of Samuel and made it the introduction to Solomon's reign in 3 Kgs 1—2. There Solomon no longer appears so much as the heir of David; he introduces the series of sinful kings. The

---

[12] R. De Vaux, *Les Livres de Samuel**, p. 11.

Books of Samuel, shortened in this manner, remained an apology of the
Davidic monarchy. The addition of the appendices confirms this
impression : by including these ancient traditions the author stressed
that David had desecrated the sanctuary of Gibeon (2 Sm 21) and
sanctified the future site of the Temple (24).

§ 4. The Book and History

In order to judge the historical value of the book, we must take into
consideration the literary genre and the age of the traditions and accounts
which it contains. Such value is often enhanced because of the antiquity
of the accounts and their nearness to the facts. These sources offer at
times the advantage of not only informing us about the events, but also
about the impression those events left in the memory of the people, and
about the religious reflection they aroused. Profane history can add
only little to the data of the book. Egypt and Assyria are dormant at
that time, which favors the success of David, but it also deprives us of
synchronisms which would allow us to establish a precise chronology.
We must be satisfied with approximate dates : about the year 1030, the
accession of Saul to power; between 1010 and 970, the reign of David.
Archeology somewhat supports the text by illustrating the civilization
of the Philistines (their pottery), their relations with Crete and Cyprus,
and their occupation of the plain between Gaza and Eqron in the beginning
of the 12th century. The excavations of Tell el-Ful, three miles north
of Jerusalem, have produced the remains of the oldest Israelite fortress,
probably that of Saul, in his residence Gibeah. Some " casemate " walls
(Tell Beit Mirsim, Beth Shemesh) go back to the time of David's struggles
with the Philistines. But the best documentation comes from the book
itself which authorizes a sound reconstruction of the beginnings of the
monarchy in Israel.

The lack of political unity particularly augmented the gravity of
the threat of the Philistines who did not hesitate to expand from the
plain, where they had established themselves in five principalities, towards
the interior of the land. The popular story of the Ark is a valuable
witness of their advance up to the mountains of Benjamin and Ephraim
(about 1050). The stele erected in Gibeah (10, 5) indicates that they
dominated the region where the Israelites had most firmly established
themselves. Just as in the times of the Judges the danger brought about
a national awakening. But this time the gravity of the situation was to
favor the union of the tribes under one leader. The influence of the
Philistine threat upon the origins of the monarchy has been retained by

the oldest account (9, 16) which also notes the charismatic character that makes Saul similar to the Judges : the irruption of the Spirit of Yahweh which is manifested by some extraordinary action (11) and answers to a divine vocation (9). But a new fact is added : the recognition by the assembled tribes (11, 15). It is here where another influence, retained by a more recent account, could come into play : the example of " the other nations " (8, 5). Beyond the Jordan, Ammon, Moab and Edom had been organized as kingdoms for a long time, and in the time of Saul the Arameans formed their kingdoms.

Of the reign of Saul the biblical text retained mainly some episodes which allow us to judge him and to explain his failure by his faults. But the text insinuates more than it says with regard to the particular style of his kingship and the importance of his historical role. There is no central organization, no capital to speak of : the king is foremost a military leader, surrounded by warriors (14, 52) among whom the men of Benjamin, his tribe, seem to enjoy special favor (22, 7). He is ready to come to the aid of every tribe that is threatened, not only those of the central region which he delivers from the Philistines (13—14), but even those of Transjordan (11; cf. 31, 11-13; 2 Sm 2, 8-9), those of the North where a new enemy, the Aramean, appears (14, 47) and of the South where thanks to his effort Juda and the related clans abandon their isolationism (15; cf. 17, 13; 23, 19). The two accounts of the quarrel which breaks out between Saul and Samuel reveal another aspect of the kingship. The new institution must adapt itself to a sacred conception of the Israelite community : the king is subject to an order of which the prophet is the interpreter. Saul is sincerely religious (cf. 14, 31 ff., 37 ff.); but he tries to make a compromise between the political interest and the respect for the religious ramifications of his power. From there flows the drama of his life and the cause of his failure. In the end, Samuel declares that Saul has been rejected. His kingship, of a charismatic nature, still lacks stability and quickly loses its prestige. He is aware of it. This partially explains the distrust and the attacks of fury which assail him.

His hatred turns against a youth from Juda, David, whom he had made one of his entourage, one of his warriors and his son-in-law. The efflorescence of traditions concerning their relationship, the anecdotal twists, at times charming, at times tragic, of these traditions indicate the popularity of David and the certainty of his ascension to the throne. He will only succeed to the throne after a national crisis during which the work of Saul runs the risk of being completely destroyed. Pursued by Saul, leader of a band of outlaws in the south of the land, then vassal of a Philistine prince, David works to gain followers among the people of Juda and succeeds in loosening their bonds with Israel. The Philistines, on their part, because of their victory of Gilboa about 1010, occupy the plain of Esdrelon, advance to Beth-Shan and cut the land in two. With Ishbaal, Saul's son, a kingship without glory is constituted anew in Transjordan, while David becomes king over Juda in Hebron. The monarchical idea, therefore, survives, but under a form which seems to consecrate Saul's failure.

But seven and a half years later, the prestige of David and a combination of circumstances which the account truthfully reports (2 Sm 2—5, 4) lead to the national unity centered around the king of Juda who also receives the crown of Israel. It is a sacred kingship indeed : David is anointed twice, and in the prophetical circles it will be told how the chosen one of God had already been consecrated secretly by Samuel. But the achieved unity remains imperfect : " He reigned over all Israel and Juda 33 years " (2 Sm 5, 5). " This is a dualistic monarchy, a united kingdom, torn by interior struggles until the schism, which will come about on the day after Solomon's death. " [13] David succeeded, at least, in giving to this kingdom a glory which it would never see again.

The account is not much interested in the great political acts of the reign. Before the account lingers on the history of David's family and on his succession, it hardly stops to mention the capture of Jerusalem, the transfer of the Ark which turns Jerusalem into a holy city, and the divine promise of an everlasting dynasty. Although the war against the Philistines preceded the conquest of Jerusalem, it receives only secondary attention (5, 17-25; cf. the appendices 21, 15-22; 23, 8 ff.). The exterior wars and the political organization of the kingdom are mentioned only in a rapid summary (8). This suffices, however, to determine the great lines of David's work.

His first task was to reconquer the Philistines and put them eventually back in their own territory. He carried the war right to their lands (21, 20) and put a definite end to their efforts of expansion. The king's guard recruited mercenaries even among them (15, 18 f.). In the interior of the land the groups of foreigners had to be integrated. The capture of Jerusalem broke down the barrier between Juda and Israel; it gave David a capital which affirmed the independence of his power with regard to the various tribes, since the city was situated on the border of Juda and Benjamin whose susceptibilities had to be respected. The understanding with the Gibeonites (21) is part of the same political endeavor

---

[13] R. De Vaux, *Les Livres de Samuel**, p. 153.

concerning interior unification as is the occupation (not told) of the Chanaanite fortresses : Megiddo, Thaanach, Beth-Shan, which we shall find in the possession of Solomon. Exterior wars, finally, subjected the Ammonites, the Arameans, the Moabites and Edomites : " From the idea of a national kingdom grows the tendency toward an empire. " [14]

The interior organization appears discreetly through a list of high functionaries (8, 15-18). They are named by the king without being delegated by their tribes. The system seems to have been patterned on Egyptian models, and the official scribe Shusha possibly was an Egyptian. Among them we notice also the two priests Abiathar and Sadok. The king may still exercise priestly functions as well as his sons. The army is formed by volunteers and mercenaries. The armies of Juda and Israel remain distinct (11, 11; 24, 9), and alarming facts show that under the personal power of the king the national unity remains fragile : Absalom, in his rebellion, finds support among the men from the North, and Sheba appeals to Israel to withdraw, using a cry which will be heard again on the day of the schism (2 Sm 20, 1 and 3 Kgs 12, 16). The unity which provisionally has been achieved is the work of David's political genius. The consequences of it will be felt beyond the schism. In Jerusalem, at least, he established a stable power : the kingdom of Juda will be one day the only seat of Israelite religion and culture; and the hope of a gathering of the Chosen People around a new David, in Jerusalem, will constitute the most beautiful homage paid by history to the grandeur of a man.

§ 5. The Religious Value

The religious value of the book appears at different levels. From the historical data which the book abundantly supplies results a vivid image of the moral and religious state of Israel at the beginning of the monarchy : very primitive practices of a still archaic religion such as the anathema, the consultation of the ephod, the ecstasies of the *nebiîm ;* a rather defaced idea of sin, often identified with an even unintentional violation of some interdiction; a summary notion of divine sanction which automatically strikes and may hit a whole group as long as a compensatory rite is not performed.... We must not examine these data in search for the contribution of Revelation, but rather we must see in them the point of departure of a progress which will be eventually achieved thanks to Revelation. Against this background stand men of exceptional religious convictions. It suffices to name David, with his uncommon magnanimity

---

[14] R. DE VAUX, *SDB**, IV, col. 745.

toward his enemies, his personal sense of sin and repentance, his already pure concept of the Ark, his submission to God and his refusal to pressure Him. We can also see, in the period of Saul and David, the origins of institutions and of religious facts which will considerably influence biblical religion : prophetism, the priesthood of Jerusalem, kingship.

In the intention of the narrators the origins of the monarchy occupy the first place, and traditions and historical memories are organized within a religious vision. The king is a sacred personality, chosen by God, and an instrument of His plans on behalf of His people. But there are obligations : the king must not flee from the divine demands nor erect a screen before Yahweh, Israel's only King. In this manner the two traditions which relate the institution of the monarchy are blended. It is repeated again and again that the political leader is the Anointed of Yahweh, be it in order to extol him or to accuse him of infidelity to his mission; and it is pointed out that he depends on the prophet who invests him and who reminds him of his duty.

The prophet signifies here Samuel, a confidant of God and a fearless executor of His will, be it in the innocence and peace of his childhood, in the strangeness of his role as seer in Galgal, or in the harshness of his interventions before the whole military camp of Saul. The king means first of all Saul, who by his life prefigures, as it were, the drama of political power versus religious statute : he lacked the faith of Abraham.

" For obedience is better than sacrifices and to hearken rather than to offer fat of rams " (1 Sm 15, 22). Abraham had heard something similar on Mount Moriah (Gn 22, 12 f.). Because he believed, the conflict between his paternal love and his religious obedience ended with a paradoxical agreement. Saul, divided between Yahweh and the favor of the people who had acclaimed him, ended by losing his people. All along the sacred history appears thus the primacy of faith over all other duties.

David, on the contrary, illustrates, in the eyes of the narrators, the ideal of the monarchy as intended by God. He has left us the memory of a king totally devoted to his God and docile to the prophets, even when they rebuke him. On the other hand, his success shows that God was with him. We admire in him a new realization of the Covenant, which takes the form of a kingdom of God on earth. In the center of the book, the oracle of Nathan opens up a new perspective for the future of the new government : Yahweh allies Himself irretrievably with the dynasty of David whose descendants He adopts as sons in order to exercise through them His kingship over His people.

In this sense the history of David is imbued with a prophetic value. What his remembrance helps to express is a faith and an expectation directed toward the accomplishment of certain values with whose introduction into sacred history David was charged. The advances of this hope will be inscribed in the portrait of the king, constantly reviewed and meditated upon; until the Exile he will be the type against which the other kings will be judged (3 and 4 Kgs). Those kings may be punished, but there is never any doubt that the dynasty will be restored (Am 9, 11; Os 3, 5). In the hours of distress, the prophets will raise up over the calamities, brought about by the infidelity of the kings, the ideal figure of a descendant of David (Is 9, 1-6; 11, 1-9; 16, 5; Jer 23, 5-6), of a new David (Jer 30, 9; Ez 34, 23-24; 37, 24-25), the Lord's Anointed, the Messias. At the return from the exile, the time is anticipated when the reconstruction of the Temple will be crowned by the restoration of the house of David, and the Messianic hopes revive around Zorobabel (Za 6, 12-13). Failure will put no end to the meditation on the promises made to David (Ps 89, 132; Is 55, 3-4; Jer 33, 14-26; Za 9, 9-10; 11, 7; 12, 6). The Book of Chronicles will place David in the center of its perspective : he will be the ideal king of the theocracy according to the sacerdotal ideas, he will be the inspired singer and reorganizer of the cult; in this glorification of the past it is difficult not to see the expression of hope. Likewise, the eulogy of Samuel and of David in the Book of Sirach ends with a note of hope (Sir 47, 11; cf. 47, 22; 36, 1-19; 51, 1-12).

The failure of the monarchy, by putting the Messianic expectation to the test, contributed to deepen it. But it is necessary in the end that Jesus come in order that the deep values of the promise made to David become manifest in their totality. Jesus announces the kingdom of God and inaugurates it already in a mysterious way. As if He were afraid to compromise the spiritual reality by using images too earthly, He remains discreet with regard to His Davidic origin. He acts on the authority, however, of the example of David (Mk 2, 25-26); " son of David, " He suggests that He is also David's Lord (Mk 12, 35-37); on some occasions He allows Himself to be greeted with the title " son of David " (Mk 10, 47-48; Mt 15, 22; 21, 9. 15). But if He exercises, when entering Jerusalem, His authority over His capital and the Temple, He does it in order to announce the destruction and to die there. By His resurrection and His enthronement before God, He separates the royal Messianism from the gangue. Henceforth His disciples will no longer hesitate, while acknowledging Him as Messias, to stress His Davidic origin (Mt 1, 1; Lk 2, 4; cf. Jn 7, 42; Rom 1, 3; 2 Tm 2, 8; Ap 5, 5; 22, 16) and the fulfilment in Him of the promise given to David (Acts 2, 30; Heb 1, 5).

Finally, it is because of its significance in the history of salvation that the account of the origins of the monarchy has been retained in the Bible. David, contrary to the kinglets of his time, has been saved from oblivion, since he had been oriented towards the realization of the kingdom of God in Jesus Christ. The Messias needed him in order to reveal Himself by surpassing him. This suffices to guarantee the permanent actuality of the Books of Samuel for the Christians. David is a part of our faith in the mystery of Christ.

CHAPTER IV

THE BOOKS OF THE KINGS

BIBLIOGRAPHY

Introductions, translations, commentaries, pp. 1 f. and 168 (R. DE VAUX, *BJ**; A. MEDEBIELLE, BPC*; BARNES, CBSC...).

A. SANDA, *Die Bücher der Könige** (Münster, 1911).

J. A. MONTGOMERY—H. S. GEHMAN, *The Books of Kings* (Edinburgh, 1951).

E. R. THIELE, *The Mysterious Numbers of the Hebrew Kings* (Chicago, 1951).

R. DE VAUX, " Israel, " *SDB*, IV, cols. 745 ff.

S. GAROFALO, *Il Libro dei Re** (Turin, 1951).

N. H. SNAITH, " The Books of Kings, " *IB* (1954).

W. F. STINESPRING, " Temple, Jerusalem, " *IDB*, IV, pp. 534-560.

A. PARROT, *Samaria, the Capital of the Northern Kingdom* (London : SCM, 1957); *The Temple of Jerusalem* (London : SCM, 1957).

D. N. FREEDMAN—E. F. CAMPBELL, " The Chronology of Israel and the Ancient Near East, " *The Bible and the Ancient Near East*, (ed.) G. E. WRIGHT (Garden City : Doubleday, 1961).

H. ROWLEY, " Elijah on Mount Carmel, " *BJRL*, 43 (1960-1961), pp. 190-219; " Hezekiah's Reform and Rebellion, " *BJRL*, 44 (1961-1962, pp. 395-431).

J. GRAY, *I and II Kings, A Commentary* (Philadelphia : Westminster, 1964).

§ 1. Content of the Book

The Books of the Kings tell the history of the kings of Juda from the death of David to the Babylonian exile : hence their title. The division into two books, just as in the case of Samuel, is artificial. The division was first made by the Septuagint which wrote Samuel and Kings on four scrolls entitled " Books of the Kingdoms. " The Latin Vulgate transmitted us this division under the title " Books of the Kings. " Thus 1 and 2 Kings according to the Hebrew correspond to 3 and 4 Kings in the Greek and Latin Bible.

The work itself suggests a division into three parts :

1. *The history of Solomon* (3 Kgs 1—11). Intrigues favor the succession of Solomon to the throne of David (1—2). The magnificence of his reign is celebrated in a triptych of glory (3—10). The wisdom which God grants to his prayer shows itself in the judgment of the two women, in the organization of his kingdom, in the abundance and quality of his maxims and parables (3—5, 14). The splendor of his constructions, especially of the Temple, showed forth his riches and his glory (5, 15—9, 25). His wealth is admired by the Queen of Sheba; his commercial relations with foreign countries are the source of it (9, 26—10). But there are shadows in the picture : foreign enemies and Jeroboam's rebellion, to punish the king for his compromising patronage of the false cults of his wives (11).

2. *The two kingdoms* (3 Kgs 12—4 Kgs 17). After the death of Solomon, the ten tribes of the North organize their own separate kingdom under Jeroboam, while Roboam, the son of Solomon, retains only Juda. The political schism is accompanied by a religious schism, condemned by the prophets (12—14, 20). The parallel existence of the two kingdoms is recalled by a series of notices dedicated to each king and arranged in chronological order : the author passes from one king to his contemporary or contemporaries of the other kingdom. The tone changes in chapter 17 where the narrative evolves in order to interest us in Elias and in the Aramean wars of Achab. From 4 Kgs 2 onwards Eliseus comes to the foreground with his superhuman powers, his interventions in the events of his time, his role in the origin of Jehu's revolution. That revolution has its repercussion in Juda when Athalia seizes the throne, is overthrown and Joas made king (11—12). Before Eliseus' death is related, notices about Joachaz and Joas are inserted into the narrative (13). The book then returns to a rapid summary of the reigns in Juda and in Israel (14—16) until the capture of Samaria by the Assyrians. This event leads to some reflections on the moral and religious infidelities which are censured (17).

3. *The kingdom of Juda until the Exile* (18—25). The account lingers gladly on the reign of Ezechias because of his religious fidelity and his relationship with the prophet Isaias (18—20). Opposed to the progress of impiety under Manasses and Amon (21) is the reform introduced by Josias, a reform based on the book of the Law discovered in the Temple (22—23, 30). But the hour of destruction has struck for the kingdom : misfortunes of Joachaz and Joakim, the capture of Jerusalem by Nabuchodonosor and the first deportation under Joakim, the revolution by Sedecias, the spoliation of the city and the second deportation

(23, 31—25, 21). The governor whom the Babylonians had appointed over Juda is assassinated (25, 22-26). A short notice takes us to a point several years later in order to mention the favor shown to Joakin, captive in Babylon (25, 27-30).

§ 2. The Unity of the Book. Its Intentions

Against a background of the summary and monotonous biographies of the kings, stand out the more developed accounts of sustained interest, such as the stories of Solomon, of Elias and Eliseus. These accounts of various literary characteristics give to the book the aspect of a work of compilation. But a rather firm framework has been imposed upon the whole work by the repetition of the same formulae and of well defined doctrinal themes, whether in the introduction or in the conclusion of each reign, or in the course of the reflections suggested by the events. This framework is the work of one author whose method reveals his intentions.

The royal biographies are drawn from the same mold. From the death of David, of Solomon, of Jeroboam we read similar phrases as for the duration of the reign, the burial of the king and the name of the successor (3 Kgs 2, 10-12; 11, 41-43; 14, 19-20). The mold becomes more evident from Roboam onwards. This personality is presented in the following terms : " Roboam, the son of Solomon, reigned in Juda; he was forty-one years old when he began to reign, and he reigned seventeen years in Jerusalem.... His mother's name was Naama the Ammonitess. He did what was evil in the sight of Yahweh " (14, 21-22). And here is the conclusion : " The rest of the history of Roboam, all that he did, is it not written in the Book of the Chronicles of the Kings of Juda?... Roboam slept with his fathers and was buried in the city of David. His son Abiam reigned in his stead " (14, 29-31). These formulae recur almost without change for each ruler just as if his life were recorded on a standardized registration card prepared beforehand and completed later by the addition of a few names and numbers. The conclusion mentions regularly the book which ought to be consulted for further details, the death and the burial of the king; the name of the successor is omitted if he is not the son of the deceased. The introduction includes the name of the king and often of his father, the duration of his reign and a judgment of his conduct. Until the destruction of Samaria, moreover, the introduction indicates exactly in what year of the reign of the corresponding king in the other kingdom the accession of each king takes place. There are some variations, however, according as the introduction deals with

a king of Juda or of Israel. The name of the mother and the age of the
king at his enthronement are only given in the former case, and while
the kings of the northern kingdom are judged unfavorably, those of the
southern kingdom are entitled to three kinds of formulae : categorical
condemnation, compliments with reservations or unreserved praise. With
the exception of these differences, the formulary recurs with evident
regularity. It suffices at times to make up a notice (15, 1-7) by freely
inserting some data (16, 24) or a short exposition (14, 25-28; 15, 16-22;
16, 1-5). If some notice is not in harmony with the preordained model,
the exception is justified by the particular conditions of the event or of the
death of the king : Joram and Ochozias, murdered by Jehu, do not need
the formula intended for the conclusion (4 Kgs 9, 22-29), neither do
the kings deposed by the enemy (Osee of Israel, Joachaz, Joakim,
Sedecias); Jehu presents himself sufficiently so that the usual introduction
can be dispensed with; the account dedicated to Athalia makes any
introduction and conclusion superfluous (4 Kgs 11).

The judgments passed upon each king reveal even better the
intentions of the author. As for the kings of Israel, the general condemnation : " He did what was evil in the sight of Yahweh " is always
expressed more precisely by adding the reproach of having adhered to
the sin of Jeroboam, that is to say, to the worship of Yahweh under
the image of the bull in the sanctuaries of Bethel and Dan (3 Kgs 15,
26. 34... etc.; this is done even in the case of Zambri whose reign did
not last more than seven days, 16, 19; also in the case of Jehu, who was
full of zeal for the Lord, 4 Kgs 10, 29-31; there is only one exception,
Osee, 4 Kgs 17, 2). Twice reference is made to the cult of vain idols, but
perhaps the same thing is meant (3 Kgs 16, 13. 26). To the sin of
Jeroboam is soon added the sin of Achab, the introduction of the worship
of Baal in Israel under the influence of Jezabel (3 Kgs 16, 31-32; 22, 53-54;
cf. 4 Kgs 3, 2; 10, 28). Among the kings of Jerusalem there were those
who did " what was evil in the sight of Yahweh " : the cult in the high
places, in the sanctuaries of the provinces is meant, a cult that imitated
pagan practices (3 Kgs 14, 23; cf. 15, 3; 4 Kgs 16, 4); or it refers to the
adoption of the religious practices of Achab's family (4 Kgs 8, 18; 8, 27),
or, finally, to the cult of foreign divinities (4 Kgs 21, 2 f. 21-22). Of
several kings it is said : " He did what was right in the eyes of Yahweh, "
but it is added : " The high places, however, were not suppressed, the
people continued to offer sacrifices and to burn incense on the high
places " (3 Kgs 15, 11-14; 22, 43-44; 4 Kgs 12, 3-4; 14, 3-4; 15, 3-4. 34-35).
Only two kings, namely Ezechias and Josias, receive the supreme praise :
" He did what was right in the eyes of Yahweh and followed in all the

example of his father David "; this means that they suppressed the high places and the practices which were considered idolatrous (4 Kgs 18, 3; 22, 2). In this way all the evils were traced back to the cult of foreign gods, to the cult of Yahweh practiced under the equivocal form in Bethel and Dan, or simply to the worship on the high places, that is to say, in Yahwistic sanctuaries distinct from the Temple of Jerusalem.

The kings, evidently, are estimated according to the norm of Deuteronomy. " The fundamental articles of this Law are : one God, one Temple, that is to say, the rejection of all forms of paganism and the centralization of the divine worship in only one sanctuary. " [1]   Deuteronomy, indeed, rebukes uncompromisingly all kinds of idolatry. It is Deuteronomy, on the other hand, which pronounces the law of only one sanctuary, and by the injunction that every other place of worship must be destroyed, it establishes the monopoly of the Temple and of the priesthood of Jerusalem (Dt 12). Not only the ideas, but also the favorite style and expressions of Deuteronomy are found in the Books of Kings (cf. for example 3 Kgs 14, 21-24 with Dt 12, 2. 3. 5. 29. 31). The " Law of Moses, " quoted several times, can only signify Deuteronomy (3 Kgs 2, 3; 4 Kgs 14, 6 quoting Dt 24, 16). Josias discovers it in the Temple and applies it in his reform : it is not surprising that this event forms the object of a detailed account (4 Kgs 22—23). The author of the book knows that the centralization of the cult in Jerusalem was not achieved before Josias. He finds an excuse as for Solomon in the fact that the Temple did not yet exist (3 Kgs 3, 2-3); but all the other kings, even the best ones, have a tarnished reputation. When the book found in the Temple is read, Josias exclaims : " Great is the wrath of Yahweh that is kindled against us, for our fathers did not obey the words of this book to do all which it commands us " (4 Kgs 22, 13). This is also the personal thought of the author.

He expresses it also in the reflections which he intersperses here and there among his work. The prayer of Solomon, on the occasion of the dedication of the Temple, received amplifications in the spirit and style of Deuteronomy : Yahweh is faithful to the Covenant whenever His servants are faithful towards Him (3 Kgs 8, 23; cf. Dt 4, 39; 7, 9), He has separated Israel from among the nations to be His heritage (3 Kgs 8, 53; cf. Dt 7, 6); He has made His Name dwell in the Temple (3 Kgs 8, 29; cf. Dt 12, 5. 11); Solomon, moreover, asks Yahweh to hear the prayer of His people when they are struck by the evils with which Deuteronomy threatens them (3 Kgs 8, 33-37; cf. Dt 28). Deuteronomy inspires also

---

[1] R. DE VAUX, *Les Livres des Rois**, p. 14.

the judgment passed upon the destruction of Samaria : the destruction is explained not only by the sin of Jeroboam who turned Israel away from the Temple of Jerusalem (4 Kgs 17, 7. 21-23), but also by having other gods besides Yahweh and by the erection of sanctuaries, stelae and sacred pillars throughout the land (4 Kgs 17, 7ᵇ-17; cf. Dt 7, 5; 9, 13; 12, 2-3; 16, 21; 18, 10). The destruction gives reality to the threats which in Deuteronomy form the sanctions for any disobedience against the precepts of the Covenant. The misfortunes of the reign of Solomon are presented as illustrations of the same theology : they punish his weakness for foreign women (3 Kgs 11, 1-2; cf. Dt 7, 3-4) and his indulgence for their idols (11, 9-13).

The estimation of the kings in the light of Deuteronomy is of such importance for the author of the book that he practically ignores all that has to do with profane history. For the most part he gives only some stereotyped data and refers his readers to other works. Even such important reigns as those of Amri and Jeroboam II receive little more than the usual schematic phraseology. If some accounts are more developed and pass beyond the usual framework, it is because they offer a religious interest. Such accounts are : the history of Solomon, the builder of the Temple (3 Kgs 3—11); the story of the schism by which the northern tribes separate themselves from the Temple (12—14); the history of Elias and Eliseus, that is to say, of the struggle against the sin of Achab and the cult of Baal (3 Kgs 17—4 Kgs 10); the end of this cult in Juda because of the death of Athalia and the repairs of the Temple by Joas (4 Kgs 11—12); the alterations introduced into the Temple by Achaz (16); the measures taken by Ezechias against the high places and his relations with the prophet Isaias (18—20); the discovery of the Law and the reform of Josias (22—23). Our attention is constantly directed toward the Temple and the prophets in their struggle against paganism. This was already the object of the worries of Deuteronomy.

This book, therefore, is less a history than an interpretation of the history in the light of the teaching of Deuteronomy. It wishes to show that during the period of the monarchy a series of infidelities to the cult of the true God and to the prerogatives of the Temple led the two kingdoms to their destruction, in spite of the efforts by which the prophets and some kings tried to bring the people back to obedience. The reference to the promises given to David leaves a ray of hope in the midst of this negative balance (3 Kgs 8, 15-19; 8, 24-26; 15, 4-5; 4 Kgs 8, 19). It is not God who has been unfaithful, but the Chosen People.

§ 3. The Sources and the Materials Used

In order to construct his synthesis, the author had various sources at his disposal. Besides the " Book of Song " from which according to the Greek translation the little poem of Solomon quoted in 3 Kgs 8, 12-13 is said to have been borrowed (probably the same collection as the " Book of Jashar " of Jos 10, 13 and 2 Sm 1, 18), the concluding formulae mention by name three works : " the Book of the Acts of Solomon, " " the Book of the Chronicles of the Kings of Juda " and " the Book of the Chronicles of the Kings of Israel. " To these works the author refers his readers who wish to have more details. We must not consider them as official chronicles, written by scribes in the service of the king and kept in the archives : the public could not consult them. It is rather a question of works easily accessible, written by private authors who might have consulted, moreover, the royal archives. As for the kings of the North and the South, these chronicles have been recorded until the destruction of the kingdoms, for they are quoted until the last kings who died in Samaria and in Jerusalem. It is conceivable that they were constantly brought up to date rather than redacted only at that time. The manner, indeed, in which our books refer to these chronicles as regards wars, conspiracies, constructions, etc., about which they do not wish to talk, reminds us of annals that recorded in succession the external acts of each reign rather than of a whole work composed by some historian.

Although the author refers to them only with regard to items which he himself does not intend to discuss, he must have drawn from them other information and also some definite facts with which at times he illustrates his remarks. But it is possible that he also had at his disposal other writings which he does not mention. By their particular style and spirit we may recognize in his book several literary units which cannot be his work and which he reproduced faithfully. These units do not always correspond to his views : for example, when Elias repairs an altar outside Jerusalem and laymen offer up sacrifices (3 Kgs 18, 30). Did he receive these texts directly or had the chronicles he quotes already been collected? It is not always possible to give an answer. It is of greater importance to appreciate the genre, the age and the value of these compositions which often preserve the oldest and most beautiful pages of Israelite historiography. Following the order of the book we will analyze them and examine at once their historical and religious value.

1. *The chronicle of the succession of David* (continuation 3 Kgs 1—2) The first two chapters of the book continue the family chronicle of David, written by a contemporary of Solomon and reproduced at least from

2 Sm 9 onwards. The author of Kgs detached these chapters from
Samuel so as to provide an introduction to the story of Solomon. He
revised slightly the testament of David (3 Kgs 2, 3-4). We know already
the literary and historical qualities of this account. [2] If the last words
of David and their execution by Solomon shock us, we must not forget
that they were men of their own time. They shared the accepted ideas
concerning the duty of blood-revenge and of removing the effect of curses
by returning them against their authors. The magnanimity of David,
during his life, with regard to his enemies appears all the more exceptional.

2. *The history of Solomon* (3 Kgs 3—11)

The hand of the Deuteronomistic redactor can be recognized in 3, 2-3;
in several verses of 8 and 11, 1-13 as well as in 11, 41-43. He also
intervened in the choice and organization of its material : he lingers on
the construction of the Temple [3]; he reports at the end, as punishments,
wars which had begun at the beginning of Solomon's reign (11, 21-25).
He certainly owes much to " the Book of the Acts of Solomon " (11, 41).
If we judge according to what he could have borrowed, that book must
have presented already the characteristics of a compilation. A copy of
official documents drawn up by the scribes of the king was found there :
a list of high functionaries in the service of the central power whose
names apparently were Judean, with the exception of two scribes who
were perhaps Egyptian, and the one in charge of the forced labor who
was a Phoenician (4, 1-6); a list of twelve prefects whose duty it was to
collect assessments for the maintenance of the national services in twelve
districts, but not in Juda (4, 7-19; cf. 5, 7-8). These are documents of
the first order which inform us concerning Solomon's political outlook,
but also about the favored treatment which Juda enjoyed and which
already contained in germ the schism of the northern tribes.

The book contained also a continuous account of the reign, a kind
of private chronicle in praise of the Great King, of his power, of his
luxury, omitting neither the reverses of his foreign policy nor his financial
obligations, such as the surrender of twenty cities to his creditor Hiram,
king of Tyre (11, 14-25; 9, 11-13). This obliges us to assign the
composition to a time not too long after Solomon's death, in the course
of the subsequent century. The account comprises exact data, of great
historical interest, concerning foreign enemies who are rising again
(11, 14-25), fortifications built for the defense of the country (9, 15-19),
the armed fleet for overseas trade (9, 26-28; 10, 11. 28), the caravans for

---

[2] Cf. above, pp. 202 ff.

[3] A. PARROT, *Le Temple de Jérusalem* (Paris-Neuchâtel, 1955).

the import of horses and chariots (10, 28-29), the dowry brought by Pharao's daughter, her house in Jerusalem, and the private sanctuaries built for the gods of the women of the king's harem (9, 16-24; 11, 7). This information permits the historian to characterize quite accurately the reign of Solomon : " While the preceding period in which the monarchy had been formed was marked by dynamism, Solomon's reign is static. Henceforth all effort is directed to preserve, to organize, and, above all, to exploit. " [4] It is no longer a question of conquering, but of defending (badly enough) David's conquests against the struggles of the Edomites and the Arameans for their independence. Egypt which had made an expedition along the coast prefers an alliance to war and seals it by a marriage. " Cities for chariots and horses " (9, 19) are built throughout the land to serve as garrison for the mounted troops, a great novelty of Solomon's army. Archeology has illustrated the text in this regard : in Megiddo stables of the time of Solomon have been discovered, carefully laid out to accommodate 450 horses. The " store-cities " put in stock the contributions in kind levied for the needs of the court, of the administration and of the army. Commercial activity flourishes in all its forms, sea trade, caravan trade, transit-duty. Here again the text is illustrated by the sensational discovery (N. Glueck, 1938) of copper refineries, built by Solomon at Ezion-geber on the northeastern end of the Gulf of Aqaba, to produce a metal valued highly on the international market. Wealth came to Israel—swallowed up, it is true, by the expenses of a luxurious court and by a plan of grandiose constructions. The most famous construction was the Temple. The details which are given concerning its construction, its dimensions, its furniture (6; 7, 13-51) point perhaps to a special source, taken from the archives of the Temple.

The Book of the Acts of Solomon, such as the author of Kings knew it and to which he refers not only with regard to external acts of the reign but also with regard to the wisdom of the king (11, 41), must have contained some narrative passages such as the story of the dream at Gibeon, the judgment of the case of the two mothers and the visit of the queen of Saba (3, 4-14; 3, 16-28; 10, 1-10). These accounts, in the style of the royal " novel " of the Ancient Orient, [5] added to the memory of Solomon the acknowledgment of the reputation he had acquired.

The Book of the Acts, it appears, does not depart from this laudatory tone. It is difficult to discover its pattern of organization. We may assign to it the three tableaux of the wisdom, the constructions and the

---

[4] R. DE VAUX, *SDB**, IV, col. 746.

[5] French ed., p. 128.

trade of Solomon the Magnificent, but we cannot say what place the Acts
accorded to his failures and to the rebellion of Jeroboam, significant
traits of the limitations of Solomon's success. The verses 11, 26-28 and 40
are only the bits of a more developed account which the author preferred
instead of another (11, 29-39). This latter account tells the action of the
prophet Ahias the Silonite who tears his garment in twelve pieces in
order to give ten pieces to Jeroboam : this is the announcement of the
schism of the ten northern tribes as punishment of Solomon's religious
infidelities. The text, without doubt, has been revised by the Deuteronomistic redactor, but it reflects an account that originated from the
prophetical milieu of the northern kingdom; they showed greater
perspicacity than the royal apologists of the South and saw also the
reverse side of the splendor (cf. 1 Sm 8, 11-18). Their diagnosis is of a
religious order. It confirms the impression which the preceding chapters
have already left : " Solomon as king of the Chosen People is too much
involved in the affairs of this world, his wisdom is chiefly profane, his
religious conviction is much less deep than that of David. "[6] The
prophets, by making us see in the future schism the consequence of
Solomon's faults, explain the religious meaning of an event that could
be observed even by a profane historian. Jeroboam, indeed, is a man
from the North and a master of forced labor; the northern tribes separate
themselves from the king of Jerusalem, because the yoke he imposes on
them is too heavy. The rebellion of Jeroboam will lead Israel in the end
to disaster, but it will be, in part, the sanction of Solomon's abuses : the
discontent of the Israelites with the burdens from which Juda was
exempt will bear its fruits. By combining these two sources the author
asserts his belief in the Temple and the dynasty as well as his disapproval
of the king's impieties.

3. *The history of the schism* (3 Kgs 12—14)

This history, without doubt, owes much to the chronicles of the kings
of Israel (14, 19). The wrongs, according to 12, 1-20, are on the side
of Roboam. This account shows forth the dualistic character of the
monarchy : the son of Solomon is easily accepted by Juda, but he must
seek the recognition of the northern tribes who do not seem to support
the hereditary principle as firmly as Juda. They ask for an alleviation
of their burdens. Roboam's lack of political experience and his intransigence do the rest : the northern tribes see their demands rejected and
choose Jeroboam as king.

---

[6] R. De Vaux, *SDB**, IV, col. 747.

The author of Kings was even more interested in the religious schism which followed, and the trace of his hand can be found in the account which describes it (12, 26-33). He did not have to stress in how far the religious innovations of Jeroboam continued previous practices, as, for instance, the worship of local sanctuaries or also a certain use of cultic images (cf. Jgs 8, 27; 1 Sm 19, 13; 21, 10). But he saw well their serious implications : by representing Yahweh under the image of a bull, the sacred animal of the Chanaanite Baal, Jeroboam encouraged the introduction of pagan practices into the cult; by establishing sanctuaries which rivaled that of the Ark in Jerusalem, he broke the religious bond which since the covenant of Josue at Sichem had engendered a certain national conscience common to all the tribes.

The condemnation of these innovations is expressed by two accounts which perhaps proceed from a collection of traditions concerning the prophets; they report the curse of the altar at Bethel by a man of God (12, 33—13, 33) and the oracle of Ahias against Jeroboam (14, 1-18). This second passage, redacted at an early time, received some Deuteronomistic additions (14, 7-11). The first account recalls the polemic waged by the northern prophets against the depraved cults (cf. Am 7, 10 f.) and its style resembles that of the traditions concerning Eliseus; but the mention of Josias in 13, 2 has been added afterwards or is an indication of a late redaction.

4. *The cycle of Elias narratives*

The amplitude of the account, found between the introduction and the conclusion of the reign of Achab (16, 29-30 and 22, 39-40), requires sources other than the chronicles of the kings of Israel. Two groups of narratives are distinguished : those which concern Elias and are violently hostile against Achab, and the history of the Aramean wars of Achab (20; 22, 1-38), much more balanced as far as he is concerned and where Elias is not mentioned. These two groups cannot have the same origin. In the second group, something of the literary characteristics of the memoirs of David's family is found : keenness of observation, psychological sensitiveness, objectivity of the author who disappears behind the men and the facts. The ruse, then the pride of Achab in the face of the humiliating conditions which Benadad wanted to impose upon him, the superstition of the Arameans who fear Yahweh, the God of the mountains, and want to fight in the plain, afterwards their trust in the mercy of the kings of Israel, all this is described with picturesque liveliness (20). Chapter 22 constitutes a short drama in several well connected scenes : consultation of the prophets who flatter the king;

intervention of Micheas, first speaking in irony, then threatening; defeat of Achab. These accounts cannot be much later than the events. This is living history. With difficulty can the spirit of the popular tradition be felt in 20, 35-43. The testimony of these accounts is of great historical value. The author agrees with the prophet Micheas that Yahweh has decided the ruin of Achab; yet he impartially presents him as a shrewd king, a courageous defender of Israel's independence, and, if not pious, at least respectful towards Yahweh and His prophets. Yahweh's prophets, indeed, live in his entourage and sustain his policy. This trait has to be retained to complete the tableau of the spiritual confusion which prevailed in the time of Elias. Only one prophet, Micheas, has the courage to separate himself from the other inspired men. He does not dispute their inspiration, however : he attributes it to a lying spirit sent by Yahweh, for nothing arrives without the order or the permission of the true God. Later, the prophets will treat their adversaries as impostors (cf. Am 7, 14; Mi 2, 11; 3, 5 ff.; Jer 23, 16 ff.; Ez 13). This fact confirms the antiquity of our writings. They are perhaps excerpts of a detailed chronicle of the reign of Achab. The author of Kings, or perhaps some compiler before him, has only retained those passages which involved the prophets.

As for Elias, [7] we have the excerpts of a more developed biography. He appears brusquely, fulminating a threat of a drought of three years against Israel, but nothing is said as to his origin or the place whence he must depart by the order of God (17, 1-3). The continuation of the account will allude to a general massacre of the prophets of Yahweh by Jezabel (18, 4. 13; 19, 10) which must have been narrated somewhere. An introduction, which the author, without doubt, was satisfied with summarizing in 16, 31-33, must have told how, prior to the drought, the impious woman of Achab attempted to substitute the cult of Yahweh with that of Baal.

The chapters 17—19 form a whole. During the drought Elias retreated to the brook Carith, then to Phoenician territory where he rewarded the hospitality of a poor widow (17). Afterwards he presents himself before Achab, who had searched for him in all the lands, and organizes on Mount Carmel a solemn contest which will decide who is the true God, Yahweh or Baal. Alone he confronts 450 prophets of Baal, and, what they cannot obtain with their cries and dances, his prayer obtains : fire from heaven, rain, the end of the drought (18). But the

---

[7] *Élie le Prophète selon les Écritures et les traditions chrétiennes** (Paris, 1956); G. FOHRER, *Elia* (Zürich, 1957).

extermination of the prophets of Baal by Elias has provoked the fury of Jezabel; he has to flee from her threats into the desert of Bersabee. Discouraged he receives from above the strength to continue his journey to Horeb, to the encounter with the living God who had manifested Himself to Moses and who gives him to recognize His presence in the murmur of a light breeze. He receives the order to anoint Hazael as king of Damascus, Jehu as king of Israel and Elias as prophet in his place (19, 18). These three personalities will be the instruments of the punishment of Achab and of his dynasty. But the account ends abruptly. Elias' return is not told nor is the execution of the mission he had received. The call of Eliseus, as servant of Elias and not as prophet, is mentioned here (19, 19-21) according to an excerpt from the Eliseus cycle. To this cycle belong also the two accounts in which we see Eliseus bringing Hazael and Jehu to the throne (4 Kgs 8, 7-15 and 9, 1-12). We cannot say whether the cycle of Elias also included something similar or whether it showed Elias entrusting Eliseus with the execution of the received orders : the interruption of the account in 19, 18, at any rate, does not seem to be normal.

Two other episodes, detached from the life of Elias, have been retained : the condemnation of Achab and Jezabel after the murder of Naboth (21), the announcement of the death of Ochozias, the son of Achab, for having consulted Beelzebub, the god of Accaron (4 Kgs 1, 2-17). The first text has been inserted between the two Aramean wars of Achab perhaps in order to put together the oracle of Elias and the death of the king narrated in chapter 22 (22, 38 stresses this by alluding to 21, 19 and by forgetting 21, 29; in the Septuagint, our chapter 21 immediately follows chapter 19).

The author of Elias' biography was skilful in the art of literary composition. We can conclude this from the arrangement of chapters 17—19 and from the dramatic tone of his narratives. His work may have received later enrichments. The oracle against Achab seems to have been commented upon (21, 21-26). The account of the resurrection in 17, 17-24 can easily be detached from the context (no allusion to the drought) and suggests at least a literary influence of the cycle of Eliseus (cf. 4 Kgs 4, 18-37; cf. especially the " mistress of the house " of 3 Kgs 17, 17 with the poor widow of the preceding verses as well as with the " wealthy woman " of 4 Kgs 4, 8; the title of " man of God, " 3 Kgs 17, 24, is the usual title of Eliseus). The account of the intervention against Ochozias is overloaded by a development (4 Kgs 1, 9-16) which does not advance the account in any way, but adorns it with episodes of popular taste (there, and there alone, the title " man of God " occurs).

The work, while taking into account these possible complements, may go back to a time about half a century after Elias' death, about the year 800. He is heard to complain about the destruction of the altars of Yahweh and we see him reconstructing the altar of Carmel : the author, therefore, ignores the Deuteronomistic reform and even the polemic of Amos and Osee against the sanctuaries of the northern kingdom. He can rely on a firm historical tradition.

The history certainly has been stylized (cf. the history of the Aramean wars of Achab). In splendid isolation Elias sets himself against Jezabel totally devoted to the cause of Baal, against Achab dominated by his wife, against the whole body of persons engaged in the shameful cult introduced in Israel, against the whole people which allows itself to be led into impiety. An implacable war is waged in which the power of God can only act through a man of faith. In him is embodied the intransigence of Yahwism with regard to every other cult and its social demands against the exploitation engendered by the government of Amri's dynasty. It is not quite exact to speak of a biography of Elias : the narrative did not only wish to tell us about his life, but also wanted to revive Israel's faith and to prolong the shock of the consciences brought on by the protestations of the prophet. It is for this reason that individual traits do not abound.

These intentions, however, do not exclude fidelity to history. The account of the rebellion of Jehu, the value of which we will try to estimate, confirms that the king Achab erected in his capital a temple to Baal (probably to the Baal of Tyre, Melkart) after his marriage with Jezabel, daughter of the king-priest of Tyre (4 Kgs 10, 18-19). This fact, if it did not imply the abolition of the cult of Yahweh (Achab gave Yahwistic names to several of his children), constituted an alarming innovation in the history of the religious infidelities of the royal house and provoked the opposition of the prophets, of Micheas and of Elias. The same account confirms also the murder of Naboth (4 Kgs 9, 25-26), another motive of opposition for the men in whom faith lived and developed its demands. The opposition, in the end, will overthrow Achab's dynasty. The history of Elias, moreover, avoids purely imaginative idealization. The marvelous does not intervene under that gratuitous form which is favored by the hagiographic literature and which is found, for example, in the cycle of Eliseus. The scene on Mount Carmel is full of allusions on which R. de Vaux [8] could shed light through what is known about the cult of

---

[8] R. DE VAUX, " Les Prophètes de Baal sur le Mont Carmel "*, Bul. du Musée de Beyrouth, V (1941), pp. 7-20.

Melkart (ritual dances with genuflections, the myth of a god taken up by multiple affairs or leaving for distant expeditions, invocations to awaken him). The mention of the ecstatic states of Elias (18, 46) introduces us to the milieu of the ancient *nebiim* (prophets). The discouragement of the prophet in chapter 19 is a touching aspect of human nature. If the similarities with Moses are deliberately stressed by the narrator (quarantine, the encounter with God in a cleft of the rock of Ex 33, 22, signs of His coming according to Ex 19, 16), they are not purely artificial : the pilgrimage to Horeb expresses, on the part of Elias, the awareness of continuing the mission of Moses and the will of keeping pure the Mosaic faith. Even the mystery which surrounds his life and the sudden character of his apparitions and disappearances (cf. 17, 3; 18, 1. 12; 4 Kgs 1, 7; 2, 16) bear witness to the impression of supernatural power which he has left behind.

As in the icons, so also here does stylization show forth the essential aspect. *Eliyahu* signifies " Yahweh is my God. " By an undivided faith, matured by trial, the prophet touched some religious souls with lasting success. They will retain only his thirst for contact with God and his refusal of any compromise : there resides the secret of his influence. His spiritual sons to whom we owe the accounts that mention him knew what they owed to his experience. Thanks to him they not only learned that Baal has no place in Israel, but also that to the exclusion of all else " it is Thou, Yahweh, who art God " (18, 37). Following him they sought God beyond the traditional signs of His manifestations, storm, earthquake, fire. Yahweh is distinct from these all too naturalistic phenomena. To herald the coming of a Spirit, who wishes to reveal himself inwardly, the breath of a light breeze passing through the stillness (19, 11-12) will be sufficient. All of which the historian would like to know more seems negligible in comparison with this spiritual discovery.

5. *The cycle of Eliseus' narratives*

The narratives concerning Eliseus present various characteristics. A first group of anecdotes shows " the man of God " in his relationship with the confraternities of " sons of the prophets " who live at Bethel, Jericho, Galgal.... They are *fioretti*, that is to say, stories told by those circles and which reveal the strong impression left by the prophet. His movements from one group to another put some order into this florilegium of traditions of diverse origins. The first scene (4 Kgs 2, 1-18) involves the principal confraternities and shows how Eliseus alone, unlike all other members, is admitted into the intimate circle of Elias and constituted his spiritual heir because of the vision he had of his mysterious translation.

The whole account is conceived for the sake of Eliseus and no longer belongs to the cycle of Elias (the latter receives in v. 12 a title which is more appropriate to Eliseus, cf. 13, 14). The other scenes exalt the thaumaturgist capable, in the eyes of his admirers, of every prodigy (2, 19-25; 4, 1-7; 4, 38-44; 6, 1-7). The marvelous tends here to evolve for itself and has not the quality of Elias' miracles which are in the service of faith. We have here a manifestation of the divine power in order to save (*Elisha*=" God saves ") and these short anecdotes illustrate the great kindness of a man willing to help in every need, even recovering an ax which had been borrowed and lost by a poor man.

In two accounts of much greater length Eliseus appears in the company of only one servant, Giezi. This is the story of the woman of Sunam, of her child born against all hope and snatched away by a sudden death : Giezi is powerless, but " the man of God, " whom the faith of a mother brings out of his retreat, restores the child to life; seven years later, the woman of Sunam profits again from the benefits of Eliseus (4, 8-37 and 8, 1-7; a redactor has separated the two parts of the account). And there is the story of Naaman, a story rich in contrasts : on the one hand, the Syrian commander who arrives with chariot and escort and causes the king of Israel great concern; on the other hand, Eliseus who does not condescend to meet Naaman and bids him to bathe in the Jordan; there is the land of Damascus with its celebrated rivers, here is Israel with its inglorious waters, whose land, however, belongs to a God unequaled; and the disinterested prophet stands in contrast with the covetous Giezi, dazzled by the riches of Naaman (5).

A third category of accounts describes Eliseus intervening in politics. The Aramean war in 6, 8-23 is of little interest to the narrator; only the prophet emerges from the anonymity, and the account only expresses its astonishment at his supernatural powers : Eliseus makes fools of the Arameans and leads them captive. The other accounts are of a different genre and abound in valuable historical information. In the war of Israel, allied with Juda and Edom, against Moab (3, 4-27) Eliseus accompanies the armies in order to consult Yahweh. He resorts to the usual devices, such as music, in order to bring himself into ecstasy and produce the oracle. The account of the military events is confirmed and completed by the stele which Mesha, the king of Moab, had erected in order to celebrate his rebellion against the house of Amri, whose tributary he had been so far, and to attribute his victory to the god Kamosh (cf. p. 19). In 6, 24—7, 19 Eliseus supports the cause of Israel, when Samaria is besieged by the Arameans. This detailed and objective account could seem to some critics to be an excerpt from some chronicle similar in its kind to that of the reign of Achab (cf. 3 Kgs 20; 22). The central role, however, attributed to the prophet indicates that it belongs rather to the cycle of traditions around Eliseus. He is magnified, but only because of the truth of his oracles : just as an Isaias, he directs rebukes to the king and demands faith in Yahweh in difficult circumstances when the leaders rely only on their policy.

According to 8, 7-15, Elias' intervention extends all the way to Damascus in order to favor the coming into power of Hazael in whom he sees the instrument of Yahweh against the house of Achab. According to 9, 1-13 he causes Jehu to be anointed as king of Israel, and Jehu's bloody revolution, lengthily narrated in 9, 14—10, marks the end of Omri's dynasty and of the cult of Baal at Samaria. It was thought that these two accounts gave a parallel version of the anointing of the two kings by Elias, according to an order received from God in 3 Kgs 19, 16. But there it was not a question of an urgent command, and the mission to anoint the two kings must not be understood in the strict sense of the terms, no more than that of anointing Elias as prophet (the prophets were not anointed). Elias had been invited to orientate by his influence the course of the events which sooner or later would involve the punishment of Achab's impiety. It is impossible to see how the older cycle of Elias could have given another version of the facts, different from that of Eliseus. The account of Jehu's revolution is counted among the best ancient chronicles of Israel (cf. the chronicle of the family of David and that of Achab). The effaced role of Eliseus does not show us a tradition concerning the prophet. This is living history, told a certain time after the events (cf. 10, 27) by a disciple of the prophets favorable to Jehu; the violences of the mercenary do not stir up his indignation (cf. some years later, Os 1, 4), for, being a convinced Yahwist, he acts as the instrument of God's judgment against the house of Achab and the followers of Baal.

A last account is added after the notices concerning the kings who succeeded in Israel and Juda between the revolution of Jehu and the death of Eliseus (13, 14-21). Already sick, the prophet still intervenes in the policy of his time. Joas, the king of Israel, relies more on him than on all his chariots of war (v. 14), and we see the man of God communicating to him by touch the divine power and causing him by a gesture abounding in effectiveness to prefigure the promised victory against the Arameans. The account also bears witness to the strong impression left by Eliseus after his death which did not put any end to his miracles.

The cycle of Eliseus, therefore, is not very homogeneous. These accounts must have formed a collection, but the diversity of their genre and origin did not allow them to be united into a well-knit composition (the Arameans no more returned into the land of Israel, according to 6, 23; in the following verse, however, they besiege Samaria; cf. also 5, 27 and 8, 4). The account of the revolution of Jehu, which is not directly inspired by the memory of the prophet, formed part of the collection because of the role played by the prophet at its beginning. It is more difficult to say whether the collection comprised the history of the fall of Athalia (11) : it is formed by two complementary Judean sources (a twofold mention of the death, vv. 16 and 20) and underlines the role of the priesthood, of the royal guard (vv. 4-12 and 18b-20), and of the people stirred up by the appeal of the priest (vv. 13-18a). The biography of Eliseus, at any rate, must have been put together in the kingdom of the North, therefore before 722. Certain accounts underwent the influence of the chronicle of Achab (cf. 3 Kgs 22, 4. 7 and 4 Kgs 3, 7. 11) or of the biography of Eliseus (cf. 3 Kgs 17, 16 and 4 Kgs 4, 1-7). The influence of the preaching of Amos and Osee, however, is not yet felt. These accounts may have been redacted between 800 and 750. It is also conceivable that a *corpus* of prophetical narratives was then constituted with the biographies of Elias and Eliseus, and of other narratives such as those concerning Ahias the Silonite (3 Kgs 11, 29 ff.; 14). The combination of two biographies, which perhaps overlap each other at the end of Elias and the beginning of Eliseus, probably explains the loss of a part of Elias' history.

The interest of the cycle of Eliseus is due to its variety. Each testimony, whether it stems from popular tradition, from a hagiographer devoted to the memory of the prophet or from a well-informed chronicler, reveals some aspect of his figure, at times so strange, and of his influence which extended well beyond his death. Eliseus, much more than Elias, is involved in political events. Although he is opposed to the house of Achab, he supports, nevertheless, the cause of Israel and pronounces his oracles with regard to precise circumstances of the national life. We are still far from the prophet Amos who will remain one from the ranks of " the sons of the prophets " and will announce the punishment and ruin of Israel. Eliseus does not surpass the ideal of national Yahwism; his interventions, at least, are inspired by the belief in the God of the Covenant. From this point of view he inherits from Elias. He does not reach the grandeur of the man from the desert, nor the absolute of his belief. It is true that the circumstances have changed. Perhaps he lacked the opportunity of being tried by persecution which kept Elias apart from political compromises and drove him into solitude, in search of God.

Another difference between him and Elias : Eliseus is in close contact with the groups of " the sons of prophets. " Without appearing as leader, he exercises a great influence upon them. The anecdotes which they spread in his praise reflect quite well the life of these groups of inspired men whom we have already met in the times of Samuel. They seem to have become wiser; we see them, at least, quite distinct from what they were in those meetings of collective trance (1 Sm 10, 9 ff.; 19, 18 ff.). It is not well known how they recruited new members. They prepared, at long range, the regrouping of the " small remnant " around the prophets of the 8th and 7th centuries. They also made the first experiment of common life in Israel, grouped in confraternities, without doubt still loosely structured, although they took their meals in common and practiced a certain poverty. We can see them swarming into the region of the Jordan which has not ceased to attract the men of God, including the Essenes, John the Baptist and the Fathers of the desert.

6. *The notices concerning Joas* (4 Kgs 12) *and Achaz* (16) are enriched by accounts of the repairs which the former made in the Temple, and by accounts of the alterations of the altar which the latter undertook. As for the origin of these passages we may assume a history of the Temple.

7. Into *the reign of Ezechias* (18—20) is inserted a new literary block dedicated to the prophet Isaias. Three accounts tell about the relations of the king with the prophet in the time of Sennacherib's invasion (18, 13-19), during a sickness of the king (20, 1-11) and on the occasion of an embassy of the king of Babylon (20, 12-19). This group of narratives is also found in the Book of Isaias 36—39 with the exception of some variants (for example, the omission of 18, 14-16 and the addition of a late psalm in Is 38, 10-20). Although the text of Isaias is in better shape, these chapters of Isaias have been borrowed from the Book of Kings. This book must have taken them from different sources : the analysis of the account of Sennacherib's invasion shows it. [9]

Some verses (18, 13-16) mention drily the attack on the strongholds of Juda by the king of Assyria and the tribute which Ezechias paid in order to be delivered. This text agrees with the Assyrian annals in which Sennacherib relates his campaign against the Philistine cities and Juda. [10] The biblical account, limited to the essential, must proceed from the archives or the official chronicles of the king.

---

[9] H. HAAG, " La campagne de Sennacherib "*, *RB*, 58 (1951), pp. 348-359.
[10] The text is quoted on p. 28.

Further on we find two combined accounts which relate the same series
of facts : an Assyrian embassy demanding the surrender of Jerusalem,
a prayer of Ezechias in the Temple, a reassuring oracle of Isaias and the
departure of Sennacherib (18, 17—19, 9ᵃ + 36-37 and 19, 9ᵇ-35). It is
evidently a question of doublets. They stress the arrogance of the
Assyrian who dares to treat the God of Juda with contempt, and they
emphasize the power of Yahweh, affirmed by Isaias and verified by the
event. There are parallel traditions narrated to the glory of the prophet.
The second account places greater emphasis upon his intervention and
attributes the failure of the enemy to the Angel of Yahweh which is a
way of signifying a scourge, or perhaps a pestilence. [11] The first account
declares simply that Sennacherib broke up camp when he heard that
Pharao Taharqa had entered into the war. The two explanations do not
exclude each other, but it is understandable that the popular tradition
preferred one of the two. Their historical value has been questioned, for
no corresponding news has been found in the Assyrian annals : but the
laudatory tone of those annals explains sufficiently their silence with
regard to the failure of Sennacherib. The mention of Taharqa, who has
not been pharao prior to 690, led one to think that the two parallel
accounts referred to a campaign distinct from that of 18, 13-16 which
according to the Assyrian texts has to be dated about 701. [12] In spite
of the difficulties raised against the role attributed to Taharqa in 701,
under the reign of his uncle Shabaka, it is a fact that our accounts know
nothing at all about a later intervention of the king of Assyria. On the
other hand, after having received the tribute of Ezechias the king of
Assyria could have demanded the total surrender of Jerusalem while
he was besieging Lachish. The intervention of Egypt, and perhaps a
pestilence, might have forced him to abandon a war which so far had been
victorious. This unexpected deliverance and the role played by Isaias
in the worst hours of the crisis would explain the birth, side by side with
the official chronicles, of accounts attentive to the religious dimensions
of the facts. Such is still the position of many historians who do not
admit a second campaign of Sennacherib against Jerusalem. The
discussion, however, is not closed.

§ 4. The Editions of the Book

At the origin of the Book of Kings, therefore, we see a certain number
of sources. Critics tried to find the continuation of two (Benzinger,

[11] Cf. p. 142.
[12] Cf. *above*, p. 29.

Hölscher) or three (Smend, Eissfeldt) great narrative strands of the Pentateuch. This hypothesis lacks any firm foundation and contributes little to the understanding of the text. Several of these sources, without doubt, had been already collected in the Acts of Solomon or in the Chronicles of the Kings of Israel and Juda : their title does not authorize us, in the name of an all too narrow definition, to reduce them to a chronicle of the external facts and to deny them any interest in the religious history. The traditions concerning Elias, Eliseus, and the prophets must have formed a separate collection. Thus the Deuteronomistic redactor, no matter how important his role may have been, did not have to create, but only to arrange and to present in the light of Deuteronomy materials already formed.

The unity of the book cannot be other than the work of a principal author. But it is probable that his work may have known several revised editions. The book ends with the liberation of Joachin by Evilmerodach who came to the throne of Babylon in 562 : in its present state, therefore, it cannot be older than that date. Other passages seem also to presuppose the destruction of Jerusalem and the deportation of 586 (cf. 4 Kgs 17, 19-20; 21, 11-15); but in their context they give the impression of being added passages, and rather clear indications lead to the conclusion that the work as a whole has been redacted prior to the Exile. After 586 it would not have been said that the Ark is still in the Temple and that Edom has freed itself from the tutelage of Juda " until this day " (3 Kgs 8, 8; 4 Kgs 8, 22). Some texts, clearly redactional, recall the promises made to David and suppose that one of his descendants is still reigning (for example, 3 Kgs 11, 36). The account of the reform of Josias fits in too well with the thesis of the author of the book to be written by another hand : his fervor suggests that there is still hope of escaping the destruction. In the present text, it is true, the prophetess Holda seems to announce the punishment of Juda as inevitable (4 Kgs 22, 15-20); but this may be a later addition. We must, therefore, place the principal redaction between 621 and 586. The reign of Josias offers the most favorable period, before the violent death of the pious king in 609 destroyed the hopes awakened by his reform. In order to sustain these hopes the author might have undertaken to show by means of the history that misfortunes in the past had as their cause the oblivion of the Law of Moses which now Josias was about to restore to its honor. The book could have ended with the restoration of that Law and with the eulogy of the king (23, 25 less the last words).

After the cruel deceptions of 597 and 586, the book was completed by the account of the new events. The reviser continues to refer to the

Chronicles of the Kings of Juda (24, 5) and to use the formulae of introduction and conclusion for each king, with less regularity, however, than
the first redactor does. He tells of the destruction of Jerusalem according
to his memory or following reliable sources (24, 18—25, 21). The
verse 25, 21 can constitute a conclusion, but this is not certain, and the
two appendices concerning Godolias (25, 22-26, summarized from Jer 40,
7—41, 18) and Joachin (25, 27-30) may proceed from the same author
who would have written, therefore, after 562. He had also to harmonize
the book with the new situation of the deported people. Through some
additions he showed that the efforts of Josias could not compensate for
the infidelity of his predecessors, and that especially since Manasses the
punishment had been decreed (3 Kgs 9, 1-9; 4 Kgs 17, 19-20; 21, 7-15;
22, 16-17; cf. 24, 2-4). He also lengthened the prayer of Solomon in the
Temple in order to ask for the conversion of those living in exile and for
their reunion (3 Kgs 8, 41-53). The grace accorded to Joachin left a ray
of hope at the end of this history of the sins and misfortunes of the nation.

The Deuteronomistic character of the book is not compromised by
the insignificant revisions, made by the sacerdotal school, which it could
have received afterwards (3 Kgs 7, 48-50; 8, 4). Certains revisions could
have been introduced even after the translation by the Septuagint which
ignores them (for example, 3 Kgs 6, 11-14; some details in 8, 1-5).

§ 5. The Book and History

We have estimated the historical value of the sources that have been
used and the quality of the information that has been retained, especially
concerning Solomon, the schism, Achab, Jehu. We also have seen that
the author sacrifices details of the profane history for the sake of his
interest in the Temple and the prophets. His information, although
reliable, needs, therefore, to be completed. This can be done thanks to
archeological excavations and thanks to the texts of other nations with
which the two kingdoms have been in contact.

I. PARALLEL EPIGRAPHIC DOCUMENTS

We have mentioned already the stele of Mesha. [13] The expedition of the
Pharao Sesac I against Palestine, in the 5th year of Roboam (3 Kgs 14,
25-28), is also testified by a list of conquered cities, inscribed on a wall
of the temple of Amon at Karnak. Apart from this exceptional fact,
Egypt, fallen from her former power, hardly had occasion to intervene

---

[13] Cf. p. 19, n. 8.

in Palestine. Conflicts placed Israel for a long time in opposition to the kingdom of Damascus, a kingdom born in the time of Solomon which had soon become the strongest state of Syria. But the Aramean inscriptions are scarce and contribute very little to our question. Damascus, just like Israel and the other Syro-Palestinian states, had to succumb to the power which since the beginning of the 9th century extended its domination toward the Mediterranean : the new Assyrian Empire. This was to be replaced by the Babylonian Empire towards the end of the 7th century. The Assyrian, and afterwards the Babylonian, texts constitute a documentation of the greatest interest to our history. We possess lists of important personalities whose names were used to designate the years (the " eponyms "), lists of kings of Babylon, a synchronized list in two columns of the kings of Babylon and of Assyria. Different chronicles, written in the Neo-Babylonian period, summarize the great events of the Mesopotamian history by giving at times their respective dates, for example : a chronicle from 745 to 668, another from 680 to 625, one from 616 to 609 of special importance for the end of the Assyrian Empire, one finally from 626 to 593 which mentions the first siege of Jerusalem by Nabuchodonosor. [14] The royal inscriptions, above all, are rich of information fixed shortly after the events and preserved in their original form. The kings, indeed, had the account of their great deeds inscribed, and when it is a question of their campaigns against Syro-Palestine, recoupments can be made as for the biblical history. These recoupments allow to complete the data of the Bible and, above all, to determine more exactly the chronology of the royal period.

II. The Chronological Problem

The chronological framework of Kings, at first sight, seems to be very exact. Not only the duration of each reign is given, but a synchronism has been established between the parallel reigns in Israel and Juda. We read, for example : " In the 18th year of Jeroboam, Abiam began to reign over Juda; he reigned for three years in Jerusalem " (3 Kgs 15, 1-2). But these two series of dates do not agree. Their respective sums are almost equal (from the schism until the destruction of Samaria, 260 years according to the absolute dates, 258 according to the synchronisms); but as to the details we encounter notable differences : Amasias, for example, has reigned 29 years, but the synchronisms give 40 years. Numerous critics have given their preference to the absolute data and consider the synchronisms to be late and artificial. But if there are synchronized

---

[14] Cf. p. 33, n. 8.

lists of Babylonian and Assyrian kings which go back to the 12th century, why should similar lists not have been drawn up in Israel? The absolute data themselves, moreover, offer surprises : if we add them throughout an equal period in Israel and in Juda, the results differ. Thus, from the simultaneous death of Joram and Ochozias by the hand of Jehu, until the destruction of Samaria, we obtain 143 years and 7 months in Israel, 165 years in Juda. Furthermore, these numbers, neither the one nor the other, correspond to the information gathered from the Assyrian inscriptions which count 121-122 years for the same period.

These discrepancies cannot all proceed from the mistakes of the copyists. Different explanations have been proposed which do not solve all the difficulties. Several causes contributed to upset the calculations of the biblical authors. The computation which was followed was perhaps not the same in the North and in the South, and it may even have varied in the same kingdom according to different periods : were the years of the reign counted from the new year which followed the accession (the Assyrian system) or from the one which preceded it (the Egyptian system) by counting the last year of a king and the first year of his successor as one year? And was the new year celebrated in the spring (the Babylonian system and the sacerdotal calendar) or in the fall (a system also known in Israel, but from what time and until when?)? The author of Kings may have imposed on the data of his sources a computation which was not theirs and thus given them an inexact interpretation. On the other hand, we know one case of co-reign : Azarias became a leper and entrusted the administration of the kingdom to his son Joatham (4 Kgs 15, 5); other similar cases, therefore, are possible. According as the first year of a king was that of his association with the throne or that of his personal government, different chronologies resulted and numbers may have been added which partly overlap each other. Finally, we must also count with the possibility of inexactitudes in the sources; later revisions which tried to remedy a confused situation have made it even worse.

In order to establish a chronology, the historian has no other way out than to address himself first to the Assyro-Babylonian texts and establish the exact date of a certain number of events common to the Mesopotamian and Palestinian history. We may consider as accurate, with variations of one year more or less, the following dates :

— 853 : at Qarqar on the Orontes, Salmanasar III won a victory over several Syro-Palestinian kings, one of whom was " Achab of Israel. "

— 841 : the same receives tribute from Jehu. This must have been in the beginning of the reign of the latter whose date we obtain in this manner.

— 738 : Menahem pays tribute to Theglathphalasar III (cf. 4 Kgs 15,20).

— 721 : the capture of Samaria, in the beginning of the reign of Sargon II; 27,290 inhabitants were deported and replaced by people from other conquered lands, under the authority of an Assyrian governor (cf. 4 Kgs 17, 5-6; 18, 9-11, which does not mention the change of the Assyrian king between the siege by Salmanasar V and the capture of the city).

— 701 : campaign of Sennacherib in Phoenicia, Philistia and Juda (cf. 18, 13 ff.; see above).

— 610 : the last Assyrian king surrenders Harran to the Babylonians; it is in order to help him that Pharao Nechao II marches towards the north, and at Megiddo he defeats Josias who tried to hinder his passage (23, 29-30).

— 605 : Nabuchodonosor defeats Nechao II at the battle of Carchemish and becomes the king of Babylon; this is the 4th year of Joakim (Jer 25,1).

— 15th-16th of March, 597 : the first capture of Jerusalem by Nabuchodonosor.

To these certain dates we can add another, thanks to two synchronisms supplied by Josephus :

— 968 : the beginning of the construction of the Temple of Jerusalem by Solomon (cf. *SDB*, I, col. 1251).

Beginning from there, strong likelihoods recommend 932-931 as the year of Solomon's death and of the schism. Finally, the biblical chronology of the last kings of Juda seems well established (data of Kgs, Jer, Ez, the Babylonian chronicle published by Wiseman) and allows us to assign the destruction of Jerusalem and the second deportation to the year 586. In order to enrich this framework and to determine more exactly the dates of each king, the biblical numbers must be interpreted by discovering the various causes which may have created the confusion. More than once the results cannot be but approximations.

III. THE FRAMEWORK OF GENERAL HISTORY

The Assyro-Babylonian texts, precious for their chronology, also complete our information concerning the royal period, either by providing us with new elements or by restoring the general history of that part of the world which often explains biblical events. Some examples suffice. About Omri (885-874) the book reports hardly anything except that he founded the new capital, Samaria. But the importance of his work is illustrated by the fact that in the Assyrian inscriptions " son of Omri " practically signifies king of Israel, as if he had been the founder of the kingdom.

The Bible is interested in Achab (874-853) because of his relations to the prophets and the favor he accorded to the cult of Baal. But an inscription of Salmanasar III reveals the might he was able to give to his kingdom : he appears as the leader of the kings allied against Assyria which threatens Syria-Palestine; he is capable of reaching a suspension of his feuds with the Arameans and to unite his forces with those of Hadadezer of Damascus and of Irhuleni of Hamath; and for the battle at Qarqar he could muster 2,000 chariots and 10,000 infantry. The religious faults, retained by the Bible, went hand in hand, with a policy of grand style and brilliant human success. The Black Obelisk of Salmanasar III represents this king as receiving the tribute of Jehu, or of his envoy, prostrate before him (841). This is the sign that Jehu, in order to establish his power in Israel, had to renounce the foreign policy of the Omrides. He is no longer on the side of the Arameans against Assyria. Israel is left isolated. But as the Assyrian threat diminishes, the Aramean pressure rises; Jehu and his son will then have to cede much of the conquests of David (4 Kgs 10, 32-33; 12, 18; 13, 7. 22).

The inscriptions of Adad-Nirari III (809-782) bear witness to the resumption of the Assyrian wars against the West and mention the capitulation of Damascus (about 800). This circumstance and the momentary eclipse of Assyria explain the reconquest by Jeroboam II (783-743) of the territories annexed by the Arameans (4 Kgs 14, 25), as well as the renewal of a material civilization, the unfortunate moral and religious consequences of which will be denounced by Amos and Osee. This renascence is also an advantage to the kingdom of Juda which regains its prosperity and its grandeur under the long reign of Azarias (781-740) : the first oracles of Isaias make numerous allusions to it (2, 1 ff., for example, 2, 7). This grandeur would be even more manifest, if we had to recognize Azarias in that Azriau of Yaudi whom the annals of Theglathphalasar III name as the leader of a Syrian coalition, eventually forced to pay tribute : the identification, however, remains doubtful. Theglathphalasar III (745-727) resumes the policy of conquest and begins a series of wars which will give to the Assyrian Empire its greatest extension. The history of Israel and of Juda will henceforth evolve under Assyria's impulse.

IV. Archeological excavations

The contribution of archeological excavations must also be indicated. The soil of Palestine has yielded some inscribed texts : ostraca of Samaria (beginning of the 8th century), witnesses of the centralized administration of the northern kingdom; the inscription of Ezechias, commemorating the piercing of the tunnel which connects the spring of Gihon with the pool of Shiloh (before 701); [15] above all, the 21 ostraca of Lachish, mostly letters, which reflect the history of the last months of the city and of the kingdom of Juda, prior to the victory of the Babylonians in 586. Numerous remains, moreover, of the material civilization have been brought to light. The excavations of Samaria, [16] Megiddo, Lachish, Tell Beit-Mirsim, Tell en-Nasbeh, Tell el-Far'ah give a clear image of the art of fortification, and even of a group of private houses in a city, in the time of Jeroboam II (Far'ah) or towards the end of the monarchy (Beit-Mirsim). In Tell el-Far'ah, the probable site of Thersa which had been the capital of Israel for a long time, an unfinished building seems to bear witness to the abandonment of the city by Omri when he decided to build his new capital in Samaria. In Samaria ivory carvings were found which had been used as inlays to decorate wooden furniture and which still speak of that luxury stigmatized by Amos. Finally, the destruction of numerous towns, in the territory of Juda, in the beginning of the 6th century, bear witness to the extension of the Chaldean invasion. Several cities, e.g., Lachish, were never again rebuilt. This was the end of a world, a time propitious for an examen of conscience such as the author of Kings was about to make.

§ 6. The Religious Value of the Book

The author wanted to write a religious history. He succeeded in evoking the spiritual drama which was the lot of Israel in the times of the kings. Here lies the principal interest of his book, always valuable for those who inquire about the nature and destiny of the people of God. He drew his inspiration from the Book of Deuteronomy. This point of view, indeed, is not that of Revelation which has been concluded. It showed neither the whole depth of the drama nor the religious transformations which will be mentioned afterwards. The balancesheet of Kings is provisional, if we wish to call it so, but it bears witness, nevertheless, to an authentic spiritual perspicacity and prepares some major acquisitions for the theology of the Chosen People.

The judicial examination of the kings is conducted with a vigor which justifies the final downfall of the kingdom. In the estimation of their work and their intentions the author may have overlooked certain nuances. The values brought into the discussion were for him the

---

[15] Text, p. 28.

[16] A. PARROT, *Samarie, capitale du royaume d'Israël* (Paris-Neuchâtel, 1956).

essential element : fidelity to the Covenant, belief in the one God of
Israel. In this regard the monarchy led to a failure even more lamentable
than the political destruction. The difficulty for the kingdom of God
of organizing within a kingdom of this world constituted the drama.
Since the time of Saul this presentiment persisted. But the experiment
had to be made so that it would contribute to an awareness of the true
attributes of the kingdom of God. The author of Kings does not renounce
the idea of a politico-religious kingdom. He considers it possible and
proposes as an example some good kings : David, Ezechias, Josias. He
affirms the permanence of the promises, a permanence already verified
by that of the Davidic dynasty. His Messianic faith passes through
the image of a king totally devoted to the service of God; the liberation
of Joachin, narrated at the end of the book, shows him that the thread
of the hope has not been broken.

Other disappointments, after the Exile, were needed in order that
the portrait of the Messias would grow more refined and would eventually
reveal its definitive traits in Jesus Christ. For a long time David had
been for one people the most expressive approximation of His expectation.
Solomon himself contributed to conceive the idea of Messianic justice
and peace (Ps 72). But someone reserved for himself the right of pointing
out, one day, the distances between the symbols and the mystery.
" Consider the lilies of the field.... I tell you, even Solomon in all his
glory was not arrayed like one of these " (Mt 6, 28-29). And again :
" The queen of the South came from the end of the earth to hear the
wisdom of Solomon : someone greater than Solomon is here " (Mt 12, 42).

By manifesting the judgment which history had pronounced on the
monarchy, the author of Kgs made himself the echo of the prophets.
He assigns to them an important place in his book by showing, as they
had done, that the action of God mingles with that of men. The incidental
events are subject to a superior plan in which the intentions of God
surpass the interests of this world : we always need to be told this. We
may regret the absence in our book of Amos, Osee, Jeremias and Ezechiel.
But our author profited by their teaching, and his book cannot but
support their criticism of the idea of Covenant.

At one time, Israel could enjoy political independence, and the
Davidic success aided in nationalizing the Covenant : God was then
with David executing His designs for Israel and favoring him against
all his enemies. Soon, however, Israel, just as the other Syro-Palestinian
States, was grappling with the forces which surpassed it and to which
it had to submit. The people still anticipated a miracle by which God
would manifest His power in their favor. But the prophets of the 8th and

7th centuries, on the contrary, proclaimed that God was about to judge His people, that He dominated all the nations, that the Assyrian and the Babylonian were instruments in His hands (cf. Is 10, 5; Jer 27, 6). If God had allied Himself with Israel, Israel would have to lend itself to the realization of God's designs for the whole universe.

By justifying the destruction of Samaria and afterwards of Jerusalem, the Book of Kings underlines the conditions of a divine Covenant. God is not bound by the concepts, all too narrow and superficial, which man conceives with regard to His gifts. Jeremias announced a new Covenant, sealed into the hearts. It cannot be said whether our author thinks likewise. But his insistence on the moral and religious content of the Covenant goes in the same direction. By setting up the prophets against the kings and against the false security built upon the divine promises, he helps to refine the idea of the Chosen People and to detach it from the nation as such in order to apply it to the community of the faithful. He is interested in the confraternities of prophets about whom it has been written that they marked " an important turningpoint in the history of religion : the emergence of a religious and spiritual society distinct from the national one " (Buchanan Gray). He maintains that around Elias " 7,000 men remain " who have not bent their knees to Baal (3 Kgs 19, 18). This is already the " small remnant " which the great prophets try to muster, a prefiguration of the Church of the later times (Rom 11, 4).

The Book of the Kings, through its ideal of a people faithful to the one God, worshiped in one Temple, prepares, in its way, that Church. The monopoly of the sanctuary in Jerusalem seems to him to be the best means of keeping the Mosaic faith intact. Without doubt, he was right : experience had shown that the cult practiced in the provincial sanctuaries was liable to be confused with the Chanaanite cults. Besides, at an hour when the political unity, already broken, seemed to disintegrate completely, the centralization of the cult in Jerusalem was meant to effect the regroupment of Israel around its religious faith : one God, one Temple, one People favored by the presence of its God. Deuteronomy and Kings prepare the postexilic Jewish community, a spiritual rather than an ethnic community, of those who from the dispersion will be united by their faith and their attachment to Sion.

In order to realize the ideal of the book, it is significant that together with the other sanctuaries also the Temple of Jerusalem had to be destroyed. After the Exile it will be restored. And in order that the sign of the Temple appear in full light, also the second Temple in turn will have to be destroyed. The Temple, symbol of the dwelling of God

in the midst of His people, will disappear when Jesus Christ, the Word
of God, will have come to dwell amongst us (Jn 1, 14). In the meantime
the Deuteronomical reform was necessary; a house of stone, unique as
the people whose glory it constituted, had to exist in order that one day
the word could be said : " I tell you, something greater than the Temple
s here " (Mt 12, 6).

PART III

THE LATTER PROPHETS

by A. Gelin

CHAPTER I

THE PROPHETS

BIBLIOGRAPHY

See the bibliography cited on pp. 5 f.

A. CONDAMIN, " Prophétisme israélite, " *Dict. apologétique de la foi cath.*, IV (1922), cols. 386-425.

E. TOBAC—J. COPPENS, *Les prophètes d'Israël*, I : *Le prophétisme en Israël. Les prophètes orateurs** (Malines, 1932).

A. GUILLAUME, *Prophecy and Divination among the Hebrews and other Semites* (1938).

J. HYATT, *Prophetic Religion* (New York : Abingdon, 1947).

M. BUBER, *The Prophetic Faith* (New York : Harper, 1949).

H. ROWLEY, *The Servant of the Lord and Other Essays* (London : Oxford, 1952).

A. C. WELCH, *Prophet and Priest in Old Israel*[2] (Oxford, 1953).

G. RINALDI, " Introduzione generale ai profeti, " *I profeti minori* (Turin, 1953), pp. 3-120.

J. CHAINE, *God's Heralds* (New York : Wagner, 1955).

A. NEHER, *L'essence du prophétisme* (Paris, 1955).

E. VOEGLIN, *Israel and Revelation* (Baton Rouge : Louisiana State Univ., 1956).

S. MOWINCKEL, *Prophecy and Tradition* (Oxford : Blackwell, 1958).

B. D. NAPIER, " Prophet, " *IDB*, III, pp. 896-919.

C. KUHL, *The Prophets of Israel* (Edinburgh : Oliver and Boyd, 1960).

J. DHEILLY, *The Prophets** (London : Burns and Oates, 1960).

E. W. HEATON, *The Old Testament Prophets* (Baltimore : Penguin, 1961), rev. ed.

O. EISSFELDT, " The Prophetic Literature, " *OTMS*, pp. 115-161.

J. SKINNER, *Prophecy and Religion*[4] (New York : Cambridge, 1961).

B. VAWTER, *The Conscience of Israel** (New York : Sheed and Ward, 1961).

A. HESCHEL, *The Prophets* (New York : Harper, 1962).

A. R. JOHNSON, *The Cultic Prophet in Ancient Israel*[2] (Cardiff : Univ. of Wales, 1962).

B. Anderson—W. Harrelson, (eds), *Israel's Prophetic Heritage* (New York : Harper, 1962).

C. F. Whitley, *The Prophetic Achievement* (Leyden : Brill, 1963).

H. Rowley, *Men of God, Studies in Old Testament Prophecy* (New York : Nelson, 1963).

J. Lindblom, *Prophecy in Ancient Israel* (Philadelphia : Fortress, 1964).

R. Clements, *Prophecy and Covenant* (London : SCM, 1965).

§ 1. Historical Considerations

I. Important terms

In Hebrew the ordinary word for prophet is *nabî'* which is a nominal form of the *qatîl* type where are ordinarily found adjectives with a passive sense : *mashîah* (anointed), *nazîr* (consecrated), *'anî* (poor).

The etymology of the word is uncertain. Some connect it with an archaic root related to *nb'* (to bubble forth noisily, to be interiorly agitated). The word would then denote the state of prophetic ecstasy. If this is the true etymology, the word, though first used of members of fanatical religious groups, modified its denotation and came to be used of the prophets in the classic sense (Tobac). Jepsen,[1] on the other hand, regards the idea of ecstasy as superimposed on the more original sense, to proclaim. Thus the prophet is one who speaks with vehemence under the influence of some superior force and makes known things hidden from men. Others relate the word to a root *nb'* (to speak), no longer used in extant Hebrew literature but evidenced in related Semitic languages. *Nabî'* is then " a speaker " (Jer 15, 19) or better " one who has been made a speaker " (by the divinity) (Desnoyers). It is difficult to choose between these two hypotheses. There are texts where the term denotes only " a spokesman " (Ex 4, 17 and 7, 1) and other texts where it denotes only the ecstatic delirium of a person under the control of an exterior force (3 Kgs 18, 28-29). Albright[2] suggests a third explanation, at once simpler and more plausible. He connects *nabî'* to the Akkadian *nabû* which from the middle of the third to the middle of the first millennium denoted " to call. " A *nabî'* is then " one called (by God). "

---

[1] A. Jepsen, *Nabi'* : *Soziologische Studien zur alttestamentlichen Literatur-und Religionsgeschichte* (Munich, 1934).

[2] W. F. Albright, *From the Stone Age to Christianity* (Baltimore, 1946), pp. 231-232.

In addition to the term *nabî'*, other related terms were also in use. *Rô'eh* (seer) was common in the time of Samuel who was the greatest of the seers. The term was regarded as archaic by the gloss of 1 Sm 9, 9. More frequently and in parallel with the preceding (Is 30, 10) the title *hôzeh* is found. This is also used in parallel with *nabî'* (Am 7, 12; Mi 3, 6-7). The same is true of *hôlem* (dreamer) Dt 13, 2). Nm 12, 6 (E) clearly shows these terms to be synonyms. The usage is quite literary in an age when all the terms had become clichés. But the gloss of 1 Sm 9, 9 poses a fundamental problem, the nature of the relationship between ancient seer and prophet [3] and further the nature of the relation between fanatical nabi and prophet. It is important to study the history of the question.

The Septuagint in translating *nabî'* carefully avoids the word μάντις (one possessed). Teresias and Cassandra were μάντεις. For the inspired man of the Bible the title προφήτης is reserved. Generally *rô'eh* and *hôzeh* are rendered by ὁρῶν or βλέπων. For the seer of lower rank (*qôsem*), regarded with disdain in the Bible, the term μάντις is used.

The particle " pro " in the Greek word " prophet " is not the temporal " pro " (to foretell) but rather the " pro " of substitution (to speak for; on the analogy of προστάτης). Thus the prophet is the spokesman or herald of someone. Condamin regards " pro " as having a local sense. The prophet is one who speaks before (a crowd), the one who proclaims, who announces. E. Fascher [4] has shown that this is the only possible etymology.

II. HISTORY OF THE PROPHETIC MOVEMENT

Origins of the movement

Though it is remarkable that the equivalent of *nabî'* has not yet turned up in Semitic texts, it is more important to pass beyond this discussion of terminology and examine the concept involved.

In Mesopotamia the seer's office seems to have been a state institution. But among these diviners, as is evident from the royal archives of Mari, there was in the time of Hammurabi a type of seer *(mahhu)* who without recourse to any divining technique presented to King Zimri-Lim oracles of the god Hadad. Here the divine intervention is closely associated

---

[3] H. JUNKER, *Prophet und Seher in Israel** (Bonn, 1927).

[4] *Prophètes : Eine sprach-und religionsgeschichtliche [Untersuchung* (Giessen, 1927).

with the ideas of election and alliance. [5] The Phoenician—Chanaanite texts of Ras-Shamra show ecstatic and oracular elements in the cult. The stele of Zakir, king of Hamat, (8th cent.) seems to present the seer's office as bound to an official sanctuary. The seer's office at Byblos (11th cent.) as presented by Wen-Amon is a royal institution. Thus prophecy in the Near East is seen to be closely connected with royal temples and practiced in the service of the king. It has both ecstatic and rational elements. [6]

---

[5] A. NEHER, *op. cit.*, pp. 24-29.

The following is a letter sent by some important official to Zimri-Lim, king of Mari. Actually the name of the addressee is lost, but it can be inferred with confidence. In the text there is an oracle delivered by a seer (literally, " one who answers " : *apilu* and not *mahhu*).

" ...In oracles Adad, Lord of Kallassu, has spoken : ' Didn't I, Adad, Lord of Kallassu, raise him on my knees and establish him on the throne of his father's house? Since establishing him on the throne of his father's house, I have given him a place of residence. Now, just as I established him on the throne of his father's house, I can deliver into his land Nihlatum. If he does not do (what is right), I am the master of the throne, territory and city. From those to whom I have given them I can take them away. But if he does (what is right) according to my desire, I will give him thrones upon thrones, houses upon houses, territories upon territories, cities upon cities and I will give him the land from the east to the west. ' That is what the seers who give oracles have said. Now the seer of Adad who is Lord of Kallassu watches over the region of Alahtum on the subject of Nihlatum. I want my Lord to know this. Previously when I was at Mari, I made known to my lord every word that the male and female seers said. Now that I am in another land, I will certainly continue to write to my lord what I hear and what I am told. If some misfortune occurs in the future, will not my lord ask : ' Why didn't you tell me what the seer who watches over the land said?' For this reason I write to my lord today. I want my lord to know this. " (Cf. A. Lods, in *Studies in O. T. Prophecy*, presented to T. H. Robinson, pp. 103-110.)

[6] Stele of Zakir (front) :

The stele which Zakir, king of Hamat and Lu'ash, has set up in honor of Iluwer, [his god]. I am Zakir, king of Hamat and Lu'ash. I was a man of no importance but Baal-Shamin [helped] me and remained with me. And Baal-Sham[in] made me king [of Ha]zrak. And Bar-Hadad, son of Hazael, king of Aram, formed a coalition against me of s[even (of a group) of] ten kings : Bar-Hadad and his army, Bar-Gush and his army, [the king] of Qoue and his army, the king of Oumq and his army, the king of Gourgou[m and his ar]my, the king of Sam' al and his army, the king of Miliz [and his a]r[my. These are the kings whom Bar-Hadad united against me]. There were sev[en kings] and their armies. All these kings planned a siege against Haz[rak, and] they set up a wall higher than the wall of Hazrak and they dug a ditch deeper than [its] d[itch]. I raised my hands to Baal-Shamin and Baal-Shamin heard me and spoke to me through seers *(hazeyin)* and diviners *('adedin)* [and] Baal-Shamin [said to me] : " Do not fear for I have made you king and I will be with you and I will deliver you from all [these] kin[gs who] have brought this siege

These facts indicate that prophecy in Israel is not to be derived simply from that ecstatic type attested to at the time of the Israelite entrance into Chanaan.

In the 9th century there appears a sort of " Hebrew Franciscanism " (Ricciotti). This was an epoch of crisis, discord among the tribes and danger from the Philistines. Groups of nabis were the resistance to every force that threatened to disintegrate the nation and cut it off from its origin (1 Sm 9—10). They associated together in bands around the sanctuaries of Yahweh. There was some organization (a leader : 1 Sm 19, 20). Perhaps they performed some role in the cult (Mowinckel, Junker). So far as can be determined the ecstasy of the nabis was a strange and irresistible frenzy that, as it were, carried a man out of himself. Under this influence he danced or sometimes walked stiffly and with jerks, rhythmically swung his body, sang and shouted. The sense of these songs and shouts was, perhaps, sometimes mysterious. There was on occasion wild gesticulating with the hands. Sometimes the nabis went about naked (1 Sm 19, 24). [7] Music with a pronounced rhythm helped to induce this ecstatic state though it was attributed to the coming of a " spirit " sent by Yahweh. The phenomenon was contagious (1 Sm 10, 5-6).

In many ways these groups of prophets resemble similar Phoenician-Chanaanite groups [8] described in biblical (3 Kgs 18) and other documents. But the resemblance is a surface resemblance. The religion of Yahweh has used for its own purposes this charismatic, Chanaanite institution. The nabis were in fact pillars of Chanaanite opposition. Like the Nazirites (Am 2, 11) and the Rechabites (Jer 35) they were a force that worked for the preservation and spread of the true religion. It is this that gives value to their activity. It is hard to say whether the prophets who received a personal call from God are connected with these groups, but the possibility is at least open. In any case the great prophets were sympathetic toward the work of their lowly predecessors (Am 2, 10-11; Jer 7, 25).

Prophecy in Israel

The explanation of 1 Sm 9, 9 equates seer with nabi. This perhaps indicates that, though the classic prophetic figure does show a remarkable

---

against you. " And [Baal-Shamin] said to me : " All those kings who have brough[t this siege against you, I will drive (?) them back] : and the wall which [they have built, I will destroy (?) it; and the ditch...].

[7] L. DESNOYERS, *Histoire du peuple hébreu*, t. III, p. 173.

[8] J. LINDBLOM, " Zur Frage des canaanäischen Ursprungs des altisraelitischen Prophetismus, " *Fest. Eissfeldt* (Berlin, 1958), pp. 89-104.

spiritual development, he is still the heir of the tradition of the seers. See, for example, the Samuel of the J-source (1 Sm 9, 7) who can be consulted about petty questions and accepts pay; or Ahias of Silo whom the wife of Jeroboam I consults about a domestic affair (3 Kgs 14, 1-16). Samuel marks a turning point. The most ancient source of his history presents him as more than a diviner. He is the pillar of the true religion of Yahweh and the founder of the royal theocracy. He it is who begins the line of the great prophets. [9]

What are these prophets? The " disturbers of Israel " (Darmesteter), the spiritual guides of the theocracy, the defenders of the covenant, the founders of the new Israel. Inspired men with a message *(dabar)*, men of spirit *(ruah)*, men ahead of their own time, they proclaim the religion of tomorrow and relate it to the religion of yesterday. They are the confidants and spokesmen of a God who reveals Himself in history. They are attuned to all the interests of the living God and have a horror of any sort of politics or casuistry that might attenuate His word. The understanding of their message was favored by the historical disorders and the climate of catastrophe in which they preached. Their work is the heart of the Old Testament.

There were prophets who preached and prophets who wrote, but the appearance of these writing prophets in the 8th century does not change the character of the movement. Their writings were only an extension of their preaching. After Amos prophets continued to appear who only preached : Jonas (4 Kgs 14, 25), Urias (Jer 26, 20-23), Holda (4 Kgs 22, 14-20).

From Samuel to Amos

It is only possible to outline the history of the prophetic movement from Samuel to Amos. David relied on two successors of Samuel; Nathan (2 Sm 7, 1-17; 12, 1-15; 3 Kgs 1—2) and Gad, who were proponents of the theocracy. Under Solomon an anti-government faction which is represented by Ahias of Silo who announced the schism of 931 (3 Kgs 11, 29-39) arose among the prophets. In their many interventions in the affairs of both kingdoms a single motive is evident. The prophets wish to maintain the old, characteristic values of the amphictyony, justice which was threatened by the royal civilization, peace which was destroyed by the division of the kingdom, the simplicity of the traditional ritual and religious unity. Ahias condemns the house of Jeroboam for its cultic innovations (3 Kgs 14, 1-19). Semeias prevents Roboam (931-913) from reconquering the northern kingdom (3 Kgs 12, 21-24).

---

[9] Some of the prophecies of Jgs 6, 7-10 and 1 Sm 2, 27-36 are later insertions.

Thus while confirming the division of the nation he calls for friendly relations between the two kingdoms. Under Jeroboam again, an anonymous prophet goes to curse the altar at Bethel (3 Kgs 13, 11-32). In the northern kingdom Jehu ben Hanani announces the end of the usurper Baasa (3 Kgs 16, 1-4. 7-13).

The dynasty of Omri (885-841) is very important for the history of the prophetic movement. It marks the beginning of the period of the great prophets. Their religious and political activity increases (3 Kgs 20, 13 ff. 28. 35 ff.). Micheas ben Jemla opposes the professional prophets (3 Kgs 22). There also appear groups of prophets, the so-called " sons of the prophets " who seem to be quite different from the ecstatic bands of the time of Samuel. These groups, whose behavior is more sober and whose organization is more definite, are located at Bethel, Jericho and Galgal. Their life is to some extent communal (4 Kgs 2; 4, 38-41; 6, 1-7) though they did marry (4 Kgs 4, 1). Some are young (4 Kgs 5, 22; 9, 4). They lived poorly (4 Kgs 4, 8; 8, 26-27; 6, 5). Their organizations were spontaneously formed to defend the religion of Yahweh against the worship of Baal which was introduced for political purposes. Among them ecstatic phenomena are not conspicuous. Elias, the defender of Yahweh, unites his own cause to that of these prophets (3 Kgs 18, 18-22; 19, 10-14). Eliseus associates with them and uses them. But neither seems to have been a member of these associations. Elias comes from Transjordan and Eliseus inherits the spirit of Elias (4 Kgs 2, 15).

The vocation of Elias was to defend the religion of Yahweh, its exclusiveness and its moral demands, against the danger of subversion by the nature religion which came to the fore with the introduction of the god Melkart from Tyre. Elias is the herald of a religious awakening in part inspired by the desert where he goes to relive the experience of Moses (3 Kgs 19, 1-18). His defense of the social order (e.g., the case of Naboth : 3 Kgs 21), his interference in the political order against both Achab and Jezabel, the threats he pronounces against the people, all spring from his loyalty to Yahweh. This powerful and solitary personality (3 Kgs 19, 10) " is an outstanding figure in the history of Israel, the most important since the period of Moses " (Jack). His political and religious work is completed by his disciple who together with the Rechabites supports the bloody revolution of Jehu who puts an end to the line of Omri (4 Kgs 10).

Thus a century before the period of the writing prophets their essential characteristics are already clear. A few further remarks will serve to situate them more precisely in the history of Israel.

III. PROPHETS AND PROPHETS

Side by side with these prophets of Yahweh there are official, institutional prophets. Prophets accompany the king when he travels (3 Kgs 22). They recite at Temple ceremonies their oracles of victory (Ps 60). They are one of the groups that make up the nation (Jer 18, 18; 4 Kgs 23, 2). They deliver oracles in the Temple (Jer 28; Neh 6, 12) where a priest was especially charged with overseeing their activities (Jer 29, 26). Their spiritual level is not necessarily low. They are open to both religious and political influences, but they are very much inclined by their position to identify Yahweh's interests with those of the king. As a result, the vocational prophets often oppose them (Am 7, 14; Micheas, Isaias, Jeremias, Ezechiel). Finally Za 13, 1-6 announces their disappearance. The rules for the discernment of spirits as given in Dt 13, 1-6; 18, 15-22 have them in view, but to regard them indiscriminately as false prophets would be an exaggerated view. The origin of the institution is obscure. Are these prophets Israel's counterpart of the divining prophets who are regular court officials in Semitic civilizations (Jer 27, 9; stele of Zakir, Mari texts)? Are they a continuation of the ecstatic nabis whose cultic character Mowinckel emphasizes? Do they belong to the cult guilds from which many of the great prophets came, as the Scandinavian school would have it? The lack of a clear answer to all these questions underlines the ambiguity of the problem.

On the other hand, the influence of the great prophets to some extent was due to these groups. We have already seen the " sons of the prophets " who were the companions of Eliseus (4 Kgs 2, 15; 4, 38; 9, 1-3). Is 8, 16 shows that Isaias gathered around himself a group of disciples. Within these groups the ideas of the prophets were conserved and developed. They are responsible for the publication of their prophecies. Within this framework the nature of the school of Isaias is easily understood. Finally it can be asked whether the concept of a continuous line of prophets is merely an artificial construction. It is true that the prophets frequently refer to their predecessors (Jer 7, 13-25; Za 7, 7) and use their prophecies. It is true that Osee and Micheas lead us back to Moses and the Sinai Covenant which gave the Israelite religion its dominant characteristics, worship of a personal God, exclusiveness, and ethical demands. This transcendence of the religion of Yahweh is the key fact underlying the existence of the prophets and the Elohist has brought their history right down to the very beginnings of the Chosen People. In fact the term *nabi'* was such that Abraham (Gn 20, 7 : E), the patriarchs (Ps 104. 105), the pagan Balaam

(Nm 22—24 : E) and especially Moses, the prophetic prototype (Dt 34, 10-12; Ex 12, 2 : E), all received this title. But it is only with the occupation of Chanaan thatthe prophet is considered a permanent institution (Dt 18, 9-22). From this point on the continuity of the prophetic line is so certain that in Second-Isaias the prophet can become a Messianic figure.

§ 2. The Psychological Problem

I. WERE THE GREAT PROPHETS ECSTATIC?

What has already been said has in fact been written to show the inadequacy of the views of some of the older critics on the development of prophecy in Israel. For some time the view most in favor was that of G. Hölscher [10] who postulated the chronological sequence : seer, nabi, prophet. The original seers of Israel would have been replaced by nabis, supposedly of Asian or Syrian origin. From this group the prophets sprang. Like the nabis they were ecstatic. According to Gunkel, " ecstasy is the basic experience of all prophecy. " By ecstasy is meant " an exaltation of the emotions together with other secondary phenomena " (Hölscher).

In this way the historical problem moves to the level of psychology. But at the same time it must be said that the word *ecstasy* is difficult to define. The problem of whether or not the great prophets were ecstatic is one that has been discussed from antiquity. Philo thought they were. Josephus denied it. The Montanists defended the absolute passivity of the prophets and some Fathers of the Church compared them to lyres plucked by the divine plectrum, or flutes which the Holy Spirit used to produce whichever sounds He would. [11]

On the other hand exegetes of the liberal school viewed the prophets as religious thinkers. Their thought processes proceeded in a rational manner and among them ecstasy played a purely secondary role. When they presented their teaching as revelations received in visions, they were adapting themselves to a kind of literary convention (Kuenen, Renan).

Some recent historians of religion have compared the inspiration of the prophets to ecstatic phenomena known among ancient peoples and have examined it from the viewpoint of modern psychiatry, e.g.,

---

[10] *Die Propheten, Untersuchungen zur Religiongeschichte Israels* (Leipzig, 1914); see A. LODS, " Recherches récentes sur le prophétisme israélite, " *RHR*, CIV (1931), pp. 279-295.

[11] P. DE LABRIOLLE, *La crise montaniste* (Paris, 1913), pp. 558-561.

G. Hölscher, [12] H. Gunkel, [13] and the physician W. Jacobi. [14] According to Hölscher the characteristic traits of the prophets are the following : violent agitation (Ez 6, 11; 21, 19); loss of physical power as evidenced by attacks of aphasia (Ez 3, 15. 25; 24, 27); paralysis (Ez 3, 25-26) or muscular spasms (Ez 9, 8; 11, 13); inability to feel wounds (Za 13, 6); loss of personality insofar as the prophet speaks as if he were God Himself; " ecstatic actions " that are both reflex and impulsive (Ez 4, 1-3, etc.); impulsive, short sayings; speaking strange languages (Is 28, 9-10); visual, audile (Ez 3, 16) and tactile hallucinations (Is 6, 6-7); the malperception of true sense data (Isaias during his inaugural vision in the Temple misinterprets true sense perceptions); ecstasy induced by suggestion (4 Kgs 6, 17) or autosuggestion (3 Kgs 3, 15).

A strong reaction against interpreting prophetic ecstasy on the basis of these secondary characteristics has set in during the last thirty years. This is illustrated by J. Fohrer's study (1952) of the ecstatic character of Ezechiel and J. Lindblom's study (1927) of the same phenomenon in Osee.

In sum the ecstasy theory is explained in different ways. According to one view it is a pathological condition. With this view we do not have to concern ourselves, for pseudoecstasy of this type is hardly an explanation of the problem in hand. The second theory speaks of ecstasy in the Neo-Platonic sense, a loss of personality through absorption in God. The third theory speaks of " concentration ecstasy " in which the prophet by focusing his attention on a single object would lose normal awareness and the functioning of the external senses.

The second theory is no explanation in the case of the great prophets. Absorption in God is a Greek rather than Semitic idea. From the Semitic point of view God is completely inaccessible. The prophet for his part makes no attempt to lose himself in God but is rather very much involved in the politics and social problems of the day. From his point of view it is his message *(dabar)* that makes him what he is. According to Causse, [15] ecstasy is not the central fact in the religious life of the prophet. " It is only the historical (?) point of departure. In the case of the great prophets it is something left over from another age. The prophets and their contemporaries could attach to it greater or lesser significance, but

---

[12] G. Hölscher, *Die Propheten : Untersuchungen zur Religiongeschichte Israels* (Leipzig, 1914).

[13] H. Gunkel, *Die Propheten* (Göttingen, 1917).

[14] W. Jacobi, *Die Ekstase der alttestamentlichen Propheten* (Munich, 1920).

[15] *RHPR* (1922), p. 354.

it remains a secondary phenomenon. " A. Lods, one of the more determined proponents of the theory, himself recognizes that it does not
account for all the facts. For him, prophetic inspiration is rather akin
to the inspiration of a poet or an artist. He offers as a comparison the
coexistence in St. Paul of the gift of tongues and a profound spiritual
life. This participation of the prophets in some of the ecstatic phenomena
of their age is one aspect of their work, but it does not explain this work
in its essence.

II. The experience of the prophet

The prophet's own explanation

One of the prophets, Jeremias, has analyzed the prophetic experience
with a precision quite remarkable for a Semite. Upon weak and fearful
man is superimposed God's majestic power. The divine revelation is an
irresistible force (Jer 20, 7. 9; Am 3, 3-8). It is accompanied by a certitude
which cannot be shaken even by the threat of death (Jer 26, 12 ff.).
Such an experience presupposes a profound intimacy between God and
the prophet. " Since both true and false prophets show signs of psychological abnormality and since both groups forecast future events, prophecy
cannot be defined in terms of these phenomena. The essential point is the
relation of the prophet and his message to God. A prophet is a man who
has known God in the immediacy of personal experience and feels himself
obliged to make known what he firmly believes is God's word. His
message is fundamentally a revelation of the nature and the will of God.
He has seen the inevitable end of this life. He makes it known to men
with the hope that they will avoid it by purifying themselves and ordering
their lives. He is a true prophet to the extent that he has experienced
God and the measure of that experience is his own receptivity and
response. " (H. H. Rowley). In short the prophets are mystics,
constructive mystics, to use the phrase of H. Delacroix.

The sense of the phrase : " Thus says Yahweh "

The whole of the prophets' lives was not filled with those awesome
events—" the abnormal element of prophetic experience " as Robinson
has called them—which occurred at their inaugural visions and were
renewed at key points in their careers. " The visions, the voices, the
interior compulsion to speak and act are always a part of the prophetic
experience, but the divine revelation is not limited to these events.
The significance of a vision makes itself a part of the thinking of the
prophet and becomes the basis for an understanding of God and the

world from which arise further new intuitions of truth and directives for action. " With these words Skinner [16] helps us to understand the sense of the affirmations which open and close the oracles of the prophets. The ancients viewed those full-blown ideas which a man conceives almost effortlessly on occasion as the gift of an exterior force rather than the fruit of slow maturation of thought. What is true of the moralists (Jb 4, 12-17; 32, 18-19; Sir 24, 31) is with all the more reason true of the prophets. Thus it is easy to see in the continual *Kô 'âmar Yahweh* of the prophets a legitimate conclusion based on their first call. [17]

The two criteria of a true prophet

It is important to note that the formula, " Thus says Yahweh, " was used by both the prophets and those who have been customarily called false prophets. Jer 28 illustrates the point well. Hananias was a prophet of Yahweh, but his conception of the Covenant was quite mechanical and materialistic. The contradiction contained in the " Thus says Yahweh " with which both he and Jeremias introduce their messages could hardly have clarified the situation for the people. For this reason Jeremias appeals to two criteria which can show the authenticity of his mission. The first is the occurrence of the events predicted (28, 15-17); the second, the conformity of the message to traditional teaching. When he says that the true prophet predicts disasters, Jeremias implicitly refers to the fact of sin, the cause of these disasters, which was always a major concern of the message of the prophets from the time of Samuel, Elias and Amos.

Deuteronomy had already presented the two criteria to which Jeremias appeals. The first, realization of the prophecies, is referred to in 18, 15-22. Since the prophets often predicted what would occur in the distant future, they had also to predict events which would shortly come to term and thus confirm their mission (Jer 28, 15-17; and doubtlessly 20, 6; 29, 32; 44, 29-30; 45, 5). The second and more important criterion was the life and message of the prophet. These had to be in accord with the traditional religion of Yahweh. In this regard the maxim of Augustine comes to mind : " Separated from the Church even the miracle-worker is nothing. " [18] As Pascal similarly observes, " Doctrine distinguishes the true miracle. "

---

[16] *Prophecy and Religion, Studies in the Life of Jeremiah* (1922), p. 220.

[17] H. W. Robinson, in *ZAW* (1923), pp. 1-15.

[18] *PL* 35, 151.

§ 3. Literary Considerations

I. The literary genres of prophecy

The prophets used several literary forms : exhortation, parable, vision, narrative, dialogue, oracle, *torah*, wisdom saying, song, prayer, " confession, " letter, hymn. It is all but impossible to find these forms in their pure state, and this is so even in the case of Amos, the first of the writing prophets. For our purposes it is sufficient to distinguish oracle, exhortation and several other genres.

The oracle

The oracle is a solemn declaration made in the name of God. In this general sense the legal decisions of the priests can be classified as oracles. Among the prophets an oracle is rather the prediction of blessing or misfortune which will occur in the proximate or distant future (Jer 19, 11; 28, 16). It is generally thought that these predictions are rather short (Gressmann, Hempel). Gressmann finds 30 such units in the Book of Amos; Kohler, 56. Recently Lindblom [19] has challenged this view. He uses as a comparison the " literature of revelation " (e.g., Bridget of Sweden) and concludes that the lack of continuity in the prophets does not indicate that the books are to be divided in this way.

Generally oracles are marked out by the use of introductory and concluding formulae. *Kô âmar Yahweh* calls to mind similar formulae used in the ancient Orient for pronouncements thought to have been made by gods (at Mari the divine word is introduced by *kiam iqbi /m*) [20] or for royal pronouncements(4 Kgs 18, 19). The same type of formula is also used for letters. The content of a letter was confided to a messenger who would then proceed to deliver the message. This is the idea behind the " And you will say " of Jer 8, 4. A letter of Taanach begins, " To Rewashsha say : Thus (says) Guli-Adad. " [21] The conclusion of the oracle is often marked by the words *Ne 'um Yahweh* (oracle of Yahweh). The term *massa* is used for an oracle that contains a threat. Jer 23, 33 shows that the use of the term is ancient.

The oracular pronouncement generally includes an explanation of its motivation. In this is revealed the essential character of the religion of Yahweh. The explanation precedes the oracle in the case of an oracle of woe (Os 9, 10-12; 12, 12). It follows when there is a question of an oracle of good fortune. In this latter case by its position the

---

[19] *Die literarische Gattung der prophetischen Literatur*, 1924.

[20] Cf. *Rev. d'Assyr.* (1948), p. 129.

[21] Pritchard, *ANET*, p. 490.

explanation centers the attention on the guarantee that what has been said will happen (Os 11, 9).

The exhortation

The exhortation according to modern critics (Hempel) is a secondary genre in relation to the preceding, but this is a question only of prehistory. Already in Amos the genre is present. The tone of the genre is that of the preacher striving to convince. For example, " Hear the word of the Lord... " (Jer 7, 2). It affirms that it is possible to avoid evil, to do what is good. It makes appeal to the emotions. This latter characteristic is very evident in Osee. Finally a formal distinction between prophetic exhortation and the priestly sermon (e.g., the sermons of Deuteronomy) is difficult to establish.

Other genres

Besides the two basic prophetic forms that have just been mentioned, there are *autobiographical accounts (Ich-Berichten)* in which the prophets describe their initial experiences or the more important events in their careers. This genre is ancient and turns up even in the accounts of Micheas ben Jemla (3 Kgs 22, 17-21). With the advent of apocalyptic literature the form becomes a literary device. *Descriptions*, especially of visions and dreams, assume an increasingly important position in prophetic writings starting with the Exile (Ezechiel, Zacharias). This form likewise becomes a fixed convention in apocalyptic literature. *Lyrics*, especially those modeled on the psalms of repentance (Os 6, 1 f.; Jer 14) and hymns (Second-Isaias), show the relation between the prophets and public worship. *Wisdom discourses* are also to be found (Jer 17, 5-11; Ag 2, 15-19). The *monologues* of Jeremias which bring to mind the " Confessions " of St. Augustine are modeled on the psalms of lamentation.

Symbolic actions [22]

The prophets customarily used symbolic actions. These should not be evaluated from a Western point of view if they are to be properly understood. The prophet wants to present his teaching to the public forcefully and to attract to it as much attention as possible. Jesus Himself uses the same technique when He curses the fig tree on the eve of His Passion (Mk 11, 12-14). That this is the correct interpretation to be given to these symbolic actions is clearly seen in the case of Jeremias' broken pitcher (19, 1-13). The mind of the Semite delights in such symbols. See, for example, Ahias tearing his new mantle (3 Kgs 11,

---

[22] G. FOHRER, *Die symbolischen Mandlungen der Propheten* (Zurich, 1953).

29-39); the iron horns of Sedecias (3 Kgs 22, 10-12); Joas shooting an arrow and beating the ground (4 Kgs 13, 14-19); Nehemias shaking out his garment (Neh 5, 12-13); Agabus binding himself hand and foot (Acts 21, 10-13). In their " prehistory " these actions were probably thought to have some influence on the future like the words of blessing and cursing, but this is not the situation in the case of the great prophets.

The lives of some of the prophets become a figure and sign of the future they announce. The classic illustration is Osee's marriage. The basis of this point of view was the total dedication of the prophet's whole being to the message he bore. Thus Isaias can say : " Look at me and the children whom the Lord has given me : we are signs and portents in Israel " (8, 18).

II. PROPHETIC LITERATURE

The prophets wrote to deepen the impact of their message upon the people (Jer 36) and to guarantee that the realization of their words could later be verified (Is 30, 8). Their works circulated at first in the form of uncollected, occasional writings. Modern critics generally distinguish three stages of development : *the uncollected writings, the first collections, the book.* Generally the last two stages are dated after the death of the prophet, but the systemization is in fact too rigid. Isaias, Jeremias and Ezechiel seem themselves to have been responsible for beginning to collect their own writings.

The complex task of editing fell to the disciples of the prophets who added certain things, broke up some of the previously collected material, and gave the books a final form according to a plan which must be specifically determined in each case. Like the redactors of the Gospels, these disciples were guided in their efforts by fidelity to their masters.

In the books of the prophets three basic types of material must be distinguished : *oracles* which are bound together by the repetition of set phrases or by a unity of theme; *biography (Er-Berichten)*, e.g., Os 1 and Is 7; *autobiography (Ich-Berichten)*, e.g., Os 3 and Is 6.

All three types are present in Amos, Osee, Isaias and Jeremias. Only the first type is present in Joel, Abdias, Nahum, Sophonias and Zacharias 9—14. In Micheas and Habacuc, especially in the former, there are traces of the third type. *Ich-Bericht* is common in Ezechiel and Zacharias 1—8. The *Er-Bericht* of Aggeus is probably artificial. The prophet may have used the third person to lend objectivity and solemnity to his words. In apocalyptic literature only the last two types of material survive, especially *Ich-Berichten*.

§ 4. The Importance of the Prophets

Even unbelievers are unsparing in their admiration for the contribution that the prophets have made to human progress. There comes readily to mind Renan's idea of the three " providential " civilizations : Greece which contributed so heavily to the progress of learning; Rome which made a similar contribution to the law; and Jerusalem which assured the maturation of the human conscience and man's sense of justice. There have been many different interpretations of this last point. Some have seen in the prophets the first socialists (K. Marx, G. Le Bon); others have understood the Messianism of the prophets as a theory of progress; others regard them as the forerunners of the encyclopedists (H. Berr).

But these are hardly adequate evaluations of the prophets. To view them with proper perspective they must be located in the religious movement of which they were the soul. Any theory that separates them from this movement distorts this perspective to the extent to which it is systematically applied. The prophets are first of all witnesses to the spiritual. Their efforts in other fields (social or political) are only the natural outgrowth of their work for religious or moral reform. This is the background against which it is necessary to measure their greatness.

I. RELIGIOUS ACTIVITY

The role of the prophets in revelation

The prophets are located at the center of the Old Testament. The heirs of the religious tradition which they continue, they faithfully develop it between the 9th and the 4th century and hand it down enriched to Judaism. They live in accord with the religious ideal fixed in the time of Moses, moral monotheism, and know well how to exploit this initial revelation faithfully and creatively. They live by it in the first place for they are mystics in whom religion takes on a warmth and authenticity that had a great appeal for their contemporaries and continue to win men's hearts.

To be more precise, these heralds of the faith and men of the Spirit are completely one with the message God transmits through them. In their own lives they incarnate this message. Their preaching which is at once God's word and their own understanding of it draws out the implications of the message. Their writings read patiently and viewed against the background of Israel's difficult history mark out the progress of the true religion toward the Christian ideal.

It is admirable to think that the prophets were the witnesses and the artisans of this catechumenate of mankind, the authorized guides for this spiritual march, and that they revealed and explained the divine design in history. They take a choice place in the immense sign of credibility constituted by the Old Testament. If there ever is a wonder which remains unshakeable, it is, as Blondel stated, " the attained and preserved miraculous purity of the faith in the one Lord and Creator, the prophetic fervor in the expectation of the Messias. "

Theological content

The theology of the prophets is vast. They have given us a better understanding of God's oneness, spirituality, transcendence, omnipotence, justice, goodness, and of that omnipresence which Augustine, more learned than Jeremias, expressed in the formula, *Intimior intimo meo.* They understood the mystery of sin and grace and retribution. They developed the understanding of God as a person who relates to men on that level. They formulated the concept of the community of the saved and looked forward to its coming. Thus they wrote the prehistory of the Church. Leaving behind the errors and theological helplessness of their age they marched gropingly toward Christ, the term and consummation of all history, and caught the first glimpse of Him.

They went right to the roots of the problem of morality showing that all morality involves the heart.

> You have been told, O man, what is good,
>   and what the Lord requires of you :
> Only to do the right and to love goodness *(hesed)*,
>   and to walk humbly with your God.

These words of Micheas (6, 8) clearly present the viewpoint of the prophets. What Yahweh wants is justice (Amos), love (Osee), faith (Isaias), a change of heart (Jeremias). Thus morality becomes something internal.

The prophets inveighed against sin. Perhaps they painted too dark a picture of their contemporaries, but of this fault many preachers are guilty (Peter Damian, Savonarola). The picture is particularly black in Jeremias (13, 23) and Ezechiel, but from this starting point both these prophets went on to discover relations between the grace of God and man's moral renovation much more profound than the understanding of their predecessors. God according to Jer 24, 7; 32, 39 will give Israel a new heart (cf. Ez 36, 26 f.). The optimism of the prophets does have a supernatural basis. They were convinced that justice and morality will triumph in this world because this is God's plan and He has the power to make it succeed. They began by making this ideal a reality in their own persons.

The prophets and worship

The prophets also directed Israel away from an understanding of worship and liturgical rites that was excessively formal and legalistic. They made clear the relation of morality to worship. They did not condemn ritualism outright as the liberal school would have it (and still Skinner, 1922). Micheas 6, 8 affirms that cult is not the essential element of the true religion. If this truth is expressed quite emphatically and even somewhat paradoxically on occasion, it is necessary to keep in view the literary character of these short, pithy sayings. Even the Gospels offer examples of this type of emphatic exaggeration (Mt 5, 30; 6, 3). On the basis of this principle should be interpreted Am 5, 24-25; Jer 7, 21-23 where the reference seems to be to the giving of the Decalogue in Ex 20; Os 6, 6 :

> For it is love that I desire, not sacrifice,
> and knowledge of God rather than holocausts.

According to the Scandinavian school, which for thirty years has reacted against the liberal school, there is an intimate relation between prophets and cult. S. Mowinckel with his *Psalmenstudien*[23] was the initiator of this revolutionary view. The presence of oracles in the psalms (Ps 60, 75, 82, 110) and conversely the presence of liturgical elements in the books of the prophets (Hb 3; Jl 1—2; Os 6, 1 f; Jer 14) indicate in his opinion that the prophets belonged to cult guilds and had an established role in Temple ceremonies. Suggestive in this regard are passages like Jer 20, 1; 29, 6; 35, 4; Neh 6, 14; Za 13, 2-6. Against this background is to be understood the great interest taken in cultic matters by Aggeus, Zacharias and Joel. The predecessors of the prophets are the ecstatic *nabis* of the time of Samuel who took charge of the ancient sanctuaries; their successors are the guilds of levites described by the Chronicler. These latter in their role as *nabis* (1 Par 25, 1-3; 2 Par 20, 14 f.) betray their origin from the ancient associations of prophets. Mowinckel's idea has been taken up, not without some exaggeration, by P. Humbert who regards the Book of Habacuc as the libretto for a ceremony directed for the most part against the reigning king, Joakim, that took place in the Temple in Jerusalem about 602.[24] The school of Uppsala has systematically applied this theory. Haldar makes Amos and Nahum members of cult guilds.[25] Kapelrud does the same for

---

[23] *Kultprophetie und prophetische Psalmen*, III (Christiania, 1923).

[24] *Problèmes du livre d'Habaquq* (Neuchâtel, 1944).

[25] *Studies in the Book of Nahum* (Uppsala, 1947).

Joel. [26] I. Engnell sees in these guilds the milieu from which emerged the great prophets. In these same guilds their oracles were conserved and redacted for future generations.

This critical reaction, despite certain excesses, was healthy. Though it is difficult to connect the great prophets to cult associations, in the future it will be equally difficult to turn them into men fundamentally opposed to cult as such.

II. INTEREST IN SOCIAL PROBLEMS

If the prophets looked to the past, it was because they sought to find there the religious ideals of Israel, better preserved in the simpler society of the nation just come to be. They did not intend to revive this society. They had quite well adjusted to agricultural, urban and royal social structures. Religion accepts these structures and tries to improve on them. The prophets were social reformers because they were first of all believers. They aimed at constructing a human society worthy of God's people and to further this end they became forceful defenders of fundamental human rights. Contracts like the wage contract are to be honored. The property of the less wealthy and influential is to be protected. Government must be humane. They promoted equality and fraternity. They were revolutionaries, but their revolution was meant to reform men's hearts. Their violent words are the product of their optimism. The intemperate character of their heated and emotional preaching was born of love and showed that they did not despair of bringing their program to fruit. Living among a people that itself was turned toward the future, they looked to God to establish the society of which they dreamed. This is the basis of their optimism. They were sure God would eventually create a truly human social order in which it would be possible for God's sons to live (Za 8; Is 11, 6-9; 19, 23-25). [27]

III. POLITICAL ACTIVITY

Because Israel was a theocratic state and because of their own position in that state, it was inevitable that the prophets took an interest in the foreign policy of the nation. During the period when Israel did have the structure of a state, they were the religious counselors of the king and his functionaries. The viewpoint of the prophets was that foreign alliances were to be avoided for they could only involve Israel in dangerous

[26] *Joel Studies* (Uppsala, 1948).
[27] B. VAWTER, " De justitia sociali apud Prophetas praeexilicos*, *VD* (1958), pp. 93 ff.

international situations and wars. More immediately there was the danger of religious syncretism since such alliances were generally sealed by marriages which introduced pagan wives into the court.

The royal theocracy did not evolve in accord with the desires of the prophets. Jeremias, one of the most eminent of their number, condemned it in all its parts—the king, Jerusalem, the state, the people, the Temple. He was even considered opposed to patriotism though in this he was completely misjudged by his contemporaries. What he aimed at was the maintenance of religious values and the royal government in the course of the centuries had showed itself incapable of maintaining them. This is why the prophets attacked the monarchy and it explains why they looked forward to a future royal Messias. This is why they cooperated after the Exile in the establishment of a theocracy that was less national in structure and which was to become an important stage in Israel's becoming the kingdom of God.

IV. THE PROPHETS AND CHRIST

The prophets prepared a people for Christ and marvelously sketched His person and work. Christ Himself cannot be understood except as their successor. He was willing to be taken for one of them returned to earth (Mt 16, 14) and He made His own their attitude toward the national religion, one of loyal criticism (Sabbath, tithes, purity, law, rabbinic casuistry). He used their forceful language (Mt 23) and their methods for attracting attention (Mk 11, 13 ff.). He understood His own mission as they had described it (Lk 4, 17-21; Mt 23, 29-38). At the Transfiguration Moses and Elias appear with Him, and, as it were, represent the whole prophetic line that preceded Him. He Himself is the great prophet, the great reformer, whose message has given history its ultimate direction (Acts 3, 22-26; 7, 37). " God, who at sundry times and in divers manners spoke in times past to the fathers by the prophets, last of all in these days has spoken to us by His Son... (Heb 1, 1-2).

CHAPTER II

THE PROPHETS OF THE EIGHTH CENTURY

We begin now the study of the writing prophets who can be chronologically arranged in four groups : those of the eighth century, those of the seventh and sixth centuries, those of the Exile, and those of the Persian period. This historical approach has the advantage of bringing immediately into focus the development of the prophetic revelation referred to in the magnificent opening of the Epistle to the Hebrews. " God, who at sundry times and in divers manners spoke in times past to the fathers by the prophets...." We see again in the lives and oracles of the prophets God's patient, progressive preparation of Israel.

This type of presentation is followed by J. Chaine, *Introduction à la lecture des Prophètes** (Paris, 1932); A. Lods, *Les prophètes d'Israël et les débuts du judaïsme* (Paris, 1935); *Histoire de la littérature hébraïque et juive* (Paris, 1950). The time-honored introductions generally follow the order of the Canon.

The pertinent bibliography for each of the great prophets is found at the head of the chapters specifically devoted to them. On the other hand, commentaries on the twelve minor prophets are frequently combined in one volume. This is the case with the important works listed below :

A. VAN HOONACKER, *Les Douze Petits Prophètes** (Paris, 1908; *EB*).

F. NÖTSCHER, *Zwölf Prophetenbuch oder Kleine Propheten** (Würzburg, 1948; *EBi*).

T. H. ROBINSON—F. HORST, *Die Zwölf Kleinen Propheten*[2] (Tübingen, 1952; *HAT*).

A. WEISER—K. ELLIGER, *Das Buch der Zwölf Kleinen Propheten* (Göttingen, 1949-1951; *ATD*).

H. JUNKER—J. LIPPL—J. THEISS, *Die Zwölf Kleinen Propheten** (Münster, 1937-1938; *HSAT*).

§ 1. Amos

BIBLIOGRAPHY

For introductions, translations, commentaries, see above pp. 1 f. and 251 (E. OSTY, *BJ**; E. SELLIN, *KAT*; A. VAN HOONACKER, *EB**).

W. R. HARPER, *Amos and Hosea* (Edinburgh, 1905).

J. TOUZARD, *Le livre d'Amos** (Paris, 1909).

L. DESNOYERS, " Le prophète Amos, " *RB* (1917), pp. 218 ff.

R. GORDIS, " The Composition and Structure of Amos, " *Harvard Theological Review*, 33 (1940), pp. 239-251.

J. MORGENSTERN, *Amos Studies, I-III* (Cincinnati : Hebrew Union College, 1941).

E. WURTHWEIN, " Amos-Studien, " *ZAW* (1949-50), pp. 10-52.

A. NEHER, *Amos, contributions à l'étude du prophétisme* (Paris, 1950).

V. MAAG, *Text, Wortschatz und Begriffswelt des Buches Amos* (Leyden, 1951).

P. G. RINALDI, *Amos** (Turin, 1953).

R. S. CRIPPS, *A Critical and Exegetical Commentary on the Book of Amos* (London, 1955).

T. H. SUTCLIFFE, *The Book of Amos**² (London, 1955).

A. S. KAPELRUD, *Central Ideas in Amos* (Oslo, 1956).

N. H. SNAITH, *Amos, Hosea, and Micah* (London, 1956).

H. E. W. FOSBROKE, " The Book of Amos, " *IB* (1956).

J. D. WATTS, *Vision and Prophecy in Amos* (Leyden, 1958).

J. L. MAYS, " Words About the Words of Amos, " *Interpretation* 13 (1959), pp. 259-272.

I. THE HISTORICAL BACKGROUND

Amos prophesied in the northern kingdom during the reign of Jeroboam II (784-744). The eclipse of Egypt and the remoteness of Assur had allowed Israel to regain precedence over Damascus. The " peace of the king " prevailed and the recent victories at Lodelar and Carnaim (Am 6, 13) were remembered with satisfaction. [1]

This tranquillity under a century-old dynasty had made progress possible. Amos was very much impressed by the luxury of the buildings of Samaria, constructed of hewn stone (5, 11), decorated with ivory (3, 15), outfitted with magnificent couches for banquets. The wealthy kept summer and winter houses (3, 15). Anointed with perfume, they dined sumptuously as they listened to the music of the harp (6, 4-6). All these things shocked the prophet who was after all a country peasant come to the city on God's mission. He was all the more appalled to find beneath all these trappings of civilization a profound moral disorder directly attributable to the privileged class. The judges who handed down judgment at the gates of the city were easily bribed (2, 6; 5, 7,

---

[1] Cf. *above*, p. 22.

10-12). The rich reduced their debtors to slavery (2, 6) or extorted from them unreasonable security (2, 8). Merchants cheated the poor (8, 4-6). All these crimes so characteristic of sinful man's social relations Amos roundly condemns.

Nor did he find the atmosphere more congenial at the sanctuaries, Dan (8, 14), Galgal (4, 4; 5, 5), and Bethel (4, 4; 5, 5; 7, 10). Bethel since the time of Jeroboam I had been a royal sanctuary where Yahweh was represented by the image of a bull. The ceremonies at these shrines were brilliant and there were many feasts (8, 5) which were attended by large crowds (5, 21). But all this magnificence was accompanied by immoral practices (2, 7) introduced from the nature religion of the worship of Baals.

Am 5, 26 perhaps contains an allusion to two Assyrian divinities and attests to a tendency toward syncretism, but the sense of the passage is not certain.

II. Biography of the Prophet

A shepherd from the desert of Thecua in Juda (6 miles south of Bethlehem), Amos used to go in the spring to tend sycamore trees. His Judean origin explains his love for Sion (1, 1) and David (9, 11 f.). To the trading caravans he owed his knowledge of neighboring countries. His own rough manner of life is the source of the scorn which he reserves for urban luxury.

In the cycle of visions in chapters 7 and 8 he recounts the story of his vocation. In 3, 3-8 he describes the experience of that call. " Compulsion was a part of the inspiration of the ecstatic *nabis*.... Saul is an example of this inability to resist prophetic delirium. But though there is this similar compulsion here, clearly the inspiration of the great prophets is more immaterial and has a more worthy source. It manifests itself with greater dignity and produces certainly much more significant results " (Desnoyers; see Jer 20, 7-9).

Though only the work of the prophet at the sanctuary of Bethel is described at any length, he certainly preached elsewhere in the country (7, 10), especially at Samaria (3, 9-11; 4, 1-3; 6, 1-7) and Galgal (4, 4). According to 1, 1 he preached prior to Osee. The Assyrian danger does not yet seem imminent (see 5, 27; 6, 14). This seems to locate his mission in the second part of the reign of Jeroboam II between 760 and 744 immediately prior to the reign of Teglath-pilessar III. At the same time 6, 2 refers to the conquest of Chalane by Assyria (738), as well as that of Hamath and Geth. This would indicate that the ministry of Amos was of short duration, but it certainly cannot be limited (so J. Morgenstern) to a single feast in 751.

The style of Amos is concrete, picturesque, direct. His images are borrowed from his experiences as a shepherd (3, 4-5. 12). Piling question upon question and affirmation upon affirmation (9, 1-4; 4, 6-12), he emphatically makes his point. When he turns aside to address, for example, the women of Samaria whom he calls " cows of Basan, " he brings to mind the manner of popular preachers like Bernardine of Siena. An important trait, characteristic of Amos as well as the other prophets, is his skilful directing of the dialogues in which he engages his listeners. So Jeremias (2, 32) asks, " Does a virgin forget her jewelry, a bride her sash? " His audience naturally enough falls into the trap and is obliged to answer with a unanimous " no. " Then the prophet concludes speaking for Yahweh, " Yet my people have forgotten me. " Such questions occur rather frequently in Amos (3, 3 f.; 5, 25; 9, 7).

III. The book

The *basic elements* include :

a) oracular material which Renan has compared to the suras of the Koran. They are short, forceful pieces. Amos himself may well be responsible for their present arrangement in some cases where the grouping is on the basis of mnemonic techniques (1, 3 f. : " For the three crimes of Damascus, and for the four, I will not revoke my word... "; 4, 6-12). His work is marked by rhythm, the neatly turned phrase, word plays (8, 2), alliteration (5, 5), all characteristics of the oral style.

b) autobiographical sections : the cycle of 5 visions (7, 1-9 + 8, 1-3 + 9, 1-4). These would seem better placed at the beginning of the book. The fifth vision apparently takes place at Bethel before Amos' expulsion from the shrine.

c) a biographical section (7, 10-17). This was probably taken from a collection of stories about Amos. The title of the book, which has certainly been expanded, also speaks of the prophet in the third person.

To the *work of compilation* the following is owed :

a) the further grouping of material according to mnemonic techniques. Note : " Hear this word " (3, 1; 4, 1; 5, 1; 8, 4) and " Woe " (5, [7], 18; 6, 1b).

b) the curious arrangement of 7—9; 7, 10-17 is introduced after the third vision because the word " sword " is mentioned in verses 9 and 17. The fifth vision (9, 1-4) is inserted in the midst of oracular material.

c) some questionable elements : the Deuteronomic piece of 2, 4-5; perhaps the doxologies of 4, 13; 5, 8-9; and 9, 5-6, since they interrupt the threats; perhaps also the conclusion 9, 13-15.

The book clearly is not arranged according to any chronological order, but it does preserve a unity of tone, characterized by threats and anathemas, which only at the end (9, 8-15) allows that there is still reason for hope.

IV. THE MESSAGE

The God of Amos is characterized by His *justice*, i.e., His power to establish that moral order which is one of the conditions of the Covenant.

Amos calls his contemporaries to a more profound understanding of that Covenant. Yahweh, the Lord of all nations (9, 7), has chosen Israel so that as a nation she might bear witness to that justice which reigns in her midst. In view of this privilege Israel's condemnation is the more terrible. God is everything; Israel, nothing. The " day of Yahweh " (5, 18-27) will come through the hands of the Assyrians and God will punish this people which has deceived itself into believing that the service of God consists in elaborate ceremony rather than the observance of justice.

Only a complete change of heart could save the nation (5, 4-6, 14-15), but Amos did not expect this to happen in his own time. All his attention is focused on the coming " day of Yahweh. " But that day will not mark the end of Israel. Amos knows that God will bring to pass His plan for Israel and he concludes his book with words of Messianic hope. A remnant of just men (9, 8-10) will survive and Israel will rise again around a descendant of David (9, 11-12) whose hut has been in ruin since the schism of 931. This passage can be considered authentic (so Hempel and Rost).

Yahweh guarantees justice among nations and the rights of peoples. In this way Amos proclaims his monotheism and universalism.

Two notes :

1) The prophets *were not revolutionaries* seeking to overthrow the established political order. They were defenders of the moral law, filled with love for the poor (in Am 2, 6 f. a synonym for " the just, " i.e., those with a just claim, *Rechtsanspruch*). They undertake their defense with an intensity often found among preachers. They use the same violent language as St. Ambrose in his little work on the vineyard of Naboth and St. John Chrysostom who describes the rich as " worse than wild beasts. " In the course of their threats the prophets envision

the final revenge of the poor (Am 9, 9-10; cf. 4 Kgs 25, 12). The approach of Deuteronomy to the same problem is more calm. It recognizes that the poor will always be present (15, 11) and is concerned with improving their lot. But both legislators and prophets start from the same premises.

2) Certain authors (Causse, Humbert) have emphasized the opposition of the prophets to the Chanaanites and to progress. In their view the prophets continue the attitude of the ancient legal codes and of the Rechabites. The Rechabites, according to Jer 35, 7, refused to drink wine and still lived in tents in the middle of the sixth century. There is a certain amount of truth in this view, but it must not be forgotten that the prophets *did become a part of their own civilization*. They were not Bedouin fanatics! Osee recognizes that the fruits of the fertile soil are God's gifts, and for Isaias agriculture is a divine science (28, 23-29). Isaias (1, 26) looks to a royal civilization as an ideal. The tendency to look back to the cult of the desert as the model of what cult should be was a form of polemic against cult practices more or less borrowed from the Chanaanites and commonly regarded as the essence of religion.

§ 2. Osee

BIBLIOGRAPHY

Introductions, translations, commentaries, pp. 1 f. and 271 (A. VAN HOONACKER, *EB**; E. OSTY, *BJ**; E. SELLIN, *KAT*; F. NÖTSCHER, *EBi**...).

W. R. HARPER, *Amos and Hosea* (Edinburgh, 1905).

P. CRUVEILHIER, " De l'interprétation historique des événements de la vie familiale du prophète Osée*, *RB* (1916), pp. 942-963.

P. HUMBERT, "Les trois premiers chapitres d'Osée, " *RHR* (1918), pp. 157-171. " Osée, le prophète bédouin, " *RHPR* (1921), pp. 97-118.

D. BUZY, *Les symboles de l'Ancien Testament** (Paris, 1923), pp. 62-93.

J. LINDBLOM, *Hosea, literarisch untersucht* (Abo, 1927).

H. S. NYBERG, *Studien zum Hoseabuch* (Uppsala, 1935).

H. W. ROBINSON, *Two Hebrew Prophets* (Oxford, 1948).

N. SNAITH, *Mercy and Sacrifice, a Study of the Book of Hosea* (London, 1953).

J. L. MCKENZIE, " Divine Passion in Osee, " *CBQ*, 17 (1955), pp. 287-299. " Knowledge of God in Hosea, "* *JBL*, 74 (1955), pp. 22-27.

G. OSTBORN, *Yahweh and Baal, Studies in the Book of Hosea* (1956).

H. ROWLEY, " The Marriage of Hosea, " *BJRL*, 39 (1956), pp. 200-233.

E. MALY, " Messianism in Osee, " *CBQ*, 19 (1957), pp. 213-225.

J. W. KRAUS, *Hosea* (Neukirchen, 1958 ff.).

A. GELIN, " Osée (le livre d')*, " *SDB*, XXXIII (1959).

W. EICHRODT, " The Holy One in Your Midst. The Theology of Hosea, "
Interpretation, 15 (1961), pp. 259-273.

I. THE BOOK

The Anglican bishop Lowth (18th cent.) compared the book to " *sparsa
quaedam Sybillae folia.* " Nevertheless there is certainly more order in
Osee than in Amos. Two parts can be distinguished :

a) 1—3 : the *conjugal life* of Osee and its prophetic interpretation.
Chapter 3 is autobiographical; chapter 1 is biographical and the work
of a disciple. Chapter 2 contains oracular material; it is less an
explanation of the matter of 1 than a free treatment of the themes of
this chapter. Jeremias makes use of the same images (Jer 2, 2; 3, 1).

The material can be dated in the second part of the reign of
Jeroboam II. According to 1, 4 the house of Jehu still holds the throne
and 2, 4-15 indicates that the nation enjoys a period of prosperity.

b) 4—14. This section makes allusion to *later kings and events* :
pronouncements (7, 16; 8, 4; 10, 3. 15); the tribute of Menahem to Asshur
and the vassal relationship with this country (5, 13; 7, 11-12; 8, 9; 10, 5-6;
12, 2); the Syro-Ephraimitic war of 735-4 (5, 8 to 6, 6); the appeal to
Egypt under King Osee (7, 11; 9, 6; 12, 2). There is nothing to show
that the prophet knew of the fall of Samaria (721).

This second part of the book contains :

— a series of threats and invectives grouped without plan and
concerned with cult and politics (4, 1 to 9, 9);

— poems (9, 10 to 14, 9) that are in fact meditations on the history
of Israel. This use of history already seen in Amos is also characteristic
of Deuteronomy with which Osee is allied.

The two collections must have been formed rather quickly for they
are certainly not extensive. Several references to Juda seem to be from
the hand of Judean scribes (1, 7; 4, 15; 5, 5) but not all (5, 8 to 6, 6).
14, 10 is a sapiential addition. On the whole the text is in rather poor
condition, but in this regard the book's dialectical differences must be
taken into account.

II. THE CONJUGAL LIFE OF OSEE

Osee was a contemporary of Amos. Both exercised their ministries in the
northern kingdom. But Osee's message is not made up solely of oracles.
His life itself becomes a symbolic expression of his teaching. He could
have said as Isaias was to say later, " Look at me and the children whom

the Lord has given me : we are signs and portents in Israel " (Is 8, 18). His married life which, so to say, incarnated his message is described, as has been indicated, in two separate accounts. The first presents Osee as married at God's command to a prostitute. He has three children who have received symbolic names (1). The second tells how he marries (again) a fallen woman. After putting her love to the test he lives together with her happily.

The first question to be asked naturally enough concerns the historicity of the events. Generally the allegorical interpretation (Origen, Calvin, Van Hoonacker, 1908, Gressmann, 1910) is not in favor today for there are aspects of the accounts which cannot be allegorized : the names of Gomer and her father, the fact that the children are two sons and a daughter, the details of the bride price *(mohar)*. Semites love concrete, living symbols. Jeremias' celibacy (16, 1) and Ezechiel's becoming a widower (24, 18) receive similar symbolic applications.

The second question concerns the order of the events. Some exegetes think that chapters 1 and 3 present two episodes from the life of Osee, either two distinct marriages (St. Jerome, Dom Calmet, Duhm, Buzy) or a remarriage with Gomer (Nowack, Marti, A. Weiser). According to this last author Gomer was rejected by Osee for her infidelity and then taken back. But a husband does not have to pay a *mohar* to get his wife back (Jgs 19, 2-4; 2 Sm 3, 14). It is consequently better to view 1 and 3 as parallel accounts of the same event with a greater wealth of detail in 3.

Was Gomer a sacred prostitute or did she submit to a matrimonial initiation rite proper to certain of the nature religions? This would explain the separation imposed as a test in 3, 3 which is symbolic of the exile of Israel (721). Nothing indicates that the marriage was not a happy one. The names given to the children are not references to the marriage but are rather prophecies for Israel.

The strict symbolism of the events would be as follows. The marriage with Gomer signifies that Yahweh is espoused to a nation that worships Baals. In the language of prophecy idolatry is in fact prostitution. The separation of Gomer from Osee is symbolic of the purification of the Exile. The woeful names given to the children indicate the punishment of Israel. The love of Osee and Gomer signifies the restoration of good relations between Yahweh and Israel.

While it is dangerous to go beyond the evidence of the text it is clear that the whole history of Osee's marriage is not found in the book and that the tone of the book is better explained if it is admitted that Osee has suffered in his marriage both as husband and father. His wife and he were not on the same spiritual level. Through this suffering he comes to that selfless love for God that characterizes his ultimate outlook.

III. The observer and critic

The political ideas of Osee evidently have a religious base. He is concerned with the politics of the day. Note, for example, the affirmations of 7, 3-7 (the allusion, according to Van Hoonacker, is to a court plot) and 8, 4 or Osee's view of foreign alliances (7, 11). The dynasty of Jehu is condemned for the bloodshed with which it began (1, 4). It is not clear that he rejected the northern kingdom as such (so Van Hoonacker), but Osee does indicate that the monarchy has been a failure (13, 10-11; 3, 4; 9, 10 f.; 10, 9 f.). In a similar way he criticizes Jacob's usurping the position of his brother (12, 4). It is hard to agree with Nyberg who understands 8, 4-10 as a polemic against idols. [2]

But Osee's primary concern is the religion of Yahweh. The ritual and religious thought of the Chanaanites were gradually introduced into popular religion. Thus Osee is forced to attack the worship of bulls or the representation of Yahweh in the form of a bull. He condemns the " heifers " to deportation (10, 5-6). The calves of Bethel are powerless idols (8, 4-6). Yahweh is unwilling to be associated with the Baals (2, 18; 13, 2). Osee goes on to condemn licentious cult practices (4, 14; cf. Am 2, 7; 4 Kgs 23, 7; Dt 23, 19) and religion become formality (8, 13; 10, 1. 5. 6; 12, 12). The priests do not do their duty but rather exploit the tendencies of the people (4, 8).

It is not always easy to determine the cult which Osee is opposing. The more generally accepted view is that it is the worship of Yahweh colored by Chanaanite practices rather than outright worship of Baals.

IV. The message

Nostalgia for the past and the desert theme

The history of Israel presents a continuous breaking with tradition. Perhaps the " disturbing figure " of Jacob, deceitful, venal, completely taken up with mundane affairs, is the incarnation of Israel's own errors. Osee looks back to Israel's glorious past, to the beginnings of that tradition, to the desert which is the witness of " the days of her youth " (2, 17) and the Covenant (13, 5). " When Israel was a child, I loved her, says Yahweh. " But in contact with materialist civilization (13, 6) Israel

---

[2] Cf. H. Cazelles, " The Problem of the Kings in Osee, 8, 4*, " *CBQ* (1949), p. 23.

forgot Yahweh. Thus Yahweh desires to lead her back to the desert and to speak to her heart (2, 16). " I will again have you live in tents, as in that appointed time " (12, 10). Osee's habit of looking back to the past and his implicit references to the decalogue (4, 2; 12, 10; 13, 4) show the direction of his thought. It has been said that the egalitarian tendencies of Israel's social legislation at base reflect a nomadic ideal. The conservatism of certain religious groups (Jer 35) is also significant in this regard. The great prophets in their turn speak of a new exodus. For Osee the desert is a place of punishment, of trial (2, 5) and of union between God and His people (2, 16). Thus he shows his understanding of suffering as a purifying preparation.

The marriage theme

When it is a question of the past, Osee refers to God as the father of Israel (11, 1 ff.; 1, 19); when it is a question of the present or future, as husband. This image which is based on the Covenant idea is taken up again by the tradition (Ez 16; Is 50, 1-3; 54, 1-6). It does not seem to have been used elsewhere by Semites. With much feeling it presents the Covenant as a work shared by both God and His people. The image reflects the profound experience of Osee himself.

The announcement of judgment

The danger which Osee foretells is the coming of the Assyrians. We have already spoken of two other enemies of Israel, the Philistines and the Syrians. The period of the Assyrian threat is about to begin and will last more than a century (734-612). " Though he (Israel) be fruitful among his fellows, an east wind shall come, a wind from the Lord, rising from the desert, that shall dry up his spring and leave his fountain dry " (13, 15). Soon (10, 15) a whirlwind will come (8, 7). Children and pregnant women will be massacred (14, 1). The city will be destroyed (8, 14). The high places will be torn down (12, 12). In this agricultural country thistles and brambles will grow (10, 8).

The key concept : hesed

With much vigor Amos emphasized the justice and omnipotence of God. Osee, a more refined spirit, is more profound. In this regard he resembles Jeremias with whom he has been compared. It is the divine goodness that explains the origin of the nation (" Yet it was I who taught Ephraim to walk, who took them in my arms... I fostered them like one who raises an infant to his cheeks... " 11, 1 ff.), and it is God's goodness which will triumph in the end (2, 21), for Yahweh is God, not man (11, 9).

But the divine *hesed*, far from being weakness, is a demanding thing Its opposite is judgment. Osee presents it as a love that is returned. God demands " *hesed* and knowledge of God " (6, 6). Religion becomes, then, a matter of the heart. The word *hesed*, like the word *pietas*, involves devotion to Someone.

It is significant to see the relationship between Osee and Deuteronomy (Dt 7, 8; 10, 15; 23, 6; 30, 6-20). The word to note is " love " *('âhabah)*. [3] The relations between Yahweh and Israel, acutely analyzed by Osee's keen insight, are similar to the relations between God and the soul. The Book of Osee becomes, then, the rough sketch of a treatise on grace.

§ 3. Micheas

BIBLIOGRAPHY

Introductions, translations, commentaries, pp. 1 f. and 271 (A. VAN HOONACKER, *EB**; A. GEORGE, *BJ**; F. NÖTSCHER, *EBi*; A. WEISER, *ATD*; E. SELLIN, *KAT*...).

J. M. POWIS SMITH, "Micah...," *ICC* (Edinburgh, 1912).

K. BUDDE, "Das Rätsel von Micha, I, " *ZAW* (1917-18), pp. 77-108; "Micha 2 und 3, " *ZAW* (1919-20), pp. 2-22.

J. LINDBLOM, *Micha, literarisch untersucht* (Helsinki, 1929).

COPASS—CARLSON, *A Study of the Prophet Micah* (1950).

L. PETTIBONE SMITH, "The Book of Micah," *Interpretation*, 6 (1952), pp. 210-227.

A. GEORGE, "Le livre de Michée, " *SDB*, V (1952), cols. 1252-1263.

R. E. WOLFE, "The Book of Micah, " *IB* (1956).

A. S. KAPELRUD, "Eschatology in the Book of Micah, " *VT*, 11 (1961), pp. 392-405.

I. THE PERIOD OF THE PROPHET

The period [4] during which Micheas lived was especially dramatic. He witnessed the progressive extension of Assyrian hegemony which was to bring such great tragedy to Israel. Samaria was destroyed (721). Then pressure was brought to bear on Jerusalem. This culminated in the siege of the city by Sennacherib (701). Juda lost territory and was forced to become a vassal of Assyria down through the whole of the reign of Manasses.

---

[3] F. BUCK, *Die Liebe Gottes beim Propheten Osee** (Rome, 1953).
[4] Cf. pp. 24-30.

II. THE BOOK

The division into four parts is artificial. Some of the oracles of woe concern Samaria; others concern Jerusalem. The terms " Israel " and " Jacob " do not always denote the northern kingdom, since 3, 9 assigns these names with an eminently religious significance to Juda. Some of the oracles are later additions.

Oracles of woe : 1—3

1, 2-7 : prediction of the destruction of Samaria (before 721). 1, 8-16 : against Juda (701; cf. Is 10, 24-34). 2, 1-11 : against social injustice. 2, 12-13 : discussion of the gathering together of the remnant, an oracle of good fortune. 3, 1-4 : against the judges (autobiographical indications). 3, 5-8 : against the prophets. 3, 9-12 : against the ruling classes and the prediction of the fall of Jerusalem.

Oracles of good fortune

There are six such pieces. Eissfeldt and Oesterley-Robinson deny their authenticity. They are regarded as original by Sellin, Gressmann and and H. Schmidt while A. Weiser and A. George accept them as authentic with some reservations.

— 4, 1-4 celebrates the glory of Sion. This oracle is also found in Is 2, 2-4. Perhaps it has been set in its place in Micheas to complete 3, 12 where the destruction of the city is spoken of. Verse 5 seems to be a liturgical addition.

— 4, 6-8 concerns the kingdom of Jahweh and the return of the Diaspora.

— 4, 9-14 describes the eschatological victory of Sion.

— 5, 1-5 on the liberator born at Bethlehem.

— 5, 6-8 which treats of the vigorous remnant seems postexilic.

— 5, 9-14 is an authentic prophecy of Micheas against Juda and against the nations.

Oracles of woe : 6—7, 6

The process of law between Yahweh and His people (6, 1-8) can be dated before 701. It is the most famous of the oracles of Micheas. The second oracle (6, 9-16) is directed against Jerusalem or Samaria (before 721, Meinhold, Lindblom). The last (7, 1-6) is a lamentation for Jerusalem.

Oracles of good fortune 7, 7-20

These three pieces (7, 7-10; 11-13; 14-20) have a liturgical form and are generally considered postexilic.

III. THE MAN AND HIS MESSAGE

Micheas was from the environs of Gath in the land of the Philistines. He was a vigorous, outspoken person (3, 8) and in this regard calls to mind Amos. Perhaps his little town had been overrun by the Assyrians during one of their raids, and as a result of this he came to Jerusalem. His preaching there is less polished than that of his contemporary Isaias. In Jerusalem he delivered the oracle against the Temple referred to by the elders in the time of Jeremias (Jer 26, 18). At Jerusalem he must have known Isaias (compare : 1, 10-16 and Is 10, 27 ff.; 2, 1-5 and Is 5, 8 ff.; 5, 9-14 and Is 2, 6 ff.). His polemic against the official prophets indicates he was not one of them. A peasant from the southwest, he was appalled by the recklessness of the policies of the rulers of Jerusalem and this is evident in his preaching.

It was his merit to sum up in 6, 8 all the preaching of his predecessors or contemporaries : justice (Amos), *hesed* (Osee), humility (Isaias).

He is above all a prophet of judgment, but like the other prophets he does give reason for great hope. His announcements of the kingdom of Yahweh use the formulas of dynastic Messianism, but the concept goes beyond them. A Messianic theme which is found in the book and which can be duplicated in Isaias is that of the remnant. [5] The beneficiary of the salvation to come will not be the nation as such but rather a religious elite derived from it. The prophets foretold the coming of this elite and prepared for it by their preaching. The disciples of the prophets are the first nucleus of this group. It will be formed definitively in the Exile.

§ 4. Isaias

BIBLIOGRAPHY

Introductions, translations, commentaries, pp.1f. and 251f. (J. STEINMANN and P. AUVRAY, *BJ**; O. PROCKSCH, *KAT*; L. DENNEFELD, *BPC**; J. SKINNER, *CBSC*...).

G. B. GRAY, " Isaiah I-XXVII, " *ICC* (Edinburgh, 1902).

A. CONDAMIN, " Le livre d'Isaïe*, " *EB* (Paris, 1905).

J. MUILENBURG, " The Literary Character of Isaiah 34, " *JBL*, 59 (1940), pp. 339-365.

E. J. KISSANE, *The Book of Isaiah** (Dublin, 1941).

G. BRILLET, *Le prophète Isaïe** (Paris, 1944).

---

[5] R. DE VAUX, " Le Reste d'Israël d'après les prophètes, " *RB* (1933), pp. 526-539; S. GAROFALO, *La nozione profetica del Resto d'Israele** (Rome, 1944).

A. FEUILLET, " Isaïe (le livre d')*, " *SDB*, IV (1947), cols. 647-688.

I. EGNELL, *The Call of Isaiah* (Uppsala, 1949).

V. HERNTRICH, *Der Prophet Jesaja. Kap.* 1-12 (Göttingen, 1950).

R. B. Y. SCOTT, " The Book of Isaiah, 1-39, " *IB* (1956).

M. BURROWS, *The Dead Sea Scrolls of St. Mark's Monastery* (New Haven : Yale, 1957).

F. MORIARTY, " The Emmanuel Prophecies, " *CBQ*, 19 (1957), pp. 226-233.

S. BLANK, *Prophetic Faith in Israel* (New York, 1958).

J. LINDBLOM, *A Study in the Immanuel Section of Isaiah* (Lund, 1958).

A. PENNA, *Isaia** (Turin-Rome, 1958).

C. H. WHITLEY, " The Call and Mission of Isaiah, " *JNES*, 18 (1959), pp. 38-48.

J. MAUCHLINE, *Isaiah* 1-39. *Introduction and Commentary* (London : SCM, 1962).

T. VRIEZEN, " Essentials of the Theology of Isaiah, " *Israel's Prophetic Hermitage*, ed. B. ANDERSON and W. HARRISON (New York : Harper, 1962).

B. ANDERSON, " Isaiah xxiv—xxvii Reconsidered, " Suppl. *VT*, 9 (1963), pp. 118-126.

I. THE MAN AND THE MANNER

Isaias, whom rabbinic tradition has made a noble of royal blood, is a personality of the first rank. Aristocratic of manner and strong-willed he deals with royalty on an equal footing (7, 11. 13; 37, 2; 39, 3). In his inaugural vision he appears as a man determined to live up to his responsibilities, and with clear and penetrating intelligence he undertakes his political activities. He has a keen, sometimes ironical gift for observation and an ever alert curiosity. " How well he knew the capital, its pools and water conduits, its towers and arsenals (7, 3; 22, 9; 29, 7), the esplanade of the Temple and its noisy crowds, its festivals spoiled by the inroads of paganism (1, 10 ff.), the pleasure houses where the rich feasted and danced while the people died of hunger (5, 8 ff.). How well he observed and precisely detailed the over-fine clothes of the elegant in the streets of Jerusalem and, half amused, half indignant, sketched their proud, sauntering bearing and their little affectations. " [6]

His feelings are less open than those of Jeremias. When he is not listened to, he retires without delay (8, 16) into the little circle of his disciples. This trait as well as his representation of the majesty of God,

---

[6] M. L. DUMESTE, *RB* (1935), p. 528.

his horror of social disorder (3, 5), and even his style would indicate an aristocratic nature and origin. Dumeste writes : " Unlike Micheas whose turbulent harangues include the deceitful nobility and Jerusalem itself in the disasters to come, this patrician of Jerusalem as he views the future never ceases to believe in the inviolability of Jerusalem and reserves a place there for its converted nobility... Isaias is a patriot, an aristocrat, a conservative. "

His style is that of a great poet. Perhaps he and the author of Job are the two great poets of the Old Testament. His descriptive powers, his ability to suggest what is not directly said, his sense of propriety and order are the most evident aspects of his literary genius.

Isaias preached from the year of the death of King Ozias during the reigns of Joatham (740-736), Achaz (736-716) and Ezechias (716-687). This period [7] saw the fall of Damascus (732), of Samaria (721) and of Ashdod (711). In short the Assyrian threat against Jerusalem was becoming more acute. It culminated in the campaign of Sennacherib (701) who was unable to take the city but did make the southern kingdom an Assyrian vassal. The oracles of Isaias which allude to these events are scattered through the book. This is in keeping with its very complex formation.

II. THE BOOK

Since the end of the 18th century (Döderlein 1775; Eichhorn 1782) modern criticism has seen in the canonical book of Isaias several blocks of material dating from different periods and joined in the editing of the book. The idea of a Second-Isaias (40—66) written at the end of the Exile became classic during the 19th century. Since Duhm's extremely important commentary (1892) the idea of a Third-Isaias (56—66) written after the return from exile has been much discussed. The Biblical Commission declared in 1908 that this hypothetical understanding of the structure of the book was not based on solid and convincing arguments; [8] it seems, however, that the work of the Catholic exegetes over the past sixty years has given more weight to these arguments.

Nevertheless, if modern criticism has thus divided the canonical book into three blocks of material, it has become increasingly aware of the continuity in its contents. Through the whole of this great work God is called the " Holy One of Israel " and His transcendence is very much emphasized. Faith, the remnant, " the poor, " are constantly recurring

---

[7] For chronology see pp. 241 f.

[8] *EB*, p. 295.

themes. Especially to be taken into account is the Messianic and eschatological viewpoint that pervades the whole book and makes it Israel's classic expression of hope. The LXX translation has further accentuated this unity. Ben Sira (Sir 48, 24-25) knew the book as a unit. Mowinckel, Engnell and Bentzen have spoken of an Isaian school similar to the Deuteronomic or sacerdotal school which expanded the great themes of Isaias and in part preserved his phraseology. In this way a unity among the various parts of the book was assured. Kissane (1943) has suggested that an anonymous prophet whose mind was completely penetrated with Isaian thought edited the book and expanded its preaching at the end of the Exile.

Second- and Third-Isaias will be studied later. [9] The following schema gives the approximate divisions of chapters 1—39 :

1—12 : Oracles on Juda and Jerusalem.

13—23 : Oracles against the nations, presented as a unit as in Jer and Ez.

24—27 : Eschatological oracles or the great apocalypse of Isaias.

28—33 : The collection of " Woes. "

34—35 : Eschatological oracles or the little apocalypse of Isaias.

36—39 : Historical appendix.

S. Mowinckel, [10] O. Eissfeldt and A. Weiser seem to have indicated the subdivisions of this general outline most perceptively. Their work is freely drawn on here.

Oracles on Juda and Jerusalem (1—12)

This part contains five sections which can be distinguished by taking into account titles, sense-breaks and connecting phrases.

1 : typical preaching of the prophet, a sort of program supplied with a title. Several fragments can be isolated : 2-3; 4-9 (dating from 701); 10-17 (in the form of Torah); 18-20, 21-26 (lamentation); 27-31. Apparently these fragments were assembled by the disciples of Isaias.

2—4 : first preaching of Isaias, inserted between two much-discussed oracles of good fortune : 2, 2-5 and 4, 2-6. It includes : 2, 6-22 (diatribe against pride); 3, 1-15 (anarchy); 3, 16—4, 1 (satire against the women). The collection has a special title (2, 1).

5 + 9, 7—11 : This section is interrupted by the insertion of the Emmanuel material. It includes : 5, 1-7 (poem on the vineyard of

---

[9] Pp. 332-342 and 349-353.

[10] Die Komposition des Jesajabuches Kp. 1-39, " *Acta orientalia* (1933), pp. 267-292.

Yahweh); 5, 8-24 + 10, 1-4 (collection of seven woes dating from different periods); 9, 7-20 + 5, 25-30 (poem of disasters); 10, 5-34 (several pieces against Assyria, about 701); the section is completed by prophecies of good fortune : 11, 1-9 (the Messias, original), 11, 10-16 (the restoration; perhaps from another inspired author).

6—9, 6 : the Emmanuel section. This section contains oracular, biographical and autobiographical material. It forms a complex literary unit. Its essential part recalls the political activity of Isaias in 735-734. 6 is the preface; 9, 1-6, the conclusion. Accounts of several different events have been juxtaposed and traces of the redactor's hand are evident in 8, 8c-10, 23 bc. The sequence is as follows : 6 (vocation of Isaias); 7, 1-9 (the reason for courage); 10-17 (the Emmanuel sign); 18-25 (judgment at the hand of Assyria); 8, 1-4 (the sign of the infant); 5-8b (the arrival of Assyria); 8c-10 (Emmanuel, much discussed); 11-15 (warning for 735-734). What follows is difficult : in 8, 16 there is the hint of a reverse suffered by Isaias. 8, 23—9, 1-6 *(Puer natus est)* speaks of the birth of an heir of David.

12 : A psalm of thanksgiving (1-3) which closes as a hymn (4-6). It serves as a concluding doxology for the section and has probably been added by a later redactor.

Oracles against the nations (13—23)
The section was put together after the Exile for it contains several non-Isaian pieces. The word *massa* (= oracle) occurs nine times (13, 1; 15, 1; 17, 1; 19, 1; 21, 1. 11. 13; 22, 1; 23, 1). The occurrence of 22, 1-14 among these oracles against the nations is explained by verses 5 ff. The same is true for 22, 15-25 : Sobna was considered a foreigner because of verse 16.

The following sections are considered original : 14, 4b-23 (705; but with hesitation), 24-27 (701); 17, 1-11 (before 732), 12-14 (701); 18, save for verse 7 (713 or 705); 19, 1-15; 20 (713-711); 22, 1-14 (701). 15-24. 29-32 (705).

The great apocalypse (24—27)
These chapters written after the Exile will be studied later. [11]

The collection of " Woes " (28—33)
The Assyrian cycle (28—31) contains oracles which are set in the years between 713 and 701 with the exception of 28, 1-4 (724). It includes : 28, 7-22 (the cornerstone); 23-29 (the ways of God); 29, 1-16 (the blindness

---

[11] Cf. pp. 352 f.

of Israel, 703-2, redone); 30, 1-5. 6-7. 8-14 (against the Egyptian alliance);
15-17 (faith); 27-33 (against Assyria); 31 (against Egypt, 703-2); 32, 9-20
(redone just before the Exile).

The following sections are considered postexilic : 29, 17-24; 30,
18-26; 32, 1-8; 33 which is a prophetic liturgy.

The little apocalypse (34—35)

These chapters written after the Exile will be studied later. [12]

Historical appendix (36—39)

Like Jer 52 this historical appendix has an apologetic purpose : history
has proved Isaias was right! Of the three accounts which were preserved
among the disciples of the prophets the last two (the sickness of Ezechias
and the embassy from Merodachbaladan) are chronologically prior to the
first (the campaign of Sennacherib). The first presents both a literary
and historical problem when it is compared with 4 Kgs 18, 13—20, 19. [13]

It is probable that the Emmanuel section and the Assyrian cycle
were the first collections to be published (6, 1—9, 6; 28—31), but it is
hard to regard the former as entirely the work of the prophet because
of chapter 7 (biography). Certain collections prepared by the disciples
of the prophet were next to be formed : 2—4; 5 + 9, 7—11, 9; 1; 13—23.
These collections grew through other additions or insertions. The great
apocalypse closes the oracles against the nations; the little apocalypse,
the oracles of hope. The historical appendix was the last piece added.

III. The essential ideas

God

The God of Isaias is the " Holy One. " Yahweh is powerful and majestic,
frightening and yet attractive. He is completely unique. Before Him
every creature senses the profundity of his nothingness and experiences a
reverential fear that is in part dread, in part awe, in part confidence.
Isaias expresses this divine transcendence with the expression " Holy
One. " When the Seraphim proclaim three times this holiness (6, 4-5),
the term also reflects the moral perfection of the divinity, but above all
else it denotes God's absolute transcendence, His ineffable mystery
before which the angels veil their faces and the prophet feels the full
weight of his nothingness. The law of holiness (Lv 17—26) also emphasizes
this divine title. But for Isaias Yahweh is also the " Holy One of Israel. "
The expression makes clear God's infinite condescension : the all-holy

---

[12] Cf. p. 351.
[13] Cf. pp. 237 f.

God is the God who acts in history through His Chosen People. This same idea underlies the divine work, the divine plan (5, 12; 10, 12; 14, 24) which Yahweh is effortlessly bringing to term in His own time (18, 4).

Faith

Isaias in his preaching insisted on the necessity of faith which he understood as the practical conviction that Yahweh alone is important. The believer must consequently reject all human alliances and all fear of foreign armies. Isaias' slogan is : " Without faith, there is no survival " (7, 9). 8, 13; 28, 16; 30, 15 also insist on the necessity of relying on God alone. Remarkably enough this idea continues to be developed in the Bible by Sophonias, the 'anawim, Nehemias, the Chronicler, and by St. Paul himself. It is difficult to say to what extent this idea has influenced the biblical accounts of Israel's heroes.

The nation

Isaias regards Sion as the inviolable palladium of the nation (28, 16). Since the future of the true religion was intimately associated with that of the people, his Messianic hopes are elaborated within the framework of a restored and renovated national life. The Messias will be the ideal king (9, 11) and Jerusalem will be the center of the future kingdom of God (1, 26). The book, which is in fact an anthology of hope, emphasizes these themes. 32, 1-8 takes up again the idea of 11 (the " poor "). 2, 2-4 and 19, 23-25 assign the other nations a place of honor.

The " remnant "

Isaias is the witness of an important development in the history of the religion of Israel. In the midst of a people that did not " sanctify " Yahweh (8, 13; 29, 23) he began a prophetic party. 8, 16 attests the emergence of this *religious* society formed from among the disciples of the prophet and distinct from the *national* society. This is the point of departure for the little " remnant, " the inheritor of the ancient promises, which the prophets described and which they began to group around themselves.

IV. THE LIFE AND ACTIVITY OF ISAIAS

The passages which can be dated with some certainty follow in chronological order.

— 740 : 6.

— between 740 and 735 : 2, 6-22; 3, 1-15; 3, 16—4, 1; 5, 8-24 + 10, 1-4; 9, 7-20 + 5, 25-30.

— 735-4 : 7; 8; 9, 1-6; 17, 1-11.

— about 724 : 28, 1-4 (perhaps the entire chapter).

— 713-711 : 18; 20.

— about 705 : 14, 4b-21; 28—32; 22, 15-17.

— about 703 : (perhaps 28, 7-29); 29, 1-15 (reworked); 30, 1-17. 27-30; 31, 1-9.

— 701 : 22, 1-14; 10, 5-34; 1, 4-9; 14, 24-27; 37, 22-25; 18, 12-14; 11, 1-9.

The inaugural vision [14]

At prayer in the Temple in 740 Isaias had a vision. Yahweh appeared to him as an oriental king surrounded by his court of supernatural beings, the Seraphim. Just as Ezechiel was to use Assyro-Babylonian imagery for the Cherubim, it is probable that Isaias uses known figures (seraphs of the Negeb or Nergal-Sharrapu) in describing his vision. These angels praise the holiness of Yahweh who reveals Himself in a theophany similar to that of Sinai (6, 3). At first the prophet is frightened (verse 5), but then becomes enthusiastic for the mission he is to undertake (verse 8). But the mission will be difficult. His own preaching will harden the hearts of those to whom he is sent (verses 9-10; see Mk 4, 11-12). The mission of Isaias is a grim mission, but verse 13 shows there is hope for the remnant or rather the dynastic trunk (Engnell). [15] This inaugural vision is like a résumé of Isaias' whole career and all his key ideas. It is very possible that the later rejection of Isaias influenced his account of the vision.

The first messages

The earliest preaching of the prophet is conserved in several passages. There stand out among these 2, 6-21, the most pathetic passage in Isaias, and 5, 1-7, the parable of the vineyard.

Between the years 740-735, during the reign of Joatham, Juda was prosperous (2, 7). From Elath (4 Kgs 14, 22) the ships of Tarshish left for Ophir (India? Yemen? the east coast of Africa?). Order reigned at Jerusalem (3, 1-3). On the walks of the city (3, 16 ff.) the prophet views the fancy clothes and can hear the music of the flute and the tambourine, which is a part of the orgies of the debauched (5, 11 ff.). His thoughts turn to the skeptics (5, 19). He promises that the day of Yahweh (2, 12; 3, 13) is coming for the monopolists (5, 3) and for the corrupt judges (10, 1). Thus far Isaias follows in the line of his predecessors, especially Amos. It is only about 735 that he begins to assume a

---

[14] P. BÉGUERIE, " La vocation d'Isaïe, " *Études sur les prophètes d'Israël**
(Paris, 1954), pp. 11-51.

[15] I. ENGNELL, *The Call of Isaiah* (Uppsala, 1949).

political role, but he has already called on Juda to consider the lesson at hand. The hand of Yahweh is stretched out against Samaria (9, 7-20), and the Assyrian menace mounts on the horizon (5, 26-30).

The political activity of 735-734

The attempt to intervene in the politics of Juda was not crowned with success. Neither the king nor public opinion were convinced and after this reverse the prophet withdrew from the scene for a time with his disciples (8, 16).

What was his message? First of all he announced the complete defeat of Samaria and Damascus. The kings of these countries—" these two stumps of smoldering brands " (7, 4)—proposed to dethrone Achaz who had refused to enter their anti-Assyrian coalition (7, 6) (see p. 25). In an interview with the king, Isaias is reassuring. The league will be defeated (7, 1-9). A little later the message is clarified still further. The prophet's own son still to be born will be the sign of the destruction of these two adversaries of Juda (8, 1-4). 732 saw the fulfilment of this threat. Damascus was conquered and a part of Samaria was annexed by Assyria.

In the midst of all this occurs a solemn promise. This concerns the dynasty which is under attack from the outside (7, 6) and unpopular at home (7, 13; 8, 6). The faith of Achaz is weak (7, 13); he has just sacrificed his son to Moloch (or as *molek*) (4 Kgs 16, 3). Isaias knows and again affirms the divine promises made through Nathan to the heir of David (2 Sm 7, 12-16). [16] Beyond this royal birth, which already bears the divine promises and where the mother plays a privileged role, [17] Isaias foresees the birth of the Messias, heir par excellence of David in later times. He evokes this birth in the same terms an ancient hymn evoked a divine birth : " the *'almah* shall conceive. " [18] He sees

---

[16] J. J. STAMM, " La prophétie d'Emmanuel, " *RHPR* (1943), pp. 1-25; J. COPPENS, " La prophétie d'Emmanuel, " *L'attente du Messie** (Bruges, 1954), pp. 39-50; A. GELIN, " Messianisme*, " *SDB*, V, cols. 1180 ff.; M. BRUNEC in *VD* (1955), pp. 257 ff., 321 ff.; (1956), pp. 16 ff.

[17] G. MOLIN, " Die Stellung der Gebira im Staats Juda, " *TZ* (1954), pp. 161-174; H. CAZELLES, " La Mère du Roi-Messie dans l'Ancien Testament, " *Maria et Ecclesia* (Rome, 1959), V, pp. 39-56; H. DONNER, " Königinmutter im Altem Testament, " *Festschrift J. Friedrich* (Heidelberg, 1959), pp. 105-146.

[18] Poem of Nikkal : *hl glmt tld b (n . . .)* in C. H. GORDON, *Ugaritic Handbook* (Rome, 1947), text 77, line 7; and in line 5 : *tld bt(.)t.* The word *'almah* (nubile girl) does not directly evoke virginity (cf. Prv 30, 19) and the prophet's insistence bears on the birth of the royal heir more than on his miraculous conception. However, later Jewish interpretation will not hesitate to speak of virginal birth : the Septuagint will translate *'almah* by ἡ παρθένος.

the child nourished with heavenly food, milk and honey, which the inhabitants will receive abundantly (7, 22), [19] thus provided with the heavenly knowledge to discern good and evil (Gn 3). This Messianic vision has probably as a sign the forthcoming birth of a child (7, 16) who before he could discern good and evil will have seen his country rid of the Syro-Samaritan threat.

However, to these Messianic outlooks the prophet must add the announcement of disasters resulting from the incredulity of the people and that of the royal court. The Messianic happiness is coupled with threats of unhappiness. Whereas the first oracle demands faith in the Davidic dynasty which the coalition wants to overthrow, the second oracle, more threatening, foresees devastations and an Assyrian invasion. The birth of the Child will be sung in a sort of liturgy (9, 5-6) but this concerns a northern kingdom already devastated, a captive Galilee, presage of further disasters for Juda. Nevertheless, Isaias offers salvation in the person of an heir of David whose names (9, 5) express the ideal of the King-Messias as also found in the royal psalms.

Is 7, 14 is, then, Messianic and it is set in a context that concerns the Davidic dynasty. To make the infant Ezechias is perhaps to interpret the text too much and to become involved in chronological difficulties. Ezechias seems to have been born in 734 (cf. the three different dates given by 4 Kgs 18, 9-10; 18, 13 and 16, 2). The Jews, however, in the time of Jerome (*PL* 24, 109) and St. Justin (*Dialogue with Trypho*, 66, 68, 71, 77) agreed that the child was Ezechias. R. Simon, Calmet, Le Hir and Steinmann have seen here an instance of a Messianic type and regarded Ezechias as a figure of Jesus Christ. This latter opinion has not been proscribed. Pius VI in 1779 condemned Isembiehl who denied the passage was Messianic in either the literal or the typical sense. [20] In our opinion there is much more.

Renewal of political activity about 724

Isaias recommended his political activities to foretell the impending fall of Samaria (28, 1-4). This event should have been a warning to equally guilty Juda, but the warning was not heeded. This was the occasion for Isaias to attack the politicians, the counselors of the government. Micheas had already inveighed against Juda's incapacity to understand

---

[19] In the Bible milk and honey are signs of the country's fertility. Same in Ugarit (Baal and Anat, GORDON, 49, iii, 13). The Mesopotamians considered these as the food of the gods.

[20] CAVALLERA, *Thesaurus doctrinae*＊ (1920), p. 59.

such clear warnings as this. " While they rely on the Lord, saying, ' Is not the Lord in the midst of us? No evil can come upon us!' " (Mi 3, 11). Isaias meets this same derisive attitude. He is regarded as a man in his dotage. The mocking words of his opponents probably do not make sense. They are only meant to ridicule the repetitiousness and solemnity of Isaias' own words. Verses 7-8 perhaps allude to a banquet at which the politicians celebrated the departure of Assyria from Palestine in 722. Isaias assures his adversaries that misfortune will strike (11-13. 18-22) and very near to Jerusalem where in former times Israel had won notable victories (21). But Yahweh will not chastise his people continuously (23-29). There is a promise of salvation for those who are worthy of it, for those who find their support in the " cornerstone " which some understand as the Messias, others, as Sion (16).

Isaias and Ezechias [21]

History has given to the successor of Achaz a reputation for being an ideal servant of Yahweh (Sir 49, 5). The record of his religious reforms is conserved in 4 Kgs 18, 1-7. 22 and 2 Par 29—30. In all probability Isaias contributed to this religious reform. Perhaps it is too much to regard him as the man behind the throne, but it is clear that his influence increased considerably. It became decisive at the moment when all seemed lost.

But a religious reform in the climate of the Old Testament could hardly be separated from a national revival. The situation was delicate. On the one side Assyria captured Gaza in 720 and Ashdod in 713-711 (Is 20). On the other side opposition to Sargon was on the increase. Merodach Baladan sent ambassadors to Ezechias (Is 39) while Egypt worked to foment revolt among the Palestinian states from the beginning of the Ethiopian dynasty (Is 18) which more or less coincided with the beginning of the reign of Ezechias (716-715). The death of Sargon (705), which is perhaps the subject of Is 14, 4b-21 (but see p. 337), was the signal for revolt to break out on all sides. Isaias repeatedly argued against succumbing to Egypt's proposals in this regard (30, 1-7; 31, 1-3). 30, 8-14 attests to the prophet's literary activity at this time. Perhaps he thought something written would be more influential than the spoken word.

The campaign of Sennacherib (701) (cf. pp. 27-30)

Ezechias succumbed to the temptation and hastily fortified Jerusalem to resist the invasion he had done nothing to avoid. The campaign

---

[21] P. DHORME, *Les pays bibliques et l'Assyrie** (Paris, 1911), p. 76.

of Sennacherib was terrible.   He did not succeed in taking the city, but
Ezechias had to pay a heavy tribute.   This is described in 4 Kgs 18,
14-16 and there is a parallel account in the Assyrian annals.   Two further
accounts are given : 4 Kgs 18, 17—19, 9a + 36-37 (Is 36, 2-37, 9b + 37-38)
and 19, 9b-35 (Is 37, 9c-36).   These parallel accounts describe with some
minor differences the same sequence of facts : the ultimatum of
Sennacherib (the letter is in the second document), the prayer of Ezechias
in the Temple, the intervention of Isaias, the departure of the Assyrian
army.   The redaction shows some of the characteristics of the Deuteronomic style.   Clearly enough the accounts were not composed on the day
after the events, but they do contain much that is important, especially
the actual words of the prophet (19, 21-34; Is 37, 22-35), and they emphasize the unforeseen circumstances that prevented Sennacherib from
capturing Ezechias and destroying Jerusalem.   Taking up a hypothesis
proposed by Winckler, Dhorme had distributed the events described
above over two campaigns, one in 701, the second in 690. [22]   The
suggestion has been supported by Albright with whom P. de Vaux is
inclined to agree. [23]   Other historians reject the hypothesis.   In any case
the Assyrian annals do not mention the setback.   This is readily explained.
The last two biblical sources with reason have understood Sennacherib's
failure as the work of Yahweh.

The oracles of Isaias dating from this period by turns attest
contrasting ideas.   The invasion is a punishment for Juda's sin.   Proud
Assyria has not understood her role as instrument.   Sion must not perish.
This does not indicate that the prophet was constantly changing his mind.
All these things remain true at one and the same time.   We connect the
following sections to the events of 701 :

— "But look! you feast... " (22, 1-14).   The departure of the
Judean forces and the enthusiasm of the people.   Jerusalem acclaims
the troops from the house tops.   The houses will fall and the city will
be put under siege.   Instead of feasting gaily Jerusalem will wear
sackcloth as in a time of mourning.

— " We will spend the night at Geba... " (10, 28-32).   Description
of the forced march of the enemy toward Jerusalem.   In point of fact the
Assyrians come from the land of the Philistines, but the description has
been dramatized.   The Assyrians are made to take a direct route through
ravines and over mountains to show the rapidity of their advance.   The
collection, 10, 5-34, can all be set in this period.

---

[22] *BASOR*, 130 (April 1953), pp. 8-11.
[23] *RB* (1956), p. 426.

— " Like a shed in a melon patch... " (1, 4-9). This important oracle describes the realization of the punishment of 5-8 and relates it to the sins of Jerusalem.

— " I will break the Assyrian in my land " (14, 24-27); cf. 17, 12-14.

— Several poems in which occur the themes of the virgin, the sword and the fire of Yahweh (30, 27-33; 31, 4-5, 8-9).

— The three oracles of 37, 22-25 which are inspired by the faith of Isaias. Like that of Abraham and Job it was strongest in hopelessly difficult situations.

— The Messianic oracle of 11, 1-9 *(Virga de radice Jesse)*. Eissfeldt doubts the authenticity of the oracle, but it is strongly defended by Bentzen. It can be dated during the period of crisis when Isaias courageously expressed his faith in the chosen dynasty (37, 35). There is here again the atmosphere of the new Eden which characterizes 7, 14. The Messianic pouring forth of the Spirit (11, 2) will be realized fully in Jesus (Mk 1, 10). " In Filium Dei... descendit, cum ipso adsuescens habitare in genere humano et requiescere in hominibus " (St. Irenaeus, *Adv. haer.* III, 17, 1).

THE PROPHETS OF THE SEVENTH CENTURY AND OF THE BEGINNING OF THE SIXTH CENTURY

The eighth century was the golden age of Assyria. [1] During the first half of the seventh century Assyrian hegemony was maintained in the fertile crescent under Sennacherib, Assarhaddon and Ashurbanipal. In 664 it reached as far as Thebes in Upper Egypt. But the great empire broke up in just a few decades after the death of Assurbanipal (632). The Scythian raids devastated Syria (about 630). Babylon seized its independence (626). Finally the Babylonians and the Medes destroyed Ninive (612) and crushed Pharao Nechao II when he attempted to help Assyria (605).

Juda follows in reverse the same historic curve. Under Manasses (687-642) and Amon (642-640) Juda was a vassal state completely dominated by Assyria and there was much religious syncretism (4 Kgs 21, 10 ff.; cf. Jer 15, 4). The spirit of the prophets smoldered under a heavy cover of ashes. It blazed forth again during the minority of Josias (640-609) who took advantage of the Assyrian decline and undertook a national and religious renewal which culminated in the reform of 622 (4 Kgs 22, 23). Israel was one again as in the time of David. Unfortunately all this was not very permanent!

§ 1. Sophonias

BIBLIOGRAPHY

Introductions, translations, commentaries, pp. 1 f. and 271 (A. GEORGE *BJ**; E. SELLIN, *KAT*; K. ELLIGER, *ATD*; F. NÖTSCHER, *EBi**...).

G. GERLEMAN, *Zephania* (Lund, 1942).

J. P. HYATT, "The Date and Background of Zephaniah," *JNES*, 7 (1948), pp. 125-133.

L. P. SMITH—E. R. LACHEMAN, "The Authorship of Zephaniah,", *JNES*, 9 (1950), pp. 137-142.

A. GELIN, *Les pauvres de Yahvé** (Paris, 1954), pp. 33-38.

[1] Cf. pp. 24-33.

C. L. TAYLOR, " The Book of Zephaniah, " *IB* (1956).

K. SULLIVAN, " The Book of Sophonias*, " *Worship*, 31 (1957), pp. 130-139.

J. H. EATON, *Obdahiah, Nahum, Habakkuk, Zephaniah* (London : SCM, 1962).

D. WILLIAMS, " The Date of Zephaniah, " *JBL*, 82 (1963), pp. 77-88.

I. THE MAN AND HIS TIME

Sophonias, " whom Yahweh shelters," has among his ancestors an Ezechias who is generally identified with King Ezechias. The list of ancestors in 1, 1 is certainly unusual, but perhaps it is meant to show that in spite of his father's name (the " Ethiopian ") the prophet was of pure Judean stock (George). Other critics have seen in his father's name an indication that he was a member of a servant family and attached to the personnel of the Temple. This view is supported by Sophonias' familiarity with the cult style (1, 7, 9; 2, 1). On this basis he is made a cult prophet (Bentzen), a fate which not even Amos has escaped! He probably preached during the regency of Josias (1, 8) between 640-630 (George). His preaching indicates the state of Jerusalem before the reform : the star worship of Assyria, cult of the Ammonite god Milkom, vestiges of Chanaanite worship (1, 4-5), foreign dress (1, 8), false prophets (3, 4), violence and injustice (3, 1-3; 1, 11). Sophonias reflects the views of the religiously-minded Judeans who welcomed and supported the reform (2, 3; 3, 12-13).

II. THE BOOK

The book can be divided into four parts :

Threats against Juda and Jerusalem (1, 2—2, 3). The first description of the day of Yahweh (1, 2-13); in 1, 2-3 as further on in 1, 18 the perspective is cosmic. The second description (1, 14-18) has inspired the *Dies irae, dies illa*. The appeal for conversion in 2, 1-3 is important because it is the first clear appearance of the vocabulary of spiritual poverty *('anawah)*.

Against the nations (2, 4-15). The direction is east to west and then south to north. It is not necessary to update the whole of 4-12. It is sufficient to admit that the section was reworked during the Exile (7 and 8-11). The oracle against Assyria is authentic (13-15).

Indictment of Jerusalem and the nations (3, 1-8). In the present text verse 8 is directed against the nations and serves as a transition

into the concluding section. In the primitive text it must have announced
the punishment of Juda like Am 3, 9-11.

Promises (3, 9-20). They are made up of oracles which often seem
later than the period of the prophet. The one which concerns the
conversion of the nations (9-10) seems to have been turned into a promise
to the dispersed Jews. Another concerns the remnant of Israel (11-13).
The psalm of joy (14-18a) seems to be of cultic origin. The conclusion
(18b-20) envisages the return of the exiles.

The Book of Sophonias was reworked and expanded into its present
form after the Exile.

III. THE MESSAGE

Sophonias has been called a follower. It is true that he depends on
Am 5, 18 and Is 2, 7 ff. for his notion of the day of Yahweh, but he has
turned it into a catastrophe of cosmic dimensions. It is true that he
depends on Is 2, 6-22 for his teaching on humility before God, but he
adds here his own notion of poverty *('anawah)* and depicts the remnant as
a poor people (spiritually) (3, 12-13). For the rest he concerned himself
with cult matters [2] and was one of the pioneers of the Deuteronomic
reform directed against pagan influence in Juda.

§ 2. Nahum

BIBLIOGRAPHY

> Introductions, translations, commentaries, pp. 1 f. and 271 (A. GEORGE,
> *BJ**; E. SELLIN, *KAT*; K. ELLIGER, *ATD*...).
>
> P. HUMBERT, " Essai d'analyse de Nahum I, 2-3, 4, " *ZAW* (1926),
> pp. 266-280. " Le problème du livre de Nahum, " *RHPR* (1933),
> pp. 1-15.
>
> A. HALDAR, *Studies in the Book of Nahum* (Uppsala, 1947).
>
> J. L. MIHELIC, " The Concept of God in the Book of Nahum, " *Interpre-
> tation*, 2 (1948), pp. 199-208.
>
> J. VAN DOORSLAER, " No Amon, " *CBQ*, 11 (1949), pp. 280-295.
>
> J. LECLERCQ, " Nahum, " *Études sur les prophètes d'Israël** (Paris, 1954),
> pp. 85-110.
>
> C. L. TAYLOR, " The Book of Nahum, " *IB* (1956).
>
> W. A. MAIER, *The Book of Nahum : A Commentary* (1959).

---

[2] NICOLSKY, " Pascha im Kulte des Jerusalem Tempels, " *ZAW*, 45 (1927),
pp. 171-190.

I. THE MAN

Only the name of the prophet is known. Perhaps it is an abbreviated form of Nahumja (Yahweh consoles). In this regard compare Menahem and Nehemias. His native town, Elcos, has been situated in the Negeb (pseudo-Epiphanius) or in Galilee (St. Jerome). The present tendency is to regard him as a cult prophet. He is represented as a precursor of Ananias, the official prophet of the Temple whom Jeremias attacked (28). His ardent nationalism is often noted.

II. THE BOOK

The divisions

The book opens with an alphabetic psalm. The alphabetic pattern is not complete (*aleph* to *kaph*), but the psalm is not a fragment. The poem describes a theophany of Yahweh who destroys His foes and protects those who trust in Him. There are in the theophany some mythological allusions (1, 1-8). In 1, 9—2, 3 there are combined words of salvation for Juda (1, 12, 13; 2, 1-3) and threats against Ninive (1, 9-11. 14). There follows abruptly a series of poems on the fall of Ninive (2, 4—3, 19). These poems are difficult to analyze, but they are remarkably forceful.

Interpretations

The majority of the critics regard the book as a series of prophecies all dating from approximately the same period : 625 (Van Hoonacker), 626 and 612 (George), about 612 (Lods). According to Weiser certain passages suppose the destruction of Ninive (2, 1; 3, 18-19) while others look forward to it, but this is to forget the convention of regarding a prophecy as virtually fulfilled when it is pronounced. The introductory psalm gives a religious and eschatological sense to the whole. To regard Nahum as its author is not farfetched even though it does seem to enlarge the significance of the fall of Ninive and to give it a symbolic value.

Humbert and Sellin have viewed the book as a prophetic liturgy actually performed on the occasion of the fall of Ninive. Against this view is the fact that much of the book looks forward rather than back to this event.

Recently Haldar (1947) has held that the book emanates from a cult group which transposed the ritual of the God-King into a piece of anti-Assyrian propaganda. There was no prophet Nahum. The name comes from 3, 7; 2, 3. The basis upon which Haldar rests his hypothesis has already been seen (p. 268). Here it goes beyond the evidence of the text.

III. The message

The book is that of a patriot who affirms the fidelity of Yahweh to his vineyard (2, 3) and emphasizes once again that it is God who directs history (2, 14). When he describes the punishment of Ninive, it is always related to the sins of Assyria (3, 1. 4; 2, 14).

§ 3. Habacuc

BIBLIOGRAPHY

> Introductions, translations, commentaries, pp. 1 f. and 271 (J. TRINQUET, *BJ**; E. SELLIN, *KAT*...).
>
> WALKER—LUND, " The Literary Structure of the Book of Habakkuk, " *JBL*, 53 (1934), pp. 335-370.
>
> W. A. IRWIN, " The Psalm of Habakkuk, " *JNES*, 1 (1942), pp. 10-40.
>
> P. HUMBERT, *Problème du livre d'Habaquq* (Neuchâtel, 1944).
>
> W. H. BROWNLEE, " The Jerusalem Habakkuk Scroll, " *BASOR*, 112 (1948), pp. 8-18; 114 (1949), pp. 9-10; 126 (1952), pp. 10-20.
>
> W. F. ALBRIGHT, " The Psalm of Habakkuk, " *Studies in Old Testament Prophecy*, ed. H. ROWLEY (Edinburgh, 1950), pp. 1-18.
>
> E. NIELSEN, " The Righteous and the Wicked in Habaqquq, " *Studia Theologica*, 6 (1953), pp. 54-78.
>
> D. M. LLOYD-JAMES, *From Fear to Faith : Studies in the Book of Habakkuk* (1953).
>
> C. L. TAYLOR, " The Book of Habakkuk, " *IB* (1956).
>
> W. H. BROWNLEE, " The Placarded Revelation of Habakkuk, " *JBL*, 82 (1963), pp. 319-325.

I. The rise of the Chaldeans [3]

Of Aramean stock, the Chaldeans came into Babylon in the eighth century. Under Nabopolassar (625-605) they assumed direction of the anti-Assyrian struggle in association with the Medes. After destroying the last Assyrian army and after defeating Egypt at Karkemish (605), Nabuchodonosor began to establish his hegemony over the whole of Syria and Palestine. From this point on, the history of Juda became the story of the progressive tightening of this control : in 597 the first siege of Jerusalem; in 586 the destruction of the city and state. This summary of events is sufficient to locate Habacuc in the period during which he worked.

---

[3] Cf. *above*, pp. 33-35.

II. The man

According to Noth the prophet's name is derived from that of an edible Akkadian plant (*hambaququ*, probably *cassia tora*). We know little of his personal history for the account of Dn 14, 33 ff. is not history in this sense. According to the LXX version of this account Habacuc is a Levite and son of Jesus. From the presence of a psalm in his work it has been concluded that he, like Nahum, was a cult prophet, but both of them could well have imitated the style of the liturgy and treated of theophanies without actually being officially involved in the Temple services. 2, 1-3 teaches us something of the psychology of the prophet's vision; 3, 16 is perhaps the prophet's reflection on a vision. For this reason Habacuc is better known to us than Nahum.

III. The book

The divisions

a) The dialogue between God and the prophet. 1, 2-4, the first complaint, concerns the prevalence of injustice in Juda and imitates a psalm of distress. 1, 5-11 is the first divine answer : the Chaldeans are coming to bring vengeance! 1, 12-17 is the second impatient complaint. It concerns the scandal of the triumph of the Chaldeans. A second divine answer (2, 1-4) announces the destruction of tyranny and the prosperity of the nation whose faith has made it just.

b) Woe for the oppressor : 5 " woes " (2, 6c-19) introduced by a brief preamble (vv. 5-6b). Verse 20 introduces the psalm.

c) The psalm (3) [4] concerns the eschatological intervention of God to bring to terms his prophecy. It calls to mind Jgs 5 and Dt 33 and uses themes from the cult tradition.

Interpretations

a) The Assyrian interpretation which posits a literary breakup.—Budde (1889) and Eissfeldt (1934) think that the two complaints were originally united and concerned the Assyrian oppression. Yahweh was to bring an end to this oppression through the coming of the Chaldeans. They posit the following order : 1, 2-4. 12-17 (Assyrian oppression); 2, 1-3; 1, 5-10 (the Chaldean avengers); 2, 6 f. (" woes " against the Assyrians).

---

[4] H. Bévenot, " Le cantique d'Habaquq*, " *RB* (1933), pp. 499-525. —P. Béguerie, " Le psaume d'Habaquq, " *Études sur les prophètes d'Israël* (Paris, 1954), pp. 53-84.—W. F. Albright, " The Psalm of Habakkuk, " *Studies in Old Testament Prophecy* (Edinburgh, 1950), pp. 1-18.—M. Delcor, " La geste de Yahvé au temps de l'Exode et l'espérance du psalmiste en Habacuc III, " *Miscellanea biblica B. Ubach** (Montserrat, 1953), pp. 287-302.

Habacuc consequently has the same perspective as Nahum. In his turn Weiser (1949) supports the Assyrian hypothesis : both complaints concern the Assyrian oppression. The answer to the first announces the coming of the Chaldeans. The second complaint is marked by impatience because nothing has yet changed! The answer to this second complaint must be sought in the psalm which was originally introduced by 2, 1-3. The premise—and the weakness— of this type of exegesis is the assumption that the text has been radically rearranged. Weiser dates Habacuc about 625-612.

b) The Babylonian interpretation which posits a plurality of authors.—Wellhausen (1893) and Nowack (1897) think that Habacuc's complaints date from about 590 and concern the Babylonian oppression. I, 5-11 which announces the vengeance to be brought by the Chaldeans was not written by him. This piece dates from about 610. Marti (1904) and Lods (1950) assign to Habacuc (about 605) only the announcement of the coming of the Chaldeans (1, 5-10. 14-15 and, for Lods, 16-17). The rest was added during the Exile with an anti-Babylonian intent. After the Exile the psalm was added because of the similarity of subject matter.

c) The Babylonian interpretation which views the book as a genuine liturgy.—Following the essays of Balla (1928) and Sellin (1929)—the latter radically changed his exegesis three times!—Humbert (1944) has interpreted Habacuc as the libretto of a liturgy. The work was written in 602-1 at the time of Nabuchodonosor's invasion. The prophet speaks out against the despotism of Joakim (2, 5b-20) who is enigmatically and satirically presented in phrases borrowed at times from Jeremias. He belonged to a cult group. But surely this anti-government posture on the part of a Temple functionary is hardly probable!

d) It seems best to regard the book as " a literary imitation of a liturgy " (Trinquet). The Chaldean presence in Juda is its principal concern. In the book there are several levels of thought based on the equivocal sense of the words " just " and " wicked " (so Junker). The first complaint is directed against the oppression that exists within Juda and which is about to be punished by the invasion of the Chaldeans. The second complaint is directed against Chaldean oppression. The divine oracle of 2, 2-4 announces the destruction of the invader. The woes give the motives for this destruction. It is also the subject of the concluding psalm. On this basis the date 602-1 can be preserved.

Importance

Habacuc is a traditionalist. In his use of the imagery of mythical combat (3) he returns to the national origins. Like Nahum he had to interpret the events of his own day. A combination of circumstances forced him to pose the problem of the justice of God in governing nations. The problem raised is similar to that raised by the Book of Job about the earthly life of individuals. There is no real solution to this problem apart from faith and in this light it is easy to understand why 2, 4 has continued to be regarded as the essence of the message of Habacuc (Gal 3, 11; Rom 1, 17).

§ 4. Jeremias

BIBLIOGRAPHY

Introductions, translations, commentaries, pp. 1 f. and 251 f. (A. GELIN, *BJ**; L. DENNEFELD, *BPC**; P. VOLZ, *KAT*; F. NÖTSCHER, *HSAT**; A. W. STREANE, *CBSC*...).

G. A. SMITH, *Jeremiah*[4] (New York : Harper, 1929).

J. SKINNER, *Prophecy and Religion, Studies in the Life of Jeremiah* (Cambridge, 1930).

H. G. MAY, " The Chronology of Jeremiah's Oracles, " *JNES*, 4 (1935), pp. 217-227.

A. CONDAMIN, " Le livre de Jérémie*, " *EB* (Paris, 1936).

H. G. MAY, " Towards an Objective Approach to the Book of Jeremiah : the Biographer, " *JBL*, 61 (1942), pp. 139-155.

A. GELIN, *Jérémie (Le livre de)**; *SDB*, V, cols. 857-889 (Paris, 1948).

H. ROWLEY, " The Prophet Jeremiah and the Book of Deuteronomy, " *Studies in Old Testament Prophecy* (Edinburgh, 1950), pp. 157-174.

A. C. WELCH, *Jeremiah, His Time and His Work* (Oxford : Blackwell, 1951).

A. PENNA, *Geremia** (Rome, 1952).

J. STEINMANN, *Le prophète Jérémie** (Paris, 1952).

A. GELIN, *Jérémie** (Paris, 1952).

A. WEISER, *Das Buch des Propheten Jeremia* (Göttingen, 1952, 1955).

G. VITTONATTO, *Il libro di Geremia** (Turin, 1955).

H. W. ROBINSON, " The Cross of Jeremiah, " *The Cross in the Old Testament* (London : SCM, 1955), pp. 115-192.

J. P. HYATT, " The Book of Jeremiah, " *IB* (1956); *Jeremiah, Prophet of Courage and Hope* (New York : Abingdon, 1958).

W. RUDOLPH, *Jeremia*[2] (Tübingen, 1958).

B. CUNLIFFE-JONES, *Jeremiah* (London : SCM, 1960).

S. BLANK, *Jeremiah : Man and Prophet* (Cincinnati, 1961).

H. ROWLEY, " The Early Prophecies of Jeremiah in their Setting, " *BJRL*, 45 (1962-1963), pp. 198-234.

J. BRIGHT, *Jeremiah* (Garden City : Doubleday, 1965).

I. Generalities

Jeremias lived through the entire drama of the last decades of the Judean state. He witnessed all the events that occurred between 626 and 586. A contemporary of Sophonias, Nahum and Habacuc, he sheds light on the whole of this troubled period only partially dealt with in each of the other three prophets.

Renan has written : " Without this extraordinary man the religious history of humanity would have followed a different course. " Yet at first sight Jeremias does not seem to have added much to the theology of his predecessors apart from a more profound understanding of sin. The concept of a " state of sin " was the point of departure for his own work. The true religion in order to survive had to be detached from the state which no longer guaranteed its preservation. His mystical experience, his continuous contact with God opened his mind to a new form of religion, and at the end of his career he could speak of the New Covenant that would replace the Old Covenant. The theology of Jeremias is less a system than a ferment. It is in the light of his influence on later generations, especially the " poor of Yahweh, " that the contribution of the prophet is to be evaluated. The theology of Jeremias was the product of a mind that is fortunately better known to us than that of any other prophet. As Bentzen has written : " A book about prophecy will always be to a large extent a book about Jeremias. "

II. The book

The basic literary facts

The differences between the Massoretic and Greek texts are considerable. The latter, shorter by nearly an eighth, is possibly a more ancient recension of the text. The tendency of the MT to gloss is easily seen in chapters 25, 27 and 28. 33, 14-26 is an addition, as also 38, 28b—39, 14. As for the quality of the respective texts in the parts that are common to both, the Hebrew text is generally superior though the Greek does preserve some excellent readings (2, 34; 46, 15). The LXX places the oracles against the nations after 25, 13c while the MT groups them at the end of the book. The form of the book attested by the Greek is certainly more ancient, but the order of the prophecies in the Hebrew recension is primitive.

The book contains a relatively small number of *interpolations*, *additions* and *amplifications*. The following are the more important : 10, 1-16; 17, 19-27; 25, 12-13c. 14; 30, 10-11. 23-24; 31, 10-11. 26. 38-40; 32, 17-23 (in part); 50—51, 58; 52. It is well known that the books of the

Bible were living books and successive generations did not hesitate to inscribe in them their own thoughts and hopes. They were books entrusted to the community and preserved within a tradition. The book of Jeremias is clear evidence of this within a limited area of the Bible. The question has been raised whether a certain number of passages composed in the emphatic style of the sermons of Deuteronomy are a reworked expansion of the preaching of Jeremias, prepared for reading in the synagogues during the Exile. The existence of synagogues during this period has not been proved conclusively, but it is certainly probable. The passages in question are : 7, 1—8, 3; 11, 1-14; 16, 1-13; 18, 1-12; 21, 1-10; 22, 1-5; 25, 1-14; 34, 8-22; 35. This opinion strongly supported by Mowinckel and Rudolph is held with reserve by Weiser and rejected by Eissfeldt and Oesterley-Robinson : " What has been called the Deuteronomic style is simply the style of Hebrew rhetorical prose during the latter part of the seventh century and the first part of the sixth century. There is no reason why Jeremias would not have used this style. " [5] The period of mass excisions from the text seems to have come to an end. Duhm (1901), the prime example of this type of criticism, left to Jeremias only 270 verses and to his biography only 200, while 850 were regarded as the work of later commentators. Jeremias apart from the letter of chapter 29 wrote only about sixty of the prayers in the elegiac rhythm of the *qînâ*! P. Volz (1922) following Schwally (1888) regarded as later additions all the prophecies against the nations. Contemporary criticism, which is more subtle in these matters, speaks of a core written by Jeremias, reworked and enlarged sometimes extensively (Weiser) at a later date. It is probable that the Messianic chapters (especially chapters 30—33) are to be interpreted with this in mind. The oracles against Babylon (50-51, 58) are an exception to this. Their inauthenticity is universally recognized.

Finally the book shows much *disorder*. This is evidenced by the number of *doublets*, the mélange of the three classic literary *forms* (oracular material, biography, autobiography), and especially the *lack of sequence* in the chronological indications spread throughout the book (3, 6; 21, 1; 24, 1; 25, 1; 26, 1; 27, 1; 28, 1; 29, 2; 32, 1; 33, 1; 34, 1; 35, 1; 36, 1. 9; 37, 5; 39, 1-2; 40, 1; 45, 1; 46, 1; 49, 34; 51, 59).

Formation of the book

The history of the formation of the book is complicated. Baruch, a professional scribe and a noble who had been won over to the ideas of

---

[5] OESTERLEY-ROBINSON, *An Introduction to the Books of the O. T.* (London, 1941), p. 298.

Jeremias and remained faithful to him through his many trials, played an important role. The long and elaborate title of the book (1, 1-3) witnesses to several stages of its formation but not all, for the dates given do not cover the material in chapters 40—44. Four stages can be distinguished :

a) The roll of 605-604

Dictated by Jeremias to Baruch and then read three times on the same day, it contained the oracles that the prophet had pronounced after 626 " against Jerusalem, Juda and all the nations " (36, 2. 29. 32). This corresponds with what we know from chapter 25. Verses 1-13b of this chapter are a summary of the oracles against Jerusalem and Juda, and verses 15 f. are the introduction to the oracles against the nations in their primitive form. The original roll can be plausibly reconstructed though the reconstruction is in part necessarily based on conjecture. Of the words of Jeremias and of the autobiographical pieces, the following must be set aside : sections dating from after 605-604; sections that do not deal with the threatening theme of the roll (promises, confessions, wisdom material); sections which concern only a particular group within the theocracy (kings, prophets). There remains : 1, 4—6, 30 (preaching under Josias); 7—20 (preaching under Joakim. The pieces listed below are to be excluded); 25; 46—49, 33 (except for 46, 13-28).

b) The additions to the roll

According to 36, 32 there were added to the original roll " many words of the same type. " The sources and the extent of these additions are not known, but it is natural to think immediately of Baruch. He could well have added to the threatening oracles other similar oracles dating from after 605-604 : 10, 17-22; 12, 7-14; 13, 12-19; 15, 5-9; 16, 16-18; 18, 1-12; 46, 13-26; 49, 34-39. He could have added other related accounts he had heard directly from his master (24; 27; 35). Thus the roll became a memoir in journal form. After the events of 586 he could have added to his manuscript the two sections against the kings (21, 11—23, 8) and against the prophets (23, 9-40) though this is less certain. Finally after the death of Jeremias, if this hypothesis is correct, he added Jeremias' precious " confessions " (11, 18—12, 6; 15, 10-12; 17, 12-18; 18, 18-23; 20, 7-18).

c) The biography of Jeremias

Besides collecting the work of his master, Baruch wrote down his own memories of Jeremias. He defends his master, affirms his faith in Jeremias' mission and lays particular emphasis on his sufferings between 608 and 586. This biography takes in the passages written in the third person. They follow in chronological order : 19, 2—20, 6; 26; 36; 45;

28—29; 51, 59-64; 34, 8-22; 37—44. Baruch probably finished his work in Egypt (43, 6). The exchanges between Jerusalem and the exiles were frequent, and it is probable that copies (not necessarily complete) arrived in Babylon by way of the holy city. This also holds true for those pieces where Jeremias' thought is given fixed form by Baruch.

d) The exilic edition

The definitive reworking of this material that has given us the Book of Jeremias must be located in the Babylonian community open as it was toward the future. Prior to this final work of compilation and synthesis, the material circulated within the community and was the object of intense study. New pieces were formed by uniting diverse elements, for instance chapters 27—29. These chapters were a sort of message to the exiles and must have been autonomous before 586. Some pieces, with proper titles, were perhaps drawn from collections made for reading in the synagogues. The " book of consolation " (30—31 + 32—33) deserved particular attention. The sections against the kings (21, 11—23, 8) and the prophets (23, 9-40) continued to be read for their own sake. All this literature was very useful to the exiles who found in it matter for reflection, repentance and conversion. The audience reached by both Ezechiel and Second-Isaias was in the first place the audience of Jeremias. Toward the end of the Exile a redactor gave the book its definitive form. Taking in hand this whole complex of material, he used the order already partly existing in it and added some passages for the edification of the community (especially 10, 1-16; 33, 14-26; 50—51, 58; 52).

Divisions of the book

The first part, 1—20, follows more or less a chronological order. This section is taken from the " roll, " except for 19, 1—20, 6 which comes from a biographical piece written by Baruch (the key word is " potter " in 18, 1 and 19, 1). For the sake of contrast, 21, 1-10 (a biographical piece) has been introduced in opposition to 20, 1 (key word : *Phassur*). The mention of Sedecias in 21, 1-10 explains why the section on the kings follows (21, 11—23, 8). Analogy of subject has caused the section on the prophets (23, 9-40) to be introduced at this point. 24 is actually connected with 21, 1-10. 25, 1-13b was the original conclusion of 1—20.

The second part introduced by 25, 15 f. is made up of homogenous material. The oracles against the nations are the center of the collection. To these there was added toward the end of the Exile an oracle against

Babylon (50—51, 58). 51, 59-64 taken from a biographical piece written by Baruch, has been joined to this oracle.

The third part artificially groups material derived from different sources and dating from different periods. In these the redactor has seen the promise of salvation.

These three parts give the book the classical order of Isaias and Ezechiel : prophecies against Juda, prophecies against the nations, prophecies of blessing. There follows a fourth, homogenous part which terminates with chapter 45. This chapter is almost the signature of Jeremias. Chapter 36 is perhaps the introduction to this fourth part because the first thirty-five chapters were thought to contain all the additions referred to in 36, 32.

The plan is as follows :

    I. Oracles against Juda and Jerusalem (1, 4—25, 13b).

   II. Oracles against the nations (25, 13c-38; 46—51).

  III. Prophecies of blessing (26—35).

  IV. The sufferings of Jeremias (36—45).

   V. Appendix : the catastrophe of 586 and the favor shown to Joachin (52).

III. THE LIFE AND WORK OF JEREMIAS

The chronological order of the narratives and discourses

626 : Vocation (1).

626-622 : Appeals for conversion addressed to Juda; the announcement of an invasion from the north (2—6, except for 3, 6-18 and 5, 18-19).

622 : Preaching for the Deuteronomic reform (11, 1-14).

After 622 : Announcement of the return of the northern kingdom (30—31, 22; 3, 6-13).

609 : Abandonment of the reform (additions to 11, 1-14). The persecution of Jeremias by the people of Anathoth (11, 18—12, 6).

608-605 : Lamentation for Joachaz (22, 10-11). Discourse against the Temple (7—8, 3; 26). Warnings to Joakim (21, 11—22, 9).

605-604 : Victory of the Babylonians at Carchemish (46, 2-12). Invasion of the Palestinian countryside (9, 9-21). Prediction of the destruction and exile that nothing save conversion can prevent (8, 4—10, 25, except 10, 1-16). Prediction of judgment brought against Juda and the neighboring nations by a people from the north (25). The main part of the oracles against the Philistines (47), Moab (48), Ammon (49, 1-6), Edom (49, 7-22), Damascus (49, 23-27), Cedar and Asor (49, 28-33). The symbolic vision of the loincloth hidden near the Euphrates. Appeal for conversion under penalty of exile (13, 20-27; 16—17, 11, except for 16, 14-15. 19-21). Prayer of Jeremias against his persecutors (17, 12-18). The discourse against Joakim (22, 13-19). Baruch begins writing down the words of Jeremias (36). Prophecy concerning Baruch (45).

About 602 : Juda besieged by her neighbors (12, 7-17; 13, 12-17). The oracles against Moab (48) and Ammon (49, 1-6) already assigned to 605 could also be located here.

Around 600 : The defective vessel; the complaints of Jeremias (18). The broken flask (19—20). The prophet's vocation reconfirmed (15, 10-21).

Sometime during Joakim's reign : The drought (14—15, 9). Against the prophets (23, 9-40).

597 : Against Joachin (22, 20-30). During the siege : the episode of the Rechabites (35). After the siege (13, 18-19).

593-592 : Struggle with the false prophets (27—28). Letters to the exiles (29). The two baskets (24). Symbolic action against Babylon (51, 39-64). Oracle against Elam (49, 34-39).

587-586 : Siege of Jerusalem (37—38). The failure to free the slaves (34, 8-22). Oracles on the fate of Sedecias (34, 1-7; 21, 1-10). The purchase of a field at Anathoth and the prediction of the return (32, except for 18-23; 33, except for 14-26). Completion of the book of consolation (30—31) with the addition of 31, 23-40. Odds and ends of prophecies of good fortune (3, 14-18; 5, 18-19; 16, 14-15, 19-20).

586 (July to October) : Events in Juda after the siege (39—43, 7). Prediction of the invasion of Egypt by the Chaldeans (46, 13-26).

General divisions of the life of Jeremias

The life of Jeremias can be divided into three stages which coincide with the reigns of Josias, Joakim and Sedecias. The beginning of the first period (626-609) is especially well known to us. He was then not yet thirty and it is not surprising to notice in his preaching some of the characteristics of youth : the full style of his preaching, the marked influence of the former prophets and the illusions which coincide with the reform of Josias in 622.

The second stage (608-597) could be called the " Gethsemane " of the prophet. It was a period uniformly bleak and somber. When it began Jeremias seems to have been about forty.

The third stage (597-586), the prophet's mature years, is crowned by words of hope and the victory of faith. When Jerusalem falls, the prophet sketches the development of Israel's religion from the phase that has passed to a new and superior phase.

Providential preparation and vocation

Jeremias was born perhaps about 645 at Anathoth four miles north of Jerusalem in the territory of Benjamin which had some connections with the old northern kingdom. Even in his first oracles Jeremias is unwilling to despair of the tribes which had fallen under Assyrian domination (31, 2-22; 30, 5-21). This attraction toward the north helps explain the affinity between Jeremias and Osee who has been called " the Jeremias of the north " (Stanley). Osee's influence on Jeremias can be seen already in Jeremias' earliest oracles. The two men also shared a similar affection toward the people to whom they were obliged to announce such woes. It is important to note this psychological struggle. Their emotional temperaments are much in evidence in their oracles. Jeremias must have assimilated the manner of Osee with all the greater facility since they were kindred spirits. In the case of Jeremias this emotive temperament was certainly refined by his priestly ancestry (1, 1). Doubtless he descended from Abiathar who had been exiled to Anathoth by Solomon (3 Kgs 2, 26-27). His love for the rural life with his family stands out in his oracles. Even his eschatology bears its stamp. With the exception of 4, 23-26 it is devoid of the catastrophic. The absence of birds, the stopping of the mills, the extinguishing of the lamp, this is what grieves the spirit of Jeremias. The period through which he lived was somber. On the international scene Assyria is still dominant and the Scythians continue their incursions. At home the tendency toward syncretism has not yet passed.

The account of the prophet's vocation opens the book. Unlike Isaias, Jeremias is not frightened by the divine presence. Jeremias' reaction gives the impression that this was not the first vision but the confirmation of a series of such mystical experiences. Jeremias is frightened by the prospect of becoming a prophet to the nations (1, 5-10); he tries to refuse; then he accepts. This will prove to be the pattern of his interior life. Two visions (vv. 11-13) complete this initiation. Yahweh explaining the second reveals to the prophet that his mission will not meet with success, but that He will support him and make the mission bearable.

The preaching under Josias (626-609)

a) The beginning

The prophet was perhaps twenty-five when he began to preach in and about Jerusalem. The religious and moral situation about him was not bright. The innate tendencies of the nation, the example of the kings, and the influence of Assyria had all contributed to the contamination of the religion of Yahweh. Yahweh was looked upon as the national God to whom appeal was made in time of peril (2, 27-28; 3, 4-10). But, as Elias had expressed it, the nation " limped on both sides " (3 Kgs 18, 21). Two groups of false gods were worshiped. The first group took in the Baals and Astartes and was of local or Phoenician origin. Its cult was conducted outside the cities (except 32, 29) on the high places. Human sacrifice was a part of this cult. The cult of the second group which took in the *army of heaven*, the astral divinities of Assyria, was conducted on the roofs of houses. These rites, the offering of cakes for example, seem to have been more simple. Like Osee Jeremias attacked the high places and the bloody and immoral cult carried on there. He regarded a " baalized " Yahweh as simply a baal. He denounced the formalism and the trafficking which were a regular part of Temple worship. He is stunned by the social injustice and the immoral lives of his contemporaries. According to him these evils were widespread (5, 1; 6, 13).

Chastisement is at the gates. In the chapters on the " enemy from the north " the prophet seems more a poet than a preacher. In no other place is the imagination of Jeremias at freer rein than here (4, 13. 15. 19-21; 6, 22-23). There is some problem as to the identity of this enemy spoken of about the same time by Sophonias (1). The prophet does not seem to have had the Scythians in mind directly, but they may well have colored his thinking (cf. p. 313).

b) The reform of 622

The cooperation of Jeremias in this reform is denied by Duhm. According to Dumeste his attitude toward the reform was one of hopeful expectancy. The majority of the critics think he actually cooperated in it. This (say Condamin and Von Rad) is not contradicted by what followed. It can be supposed that he joined the army of voluntary missionaries who helped promote the king's reform and that he settled at Jerusalem as permitted by Dt 18, 6. [6] Probably Jeremias cooperated in the reform, but he did not play a leading role. This view is supported by the following facts : 1) 25, 3 supposes that he has not interrupted his ministry; 2) 26, 24; 29, 3; 36, 11-19; 39, 14; 40, 5. 6 attest the friendship of Jeremias for the

---

[6] H. CAZELLES, " Jérémie et le Deutéronome*, " *RSR* (1951), pp. 5-36.

family of Saphan, one of the promoters of the reform (4 Kgs 22, 8-14);
3) the sentiments he expresses toward the reforming king support this
view; finally the terminology and doctrine of Jeremias are often Deuteronomic (circumcision of heart, love of God) and 11, 2-8 (in part) must
have been pronounced under these circumstances. During the following
years Josias extended his power over the old northern kingdom (4 Kgs 23,
19); a united Israel is outlined; then Jeremias affirms his hope in a series
of oracles (30, 1—31, 22) which originally concerned the northern kingdom
(Weiser).

c) The scandal of 609 (cf. p. 33).

The religious reform was accompanied by a policy of national independence. In 609 Pharao Nechao II hastened to the aid of Assyria which
was on the point of collapse. Josias tried to stop the expedition which
could have saved the former suzerain of Juda and was killed in the
attempt at the battle of Megiddo (2 Par 36, 20-35). His death must have
been a severe blow to the reformers. The king who had been so sincerely
attached to the prescriptions of Deuteronomy had not enjoyed the
temporal prosperity promised to the true servants of Jahweh. The
lamentation which Jeremias composed for Josias (22, 15-16) is mentioned
in 2 Par 35, 25.

His ministry under Joakim (608-597)

a) The philippic : 22, 13-19

The discourse presents a by-no-means flattering portrait of the new
sovereign who was a creature of Pharao. A typical oriental despot,
unjust, fond of ostentation, Joakim seems capable of taking a place
among the unholy trio, Achaz, Manasses, Amon, though 4 Kgs 24, 4
implicitly recognizes that he did not match the worst of their crimes.
It is not known whether Joakim made an official place for idolatry in
Israel (cf. 7, 31), but it was sufficient for him to relax the measures taken
by his father against idolatry for the popular practices to begin to reappear
(7, 31).

b) The false guarantees

Before a stiff-necked people Jeremias argues that it is foolish to base the
security of the nation on tottering foundations. Circumcision, cult,
the prophets, the State, the Temple, all are such. Only one thing counts,
" the knowledge of Yahweh " (9, 23; 22, 16). What Jeremias says about
the Temple is important (7 and 26) : Yahweh is no more bound to Sion
than He was to Silo. The inviolability of the Temple had become a
popular " dogma " and this was in part under Isaias' influence. Probably

it was the violence of his words that caused Jeremias to be barred from the Temple for several years.

c) The announcement of invasion and exile

The words of the prophet are progressively more clear. Babylon is the instrument of Yahweh to punish the whole of the Near East (25, 17-38). Prior to this Jeremias had spoken about the defeat of Egypt at Carchemish. The keystone of the arch of the " fertile crescent " had collapsed, and Nabuchodonosor was free to continue his victorious march westward. At this moment Jeremias gives a concrete significance to the poems about the enemy from the north which date from the first days of his mission. It has been held that for both Sophonias and Jeremias a raid by hordes of Scythians was the occasion of these poems. Lods has seen in this raid the event which was the basis for Jeremias' vocation. Today the tendency is to underline the mysterious element in the idea of unchained forces coming from the north or the end of the world (see also Ez 38—39; Jl 2, 20). In any case, the enemy from the north does have a name in 605.

Joakim knew where to turn to save Juda. But he was a creature of Pharao and could not hold himself back from seeking his help. This resulted in Nabuchodonosor's sending punitive expeditions against Juda about 602 (4 Kgs 24, 1-7). Finally, in 598-7 he came himself to lay siege to Jerusalem.

d) The " confessions " of Jeremias

Jeremias, like some of the authors of the psalms who were to follow him, has left us insights into his most personal thoughts, prayers, and almost a dialogue between himself and God. In this regard he imitates the psalms of lamentation. The personal character of his work makes him seem a literary creator. He writes of the sufferings he experienced in his mission. The misinterpretation of his threatening sermons, the failure of his ministry, official and less open persecution, sickness (17, 14), moral isolation, all were occasions of suffering, and he mentions them by turns. He was temperamentally disposed to feel these things deeply. In his writings he appears as a sensitive man who never desired evil for his people. Though he was quite timid, fierce words continually burst forth from his mouth (13, 23). He was easily discouraged (15, 19). Several times he is seized by a paroxysm of sorrow; in 12, 1-6 where he poses for the first time in the Bible the problem of the relation between God's government of the world and the conduct of individuals; in 15, 10-11, 15-21 when in the midst of Jeremias' career Yahweh calls him a second time and invites him to moral effort and spiritual progress.

The suffering of the prophet made him more open to God.   When the Temple is about to fall, when he is far from Jerusalem, his personal sufferings prove the occasion for growth in holiness.   His piety is not without its defects (pride : 12, 3; self-interest : 20, 12), but it approaches the piety taught in the Gospels.   Jeremias is the father of the " clients of Yahweh " who were later called the " poor of Yahweh. "

His ministry under Sedecias (597-586)

a) The period between the two sieges (cf. p. 33f.)
Joakim died before the fall of Jerusalem in 597.   Nabuchodonosor removed from the throne his son, Joachin, whom he carried off into captivity.   In his stead he appointed King Sedecias, son of Josias. Deprived of the advice of the royal counselors deported to Babylon with Joachin and personally weak, Sedecias let himself get involved in an anti-Babylonian coalition.   This political folly brought on the second siege of Jerusalem (587-6).

Between the two sieges there arose a nationalist movement which Jeremias opposed.   For him the center of gravity of the nation had shifted from Jerusalem to the exiled community in Babylon where the Israel of the future was being prepared (29 and 24).   In the capital numerous prophets argued against his view.   They advocated revolt against Babylon in concert with the smaller nations of western Asia who dreamed of revenge in accord with the advice of their own prophets. Jeremias seems to have been successful against this propaganda.

b) The siege of 587-586
The chapters from the pen of Baruch which recount the siege are among the most vivid in the Bible.   An initial oracle to Sedecias dates from the first battles around Jerusalem.   Jeremias offers a choice between " the way of life and the way of death. "   Jerusalem must surrender or perish (21, 1-10).   A second oracle (34, 1-7) announces to the same king that he will go to Babylon and allows for the possibility of a nonviolent death. A third oracle dates from the interruption of the siege that followed Pharao's intervention (37, 3-10).   Then follow :

Revocation of the liberty of the slaves originally freed to draw down on Jerusalem God's favor and doubtless to augment the number of fighting men (Jer 34, 8-22).

Jeremias incarcerated for treason in a dungeon (37, 10-16).

The siege taken up again.   The fourth oracle to Sedecias.   Jeremias put in the court of the guard (34, 17-21).

Complaints of the princes over the defeatism of the prophet.   Jeremias put in a cistern.   The king saves him (38, 1-13).

Jeremias incarcerated again in the court of the guard. A fifth oracle for Sedecias. It is necessary to surrender (38, 14-28).

Purchase of a field at Anathoth and the prediction of the return (32).

c) The oracles on the future of the people and religion

Precisely during the most tragic period of his life Jeremias pronounces the majority of his prophecies of good fortune (contained namely in 30—31 + 32—33). The first group takes up again the theme of the oracles pronounced in favor of the exiles of the kingdom of Israel. Previously when Josias had extended his power toward the north, Jeremias had spoken of the return of these exiles and the restoration of a kingdom united around Sion as in the time of David. It is to be noted that in Jeremias' view this promise can be fulfilled only after an adequate expiation. This is true for the northern kingdom in exile since 721, for the exiles of 597 for whom the sojourn in Babylon is a purification (24; 29), and especially for the generation that witnessed the horrors of 586.

Jeremias speaks of a Palestinian restoration with Jerusalem as the religious center and a descendant of David upon the throne. The ancient alliance which has ended in failure will be replaced by a new one. In the future God will act directly on the hearts of men (31, 33). He will give them hearts (24, 7). The law will no longer be graven on tables of stone, but in the hearts of men. God Himself will teach men His law. There will be no need for men to teach it (31, 32-34). Yahweh will be known to all (31, 34). Though religion will still remain something national, it will be very much personalized. The disappearance of the Ark (3, 16) anticipates the words of Jesus about the true adorers of the Father (Jn 4, 23). Commenting on the key passage, 31, 31-34, Nötscher writes : " No one has expressed better than Jeremias the idea that religion is an interior union between God and the individual. God freely makes this union possible; man must use the opportunity given him. "

In short, God first caused Jeremias, His prophet, to intensely live what was going to become His essential message in view of the future.

The end of Jeremias

Nabuchodonosor appointed Godolias, a friend of Jeremias, governor (39, 14; 26, 24). Jeremias supported the policies of the new governor : submission to Babylon, peace and work. The remnant left in Juda grouped together around Maspha. There followed a period of calm and an abundant harvest (40, 12) which seemed a blessing from God. But in October Godolias was assassinated by Ishmael, a member of the dethroned royal family. Ishmael, a fanatic (31, 3) and insanely jealous, was spurred

on by the Ammonites, neighbors of Juda (40, 12). The anniversary of
Godolias' death was kept as a day of public mourning in the Exile (Za 8,
19). Many Jews were completely discouraged by these events. Failing
to apprehend the murderer and fearing to be accused of complicity in the
plot (41, 8) they fled to Egypt and forced Jeremias to accompany them.
Not long after this, so it seems, the prophet died there. Chapter 44
indicates that this is where he pronounced his last known words.

The principal glory of Jeremias is to have given Old Testament
thought a decisive push in the direction of the New Testament and to
have foreshadowed much that is distinctively Christian. Numerous
New Testament passages make reference to 31, 31-34 (2 Cor 3, 3 ff.;
Heb 8, 8 ff.; 10, 11-17). St. Augustine has clearly indicated this New
Testament turn of Jeremias' thought : " The difference between the
Old and New Covenants is easily seen. In the former the law is written
on tables of stone; in the latter it is written in the hearts of men. The one
concerns externals and inspires fear; the other concerns the heart and
fills it with joy. The old law makes man a prevaricator by the letter that
kills while the new law induces men to love the law through the spirit
which vivifies. It is thus not true to say that God helps us to do what is
just by giving us the desire and the ability to observe the law (Phil 2, 13)
only because He leads us to observe its precepts exteriorly. Rather He
causes us to grow interiorly (1 Cor 3, 7) and through the Holy Spirit
who has been given to us (Rom 5, 5) puts love in our hearts " (De Spiritu
et littera 24, 24).

CHAPTER IV

THE PROPHETS OF THE EXILIC PERIOD

The catastrophe of 586 was an important turning point in the history of the Chosen People. For the dream of a temporal empire was substituted the ideal of a community whose scale of values is no longer political but religious : the " people of the saints of the Most High. " This change did not take place in a day, and thus the prophets continued to play their role within Judaism as the men directing Israel toward her destiny.

The period of the Exile was important for both literary and doctrinal development in the Bible. Jewish life in Palestine was in decline; the true nucleus of the nation was in Babylon. A part of the exiles adapted well to this new life in a strange land; the others, the idealists, would fill the ranks of those who were to return. Two prophets, one at the beginning of the Exile, the other toward the end, worked among these exiles so open to delusion, to discouragement and to hope.

§ 1. Ezechiel

BIBLIOGRAPHY

Introductions, translations, commentaries, pp. 1 f. and 251 (P. AUVRAY, *BJ**; A. G. COOKE, *ICC*; L. DENNEFELD, *BPC**; A. LODS, B. CENT; A. B. DAVIDSON, *CBSC*...).

C. C. TORREY, *Pseudo-Ezekiel and the Original Prophecy* (New Haven : Yale, 1930).

J. B. HARFORD, *Studies in the Book of Ezekiel* (London, 1935).

A. BERTHOLET, *Hezechiel* (Tübingen, 1936) *(HAT)*.

I. G. MATTHEWS, *Ezekiel* (1939).

M. GRUENTHANER, " The Messianic Concepts of Ezekiel*, " *TS*, 2 (1941), pp. 1-18.

W. A. IRWIN, *The Problem of Ezekiel* (Chicago, 1943).

H. W. ROBINSON, *Two Hebrew Prophets* (Oxford : Clarendon, 1948).

P. AUVRAY, *Ezéchiel** (Paris, 1947).—" Le problème historique du livre d'Ezéchiel*, " *RB* (1948), pp. 503-519.

C. G. HOWIE, *The Date and Composition of Ezekiel* (Philadelphia, 1950).

J. STEINMANN, *Le prophète Ezéchiel et les débuts de l'exil** (Paris, 1953).

H. H. ROWLEY, "The Book of Ezechiel in Modern Study," *Bull. J. Rylands Library* (Manchester, 1953), pp. 146-190.

W. A. IRWIN, "Ezekiel Research since 1943," *VT*, 3 (1953), pp. 54-66.

H. ROWLEY, "The Book of Ezekiel in Modern Study," *BJRL*, 36 (1953-1954), pp. 146-190.

A. GELIN, "Ezéchiel*," *Catholicisme*, IV (Paris, 1954), cols. 1021-1028.

D. N. FREEDMAN, "The Book of Ezekiel," *Interpretation*, 8 (1954), pp. 446-471.

G. FOHRER, *Die Hauptprobleme des Buches Ezechiel* (Berlin, 1952). *Ezechiel* (Tübingen, 1955) (*HAT*).

W. ZIMMERLI, *Ezechiel* (NEUKIRCHEN, 1955-1959).

H. G. MAY, "The Book of EZEKIEL," *IB* (1956).

I. THE PROBLEM OF THE BOOK

Ezechiel, a prophet of the Exile?

The past half century has profoundly changed the problem of the Book of Ezechiel.   At the beginning of the century there was general agreement among the critics that the prophet was a personage of the Exile and that "no book of the Old Testament was more clearly the integral work of one author" (G. B. Gray).   This exegetical tradition has now been broken by a number of authors.

On the one hand the generally accepted date has been challenged; on the other the Babylonian setting has been interpreted as a literary fiction.   According to C. C. Torrey (1930), N. Messel (1945) and L. E. Browne (1952), the book was written after the Exile.   These critics stress the unity of the book.

G. Hölscher (1924), whose scissors-and-paste criticism calls to mind Duhm's work on Jeremias, rejects the unity of Ezechiel.   He regards as authentic only a sixth of the book, i.e., the poems.   A later redactor is responsible for the prose.   W. A. Irwin (1943) enlarges a bit this precious nucleus and he distributes it between a Palestinian and exilic ministry. V. Herntrich (1932) and J. B. Herford (1935) argued for a ministry that was limited to Palestine before the fall of Jerusalem.   In their view an exilic redactor thoroughly reworked the book about 573.

It is evident that the question of where the prophet exercised his ministry came to the fore by slow stages.   V. Herntrich, proponent of a ministry limited to Jerusalem, has very much influenced subsequent criticism.   The Oesterley-Robinson manual (1934) accepts a Palestinian ministry beginning in 602 and holds that the exilic ministry began in 597.

A. Bertholet (1936) gave a classic form to the theory of the double ministry. Auvray (1947), Van den Born (1947), W. Robinson (1948), J. Steinmann (1953) have all followed him. Bertholet finds two distinct divine vocations in chapters 1—3 : the first (1, 4—2, 2) opened the Babylonian ministry in 585; the second (2, 3—3, 9), the Palestinian ministry in 593. An editor transferred the whole of his ministry to the Exile, but the entire Book of Ezechiel survived the process. The commentary of Bertholet is on the whole quite conservative and he has even influenced those who do not share his overall view. Certain texts like 11, 13 seem to suppose the presence of Jeremias at Jerusalem. On this basis A. Bentzen (1948) has suggested a return of the prophet to the capital. Supposedly he was allowed to return as a member of a " fifth column. " But it is hard to understand how the prophet escaped the fate of Jeremias if this is true.

All these discussions have not prevented more conservative exegetes from maintaining the traditional understanding of these matters. Reacting to Bertholet's position, they have offered new evidence supporting their own. These exegetes include O. Eissfeldt (1934), G. A. Cooke (1936), L. Dennefeld (1946), F. Spadafora (1948), J. Ziegler (1948), C. G. Howie (1950), A. Lods (1950), G. Fohrer (1952) and finally H. H. Rowley (1953) who summarizes his views as follows : " I find a greater unity in this book than in either Isaias or Jeremias. Nevertheless, I do not think that the book in its present form ought to be regarded as edited by the prophet himself though the contents of the book probably go back to him or to his disciples. It was put in its present form by an editor who to a very minor extent supplied for what he did not find in his sources. I would locate the entire ministry of Ezechiel in Babylon during the period immediately before and after the fall of Jerusalem. "

Towards a solution

The following series of arguments assembled by Fohrer favors the traditional view :

1) The public whom Ezechiel addresses appears rather vague at first. He seems to be speaking to the soul of the nation. Actually he indicates his audience quite clearly. " The rebellious house " corresponds to what Jeremias says in his letter to the exiles (Jer 29, 21 f.). These exiles are presented as men who believe in Yahweh, but they fail to understand the lessons of the events at hand and are ever ready to listen to the prophets of good fortune in their midst (Jer 29, 15; Ez 13, 3. 6. 9). When he addresses Jerusalem, Ezechiel's technique is that of Is 52, 1, 7-9; 54, 1 f. He seems to speak from far off to the foreign nations to which

he has not gone (Ez 25). He makes a distinction between the exiles whom he addresses in the second person and those at Jerusalem against whom he threatens punishment in the third person : 5, 1-17; 11, 17-20; 14, 12-23.

2) There are not two inaugural visions. 1, 2—2, 2 is not a divine call but rather the account of a theophany. The fact that a rabbinic tradition [1] has the career of Ezechiel begin in Palestine has been used as an argument. This is easily explained. The Targum and the rabbis could easily have altered the tradition to make Palestine the source of the divine message.

3) Supplementary indications. Had Ezechiel been at Jerusalem, he would, like Jeremias who was also without hope, have preached conversion. The schematic treatment of what concerns Jerusalem is not that of an eyewitness. This is true of descriptions of the religious and moral life as well as of accounts of events in the city. The absence of prophecy against Babylon is significant. The Babylonian influence on the mode of expression and thought in Ezechiel is noteworthy. [2] Finally, literary dependence on Jeremias would be limited to six passages from the roll of 605-604 (Jer 1, 8, 17-18 and Ez 3, 8-9; Jer 4, 13 and Ez 38, 9ª; Jer 6, 14ᵇ; 8, 11 and Ez 13, 10; Jer 6, 26 and Ez 27, 30-31; Jer 14, 12 and Ez 6, 12; 5, 12; Jer 18, 21 and Ez 35, 5). This would indicate quite well the time of the contacts between the two prophets and situate these contacts before the beginning of the prophetic career of Ezechiel.

The formation and plan of the book

The literary unity of the book, so strongly affirmed by both traditional criticism and the more radical criticism which has seen in Ezechiel an instance of pseudepigraphy, seems to be a myth. Cooke (1936), otherwise so restrained, concurs. There are artificial groupings, evident displacements (Cooke, Eissfeldt, Bertholet, Bentzen, Fohrer agree on the sequence : 3, 22-27; 4, 4-8; 24, 25-27; 33, 21-22), doublets, secondary developments and unauthentic passages. Throughout the book passages without dates are joined to dated passages.

On the basis of these facts we will attempt to establish the progressive formation of the book. In the attempt we follow Fohrer :

a) The stage of detached pieces *(löse Blätter)*

Ezechiel was not the same type of writer as the author of the Book of Daniel, a literary man, a writer by profession. Ezechiel's mission was to speak, to give advice. This he did before a large public or before

---

[1] *RB* (1948), p. 514.
[2] See R. TOURNAY, *RB* (1953), p. 149.

smaller groups. " For them you are only a ballad singer, with a pleasant voice and a clever touch " (33, 32). But he wrote down his ecstatic experiences (eight), the symbolic actions he performed (twelve), the words of Yahweh. These divine words are the important part of the book. They include threats (simple and motivated), lamentations, exhortations, promises, words occasioned by a discussion, instructions *(tôrôt)*, directives which concern the prophet personally. At times Ezechiel began by writing his message before proclaiming it (1—3, 15; 3, 16ᵇ-21; 33, 1-6; 33, 10-20). At times he preached first and then wrote (a response to a question; literary pieces : 16, 1-43; 18, 1-20; 23, 1-27; 36, 16-38). He reworked and enlarged this material on occasion. This supposes that the pieces existed independently for a time.

b) The stage of the initial groupings

Various collections have grouped materials according to origin (ecstatic experience, symbolic action) or around key words (" idols "in 6; " sword " in 21). More often the grouping is on the basis of related content. Some sequences have been broken; pieces of different dates have been joined; prophecies of good fortune and threatening oracles have been juxtaposed (an indication of redactional work : 11, 14-21; 16, 22. 24). It is to be remembered that according to some critics the prophet himself is in part responsible for this redactional work.

The units distinguished by Fohrer are : 1, 1-3. 15 (vocation); 3, 16ᵃ—5 (symbolic actions; 3, 16ᵇ-21 is an interpolation); 6 (idols); 7 (judgment); 8—11; 21 (ecstatic visit to Jerusalem; 11, 14-21, added promises); 12, 1-20 (symbolic actions); 12, 21—13, 21 (words about the audience of the prophet; 14, 1-11 and 12-23 have been added); 15—16, 43 + 20, 1-31 (shortcomings of the nation; 16, 44-63 and 20, 32-44 were added after 587); 17—19 (the sins and punishment of the kings; 17, 22-24, a Messianic promise, has been added; 18 has been inserted here to clarify the fate of Sedecias spoken of in 17); 21 (words grouped around the word " sword "); 22 (crimes concerning blood); 23 (Ohola and Oholiba); 24, 1-27 (symbolic actions; before the work of redaction, 4, 4-8; 3, 22-27 and 33, 21-22 were located here); 25 (the neighbors of Juda); 26—28 (Tyre; 28, 20-26 is disputed); 29—32 (Egypt); 33, 1-20 (the work of a prophet; 3, 16ᵇ-21 was previously connected with this section; 33, 23-29. 30-33 have been introduced into the section); 34 (shepherd and flock); 35 (Edom); 36—39 (words, ecstatic experience, symbolic action concerning the restoration of Israel; 38—39, 20, a section concerning Gog, is an interpolation and breaks the sequence between 37, 28 and 39, 21; its authenticity is questioned); 40—48 *(Torah* of Ezechiel).

c) The book

The third stage more or less contemporaneous with the preceding involved the combination of the previously grouped materials to form the book. The sequence of the materials in the book was both chronological and logical and corresponded to the actual development of the career of the prophet. The prophecies against the nations seem to have been the last section to be inserted in its present position where it interrupts the sequence between 24 and 33. The book was certainly completed before the end of the Exile since the temple of Ezechiel is not that of Zorobabel.

The plan of the book is similar to that of Isaias and Jeremias (Greek) : a) 1—24 : oracles against Juda; b) 25—32 : oracles against the nations; c) 33—39 + 40—48 : eschatological oracles.

II. Ezechiel, the man

A complex person

Like St. Paul and Theresa of Avila Ezechiel was perhaps afflicted with epilepsy, but he was certainly not a deranged person. With St. Paul he shared a profound encounter with God and played an important role in the divine plan for men. The hand of God was upon him (1, 3; 3, 14-22; 8, 1; 33, 22; 37, 1; 40, 1); the spirit of God took hold of him (2, 2; 3, 12. 14. 24; 8, 3; 11, 1; 37, 1); he fell on his face (1, 28; 3, 23; 9, 8); he became dumb (3, 22-27; 24, 25-27) and seemed a man deprived of reason (3, 15) after an encounter with God. Divine possession is an important part of this ecstasy. This seems to be indicated by 3, 22-24 and 37, 1 f. (the " plain " where the " glory of Yahweh " is revealed corresponds to the void spoken of by mystics) and by the inaugural vision and the visit to Jerusalem (8 f.).

Kittel [3] has described Ezechiel as a man with two souls. It is easy in fact to point out contrasts in Ezechiel. He is priest and prophet; preacher and writer; herald of disaster and salvation; visionary and a man of incisive logic; a reflective person endowed with intense feelings; dreamer and realist; strong but pitiable. All these contrasts are resolved in the unity of his vocation. He was conscious of having been sent by God at a critical moment in history. Israel reflecting on her destiny found herself like Ezechiel divided. Several voices cried out within her, pride and nostalgia, faith and hope, discouragement and remorse, cowardice and courage. Ezechiel, like the prophets of the Exile, outlined for his people the foundations of the new nation. But like the nation itself Ezechiel is baffling. Living between two worlds, that which had

---

[3] *Geschichte des Volkes Israel*, III, p. 146.

collapsed and that which was coming to be, he is full of memories, full of " points of departure. " He is a person not easily described. When the nation was at this great turning point in its history, God raised up a man as complex as the period in which he lived. Ezechiel was a man of his age.

The priest

Ezechiel was a Sadoqite priest and was supposed to serve in Jerusalem. Far from the city he directs his thoughts constantly toward the Temple. He knew its every nook and corner (8). Sometime after 586 he gives an extremely detailed description of a new temple constructed according to the pattern of the old (40—42). Even the dimensions of the stalls for the animals are included! He is certainly not reflecting the popular idea (11, 15) that Yahweh's presence is limited to the Temple. In an awe-inspiring tableau he even represents Yahweh as departing from His dwelling (11, 22-23), but this situation is extraordinary and in the Messianic period Yahweh will return to Jerusalem which will then have the name, " The Lord is here " (48, 35 : the name indicates the divine presence in the city).

The fact that Ezechiel was a priest explains other things. It explains for instance his dependence on Deuteronomy which also witnesses to this union between prophecy and cult. The temple of Ezechiel is the sanctuary of Deuteronomy, the one center of cult for the nation. The position taken by Ezechiel regarding priests and levites (44, 10 ff.) supposes the legislation of Dt 18, 6-8 which it corrects. In both Ezechiel and Deuteronomy there is the same defiant attitude toward royalty (Dt 17; Ez 46), the same legislative bent, the same understanding of history. In addition Ezechiel is dependent on the code of holiness (H, Lv 17—26) which on the whole is more ancient than Ezechiel though in part it dates from the same period (Lv 26). On the other hand Ezechiel is older than the priestly code (P). His *Torâh* differs from it in several respects : the form of the altar (Ez 43, 13-27; Ex 27, 1-8); the matter for sacrifices. Ezechiel does not mention the high priest. The editors and glossators of the book come from the priestly circles of the Exile. Ezechiel's penchant for legal codes and perhaps for dates can be connected with his position as priest.

His piety

His sensitiveness does not influence his prophetic ministry (24, 16). To be sure he suffered deeply, but a keen sense of responsibility (3, 18 f; 33, 1-9) gave him the appearance of a rigidly insensible person. He announces the coming of Esdras. He has a marked penchant for theology! " He was the first dogmatist of Judaism " (Lods). Perhaps nowhere

more than in Ezechiel are the magnificence of " Adonai Yahweh" and
the nothingness of man (" son of man, " 87 times) emphasized. Rarely
does he speak to God after the manner of Jeremias. Three typical
expressions show this stress on the majesty of Yahweh :

— " They will know that I am Yahweh. "

— " I will sanctify Myself among you (them). "

— " I act for the sake of My Name that it might not be profaned
among the *goyim*. "

The author

Ezechiel's fertile imagination nourished on the splendors of Babylon and
attracted by what glittered (cf. 28, 13-14; 1, 27) was capable of painting
grandiose tableaux which sometimes are overdone. He piles images one
upon another (32, 2-7 : Pharao is a lion, a monster, a star) without drawing
back even from the precipice of incoherence (17) or triviality (16, 23).
Carefully controlled, Ezechiel's ebullience can produce allegory of a high
caliber (the ship of Tyre, 27). It excels in drawing awesome scenes : the
people of Sheol (32), Yahweh's visit to the Temple (8—10), the resurrection
of the bones (37). Yet this turbulent, somber, fantastic imagination is
capable of envisioning the future in a geometric dream (40 ff.). It can
use erudite and historical materials—even in poetry, a sign of the
beginnings of apocalyptic literature.

III. The life and activity of Ezechiel

Chronological order of the sections of the book

593, summer. Call of Ezechiel in Babylon (1—3, 15). First symbolic
action (3, 16ᵃ — 4, 1-3. 7); certainly some other symbolic actions date
from this period and are connected with the agitation in Jerusalem
(4, 6, except 4, 4-8).

591, summer. Ecstatic visit(s) to the Temple (8—11, 13).

590, summer. Consultation on cult questions (20, 1-31). Certain
historical summaries and threats dating from some time before the siege :
6; 7; 12; 13 (in part); 14, 1-11 (in part); 15; 16, 1-43; 22, 1-22; 23; 14,
12-23 and 18 probably date from about 587.

588. 21, 23-32 (perhaps 21, 1-22).

587. Beginning of the siege : 17 (against Sedecias; except verses
22-24). Two symbolic actions (24, 1-24; January).

586. Before the fall of Jerusalem certain symbolic actions : 3, 22-27;
4, 4-8; 24, 25-27. Prophecy against Hophra (29, 1-16 : January). Two
other prophecies against Egypt (30, 20-26 : March; 31 : May). An oracle

against the king which reviews recent history and was occasioned by the disaster of 586 : 19 (also certain additions to 12).

586, August. The fall of Jerusalem.

585, January. The fugitive reports to Ezechiel (33, 21-22). Pastoral ministry : 3, 16ᵇ-21; 33, 1-20. First prophecy against Tyre : 26 (LXX). Two prophecies against Egypt (32, dates based on LXX and several Hebrew manuscripts). Most probably, the oracles against the neighboring nations (25).

After 586. 11, 14-21; 13, in part; 14, 1-11 in part; 16, 44-63; 17, 22-24; 20, 32-44; 22, 23-31 and especially 34 to 37.

572, March. The Torah of Ezechiel (40—48).

570, March. Ezechiel changes his views on Tyre and Egypt (29, 17-20. Verse 21 is probably the last written by the prophet).

From Jerusalem to Tel-Abib

Some scholars think Ezechiel actually was a priest in the Temple (R. H. Kennett); others, that he was called to be a prophet at thirty, the age at which levites customarily began their service (Nm 4, 3. 23). This second hypothesis supposes that 1, 1 reads " in my thirtieth year " (so J. A. Bewer who compares Lk 3, 23). The date of his arrival in Babylonia is not known. Possibly he arrived with Joachin and the other exiles of 597 following the revolt against Nabuchodonosor (4 Kgs 24, 8-17).

His inaugural vision took place in 592 near *nâr Kabaru*, an artificial canal that is now dry. The canal started at the Euphrates somewhat north of Babylon, passed through Nippur and met the river again just south of Ur. The exiles were located in the region and enjoyed a certain amount of freedom. Perhaps they worked on the Babylonian irrigation system.

Ezechiel witnesses a grandiose theophany coming from the north. The glory of Yahweh, described with restraint (1, 27-28), appears in the midst of a storm cloud. The vision includes four *Cherubim* standing back to back and facing all directions. These spirits, each with four faces, are the mobile throne of Yahweh. Their wings support the platform on which He sits. The complex symbolism indicates the divine intelligence, power and swiftness. This idea of transcendence is accentuated by the first words with which God addresses Ezechiel, " son of man " (2, 1). The expression, in the present context the equivalent of " mortal, " occurs 87 times in the rest of the book. The theophany is the initiation of the prophet. During it the destructive and vindictive word of Yahweh is confided to him. Since this is the age of the book, the word is written on a scroll which Ezechiel is told to eat (3, 1; see Jer 1, 9) so that he may be able to preach its content. Like Jeremias (Jer 1, 8, 17-18) Ezechiel will be forceful and determined (3, 8-9), thus living up to his name (" God is strong " or " God is my strength "), before an audience whose dispositions have already been described. At Tel-Abib (Tell-Abubi : hill of the inundation) among the sandy dunes around Nippur he begins his work. God does not abandon His exiled people.

Delenda est Jerusalem!

Ezechiel's vision came at a moment of political unrest. When Psammetichus II ascended the throne in Egypt, thoughts turned toward an anti-Babylonian coalition between Jerusalem and Egypt (Jer 27—28). In point of fact Pharao intended to maintain the peace and Sedecias also hastened to reassure his suzerain (Jer 51, 59). But both at Jerusalem and among the exiles the situation was regarded as intolerable and men dreamed of the rapid reestablishment of an independent Juda (Jer 29). Ezechiel did his best to open the eyes of his fellow exiles. During the five years that preceded the fall of Jerusalem he multiplied his threatening predictions that Jerusalem was to be destroyed.

Some of his symbolic actions perhaps give concrete expression to these threats as early as 592 : the siege of the clay tablet (3, 16ª + 4, 1-3. 7), the meager rations (4, 9-11, 16-17), the razor (5), the unclean bread (4, 12-15). The first three concern the coming siege; the last, the exile.

In the following year, taken in ecstatic transport to Jerusalem, Ezechiel details the various types of idolatry carried on there (8). He also sees a council of notables who are reassuring the people (11, 1-13ª). But the city is lost and Yahweh is about to leave it (11, 22-24); only the just who bear the mark of a *taw* (letter in the form of a cross) will escape. This idea of a selective punishment hardly lessens the terrible chastisement to come.

In 590 a consultation on the questions of cult is the occasion for listing the charges against the nation. This takes the form of a review of Israel's history (20, 1-31).

Characteristic of Ezechiel are the panoramic frescoes he paints of the distant and recent past of his people. In these frescoes he outlines the sins of the nation, especially those concerning cult, from the period of the desert on down. In this Ezechiel differs from his predecessors who made the period of the desert the ideal period of Israel's history. Sin is at the center of his understanding of history as it is in *Romans*.

The allegorical history of Israel (16 and 23) affirms the necessity of a corporate punishment.

Chapter 18, written at a time when events seemed to call into doubt divine providence, is important. In this chapter Ezechiel shows that in the moral order the individual is distinct from the nation and even, on condition that he be converted, distinct from his own past. This *torah* (cf. 14, 12-23) shows the development of moral thought in Israel. It marks the advent of religious personalism. The individual reaps the fruit of his own actions; no longer are the teeth of children set on edge because their fathers ate green grapes. Though this retribution is no longer regarded as collective, it is still understood as something accomplished on earth. This further problem is the basis for the great discussions of Job and Ecclesiastes.

At the same time Ezechiel preached the necessity of expiation for sins committed through the ages. How was he able to juxtapose these concepts of personal and collective retribution? Collective retribution concerned the terrible events of the present moment. It was applicable to the mass of men still in Palestine, but it had been abrogated for the immediate future for which the terrible events of the day were an introduction and a preparation. The present Jerusalem was a city of blood (22). The day of Yahweh was at hand (6—7). He attacks the prophets, prophetesses and sorceresses of the Exile (13). It is not possible to date all these pieces precisely, but they certainly precede 586. The same is true of 12 (two symbolic actions) and 14, 1-11 (consultation by certain idolaters).

The fall of Jerusalem and the message of hope

Events press on. In 587 Nabuchodonosor undertakes a campaign toward the west (21). Ezechiel thunders against Sedecias who has broken the oath made to his suzerain (17, 1-21). The beginning of the siege of Jerusalem is marked by two symbolic actions (24, 1-24). Just before the fall of the city Ezechiel becomes mute and thus bears symbolically the sins of his people (3, 22-24. 26; 4, 4-6. 8; 24, 25-27). Previously he had prophesied against the new pharao, Hophra, and against the interference of Egypt in the affairs of Palestine (29, 1-16 : January; 30, 20-26 : March; 31 : May) and delivered an oracle against the house of Juda in which he reviewed the history of the royal house (19).

Ezechiel's dumbness is brought to an end by the arrival of a fugitive from Jerusalem. The fugitive must have spent some time in Palestine for he arrives in Babylonia six months after the disaster (according to several Greek and Hebrew manuscripts). From this point on there is

a change in the prophet. His attitude becomes pastoral (3, 16ᵇ-21).
He feels himself personally charged with the care of each one of his
brothers. During this period he pronounced the greater part of his
oracles against the nations : neighboring peoples (25; 35), Egypt (32),
Tyre (26—28).

The pieces on Tyre are well known because of the information they
give concerning the international commerce of the day. The elegy on
the fall of the king of Tyre (28, 11-19) opens the way to some interesting
speculation. " The parallelism between Gn 2—3 and Ez 28 extends even
to the use of the same borrowings from popular traditions. In Ezechiel
the paradise theme illustrates the history of an act of open rebellion
against God, the rebellion of the king of Tyre whose sin in certain respects
can be compared with that which involved the fall of mankind....
Clearly Ezechiel knew how to distinguish in the Genesis accounts between
the essential doctrine and the ornamental veneer borrowed from legendary
traditions concerning the garden of the Elohim. The Catholic exegete
consequently has the right to base his interpretation on that of an inspired
author. " [4]

During this period Ezechiel works to form soul by soul the new
Israel. He announces the restoration of the nation. Yahweh will be its
shepherd (34). The new Israel is described in a series of visions : salvation
in a regenerated land (36), resurrection symbolized in the vision of the
bones (37, 1-14), unification of the kingdom under a new David (37, 15-28).
From this same period date the reworking of older pieces (11, 14-21) and
certain verses of 13; 14, 1-11; 16, 44-63; 17, 22-24; 20, 32-44; 22, 23-31.

In a magnificent vision, which has affinities with Plato's *Republic*
and Utopian literature in general, Ezechiel legislates for the future as
he describes successively the city of the Temple (40—43, 17), the divine
cult (43, 18-46) and the Holy Land (47—48). His interest is to distinguish
clearly God's kingdom, to make the Sadoqite priest the living center of
the community, to reduce the future princes to a purely administrative
role. His symbolic description of the land made fertile by the Temple's
spring and divided up among the tribes (note the order based on proximity
to the Temple) culminates in a description of Jerusalem, the perfect city,
which bears the name " Yahweh is there. "

This *Torah* dates from 572. In 571 Ezechiel corrects himself with
regard to Tyre (29, 17-21). These are his last words. There is some
question as to whether the eschatological prophecy, sometimes referred
to as the *Apocalypse of Gog* (38—39), is to be attributed to Ezechiel.

---

⁴ J. COPPENS, *Le chanoine Albin Van Hoonacker** (Paris, 1935), p. 19.

The imagery of the piece is apocalyptic. It presents a second phase in the establishment of God's kingdom. After the restoration of Israel which is the initial victory of Yahweh upon the earth there will be a second and definitive victory. This time Israel no longer struggles against her traditional enemies but rather against the massed companies of an invading enemy coming from afar (see p. 313). The law of the prophecy without perspective thus begins to be broken. Still later another phase will be distinguished in this age to come, the resurrection of the dead (Dn 12, 1-3).

The idea which underlies the imagery of the section is that mankind up until the very end will place an obstacle in the way of the establishment of the true religion. John's Apocalypse takes up the same imagery and idea (Ap 20, 8 ff.).

IV. THE THEOLOGY AND INFLUENCE OF EZECHIEL

The theocentric aspect of his thought

The theocentric aspect of Ezechiel's thought is very much in evidence in his writing. Yahweh's transcendence is marked in the inaugural vision (the omnipresence, omniscience, omnipotence of the Completely-Other); in the title, " son of man "; in the denunciation of the sin of pride (28); in the numerous phrases that express the honor of the name of Yahweh; in the fact that the Temple is first of all Yahweh's abode and, as it were, the introduction to his " holiness "; in the concept of the catastrophic history of the " days of Yahweh "; in the fact of his creative grace of which St. Paul speaks. Once reestablished, the nation will be converted (36, 28-31). This shows the conversion is gratuitous.

The people of God, a religious concept

a) The liquidation of the past

From its beginnings the nation had sinned. It was corrupt at its source. Even in Egypt it had not understood that Yahweh is a jealous God. The image of marriage and adultery is used to describe the history of the covenant; also the image of uncleanness *(tame')* : the history of Israel is that of her sins to which she remains attached. The present generation remains bound to the sins of preceding generations and has even added to them. Jerusalem is the place where this sin is concentrated. Judgment will be absolutely without pity. Ezechiel is the one to record this act of God. In this he resembles Amos. Nevertheless, he has added to this first idea the concept of a selective punishment (14, 21-23; 8, 6). This is, as it were, an indication of the direction in which his thought will develop.

b) The " remnant "

Shortly before the inevitable catastrophe Ezechiel's thoughts turned to the qualifications necessary for membership in the new people (18). He declared abolished the axiom that the sins of fathers reverted to their children and established the theory of reward and punishment based on individual merits. This transference of guilt from father to son had long since been abrogated by the civil code (4 Kgs 14, 5-6; Dt 24, 16); the understanding of the divine government is the heir of this progress. The preaching (appeal for personal repentance) and life of the prophets (especially Jeremias) had already done much to show the value of the individual. After 586 the ministry of Ezechiel becomes almost pastoral. In the future man must have a new heart (18, 31). Jewish voluntarism, which one day will speak of the joy of observing the commandments, has arrived. In point of fact the observance of the commandments tends to become the essence of religion. Ezechiel loves to call attention to the decalogues which list without order religious and moral directives and sexual prohibitions (see the code of holiness, Lv 19). This leads to a moral rigorism which will be characteristic of the Jewish spirit. Religion becomes a matter of observances. Still later the liturgy of expiation will have the daily function of effacing sin. Among these observances great importance will be given to the Sabbath observance.

c) The new heart (36, 23-28)

God will make it possible for each Israelite to enter into the New Covenant. This includes pardon and the conferring of a new " spirit " which makes possible the observance of the law. These formulae reflect the thought and expression of Jeremias (p. 315). They are the heart of the message of Ezechiel. His concern is the people of tomorrow, but like Isaias and Sophonias, Ezechiel worked to form this people in his own day. Psalm 51 *(Miserere)* perhaps is a reflection of Ezechiel's thought.

The people of God, a Messianic people

a) " Israel "

The name, " Israel, " which occurs so frequently in Ezechiel, has a religious rather than a political denotation. It is the name of the people of the covenant in the period of the desert as well as in the period of salvation. It signifies the *Gola*, the exiled Judeans. They are the *pars potior* of the new people. Only in two places in Ezechiel does the expression designate the northern kingdom : 4, 4-6, where the mention of Juda seems secondary, and 37, 16.

b) The Messias

The Israel-Juda division appears only in the latter reference. There the future king *(melek)* is the subject, for David easily comes to mind in this representation of the double monarchy. It is important to note in this regard that " the references to David are rather automatic and lack the warmth they have in Isaias " (Steinmann). This division did not have much appeal for Ezechiel.

c) The church of Israel

On the contrary Ezechiel speaks of the restoration using the twelve-tribe division. Perhaps the designation of the prince of the restoration as *nasi* is related to this division. As has been seen, the *Torah* of Ezechiel (40—48) indicates that " at base his true Messias is the Temple " (Stein-mann). Yahweh Himself dictates its outline and its laws. This was the attitude of the editors of the priestly code when they bound the ritual rules of the Temple to the theophanies of Sinai. Ezechiel's view of the Temple profoundly influenced the future of Israel.

Universalism and particularism

What Yahweh does for Israel concerns the other nations. Israel is a people of witness. But unlike his disciple Second-Isaias, Ezechiel does not make Israel a missionary people. The return of Israel to her land will cleanse the name of Yahweh from dishonor, but it will not lead to the conversion of the *goyim*. Likewise, triumph over the other nations is part of Yahweh's plan of vengeance. This is a " service " Yahweh will demand from a people who will be the scourge of God. The descendants of Ezechiel will not forget this!

Ezechiel, father of Judaism

On many counts Ezechiel merits the title " father of Judaism. " Still it is difficult to measure his personal contribution for sometimes he developed ideas already advanced. He enlarged upon Jeremias 31, 31-34 as well as the prescriptions of the code of holiness. He was the herald of grace, the herald of voluntarism, the bearer of a complex tradition that he has transmitted to us enriched and clarified by his own theological genius. The priestly circles of the Exile, Esdras, the apocalyptic writers will all be his disciples. To him is owed in part the cult of the Temple and of the law, concern for " holiness " and a horror of " uncleanness, " the view of Israel as church, particularism, the apocalyptic theme and style that characterize the visions of Zacharias and Daniel. The wisdom writers inherit from him the problem of reward and punishment, but Job and Coheleth go beyond him in their investigation of the problem.

§ 2.   Isaias 40—55, or the Consolation of Israel

BIBLIOGRAPHY

Introductions, translations, commentaries, pp. 1 f., 251 f., and 283 f.
(J. STEINMANN and P. AUVRAY, *BJ**; L. DENNEFELD, *BPC**;
J. SKINNER, *CBSC*; P. VOLZ, *KAT*...).

A. CONDAMIN, *Le livre d'Isaie** (Paris, 1905).

R. LEVY, *Deutero-Isaiah : A Commentary* (Oxford, 1925).

C. C. TORREY, *The Second Isaiah. A New Interpretation* (Edinburgh, 1928).

J. FISCHER, *Das Buch Isaias II** (Bonn, 1939).

S. BLANK, " Studies in Deutero-Isaiah, " *HUCA*, 15 (1940), pp. 1-46.

E. J. KISSANE, *The Book of Isaiah II** (Dublin, 1943).

J. P. HYATT, " The Sources of the Suffering Servant Idea, " *JNES*, 3 (1944), pp. 79-86.

A. FEUILLET, " Isaïe (le livre d')*, " *SDB*, IV (1947), cols. 689-714.

R. MURPHY, " Second Isaias : The Servant of the Lord*, " *CBQ*, 9 (1947), pp. 262-274.

I. ENGNELL, " The Ebed-Yahweh Songs and the Suffering Messiah in Deutero-Isaiah, " *BJRL*, 31 (1948), pp. 54-93.

C. LINDHAVEN, *The Servant Motif in the Old Testament* (Uppsala, 1950).

J. LINDBLOM, *The Servant Songs in Deutero-Isaiah* (Lund, 1951).

H. ROWLEY, *The Servant of the Lord and Other Essays* (London : Lutterworth, 1952).

S. MOWINCKEL, *He That Cometh* (New York : Abingdon, 1954).

H. W. ROBINSON, " The Cross of the Servant, " *The Cross in the Old Testament* (London : SCM, 1955), pp. 55-114.

L. G. RIGNELL, *A Study of Isaiah, Ch. 40-55* (Lund, 1956).

C. R. NORTH, *The Suffering Servant in Deutero-Isaiah²* (London : Oxford, 1956).

J. MUILENBURG, " The Book of Isaiah, 40-66, " *IB* (1956).

J. MORGENSTERN, " Jerusalem—485 BC, " *HUCA*, 27 (1956), pp. 101-179; 28 (1957), pp. 15-47; 31 (1960), pp. 1-29.

P. A. H. DE BOER, *Second Isaiah's Message* (Leyden, 1956).

H. RINGGREN, *The Messiah in the Old Testament* (London : SCM, 1957).

C. F. WHITLEY, *The Exilic Age* (Philadelphia : Westminster, 1957).

J. MORGENSTERN, " The Message of Deutero-Isaiah in its Sequential Unfolding, " *HUCA*, 29 (1958), pp. 1-67; 30 (1959), pp. 1-102.

C. STUHLMUELLER, " The Theology of Creation in Second Isaias*, " *CBQ*, 21 (1959), pp. 429-467.

J. MORGENSTERN, " The Suffering Servant—A New Solution, " *VT*, 11 (1961), pp. 292-320, 406-431; 13 (1963), pp. 321-332.

B. ANDERSON, " Exodus Typology in Second Isaiah, " *Israel's Prophetic Heritage* (New York : Harper, 1962).

C. R. NORTH, *The Second Isaiah, Introduction, Translation, and Commentary* (New York : Oxford, 1964).

W. ZIMMERLI—J. JEREMIAS, The Servant of God (London : SCM, 1965)·

I. THE PROBLEM OF SECOND-ISAIAS

Is Second-Isaias a distinct section?

Since the end of the eighteenth century (Döderlein, 1775; Eichhorn, 1782) criticism has tended more and more to distinguish Is 1-39, on the whole the work of the prophet of the eighth century, from Is 40 ff. (see p. 285). Chapters 40—55 are attributed to an anonymous prophet of the Exile, Deutero-Isaias or Second-Isaias. With chapter 56 the setting of the book becomes postexilic and for this reason it is attributed to a Third-Isaias. Only the problem of chapters 40—55 is under consideration here. There are many reasons for distinguishing these chapters from the work of Isaias himself.

a) Historical reasons

The center of interest for Second-Isaias is the end of the Exile, the period between the victories of Cyrus against Lydia (546) and the fall of Babylon (539). These victories against Lydia are regarded as the guarantee of the question of what interest an eighth century public would have taken in the prediction of the fall of Babylon. There is a further question as to how these prophecies could have been closed secrets to the prophets of the seventh and the first part of the sixth century. The prediction of a precise event in the distant future is not an impossibility, but it is a fact that the prophets generally concern themselves with the problems of the period in which they work. Is the present case an exception to this general rule?

b) Doctrinal reasons

The book's formulation of the doctrine of monotheism is perfectly clear. There is no intention here to deny the antiquity of monotheism in Israel, but in Second-Isaias the theological elaboration of the doctrine and the precise terminology in which it is formulated surpass anything that preceded it. Besides, the Messianic teaching of Second-Isaias is on a level quite different from that of Isaias himself, and it develops along other lines as will be seen. The attitudes of the prophet toward the foreign nations also differ. Second-Isaias speaks of their conversion with a clarity previously unknown.

c) Literary reasons

The message of Isaias was presented in brief, brilliant oracles. His style was concise and brilliant. The language of Second-Isaias is rich, copious, solemn, now verging on sapiential discourse, now verging on the style of hymns. Thus the styles of the two works are as different as for example the sayings of Jesus in the Synoptics and the discourses recorded in the fourth Gospel (Bentzen).

Origin of the book

It cannot be denied, however, that the two sections have much in common (for example : the title, " Holy One of Israel "; the doctrine of humility). These constants are even more clear in the Septuagint translation where the book was regarded as a unit. As has already been indicated, today reference is frequently made to a school of Isaias. Perhaps this fact explains why material of the type that is characteristic of Second-Isaias and even Third-Isaias (13—14; 34—35) turns up in chapters 1—39. Jewish tradition accepted the unity of authorship of the book. Sirach reflects this tradition about 200 (Sir 48, 23-24) and the New Testament assumes it. But these references to a traditional view are not a determining argument. They do not resolve the problem at issue, a problem of literary and historical criticism [5] which does not directly concern faith. In 1908 the Biblical Commission affirmed that the weight of the arguments advanced for the view put forward here was not sufficient. The work of Catholic exegetes during the past fifty years seems to have amplified these arguments adequately. In any case, Is 40-55 must be read against the background of the Exile.

II. COMPOSITION OF THE BOOK

General divisions

Besides an introduction (40, 1-11) and a conclusion (55, 10-13), both of which celebrate God's creative word acting in history to bring about the return from exile, the book is generally regarded as having two broad divisions : 40—48 which concerns Israel exiled in Babylon and 49—55 which concerns the restoration of Sion. The first section contains the cycle dealing with Cyrus (44, 24—48, 12) and is situated against the background of his first victories. The second section speaks neither of Cyrus nor of Babylon and is situated in the period immediately preceding 539.

---

[5] Cf. J. SCHILDENBERGER, in *Alttestamentliche Studien**, Festschrift Nötscher (Bonn, 1950).

Generally the Servant Songs are considered a distinct section (42, 1-4; 49, 1-6; 50, 4-9; 52, 13—53, 12; Bentzen adds 51, 9-16). We accept these divisions but maintain they are to be attributed to the author of the rest of the book.

The material

The book is made up of about fifty units of various literary genres : oracles of good fortune (40, 1-2; 43, 1-8) or of woe (48, 1-11), exhortations (51, 1-8), messages (40, 9-11), controversies (41), satires (44, 9-11; 47), accounts of visions or voices (40, 3-5. 6-8), historical reviews (43, 22-28). The hymn (44, 23; 49, 13), sometimes in a new form in which Yahweh praises Himself (44, 24-28), is particularly characteristic of Second-Isaias, the herald and poet of God's majesty.

These elements are not simply juxtaposed without order. If it is not possible to restore five great poems each concluding with a doxology (so Kissane), there is a general order based on chronology and subject matter. But if on the whole the book shows progression, the order is based especially on a unity of themes. The same themes recur again and again : important moments in the history of Israel, Palestinian restoration, the ecumenical role of Israel, conversion of the nations, Yahweh as the one God, as creator, as master of history.

Origin of the collection

Was it Second-Isaias himself or an editor who collected these pieces which had been previously preached in Babylonia, perhaps at the Sabbath assemblies (Weiser)? The analogy of the other prophetic books would indicate the second solution is to be preferred. This is supported by a detailed study of the collection.

III. Yahweh's glorious establishment of his kingdom

The vocation of Israel

Never did Israel reflect so much on her vocation as during the Exile : the vocation of a nation comes to be understood through the nation's history. For Second-Isaias three landmarks distinguish the stages of that history : Abraham (41, 8-9; 51, 2); the exodus and conquest (passim); David (55, 3). This history is a heritage with which the new Israel is charged. In her heritage the privileges and the missions of Abraham, Moses and David live and are extended to all.

It is to be noted that Israel has here the mission of *witness* and *mediator*. Israel at the center of history witnesses to monotheism which has never been so clearly formulated (40, 18. 25; 43, 11; 44, 7; 45, 5. 6. 18-22; 46, 5. 9). It is a question here of veritable formulae of faith

(44, 6; 54, 5). A characteristic of Second-Isaias is the clear relation he draws between Yahweh's creative and salvific activity. The creation of the world and the destiny of Israel are two great divine works presented together (44, 24-28; 42, 5-6; 45, 12-13; 51, 9-10). Before Yahweh idols like Marduk (Bel) and Nebo are nothing (46, 1-2) and the old title, " Lord of hosts, " takes on a polemical significance (45, 12-13). Israel witnesses to those predictions in which Yahweh had spoken of His plan (43, 10 ff.). It witnesses to the deed through which Yahweh is going to establish His people. This reestablishment will have such repercussions that it will prove the beginning of the conversion of the nations (40, 5; 42, 10; 45, 14; 52, 10; 54, 5). 45, 22-24 is an appeal for the conversion of the world and 44, 5 shows this new proselytism. Certainly this universalism is not that of Jesus or Paul. There is question here of salvation through Israel, in her wake, under her domination. But it had never been so clearly emphasized before that the covenant was for the benefit of all men.

The Israel which has the honor to be responsible for all this is a community defined in religious terms. It is the remnant (41, 14; 46, 3), the " poor of Yahweh " (49, 13), those who have the law in their hearts (51, 7), the servants of Yahweh (44, 1; 54, 17), those who hope in Yahweh (40, 31), the race of Israel (Jacob) (44, 3). Thus the word race *(zera')* takes on a religious sense.

The missionary idea begins to appear and proselytism is spoken of (44, 5). The other nations animated by religious hope (51, 5) exclaim :
> " With you only is God, and nowhere else;
>   the gods are nought.
> Truly with you God is hidden,
>   the God of Israel, the Saviour! " (45, 14-15)

Cyrus as Messias (45, 1) (*above,* pp. 333 f.)

Precisely at the time when the prophet addressed his compatriots the Middle East was in the process of rapid change. [6] Cyrus had united under his scepter the Medes and the Persians (549). Victorious over the Lydians (546) he directed his march toward Babylon.

Is 41, 2-3. 25 mysteriously presents at first the conqueror whom Yahweh loves; then he is expressly named (44, 28—45, 13). The investiture formulae which the prophet uses to make Cyrus " the Messias of Yahweh " resemble those found on a Babylonian cylinder : " Marduk sought a just king, took by the hand the man he desired, named him Cyrus, king of Anshan, gave him dominion over all things. " The prophet notes three landmarks in the rise of Cyrus : Ecbatana-Sardis (41, 2-3. 25),

---

[6] Cf. pp. 36 f.

Babylon which he will seize, Jerusalem which he will rebuild together with its temple (44, 28; 45, 13). As in the former prophets, the great pagan kings serve the true God as instruments of punishment and restoration.

Announcement of the fall of Babylon

Is 47 describes in advance the disaster in five strophes (1-4; 5-7; 8-10a; 10b-12; 13-15). It is evident that the prophecy is concerned rather with the fact than the manner in which it will occur. It contains an ironical allusion to the feast of *akitu* (verses 1-2). In fact the idols were not removed; the conqueror surrounded the temples with honor : " No weapon was placed in the *e-sag-il* and the other temples; no battle standard was carried there. " From December to March 539-538 Cyrus restored to the cities their statues and had " eternal dwellings " built for the gods. He had liberal tendencies in religious as well as political matters.

The other anti-Babylonian poems probably date from the same period. Without doubt reasons of prudence explain why such poems are lacking in Ezechiel. As the inevitability of the fatal day became more clear, the exiles became bolder. Jer 50—51, 58 presents a collection of oracles, satires, maledictions against Babylon in this perspective of the approaching end (cf. p. 305). But it is in Is 13—14, 23 that the most famous examples are found. A first poem (13) announces the threat of the coming of the Medes (vv. 17-18). Babylon will be turned into a desert (vv. 19-22); an introduction in the apocalyptic style (vv. 1-16) describes the day of Yahweh and its significance for the arrogant and for tyrants. This perhaps dates from 550. A second poem (14, 4b-21) contains a lamentation for the king of Babylon, either Nabuchodonosor or Nabonidus. This, at least, seems to be the interpretation indicated by the prose introduction (vv. 1-4a) and conclusion (vv. 22-23); but it is still possible that the poem, which lacks any specific references, was composed by Isaias to celebrate the death of Sargon II (*supra*, p. 293). Thus the announcement of the impending fall of Babylon by Second-Isaias is not an isolated phenomenon. It fits into this larger literary framework and dominates it by its own doctrinal orientation.

The new exodus and salvation

Israel will be delivered and will return to Jerusalem across the Syrian desert by the shortest possible route. The procession will be slow and majestic. Yahweh will march at its head (52, 11-12). To facilitate Israel's journey the desert will be transformed (40, 3-5; 41, 17-19; 43, 19-20). Yahweh will enter Jerusalem as king (52, 7). The nations will see all this, be converted, and associate themselves with the Chosen People (44, 5).

The return from the exile is the sign of pardon from sin, a key aspect of the salvation granted Israel. Yahweh, Israel's *Goel*, saves His people (43, 22-24; 48, 9-11). Yahweh will reign (52, 7) over the land from the rebuilt capital and Temple (44, 26-28; 49, 16). Israel will multiply (49, 19-20; 54, 1), live long (51, 6-7) in an alliance of peace (54, 10) and in the knowledge of Yahweh (54, 13; 51, 7; 48, 17) and be served by the other nations (45, 14; 49, 22-23; 54, 46).

IV. THE KINGDOM OF GOD ESTABLISHED BY PREACHING AND MARTYRDOM

The literary problem of the songs of the servant of Yahweh [7]

In the texts studied thus far Israel has been referred to as " servant of Yahweh " (for example : 41, 8-9; 42, 19; 43, 10; 44, 1-2, 21; 48, 20). The title was used in the same way as in Ezechiel 28, 25 and 37, 25. In the songs of the servant of Yahweh the problem appears in a different light. The critics include the following passages in this group :

1 : Oracle of solemn investiture (42, 1-7; 8-9 is discussed).

2 : Autobiographical account of the servant's vocation (49, 1-6).

3 : Confession after the manner of Jeremias (50, 4-9; 10-11 is discussed).

4 : Collective lamentation of the kings of the earth, preceded and followed by an oracle of Yahweh (52, 13—53, 12).

In these songs the servant is presented as a mysterious person favored by Yahweh who has poured out upon him His spirit (42, 1) and given him a task that is at once national and universal in scope. On the one hand he is to lead back Jacob (49, 5-6) and be the instrument of the final covenant (42, 6); on the other hand he is to be a light to the nations (49, 6) in the sense that he will win them over and teach them the true religion. His mission is to teach (50, 4-5); he will not meet with success in his lifetime (49, 4), but he is to persevere in spite of outrage and persecution. His sufferings and death have a redemptive significance (53, 5).

This servant contrasts with the servant (Israel) spoken of in the rest of the book. Israel is deaf and blind (42, 19-20); this servant listens

---

[7] C. NORTH, *The Suffering Servant in Deutero-Isaiah* (Oxford, 1948).—H. H. ROWLEY, *The Servant of the Lord* (London, 1952), pp. 3-88.—J. S. VAN DER PLOEG, *Les chants du Serviteur de Yahvé dans la seconde partie du livre d'Isaïe** (Paris, 1936).—J. LINDBLOM, *The Servant Songs in Deutero-Isaiah* (Lund, 1951).—R. J. TOURNAY, " Les chants du Serviteur dans la Seconde partie d'Isaïe*, " *RB* (1952), pp. 355-384, 481-512.—H. CAZELLES, " Les poèmes du Serviteur, leur place, leur structure, leur théologie*, " *RSR* (1955), pp. 5-55.

(50, 4-5) and illumines (49, 6).   Israel is sinful (42, 18-25; 43, 22-28);
this servant is just (43, 9, 11).   Israel has need of strength (41, 9-10);
this servant has a courageous faith.   He has the mission of bringing
about the restoration of Israel (49, 5-6).   He serves the other nations
while Israel aspires to be served by them (51, 22-23).   But at the same
time it is clear that several expressions used of the servant are also
applied to Israel (" to call by name, " " to take by the hand ") and that
the key themes of Second-Isaias appear in passages dealing with the
servant and in passages dealing with Israel : theocentric monotheism,
the missionary idea, conversion of the nations.

The question of unity of authorship

The problem of the songs is precisely the fact that they resemble and at the
same time differ so strikingly from the rest of the book.   Duhm (1892)
was the first to offer a systematic solution to this problem.   He regarded
the songs as a distinct unit which does not fit into the context of the
rest of the book.   He attributed them to an author of the first half of the
fifth century.   This point of view of Duhm has influenced later exegesis
even when this reacted strongly against his views as is true today.   The
following are several opinions that have been put forward.

1) If the stylistic unity of the songs and the rest of the book is more
and more generally admitted (North, Rowley), some reject unity of
authorship (Steinmann, Auvray).

2) Some exegetes continue to regard the songs as a literary cycle
independent of their present context (Kittel, Volz, Fisher, Dennefeld,
van der Ploeg, Feuillet, Coppens).   It is difficult not to discern the difference in tone between the songs and the rest of Second-Isaias.   The
marvelous element is missing and there is only the humble preaching of
redemption through martyrdom.   Nevertheless, some exegetes have
recently been impressed by the close relationship between the songs and
their present context (Lods, 1950; Tournay, 1952; Cazelles, 1955).

3) Some exegetes have rejected the unity of the cycle of songs.
In their view the songs describe several different persons (Kissane, Volz)
or, at least develop a " many-sided theme " in which there is progression
from Israel to the Messias (H. Wheeler-Robinson, 1926; O. Eissfeldt, 1933;
Tournay, 1952; H. H. Rowley, 1953).

Identification of the servant : a summary

An exhaustive review of the opinions held would indicate the difficulty
of the problem.   An exegete of such importance as Mowinckel has changed
his opinion three times in thirty years.   It would also show a progressively

more evident return to the eschatological and Messianic interpretation. These are some of the views :

a) Collective exegesis

This predominates in the school of Wellhausen. It identifies the servant with historical Israel (Budde, 1900; Lods, 1935, 1950), or an ideal Israel (Driver, 1893; Skinner, 1902), or an Israel to be formed in the exile (E. König, 1926). But historical Israel does not fit since the songs contrast historical Israel with the servant. Ideal Israel is incapable of real action. The servant is given a mission to the Israel to be formed in the exile (49, 6). For this reason the attempt is made to pass from one nuance to the other (Lods) and today research is generally oriented in the direction of *corporate personality* (cf. *below*).

b) Individual, non-Messianic exegesis

The servant is some personage of the past : Moses (Sellin, 1922), Jeremias (Saadiâ Gaôn, in the Middle Ages; Duhm, 1922); or a personage of the present : either a contemporary of Second-Isaias (Rudolph, 1925; Kittel, 1926) or Second-Isaias himself (autobiographical theory : Mowinckel, 1921; followed by Sellin, 1930 and Volz, 1932, who exclude the fourth song which they regard as written by another author. Volz interprets this song eschatologically). But it is clear that Second-Isaias could not have spoken of himself in such glowing terms. As for a contemporary, it can be asked how such an important person could have remained unknown to history. Besides how could 42, 1-4 and 49, 1-6 have remained unchanged even though contradicted by history?

c) Individual, eschatological exegesis

Starting with an historical individual, a figure of the future has been constructed : Joachin, the exiled king (Rothstein, 1902; Van Hoonacker, 1916); Josias (at least in some respects : Gressmann, 1929; Lagrange, 1931); the Babylonian king as suffering on the feast of *akitu* (Dürr, 1925). It is true that the figure of the servant does have certain royal characteristics (Van de Leeuw, Coppens [8]). Nevertheless, the vocation of the servant is not that of a king but rather that of a prophet or even a sage. For this reason he has been understood as a prophetic figure (Gunkel, 1912 : the perfect prophet; Bentzen, 1948, who combines the reference to Moses with the autobiographical theory of Mowinckel, 1921). For some the figure of the servant is *Heilsgestalt* which uses categories borrowed from the cult of Tammuz and the view of the king prevalent in the Middle East (Gressmann, 1929; Engnell, 1948). But there is not in any of

---

[8] Cf. CERFAUX-COPPENS, *L'attente du Messie**, pp. 51-56.

these so-called models any idea of active redemption. Fischer (1916) and O. Procksh (1938) understand the poems in a strictly Christological sense.

S. Mowinckel (1951) thinks of a person coming after Second-Isaias who died in the accomplishment of his missionary task. His resurrection is expected. His memory, almost his presence, is preserved in the circle of his disciples. Thus the servant again becomes an eschatological figure as the mediator of salvation.

d) Fluid exegesis

Gradually passage is made from Israel to her most worthy representative, the Messias, in virtue of the biblical concept of " corporate personality " which reconciles the two types of exegesis. So Wheeler-Robinson (1926); O. Eissfeldt (1933, emphasis on the collectivity); Tournay (1950) and also North (1948, emphasis on the individual).

Two types of explication

The first is linear and psychological; it is very much indebted to North. The second is inspired by Rowley and a type of fluid exegesis. Both in the end see in the servant Messianic significance.

a) The servant is the eschatological projection of the prophets.

Second-Isaias witnessed a grave setback for Israel. The return from exile was without marvels and the repatriates were limited in number. A hundred years after 538, Esdras was to bring back another important caravan; meanwhile it was the custom to look forward to and to predict this return (Is 57, 19; Ag 2, 7-8; Za 8, 7; 10, 10). At the same time the nations were not converted. Ag 2, 22 and Za 2, 15 look forward to this conversion. All this appears as the essence of the divine plan as presented by Second-Isaias. He deals with these themes but gives them a new perspective.

This time God's plan will be a complete success (53, 10); Israel will be reunited and the nations will be converted. The instrument by which God will bring to term His plan will be a man of the future. No longer is this instrument Cyrus (44, 28) but a man taken from Israel who incarnates and represents in himself the true Israel (49, 3). He is described as a man like Moses, like Jeremias, especially the latter (ministry of intercession, of the word, of the covenant, struggle against sin in the face of strong opposition). His martyrdom is foretold in liturgical formulae (sacrifice of expiation). Borrowings from royal-messianic themes (42, 1; 53, 12) make it clear that he is also a figure of the Messias, but he is rather the Messias-prophet than the Messias-King. This new type of Messias was born of a spiritual expectation lived especially on the level of Jeremias and Ezechiel. These prophets created the possibility of conceiving a mediation of a new type which replaced royal mediation once the monarchy passed from the scene. [9] It was only necessary to give this mediation an eschatological dimension.

Thus Second-Isaias explored more deeply his earlier points of view. These new perspectives he bequeathed to the circles of his disciples who inserted them in the collection of his works and supplied the necessary connections. In this way was conserved what North has called " the living heart of his message. "

Exegesis of this type is resolutely individualistic and Messianic, but it does not pretend to be Christological in the strict sense. Prophecy did not photograph centuries before time the reality which was to come. It foresees its coming; it orients men's minds and hearts in the right direction. In point of fact Jesus did identify Himself with the figure of the servant. He clearly applied to Himself 53, 12 (Lk 22, 37), and John the Baptist (Jn 1, 29) evidently alludes to 53, 6-7. This whole chapter, which " seems to have been written under the cross of Golgotha " (Delitzsch), is an introduction to the expiatory work of Jesus. It has been called the fifth Gospel.

b) The servant is the Israel of tomorrow fulfilling her vocation and embodied in an eminent personage.

In this type of exegesis the point of departure for the poems is Second-Isaias' reflection on the vocation of Israel in the terms already indicated. The mission of Israel is the corollary of her election by the one God. Her mission is consequently universal. This awareness is expressed in a series of varied and pregnant conceptions that develop along the following lines. Israel is charged with introducing the true religion to the world (first song). But only a purified remnant can lay claim to this role. This remnant must first convert Israel (second song). The mission will be difficult for Israel or, at least, for the guide who symbolizes Israel (third song). This suffering will not be accidental to the mission, but it will be the means by which the mission will be fulfilled by a man who will surpass in dignity and power every historical figure. In this person Israel is perfectly represented in such a way that the thought of Israel is never far from the presentation of him. This contraction and expansion remarkably foreshadow the mystery of Christ and the Church.

The essential thing is that modern exegesis find Christ at the term of its labors and thus be in harmony with patristic exegesis. " Quia laboravit, (Christus) videbit ecclesias in toto orbe consurgere et earum saturabitur fide " (St. Jerome, on 53, 10-11; *PL* 24, 511).

---

[9] Cf. A. FEUILLET, " Isaïe*, " *SDB*, IV, cols. 709-714; A. GELIN, " Messianisme*, " *SDB*, V, col. 1194.

CHAPTER V

PROPHECY DURING THE PERSIAN PERIOD
(538-332)

§ 1. Historical Introduction [1]

Cyrus' edict of 538 is a turning point in sacred history. Several caravans of Jews return from exile and settle in Jerusalem. After some difficulties with the Samaritans, they succeed in reconstructing the Temple which is inaugurated in 515. From this point on Judea is a small, unimportant province in the interior of the fifth satrapy, but Judaism throughout the Empire has found again a center (Jerusalem) and a head (the high priest). This state of things will last down to the period of Alexander's conquests (333). In the religion of the period there is a threefold evolution.

The evolution of prophecy

There is greater optimism than among the preexilic prophets. The promises tended to overshadow the threats. The definite orientation toward cult (Za, Mal) derives from Ezechiel; the Temple is the major center of interest of the community. A progressive eschatology is formed : last judgment (Jl 3—4; Za 12—14); return of Elias (Mal 3); gehenna (Is 66, 24); resurrection (Is 26, 19). The less and less spontaneous character of prophecy is also evident. Ezechiel had already taken care to form a list of regulations, a *torah* (Ez 40—48). He used the texts of his predecessors when he wrote, and there are already in his writings examples of the " *style anthologique.* " [2] The age of the book, the age of the scribe, has arrived.

Progress in doctrine

Both Ezechiel and Second-Isaias had stressed God's transcendence. Soon he will be considered inaccessible. This leads to a development of angelology. Ezechiel multiplied the number of angels who explain and carry out the divine commands. Zacharias carries the process further. Ezechiel had dealt with the problem of reward and punishment completely within the framework of this world though he did progress to the concept of reward and punishment based on individual merits. Some thoughtful

---

[1] Cf. *above*, pp. 36-47.
[2] Cf. A. ROBERT, *RB* (1946), pp. 135-140.

Jews (Job and Ecclesiastes) hasten the evolution of this doctrine which is paralleled by a related development of Jewish piety (Pss 16, 49, 73). The term of this development will be a concept of reward or punishment after death, in heaven or hell.

The evolution of piety

Ezechiel's line of thought, which emphasized a detailed ritualism illumined by ideas of sanctity and expiation, continues. The piety of the psalmists opens perspectives of an interior piety. Their voice is the voice of the *'anawim*.

§ 2. The Prophets of the Restoration

I. AGGEUS

BIBLIOGRAPHY

Introductions, translations, commentaries, pp. 1 f. and 271 f. (A. VAN HOONACKER, *EB**; A. GELIN, *BJ**; F. NÖTSCHER, *EBi*; E. SELLIN, *KAT*...).

J. TOUZARD, " L'âme juive au temps des Perses*, " *RB* (1923), pp. 66-68.

P. F. BLOOMHARDT, " The Poems of Haggai, " *HUCA*, 5 (1928), pp. 153-195.

A. BENTZEN, " Quelques remarques sur le mouvement messianique parmi les Juifs aux environs de l'an 520 avant J.-C., " *RHPR* (1930), pp. 493-503.

P. ACKROYD, " Studies in the Book of Haggai, " *Journal of Jewish Studies*, 2 (1951), pp. 163-176; 3 (1952), pp. 1-13, 151-156.

T. CHARY, *Les prophètes et le culte à partir de l'Exil** (Paris, 1955), pp. 118-159.

D. WINTON THOMAS, " The Book of Haggai, " *IB* (1956).

P. ACKROYD, " Two Old Testament Historical Problems of the Early Persian Period, " *JNES*, 17 (1958), pp. 13-27.

A. ALT, " Die Rolle Samarias bei der Entstehung des Judentums, " *Kleine Schriften*..., II, pp. 316-337.

The historical context

Immediately after the return from exile the work of rebuilding the Temple was begun with enthusiasm (Esd 3). Then apathy and lack of interest set in and for eighteen years the project was put aside. In the summer of 520 two prophets, Aggeus and Zacharias, determined to begin the work again. The times seemed favorable. The political difficulties that marked Darius' taking the throne were the signal for a religious revival. Though checked by the Great-King (inscription of Behistun), they seemed to foreshadow an even greater, worldwide upheaval (Ag 2 21-22) and to signal the arrival of the kingdom of God. At Jerusalem Zorobabel, the Davidic *peha*, was greeted in Messianic terms (Ag 2, 23; compare Jer 22, 24). Together with Josue, the high priest, he undertook the rebuilding of the Temple. The labors lasted less than five years : from August 520 to March 515. This reconstruction was regarded as a sign of the arrival of the Messianic era.

All Aggeus' (*Haggai = Festus*) concern seems to have been concentrated on this sanctuary. It is possible that he was a cult prophet. He does not describe his entire career in his book which only deals with his activities from August to December 520.

The book

The book was written either by Aggeus himself or by a disciple working shortly after the prophet's efforts on behalf of the Temple. It contains five dated *exhortations*.

a) 1, 1-11. An appeal for the rebuilding of the Temple. Agricultural promises connected with this reconstruction (beginning of August 520). An added note indicating that the appeal was successful and the reconstruction begun at the end of August (1, 12-15a).

b) Probably 2, 15-19 belongs here. It refers to the event dated in 1, 15a but has been located three months later by an inexact gloss. This has curiously caused the section to be attached to 2, 10-14 (Rothstein).

c) 1, 15b-2, 9 : the future glory of the Temple (October 520).

d) 2, 10-14 : consultation before the priests about Samaritan participation in the work (December 520).

e) 2, 20-23 : promise to Zorobabel. It probably dates from August 520 (1, 15a) like 2, 15-19.

The message

The delay in the reconstruction of the Temple explains present misfortunes. The reconstruction gives men a glimpse of the Messianic era to come which is described in the manner of the period : apocalyptic theme of the overthrow of heaven and earth (2, 6, 21; see Is 51, 6; 66, 22), theme of the service of the nations (2, 7-9), theme of peace (2, 9. 22), theme of the Davidic Messias actualized in the person of Zorobabel (2, 23). Non-Jews are excluded from the work of reconstruction (2, 10-14). This solicitude for ritual purity and the Temple perhaps indicate Aggeus was a disciple of Ezechiel.

II. ZACHARIAS (1—8)

BIBLIOGRAPHY

See the bibliographie for Aggeus, p. 344.

D. BUZY, *Les symboles de l'Ancien Testament** (Paris, 1923).

A. RÉGNIER. " Le réalisme dans les symboles des prophètes*, " *RB* (1923), pp. 383-408.

H. G. MAY, " A Key to the Interpretation of Zechariah's Visions, " *JBL*, 57 (1938), pp. 173-184.

C. L. FEINBERG, " Exegetical Studies in Zechariah, " *Bibliotheca Sacra* (1940-1949), pp. 97-103.

D. WINTON THOMAS, " The Book of Zechariah, 1-8, " *IB* (1956).

D. R. JONES, *Haggai, Zechariah, and Micah. Introduction and Commentary* (London : SCM, 1962).

The prophet in his historical context

Zacharias was a contemporary of Aggeus and of priestly descent (family of Addo : Esd 5, 1; 6, 14; Neh 12, 16). He must be regarded as a priest-prophet after the manner of Ezechiel by whom he was considerably influenced (position of the priesthood in the Messianic hope; the concept of purity of the land; transcendence of God). His oracles date from November 520 to December 518. They give a clear insight into the frame of mind of the inhabitants of Juda. After the glowing promises of the prophets of the Exile, the reality seemed a terrible scandal. Darius had restored peace everywhere (1, 11), but Juda did not seem to share in it : poor crops (8, 10), an inadequate population (7, 7), hostility from certain quarters (4, 10; 8, 10), the stain of sin (3, 9; 7, 4-6). Salvation was delayed and the people grew impatient (1, 12).

Zacharias met the situation head on and guaranteed that the Messianic program would be accomplished at once. He differs from Aggeus in the extent of this program.

The book

Only Za 1—8 is under discussion here. The remaining chapters, Second-Zacharias as the critics say, date from the end of the Persian period or the beginning of the Greek period.

Za 1—8 seems to be a dated, autobiographical " journal. " Its beginning has been made more solemn by the use of *Er-Bericht*. [3] Aggeus and Zacharias like Ezechiel (p. 321) sketch their visions and oracles with great care. They include : 1, 1 to 2, 9 + 3, 1-7, 9 + 4, 1-6a, 10d-

---

[3] See p. 265.

14 + 5—6, 8, 15 + 7, 1-3; 8, 18-19. Within the "journal" have been inserted pieces without dates but preceded by auto-biographical introductions : 4, 6b-10c; 6, 9-14; 7, 4-14. Finally there are various, undated words presented with a brief introduction : 2, 10-17; 3, 8, 9c-10; 8, 1-17, 20-23.

In the editing of the book, which was perhaps extensive, the other two groups of material were inserted in the "journal" because of similarity of subject matter. The promises were also added.

Basically the journal is made up of eight visions dating from February 519 (1, 7). They all apparently occurred during the same night. They are symetrically arranged according to the following schema in groups of two : a-h, b-c, d-e, f-g. All treat the same subject, the coming of the Messias. The plan is as follows :

1, 1-6 : appeal for conversion (November 520).

1, 7—6, 8 : the eight nocturnal visions [4] :

a) 1, 7-17 : the four horsemen : the peace of the empires is coming to an end.

b) 2, 1-14 : the four horns; those who have destroyed Jerusalem will themselves come to ruin.

c) 2, 5-9 : the surveyor; Jerusalem will be protected. Two appeals to the exiles (2, 10-13, 14-17) have been inserted here.

d) 3, 1-10 : the changing of the garments of the high priest Josue; the priesthood is associated with him in saluting the Messias-shoot : in 3, 9 (cf. 6, 11) read Zorobabel in place of Josue.

e) 4, 1-6a + 10c-14 : the lampstand and the olive trees; the twin powers at the service of the Lord (three words about Zorobabel have been inserted here : 4, 6b-10b).

f) 5, 1-4 : the scroll of curses flying over the land; destruction of the impious in Palestine.

g) 5, 5-11 : the woman in the *'epha*; sin transported to Babylonia to draw down punishment there.

h) 6, 1—8, 15 : the four chariots that bring destruction; one especially directed against Babylonia, the seat of Persian power.

6, 9-14 : a symbolic action, the crowning of Zorobabel and the bestowal of a Messianic title upon him.

---

[4] L. G. RIGNELL, *Die Nachtgesichte des Sacharja* (1950).—H. SCHMIDT, " *Das vierte Nachtgesicht des Propheten Zacharja,* " *ZAW* (1936), pp. 48-60.—ROTHSTEIN, *Die Nachtgesichte des Sacharja* (1910).

7, 1-3 and 8, 18-19 : a question about fasting (November 518) posed by the inhabitants of Bethel; it is not necessary to continue the fasts commemorating the events of 586.

7, 4-14 : reflections on the fasts of the Exile and a review of the nation's history.

8 (except 18-19) : a collection of oracles of salvation.

The message

Zacharias was a member of a family which had returned from exile and had preserved contacts with the exiled community (6, 10). His ideas bear a close resemblance to the thought of Ezechiel. God is transcendent. For this reason he introduces a host of intermediary figures who personify the divine activity. God is demanding. Thus conversion must precede salvation (1, 3; 8, 14-17).

Promises predominate. They present a tableau of the Messianic era : humiliation of the nations who oppress Sion (2, 1-4; 10-13); rebuilding of the Temple (1, 16); rebuilding of Jerusalem and the giving of new names to the city (8, 3); the coming of God to His city (8, 3; 2, 14); the repopulation of the city (2, 8; 8, 4-5); the return of the dispersed (6, 15; 7, 7-8); conversion of the nations (2, 15; 8, 20-23); prosperity and peace (3, 10; 8, 12); the end of sin (3, 9; 5).

The institutional tendency of Ezechiel continues in Zacharias. He thought that the previously predicted harmony between the *nasi* and the priesthood would be incarnated in history. The *peha* and the high priest are to bring it about. The *peha* is given a Messianic title (3, 8; 4, 14; 6, 11-13; cf. Is 4, 2; Jer 23, 5; 33, 15). But the fact that he will have descendents (6, 12) shows that Zacharias had in mind only a royal Messianism *redivivus*. [5]

III. THE ADDITIONS TO THE BOOK OF ISAIAS

These additions include first of all chapters 55 to 66. It is also generally agreed that some insertions have been made in the first part of the book (1—39). These include glosses of inspired editors who clarify the oracles of the prophet with more recent texts and thus complete his message, and anonymous oracles written in a style that contrasts sharply with the contexts in which they appear. In the first group can be placed 11, 10-16 and 19, 16-24. [6] Chapters 34—35 (the " Little Apocalypse ") and 24—27 (the " Great Apocalypse ") fit into the second group. Both these apocalypses will be treated after the discussion of chapters 56—66.

---

[5] " Messianisme*, " *SDB*, V, col. 1187.

[6] Is 13—14 has already been examined.

Isaias 56—66 (Third-Isaias)

BIBLIOGRAPHY

Introductions, translations, commentaries, pp. 1 f., 251 f. and 332 f.

J. MARTY, *Les chapitres 56-66 du livre d'Isaïe* (Nancy, 1924).

C. C. TORREY, *The Second Isaiah. A New Interpretation* (Edinburgh, 1928).

H. ODEBERG, *Trito-Isaiah (Isaiah 56-66). A Literary and Linguistic Analysis* (Uppsala, 1931).

K. ELLIGER, *Der Prophet Trito-Esaja* (Stuttgart, 1931).

L. GLAHN, " Quelques remarques sur la question du Trito-Isaïe en son état acuel, " *RHPR* (1932), pp. 34-46.

S. McCULLOUGH, " Reexamination of Isaiah 56-66, " *JBL* (1948), pp. 27-36.

J. MORGENSTERN, " Isaiah lxiii, " *HUCA*, 23 (1950-1951), pp. 185-203.

" Two Prophecies from the Fourth Century BC and the Evolution of Yom Kippur, " *HUCA*, 24 (1952-1953), pp. 1-74.

T. CHARY, *Les prophètes et le culte à partir de l'Exil** (Paris, 1955), pp. 93-112.

J. MUILENBURG, " The Book of Isaiah, 40-66, " *IB* (1956).

M. DAHOOD, " Some Ambiguous Texts in Isaiah*, " *CBQ*, 20 (1958), pp. 41-49.

a) A history of the criticism

Duhm (1892) was the first to recognize here an independent section coming from the hand of a distinct author whom he named Third-Isaias. He dated the work about 450. The book addresses the people in Palestine. The centers of interest are the theocratic institutions. Danger does not threaten from abroad. The danger that threatens is the danger of unfaithful Jews seizing control of the community. The optimism is less evident than in Second-Isaias for salvation seems always delayed. A study of the vocabulary and style also indicates the autonomy of Third-Isaias. It is important to note how citations from Second-Isaias are given a new interpretation (compare 57, 14 and 40, 3; 60, 13 and 41, 19b; 60, 16 and 49, 23a). Littmann (1899), Marti (1900), Hölscher (1914), Causse (1924) have followed Duhm.

The hypothesis generally favored today posits a plurality of authors. The pieces of the book date from the entire period of the restoration. The evidence for this is the differences in style, thought and historical contexts within the book. So Cheyne (1895), Kittel (1898), Abramowski (1925), Volz (1932), Eissfeldt (1934), Lods (1950), Auvray-Steinmann

(1951), Weiser (1949). Weiser supposes that the majority of the pieces were written a little after the return from exile. He dates 63, 7—64, 11 in the period of the exile and 65 and 66, 3 f. in the Hellenistic period.

A reaction has set in favoring Duhm's position but dating Third-Isaias between 538 and 510. The prophet was the spiritual guide of those who returned. He was a minor figure indebted to both Ezechiel and Second-Isaias. His writings present a tableau of the resettlement of the Holy Land. The pious minority (the poor of Yahweh) is joined by a small part of the population of Juda and Benjamin, but the majority remains in a state of semi-paganism. This gives rise to a polemic between the two groups and the invitation to the latter to be converted. The Temple which was rebuilt between 520 and 515 is not always regarded as reconstructed. This leaves a certain elasticity in dating the pieces. The conversion of the population of the country and the return of the Diaspora to constitute the new Israel, a religious people, are looked forward to with expectation. Theological and stylistic constants, especially with reference to the vocabulary of the covenant, justice and poverty, support this interpretation. It has been proposed by Elliger (1928-1933) and Chary (1954) and is the interpretation we favor.

Glahn (1934) argued that Third-Isaias is Second-Isaias preaching in Palestine after the return.

b) Divisions of the collection

56, 1-8 : Instruction *(torah)* on the conditions for belonging to the people of God. Promises to eunuchs and proselytes show its universalist tendency. It emphasizes the Sabbath which had become during the exile a criterion for religious orthodoxy. The Temple seems rebuilt (vv. 5, 7). The piece seems to have been written for one of the numerous groups to return (v. 8).

56, 9—57, 21 : reproaches and promises. 56, 9—57, 2 : against the leaders. 57, 3-13a : against " prostitution "; the nature cults, always a temptation, are denounced. 57, 13b-21 : promises to a humble and " poor " people. These different pieces can all be dated after 515.

58 : the fast that Yahweh approves; an attack on religious formalism. According to verses 2 and 3, service in the Temple seems to have begun again. Verse 12 indicates that the city has not yet been rebuilt.

59, 1-15a : the delay of salvation is due to the sins of Israel; the complaints of the people.

59, 15b-20 : Yahweh crushes the nations (compare Is 24—27); verse 21 is a gloss in prose on the spiritual Israel.

60 : the future glory of Sion. The Temple is rebuilt (v. 10) but not yet furnished. The pilgrimage of the nations supplies for this lack (vv. 3-9). Condamin and Van Hoonacker attribute this poem to Second-Isaias, but the universalism here is less pure. The nations will be subjected to Israel rather than converted.

61 : The mission of the prophet is to announce the rebuilding of Jerusalem and Juda and the advance of Israel among the nations. The announcement is made to the poor of Yahweh. Verses 10 and 11 contain Jerusalem's hymn of thanksgiving. It is not the servant who speaks (against Van Hoonacker) for there is no appeal to the nations.

62 : a new age for Jerusalem and Israel.

63, 1-6 : the day of the vengeance of Yahweh against the nations (apocalyptic genre).

63, 7—64, 11 : national lamentation for the Temple in ruins (63, 18; 64, 10) and the devastated villages. Before 520.

65 : criticism of the nation and promises of good fortune to the faithful. The new heavens and the new earth (vv. 17-25).

66, 1-2a : Yahweh refuses a Temple. Before 520.

66, 2b-4. 17 : false piety.

66, 5-16 : salvation. The prose section (vv. 18-24) describes the pilgrimage of the Diaspora to Jerusalem. It seems to be an addition.

c) The message

Third-Isaias " has vitalized the message of Ezechiel with the force of Second-Isaias " (Chary). From Ezechiel he took his interest in the sanctuary and he extends the holiness of the sanctuary to the city. Like Ezechiel he insisted on fasting and the Sabbath. To Second-Isaias he owes his anxiety for the pagan nations and for a religion of the heart. The idea of the glory of Jerusalem (60—62) is also derived from Second-Isaias. From both prophets comes the idea of a purified Jerusalem given to Israel as a great gift. Third-Isaias also inherits from both prophets his horror of idolatry which he is the last prophet to denounce.

Isaias 34—35 : *the " Little Apocalypse "*

BIBLIOGRAPHY

Introductions and commentaries, pp. 1 f. and 283 f.

W. CASPARI, " Jesaja 34 und 35, " *ZAW* (1931), pp. 67-86.

C. C. TORREY, *The Second Isaiah* (New York, 1928), pp. 270 ff.

A. MAILLAND, *La petite Apocalypse d'Isaïe* (Lyon, 1956).

The two chapters form a unit. In several respects they resemble the apocalyptic genre soon to develop from literary current in prophetic literature : vision, oracle against the nations, eschatological oracle. Though the genre is not fully formed here, this small, anonymous composition has frequently been termed " the Little Apocalypse of Isaias. "

First of all (34) it describes the vengeance of Yahweh against the nations. He vows to destroy them; the stars fall from the sky to make place for the new heavens. Edom is the model of the nations to be crushed. Yahweh sacrifices the Edomites in Bosra. The earth becomes sulphur, and wild beasts, satyrs, and Lilith (the nocturnal phantom with which the Talmud and Victor Hugo are so concerned) inhabit the ruins. Then follows the triumph of Israel (35). After a new exodus in a desert that has been completely transformed the people return again to Sion, an enchanted land. The vast return of the Diaspora is described in terms of a solemn pilgrimage.

It is clear that these chapters are based, at times to the letter, on the literature of the Exile (34, 11-14 and Is 13, 21-22; 35, 10 and Is 51, 11). Chapter 35 is written in the style of Second-Isaias (35, 1-2 and 41, 18-19; 35, 8 and 40, 3; 43, 19; 49, 11; 35, 6 and 43, 19-20), but the return described is more extensive and less precise than that from Babylon. The Edomite theme in chapter 34 calls to mind Abdias and Third-Isaias (Is 63, 1-6); the allusion to the book of Yahweh (v. 16) and the images of verse 4 are found frequently in apocalyptic writing.

Possibly 35 was a liturgy like that supposed by the psalms of the kingdom (so Caspari). 34 in its turn opens with an invitatory reminiscent of the psalms. It is perhaps better to speak of the imitation of a liturgy. Probably this apocalypse dates from the fifth or fourth century.

Isaias 24—27 : the " Great Apocalypse "

BIBLIOGRAPHY

Introductions and commentaries, pp. 1 f. and 283 f.

P. LOHMANN, " Die selbstandigen lyrischen Abschnitte in Jes. 24-27, " *ZAW* (1917-1918), pp. 1-58.

W. RUDOLPH, *Jesaja* 24-27 (Leipzig-Stuttgart, 1933).

J. LINDBLOM, *Die Jesaja Apokalypse : Jes.* 24-27 (Lund, 1938).

J. COSTE, " Le texte grec d'Isaïe XXV, 1-5*, " *RB* (1954), pp. 36-66.

The subject of this book, sometimes called the great apocalypse by comparison with chapters 34—35, is the eschatological judgment, the establishment of God's kingdom, His victory over the forces of heaven and earth, the salvation and return of Juda in the midst of universal catastrophe, and finally the resurrection of the just (26, 19). This descriptive part is interrupted by a cycle of poems which has for theme the triumph of God's city over the city of evil (24, 7-12; 25, 1-5. 9-12; 26, 1-3. 4-6. 7-11; 27, 2-6. 10-11). There does not seem to be any organic relation between the apocalyptic sections and this cycle of poems. Perhaps lack of logical structure in apocalyptic literature is not a sign that several authors are responsible for the book.

The horizon of the hymns which forcefully express Israel's national aspirations is narrower than the horizon of the apocalyptic sections. The apocalyptic sections deal with the coming of the new world; all humanity, the angels and the universe are involved. The earth and its inhabitants are under a curse (24, 6). The situation is destined to become more and more catastrophic (24, 16b-20). Yahweh will punish the angels and the kings (24, 21) and will reign on Sion (24, 23). All nations are invited to the feast which inaugurates this kingdom (25, 6-8). Israel will rise from the dead (26, 19). He is to hide while Yahweh chastises the earth (26, 20-21) and punishes Leviathan, symbol of pagan power (27, 1). Then the return of the dispersed to Jerusalem will be possible (27, 12-13).

During the period when the apocalypse was written there existed a Diaspora spread far and wide (24, 14-16; 26, 13; 27, 12-13). The idea of the judgment of the angels and of the resurrection of the dead (on a selective basis as in Dn 12, 1-3) indicates a rather late date. The destruction of an anonymous city alluded to in the cycle of poems (24, 10. 12; 25, 2. 12; 26, 5; 27, 10) is the concrete fact on which attempts to date the section are based. Lindblom suggests the fall of Babylon to Xerxes in 485; Rudolph, the conquest of the city by Alexander in 331. It is difficult to decide.

§ 3. The Prophets of the Fifth and Fourth Centuries

Particularism and universalism are the principal and contrasting themes of the prophetic literature of this period. Particularism dominates. It has its origins particularly in Ezechiel and reappears in Second-Zacharias and especially in Joel and Abdias. The pagans will be annihilated on the day of Yahweh. At very least they will be subjected to the Chosen People. This idea already clear in Third-Isaias is met again in Second-Zacharias. The discourses of Malachias witness to a calculated mistrust of strangers; at times, however, a word of admiration for them escapes (Mal 1, 11). The universalist tendency so clear in Second-Isaias appears again in a pure state only in the Book of Jonas and in Is 19, 23-25 (if it is separated from its present context).

The center of interest that has been indicated is not the only one which can help guide the reader through these prophets, but in our opinion it is the principal one.

I. MALACHIAS

BIBLIOGRAPHY

Introductions, translations, commentaries, pp. 1 f. and 271 (A. VAN HOONACKER, *EB**; A. GELIN, *BJ**; E. SELLIN, *KAT*; K. ELLIGER, *ATD...*).

C. LATTEY, *The Book of Malachy** (London, 1935).

A. ROBINSON, " God the Refiner of Silver, " *CBQ*, 11 (1949), pp. 188-190.

E. TOBAC, " Malachie*, " *DTC*, IX-2, cols. 1745-1760.

R. PAUTREL, " Malachie*, " *SDB*, V (Paris, 1953), cols. 739-746.

T. CHARY, *Les prophètes et le culte à partir de l'Exil** (Paris, 1955), pp. 160-189.

R. C. DENTAN, " The Book of Malachi, " *IB* (1956).

The period

It is generally admitted that the Book of Malachias is an anonymous work. Malachias is rather a name based on 3, 1 (= my messenger) than a proper name as the LXX understands it. This anonymous prophet worked after Aggeus and Zacharias and before the mission of Esdras. The Temple has been reconstructed (Esd 6, 13-22) and regular services are held. Tithes given reluctantly (2, 17; 3, 7, 10-14; Neh 10, 32-39; 13, 10-13), the custom of mixed marriages (2, 10-16; Neh 10, 28-30; 13, 23-31), the laxity of the priests (1, 6-8), social injustice (3, 5; Neh 5, 1-13) are the traits of the period. Malachias prepared the way for the great reformer of Judaism. Possibly he worked between the two missions of Nehemias about 430. His manner of speaking of the priesthood depends on Deuteronomy. " Priests " and " levites " are titles that recur; there is not yet question of the sons of Aaron. Thus the book precedes the promulgation of the sacerdotal legislation of Esdras (Neh 8) though the date of this promulgation is controverted.

Structure and content of the book

The title in 1, 1 corresponds to Za 9, 1 and 12, 1. Thus the three anonymous collections set at the end of the Minor Prophets open in the same way.

Characteristic of the book is its use of a dialogue. This must be the echo of real controversies between the prophet and his contemporaries. God through His spokesman makes an affirmation; those listening object; brief objections and responses follow and lead into a prophetic discourse. Six pieces are built up in this way.

I, 2-5 : Jacob preferred to Esau. Directed against those who pretend that Yahweh does not love Israel. This passage evidently alludes to the Nabatean invasion of Edom (p. 360).

I, 6—2, 9 : This indictment of the priests contains the passage (1, 11) about the sacrifice offered among the pagans which proved to be a type of the perfect sacrifice of the Messianic era (DB, 939).

2, 10-16 : against mixed marriage and divorce.

2, 17—3, 5 : the day of Yahweh. Against those who pretend that Yahweh is not just in administering reward and punishment. On that day priests and people will be purified from their sins.

3, 6-12 : failure to pay tithes.

3, 13-21 : Yahweh will distinguish the just from the unjust on His day.

Two appendices have been added : one on the practice of the law (3, 22, a Deuteronomic warning); the other, an exegesis of 3, 1 which treats of the return of Elias. This closing has been commented on in the Gospels (Lk 1, 17; Mt 17, 12). According to these texts the prophecy is not to be understood in a strict and literal sense of the ancient prophet but rather of a prophet who by the grandeur of his mission would in some way be the incarnation of the spirit and power of Elias (Van Hoonacker).

Rabbinic and popular understanding of the passage seems to have been more concrete (Mt 16, 14; Jn 1, 21). Trypho, the Jew, makes this objection to Justin : " If Christ has been born and if He exists somewhere, He is unknown. He does not even know that He is Christ and He has no power since Elias has not come to anoint Him and to manifest Him to all " (*Dial. Trypho*, VIII, 4).

The texts on the precursor are to be read in the following order :

1) Mal 3, 1 : a messenger prepares for the day of Yahweh (cf. Is 40, 3).

2) Mal 3, 23-24 : identification of the messenger. Sir 48, 10-11 and the rabbinic texts (see also *Dial. Trypho*) are even more precise.

3) Explanation of the Gospels (see above).

The message

Malachias is very much dependent upon Deuteronomy. Religion culminates in cult. If the details into which the prophet enters in this regard seem to us trivial, we perhaps forget the demands of the virtue of religion. The day of Yahweh is described in a cult context. Cult will be perfected in the world to come (3, 4). The particularism of Malachias is evident in his judgment of Edom and in his solicitude for the purity of Jewish blood (2, 11).

But Malachias is a man of contrast. He is also capable of profound reflections on the responsibilities of priests (2, 6-7), on the moral foundations of the true religion (2, 10-13), against the divorce law (2, 16). This last point, which foreshadowed the condemnation of Jesus, illustrates the authority of the prophets in matters of this type. His affirmation of the universal reign of Yahweh (1, 14) and his sympathetic view of " the pure oblation offered in every place " by the Jews of the Diaspora (according to some exegetes, by pagans) (1, 11) are not less noteworthy.

II. The book of jonas

BIBLIOGRAPHY

Introductions, translations, commentaries, pp. 1 f. and 271 (A. van Hoonacker, *EB**; A. Feuillet, *BJ**; T. H. Robinson, *HAT*; F. Nötscher, *EBi*; E. Sellin, *KAT...*).

L. Dennefeld, " Jonas*, " *DTC*, VIII-2 (Paris, 1925), cols. 1497-1504.

A. Feuillet, " Jonas*, " *SDB*, IV (Paris, 1948), cols. 1104-1131.

Aalders, *The Problem of the Book of Jonah* (1948).

B. Trépanier, " The Story of Jonas, " *CBQ*, 13 (1951), pp. 8-16.

S. Blank, " Doest Thou Will to be Angry? A Study in Self-Pity, " *HUCA*, 26 (1955), pp. 29-41.

J. D. Smart, " The Book of Jonah, " *IB* (1956).

G. Knight, *Ruth and Jonah²* (London : SCM, 1956).

Analysis of the book

Called by Yahweh to preach repentance at Ninive, Jonas rebels and flees toward Spain. A tempest sent by Yahweh engulfs the ship. The sailors learn that Jonas is the cause of their distress and toss him overboard. The sea immediately becomes calm (1). A great fish swallows the prophet and he remains in the belly of the fish three days. Jonas recites a psalm of thanksgiving and the fish vomits him up on the shore (2). God orders Jonas a second time to go and preach penance at Ninive (3). The city is converted by his preaching and receives God's pardon. Jonas is very much put out by this manifestation of divine mercy and God teaches him a lesson. His shelter formed by a miraculous castor-bean plant is suddenly destroyed. Jonas is vexed. The lesson : God has even more reason to be concerned over the great city, Ninive.

The psalm of thanksgiving supposedly recited in the belly of the fish (2, 3-10) is manifestly an addition to the narrative. It does not fit the context. Some exegetes think that 4, 5 is to be read after 3, 4.

Date, literary genre, purpose

There are notable Aramaisms (1, 6. 7. 12; 3, 7; 2, 1; etc.) and certain of the characteristics of late Hebrew in the book. It takes up once more the missionary idea of Second-Isaias and gives it an even clearer presentation. The author seems to be trying to overcome the resistance to the idea, to undermine the exclusivism and particularism prevalent since the days of Nehemias and Esdras. Several voices made themselves heard about the same time in this attempt to restore the universalism characteristic of the first chapters of Genesis : Is 19, 23-25 and Ruth are likely from the same period as the Book of Jonas.

The book is not genuine biography but rather didactic fiction (3, 10; 4, 10-11). History certainly knows nothing of this conversion of Ninive which in any case would put us " in the presence of a miracle unequaled in the history of mankind and superior even to that of Pentecost " (Feuillet). The dimensions attributed to the great city (at least fifty miles in diameter : Jon 3, 3) are not verified by modern archeology. The Ninive of the book is an allegorical Ninive. The folklore of all peoples knows the theme of the fish who swallows and saves. The same theme appears in Lucian. Biblical literature knows the theme of the prophet who resists Yahweh and then is vanquished by Yahweh (2 Kgs 19, 4; Jer 15). There existed in the time of Jeroboam II a prophet by the name of Jonas (4 Kgs 14, 25) (the name signifies " pigeon, " that is, a person who remains at home). These facts lay the foundation for the development of a *midrash*. This literary genre which developed widely after the Exile includes edifying stories based on facts or a fact taken from the Scriptures.

The lesson in the present case is one of the most lofty in the Old Testament : all men—even the fiercest enemies of Israel—are called to salvation. This is taught in a magnificent story which gave men reason to rejoice and must have born fruit.

III. JOEL

BIBLIOGRAPHY

Introductions, translations, commentaries, pp. 1 f. and 271 (J. TRINQUET, *BJ**; A. VAN HOONACKER, *EB**; F. NÖTSCHER, *EBi**; E. SELLIN, *KAT* ...).

L. DENNEFELD, *Les problèmes du livre de Joël** (Paris, 1926).

A. KAPELRUD, *Joel Studies* (Uppsala, 1948).

R. PAUTREL, " Joël*, " *SDB*, IV (Paris, 1948), cols. 1098-1104.

L. MARIÈS, " A propos de récentes études sur Joël*, " *RSR* (1950), pp. 120 ff.

J. STEINMANN, " Remarques sur le livre de Joël, " *Études sur les Prophètes d'Israël** (Paris, 1954), pp. 147-173.

J. A. THOMPSON, " Joel's Locusts In the Light of Near Eastern Parallels, " *JNES*, 14 (1955), pp. 52-55. " The Book of Joel, " *IB* (1956).

M. TREVES, " The Date of Joel, " *VT*, 7 (1957), pp. 149-156.

Analysis of the book

a) The plague of locusts (1—2)

The prophet calls the people to pray and to do penance on the occasion of an invasion of locusts. He uses the form of a liturgy. This liturgy is repeated twice. 1) The prophet first invites the people to consider the ravages of the plague (1, 2-12). Then he urges the priests to assemble the community for a solemn fast (1, 13-14). 1, 15-20 is the prayer of this fast. 2) Again (2, 1-11) the prophet calls for the sounding of the alarm on Sion and describes the plague of locusts, comparing them to an army. 2, 12-14 is an exhortation to repentance. 2, 14-17 repeats the invitation to a solemn fast and gives the theme of the supplication. There follows an oracle in which Yahweh announces the end of the scourge (2, 18-20). A hymn of thanksgiving (2, 21-23) and the promise of abundant harvests conclude the first section. It is to be noted that the expression, " day of Yahweh " (1, 15; 2, 1. 2. 11) here involves woe for Juda.

b) The description of the day of Yahweh (3—4)

The first sign of its arrival : the pouring forth of the spirit (3, 1-2) in the manner of Nm 11, 29; no time of life, no social level will be deprived of this gift which the text limits to Israel. The second sign of its arrival : prodigies in the heavens (3, 3-5) which will not frighten the Jews for they will have a refuge in Sion (3, 5, borrowed from Abd 17). Then there will follow the drama of Josaphat (4, 1-17). All nations will come together from all parts of the world (4, 2, 11. 12) to war against God's angels (4, 9). The grievances of Yahweh against these nations are summed up in their indictment for hostility toward Israel (4, 2 f.). All this will occur in the valley of " Yahweh-Judge " as in Ez 38—39 and Za 14. The place of punishment is near Jerusalem. It has been identified with the ravine of the Cedron which since the fourth century after Christ has been called the Valley of Josaphat. The judgment of Yahweh is an execution. This scene, the divine harvest and vintage (4, 13), is presented again in Ap 14, 14-20. The sentence of execution, received with the words " Turmoil! Turmoil! " (4, 14a), is accompanied by disturbances in the heavens. Finally in 4, 18-21 there is a description of the new earth, of the magnificent and peaceful land where the wadies will be replaced by rivers always filled with water (4, 18c). One of these will flow from the Temple (cf. Ez 47, 1 f.; Za 14, 8) to make the land fertile. The Jews will live perpetually with Yahweh who dwells on Sion. The conclusions of Joel and Ezechiel resemble one another.

Critical problems

a) Literary unity

The idea of duality of authorship first put forward by M. Vernes (1872) and Rothstein (1896) was taken up by Duhm (1911). The Second-Joel who wrote 3—4 is a " preacher in a synagogue. " He combined his own piece with the first section and inserted in it mention of the day of Yahweh (1, 15; 2, 1b-2a; 2, 11b). Duhm has been followed by Hölscher (1914), Eissfeldt (1934), Baumgartner (1947), Trinquet (1953), T. H. Robinson (1938). Robinson follows Bewer (1912) in dividing up the second part and in indicating a special author for 4, 4-8 which limits the international horizon. On the other hand recent critics have favored literary unity (Bentzen, 1940; Lods, 1950; Weiser, 1940; Kapelrud, 1948). Though the two parts are admittedly quite different, this is due to the fact that a concrete event is described in the first part while the second part is based on more impersonal, eschatological themes. This second part is " a compendium of Jewish eschatology " (Dennefeld).

b) The date

Contemporary commentators generally date Joel about 400. Interest is centered on " Juda and Jerusalem " (a favorite expression of the Chronicler). The Greeks (4, 6), the return of the Diaspora are mentioned. There are borrowings from books generally regarded as late (Jl 2, 11 and Mal 3, 2; Jl 3, 4 and Mal 3, 23; Jl 1, 15 and Is 13, 6; Jl 2, 10 and Is 13, 10). Particularism and the emphasis on cult are much in evidence. All these indications form a solid foundation for this position. Recently, however, it has been challenged by Kapelrud. He situates Joel about 600 and emphasizes the contacts between Chanaanite cult vocabulary and that of the prophet. In this study he has especially relied on the Ras-Shamra texts. These stereotyped formulae which have lost much of their original force could, however, just as readily date from 400 as from the time of Jeremias.

c) The literary genre

The circumstances which occasioned this prophecy may well have been an agricultural calamity. The prophecy suggested (1, 15; 2, 1-2a) the eschatological themes set forth in 3 and 4 which are the heart of the book. Only Engnell (1948), followed by Steinmann (1953), argues for a liturgy properly so called.

The message

Joel is a prophet whose main interests are particularism, cult and eschatology—all themes from Ezechiel. He emphasizes eschatology. The eschatological section is clearly detached from history and historical perspective. The resulting tableau is nuanced in the direction of cult : eschatological promotion of cult prophets (3, 1-2), cultic structure of the eschatological community (4, 17), fecundity of the country based on the presence of the Temple (4, 18; cf. Ez 47, 1-12 and Za 14, 8), perhaps (Kapelrud) mention of acacia trees in 4, 18 as matter of cult objects.

IV.   ABDIAS

BIBLIOGRAPHY

Introductions, translations, commentaries, pp. 1 f. and 271 (A. VAN HOONACKER, *EB**; J. TRINQUET, *BJ**; E. SELLIN, *KAT* . . .).

T. H. ROBINSON, " The structure of the Book of Obadiah, " *JTS* (1916), pp. 402-408.

W. RUDOLPH, " Obadja, " *ZAW*, 49 (1931), pp. 222-231.

F. E. GAEBELEIN, *The Servant and the Dove : Obadjah and Jonah* (New York, 1946).

J. STARCKY, " The Nabateans, " *BA*, 18 (1955), pp. 84-106.

N. F. LANGFORD, " The Book of Obadiah, " *IB* (1956).

The book

Introduced by the technical word " vision " which designates first of all prophetic ecstasy, then the message received, then the writing in which the message is contained (cf. Is 1, 1), the Book of Abdias, the shortest in the Old Testament, is divided into two parts :

1-14 + 15b : curse against Edom based on her conduct during the events of 587. It is reminiscent of the stereotyped literature inspired by the fall of Jerusalem found in Lam 4, 21-22; Ps 137; Ez 25, 12 f.; Is 34. Wellhausen followed by van Hoonacker and Trinquet sees in the curse evidence of the gains of the Arabs at the expense of Edom (v. 7).

The progressive retreat of the latter is climaxed in 312 when the Nabatean Arabs seize Petra. There are certain similarities between this first part and Jer 49, 7-22. The text of Jeremias seems more ancient for the thought sequence is better. It is, however, impossible to guarantee the authenticity of the passage in Jeremias and consequently it is not a criterion for dating the present passage with precision.

15a + 16-21 : an apocalyptic expansion. The destruction of Edom is the sign of the coming of the day of Yahweh for all the pagan nations. The expressions and the spirit of the section are close to Joel. This may be the reason why Abdias follows Joel in the LXX. Verse 17 on Sion as a refuge for the Jews has been taken up in Jl 3, 5. The description of the new Israel (19-21) presents rather modest territorial ambitions. The section closes with mention of the kingdom of Yahweh as coinciding with the suzerainty of Israel. Just as it is not necessary to suppose duality of authorship for Joel where there is a similar plan, it is not necessary to suppose a new author for the second part of this book (with Rudolph, 1931; against Sellin, 1929, T. H. Robinson, 1916, and J. Trinquet, 1953, who situates the first part between 550 and 450 and the second part before Joel which he dates between 400 and 200).

The message

The book presents a nationalism similar to that of the Book of Joel. It reflects the ambitions of the Palestinian, Jewish milieu afflicted with such bitter memories and looking forward to future grandeur. There is faith in God's fidelity toward Israel, but there are hints of a moral disorder that an Amos would have denounced emphatically. The missionary emphasis met in the " servant of Yahweh " of Second-Isaias gives way in the work of this " servant of Yahweh " (Abdias = Servant of Yahweh) to a bitter and vindictive attitude toward foreign nations. Clearly the book does not suffice in itself and must not be isolated from the ensemble of the prophetic books.

V. ZACHARIAS 9—14

BIBLIOGRAPHY

Introductions, translations, commentaries, pp. 1 f. and 346 (A. VAN HOONACKER*, A. GELIN*, E. SELLIN...).

A. JEPSEN, " Der Aufbau des deuterosachar janischen Buches, " *ZAW* (1939), pp. 242-255.

T. JANSMA, " Inquiry into the Hebrew text and the ancient versions of Zach IX-XI, XIV, " *Oudtestamentliche Stüdien*, VII (Leiden, 1950), pp. 1-141.

A. GELIN, " L'allégorie des pasteurs, " *Mélanges Vaganay** (Lyon, 1950).

K. ELLIGER, " Ein Zeugnis aus der jüdischen Gemeinde im Alexanderjahr 332 v. Chr., " *ZAW* (1949-1950), pp. 63-114.

M. DELCOR, " Les allusions à Alexandre le Grand dans Zach, IX, 1-8*, " *VT* (1951), pp. 110-124. " Un problème de critique textuelle et d'exégèse, Zach. XII, 10*, " *RB* (1951), pp. 189-199. " Deux passages difficiles, Zach. XII, 11, et XI, 13*, " *VT* (1953), pp. 67-77.

P. ACKROYD, " Criteria for the Maccabean Dating of Old Testament Literature, " *VT*, 3 (1953), pp. 113-132.

R. C. DENTAN, " The Book of Zechariah, 9-14, " *IB* (1956).

F. BRUCE, " The Book of Zechariah and the Passion Narrative, " *BJRL*, 43 (1960-1961), pp. 336-353.

D. JONES, " A Fresh Interpretation of Zechariah ix-xi, " *VT*, 12 (1962), pp. 241-259.

Content

Zacharias 9—14 is divided into two parts, each introduced by the same formula *(massa debar Yahweh)* which is also found at the beginning of Malachias (p. 354).

First part (9—11 + 13, 7-9).

This first part treats of the salvation of the people. The rather frequent repetition of the words, " shepherd " and " flock " (9, 16; 10, 2-3; 11, 3. 4. 5; 13, 7), indicates an artificial unity. The following sections can be distinguished.

1) Jews and the nations : 9, 1-8 (Yahweh comes to the Near East and prepares the new land of Israel); 9, 9-10 (the humble Messias); 9, 11-17 (the Diaspora will return); 10, 1-2 (fidelity to Yahweh); 10, 3—11, 3 (liberation and reestablishment of Israel).

2) The struggles within Judaism, 11, 1-17 (the allegory of the two shepherds [7]; 6 and 8a are probably later glosses). Since Ewald (1840) 13, 7-9 have been added to this section. These verses salute the new people which has been tested and then blessed with the benefits of the covenant.

Second part (12—14)

The center of interest is eschatological Jerusalem. It is a question of the final struggle and glorification of Judaism. The theme recurs twice : 12—13, 6 (the nations attack Jerusalem; lamentation for the one who has been pierced; the fountain which purifies from sin; the end of idols and prophets); 14 (the nations attack Jerusalem; Yahweh intervenes; transformation of the country; the total consecration of Juda).

The date

a) Za 9—14 distinct from Za 1—8.

From the historical point of view there is no longer question of the rebuilding of the Temple; the leaders of the people are anonymous and nations other than those who had relations with the Jews in 520 are prominent in the book. From the religious point of view the Messianic perspective is not that of 520. Zorobabel was then the concrete expression of Messianic hopes; there is question here of a many-faceted dream of an eschatological theocracy. From the literary point of view Za 1—8 contains dated and signed oracles in an original prose; the oracles of Za 9—14 are without dates and unsigned. They are generally written in verse in the anthological style.

Independent critics are unanimous in distinguishing between the two sections of Zacharias. Catholic exegesis tends in the same direction : Lagrange (1906), Nötscher (1948), and Gelin (1948). Van Hoonacker (1908) and Junker (1938) defend unity of authorship.

b) The problem of dating Second-Zacharias.

The first critical studies during the eighteenth century dated 9—11 before 721 because of the mention of Ephraim (understood as the northern kingdom), Assyria, and Egypt (9, 10. 13; 10, 6. 7. 10. 11). Chapters 12—14 which speak only of Juda and contain an allusion (12, 11) to the death of Josias (609) are dated between 609 and 586. Against this opinion (cf. Dillmann, König) it is necessary to take into consideration the artificial character of the archaisms in the eschatological, apocalyptic style. Egypt and Assyria have a symbolic and typical sense as in Is 19, 23-25 and 27, 13. They are used to designate the Ptolemies and the Seleucids. At best it is possible to speak of the use of older material, but the mention of the Exile and the Diaspora (9, 11-12) clearly indicate a postexilic date.

The essay of Stade (1881-1882) has decisively influenced consequent studies of Second-Zacharias which he dated from the period of the first of the Diadochi. Second-Zacharias is a bookish author and even at this early date shows signs of collecting into his own work selections from other authors. Lagrange (1906), Abel, Gelin (1948), Chary (1955), Delcor have followed Stade.

Stade's study has been modified on two points : the unity of 9—14 and the date. The pieces have been assigned diverse origins. Steuernagel

---

[7] KREMER, *Die Hirtenallegorie im Buche Zacharias auf ihre Messianität hin untersucht* (1930).

(1912) thinks 9—11 date from before 722 and were reworked during the Greek period. He assigns 12—14 to the period of Alexander. Eissfeldt (1934) postulates two anonymous, practically contemporary collections. Their collector lived about the time of the author of Daniel. The allegory of the shepherds refers to the struggle for the office of high priest at the beginning of the Machabean period. It dates from about 160 (Marti) or 150 (Sellin). The pierced person of 12, 10-14 could be the high priest Onias III (170) (Sellin) or Simon (1 Mc 16, 1-22) (134) (Duhm). But this late date, accepted by Weiser (1949), clashes with the fact that the collection of the twelve minor prophets was closed about 200 (Sir 49, 10). It seems best to accept Stade's date, even if we should allow for a complex origin of the pieces of the book and consider 11, 8a, the *crux interpretum*, as a gloss from Machabean times.

The message

Second-Zacharias is a compendium of eschatology. At the collapse of the Persian Empire hopes of every kind flourished. The presentation of the final struggle is almost what it was in Joel (10, 2—11, 3) though here there is the addition of the pierced person whose death has a salvific value in the eschatological battle. The ideal of a theocracy based on cult (14) calls to mind Ezechiel, but the perspective is broader. There is grouped around the Temple a religious community which sees in itself the religious center of the world. The house of David is revitalized (12, 7 ff.—13, 1). The meek and gentle Messias (9, 9-10) combines the ancient royal hopes with the expectations of the 'anawim.

The Gospels insist that this prophecy was fulfilled on the day of Our Lord's triumphal entry into Jerusalem (Mt 21, 2-7) : " Exultat ergo Sion... quia venit ei Rex suus qui omnium prophetarum vaticiniis repromissus est : Justus et ipse, Salvator id est Jesus, sicut angelus interpretatus loquens est ad Virginem " (St. Jerome, *PL*, 25, 1483).

PART IV

THE KETUBIM OR SACRED WRITINGS

The books which make up the third part of the Jewish canon are, generally speaking, the ones that were composed and accorded canonical recognition later than the rest. They belong to widely different classifications. After the *Psalms*, which must be given a special place, come books that treat the subject of wisdom; namely, *Proverbs* and *Job*. Five scrolls *(Megillôt)* form a collection of liturgical prayers for five great feasts *(Canticle of Canticles, Ruth, Lamentations, Ecclesiastes, Esther)*. *Daniel* occupies a special place. The Jewish canon closes with the Books of *Esdras, Nehemias,* and *Paralipomenon*. In these last three books the mind of a single writer can be recognized. Each of the other books belonging to the Ketubim should be studied as a separate unit.

SECTION I

THE PSALMS

by P. Auvray

For introductions, translations, and commentaries, see pp. 1 f.

D. C. SIMPSON, ed., *The Psalmists* (London, 1926).

H. GUNKEL, *Einleitung in die Psalmen* (Göttingen, 1933).

N. H. SNAITH, *Studies in the Psalter* (1934); *The Jewish New Year Festival* (1947).

G. WIDENGREN, *The Accadian and Hebrew Psalms of Lamentation as Religious Documents* (Uppsala, 1936).

J. H. PATTON, *Canaanite Parallels in the Book of Psalms* (1944).

J. J. WEBER, *Le Psautier du Bréviaire romain** (Paris-Tournai, 1944).

E. PODECHARD, *Le Psautier**, 3 Vols. (Lyon, 1949-1954).

H. DUESBERG, *Le Psautier des malades** (Maredsous, 1952).

E. J. KISSANE, *The Book of Psalms**, 2 Vols. (Dublin, 1953).

W. O. OESTERLEY, *The Psalms* (London, 1953).

G. CASTELLINO, *I Salmi** (Turin, 1955).

J. J. STAMM, " Ein Viertelyahrhundert Psalmenforschung, " *Theologische Rundschau*, 23 (1955), pp. 1-68.

M. TSEVAT, *A Study of the Language of the Biblical Psalms* (1955).

C. GORDON, *Ugaritic Manual* (1955).

S. MOWINCKEL, *The Psalms in Israel's Worship, I and II* (New York : Abingdon, 1962); " Psalm Criticism Between 1900 and 1935, " *VT*, 5 (1955), pp. 13-33; " Traditionalism and Personality in the Psalms, " *HUCA*, 23 (1950-1951), pp. 205-231.

A. R. JOHNSON, " The Psalms, " *OTMS*, pp. 162-209.

P. DRIJVERS, *Les Psaumes. Genres littéraires et thèmes doctrinaux** (Paris, 1958).

J. GRAY, " The Kingship of God in the Prophets and Psalms, " *VT*, 11 (1961), pp. 1 ff.

A. WEISER, *The Psalms, A Commentary* (Philadelphia : Westminster, 1962).

T. WORDEN, *The Psalms are Christian Prayer* (New York : Sheed and Ward, 1962).

P. A. H. DE BOER, *Studies on Psalms* (Leyden, 1963).

G. W. ANDERSON, " The Psalms, " *Peake's Commentary on the Bible*, ed. M. BLACK—H. ROWLEY (New York : Nelson, 1963), pp. 409-443.

H. RINGGREN, *The Faith of the Psalmists* (Philadelphia : Fortress, 1964).

C. WESTERMANN, *The Praise of God in the Psalms* (Richmond : Knox, 1965).

P. DRIJVERS, *The Psalms, Their Structure and Meaning** (New York : Herder and Herder, 1965).

M. DAHOOD, *The Psalms, 1-50** (Garden City : Doubleday, 1966).

CHAPTER I

THE BOOK OF PSALMS

§ 1. Title and Place in the Bible

The Book of Psalms comes at the beginning of the *Ketubim* (Writings), which is the third section of the Hebrew Bible. In the Greek Bible it is also found at the beginning of the third section, that consisting of the didactic books. But the Latin Bible, as far back as we can go (Council of Hippo, A.D. 393), places the Book of Psalms after Job.

In Hebrew Bibles the book is called *tehillim* or *sefer tehillim*. This is an irregular [1] plural form of the feminine noun *tehillah* (root : *halal*, praise), which has a specialized meaning; it refers to a certain kind of psalm, namely *praises* or *hymns*. The word which corresponds exactly with our word *psalm* would be *mizmor* (root : *zamar*, to sing with accompaniment); it refers to a poem to be sung to the accompaniment of stringed instruments. This word is found in the titles of 57 psalms.

As a rule the LXX gives this book the title *Psalmoi* or *Biblos Psalmon*, a title which is borne out by the New Testament also (Lk 20, 13; 24, 44; Acts 1, 20). The LXX codex Alexandrinus gives it the title *Psalterion* (a word which generally means a musical instrument).

The Latin Bible also uses two titles, *Liber Psalmorum* and *Psalterium* (or *Liber Psalterii*), from which we have the French titles *livre des psaumes* and *psautier* as well as the English *Book of Psalms* and *Psalter*. *Psalter* is the title preferred in liturgical usage.

§ 2. Content

If we consider the Book of Psalms as it has come down to us, with its individual psalm titles and its musical and liturgical markings, it seems to be a more or less official collection of songs used in the Jerusalem liturgy during the period of the second Temple.

The collection contains 150 psalms, there being no reason to include a 151st psalm which is found as an extra in the LXX. This 151st psalm

---

[1] EHRLICH thinks that this plural form *im* instead of the normal *tehillot* was characteristic of titles given to books or collections. See Esd 2, 10, *qinim* instead of *qinot*. But this is uncertain.

is not in the Hebrew nor in the Latin Vulgate, and it does not belong to the canonical text.

Although the number of psalms (150) is agreed to, the sources of the Book of Psalms do not all give the same divisions. Twice the LXX, followed by the Latin Vulgate, divides a single Hebrew psalm in two. Twice again two Hebrew psalms correspond to one in the LXX. In numbering the psalms this difference can be represented as follows :

Hebrew		LXX and Latin Vulgate
1—8	—	1—8
9	—	9, 1-21 ⎱
10	—	9, 22-39 ⎰
11 to 113	—	10 to 112
114	—	113, 1-8 ⎱
115	—	113, 9-26 ⎰
⎰116, 1-9	—	114
⎱116, 10-19	—	115
117 to 146	—	116 to 145
⎰147, 1-11	—	146
⎱147, 12-20	—	147
148 to 150	—	148 to 150

Most of the time it is difficult to decide which of these traditional ways of dividing is correct. An exception is the LXX psalm 9, which is psalms 9 and 10 in Hebrew. It seems that the LXX tradition is the better one here, since the whole composition forms an alphabetical psalm. The problem of these divisions will be met in particular instances in commentaries.

We cannot say exactly when this collection of psalms was put together. The collection existed as part of the canon and was already translated into Greek when the grandson of Ben Sira attached a prologue to his translation of the Book of Ecclesiasticus (about B.C. 117). In three places this prologue mentions the three parts of the Hebrew Bible, and the third part certainly begins with the Book of Psalms. The writer of this prologue further implies that the psalms were already a part of the Bible in his grandfather's day, thus at the beginning of the second century B.C.

The Book of Ecclesiasticus (47, 8-10) as well as the citation of a psalm as
" scripture " in 1 Machabees 7, 17 afford some support to this early second
century B.C. date for the collection of the psalms. This date may be set
a little farther back. In 1 Par 16 we find a song that is made up with
parts of psalms 105, 96 and 106. And 1 Par 16, 36 gives the doxology
which concludes the fourth section of the Book of Psalms. Although
there are some uncertainties here, and complete precision is impossible,
we may be right in saying that this collection of psalms already existed
in the third century B.C.

§ 3. Subdivisions

Like the Law (Torah), the Psalter is divided into five books, and each one
ends with a doxology :

Part I : psalms 1-41

Part II : psalms 42-72 (note psalm 72, 20 " The prayers [LXX : the
hymns] of David, son of Jesse, are ended ")

Part III : psalms 73-89

Part IV : psalms 90-106

Part V : psalms 107-150 (psalm 150 is a kind of doxology)

A close study of the psalms shows up many repetitions or doublets.
Psalm 14 appears again as psalm 53. Psalm 70 is a reworking of psalm 40,
14-18. Psalm 108 is a reconstruction of psalm 57, 8-12 and psalm 50,
8-14. There is a very uneven use of the divine names in the psalms.
The first part of the Psalter is predominantly " Yahwist " (the name
Yahweh is used 272 times, Elohim 15). The second part is " Elohist "
(Elohim is used 164 times, Yahweh 30). The third part divides the names
rather evenly (44 to 43). The fourth and fifth books are clearly Yahwist
(103 and 236 respectively against none and 7). Whatever may have been
the motive for substituting the name Elohim for Yahweh, the fact that
such a characteristic is present, along with the doublets, clearly proves
that there were partial collections of psalms in existence earlier than the
actual Psalter which we have, collections made in different places and at
different times. The study of editorial notes such as the one in psalm 72,
20 and of the individual psalm titles will lead to the same conclusion.

§ 4. Titles

Many of the psalms have titles, although in giving titles the Massoretic
tradition does not agree perfectly with that of the LXX. In general the

LXX has more titles. While 34 psalms have no titles in Hebrew, only 19 lack them in Greek. In the Hebrew 73 psalms are attributed to David, in the LXX 84. Whatever may be the solution to this minor textual problem, the titles have their importance and deserve close study.

I. The various kinds of psalms

Some are called psalms (*mizmor*, 57 times), others are called songs (*shir*, 30 times), others prayers (*tefillah*, 5 times) or hymns (*tehillah*, once, Ps. 145). Related to this last title (tehillah) is the acclamation *Halleluyah* which some psalms have at the beginning (10 in all) and some at the end (13) [2]; these are classified as hymns. Some of the names of the psalms are obscure : *miktam* (6 times), which was understood by the LXX as " inscription poem " and by others as " poem of gold "; *maskil* (13 times) was generally taken to mean " didactic piece "; *shiggayon* (once, Ps. 7; cf. Hb 3, 1) might mean " prayer of repentance. " These classifications are not complete, and they are not very exact. Therefore, they are not decisive in classifying the psalms according to their different literary forms.

II. The initial lamed

This *lamed*, which is called the *lamed auctoris*, is ambiguous. Its actual meaning is so uncertain that some recent writers have denied the very existence of a real *lamed auctoris*. Let us look at the data.

Fifty-five psalms have the title *lamenasseah* (in Greek : *eis to telos*), which is generally translated " of (or) for the songmaster. "

Seventy-three psalms have the formula " for David " (in Greek : *to David*, 84 times).

Twelve psalms have " for the sons of Asaph. "

Twelve psalms have " for the sons of Core. "

One psalm has " for Moses. " (Ps. 90)

Two psalms (72 and 127) have " for Solomon. "

One psalm (88) has " for Heman the Ezrahite. " This psalm also has " for the sons of Core. "

One psalm (89) has " for Ethan the Ezrahite. "

One psalm (39) has " for Yedutun. " It also has " for David. " Psalm 62 has " over Yedutun, for David. " Psalm 77 has " over Yedutun, for Asaph. "

---

[2] In the LXX the *alleluia* always comes at the beginning, with the exception of Ps 150 which has two *alleluias*, one at the beginning and one at the end.

Many of these persons are known—David, Moses, Solomon. The mention of the levites Asaph, Heman, etc. is a witness to the organization of liturgical song and worship as we know it from the priestly tradition. After the Exile liturgical song seems to have been the monopoly of the sons of Asaph (Esd 2, 41; 3, 10; Neh 7, 44; 11, 17. 22.). But during the period of the monarchy, starting from the time of that organization of liturgy referred to as the work of David (1 Par 6, 16-32), the priestly author of Par mentions three corporations of singers. Heading these groups were Asaph, Heman, and Ethan (who is identified with Yedutun, 1 Par 15, 16-24; 25, 1-6; 2 Par 5, 12; 29, 13-14; 35, 15). The older and larger group, which was called the sons of Core (ancestor of Heman, 1 Par 6, 7-12. 18-23), acted in various capacities such as porters (1 Par 9, 17-19; 11, 19) and bakers (1 Par 9, 31). They were linked to the levite Core of the time of Moses. Core's revolt was punished severely (Nm 16, 1-35), but he still had some descendants (Nm 26, 11).

The term *menasseah* is generally taken as a common noun (more accurately a piel participle of the verb *nasah*, to guide; see 1 Par 15, 21). Fifty-three of the fifty-five psalms which begin with this word are at the same time attributed to a specific person: 39 to David, 9 to the sons of Core, 5 to the sons of Asaph (see a similar case in the psalm of Habacuc, Hb 3, 19). The meaning of the expression is disputed.

These remarks as well as those made earlier regarding the Asaphite and Coraite professional singers, and reference to the Ras Shamra tablets with their titles *(lebaal, lekeret)* which indicate the poem or cycle of poems to which they belonged, along with the testimony of the Book of Par (2 Par 29, 30)—all these items have led scholars to speak of partial collections older than our actual Psalter or even older than the five books which it contains. There must have been Asaphite and Coraite collections of psalms as well as a collection prepared for the songmaster. In all these instances, the phrase " for Asaph, " " for Core, " etc., placed at the beginning of a psalm, shows that the psalm in question belonged to one or the other of these collections. The phrase, however, does not necessarily say anything about the author of the psalm. The same can be said about the title " for David. " This title shows that " Davidic " collections were in existence, a fact already suggested by the editorial note of Ps 72, 20 and by the testimony of 2 Par 29, 30.

There are instances, however, in which such titles do not suggest the existence of a special collection. One psalm (90) has the title " for Moses, " and two psalms (72 and 127) have the title " for Solomon. " There is no question here of relating these psalms to a collection, but rather of attributing them to an author. The same should be said about those " Davidic " psalms in which the title " for David " is followed by a description of circumstances which are regarded as providing the occasion for the composition of the psalm. It doesn't matter much whether this understanding of titles led to the idea that the whole Psalter was the work of David, or whether the conviction that the whole Psalter was David's suggested this interpretation of the titles. The essential point here is that these two factors coincide. We conclude that the *lamed* was certainly understood by later tradition as a *lamed auctoris*.

III. MUSICAL DATA

Certain obscure expressions in the Book of Psalms are generally included under this heading of musical data. The expressions refer to the following :

—instruments for musical accompaniment : *bineginot*, with stringed instruments (Ps 4; 6; 54; 55; 61; 67; 76); *el nehilot*, for flutes(?) (Ps 5); *al haggitit*, on the Gath harp (Ps 8; 81; 84; according to others : on the melody of the Gattite).

—the musical mode : at the octave (Ps 6; 12; according to others : on the eight-stringed harp); for the voice of sopranos(?) (Ps 46; see 9, 1 and 48, 15 and the commentaries).

—the melodies to be used : " to the melody of *Do not destroy* " (Ps 57; 58; 59; 75; see Is 65, 8); " to the melody of *The dove of the distant terebinths* " (Ps 56); possibly also : " to the melody of *The death of the son* " (Ps 9); " to the melody of *The Gattite* " (Ps 8; 81; 84); and many others— see Ps 45; 69; 60; 80.

The meaning of these phrases is often unclear. Even less clear is the sense of the formulae *lelammed* (" for teaching, " Ps 60; see 2 Sam 1, 18) and *le annot* (" for answering, " Ps 88).

We should mention here the puzzling word *selah*, which is used 71 times in 39 psalms, 37 of these 39 psalms being in the first two books. *Selah* could mean " raise of voice " or " pause " or " interlude " (Greek : *diapsalma*).

The obscurity of all these expressions is proof of their great age. Most of them were already unintelligible in the period of the LXX translation. One may speak of preexilic notations, the meaning of which was lost during the long period when the Temple lay in ruins. But this is only hypothesis.

IV. LITURGICAL CLARIFICATIONS

The main one is found in the title " song of the steps " (Ps 120—134) which must be an allusion to the *ascent* of the pilgrims towards the Temple of Jerusalem. Others are the " song of the dedication of the Temple " (Ps 30), the " song for the Sabbath " (Ps 92), and the expressions " for commemorating " or " in memory of " (Ps 38; 70; see Lv 2, 2, etc.).

The LXX has many more notations of this kind indicating that a psalm is for the first or second or fourth or sixth day after the Sabbath (Ps 24 [23]; 48 [47]; 94 [93]; 93 [92]; or also " for the last day of the feast of tents " (Ps 29 [28]). These LXX notations are confirmed and sometimes expanded by the Mishna.

The fact that the LXX has this greater abundance of titles does not mean that they are more recent. The form of these titles rather shows that they were translated from the Hebrew. The Greek translation was using a Hebrew edition which was different from the one we have, but just as old. And like the one we have, that edition had Palestine for its place of origin.

V. HISTORICAL INDICATIONS

These historical indications fill out the details for the psalms attributed to David. They allude to his flight from Saul (Ps 7; 18; 34; 52; 56; 57; 59; 63; 142), to his repentance after his sin (Ps 51), to his wars (Ps 60), to his flight from Absalom (Ps 3).

All these indications of historical detail are found in the LXX as well as in the Hebrew Psalter. The LXX has in fact about a dozen more such indications than the Hebrew. They refer the psalms in question to David or other authors. Examples are : " Of David, before his anointing " (Ps 27 [26]); " For David, poem of Jeremias and Ezechiel, about the captivity, when they were going to leave " (Ps 65 [64]); " For David, of the sons of Jonadab and the first exiles " (Ps 71 [70]); " When the Temple was rebuilt after the Exile, poem of David " (Ps 96 [95]; " Over the Assyrians " (Ps 80 [79]); " For David, against Goliath " (Ps 144 [143]), and many others.

CONCLUSION

What can be said about the question of the inspiration and authority of these psalm titles? Although patristic tradition often favored the idea of taking these titles as canonical and inspired, the practice of the Fathers is not unanimous on this point. Besides, this tradition was built for the most part on the insufficient criterion of literary authenticity; that is, these titles would be taken as canonical in the degree that they were thought to go back to the very authors of the psalms. The almost unanimous practice of the Fathers was to discuss the authenticity and then the veracity of these titles.

Many recent theologians have come to doubt the inspiration of these titles. Dom Calmet [3] already in his day mentioned his contemporaries Noel Alexandre and L. Ferrand as doubting their inspiration. In our day, the great majority of exegetes who have faced the question have arrived at the same conclusion. [4] The answers of the Biblical Commission of May 1, 1910 (answers II and III), by the very fact that they do not oblige the Catholic exegete to consider the titles of the psalms as having unquestionable authority, seem to adopt the same position.

However, the titles of the psalms should not be undervalued. They provide positive data which bear witness to a tradition. Only good arguments to the contrary can oppose them in particular cases.

---

[3] *Dissertation sur les titres des Psaumes*.

[4] Most of these theologians are content simply to mention the fact that this is their position, without bothering much about the reasons for it. Basically, the idea guiding them is that these titles are editorial insertions, late, and external to the sacred text. The relation of psalm title to psalm is similar to the relation of the prologue to the Book of Ecclesiasticus.

CHAPTER II

THE TEXT

The question of textual criticism is a very touchy one in the Book of Psalms, more so than for any other book of the Bible.

I. THE HEBREW TEXT

Frequent flaws are found in the Hebrew text. From a literary standpoint, the Hebrew text has often been reworked or glossed to adapt it to changing circumstances. Besides, a text used as much as the Psalms must be copied often. This leads to errors on the part of those copyists who are not well trained in a difficult language. The comparison of doublets such as Ps 18 and 1 Sm 22 or of Ps 14 and Ps 53 points up some of the textual difficulties and leads us to suspect similar ones even in those places where there is no comparison to be made which would give concrete proof of the difficulty. If we compare the Hebrew text with the Greek version, we may conclude that in places the Hebrew text was corrupted beyond remedy even before the Greek translator got to it. Still, in practice great prudence is called for in making textual emendations.

II. THE VERSIONS MADE FROM THE HEBREW

One of the poorest translations in the entire LXX is its version of the Book of Psalms. The reason is the difficulty of the Hebrew text and its poor condition on the one hand, and on the other the mediocre talents of the translators. There are many instances of countersense in the LXX, and some of nonsense. The verbs are translated mechanically, Greek aorist translating Hebrew perfect and Greek future translating Hebrew imperfect. The supposed vocalizations are often erroneous. All things considered, the Psalm text of the LXX is practically useless as a translation.

Even so, the LXX is valuable as a witness to a Hebrew text that is not always identical with our Massoretic text. And from this standpoint the very ineptitude of the translator is sometimes welcome, since it gives us more information than a more careful translation ever would.

Other primary versions worth mentioning are the following : 1) The Syriac (peshitto) version, which was made from a Hebrew text which can be easily identified with our Massoretic text, although the Syriac version was also heavily influenced by the LXX; 2) the three Greek versions or revisions of Aquila, Symmachus, and Theodotion, the partial preservation of which we owe to the hexapla of Origen—these versions are not too important; 3) the remarkable version of St. Jerome which is called *iuxta Hebraeos* [1]; it was made from a Hebrew text that was identical with our Massoretic text and was an excellent translation for its time.

III. The secondary versions

Among the secondary versions (made from the Greek), we mention only the following : the *vetus latina*, [2] which after a quick revision on St. Jerome's part gives us the *Roman Psalter*, [3] and after a more thorough revision and correction gives us the *Gallican Psalter*. [4] It was this latter version that became the text of our Sixto-Clementine Vulgate.

---

[1] Dom Henri de SAINTE-MARIE, *Sancti Hieronymi psalterium juxta Hebraeos. Édition critique* (Collectanea biblica latina, Vol. XI) (Rome : Abbey of Saint Jerome, 1954).

[2] Of the *Vetus Latina Hispanica* (edited by T. A. MARAZUELA : I *Prolegomena*, Madrid, 1953), Vol. 21 has already been published, *Psalterium Wisigothorum-Mozarabicum** (Madrid, 1957).

[3] A rather recent edition is the one by Dom Robert WEBER, *Le psautier romain et les autres anciens psautiers latins. Édition critique** (Collectanea biblica latina, Vol. X, Rome, Abbey of Saint Jerome, 1953). The identification of the *Roman Psalter* with the first psalm revision made by Jerome has recently been contested by Dom D. DE BRUYNE in *Le Problème du Psautier Romain** (*Revue Bénédictine*, 42, 1930, pp. 101 ff.). This learned Benedictine holds that the text of the Roman Psalter existed before St. Jerome and was not touched by him. But Father Vaccari has made serious objections to this position (*Scritti di Erudizione e di Filologia** [Rome, 1952], I, 211). And Dom Weber, in his edition of the Roman Psalter (p. ix) does not commit himself completely in favor of de Bruyne's position.

[4] *Biblia sacra juxta vulgatam versionem ad codicum fidem... X. Liber psalmorum ex recensione sancti Hieronymi**, (Rome : Tipografia polyglotta vaticana, 1954).

CHAPTER III

LITERARY FORMS OF THE PSALMS

People have always noticed differences both of spirit and of form among the various psalms. The very psalm titles such as hymn, song, thanksgiving, etc. are an invitation to recognize these differences.

About 30 years ago, [1] with the increase of knowledge about the psalms and the improvement in methods of studying them, the problem of classifying the psalms was posed in a new way.

This kind of study must be placed on as broad a base as possible. This is done when we put alongside the 150 psalms of our Psalter a number of similar poetic pieces which are scattered through the other books of the Bible; for example, the song of Moses (Ex 15), the song of Anna (1 Sm 2), the song of Ezechias (Is 38, 10-20), the hymns inserted into the passage in Isaias 24—27, the song of Habacuc (Hb 3), the hymn of the three young men (Dn 3, 52-88), [2] the psalms inserted into the Book of Ecclesiasticus (46, 1-17), many of the Lamentations of Jeremias, etc. To all this we may add certain pieces of non-biblical literature such as the Psalms of Solomon and the thanksgiving psalms of Qumran.

Besides all this, the religious poetry of neighboring peoples can be studied with profit. Such comparative study is a difficult one and calls for much caution. It can shed welcome light on certain Israelite institutions. For a long time it has been pointed out that some of the Assyro-Babylonian religious texts are worthy of close study in connection with certain passages of the Bible. Similarities as well as differences that can be noticed will help us in our understanding of the psalms. The still recent discovery of Sumerian literature allows us to go even farther back. Even though the study of this literature is still in its rough stages, it is full of promise. When we turn to Egypt we find that, in spite of some impressive contacts (the hymn of Akhenaton and Ps 104), Egyptian literature seems on the whole to have few comparisons to offer. These few should not be neglected. Finally, in the area of Phoenicia the Ras

---

[1] This was true especially after the appearance of Gunkel's Introduction to the Psalms (1933).

[2] In many manuscripts of the LXX several of these canticles are united under the title of " Odes " and placed after the Psalms.

Shamra texts which were discovered and published about 30 years ago give us an insight into the religious ideas and their manifestation in the literature of a country very near to Chanaan before the Israelites arrived. [3] There is no question of finding among these neighboring peoples the source of the Bible's lyric poetry nor of pointing out comparisons that would suffice to explain the origin of that poetry. However, such an investigation of the larger literary context will give us a better grasp of certain characteristics of biblical poetry and will help us to appreciate its remarkable originality.

§ 1. Variety of the Psalm Form

After the general area of the psalm form has been determined, the exegete is soon impressed by the limitless variety within this form. It is very difficult to put order into so rich a variety. It isn't as if we could sort out and classify these different psalms on the basis of clear signs as to their origin or form or subject. In the literary world of the psalms, a world alive with all sorts of inspiration and showing widely different characteristics, divisions must be created in somewhat the way paths are traced in an unexplored forest. This means that the results may be disappointing to exact minds looking for order and logic. The forms that we will try to define are not always clearly marked off. Many psalms remain more or less outside any classification. Several forms seem to overlap one another and mix. The attempt at classification is none the less a first step in the direction that leads to a more perfect understanding and explanation of the psalms.

It is immediately clear that there is a distinction to be made between individual and collective psalms. Whatever may be the precise form and content of a prayer, it can come from an isolated individual or from a group. It can be expressed by an I or a We. This point is important and is not merely a question of the form in which the prayer is cast. Collective prayer usually develops in a situation of worship. The collective psalms may be liturgical prayers that originated in Israel's sanctuaries and were used in them in connection with feasts and Israel's life of worship. On the other hand an expression of individual piety can be isolated and exceptional, and it may only instruct us about the personal piety of its author. As we will see later, however, the matter is not quite that simple. The I can itself be collective; for example, in the case of a king or priest speaking in the name of a whole group, and especially in the case

---

[3] All these texts are brought together in the anthologies referred to on pp. 1 f.

of the " individual lamentations "—it is practically certain that these lamentations originated in a cultic and therefore collective situation. The exegete must be sensitive to shades of meaning here, his main duty being that of giving his attention to objective data. When he attempts to place the psalms back into their living context, the first question he must ask is whether their orientation is individual or collective.

§ 2.   The Hymns

The hymn form is found throughout the history of religious poetry in Israel, from the song of Miriam (Ex 15, 21) and the song of Debora (Jgs 5) to the New Testament's *Benedictus* and *Magnificat*, two hymns that draw all their inspiration from the earlier Israelite poetry. The hymn form is found in many parts of our Psalter; for example, Ps 8, 19; 29; 33; 67; 100; 103; 104; 105; 111; 113; 114; 136; 145; 146; 147; 148; 149; 150. [4] There are also elements of hymns in psalms that are more or less composite. And there are special forms like the royal hymns or the hymns to Sion. These will be considered later.

The hymn is characterized clearly by its tone of praise. It glorifies God above all for His own sake rather than for the sake of some personal benefit to the one who is praying it. The person who prays a hymn does not ask favors for himself or for those dear to him. He does not reflect on himself but keeps his attention centered in God. Since the hymn is completely involved with Yahweh and His glory, it is a very pure expression of religion.

Among all the psalm forms, the hymn has the most consistent structure. Although this structure does not exlude the use of imagination in expressing one's devotion, the variations that result from this use of imagination seem to fit into a rigid system that can be recognized easily.

The hymn has an *introduction*. It is a brief invitation to praise Yahweh. The introductory invitation is usually a plural imperative joined with an expression referring to those who are uniting in the act of praise *(Praise the Lord, you children; Praise the Lord, all you nations)*. The invitation can also be expressed in the first person and in the future tense *(I will praise you, O Lord; we will praise you, O God)*.

After the hymn's introduction comes a *development*. This part generally begins with " because " (Hebrew : *ki*) or some similar word. Sometimes it begins with active participles or relative clauses. The

---

[4] These lists of references are not complete. They aim only to point out characteristic examples.

" development " names and describes the attributes of God, retells His powerful actions in favor of Israel and other men. Sometimes it lengthens out into fuller narratives (Ps 104, 6-9) or repeats the story of historical events (Ps 105; 106). In doing all this the hymn uses a wide range of forms; for example, exclamations or questions, comparisons drawn between Yahweh and the nothingness of false gods, wishes and blessings, refrain-like repetitions of ideas or formulae that have already appeared in the introduction.

Ordinarily it is Yahweh who is the direct object of this praise, whatever may be the name by which He is called or the epithets that are applied to Him. But some of the psalm hymns are addressed to Sion (Ps 48; 84). It also happens that the praise which is given to God is blended with the glorification of His sanctuary or of the holy city.

The hymns usually end with a short *conclusion*. This can be a more developed or more personal restatement of the introductory formula. It can be a short blessing, a promise, or a prayer. Sometimes it is a simple " Praise Yahweh " or " forever, " which could be said by the whole crowd in answer to the longer expressions used by the choir.

We can gain some idea of the variation of tone among the psalm hymns if we look at certain " cosmic " hymns such as Ps 8; 19; 29; 104. Psalm 29 is a kind of litany to the God of the storm. After a short invitation to rejoice in God's glory (1-2), the author gives a detailed description of the manifestations of " Yahweh's voice. " This voice makes His glory brilliantly visible and it terrifies the proudest creatures (3-10). Finally, a short conclusion (11) mentions Israel, the people for whom God has a blessing.

Psalm 19 is a hymn to the beauty of the skies, and especially to the beauty of the sun because it tells the glory of God in a special way (2-7). The psalm ends with a long meditation on the Law. Like the sun, the Law gives light and warmth to men (8-15). This conclusion may be a later addition.

The greatest cosmic psalm is Ps 104. Many comparisons have been made between this psalm and the famous hymn of Amenophis IV to the glory of the solar disc. There are, in fact, striking points of comparison between the two texts, and a similar motif for the two pieces is admitted by all. But there is probably no literary dependence to be uncovered here, not even of an indirect kind. Within the Bible itself two passages, Gn 1 and Jb 38—40, invite comparison with Ps 104. All three pieces have the same point of departure; namely, the contemplation of nature by a keenly observant man. With a sense of wonder the man in each case discovers harmonious order in the world. But each one's manner of expressing this wonder is different. Gn 1 is the product of a mind aiming vaguely at scientific expression. Its presentation is didactic, in rhythmic prose. Jb 38—40 is a grandiose page of " theodicy " read out in epic style. It is an enthusiastic picture of God's greatness seen in the wonders of creation. Ps 104 seems to stand midway between the two. It has neither the cold exactness of the first account of creation nor the fantasy of the passage in Job. Ps 104 is a good example of genuine religious lyric poetry. The author speaks admiringly to God as he describes the visible world with fine feeling for what is picturesque and colorful and for movement. It is true that at the end (32-35) he mentions the wicked, and in doing so he points out the disorder that has found its way into the world; but this is only a passing reference. The author of Ps 104 is a religious optimist. He understands and loves nature, including fierce animals and catastrophic events. Everything is for him a way of rising towards God.

In contrast with the " cosmic " hymns are the " human " hymns, which show interest in man rather than in things. They move from man to God without the help of other creatures. Ps 8 mentions the majesty of the Lord above the skies (2) and the work of God in the sky, the moon and the stars (4) only as an introduction to the contemplation of man who was created " a little less than a god " and set up as master of creation (6-9).

Ps 113, the first of the *hallel*, also mentions the glory of God " above the skies. " But the author of this psalm is particularly interested in the praise of God on the lips of man and in God's generous actions in favor of men. Here the impression is given that God's glory lies mainly in His mercy. God is greater for having raised Job from his dung hill than for having created sky and earth. This kind of hymn, which is usually quite solemn, lets the human sounds of pleading and thanksgiving come through.

In this connection the most striking psalm is Ps 103. It has been compared with Ps 104, and a similarity of structure and tone seems to be intentionally emphasized by the fact that they have the same introduction and conclusion formulae. But there is a big difference. The author of Ps 104, a nature poet, goes from the exterior to the interior, from the world to God. The author of Psalm 103 has only a moderate interest in nature, but a very keen insight into the moral world of man. And he shows deep religious feeling in his praise to the Lord in connection with that world. He sees the greatness of God in man's lowliness and in all the manifestations of divine mercy. Although as a poem it is not as fine as Ps 104, it has a greater psychological and religious depth.

Most of the hymns give the impression of being impersonal, and they appear to be expressions of Israel's collective piety. Many allusions to the sanctuary and to God's presence there can be found in these hymns. They contain indications of liturgical actions such as prostrating, lifting the hands, shouting. In them we find traces of dialogue, invitations and responses, references to processions and to sacrifices. All of this, when taken in connection with scattered descriptions in the historical and prophetic books, gives us a picture of the liturgical context in which these hymns originated and in which they were used. Unfortunately we have no ancient ritual that would give us more detailed information. We know only that the psalms of the *hallel* (Ps 113—118) [5] were recited in later centuries at the three great feasts, particularly during the paschal meal (see Mt 26, 30; Mk 14, 26).

§ 3. Supplications

The term " lamentation " is often used for this psalm form. But it seems that the name " supplication, " which is broad enough to include the dirge character of the lament as well as other elements in this kind of poetry, is the better term.

Collective supplications (Ps 44; 79; 80; 83; etc.) are not as common as individual supplications (Ps 3; 5; 13; 22; 25; etc.). The two kinds of supplication are distinguished only by the particular grammar proper to each. At base their forms are the same. They both grow out of the reaction of the religious person in the presence of enemies or evils that assail him. When persecuted or hurt, the devout Israelite turns to God to tell Him his troubles and to ask for help.

The structure of the supplication is much like that of the hymn. But it is not as rigid as the hymn, especially in the case of the individual supplications.

The *introduction* in supplication psalms is very brief. It is an appeal to God. Sometimes it is cut down to a simple vocative; at other times it is a little more developed. It recalls God's unfailing goodness towards those who cry to Him.

---

[5] This is the *hallel* par excellence, also called the *hallel* of Egypt. The tradition of the Talmud gives the name *hallel* also to Ps 136 (great *hallel*) and to Psalms 145—150.

The *development* in supplication psalms, in contrast to that of the hymns, is always concrete and personal. The psalmist describes his situation and admits that he is helpless. Thus the one who prays the supplication psalm puts himself forward and speaks in the first person. He describes his troubles, points out and judges his enemies, and makes his cry of distress with all the art of impassioned rhetoric. Sometimes he ends his piece by insisting again on the fact that he is weak and that none but Yahweh can save him. This avowal serves as a kind of step by which he moves to the supplication proper.

The psalmist's purpose here is to get Yahweh to intervene. Most of the time he solicits this intervention directly (" Rise up, Yahweh, save us! " Ps 44, 24, 27). But often he tells God reasons why he should intervene. These motives are Yahweh's power (and here the supplication will sound much like a hymn) and His goodness as shown in past interventions; and also the innocence and weakness and confidence of the one who is praying. The reason put forward to God can also be the opinion of onlooking strangers and Yahweh's concern for His name's honor and glory.

The *conclusion* to the supplication psalm usually expresses confidence and is marked by a conviction that God will listen and answer. Sometimes the supplication ends with words of thanksgiving.

The psalms that are dearest to the devoted faithful belong to this classification. The *De Profundis* (Ps 130) belongs here. Private devotion has made it a prayer for the souls in purgatory. Originally it was the supplication made by a man who was sick and discouraged. He made his appeal to Yahweh (1-2) by pointing out the motives he had for despairing (3-4) and by making his act of faith (5-8). The last strophe (7-8) could be the result of a later transformation of the psalm which aimed at applying it to all Israel even though originally it had been the prayer of an individual.

The *Miserere* (Ps 51) is similar in spirit to the *De Profundis* and is still more moving. The psalmist lays great stress on the sin he has committed (5-8) and on the pardon which he has asked for and expects to receive (3-4; 9-14). He says emphatically, " Create a clean heart in me. Give me once more a strong spirit " (12). These words give a more complete and precise expression to the rather flat idea of a fault being " covered " or " erased. " (11) The psalmist is sure of God's pardon. He promises to express his grateful recognition in hymns (17) and to spell it out still more by offering a personal sacrifice (19). Here again, as in the case of Ps 130, the conclusion (20-21) enlarges the content of the psalm.

Ps 22, although it is not used as much as these other two in modern devotion, is famous because of the use made of it by Jesus and the evangelists. It too is a complaint. But it is the complaint of a just man who is aware of his innocence. He makes his cry of hope to God in the midst of the cruelest sufferings. The tone of his appeal and certain concrete details in his expression have led some to relate this psalm to the last of the Servant Songs in Isaias (Is 52—53). The first part (2-12) is a mixture of complaint and confidence. The second part (13-22) is a pure lamentation which describes the miserable condition of the persecuted just man. This part ends with a heart-rending appeal (20-22). In a long conclusion the psalmist makes promises. When he is delivered, he will publicly acknowledge his debt to the Lord. He will be very generous with his benefits. He will work for the conversion of the world to God. His outlook is full of hope. Moving beyond his own personal experience, he opens up still larger religious perspectives. At this point the tone of the psalm becomes that of a hymn. The psalm becomes Messianic and even eschatological. The conclusion gives to Ps 22 a prophetic and universalist meaning which is rare in the Psalter. It is easy to see why it was used so much by the New Testament writers.

The usual context or life situation of these supplication psalms was evidently the occurrence of national or individual catastrophes and the dirge ceremonies that followed them. The historical books of the Bible do not place psalms similar to those in our collection on the lips of historical persons, although the elegy spoken by David at the death of Saul and Jonathan (2 Sm 1, 17-27) is not altogether unlike them. Still, these books refer to actions of mourning (Dt 9, 18; Jos 7, 6), and they also stress the fact that mourners " wept in the presence of Yahweh " (Jgs 20, 23. 26). Sometimes the short prayers of the mourners are mentioned (Jgs 21, 3; 4 Kgs 8, 33). We also know that on certain occasions a fast was decreed and all the people were invited to make their lament in the presence of Yahweh in a cry for pity (Jl 2, 15-17). In the period after the Exile, the prophet Zacharias mentions many annual fast days such as those for the fourth, fifth, seventh, and tenth months (Za 8, 19). At least two of these solemn fast days date back to the time of the Exile (Za 7; 5). At about the same period, the feast of Expiation (kippurim), which was kept on the 10th of the month tishri and the days immediately following, took on an importance that was to continue in Judaism. It is very likely that the ritual for these fasts provided for lamentations in the presence of Yahweh as well as for sacrifices and purification rites. Many of our supplication psalms are more clearly intelligible in this situation.

§ 4. Thanksgiving Psalms

Like supplication psalms, these thanksgiving psalms belong mostly to the area of individual devotion (Ps 18; 32; 34; 40; etc.). There are only five or six instances of collective thanksgiving psalms (Ps 66; 67; 124; 129).

Thanksgiving psalms have something in common with the hymn and with the supplication psalm. The attitude of the faithful person who gives thanks to God is expressed easily in words of praise. This makes his prayer like a hymn. When an appeal addressed to God in a supplication psalm has been answered, the one who has prayed will move on to acts of thanksgiving. And so the connection between the two psalm forms is evident.

The *introduction* to thanksgiving psalms is something like the introduction to hymns. We find the following : " I will sing... "; " I will praise... "; " Shout to God... " This introduction is sometimes addressed to God, who is to be thanked. Sometimes it is addressed to the community, which is invited to join the psalmist as witness to God's favors.

The *development* in thanksgiving psalms is usually a narrative. The psalmist begins this development by recalling the dangers he has experienced and the attacks or persecutions that have been aimed at him. Sometimes he admits his faults and confesses his weakness. At other times he claims he is innocent and makes a protest against unjust persecution.

Then he makes his request in terms similar to those used in supplication psalms.

At this point the thanksgiving psalm tells about the saving intervention of God. This saving intervention is the element of originality in the thanksgiving psalm. By proclaiming the power of Yahweh the psalmist shows himself sure of the victory to be enjoyed by the person who places his trust in Yahweh. For this reason the thanksgiving psalm usually ends with a hymn motif.

The *conclusion* of a thanksgiving psalm, when there is one, generally looks to the future. Man's confidence in God is renewed and strengthened. He promises to give glory to Yahweh forever. He invites the community to make a perpetual act of thanks to God. Sometimes the conclusion is a simple blessing formula.

Ps 30 is a thanksgiving psalm that has mixed elements. It glorifies God (verses 1 and 5), it narrates the psalmist's experience of danger and his rescue (3-4; 7-8), and it makes general observations about God's

mercy (verses 6 and 10). Its title indicates that it was once used for
the feast of the dedication of the Temple. It was applied to Israel or to
the Temple of Yahweh, Israel having been at first happy and the Temple
full of splendor but afterwards put to the test and persecuted and finally
rescued by the intervention of God.

The first part of Ps 34 (1-11) is also a thanksgiving psalm, and it
looks like a completion of the supplication Ps 25. After a hymn-like
introduction (2-3), which is taken up again by the crowd in verse 4, there
is a short description of the psalmist's rescue (5). Then the psalm becomes
a kind of meditation on God's goodness (6-11). The second part of this
alphabetical Ps 34 is a long *development* of a wisdom theme. This makes it
sound like a teacher's instruction to his disciple. This psalm must be
taken as a unit. Its wisdom development shows the turn which traditional
devotion took during the period that was dominated by the scribes.

The thanksgiving psalm appears to be as old as the thanksgiving
sacrifice and as old as the feasts that commemorated the great events of
Israel's history. Commemorative ceremonies, great yearly feasts,
dedications, anniversaries of victories—these were the situations in which
many of these thanksgiving psalms originated and in which they are to be
given their liturgical setting. This kind of psalm accompanied the
sacrifice. It was sung in processions, perhaps alternately with hymns.
However, we cannot be very precise here. The discoveries at Qumran
have given us about 20 thanksgiving psalms which are full of biblical
reminiscences. It is clear that they are imitations of our canonical
psalms. But these Qumran psalms have a rather new spirit [6] about them
and are filled with allusions to the history of the Qumran sect. They tell
us nothing about how they were used.

§ 5. Royal Psalms

Although the phrase " royal psalm " is ambiguous, it refers us to still
another kind of psalm. The term actually covers two rather different
kinds of psalms; namely, those which are built on the idea of the kingship
of Yahweh and those which honor the Israelite king.

The psalms about the kingship of Yahweh are represented by Ps 47
and by the series of Ps 93—100. These are basically hymns with an
eschatological turn (Ps 47; 97; 98; 99). And they draw a great deal of

---

[6] The materials to be studied in isolating this new spirit more exactly are the
hymns collected in Is 24—27 and the *hôdayôt* of Qumran.

their inspiration from the second part of Isaias. During the period of the return from Exile, Israel developed its idea of God as Ruler along with its universalist hope. Israel's devotion was moved to sing of God as the true King of Israel and Master of the whole earth. It seems unnecessary to hold with Mowinckel [7] that there was a New Year's day feast of the enthronement of Yahweh. The Bible does not give any hint of such a feast.

Other psalms have as their theme the individual *Israelite king* (Ps 2; 20; 21; 45; 89; 110; 132). These psalms do not present us with a new literary form. They are hymns, thanksgiving songs, supplications, etc. But the important place occupied in these psalms by the king gives them a special character which should be noted. The king held a privileged position in the religion of Israel. His function was not simply to serve as a guide in nonreligious matters for a people called by God to a supernatural destiny. He was himself the instrument of God's plan. He shared in the promises and in the supernatural character of the history that was unfolding in and through his life. [8] He was God's representative in guiding the people, and he was their spokesman in God's presence. It is natural that some of the psalms should give the king this special attention.

Among these royal psalms we will look particularly at two, Ps 110 and 2, which resemble and complete one another. Both appear to refer to a similar ceremony; namely, the anointing or enthronement of a king. Ps 110, which has a very difficult text, shows possible points of contact with Egyptian, Assyro-Babylonian, and Ugaritic texts. Its references to the priestly character of the king and its mention of Melchisedech underline its archaic quality as well as its religious content. The fact that the recitation of this psalm was continued even after the dynasty was a thing of the past, and the fact that it was quoted many times by the New Testament writers, are signs that the Messianic meaning of this psalm was recognized very early. Ps 2 is simpler than Ps 110 and more recent. It is presented as a proclamation by a king on the occasion of his enthronement in the midst of difficult circumstances. Here too, the Messianic bearing of this psalm is emphasized by the use made of it in the New Testament and throughout Christian tradition. Ps 2 looks to the Messias in his temporal reign (Acts 4, 25. 26), or in his Church (Ap 12, 5; 19, 15), or in his end-time appearance.

---

[7] *Psalmenstudien* II (Kristiana, 1932).

[8] See J. DE FRAINE, " L'aspect religieux de la royauté israélite, " *Analecta biblica*, 3 (Rome, 1954).

§ 6. Messianic Psalms

The Israelite king was the representative of a dynasty. And the dynasty was the object of divine favors, the possessor of divine promises (2 Sm 7). When some psalms insist on the glory of the house of David and its representatives, when they sing about the greatness of this house in terms that go beyond even the exaggerations of oriental court style, when they stress the moral virtues and the priestly prerogatives of the son of David, they are thinking not only of the reigning king. These ideas look also to the future king who will " increase the empire for the sake of endless peace " (Is 9, 6). Jesus and the authors of the New Testament were not deceived. They often quote the psalms as Messianic prophecies that were fulfilled in the person of Jesus. (Mt 21, 42 and Ps 118, 22; Mt 22, 44 and Ps 110, 1; Jn 13, 18 and Ps 41, 10; Acts 2, 25-28 and Ps 16, 8-11; Acts 2, 34 and Ps 110, 1; Acts 4, 25 and Ps 2, 1; see also Jesus' more general declaration in Luke 24, 44). Ancient Christian tradition has taught the same doctrine almost unanimously, with the possible exception of Theodore of Mopsuestia. The existence of a certain number of Messianic psalms is a revealed doctrine, as the Catholic Church has recognized. [9] This does not mean that all the psalms mentioned by the Fathers of the Church as Messianic—or even by the New Testament—are necessarily Messianic in the literal sense. This is a touchy problem for exegetes, and it can be resolved only after a careful examination of particular cases. But Messianism is a phenomenon of such importance in the history of Israel that the absence of psalms representing this religious attitude would be incomprehensible.

Next to these Messianic royal psalms we can place certain songs about the glory of Sion and Jerusalem. Even if the Messias is not named in them and described as he is in the royal psalms, their perspective none the less places us in a future which is clearly of the end-time. Like some of the psalms about the kingship of Yahweh, many of the songs of Sion should be studied in connection with the last chapters of the Book of Isaias. (Ps 46; 38; 76; 87) They are testimonies to Israel's expectation.

§ 7. Didactic and Wisdom Psalms

This kind of psalm, which is quite different from the rest, was designed with a view to instruction rather than liturgical use. These wisdom psalms show certain special characteristics both in form and

---

[9] This is affirmed by the 8th response of the Biblical Commission on May 10, 1910 (*EB*, 351 : " Agnoscendi sunt ").

content. For one thing, they are filled with reminiscences of earlier texts. Because of this we may speak of the anthological method in which the writer is more a collector than an author. Such writers made use of other ordinary procedures of composition followed in the scribal schools; for instance, they use the alphabet as a kind of frame for the psalm (Ps 9—10; 25; 34; 37; 111; 112; 119; 145). The subjects of these psalms are usually the Law, wisdom, the moral life. All these are regular themes in the Old Testament wisdom books. Sometimes we find in these psalms a tendency to make historical digressions and moral reflections. Now and then they raise problems, such as that of retribution. But the writers of these wisdom psalms seldom dare to propose a doctrine that was unknown to their predecessors. For instance, we find that allusions to the expectation of immortality are rare in the psalms. And when such allusions are made, they are deliberately vague (Ps 16; 37; 49; 73).

§ 8. Other Classifications

Can we speak of prophetic psalms, oracle psalms, psalms of blessing or cursing, victory psalms, as special classifications? These themes appear often in the Book of Psalms. But they do not come with enough consistency or exactness for us to see in them any independent literary forms. They are rather the different shapes assumed by hymns or supplications to fit different occasions. We should not pass over these differences when we attempt to explain particular psalms, but neither should we make too much of them.

Much the same thing is to be said of those psalms that are called *mixed*. There are cases where the psalm seems to change its form and to pass from supplication to hymn or thanksgiving, or vice-versa. There are cases of brusque change in rhythm midway in a psalm that seems to cut it in two (Ps 19; 24). From this fact some have concluded that new and complex psalm forms were used in certain cultic ceremonies. Some speak of " liturgies, " that is, composite pieces in which a question posed by the faithful called forth from the priests an " oracular " response, the whole ending with a blessing (Ps 14; 24). But when we look closely at the texts, the problem does not appear to be so simple. Sometimes the explanation of the *mixed* form may lie in a purely accidental union of two different psalms. We must also allow for the liberty of the psalmist, who did not feel himself bound by our stricter ideas of literary form. It remains possible that cultic ceremonies did result in some consistent psalm pattern. But the examples brought forward so far as evidence are too uncertain to establish this theory. The idea that these composite psalms are patterned on a special literary form remains a fragile supposition, and it should not be pushed too far.

Finally, two psalms must be mentioned which stand outside any classification. This very originality gives them a special place. Psalm 137 *(Super flumina Babylonis)* is a strong and pathetic evocation of history which gives us a glimpse into the Jewish soul at the time of the Exile. The psalm's conclusion seems cruel. But this understandable harshness must not make us forget the central idea; namely, the attachment of the Jewish exile to Jerusalem. Psalm 45 takes up the theme of a royal marriage and reminds us of the Song of Songs. This psalm does, in fact, present some of the same problems as the Song of Songs, and it has received as many different interpretations. Tradition has seen in both a parable or an allegory celebrating the nuptials of the Messias King with the Chosen People and with the Church.

CHAPTER IV

ORIGIN AND HISTORY OF THE PSALMS

Our knowledge of religion in ancient Israel, the many allusions in the psalms to the sanctuary and to liturgical acts, the probabilities that emerge from a comparison with neighboring peoples, as well as general observations about the history of religions—all this has led recent authors to insist on the liturgical and therefore the collective origin of many of the psalms.

However, it is a very difficult and risky matter to attempt to describe the precise circumstances in which these psalms originated. Indications in the psalm titles are rare and not altogether sure. With few exceptions (Ps 24 is one) the data of internal criticism, such as allusions to sacrifices and liturgical actions, references to processions and dialogue recitations, are usually vague. These items call for close attention, but they simply do not tell us very much. We have already pointed out that there is no solid reason for imagining the existence of liturgical feasts when tradition tells us nothing about them. Even when we extract from the psalms themselves and from the historical books of the Bible the maximum of information that they have to offer, we must admit our ignorance about the earliest source and the original context of most of these ancient pieces.

So it would be an exaggeration to attribute a liturgical origin to all the psalms. Even if we suppose that the individual who appears in some of them is fictitious and that the one who prays is in reality a king, priest, or levite, who speaks in the name of the people, it is still certain that many of the psalms are the pure products of individual devotion. [1]

The tradition which is represented by the psalm titles placed these psalms on the lips of certain known personages of the Old Testament. The tradition, therefore, understood these psalms as being the expression of individual devotion. And even though the psalm titles are not above suspicion, it remains highly probable that in the period of the prophets, even as early as Samuel and David, individual devotion was expressed in pieces of this kind and that they were later introduced into the liturgy.

---

[1] See A. ROBERT, " L'exégèse des Psaumes selon les méthodes de la Form-geschichteschule, " *Miscellanea Biblica B. Ubach** (Montserrat, 1953), pp. 211-226; A. FEUILLET, *Les psaumes eschatologiques du Règne de Yahweh**, NRT (1951), pp. 244-260; 352-363.

We must above all stress the fact that the psalms, whatever their precise origin, remained for a long time living realities capable of adaptation to new circumstances and to new religious conceptions. It happens often that, when an " individual " psalm passes into the liturgy, it changes or loses some of its most concrete expressions. There must also have been cases where psalms that originated in a provincial sanctuary were later adapted to the liturgy of Jerusalem. Psalms that were purely royal in their origin took on later a clearly Messianic meaning. Historical perspectives were transformed into eschatological visions. The reflections of scribes filled out or corrected more ancient ideas.

The psalms which we recognize as canonical and inspired are the psalms in their final form as they have come down to us. It would be a bad kind of archeologism to disregard or exclude every " addition " or " explanatory gloss. " Still, if we are to have a better understanding of the psalm's whole meaning, it is important to reconstruct the history of the text as well as we can. Pointing out a gloss or disengaging from the text a later development often provides the answer to a difficulty and makes for a better understanding of the psalmist's mind. All this helps the modern reader to handle the ancient text better.

Then too, there is some value in following the successive interpretations of the psalms as well as we can, even when these interpretations move a long way from the literal sense. These " successive readings " [2] of the psalms are sometimes clarified by the LXX, by New Testament citations, and also by quotations made by the Fathers of the Church. They allow us to retrace the progress of revelation and the development of ideas across the centuries. The modern reader has something to learn from them.

§ 1. Antiquity of the Psalms

After what we have said, it will be seen how problematical is this matter of the age of the psalms. [3] It is extremely difficult to reconstruct the life situation of pieces of liturgical literature which are by definition anonymous and impersonal. Even when we think we have found a precise and concrete origin for individual psalms, they have usually been too much polished by usage for anyone to recognize in them any indications

---

[2] See A. GELIN, *Problèmes d'Ancien Testament** (Lyon, 1952), pp. 93-110; and the same author's " Les quatre lectures du ps. XXII, " *Bible et vie chrétienne*, 1, pp. 31-39.

[3] See R. TOURNAY, " Recherches sur la chronologie des Psaumes, " *RB* (1958), pp. 321-357.

that would point to the circumstances of their origin. Only the psalm titles, about which we will say more later on, might be able to satisfy our curiosity. In spite of this scarcity of information, the actual evolution of the positions of biblical criticism over the past half-century has been remarkable. At the end of the 19th century, many scholars thought that the Psalter as a whole was postexilic and that it reflected the Jewish religion rather than the preexilic religion of Israel. These scholars confidently assigned a great number of psalms to the Machabean period. [4] Recently, however, I. Engnell of the Scandinavian school wrote, " I frankly admit that there is only one psalm in the whole Psalter which appears to me to be certainly postexilic; this is Ps 137. No matter where I look, I cannot find another psalm that is comparable to it in content and style. How is this to be explained? " [5] Not all authors would go this far. But there is a rather common tendency now to consider many of the psalms as dating from the period of the monarchy. Some psalms may date from the earliest part of that period. As for the alleged Machabean psalms, there is no a priori argument against them. But neither has anyone made a convincing argument for them. What we have already said about the formation of the Psalter as a collection would favor exclusion of pieces written as late as the second century before Christ.

§ 2. Authors of the Psalms

The tradition of Davidic origin for the Psalter no longer appears to be in open contradiction to the stand taken by the majority of critics. However, the tradition is not being accepted in any simple form, and important adjustments will have to be made in regard to it.

There is a broad historical tradition claiming that David was a musician (1 Sm 16, 18-23; 18, 10; Am 6, 5), and that he organized the liturgy (2 Sm 6, 5-16; 1 Par 15, 28; Esd 3, 10; Neh 12, 24. 36). This tradition attributes several important poems to David (2 Sm 1, 19-27; 3, 33-34; 2 Sm 22 (Ps 18); 23, 1-7).

There is also the fact that 73 psalm titles (84 in Greek) assign psalms to David. Some of these titles grow more precise by proposing the circumstances in which the psalm was supposedly written. Even if these

---

[4] The most radical exponent of this opinion was B. Duhm (1899, second edition in 1922).

[5] I. ENGNELL, *Studies in Divine Kingship in the Ancient Near East* (Uppsala, 1943), p. 176, note 2. He is quoted by A. BENTZEN in *Introduction to the Old Testament* (Copenhagen, 1948), II, p. 167, note 2.

psalm titles are not canonical and do not go back to the psalmist himself, and even if they were not originally understood as referring directly to the psalmist, it remains true that at one time they were for the average reader expressions of an accepted tradition that claimed David as author of the Psalter.

New Testament citations bear witness to this same tradition, not for the whole Psalter but for a certain number of particular psalms (Mt 24, 43; Acts 1, 20; 2, 25; 34; 4, 25; Rom 4, 6; 11, 9).

Such are the ancient witnesses which have led Jewish or Christian authors to consider " the psalms " as being the psalms " of David. " Here we have an explanation of the formula used by the Council of Trent, " *psalterium davidicum.* "

We must note here the fact that St. Hilary and St. Jerome protested against the idea of attributing all the psalms to David. And the Council of Trent would not use the expression, " the 150 psalms of David. " These items, along with indications in the Psalter itself, show that the attribution to David is to be understood in a general way. When it comes to particular psalms, the tradition of Davidic authorship may be questioned. And in any case it should not be exaggerated.

It is perhaps unfortunate that the only way to begin the discussion of this question about authorship is to consider the data of internal criticism. This is a difficult thing to manage, and in many instances the search will turn up no decisive argument either for or against Davidic authorship. Besides, the exegete must take into account the possibility of additions and transformations in the history of the psalms. Even a precise reference to an event, or a formula which is characteristic of a certain period, will be too slight an indication to date the whole psalm.

This is no reason for exaggerated skepticism or for renouncing all research into the history of the Psalter. While it is difficult to prove that these poems go back to a certain author or point to a certain event, it is fairly easy to assign them their true places in the development of the religious thought of Israel. A certain psalm will reflect the influence of Deuteronomy. Another shows a relationship to one of the great prophets. Many psalms present a conception of the monarchy that the careful historian will be able to situate in time and place. Some psalms appear to be full of borrowings from earlier texts. All these items can lead to fairly certain conclusions about the history of the Psalter.

If we look at modern commentaries on the psalms, we find a tendency on the part of exegetes to date the great royal psalms to an ancient period, at least to the period before the Exile (Ps 2; 45; 72; 110). The same is true of the most beautiful pieces of hymn poetry (Ps 8; 19A;

29; 84; part of 89; etc.), some of the supplication psalms (Ps 28; 61; 63), and some of the thanksgiving psalms (Ps 18). But the last word has surely not been said on this difficult problem, and the door should be left open for further studies.

In addition to the problems already mentioned, it should be said here that there are some psalms whose age is very much disputed, either because they belong to an intermediate and ill-defined period or because opposite ways of approaching them lead to opposite solutions (see Ps 42; 68; 78; 104). We have to resign ourselves to having a partial knowledge, and we should keep in mind that a religious text can be very useful without our knowing exactly how old it is.

CHAPTER V

DOCTRINE OF THE PSALMS

§ 1. Question of Method

Speaking of the doctrine of the Psalms is somewhat difficult. It is true that a number of " theologies of the psalms " can be found. These studies take the Psalter as a homogeneous whole. Wisdom psalms and royal psalms are brought together. The most ancient hymns and the more recent instructional pieces are placed side by side. This method is not to be condemned out of hand. If it is used carefully, it can provide a useful reconstruction of an important moment of history that is the climax of many centuries of evolution. The synthesis offered by this method is a part of the theology of Judaism in the period when the Psalter as a whole was fixed in its present form; namely, the period immediately preceding the Christian revelation.

But this method of constructing a theology of the psalms runs the risk of misleading those who have a tendency to project a relatively late picture back into the distant past. From what we have said about the great variety in the psalms, their different ages, their suppleness in being fitted to new circumstances, in a word, their *living* character, we can see that so static a presentation cannot satisfy those who have a sense of history.

Does this mean that we have to hold a purely evolutionary view of the psalms and attempt to trace in successive pictures the different stages of the religious thought expressed in them? Such a task would be very difficult. And even if it proved successful, the results might be deceptive. For one thing, there is great uncertainty about the date of the psalms and about the shifting paths of their development. A beginning would have to be made on the basis of an a priori outline of Israel's religious history. This would result in an arbitrary and questionable picture. Besides, the wish to stress the element of change, if carried too far, would obscure the fact that there is in the psalms a real continuity of doctrine. Revelation progresses step by step. But the progress is similar to that of a river valley increasing its soil by flood deposits. It is a matter of repeated enrichment. The past is not wiped out when history unfolds; the present is rather an organic development of the past.

Between these two opposite methods of constructing a synthesis of the doctrine of the psalms, that of a purely historical and " evolutionary " presentation on the one hand and on the other a collection of " pegs " of doctrine gathered and logically classified, we must find a middle way. This middle way must answer the demands of the historian as well as those of the theologian. [1] So much for methodology. [2] We move now to the question of the doctrine of the Psalms.

§ 2. Popular Devotion and Liturgical Life

The Psalter has been aptly named the " mirror of biblical devotion. " We must note that, in the distant period when the Psalter was formed, it would be meaningless to make a distinction between devotion and theology or between dogma and moral. It is the whole religious soul of Israel that finds expression in the 150 psalms, and a very clear expression it is.

It is true that other biblical books, like Judges, Samuel, and the Prophets, tell us about the ordinary manifestations of popular devotion in Israel. Many expressions of Israel's life of worship are known to us also from Leviticus, Numbers, and parts of Paralipomenon. Popular devotion seems most often to be that of an individual. It is spontaneous. It is charged with feeling and sometimes passion. On the other hand, expressions of cult are described in connection with priestly ceremonies where everything is planned and regulated. Cultic expressions seem particularly impersonal.

It is not that these two aspects of religious life are totally different. They sometimes flow together in episodes that are congenial to both. Such would be the episode of Anna at the sanctuary of Silo (1 Sm 1—2), and that of the transfer of the Ark of the Covenant (2 Sm 6). In this same line of thought, we may also find certain allusions to popular feasts and pilgrimages. But these items are relatively rare. The two forms,

---

[1] This is a general problem of biblical theology. The following works can be consulted : P. VAN IMSCHOOT, *Theology of the Old Testament*, I (New York : Desclée, 1965); P. HEINISCH, *Theology of the Old Testament* (Collegeville : Liturgical Press, 1956); W. EICHRODT, *Theology of the Old Testament* (Philadelphia, 1961); E. JACOB, *Theology of the Old Testament* (New York, 1958).

[2] In this exposition many more references and quotations could be given. Since it is impossible to give them all, it seems more useful to keep them brief and to ask the reader to look into the more developed syntheses such as the article " Psaumes " in the *DTC*. He should also be encouraged to make his own personal effort at doctrinal synthesis.

popular devotion and cultic expressions, are generally separated in the Bible.

Perhaps the psalms can serve as a bond of union for these two forms of religious expression, the personal and the cultic. On the one hand, the psalms grew out of the soul of the people and they express the deepest feelings. On the other hand, it is becoming more and more certain that they were introduced into the liturgy of Israel. They express the very soul of certain liturgical ceremonies, the external rites being simply the shell enclosing it.

We can note a certain harmony between some well-known liturgical ceremonies and the psalm forms. Processions and pilgrimages call to mind the gradual psalms, the psalms of Sion, and in general the hymns to the glory of Yahweh and His dwelling place. The thanksgiving psalms correspond to the holocaust, which was the ancient thanksgiving sacrifice. The sacrifice of expiation and the days of fast and penance were surely accompanied by lamentations. The peace sacrifice and the communion sacrifice seem to call for the collective hymns and in general for the hymns which evoke Israel's past greatness or its deepest hopes. These are only hints. But we could push our search further and gain a more precise knowledge of the *Sitz im Leben*, the life context, of most of our psalms. And this would surely help us to understand better the ideas enshrined in them.

However, we should bear in mind that the psalms range over an area much wider than the liturgy. In the most ancient period this variety, the degree of which we cannot determine precisely, can be seen in the fact that the psalms often reflect strictly individual religious experiences and forms of prayer. In the more recent periods the psalms introduce into liturgical life expressions that were not originally meant for it. The devotion of the scribes, for example, which the wisdom books make known to us, is essentially individual devotion. But its main themes, such as love for the law and meditation on it (Ps 19) and the interpretation of history (Ps 78; 105; 106), form the subject of the many psalms which introduce these themes into the liturgy.

The same is true of that devotional movement which is represented by the *anawim*, the " poor ones of Yahweh, " who had so important a place in the religious life of Israel after the Exile. Certain psalms appear which are the purest expression of this new spirituality (Ps 34; 37; 9—10). This spirituality, which came from the prophets, was to undergo an important development in Christianity.

§ 3. Main Doctrinal Themes

I. GOD

The hymn is the most characteristic as well as the oldest and most permanent literary form in the Psalter. The main subject of the hymn is God in His greatness and perfection. All the hymns are addressed to God. They speak only of Him. Every other object is related to Him, the world which owes its existence to Him, Israel whom He had chosen and guided, loved and punished in the course of its history, each believer whose steps follow His path. In the supplication and thanksgiving psalms, the relations between God and His own are presented in more varied style. Anthropomorphism is evident in them. In the more distant periods, God is often represented as having human feelings. But these are images, and in reality the psalmist knew that God was completely above His creatures.

God is unique. In spite of some surprising formulae which seem to affirm only the superiority of Yahweh over the other gods (Ps 136, 2-3; 97, 7-9), the Psalter as a whole is clearly monotheistic. Even when it borrows from surrounding literature and ideology, these borrowings have undergone a thorough expurgation. The nothingness of idols and the emptiness of false gods are frequent themes. The psalmists do know of the existence of spiritual beings and sometimes call them divine (*elohim* Ps 8, 6). But these are creatures and servants of the sovereign Master. As for demons, they are never mentioned explicitly in the Hebrew text. But the psalms do refer to enemies and evil powers who threaten and persecute the faithful man, and these expressions can mean evil spirits.

God is not only above every creature, He is also in constant relationship with every creature. He is the Providence that not only secures the order of the material world but also the rule of justice. He is the defender and avenger of the just. He is the refuge of the repentant sinner. In the case of the poor and the lowly, His goodness becomes mercy and beneficence and love *(hesed)*.

II. SALVATION

God has promised men salvation. He will one day intervene to assure the just man's triumph over the sinner and sin. He will inaugurate His true reign over a world renewed. These promises are vague in the older texts, but they grow clearer all the time. Salvation will come on Sion, the holy mountain. It will be brought by the Davidic dynasty. One of the members of this dynasty will be the Messias, king and priest at the same time. He will make all the promises a fulfilled reality. Although the Messias will be persecuted, he will also be the great conqueror. At the same time he will be the peaceful ruler equipped with all the virtues of the ideal king and charged with the office of governing and judging the whole world. The latest pictures of the Messianic age give us a glimpse of the Messias's universal reign. All the nations will converge on Sion and will prostrate themselves in the presence of Israel's God.

III. MAN

In the presence of God man seems slight and full of misery. Man's cry of distress only highlights his dependence. But man is not left all alone. By prayer he obtains his Creator's blessing and help. God rescues him, and then receives his praise and thanksgiving.

Moral life means practicing justice, observing the law, and taking part in worship. These are not unrelated realities. They are simply different aspects of one same ideal. The most ancient as well as the latest psalms mention the Temple. In the late period of Judaism, the study and meditation of the law took on an exceptionally important place in the just man's life. This was not properly speaking a novelty, but rather a new stress placed on an already existing element in the religion of the Fathers.

IV. RETRIBUTION

The history of religion in Israel is dominated by the problem of retribution. So there is nothing surprising in the fact that this problem shows up in the Psalter. In most of the psalms we find a more or less explicit reflection of the ideas of the Israelite people. For them, it seemed that devotion to God and happiness ought to go hand in hand. Reversely, unhappiness was thought to be necessarily a punishment for evil. But attentive observers and alert moralists were not satisfied with a theoretical answer of this kind that often contradicted their experience. Sometimes they gave explanations which suppressed or reduced the shock. So we find a psalmist affirming that the failure of justice is only apparent, that the happiness of the wicked man is only a passing happiness and more or less illusory (Ps 37; 49). Sometimes he excitedly expresses his indignation. He complains to Yahweh and asks him to intervene. He lets fly curses against the victorious wicked ones. Sometimes he resigns himself to the apparent injustice of the present and waits for the Lord to provide an equitable retribution in a more distant future.

However, many reservations have to be made when we talk about a belief in the future life expressed in the psalms. For the most part the psalms hold fast to the traditional ideas on this subject. In sheol the soul enjoys a kind of half-life, without activity, almost without personality. It is the land of forgetfulness where no one experiences joy and no one gives praise to God. In sheol there can be neither a true reward nor true punishment. And so, according to this traditional idea, God's justice must be exercised here below by an immediate intervention in favor of the just man. Later is too late. This is what explains the indignation or the despair of the persecuted just man when God's intervention does not take place or is delayed. The great prophets and the author of Job did not await a resurrection or a survival of the soul after death. This is also the general attitude of the psalmists.

Even so, there are some psalms which seem to have a presentiment of a later revelation. This presentiment is seen in the psalms which have the faithful proclaiming by a bold image that God will " rescue " them or " make them come up " from sheol (Ps 30, 10; 86, 13). Sometimes the psalmist staunchly asserts that not even death is strong enough to separate him from his God, and therefore that another destiny lies before him (Ps 16, 10; 49, 16; 73). But these texts provide only a glimmer of light, and their precise bearing on this subject is not beyond dispute. The New Testament will enrich and complete their meaning.

Conclusion

We have looked at the main themes which a reading of the psalms will offer to our meditation. Each of the psalms can, without much need of readjustment, express the feelings of the Christian. However, there are some passages which are somewhat difficult to use. The rude feelings sometimes expressed in the psalms are at odds with the law of the Gospel. Such pieces are rare, and they often represent small fragments inserted into a context of quite different spirit (Ps 59; 69). If these problematical pieces are placed in their cultural and doctrinal background, an explanation can be found for them and their positive value can be seen. This will not, of course, make them congenial to the Christian. But such an effort will give him a better understanding of the soul of the ancient Israelite. This Israelite was impatient and did not wish to wait for a justice that was passing him by. He had confidence in God. But God was not fully revealed to him. In such a frame of mind, he revolted against the triumph of evil. When the Christian reads passages where the psalmist's excessive language appears unacceptable, he will gain a better appreciation of the newness of the Sermon on the Mount.

In any case these difficult psalms make up only a small part of the Psalter. As a whole it gives us a remarkable synthesis of religious doctrine.

This insight was expressed very well by the Fathers of the Church. Without making as close a distinction as we do between the literal and the spiritual sense, they found in the Psalter a teaching that went beyond the historical context of the psalms. " The divine scripture does not make use of historical narratives just to give us knowledge of the facts which we learn from the actions and feelings of the ancients. It uses these narratives in order to offer us a teaching that will guide us in our life of virtue. The history must be accompanied by this higher meaning " (St. Gregory of Nyssa, *Homilies on the Inscription of the Psalms*, II). This is why St. Ambrose wrote, " In the psalms we not only assist at the birth of Christ, but we also see him enduring His saving passion, dying, rising, ascending to heaven and sitting at the right hand of the Father " *(In Ps 1, 8)*.

St. Augustine, especially in his *Enarrationes in Psalmos*, [3] found in the psalms the richest and most coherent synthesis of doctrine. For him the psalms announce not only the life of Christ but also the life and history of the Church. " Our method is not to stop with the letter alone, but to search through the letter for the mysteries. Your charity well knows that in all the psalms we hear the voice of a man (Christ) who alone possesses the head and the members " *(In Ps 131, 2)*. For Augustine, the psalms already provide an answer to all the great problems of history. " The wicked are prosperous and the good are tested. How can God look on this scandal? Take and drink. Every sickness of the soul finds its remedy in the Scripture " *(In Ps 36)*. The *Enarrationes* is a first attempt at writing the *City of God*.

[3] See M. PONTET, *L'exégèse de saint Augustin prédicateur** (Paris : Aubier, 1945), chap. VII, pp. 387-418.

SECTION II

THE OTHER HAGIOGRAPHERS

by Msgr. H. Lusseau

CHAPTER I

PROVERBS

BIBLIOGRAPHY

On Wisdom and Wisdom writings in general :

E. TOBAC, *Les cinq livres de Salomon** (Brussels, 1926).

W. O. E. OESTERLEY, *The Wisdom of Egypt and the Old Testament* (London, 1927).

A. VACCARI, *De libris didacticis (Institutiones biblicae)** (Rome, 1929).

H. DUESBERG, *Les scribes inspirés**, 2 Vols. (Paris, 1938).

A. M. DUBARLE, *Les Sages d'Israël** (Paris, 1946).

J. C. RYLAARSDAM, *Revelation in Jewish Wisdom Literature* (1946).

H. RINGGREN, *Word and Wisdom* (Land, 1947).

M. NOTH—D. WINTON THOMAS, eds., *Wisdom in Israel and in the Ancient Near East* (Leiden, 1955).

R. MURPHY, *Seven Books of Wisdom** (Milwaukee : Bruce, 1960).

W. MCKANE, *Prophets and Wise Men* (London : SCM, 1965).

W. BAUMGARTNER, " The Wisdom Literature, " *OTMS*, pp. 210-237.

R. GORDIS, " The Social Background of Wisdom Literature, " *HUCA*, 18 (1843-1944), pp. 77-118.

M. P. STAPLETON, "Ancient Wisdom and Modern Times, " *CBQ*, 4 (1942), pp. 311-322; 5 (1943), pp. 47-62.

On the Book of Proverbs :

Introductions, translations, commentaries, pp. 1 f. (H. RENARD, *BPC**; H. DUESBERG and P. AUVRAY, *BJ**; C. H. TOY, *ICC*...).

H. WIESMANN, *Das Buch der Sprüche** (Bonn, 1923).

W. O. E. OESTERLEY, *The Book of Proverbs*, (London, 1929).

B. GEMSER, *Sprüche Salomos* (Tübingen, 1937).

J. J. WEBER, *Le livre des Proverbes, le livre de la Sagesse et le Cantique des cantiques** (Paris, 1949).

E. JONES, *Proverbs and Ecclesiastes* (London : SCM, 1962).

M. DAHOOD, *Proverbs and Northwest Semitic Philology** (Rome, 1963).

R. B. Y. SCOTT, *Proverbs and Ecclesiastes* (Garden City : Doubleday, 1965).

R. N. WHYBRAY, *Wisdom in Proverbs* (London : SCM, 1965).

A. ROBERT, " Les attaches littéraires bibliques de Prov. 1-9, " *RB* (1934), pp. 42 ff., 172 ff., 374 ff.; (1935), pp. 344 ff., 502 ff.

P. SKEHAN, " Single Editor for the Whole Book of Proverbs, " *CBQ*, 10 (1948), pp. 115-130.

G. R. Driver, " Problems in the Hebrew Text of Proverbs, " *Biblica*, 32 (1951), pp. 173-197.

C. T. Fritsch, " The Book of Proverbs, " *IB* (1955).

§ 1. Title

The title of this book in the Hebrew Bible : *Mešalim* fits the content well. The " mašal " is actually a very flexible literary form : it is applied to different poems (Nm 21, 27-30; Ps 49, 5; 78, 2), oracles (Nm 23, 7. 18, etc.), satires (Is 14, 4; Mi 2, 4), discourses in which the comparative element dominates (Ez 17, 2; 21, 5; 24, 3), popular sayings, maxims or proverbs that are frequently artistically patterned (1 Sm 10, 12; 24, 14; Ez 12, 22-23; 18, 2-3). Now, the Book of Proverbs, undoubtedly characterized by its comparisons and its artistically labored sayings, contains also different forms of poems about select and profound themes that are not without a religious and moral import (1, 8-9; 31, 10-31).

The Greek (παροιμιαι) and the Latin *(proverbia)* connote too exclusively the idea of *sayings* or *maxims* to do justice to the Hebrew word or the content of the work. They can be considered only as *a potiori* labels.

It is difficult to find an exact word in our modern languages that has the different meanings of the word *mašal*. If it were possible to resort to the root *mšl III*, to govern, (Pedersen, Boström, cf. Bentzen, *Introd.*, I, 168), in relation to the Arabic : *to be more valuable or superior*, the substantives : *directive, instruction, rule* would seem to be indicated. But the verbal root *mšl III* has as nominal derivatives only *mimšâl* and *mêmšâlâh* meaning *government, rule*, whereas for the block of Semitic languages *mâšâl*, coming from the root *mšl I*, always carries the idea of *comparison, fable, proverb*. The English translation does not avoid the etymological difficulty. Perhaps the term *sayings* with its broad usage would be more suitable.

Be that as it may, *mešâlîm* are usually, considering the external literary form, defined as : generally religious or moral teachings founded on common observation, and usually expressed in images, open or veiled, which demand reflective effort to understand.

§ 2. Historico-Literary Context of the Work

The Book of Proverbs is a work of Wisdom. In general, the term Wisdom designates a mentality preoccupied with the practical. The Books of the Bible which are classified as sapiential are but a part of the abundant sapiential literature found especially in the Orient. They must be situated in that context in order that their provenance and originality be better understood.

I. WISDOM IN THE ANCIENT ORIENT

It is commonly known that there were Wise Men in Egypt, Babylonia, Phoenicia, and in all of the ancient Orient. The Bible makes many allusions to them (3 Kgs 4, 30-31; Jer 49, 7; Abd 8), which is confirmed by the Greeks' esteem of wisdom, mother of their own culture. And the literature of the Middle East, recently enlarged by the discoveries of Ras-Shamra (Ugarit), gives abundant witness to the existence of a widely popularized Wisdom literature.

The Wise Men of the Orient are found mainly among the ruling classes—more precisely among the members of the court, the king's ministers, advisors, secretaries and archivists. Their position, by reason of their role, demanded that they be cultured men of some philosophical and moral refinement, accomplished in the art of speaking well, but even more in the art of worldly prudence : how to live and act. They were capable of reflecting on the facts of life and human conduct. The religious aspect of life, however, was not excluded from their observations; humanism for them was not atheistic.

Naturally they tried to communicate to others the *results* of their experience, the *principles* they used, and the *means* to succeed in their careers. Thus they were inclined to draw from Wisdom writings—opinions and instructions from Egypt, philosophical fables and allegories from Babylonia, picturesque maxims and parables from Chanaan and Phoenicia. These writings were destined for the scribe class, whose role it was to transmit sound traditions of advice and prudence suitable for the royal household, magistrates and functionaries. Sometimes the driving force of their literary activity was to facilitate their sons' access to positions of influence. They had to " form " their successors to " assume a position. "

Such was the case of the Wise Men of Egypt [1] : Ka-Gemni, son of a Visier of King Ouni (3rd dynasty; beginning of the 3rd millennium), the son of Ptah-hetep, Visier of King Issi (5th dynasty; about 2300), Meri-Ka-Re, son of a certain Kheti, monarch of Herakleopolis (9th dynasty; about 2150), Sesostris, son of Amen-em-hat I (founder of the 12th dynasty; 1993-1970). One does not know if these Wise Men are authentic or

---

[1] P. HUMBERT, *Recherches sur les sources égyptiennes de la littérature sapientiale d'Israël* (Neuchâtel, 1927).

merely creations of literary fiction : the personal tone and the concrete circumstances of the instruction for Meri-Ka-Re warrant authenticity. Other Wise Men stories come from Sumer and Mesopotamia. [2] Closer to the Israelite royal age is the Wisdom writing that Amen-em-Ope [3] himself gave to his son (of uncertain date; between 18th and 26th dynasties : probably between 1000 and 600). In Assyria, Ahiguar, who perhaps wrote under the reign of Sennacherib (705-681) or of Asarhaddon (681-669), may well be only a legendary hero. Be that as it may, several collections have come down to us under his name. The most ancient of these is an Aramaic version discovered in the archives of the Elephantine Jews (5th century B.C.). The Bible itself presents Tobias as one of his relatives. Lastly the material of Ras-Shamra gives us the name of a Phoenician Wise Man (historical? or fictional?) : Daniel. Ezechiel very probably mentions this Daniel three times (Ez 14, 14. 20; 28, 3).

One might ask to what extent the priests belonged to the class of Wise Men. The fact is that priests and Wise Men are identified in Babylonia. But Engnell certainly exaggerates in generalizing this identification. Although it is true that Wisdom literature has an indiscutable relation to cult, as is proven from religious poems, notably the Psalms, it would be very difficult to establish that in Egypt the statesmen and royal household were all of the priestly class, and that in Israel the position of Esdras, priest and scribe, would have to be considered as the rule. It must be admitted, however, that Wisdom literature developed on a parallel with the progress of religious sentiment. Wisdom and "theology" formed a pair, but the Wisdom themes were not restricted to moral laws and cultic formulas.

The high positions occupied by the Wise Men, [4] the international relations in which they were involved, and the competition in which they undoubtedly engaged (cf. 3 Kgs 10, 1-3) made Wisdom an article for export. It became an international commodity.

II. WISDOM IN ISRAEL

Israel would borrow freely from this common commodity, as it drew from the sources of oriental codes of law, from rituals of neighboring peoples, as it absorbed, especially at the beginning of the institution,

---

[2] J. J. VAN DIJK, *La Sagesse suméro-accadienne* (Leyden, 1953).

[3] A. MALLON, " La Sagesse de l'Égyptien Amen-em-opé et les Proverbes, " *Bi* (1927), pp. 3-30.

[4] A. ROBERT, " Les scribes du roi et l'origine des Proverbes, " *Revue Apologétique* (1938), pp. 461-467.

some of the ways of Syro-Chanaanite *nabism*. [5] But in the domain of
Wisdom, as in the fields of legislation and prophecy, it surpassed them.
Israel knew how to mint its own gold coin from many streams.
The more that we study the Israelite Wisdom literature, the more
we note its transcendent originality. Let it suffice for now to give some
general indications.

Solomon is presented as the originator of sapiential literature, just
as Moses is of juridical literature, and David of psalms. The court of the
great King, patterned after the model of foreign courts, abounded with
counselors, archivists and scribes, [6] and these functionaries, as their
counterparts in Egypt, Phoenicia, and Babylonia, were Wise Men
(3 Kgs 4, 3). Solomon preached by example (3 Kgs 4, 30-34). He
was a master of Wisdom, just as he was in some respects a born
administrator.

Two traits characterize Israelite Wisdom. Even though it bases its
teaching on *experience*, it also gives of its soul by animating its Wisdom
with its faith in Yahweh, sovereign master of all Wisdom (3 Kgs 3, 4-15).
" Even in the most ancient collections of Proverbs, " writes A. Robert,
" maxims that seem neutral are profoundly religious and subtly refer to
the Torah. " It is furthermore established that the Wise Men have also
used the prophets, from whom they borrowed the vocabulary and the
themes that were compatible with the laws of the genre. But precisely
if they had such openness it is because, while accepting the points of
view and methods from international Wisdom, from the beginning they
remained in their hearts disciples of Moses. Their impassivity then was
simply conformity to the laws of the genre.

The postexilic Wise Men of Israel likewise orientated their thought
toward divine Wisdom. They described it by detailing its works in the
cosmic order and in the context of the historical and religious evolution
of the nation. Moreover the literary personification of this sovereign
Wisdom would go to the limit of personification, that the New Testament
will propose to our faith in revealing the Wisdom Incarnate.

Thus the Wise Men of Israel, in their way, according to the laws of
the genre, and despite some legalistic rigidity, helped to prepare, through
their religious humanism, for the coming of the Messias. They were,
with the prophets, the spiritual guides who supported Judaism in its
ascent toward the Gospel.

---

[5] See also the inscriptions of the tomb of Petosiris (B.C. 4th century);
G. LEFEBVRE, " Égyptiens et Hébreux, " *RB* (1922), pp. 481-488.

[6] Cf. p. 18 f.

§ 3. Composition of the Book of Proverbs

Many indications of internal criticism (attribution to different authors, the variety of subjects treated, the diversity of literary forms) enable us to distinguish eight sections in the Book of Proverbs. They are presented in the following table. [7]

Sections	Subjects treated	Literary Forms	Authors
1, 8—9, 18	Invitation to acquire Wisdom. The author points out its fruits and praises it.	Strophes of about 10 verses each	Anonymous
10, 1—22, 16	Rules of conduct	Mešalim : two parallel members, either antithetic (10-15) or synonymous (16-22)	" Solomon "
22, 17—24, 34	Duties toward neighbors. Rules of temperance. Concerning idleness.	Four-membered synonymous parallelism.	" The Sages "
25—29	Various maxims	Two-membered. Comparisons. Antithesis.	" Solomon " and the scribes of Ezechias
30, 1-14	Divine Wisdom. The smallness of man.	Four-membered synonymous parallelism.	" Agur "
30, 15-33	Numerical mešalim	Synthetic and synonymous parallelism	Anonymous
31, 1-9	Counsels for kings	Four-membered synonymous parallelism	" Lamuel "
31, 10-31	Praise of the valiant wife	Alphabetic poem in synthetic parallelism	Anonymous

[7] Cf. *Institutiones Biblicae* (Rome, 1929), p. 51.

A double collection of the " maxims of Solomon " forms the basis of the work (2nd and 4th sections). Five appendices were added to this, one to the first collection (3rd section), " remarks of Sages, " and four to the second collection (5th to the 8th section). The introduction (1st section) is of a more recent date. The Greek version of the LXX adopted a different order : the appendices are placed between the two collections of the maxims of Solomon—except the praise of the valiant wife which serves as the conclusion of the work.

A certain number of repetitions (10, 1 and 15, 20; 10, 2b and 11, 4b; 10, 6b and 10, 11b; 10, 8b and 11, 10b; 10, 13b and 19, 29b) could suggest the idea that section 10—22, 16 is itself a collection of smaller collections, compiled by the last editor. This hypothesis is admittedly very probable, and could be applied to other sections, especially to the collection 25—29 on which the scribes of Ezechias worked. But the material is too fluid to permit a well-founded exact reconstruction of the text.

§ 4. Origin of the Sections and the Book

The two major sections (10, 1—22, 16 and 25—29) are attributed to Solomon, the second with this precision that it was collected under the reign of Ezechias (about 700). If it is not certain that the son of David, whose renown for Wisdom is amply established (3 Kgs 3, 4-15; 4, 29-34; 10, 1-10), is the author of all the maxims, it is at least very probable that a number of them could have been composed by him and collected by the court scribes. It is only natural to suppose that the monarch would make it a point of honor not to be surpassed in this art by members of his household. Moreover, the collections listed under his name seem to be the oldest in the work : the predominant literary form is the simple and primitive doublet. The maxims are generally the fruit of daily experience or current customs. The terms in which they speak of the king (14, 28-35; 16, 10-15; 20, 2. 8. 28; 25, 1-6; 29, 4 etc.) and the allusions to the life of the court (10, 8; 11, 2; 15, 1; 16, 14. 15. 18; 19, 12; 22, 11; 25, 6-7; 29, 23) have led some to think, perhaps too readily, that their setting is royalty at its most flourishing moment.

Nevertheless, some Aramaisms, sometimes explicable by the fact that certain outlying countries (Edom on the border of Arabia) were Aramaized quite early, lead one to believe that additions and retouchings were done at a late date. Moreover several maxims are related to the Prophets and Deuteronomy. It would not exceed scientific limits to argue that at the time of the captivity sapiential reflection enjoyed a renaissance, and that if at such time all that remained of the Solomon tradition was collected, new sayings would have been added to the older works. Thus in all probability the Solomon collections grew with the centuries, especially the second collection, for which the Exile would provide a favorable terrain.

The identity and age of the Wise Men remain unknown to us. There is, on literary grounds, an obvious comparison to be made between the 3rd section of the Book of Proverbs (especially 22, 17—24, 22) and the Wisdom of the Egyptian Amen-em-Ope, a high official of Egypt living at Panopolis. The papyrus that contains his work was published in 1923-1924 by Sir Wallis Budge, director of the British Museum's Service of Egyptian Antiquities. There are, however, problems to be solved before it will be possible to date the works of the Wise Men by means of this papyrus. On one hand, the dating of Amen-em-Ope's writing oscillates between B.C. 1000 and 600; on the other hand, the relation of the two works is still an open question. While Fr. Mallon holds that the quartains of the Wise Men depend on Egyptian Wisdom, others assert that the two works depend on a common source, whether Egyptian or Hebrew. Dhorme considers the similarities accidental, and Fr. Humbert, with Duesberg, insists on the transcendence of the biblical quatrains regardless of the influence of foreign literature.

The names of Agur and Lamuel seem to designate Wise Men of the tribe of Massa (Gn 25, 14), unless the expression is part of the literary genre (oracle, vision, cf. Is 13, 1). We know nothing, however, of the age in which they lived. The position of their writings in the work and the numerous Aramaic expressions of the piece attributed to Lamuel would seem to indicate a postexilic period.

It is the last editor who added, by way of conclusion, the 8th section (31, 10-31), and who added the 1st section (1, 8—9, 18) as an introduction.

During the age of Sirach (about B.C. 200), the Book of Proverbs existed in its present form (cf. Sir 47, 17; Vulg 18, and Prv 1, 6). It may even have been translated into Greek (cf. Sir Prologue).

§ 5. The Doctrine of Proverbs

We will consider the general doctrine found in the work as a whole, and then the peculiar aspects of the various collections.

I. GENERAL DOCTRINE OF THE WORK

The scribes of the Law

The reader of Proverbs can easily find himself fascinated by the sharp, incisive, enigmatic character of the statements. It is necessary to rise above this plane to arrive at the level of doctrine in which the Wisdom writers of Israel transcend their foreign colleagues.

The Israelites, in fact, already possessed a treasure acquired in the desert. They received from Moses a body of principles from which their religious, moral, and social obligations sprang. The teachings of the prophets and the organic development of the Torah anchored and made more profound the old codes. For centuries and centuries they had already gathered insights concerning God, the world, society, the family, the human person. When they undertook to express themselves in Wisdom language, they not only added to their acquired treasure the rules of good conduct drawn from a foreign culture and adapted them to their new conditions—as for example the sayings especially destined for members of the court, functionaries, statesmen—but they animated all that imported material with their profoundly monotheistic and Mosaic spirit. They were not ostentatious in their beliefs, observances, and piety. They were not devout as Ani, nor members of several brotherhoods as Amen-em-Ope. They did not encumber themselves with theological speculation as Kheti, nor multiply prayers to Yahweh as did the Prince of Herakleopolis to Thoth. But they did retain well a sense of the divine, a supernatural orientation, and an awareness of the authentic providential order. They were scribes of *the Law*.

Good conduct of life

They knew that everything good comes from God (10, 22); it is necessary then to avoid whatever He abhors and to do what pleases Him (11, 1; 12, 22; 15, 3. 8; 16, 1-9). The fear of Yahweh is the beginning of wisdom and justice (1, 7; 14, 2); it is the source of life and the assurance of happiness (12, 28; 14, 27; 16, 20; 18, 10; 29, 6. 25). One must further love and practice the Law (29, 18), hold in high regard justice and equity (21, 3).

It is Wisdom which is the foundation of the authority of kings, and inspires their actions (8, 15-16). The prince is not to be greedy (29, 4) nor intemperate (31, 3-5), but just and loyal (14, 34; 16, 12; 17, 7; 25, 5; 29, 4. 12; 31, 9) and kind to the needy (20, 28). He should know how to surround himself with good counselors (14, 35; 25, 13), to be prudent in war (20, 18; 24, 16) and distrust liars (29, 12). He should, in exchange, be able to count on his collaborators, on the integrity of the judges and the respect of his subjects (17, 15. 23; 18, 5; 20, 2; 24, 21. 23; 28, 21).

For the rest, individual, family and social virtues are the object of precise and concrete recommendations. One should practice justice and charity toward his neighbor (11, 17; 14, 9. 21; 17, 17; 21, 3), generous fidelity toward a true friend wisely chosen (3, 28; 11, 13; 13, 20; 22, 4; 25, 9; 27, 10). Almsgiving and the pardon of injuries call down the blessings of God (14, 31; 19, 17; 22, 9; 28, 27).

Spouses should be faithful (5, 15-21). The husband should provide for the family (27, 23-27). The ideal companion and mistress of the house is honored with resounding praise (31, 10-31). A husband can measure his happiness by the degree of misfortune caused by a senseless wife (14, 1), by a wicked one, a quarrelsome one, an unfaithful one (7, 6-23; 12, 4; 14, 1; 19, 13; 21, 9. 19; 25, 24; 27, 15-16). The education of the children is a life-long work (22, 6) : who loves well punishes well (13, 24; 23, 13); in exchange the children will be docile (1, 18; 6, 20; 23, 22), in order to avoid many miseries (19, 26; 20, 20; 28, 24). Although it is fitting to be firm with servants (29, 21), one must not neglect them in their need (31, 15-21).

At times the generally vigorous condemnation of vices is the occasion for picturesque descriptions. It is thus that pride (6, 17; 11, 2; 13, 10; 15, 25; 16, 18; 25, 6-7; 29, 23), avarice (15, 27; 23, 4-5; 10, 12; 11, 4. 28), lust (5, 1-14; 6, 20—7, 27), envy (14, 30), gluttony (23, 29-35; 21, 17), anger (15, 18; 26, 21; 29, 22; 30, 33), sloth (6, 6-11; 10, 4-5; 24, 28-34; 26, 13-16) are censured.

Life is subject to many trials (24, 16). Certainly God is the sovereign master of existence (16, 1. 33; 19, 21). We are, nevertheless, most often the shapers of our own happiness or misery. The sayings aim generally to orientate us on the way of success by turning us away from obstacles.

Proverbs and the ancient traditions of Israel

In all these respects the teachings of Proverbs, as indeed all of the Wisdom literature, harmonize well with the pedagogy of the narrators who have left us the precious accounts in which the basic maxims of religious, social, and professional life are actualized by being situated in real life. For example, the heroes of patriarchal history, notably Joseph, conform in their conduct to a practical wisdom which is essentially religious. They show themselves in every circumstance attentive and submissive to the management of Providence (Gn 12, 4; 15, 6; 22, 1-3; 24, 10-14. 21. 26-27. 31. 40. 42. 48. 50-52. 56; 31, 9. 12-18. 49. 53; 40, 8; 41, 16. 25; 43, 23; 45, 5-13; 46, 3; 48, 9. 11. 15-16. 21; 50, 19-20. 25), penetrated with a reverential fear of Yahweh (Gn 17, 3; 39, 9; 42, 18; 44, 7. 17), at ease with confident prayer (Gn 18, 16-33; 19, 17-22; 24, 12-14; 28, 16-22; 32, 10-13; 48, 15-16, 20; 49, 24c-26), well able to take care of their personal or family interest (Gn 13, 2; 21, 25; 23, 17; 25, 31; 26, 12-14. 18-22; 30, 29. 43; 31, 36-42; 33, 9; 39, 2-6; 40, 14; 41, 34-46; 46, 31-35), but respectful, with some exceptions (Gn 27, 6-40; cf. 35; 30, 42—31, 1), of the rights of others (Gn 13, 8-9; 14, 23; 23, 1-18; 30, 33; 31, 45-53; 33, 9; 43, 11-12). The examples of conjugal fidelity, still tainted with polygamy (Gn 16, 2-3; 25, 1; 29, 30), the candid views of mutual devotion of spouses, the perfect honesty of Joseph in warding off the advances of a loose woman (Gn 39, 7-12), the integrity, savoir faire, and administrative talent of Pharao's minister (39, 7-20; 47, 13-26), the prudence and shrewdness with which he treated his brothers (Gn 42—45), the generous pardon he granted them (45, 3-7; 50, 15-21), the tender affection he showed his father (46, 28-29) : these are so many concrete teachings which play on very basic themes, less overtly religious, but all the more accessible to the profane. The Book of Proverbs develops and casts them in metal. What harmonious agreement, soundly pedagogical, between rule and application! It underscores the profound connection between the sapiential and historical genre in Israel.

II. PARTICULAR ASPECTS OF THE COLLECTIONS

The Solomon sections

The sections attributed to Solomon, but which in fact largely overflow into subsequent centuries, are especially distinguished by the richness of observation they contain. Sometimes the concrete observations, metalic in their resonance, imply no evaluation, but are content to fix an experience, somewhat as one sets choice gems : success of the rich, the crafty (14, 35), the flatterers (19, 6), unscrupulous merchants (20, 14); the powers of the tongue (15, 2. 4); the efficacy of bribes (17, 23). These finely applied touches let one nevertheless see, here and there, in caricature (19, 24; 20, 4; 26, 13-16 : sloth; 27, 15 : quarrelsomeness), or with discrete approval (25, 4 : refined silver; 11 : apples and rings of gold), a hint of judgment in the practical order.

Critical evaluation in most cases confirms this observation. There is a well-defined line between the good and the evil, the wise and the foolish. The authors delighted in discovering and multiplying a veritable flood of contrasts in which these extremes clash, and inserted them in the framework of arresting antithetical parallels (10, 3. 6. 7; 21, 26; 29, 6-11) : the praise of virtuous people (10, 31-32; 12, 5. 15. 16; 15, 18; 19, 11; 29, 11), of exemplary children (10, 11; 15, 20), of wise and reserved women (11, 16; 18, 22; 19, 14) and reproach of perverse men, whom he vigorously takes to task (12, 5. 17; 13, 5. 10; 16, 28. 29; 21, 24; 28, 24. 25; 29, 11), for unruly women, whom he mercilessly unmasks (11, 22; 19, 13; 21, 9. 19; 25, 24), for perverse children, whom he covers with shame and curses (19, 26; 20, 20; 28, 24).

The moral criterion used by the Wise Men does not seem to rise above *personal interest* and the domain of the present life. It is with that reservation that one should note the parallelism of the two ways : the way of virtue leads to success and to life (10, 11; 13, 4; 16, 22; 12, 31), the way of evil leads to ruin and death (10, 16-17; 11, 19). Virtue and happiness, vice and misery go hand in hand. Is this thesis well founded? Undoubtedly, order generates good, disorder evil. But the Wise Men usually limit themselves to assertions of an experimental nature. Now these are often such as to lead to the opposite conclusion. The equation is often inverted. The authors of Proverbs might well have raised the problem of the suffering of the just and the prosperity of the impious. If they avoid it, it is due to the fact that beyond the data of experience to which they make appeal, they place their *faith in God* who blesses the good and confounds the wicked (10, 3. 6. 27. 29; 22, 12), who probes hearts (15, 3. 11; 16, 2; 17, 3; 20, 12; 21, 2) and lays bare intentions (21, 3. 27; 28, 9). It is He who holds in His hands the progress of the universe (19, 21), the stream of human destinies (16, 1. 9. 33; 21, 31), the conduct of all life (20, 24; 21, 1). The enigma of the suffering just and the wicked who prosper remains an exception, no matter how numerous the incidences. At most, the author of the introduction, who wrote at a much later date, suggests that God tests the just out of love (3, 12). Job will prove more demanding. But the answer that Yahweh gives him invokes practically the same confidence which the Wise Men had in Him. The hour to reveal sanctions in the next life has not yet arrived.

Supplementary sections

The supplementary sections attributed to the Wise Men (22, 17—24, 34), to Agur (30, 1-14), to Lamuel (31, 1-9) and those lacking all indication of authorship (30, 15-33; 31, 10-31) present more special themes.

The collection of the Wise Men intends to educate the ideal functionary. We can understand that the Egyptian influence is preponderant here (Amen-em-Ope) and that the practical advice concerns the main qualities of the " honest man, " who is upright (22, 22-23; 23, 10-11), friend of good manners (13, 14. 22; 23, 1-2), sober (23, 20-21, 29-35), orderly (23, 26-28). This is the same kind of advice that Lamuel, candidate for the throne, received from his mother.

Agur gives the impression of a more rough nature, but the accent of his enunciations is profoundly religious; it is the faith of a peasant which is expressed, inspired by nature and blossoming in prayer (30, 1. 4; 7, 9).

The *numerical mešalim* (30, 18-33), which are not peculiar to the Book of Proverbs (cf. Ps 61 (62), 12; Jb 5, 19; Mi 5, 4; Eccl 11, 2; Sir 23, 16; 25, 7; 26, 5. 19 etc.), aim to attract attention and aid the memory. The praise of the *valiant wife* (31, 10-31) is an alphabetic poem (cf. Ps 9A; 9B (10); 24 (25)...; Lam 1—4; Na 1, 2-10; Sir 51, 15-29) of a high moral and religious plane. The lines that etch this portrait, borrowed from the customs of the surroundings, testify that the Wisdom writers remained perseveringly faithful to the observation of the world, and that their fine and penetrating psychology attained to a classical ideal of universal application. They penetrated the inner secrets of the human heart.

The introduction

The introduction to the Book of Proverbs, with its unity of composition and thought, stands in contrast to the Solomon collections. This literary and doctrinal block is almost entirely composed of the exhortations of a master who aims to arm his disciple against bad companions (1, 8-19) and corrupt women (5, 1-23; 6, 20—7, 27) and to develop in his heart the cult of Wisdom, whose usefulness (2, 1-22), practice (3, 1-35) and advantages (4, 1-27) are dwelt on at length.

It is evident that the author of these paternal exhortations is much closer to the stream of biblical tradition than to any foreign wisdom whatsoever. He lives, thinks, meditates, in an atmosphere, an ideological climate, the components of which are the doctrines contained in the more ancient sections : such as his advice concerning loyalty (4, 11), mercy (3, 27-30), docility (1, 8; 5, 13), greed (1, 19), violence (1, 11. 16; 3, 29-31), bad company (1, 10-16). He is also in the tradition of earlier proverbs in his exhortation to knowledge, prudence, fear of God (1, 1-7) and the passages concerning misconduct and adultery (2, 16-19; 5, 3-23; 6, 20-35).

Moreover the Wisdom writer used especially, although in different degrees, Deuteronomy, the writings of Jeremias and Second-Isaias. He was not tied to the letter of his sources, but he arranged the formulae and adapted them to his own purpose. He introduced elements of these ancient sources, transforming them into the structure of his composition. He thus obeyed the genius of the race, which, moved by an ever watchful instinct, delighted, just as in the midrashim, [8] in provoking doctrinal developments within the organic unity of a single current of living thought without breaking with the past.

We have not pointed out the passage 6, 1-19, a sort of parenthesis which interrupts the uniformity of the exhortation, and must be compared

---

[8] See p. 498.

to the sections attributed to Solomon. We have yet to consider the
pericopes in which Wisdom itself speaks (1, 20-33; 8, 1-9. 12). These
celebrated passages give us the occasion to conclude our work by treating
of Wisdom in the Book of Proverbs.

§ 6. Wisdom in the Book of Proverbs

The technical term in Hebrew is *hokmâh*. He who possesses it, or at
least seeks to acquire it, is a *hâkâm*.

I. THE WISDOM OF MAN

Applied to man, *hokmâh* appears as a complex quality, thanks to which
human acts are oriented to their true end. It is situated, then, in the
order of action limited to the domain of morality. Its components are,
however, diverse : *hokmâh* is the result of *attentive observation* (*bînah,
tebûnah :* cf. 1, 2. 6; 2, 5. 9; 8, 5-9; 14, 8; 19, 25; 20, 24; 28, 5; 29, 7...),
judicious reflection (*sekel :* cf. 16, 20; 21, 12...), *foresight* (*tušiyyah :*
cf. 3, 21; 6, 14), *cleverness*, astute when necessary ('*ormah :* cf. 12, 16. 23;
13, 16; 14, 8. 15; 22, 3; 27, 12), *perspicacity* (*mezimmah :* cf. 1, 4; 2, 11;
3, 21; 5, 2; 8, 12), every disposition that ultimately informs, elevates and
adapts to action " the knowledge of Elohim, " the *practical knowledge*
whose source is the Creator (*da'at :* cf. 1, 2. 4. 7. 29; 2, 5, 9. 10; 3, 20;
4, 1; 5, 2; 8, 10. 12; 14, 10; 17, 27; 31, 23...). When it arrives at this
degree, Wisdom attains perfection : it lets itself be guided by reverential
fear of God (15, 33) or filial piety (*yir'ah*), the principle of *hokmâh* (1, 29;
2, 5) and source of all the advantages that, along with justice (*sedeq* or
sedaqâh : cf. 1, 3; 8, 8. 15), Wisdom promises its disciples (long life :
10, 27; security : 14, 26; abundance of wealth, honor and life : 15, 16;
22, 4; cf. 10, 3. 6. 7. 11. 20. 21. 31. 32; 11, 21. 28; 12, 3. 5. 7. 10; 13, 5;
15, 28; 20, 7; 21, 26; 29, 7...).

II. WISDOM PERSONIFIED

Now Wisdom does not appear only as a quality : it disengages itself from
conceptual trappings and assumes the physionomy of a living being. It
stands in the wide open, in busy places, at noisy crossroads, at the city
gates (1, 20-21; cf. Jer 7, 2; 11, 6; 17, 19-20; 22, 2-6; 26, 2)—like a prophet.

By its calls it endeavors to attract attention. Like the prophets it
addresses sinners first of all, the ignorant in this context (1, 22a : *petayim :*
babblers; 1, 4; cf. 20, 19; 7, 7; 8, 5; 9, 4. 16; 14, 15. 18; 19, 25; 21, 11;

22, 3), scoffers (1, 22b : *lesim* : cf. 3, 34; 9, 8; 15, 12; 19, 25; 21, 11), the inane (1, 22c : *ewilim* : cf. 15, 5; 17, 28; 22, 15). Its call, at first plaintive (1, 22), changes to a pressing, friendly, engaging invitation (1, 22-23). It speaks the language of prophets, which is that of God (1, 23b; cf. Ez 36, 24-27; especially Is 44, 3) and like prophets it reacts with menaces (1, 24-27; cf. Is 28, 7-22; Jer 7, 24-29; 11, 8; 17, 23; Is 65, 2. 12; 66, 4). It will have its day of vengeance when, faced with misery, the recalcitrants will turn to their divine messenger (1, 28-31). Too late!

Prophet that it is, Wisdom also takes on the traits of a generous hostess (9, 1-6). In the house that she builds she invites her own to feast. All men are invited there. One can imagine, inspired by the imagery (building, victims, meals) borrowed from the service of the material temple, a prefiguration of a transcendent feast in a spiritual sanctuary. Wisdom here fulfills a doctrinal function. In any event, its teaching is presented to us as tasty and substantial. Dame Folly, who runs a hotel across the street (9, 13-18), can only exalt, by the contrast of her behavior, the marvelous invitation of provident Wisdom.

Also, *hokmâh* is capable of self-praise (8, 1-21) and sets forth its claims to nobility (8, 22-36). It places itself before all men; its mission is decidely *universal* (8, 1-3; cf. Is 40, 9; 49, 6; 52, 7-9; 55, 5). The goods it promises are so surpassing that all mortals are attracted to it. It is its own dignity that confers on these goods their exceptional value. For that which man has by effort, Wisdom possesses by nature (8, 12-14) : savoir faire, knowledge, perspicacity, reflection, foresight, penetration, power (cf. Is 11, 2; 35, 6). It confers moral rectitude and authority upon leaders (8, 15-16). It loves those who love it; those who search for it find it (cf. Mt 7, 7-8; Lk 11, 9-10), and have their fill of it (8, 17-21).

III. DIVINE WISDOM

How can such pretentions be justified? Wisdom is intimate with God, who gave it being in all eternity. He gave it birth, enthroned it (8, 22, 26) : Yahweh was always wise. During the whole of creative activity, *hokmâh* was master of the work, bringing into effect, as if at play, the building of the universe (8, 27-31a), seeking with pleasure the company of men (8, 31b).

For this reason, listening to its instruction *(torâh)* is for them a question of life or death (8, 32-36).

Many exegetes view the labeling of Wisdom with the traits of prophet and hostess as simple literary personifications. Others (Lagrange, Gressmann, Procksch, Eichrodt, Robert, Jacob) consider, not without solid reasons, that the sacred author goes much further. One must at least concede that the path is opened that permits authors of the New Testament to make explicit the relation of Wisdom Incarnate to the Father. The description uses terms such that one cannot fail to compare it with the prologue of St. John. Thus, in light of the New Testament, the Fathers of the first centuries and the great majority of exegetes have applied this passage to the second person of the Trinity. In a broad sense, this interpretation cannot be called into doubt.

By way of accommodation, the Church in its liturgy applies the entire passage describing eternal Wisdom to the Blessed Virgin Mary, predestined in all eternity in the divine mind to the role of Mother of the Incarnate Word : *Sedes Sapientiae*. [9]

§ 7. Canonicity and Liturgical Use

The Book of Proverbs is protocanonical. The rabbinical discussions about it were terminated at the Council of Jamnia. It is not certain that Theodore of Mopsuestia formally denied its inspiration, but he certainly underestimated this work by stressing that it could be explained by human wisdom alone. To be noted, however, is the fact that the biblical opinions of Theodore of Mopsuestia were discussed at the Council of Constantinople, in a context that examined them, but one can not maintain, as is generally the case, that they were the object of a formal condemnation. [10] To the same type of objection put forward by Spinoza and Leclerc, Richard Simon answered that numerous inspired books would fall into the same category, if one must exclude, in order to assert their divine origin, the ability of the human author to compose them by himself.

The Book of Proverbs is frequently cited in the New Testament. It was nevertheless scarcely commented on by the Fathers of the Church. Besides the passages applied to the Blessed Virgin, the liturgy uses the poem of the valiant wife (Common of Holy Women and feast of St. Anne).

---

[9] A number of the Fathers and the Scotists apply the Wisdom passage specifically to the Second Person Incarnate; hence the aptness of liturgical accommodation to Mary, predestined with her Son by the same decree. *(Translator's note)*.

[10] See the councilar texts in MANSI, and the article of Fr. DUBARLE in *RB* (1954), pp. 68-69. Cf. also below the note concerning the Canticle, p. 439.

CHAPTER II

JOB

BIBLIOGRAPHY

Introductions, translations, commentaries, pp. 1 f. and 407 (P. LARCHER, *BJ**; A. B. DAVIDSON, *CBSC;* S. R. DRIVER—G. B. GRAY, *ICC*...).
P. DHORME, *Le livre de Job** (Paris, 1926).
G. HÖLSCHER, *Das Buch Hiob* (Tübingen, 1937).
E. J. KISSANE, *The Book of Job** (Dublin, 1946).
W. B. STEVENSON, *The Poem of Job* (London, 1947).
J. J. WEBER, *Job et l'Ecclésiaste** (Paris, 1947).
S. R. DRIVER—G. B. GRAY, *A Critical and Exegetical Commentary on the Book of Job*² (New York : Scribner, 1950).
A. WEISER, *Das Buch Hiob* (Göttingen, 1951).
T. H. ROBINSON, *Job and His Friends* (London, 1954).
F. STIER, *Das Buch Ijjob* (Munich, 1954).
S. TERRIEN, " The Book of Job, " *IB* (1954).
"   *Job, Poet of Existence* (New York, 1957).
J. DANIÉLOU, *Holy Pagans of the Old Testament** (New York, 1957).
M. BOURKE, *The Book of Job, I and II** (New York : Paulist, 1962-1963).
M. POPE, *Job* (Garden City : Doubleday, 1965).
A. LEFÈVRE, " *Job,* " *SDB*, IV (Paris, 1948), cols. 1073-1098.
E. SUTCLIFFE, " Notes on Job, Textual and Exegetical, " *Biblica*, 30 (1949), pp. 66-90.
O. J. BAAB, " The Book of Job, " *Interpretation*, 5 (1951), pp. 329-343.
H. W. ROBINSON, " The Cross of Job, " *The Cross in the Old Testament* (London : *SCM*, 1955), pp. 9-54.
H. ROWLEY, " The Book of Job and Its Meaning, " *BJRL*, 41 (1958), pp. 167-207.
R. A. F. McKENZIE, " The Purpose of the Yahweh Speeches in the Book of Job, " *Biblica*, 40 (1959), pp. 435-445.
P. SKEHAN, " Strophic Patterns in the Book of Job, " *CBQ*, 23 (1961), pp. 129-143.

§ 1. The Book

I. POSITION IN THE BIBLE AND GENERAL THEME

Always listed among the *ketûbîm* in the Jewish catalogues, the Book of Job is found in different places within that group.   It is found sometimes in the second place, sometimes in the third place of the block it composed with the Psalms and Proverbs. The Psalter usually headed this three-membered group. If one notes that in the Catholic canon the location of Job is likewise variable (between the Pentateuch and Josue in the Syriac version, at the head of the didactic books in the Vulgate), one is led to think that in part at least these differences are a result of uncertainty about the origin of the work and the era of the hero.

The general theme of the work is relatively simple. Job is presented as a just man whom God permits Satan to test. Three of his friends take it upon themselves to convince him that he suffers because he is a sinner. But the unhappy man energetically rejects the opinion of his accusers. A fourth person intervenes and pretends to solve the enigma by affirming the instructive power of suffering. At last Yahweh appears. He unrolls, like an immense film, the marvel of creation, and reproaches Job for the indiscretion of his complaints. The book closes with the restoration of the proven just man to his original happiness, blessed moreover with new benefits.

II. LITERARY STRUCTURE

The work is obviously complex. Two parts are in prose : the prologue (1—2) and the epilogue (42, 7-17). Between these two sections a long poem intervenes (3, 1—42, 6). It is itself a compilation. There is first an argumentative dialogue instigated by a monologue of Job (3, 1-26). The dialogue develops in three series of discourses, each containing three exchanges : one of Eliphaz (4—5; 15; 22), the second of Baldad (8; 18; 25 and 26, 5-14), the third of Sophar (11; 20; 27, 13-23 and 24, 18-24). Job replies to each of these nine discourses with a defense of his cause (6—7; 9—10; 12—14; 16—17; 19; 21; 23—24, 17 and 24, 25; 26, 1-4 and 27, 1-12; 29—31). It must be noted that the end of the dialogue is not presented clearly in the book in its present form. The texts must be rearranged to assure harmony of ideology and composition.

Chapter 28 is a special problem. It is inserted as an interlude between the third intervention of Sophar and the last answer of Job (29—31).

The dialogue is immediately followed by a series of discourses (32, 6-33; 33; 34; 35; 36, 1-21; 36, 22—37, 24 : the harangues of Elihu).

The poem ends with two discourses of Yahweh (38, 1—40, 2 and 40, 6—41, 26) each followed by a response of Job (40, 3-5 and 42, 1-6).

III. THE ORIGIN OF THE COMPOSITION

The apparent unity of the book

It cannot be denied that a certain homogeneity emerges from the complexity of the work in its present form. But it is a unity of the doctrinal order : the problem of the suffering of the just confronted with the prosperity of the impious constitutes the work's central object.

This homogeneity is also founded on considerations of the psychological and literary order. The attitude of Job is discernably the same in the prologue-epilogue and in the poem, granting a heightened vividness of language used by the hero in the dialogue. This is accounted for by the laws of the literary genre used, the necessity to stand up to the impertinency of the accusers, and to bring out clearly the agony of the trial.

The consistency with which the divine names are distributed and grouped should be noted. That of Yahweh is never placed on the lips of Job (except in 1, 21 : a common formula), nor on the lips of his friends; the names Elohim (five times in the poem), El, Eloâh, and Šadday (more frequent) are artfully distributed in the poetic work.

Finally, the mutual references of the prologue and epilogue (1—2 and 42, 6-17; compare 1, 5 and 42, 8; 1, 11 and 42, 7-9), of the dialogue and the theophany (implored by Job : 13, 3-12; 15, 27; 16, 19-21; 19, 25-29; 31, 35-37 and by his friends : 5, 8; 8, 5; 11, 5-6; compare 19, 27 and 42, 5), the discourses of Elihu and the dialogue (Elihu recalls the talk of the friends and Job : 31, 1-22; 33, 9-11—cf. 10, 7; 16, 17; 23, 10; 27, 5;—34, 5-6—cf. 27, 2; 29, 15; 30, 21; 35, 3—cf. 7-20), of the dialogue and sapiential references (inaccessible Wisdom is alone capable of solving the enigma) constitute so many ties that associate and bind the different elements of the writing. It is not surprising then that the unity of the Book has been defended by the majority of critics.

Traces of revisions

In any event it is not a question of a unity without fault. There is evidence against the perfect homogeneity of the Book. The absence of Satan and Job's wife (42, 7-17) is to be regretted as a flaw in the harmony of the prologue and epilogue. There are more nuances in the attitudes of Job in the prologue-epilogue and in the poetic dialogue than one would suspect. Even in the dialogue there are indications of disorder in the last discussions (24, 18—27, 25) that, although reparable, disturb the harmony of the overall beautiful order.

But it is especially the calling upon Wisdom, and the present form of the discourses of Yahweh and the harangues of Elihu which cause difficulty.

The invocation of Wisdom seems to be an interpolation. The initial conjunction " for " hardly fits in the context where we read it. One might even say that the theme does not seem to be occasioned at all by the statements of Job and his friends. To see here, with Budde, a reproach of God by Job for not having revealed to him the plenitude of Wisdom (28) seems to be a poorly founded conjecture. One would well be more tempted to affirm that neither Job nor his friends, in spite of 11, 6; 15, 8; 26, 3, thought of any other intervention than God's.

Likewise it would be very unreasonable not to consider the divine intervention as an essential element of the poem. One must however agree that the discourses of Yahweh in their present form suggest that there have been additions and revisions. It is possible that God held only one discourse (38, 1—40, 2); even so it is not certain whether the description of the ostrich and the horse (39, 13-24) were part of the original passage. To this discourse one would have added the powerful reference to Behemoth (the hippopotamus : 40, 13-24) and to Leviathan (the crocodile : 40, 25—41, 26). Thus a break would have resulted that would have necessitated the introduction that we read in 40, 6-14 (compare 40, 6 and 38, 3) and Job's second answer (42, 1-6).

It must be admitted that the harangues of Elihu are an addition to the original plan. Elihu was not expected at all. He speaks and reasons in an entirely different manner from the accredited accusers. He seems to refer to the preceding discourses, but a later author could have used that device. Above all he delays the intervention of Yahweh who speaks over his head directly to Job (compare 31, 35 and 38, 1-3) and ignores the pretentious babbler in 42, 7-17.

Conclusion

To conclude, we find that there are clear indications of unity and signs of disunity, the latter being more pronounced. But the differences notwithstanding, the fundamental theme is consistent. Thus we think that while admitting a lack of literary unity, we must admit an organic unity. The poet found himself with a popular work *(Volksbuch)*, the substance of which is contained in the material of the present prose section. To it he probably added the friends of Job (2, 11-13), composed the poetic dialogue and the discourses of Yahweh, and to conclude reintroduced the three accusers as a necessary denouement (42, 7-9).

The same author, or another one, finding the work in that condition, probably balanced it by lengthening the discourses of Yahweh, and then introduced the character of Elihu, who seems to bring a new element into the discussion (33, 19-30). Elihu could not be placed after Yahweh; he actually serves as a prelude to Him (36, 22—37, 24) in a hymn to divine Wisdom. Perhaps it seemed well to a later editor to close the discussion with a similar procedure. It was probably at the same time that the praise of Wisdom in 28 assumed its present place. At that time it seemed to fit well, if not in the literary and psychological context, at least in the ideological context.

It is thus possible to explain the organic unity by a process of growth beginning with a basic work (the prose book, dialogue, theophany), which its author, or another, enriched with new elements quite artistically joined to the original.

§ 2. The Problem

I. A COMMON THEME IN ANCIENT LITERATURE

The problem is that of the suffering of the just, along with the related one, which serves to accentuate it : the prosperity of the sinners.

It is a perennial problem, but it becomes more pressing in proportion as the demands of morality are more deeply felt. From the time of the Middle Empire, Egyptian thinkers had deplored in vehement terms the misery of the poor *(Plaint of the Poor Peasant)*. In the measure that they accepted or rejected the efficacy of funeral rites, they celebrated death as an entering into happiness (*Dialogue of the Despairing :* poetic section), or as a fall into nothingness (same work : prose section), on occasion ridiculing the cult of afterlife *(Antef)*. Around 1350 a poet composed an unqualified praise of death, slanted toward a criticism of skeptics.

But it does not appear that anyone in Egypt sought to resolve the anguishing problem. One the other hand, already in the year 2000 the problem challenged the wisdom of a great poet of Akkad, probably a king : Shushi-Meshri-Nergal (gather-riches-Nergal). Fallen from power, inflicted with illness, the unfortunate professes his justice, and ends, by virtue of moving prayers, by obtaining his cure from Marduk. About ten centuries later another afflicted man converses with a friend, whom he moves to pity by proclaiming his innocence.

Greek philosophical works and tragedies, contemporary with the Book of Job, raised the same question. Prometheus is certainly not innocent, but his excessive punishment embitters him and makes his despair. Oedipus Rex, for an offense against the gods for which he was not responsible, undergoes an accumulation of misfortunes, a Machiavellian destiny. Heracleus, though, is a just man, and it is the sadistic cruelty of the gods which crushes him. There is no way out of the pessimism which fatalism engenders. The philosophers, notably Plato, did succeed in giving the insoluble question its precise form, without arriving at any other solution for it than a recourse to some evil divinity.

If it remains difficult to place the Book of Job in the exact framework of these oriental writings, it is at least certain that the sacred author first of all shared the properly human preoccupation which they reveal, and undoubtedly captured some of the sense of suffering which they suffuse. It might even be possible to assert an external dependence (material similarity of thought and expression) of the canonical writing upon the Babylonian poems. Most likely this dependence reached its high point by way of the Accadian " Suffering Just Man, " which the author of Job could have known through Chananeo-Phoenician tradition. But it is above all biblical speculation which gave birth to the inspired work. [1]

II. THE PROBLEM OF RETRIBUTION IN THE BOOK OF JOB

The biblical context

It will be recalled that in the Old Testament, retribution of good and evil, considered at first as collective (Ex 20, 5-6; cf. Nm 16, 31-33; Jos 7, 1c-5; 2 Sm 3, 2; 21, 1-5; 24, 11-17, etc....), then as individual (Dt 24, 16; cf. 4 Kgs 14, 1-6; Ez 18; 33), is situated, until the last centuries of Judaism, in an earthly perspective, and in a framework of temporal sanctions. It is only since the first half of the second century that we find belief in spiritual and eternal sanctions manifested (Dn 12, 1-3; 2 Mc 7, 9. 11. 14. 23; 12, 43-46; Wis 1—5). The progress achieved in proportion as the historical situation evolved seems to have been the result of critical reflection, which, under the light of revelation, directed tormented spirits (cf. Ez 18, 2; Jer 31, 29; Mal 2, 17) little by little toward conceptions more and more in conformity with reality. The Book of Job finds its fitting place in the age when individual and earthly retribution came to grips with insoluble difficulties of the experimental order.

The propositions in the book

The friends of Job defend the commonly accepted opinion.

Eliphaz, like an Idumean Wise Man (Abd 8. 9; Jer 49, 7; Bar 1, 22-23), in a calm, magisterial, and slightly pretentious tone, expounds it at greatest length. His personal reflections (4, 8. 12; 5, 3. 27), confirmed by a revelation in a dream (4, 12-16) and by the witness of the ancients (15, 17-19), lead him to affirm that the innocent will not perish (4, 7), that sin calls down punishment (4, 8. 9), and that God finds fault with all men

---

[1] J. STEINMANN, *Le Livre de Job*, chaps. II and III, has conveniently brought together the principal extrabiblical texts relating to the problem.

(4, 17-19; 15, 14-16), Job included (22, 6-10). To be sure, punishment is
for correction (5, 17-18), and the latter restores prosperity (5, 19-26).

Baldad is more spontaneous and direct. He poses as an apologist
for God, to whom he thinks it would be injurious to admit mysteries in
the rule of providence (25, 1-6; 26, 5-14). Tradition is enough for him
(8, 8-10). However, he occasionally emphasizes the current doctrine in
a somewhat fatalist accent (18, 2-21). He insists upon the lot that awaits
the just and the wicked (8, 11-22). He acknowledges, just as Eliphaz,
that conversion brings about a return of good fortune (8, 6-7).

Sophar is decidedly aggressive, subtle, pessimistic. He appeals only
to his own authority (20, 2; 24, 25), is determined to sting Job (11, 2-4),
holds that there is no remedy for the sinner's punishment (20, 5-29), and
goes so far as to admit unconscious sins (11, 5-12). Nevertheless, he too
considers conversion the principle of restoration (11, 13-20).

Job stands out for the firm, constant defense of his cause. He
opposes his personal case to the current doctrine : he is innocent and he
is suffering (9, 21; 13, 23; 16, 16-17; 30, 25-37). His final answer (29—31)
poses the problem in all its sharpness. But how to resolve it? The
anomaly incarnate in him is explained, in his view, by a violent persecution
of God who relentlessly pursues his servant (7, 11-12; 10, 2-4; 13, 24-28;
14, 16-17; 16, 7-14; 19, 6-12. 21-22; 30, 19-23). Admittedly he puts
forward a quite bold conception of God, in that he attempts to link divine
Wisdom with a kind of tyranny that would constitute His essential
property. God is always just, whether He strikes the innocent or makes
the culpable prosper. His omnipotence seems arbitrarily to create its
own morality. The conclusion of this singular theodicy is that man must
remain silent before God. He is inaccessible to human reason, based on
a concept of morality that divine transcendence surpasses (9, 2. 3. 12.
19-20).

There are in this some excessive statements, whose intent, however,
is to safeguard the sanctity of Yahweh. " Job fights to rediscover God, "
writes Fr. Larcher (*op. cit.*, p. 21), " feeling that he is cut off from Him,
while the others content themselves with speaking well of Him. And it
is Job alone who faces the problem of God.... " Finally, after having
given up all hope of satisfaction, he takes refuge in confidence in Him
who remains, beyond suffering and death itself, his ultimate goel and his
friend (19, 25-27). [2]

---

[2] A difficult passage. It would be profitable to read the study Fr. LARCHER
has made of it (*op. cit.*, 27-31). It is certain that Catholic tradition is unanimous in
proclaiming the dogma of the resurrection of the body. But it is equally incontestable that tradition has not been unanimous in so interpreting the famous text

The statements of Elihu intend to point out the inaccuracies of Job and his friends. It likewise delights this singular speaker to place in relief those elements of a solution which the dialogue presents : God instructs men not only by dreams (33, 15-18), but also by suffering (33, 19-23). Is this not an instrument of salvation (36, 15)? If He does not seem to listen to the outcries of those under trial, the reason is that they have neglected to call upon Him as Creator and Lord (35, 9-13). Should a mediator intercede for them, His benevolence would show itself (33, 23-30)! To be sure, God saves the penitent (34, 31-32; 36, 11). Job will be delivered from his anguish (36, 16), but he must beware of falling back into sin (36, 18-21).

God's intervention does not bring the solution which might be expected of Him to whom Job and his friends had appealed. The reason is that Yahweh is not a gambler who takes up the challenge. He speaks as God and not as man. In this respect He grants several points to Job, who better grasped the mystery of divine transcendence. It is precisely this transcendence which bursts forth when the Creator and Arranger of the universe unfolds the panoramic spectacle of His enormous works (38, 1—42, 6). His power and His wisdom overcame the forces of chaos and brought stability to the cosmos. Is it not an unavoidable conclusion that such wisdom and power cannot fail to resolve the problems which the spirit of man is not capable of solving?

Further development

The response to the problem posed remains therefore hidden in God. But one senses in advance that there is an answer. Only its revelation is deferred. Daniel's last vision (12, 1-3), the Second Book of Machabees (7, 9. 11. 14. 23; 12, 43-46), and the Book of Wisdom (1—5) will unveil the eternal destiny reserved for the just and sinners, and the New Testament, in developing the teachings of the Servant Poems (Is 53, 1-12), will succeed in giving the solution which the just man who suffers could still find desirable on the plane of life here below : the suffering of the just has redemptive value (Rom 5, 6-19; 1 Cor 15, 3; 2 Cor 5, 15; Col 1, 14. 20. 24, etc.).

---

of Job. The Vulgate's translation is influenced, here as in many other passages, by the theology of the age.

Contemporary exegetes are for their part far from agreement on the object of the patriarch's vehement declaration. Some allege the object is a cure (Bickell, Hudal, Bigot, Szcygiel); the assurance of well-being that Yahweh will promulgate, either here below (Vetter, Peters, Ceuppens, Beel), or after the resurrection of the body (Knabenbauer, Royer, Hontheim, Sales, Vaccari, Lagrange); the separated soul's vision of God (Dillman, Welte).

§ 3. Date, Author, Literary Genre

I. DATE

The patriarchal coloring of the prose passage leads one to think that the foundation of the popular legend sinks its roots into the far distant past. Still it is right to observe that the character of Satan is not mentioned until late in the Bible (Za 3, 1, where he is matched, to one side of the throne of God, with the " angel of God " who stands on the other side; cf. also 1 Par 21, 1 : Satan there has replaced the anger of Yahweh of 2 Sm 24, 1). In any case, the principal part of the work, of incontestable literary perfection, is certainly of more recent compostion.

The art demonstrated by the plan, the power of expression, the elegance of style—these traits have led some to suggest the golden age of Hebrew literature (10th—8th centuries) : from the reign of Solomon to that of Ezechias. But does this dating, forcibly obtained by way of comparison, take into sufficient account the fact that many works not long ago attributed to ancient writers are commonly regarded as having acquired their definitive form in a more recent age? And moreover the literary perfection of the work must be able to be reconciled with the Aramaisms which, taking into account the liberties which a poet familiar with several dialects could have permitted himself, of themselves impose as probable the end of the royal period (Pfeiffer).

But there is more. A number of literary ties, implied in historical references, encourage one to go further along this path. The figure of the " just man who suffers " which dominates the Book of Job, suggests a relation to the Book of Jeremias. Is it not quite possible that there is some relation between the reference to the prosperity of the wicked (Jb 21, 7-34) and the strong protest against God over the happiness of the evildoer (Jer 12, 1-3)? The same holds for the bitter complaints of Job (3, 3-26) and the morbid curses of Jeremias (20, 14-18).

More discretion is necessary in comparing the " suffering servant, " whose traits are described by Isaias (42, 1-7; 49, 1-9; 50, 4-10; 53, 1-12), with the patriarch misunderstood by his friends. The problem is stated in Job in a more pointed way, but it is in Isaias that the solution is given (Is 53, 4-6. 8. 10-12) : the just man suffers to save the many.

As far as other claimed relationships are concerned (Ps 107 (106) and Jb 5, 16; 12, 24; Prv 13, 9; 24, 20 and Jb 18, 5-6), they are not sufficiently clear to be of help in solving the problem at hand.

No matter what relationships might be suggested by comparisons and references, it is certain that the historical background which agrees with the preoccupation of the characters of the Book of Job is one not prior to the Exile.

We must go further and state that it is posterior to the Exile. Without insisting too much upon the allusions to the deportations which we read in Job (12, 17-25; 36, 7-12), it might not be amiss to suppose that the morale of Ezechiel (18; 33) could have appeared insufficient only after the accumulation of trials undergone by the best of the sons of Israel, those who returned to Juda from Babylonia. Aggeus and Zacharias sustained their courage for a while. But after the disappearance of these prophets, the unhappy Jews felt dearly the insufficiency of the solution of the son of Buzi. Might it not be during the course of this crisis that the Book of Job was written?

It would be further from the truth, it seems to us, to go back further than the age of Esdras and Nehemias. The Prophet Malachias, a contemporary of the pioneers of the restoration, was certainly not ignorant of the complaints of the people (2, 17; 3, 13-15), but he was better instructed than the characters of the Book of Job concerning the outcome of the painful situation (3, 16-20). With more reason, then, the reader will note, as Dhorme does, some connections between Malachias and the discourses of Elihu.

In any case, there is no reason to situate the book in the Hellenistic age, whatever possible relations there might be between the biblical writing and the tragedies of Aeschylus and Sophocles or the dialogues of Plato. We have already said that the Book of Job belongs more to the family of Babylonian rather than to Greek writings.

In sum, we place the redaction of the work between the return from captivity (538) and the Hellenistic invasion (330). The end of the fifth century would seem the most appropriate date.

II. THE AUTHOR

The author has not told us his name. But he did at least reveal the high character and outstanding quality of his spirit, profoundly religious and moral, capable of sharp psychological reflections, endowed with moving sympathy for the unfortunate. He most probably experienced sadness himself. Many traits of his writing lead one to believe that he was an intellectual : even if the imagery he employs is Palestinian, the Assyro-Babylonian, Phoenician and Egyptian associations justify the conclusion that he was a writer of vast culture. Quite a number of details of the Book of Job clearly suggest the notion of some relation to the Egyptian world (28, 1-11 : the mines of Sinai; 40, 15—41, 26 : Behemoth and

Leviathan; 9, 26 : boats made of reeds; 8, 11 : papyrus; 40, 11-12 : lotus).
Nevertheless, these relations have been contested recently by Tournay. [3]

III. THE LITERARY GENRE

The Book of Job is fundamentally a didactic writing. It is not however
impossible that the hero did exist. And it is not only the discovery of
his name under the form *'ayyab* (El-Amarna : A-ia-ab, king of Pi-hi-lim,
today Fahil) that suggests this. The allusion of Ezechiel (14, 14. 20)
refers only to a proverbial Wise Man. On the other hand, the absence of
a genealogy would not appear to be an unfavorable sign : Job is presented
to us as a stranger to the people of Israel. The appendix of the LXX
rightly places the land of Us on the border of Idumea and Arabia. But
it is easier to draw from these geographical particulars an argument for
the homeland of the author than for the historicity of the hero. Many
modern authors, Pfeiffer among them, actually hold that the poem has
deep roots in Idumean soil; without going so far, it is not out of order
to ask oneself to what extent Idumean wisdom, which is called to mind
by the origins of the characters, influenced Israelite Wisdom. The origin
of oriental traditions, which are generally the products of real facts,
perhaps warns against rejection of the absolute historicity of Job and the
basic elements of the prose section; but in the book the case at hand is
generalized and raised to the level of a type.

As a Wisdom writing, the Book of Job belongs by its literary form
to various genres. The question treated gives the dialogue a philosophic
turn; the interacting characters and the development of the action make
it a sort of drama; the sentiments expressed, the bold imagery, the
evocation of the miraculous raise it to the heights of lyric and epic.

§ 4. Job in the Progression of Revelation

If one reads the Book of Job after that of Proverbs, he discovers at once
that reflexive questioning, which calls easy solutions into doubt, follows
the simple teaching founded on observation. It is also easy to see that
a self-seeking morality gives way to an investigation of the causes which
would be capable of justifying the failures which this morality records.
The questioning takes the form of a long emotional complaint. So it

---

[3] *RB* (1956), p. 134, in reply to Fr. HUMBERT, *Recherches sur les sources
égyptiennes de la littérature sapientiale d'Israël*, pp. 75-106; see also the moderate
conclusion of Fr. LEFEVRE, *SDB*, IV, art. *Job*, cols. 1074-1075.

pleased the Spirit of God to lead the spirit of man toward a solution of the mystery that causes him most anguish. The cry of Jeremias echoes throughout Job. The insufficiency of personal and earthly retribution breaks forth. The author of Ecclesiastes may try to stop the quest by affecting the attitude of a disillusioned sage; his apparent skepticism only deepens the emptiness which he himself suffers.

The liberating solution, which the Servant of Yahweh songs had incidentally sketched by proclaiming the redemptive value of the sufferings of the just, will find its full expression in the eschatological revelations of Daniel (12, 1-3) and the Book of Wisdom (2—5). The trials of the just, already worthwhile on account of their expiatory value, will be transformed into eternal happiness, while the prosperity of the impious will give way to eternal damnation. We who are more blessed than Job, who live in the brightness of the New Testament, can contemplate in Christ, who suffered for us before entering into glory, the perfect example of the solution to the never ending—but forever solved—problem.

CHAPTER III

THE CANTICLE OF CANTICLES

BIBLIOGRAPHY

Introductions, translations, commentaries, pp. 1 f. (A. MILLER, *HSAT**; A. ROBERT, *BJ**; J. FISCHER, *EBi**; D. BUZY, *BPC**...).

G. RICCIOTTI, *Il cantico dei cantici** (Turin, 1928).

M. HALLER, " Das hohe Lied, " *Die fünf Megilloth* (Tübingen, 1940), pp. 21-46.

H. ROWLEY, " The Interpretation of the Song of Songs, " *The Servant of the Lord and Other Essays* (London : Lutterworth, 1952), pp. 189-234.

A. BEA, *Canticum canticorum** (Rome, 1953).

A. FEUILLET, *Le Cantique des Cantiques** (Paris, 1953).

R. GORDIS, *The Song of Songs* (New York, 1954).

G. KNIGHT, *Esther, Song of Songs, and Lamentations* (London : SCM, 1955).

H. SCHMÖKEL, *Heilige Hochzeit and Hoheslied* (Wiesbaden, 1956).

A. M. DUBARLE, " Le Cantique des cantiques, " *RSPT* (1954), pp. 92 ff.

R. MURPHY, " Recent Literature on the Canticle of Canticles, " *CBQ*, 16 (1954), pp. 1-11.

J. P. AUDET, " Le sens du Cantique des cantiques, " *RB* (1955), pp. 197-221.

T. J. MEEK, " The Song of Songs, " *IB* (1956).

"   " Babylonian Parallels to the Song of Songs, " *JBL*, 43 (1924), pp. 245-252.

M. SEGAL, " The Song of Songs, " *VT*, 12 (1962), pp. 470-490.

B. ULANOV, " The Song of Songs : the Rhetoric of Love, " *The Bridge*, 4 (1962), pp. 89-118.

In the present Hebrew Bibles, the Canticle of Canticles is placed at the head of the *Megillôt*. [1] The name it bears expresses its eminence; it is a *superlative*, akin to the superlatives which were used to designate the most sacred part of the Temple (the Holy of Holies), the greatest king (the King of Kings), the ultimate nothingness (vanity of vanities). " All the Sacred Writings are holy, " wrote Rabbi Aqiba in the 2nd century,

---

[1] See p. 366.

" but the Canticle is sacrosanct. " The Pesshita even carries this subtitle :
" *Wisdom of Wisdoms of Solomon.* " In the synagogues the Canticle is
recited on the octave of the Passover.

§ 1.   Historico-Literary Content of the Canticle

The Canticle is a love song. Before starting our study, it would not be
useless to place it in its historical and literary milieu, even if it soars
above the other examples of the genre.

The fact is that the milieu of the Canticle is first of all profoundly
human, and as such, universal in time and space. Nevertheless its
characteristics relate it more strictly to the customs and love songs of
the Orient. [2] Week-long marriage feasts, jubilant and expressive, are
still known there today. It was no different long ago. Nuptial songs
constituted a specific and richly varied genre : these were popular songs,
often risqué and derisive, and higher class poems, sometimes artistically
composed.

It was an unwritten law to praise the beauty of the spouses. The
existing Syrian *wassf* is a very ancient legacy. Not that hackneyed
expressions were always lacking. Some descriptions smack of artificiality.
They have nonetheless this peculiarity that they associate nature with
the well-being of the spouses. Moreover any real ugliness perceived
during these days of rejoicing served as point of comparison with the
physical beauty of the bride and groom. To praise of physical charms
were always added good wishes, among which that for fecundity was
never lacking. In this way, the songs rose to a religious plane, becoming
veritable nuptial blessings, matching the incantations to ward off the
effects of sorcery, the " evil eye. " It happened that in this context
obscenities or at least realistic expressions, tempered by euphemisms,
were not at all excluded. A number of Egyptian pieces (cf. Pap. Harris,
about B.C. 1200) nevertheless extol love, the joy of loving, lovesickness,
and love potions without shocking expressions. They often expressed,
notably in the case of marital misfortunes, tender and affectionate
sentiments, mixed on occasion, if jealously intervened, with accents of
indignant anger.

The love songs of the Chester Beatty I papyrus deserve special
consideration. " They do not lack agreement down to detail with the

---

[2] S. Schott, *Les chants d'amour de l'Égypte ancienne,* French transl.
Fr. Krieger (Paris, 1956).

material form of the Canticle, " writes E. Suys. [3] " One especially merits attention because of an obvious similarity of plan, although the basic ideas differ. It is a question of a complex and somewhat artificial composition in seven couplets... The author is " the grand amuser, " in other words, the woman in charge of entertainment. At first glance it is astonishing that the author is a woman. But it must be recalled that on the bas-relief of El-Amarna representing dramatic, or if one prefers, orchestral performances, it is a woman who is directing " (p. 209-210).

Israel, placed as it was at the crossroads of the great oriental nations, could not ignore the literary genre of wedding chants and love songs. The week-long wedding feasts which unfolded at Harran (Gn 29, 27. 28) must have found a place in the family ritual of the descendants of the patriarchs (Jgs 14, 10-18). Jeremias (16, 9; 25, 10) prophesied that these joyful melodies would soon cease in the face of invasion. Psalm 44 (45) has preserved the record of a marriage feast in which the groom seems to be a real prince and not just king for a week. The description of the royal couple is the work of a delicate writer. This piece puts us on the path to the object of our present study.

§ 2. General View of the Canticle

At first reading the Canticle appears to be a poem of married love, presented in alternating chants whose plan resists rigorous and precise determination. Thus analysis differs according to the opinion one holds concerning the unity of the work and its literary genre. Fortunately, it is not necessary to take a stand in order to acquire a general understanding of the work.

Whether one divides it into five sections (C. a Lapide), five poems (Robert), six scenes (Kaulen, Pelt, Muntz), seven songs (Bossuet, Calmet, Lorath), or even more (Budde finds twenty-three of them), it is apparent it concerns two separated lovers who are avidly searching for one another. They proclaim their mutual love, they are reunited and separated again, waiting to succeed, after a trial over which the lover triumphs, in possessing one another definitively.

The absence, at least apparent, of a logical thread through the poems, the diversity of *places* where the events take place and of *situations* in which the characters are placed, the repetitions of themes, images and

---

[3] *Bi* (1932), pp. 209-227.

words—all these factors do not succeed in destroying the unity which results from the development of the plot, and from the likeness of spirit and form of the various songs. The striking color and richness of imagery, spread through the whole work, is convincing evidence that the work should not be denied a basic homogeneity.

§ 3. Diverse Interpretations of the Canticle

A deeper study of the Canticle can only be done within the framework of an interpretation. The best must be selected from among many. We will first present a historical summary of the systems proposed. As a preparation, a few notions from the science of interpretation will be helpful.

Every *inspired* book has a *literal* sense, proper or figurative, which emerges from the terms of the text, interpreted according to the ordinary rules of human language, taking into consideration time, place, and literary genre. The *figurative literal sense* can assume various modalities : it can be parabolic or allegorical; allegory itself can be subdivided, being capable of attaching itself to a historical foundation, or merely providing its own foundation. A *typical* sense can be added to the literal sense, proper or figurative. It pertains to Revelation to make it known to us, since the typical sense is itself inspired : God may, in effect, will that persons, situations, or events signify higher realities as a prefiguration of future events. The Canticle has given rise to interpretations corresponding to these various classes of senses.

I. Ancient interpretations

It has been doubted whether the Jews admitted any other interpretation than the allegorical. How else could they have overcome the difficulties which arose, at the end of the first century of our era, concerning the canonicity of an apparently profane book, if this book had been, in their tradition, an anthology of radically sensual songs? The author of the Apocalypse of Esdras is a witness in favor of this figurative interpretation when he calls the people of Israel garden, lily, dove (4 Esd 5, 24. 26; cf. Ct 2, 2. 10; 4, 12). That is also the interpretation of the Targum [4] and the Talmud, which consider God the Beloved, and the nation of Israel the spouse of Yahweh. The substance of this explanation has remained intact among the best Israelites down through the centuries.

---

[4] E. VULLIAUD, *Le Cantique d'après la tradition juive* (Paris, 1925).

A few exegetical blunders, more or less fantastic, did not succeed in obscuring the essential idea the Jews had of the Canticle : *the work sings of the mystical marriage of the Lord and the Chosen People.*

In the beginning the Christians' way of thinking was no different. They merely adapted the allegorical interpretation to the conditions of the New Testament. The name of Christ was substituted for that of Yahweh and the Christian people for the people of Israel. The Canticle, celebrates the mystical marriage of Christ and the Church. A normal evolution took place in exegesis; it took on more particular applications according as the spouse became all mankind, the faithful soul, or, in the Middle Ages, the Virgin Mary (St. Bernard). There was no departure from the line laid down by Jewish exegesis. At most, one could conclude that the evolution, without breaking with the allegorical interpretation, leads toward the superimposition of meanings of the kind tinged with typology, and toward applications in an evidently *accommodated sense.*

Nevertheless, there was a discordant voice : Theodore of Mopsuestia (350-428) interpreted the Canticle as a souvenir of Solomon's marriage to an Egyptian princess—a prelude to the " Banquet " of Plato. The interpretation of Theodore, which granted the work only a proper literal sense, was dealt with unfavorably at the Fifth Ecumenical Council. [5] It was proposed again in the 16th century, and the Jewish exegete who revived it, Sebastian Castellion (1547), had no followers. It is evident though that there was a movement toward making the literal sense more *concrete.* In 1621, Panigarola was a spokesman for the movement when he proposed to see in the Canticle an idyllic drama between a shepherd and a shepherdess. For Catholics anxious to conciliate, the door was open to a more complex interpretation.

It was this path, already indicated by Honorius of Autun (*PL* 172, 347-496), that P. Sherlog (1633-1640), F. Q. de Salazar (1642), Bossuet (1693) and Dom Calmet (1726) followed. According to them, the Canticle recalls the love of Solomon and one of his wives (the daughter of Pharao or Abisag the Sulamite). But the marriage of the prince was ordained by God to signify the mystical union of Yahweh with Israel and of Christ with the Church. The typical interpretation was born.

---

[5] Fr. DUBARLE makes a point of calling the condemnation of Theodore's opinion into question (*RB*, 1954, pp. 68-69). Cf. VOSTÉ, *RB* (1929), pp. 390-395; R. DEVREESSE, *RB* (1930), pp. 362-377; *Studi et Testi*, Bibl. Apost. Vat., 141 (1948), pp. 34-35. L. PIROT (*L'œuvre exégétique de Théodore de Mopsueste*, Rome, 1913, pp. 134-137) does not mention any condemnation. But the judgment of the Fathers was decidedly contrary : the " *commenta* " of Theodore are " *infanda Christianorum auribus.* "

II. FROM THE 18th CENTURY TO MODERN TIMES

From the 18th century on, then, there were three currents. The old allegorical tradition always had adherents. But the *boring genre* (A. Robert) which marks them all, leaves room for philosophical and political variations : the marriage of Solomon to Wisdom (Rosemüller : cf. Prv 7, 4; 9, 5; Wis 8, 2-9; 9, 1-10; and Ct 5, 1); the attempt to unite Israel and Juda (L. Hug, 1813, followed by I. G. Herbst); conflict followed by pacification of Yahwism and human civilization (A. Torelli, 1892). Fr. Joüon (1909) strove to put an end to these products of the decadent age by introducing into the ancient theme precise historical references : according to him the Canticle recalls the various phases of the Alliance from the Exodus to the coming of the Messias.

Alongside the allegorical interpretations developed that of Theodore of Mopsuestia. In 1771 Jacobi revived Panigarola's opinion in a new form : the shepherdess was stolen from her fiancé and placed in Solomon's harem. But she refuses the king's advances and gifts, and he is forced to free her. Renan was the champion of this interpretation in France, while the observations collected by Wetzstein, German consul at Damascus, concerning wedding feasts in Auranitis, gave K. Budde the idea for a folklore explanation : the Canticle is a collection of love songs destined to celebrate the new spouses, king and queen for a week (Week of the king).

The typological current likewise holds its own. Its promoters were Casazza (1846) and P. Shegg (1865). Then after the interpretation of Budde became popular and predominant, Zapletal (1907), J. Hontheim (1908) and A. Miller (1927) modified the figurative element, which ceases to be a marriage of Solomon, in order to draw nearer to the current opinion, which was considered sufficiently founded upon details of the Canticle. But they firmly retained the reference to the reality represented in figure : mystical union, which pure allegorism had found just beneath the letter. According to A. Miller, the literal sense of the Canticle is to be applied to an ideal marriage typically prefiguring the union of God and man. [6]

III. PRESENT POSITIONS

It is apparent, therefore, that the substance of the primitive interpretation has held its ground. Neither the revival of Jacobi's interpretation, which

---

[6] Cf. *op. cit.*, p. 89.

for the rest was unmasked by Pouget and Guitton (1934), [7] as at least an accommodated interpretation, nor, even more so, the efforts of a poorly conceived comparative method undertaken by Meet (1922) and Wittekindt (1925), seem to have been successful in eliminating the inspired allegorical sense, at least typical.   Moreover Fr. Buzy (1950) thinks that the literary genre of the Canticle is a descendent of pure poetry, allowing for parabolic reflections, while A. Robert and A. Feuillet, having rejected all parabolic interpretation, hold that the poem signifies immediately the union of Yahweh and Israel.   R. J. Tournay agrees with this exegesis.   On the other hand, A. M. Dubarle (1954) and J. P. Audet (1955) have turned to an [exactly opposite opinion : the Canticle celebrates human love just as God willed it; it took its normal place in the wedding celebrations of Israel until the rabbis, at a more recent date, interpreted it allegorically.

What conclusion is to be drawn?   Admittedly, those interpretations which welcome an appeal to the material, the worldly, the profane, remain acceptable if they do not reject all religious significance.   They are all the more acceptable if they admit the existence of a typical sense.   It is not contrary to inspiration to admit that in this case, as in others, likewise disputed (Gn 3, 15; Is 7, 14; Ps 44 [45]), historical events can be raised to the dignity of symbols which point to supernatural realities.   And if some rearrangement or reinterpretation was necessary right from the beginning to obtain the desired result, we do not think such a purification impossible.   Who knows whether the Jewish doctors were not the first to effect this transposition, thus qualifying human love songs, purified of all profane meaning and elevated under divine influence, to take their place in the canon of sacred writings?

Still we find it preferable to settle for the figurative literal sense, that is, the allegorical.   Thus we take into account the extension that this sense can acquire when under the proper circumstances the mind rises from the union of Yahweh and Israel to that of Christ and the Church, Christ and the individual soul, and the Holy Spirit and the Virgin Mary.

---

[7] According to POUGET-GUITTON, in the proper literal sense, the only one intended by the sacred author, the work declares the doctrine of marriage (indissolubility, conjugal fidelity, monogamy), under the form of a dramatic presentation; but the proper literal sense contains the germ of the spiritual sense (union of God and Israel).   In the course of time this germ developed and blossomed into the allegorical sense.   (Cf. *op. cit.*, pp. 126-127.)

§ 4. A Brief Analysis of the Canticle

We can now analyze the plan of the work. With A. Robert we distinguish five poems, preceded by a prologue and followed by two appendixes.

In the prologue (1, 2-4) the bride is searching for her bridegroom.

The first poem (1, 5—2, 7) describes the anxiety of the separated one (1, 5-7); the chorus urges her not to lose hope (8). The bridegroom appears; he allows himself to give in to the charms of the beloved (9-11). A dialogue informs us of their sentiments of mutual admiration (1, 12—2, 5). Their union, however, is not yet assured (6-7).

The second poem (2, 8—3, 5) depicts the mutual search which the two spouses renew. The bride describes the beloved running toward her (2, 8-16); she rushes to search for him and meets him in the city (2, 17—3, 4). Is possession achieved? Not yet (3, 5).

The third poem (3, 6—5, 1) opens with a description of a triumphal procession presided over by Solomon (3, 6-11). The bridegroom demonstrates more and more that he is in love (4, 1—5, 7). He establishes a meeting place (6) and invites his beloved there in passionate terms (8-15). The bride accepts. One gathers that she will soon yield (4, 16—5, 1).

The fourth poem (5, 2—6, 3) presents a still withdrawn bride (5, 2-3). She finally opens the door, but too late! The bridegroom has left (4-6ab). The exasperated bride searches for him again (6c-8) and describes him to the chorus which is struck by so forceful an attachment (9-16). There is another meeting. Mutual possession is now very near (6, 1-3).

The fifth poem (6, 4—8, 4) leads to the denouement. The groom again describes the beauty of his beloved (6, 4-12). He replies to the chorus, which invites him to turn around (7, 1a), with ever more vehement declaration of love (1b-10a). Then the bride expresses her passion (10b—8, 3). But she has not achieved her dream (4).

The denouement is reached (8, 5-7). It is the bridegroom who awakens her (5). He demands eternal love (6-7).

Two appendixes, which were added later, seem to be reflections suggested by the Canticle (8, 8-14).

§ 5. The Bible as Milieu of the Canticle

The allegorical sense of the Canticle seems to us to be required by its vital relation to a long biblical tradition of which it is the product. What is spread over its pages under a form that reaches the heights of poetry are those same themes that are spread through the Bible, and whose common object is the mystical conjugal union of Yahweh and Israel.

One has only to read the sacred book. Yahweh has married Israel (Os 2, 2; Ez 16, 8), but the nation did not remain faithful (Os 2, 7; Jer 2, 20-25; 3, 2. 6. 8b-10; 13, 27; Ez 16, 15-34; 23, 2-8. 11-21), God repudiates her as an adulteress (Os 2, 4-6; Jer 3, 8a). The rejection was not definitive : Israel does not cease to be a bride dear to her bridegroom. In order to correct her, He gives the nation over to the infamy and adventures of a vagrant life (Os 2, 8. 9. 11-13; Ez 16, 35-41; 23, 9-10. 22-26. 28-35. 45-48). So great is His desire to bring the unfaithful back to Himself (Jer 3, 7b. 12-18; 4, 1-4; Ez 3, 26-27)! He knows that the sinful people themselves want to return (Os 2, 9; Jer 3, 4. 5a. 22; 4, 31). Pardon must however be delayed (Jer 3, 1. 5b. 22), because God will not be satisfied with empty promises (Jer 2, 29-37). The people must be constrained besides to confess their insufficiency (Jer 31, 19; Is 63, 15—64, 11). Yahweh must intervene with the fullness of His power and mercy (Os 11, 8-9). He will Himself bring about the reconciliation, and will restore to His spouse all her rights (Os 2, 16-25; Ez 36—37; Jer 31, 20-40; Is 51, 52, 54, 60, 61, 62). Then the idyl of the desert will live again (Os 2, 16-17. 21-22) : the bride and groom will possess each other forever.

Is this not the theme of the Canticle? The only difference is that in this book the bride has to yearn for a long while before realizing the final outcome, which God will transform, by an act of His omnipotence, into a definitive conversion.

That is the process described for us. Each of the sections, as A. Robert notes, could be summarized in two words : *tension* and *repose*. " The tension is expressed in the admiring contemplation, the openly expressed desire, the appeals and their response, the anxious search "— all elements whose order can vary. " By repose, one should understand ' mutual possession ' (Buzy) : the goal of each section. "

To thematic connections must be added the climate created by the style. It is a very biblical climate, one in which sumptuous images spring up spontaneously : perfume, oil, nard, myrrh, aloe, clusters of grapes, vineyard, narcissus, cinnamon, Lebanon, flocks, shepherd, king, tower of David.... If the Yahwist influence does not appear explicitly, is it not there in filigree, in the complex of thought and expression? Is this not the way, without revealing itself expressly, that it informs the development and the doctrine of the classic works of Wisdom?

It is understandable, therefore, how well the originality of the Canticle stands out when compared with the writings which have been invoked in order to give it a naturalist interpretation. It is only natural that love poems show a similarity of expression. Besides, we can well imagine that oriental imagery would illustrate isolated works of this genre in the same glistening colors in Palestine, Assyro-Babylonia, Egypt and Arabia. Just as Wisdom literature spread throughout the Orient and encountered Israelite thinkers on its way, so it should not be surprising that this or that type of love-litterature—we are thinking especially of the Egyptian—may have provided the author of the Canticle some technical suggestions (dialogue, romantic intrigue, couplets recited by a chorus, etc.). To go further would prove that one has not understood the genius of the Canticle. It is not a common imitation, nor a skillfully handled borrowing or recasting : it is a true creation. Its transcendence is evident.

§ 6.   Literary Genre of the Canticle

Despite appearances, the Canticle is not an anthology of poems, in which each is complete in itself, and all together leave the work a mere accidental unity. There is at least an *organic unity*, which our analysis revealed.

Does this unity justify the conclusion that the writing belongs to the dramatic genre? Some, following Panigarola and Jacobi, have thought so. J. Guitton shares this view. As a matter of fact the Canticle does contain a plot, crises, a denouement. It draws characters, particularly the bride and groom on whom it concentrates its attention. In our estimation, we would be dealing with no more than a lyric drama, a cantata in dialogue, composed of long recitations and interludes more sentimental than dynamic.

Besides, it is not a question of history. Even if the Canticle directs one's thought toward an idealized synthesis of the relations of Yahweh and Israel, it does not permit one to extract from it a detailed evolution of this union. It would not be amiss, however, to see there a future projection of God's fidelity to His promise, and consequently to allow the work a prophetic character. Would it be unreasonable to compare the Canticle with Daniel and the Apocalypse, two works which in like manner applied the past to the future? The eschatological flavor of a number of passages of the Canticle (2, 11-13; 3, 6-11; 8, 1-2) incline one to accept this view.

§ 7.   Date and Author of the Work

Attribution of the Canticle to Solomon is obviously a literary fiction. As in the case of Proverbs, Ecclesiastes, and Wisdom, it proves no more than that the son of David was considered the originator of the sapiential genre. Besides, the language of the Canticle is full of expressions belonging to the Hebrew of a later age : Aramaisms are numerous. On the other hand many indications point if not to the Greek period (Hellenistic influence is contingent), at least to the Persian period, which is evidenced in several expressions (*'egôz*, nut : 6, 11; *pardes*, garden : 5, 1; *nerd*, nard : 1, 12; *karkom*, saffron : 4, 14, etc...).

Moreover, is not the postexilic age sufficiently indicated by the basic theme of the work, which supposes a certain reflection upon prophetic data from which it borrows its general development? The age of trials that gave birth to the Book of Job was an apt time to emphasize the irreversibility of the design of God and the depth of His attachment to Israel. The " optimistic bent " of the Canticle too reflects very well the religious fervor which resulted in the reforms of the Jewish community under Nehemias and Esdras. The tone of the work also accords with the era of political peace of the first half of the 4th century. Dussaud, Tobac, Ricciotti, and Buzy likewise consider this epoch the literary period of the Canticle.

§ 8. Canonicity and Liturgical Use

The silence observed by the Canticle in regard to God, to the *legal covenant*, to *prophetic preaching*, and to the *great events* of Israel's history led some rabbis to doubt its inspiration. But the synod of Jamnia considered it necessary to decide, not its introduction, but its maintenance in the Hebrew canon. Rabbi Aqiba strongly defended this decision in the second century.

With the exception of Theodore of Mopsuestia, whose interpretation tended to minimize the inspiration of the writing, the Canticle was always regarded as canonical, even though it is not cited in the New Testament.

The Protestant tradition is equally favorable to its canonicity, even though many contemporary Protestants consider it a purely profane work.

The missal and breviary frequently cite passages of the Canticle which they apply, in an accommodated sense, to the Blessed Virgin and to holy women. Especially to be noted is the use made of it in the Office and Mass of Mary Magdalen. That is certainly a precious argument in favor of the allegorical, or at least typical, sense of this work.

Every Christian soul can draw salutary lessons from it. There is the drama of sin, of repentance, of the conversion (never ending here below) which shines through the symbols of the marriage life of Israel and Yahweh. Sin breaks the bond of love; repentance is necessary to resume intimate relations with God. Justification is a gratuitous gift, and the return to favor is perfect joy. [8]

---

[8] The exegesis of the Canticle which we propose seems to receive valuable confirmation in the New Testament. In Ap 12, 1 the woman clothed with the sun and with the moon under her feet is considered by most commentators, including Fr. DUBARLE (Cf. *Mélanges bibliques rédigés en l'honneur de A. Robert*, Paris, 1957, pp. 512-518), as a recollection of Ct 6, 10. The liturgy itself associates the two texts and applies them to the Blessed Virgin. Now Ap 12, 3 clearly brings to mind the ideal Sion of the prophets, spouse of Yahweh, and mother of the people of God in the age of grace (cf. especially Is 60, 19-20; 66, 7-8). Cf. *RB* (1959), pp. 67-72. Ap 3, 20 would seem to refer to Ct 5, 2, and constitute another New Testament confirmation of the allegorical interpretation of the mysterious love poem.

CHAPTER IV

RUTH

BIBLIOGRAPHY

Introductions, translations, commentaries, pp. 1 f. (A. VINCENT, *BJ**; R. TAMISIER, *BPC**; A. SCHULZ, *HSAT**...).

P. JOÜON, *Ruth** (Rome, 1924).

C. LATTEY, *The Book of Ruth** (London, 1935).

W. RUDOLPH, *Das Buch Ruth* (Leipzig, 1940).

H. H. ROWLEY, " The Marriage of Ruth, " *The Servant of the Lord and Other Essays* (London, 1952), pp. 163-186.

J. M. MYERS, *The Linguistic and Literary Form of the Book of Ruth* (Leiden, 1955).

G. KNIGHT, *Ruth and Jonah*[2] (London : SCM, 1956).

A. CLAMER, " Ruth, " *DTC*, XIV, 1 (Paris, 1939), cols. 373-382.

M. HALLER, " Ruth, " *Die Fünf Megilloth* (Tübingen, 1940).

L. P. SMITH, " The Book of Ruth, " *IB* (1953).

THORNHILL, " The Greek Text of the Book of Ruth, " *VT*, 3 (1953), pp. 236-249.

G. GLANZMAN, " The Origin and Date of the Book of Ruth, " *CBQ*, 21 (1959), pp. 201-207.

In the LXX and the Vulgate the Book of Ruth stands between the Book of Judges and the first Book of Samuel. The modern Hebrew Bible places it in the canon of the *Ketûbîm*, among the *Megillôt*, between the Canticle and Lamentations. It is difficult to determine which of these traditions represents the order of the primitive Hebrew canon.

Origen and St. Jerome claimed that originally Ruth was joined to Judges as a kind of third appendix. Melito of Sardis and St. Athanasius likewise placed it in their canons after Judges. The order of the modern Hebrew Bible, which is of recent date, especially concerning the *Ketûbîm* (cf. Bentzen, *Introd.* I, 32), is not a decisive witness against these assertions.

Nevertheless it would be difficult to admit that the Book of Ruth was transferred from the more esteemed canon of the prophets to the less esteemed canon of the holy writings. It would be better to grant its insertion among the " former prophets " as retrospectively justified by the opening words of the work (1, 1 : " Once in the time of the Judges ") and the purpose of the story (the ancestry of David). Moreover, the Babylonian Talmud (Baba Bathra, 14b), which holds that Ruth was written by Samuel (and that Job was a contemporary of Moses), did not dare to list Ruth outside the canon of the *Ketûbîm*, where it places it at the head of the group, ahead of Psalms. Is this not a proof that the authentic place of the Book of Ruth was among the Writings?

§ 1.   Content of the Work

In the age of the Judges, Elimelech of Bethlehem was forced by a famine to emigrate to Moab with his wife Noemi and his two sons Mahalon and Chelion. He dies there, and the two sons marry Moabites, Ruth and Orpha. Then they too die.

After the famine had ended, the three widows leave Moab for Juda. But Orpha accedes to the entreaties of her mother-in-law, and returns to her fatherland. Ruth, however, stays at Noemi's side and goes to Bethlehem with her. It is the time of the barley harvest.

Since the two women had only meager means, Ruth gleans where the harvesters have passed. In doing this she meets Booz, a rich owner and relative of Elimelech. He is very considerate of her.

Heeding the suggestions of her mother-in-law, Ruth musters courage to ask Booz to exercise his right of " goel " in her favor. One night she goes up to her benefactor while he sleeps on his floor, and covers herself with a corner of his cloak.

Booz understands Ruth's gesture, and promises to accede to her wishes, if a closer relative of Elimelech is willing to forfeit his right to him. After this other relative forfeits his right at the city gate in the presence of the ancients, Booz solemnly takes possession of Elimelech's land and takes Ruth as his wife with the obligation of providing legal offspring for the deceased. Of this union is born Obed, father of Jesse and grandfather of David.

§ 2.   The Characteristics of the Writing

For anyone who reads it after Josue and Judges, the Book of Ruth evokes an emotional idyl that rests the spirit from the intensity of combat and the brutal scenes he has just witnessed. The simple and candid atmosphere of the patriarchal age comes again into its own. The account of Samuel's birth too belongs in such a climate.

The noble simplicity of family life, all fidelity and mutual devotion, is described with sober magnificence. Elimelech accepts expatriation in order to provide a living for his family (1, 1); Noemi is more preoccupied about the future of her daughters-in-law than about her own affairs (1, 8-13); Ruth places her attachment to her mother-in-law above all other considerations (1, 14-18); Booz is kind and charitable toward his relative (2, 8-17).

But the principal center of interest of the work goes beyond this framework, or better, brings to it a new dimension. The Book of Ruth allows us to grasp in the concrete the procedure called " goel, " the law of solidarity of the clan. It is not a matter here of freeing a relative who has fallen into slavery (Lv 25, 47-49), nor of revenging the blood of a member of the group (Nm 35, 19; Jgs 8, 18-21), but of redeeming the land of Elimelech (Lv 25, 25-28) and marrying Ruth (Dt 25, 5-10). This last obligation was known under the name of " levirate law. " It pertained to the next of kin—normally a brother of the deceased—to exercise the rights and duties of goel. The words " near relative " and goel were used interchangeably (cf. 3, 12 : " if I am goel... "). Thus we see that when Ruth, at the urging of her mother-in-law, pleads with Booz to assume the classic obligation, the latter accepts only after the nearer relative forfeits his right (3, 12-13; 4, 1-12).

We conclude likewise from the Book of Ruth that marriages between Israelites and foreigners were not so strongly prohibited by law. Neither Mahalon nor Chelion is reprehended in the least for marrying a Moabite, and it would require a lack of feeling to protest the action of Booz who, by introducing Ruth into the people of Yahweh, was to assure the birth of David and become a link in the ancestral line of the Messias (Mt 1, 5).

§ 3. Date of the Work

Faced with a writing that seems so classical and natural, we are tempted to accept the opinion suggested by the LXX and the Vulgate and to date the Book of Ruth, with the Talmudists, in the age of Samuel. Have not some ancient and modern commentators (Keil, Cassel, H. Weiss, Schenz, Cornely-Hagen) subscribed to this opinion?

Lamy, Kaulen-Hoberg, Seisenberger, Goettsberger did not consider it certain. Anyone who has examined the text in depth cannot reasonably hold that opinion.

A few superficial observations suffice to place the redaction after the end of the age of the Judges (1, 1) and by no means before the reign of David (4, 18). The archeological parenthesis between 4, 6 and 4, 8, which does not seem an editorial addition, makes it apparent that the symbolic removal of the sandal had not been in use for a long time when the author wrote. But it would be hazardous to allege on the basis of this short verse that the Deuteronomic era was already long passed (Lods), because the event recorded in Dt 25, 9 does not have the same meaning as that in Ru 4, 8 (Vincent) : it could be considered an addition to the custom which it supposes. If the goel does not remove his shoe, the offended widow removes it by force and spits in his face. Accordingly Dt 25, 9 presupposes the ceremony recorded in Ru 4, 7 (Rudolph).

Nevertheless, other indications suggest a date later than Deuteronomy. Thus in Ruth (1, 9-13; 3, 1) the remarriage by levirate law seems to have as principal aim the happiness of the widow, while in Dt 25, 5-10 the aim was first and foremost to keep the name of the deceased husband from falling into oblivion (cf. Ru 4, 9-10).

Even though the Aramaisms are not so numerous that their presence alone would suffice to consign the work to a recent age, certain neologisms (1, 13 : *nâsâh nâšîm*, to take a wife, instead of the classic *lâqah'iššâh*, Gn 4, 18; 6, 2; 11, 29; 12, 19; 24, 4. 7, etc...; *âgan*, in niphal, to forbid (marriage), a Talmudic formula of Aramaic origin; 4, 7 : *qiyyam*, to validate; cf. Est 9, 31-32; Ez 13, 6, in place of *qômêm;* 1, 13 : *sibber*, in the sense of to hope for, to expect, instead of to reduce to pieces, to break, Ex 32, 19 (E); 34, 1 (J); *hâlahên*, what is the reason for...; cf. Dn 2, 6. 9; 4, 24, in place of *lâmâh* or *lammâh*, Is 1, 11) leave no possibility of considering a preexilic date.

Finally, the place that Ruth seems te have occupied in the primitive Jewish canon is convincing evidence that its redaction was postexilic. Its exterior aspect and its object, however, led it to be placed among the " former prophets. "

§ 4. The Author's Purpose

We grant that the hypothesis of a recent date favors the opinion that finds in the author's plan a somewhat aggressive intention underlying the calm surface of the account.

Without doubt not all historical preoccupation should be excluded. Even if one admits that the book's conclusion (4, 18-22; cf. 1 Par 2, 10-15) is an obvious addition (because Obed does not appear to be the offspring of Mahalon or of Elimelech, despite 4, 10. 17), and that the conclusion of the story (4, 17) could have been revised (because the text does not present the expected formula or name), nevertheless the author certainly wanted to make known a tradition about the origins of David.

It is equally incontestable that an intention of illustrating family virtues was not alien to the author's perspective. The description stands out too well not to have been intentional. We encounter here a " morality story. "

This stage of thought, at which Gunkel and Gressmann stop, should be further developed. Beneath the story, so simple in appearance, lies a polemic concern : *non sine felle columbinus*. Has it been sufficiently observed that Ruth " the Moabite " is insistently presented as a foreigner to the Chosen People? Notwithstanding that, she enters into an Israelite family; she accepts Yahweh as her God; she conducts herself with the utmost loyalty towards her relatives; she merits the praise of her neighbors and divine favor. She will be David's great-grandmother!

Certainly Ruth is a special case. It is by the way of goel and the levirate law that the foreigner becomes an Israelite citizen. But precisely, is there not in this an indication in favor of some mixed marriages, an insistence on the validity of the practice, at least when it is in accord with family virtues? All the more so since the writer seems to take pleasure in recalling a whole group of customs : redemption tied to the levirate law, the shoe ritual, adoption... It would seem that that is enough to suggest that the story is the author's protest against a certain contemporary rigorism. One is imperceptibly led to consider the Book of Ruth as an appeal for moderation in the application of the measures taken by Esdras and Nehemias against mixed marriages (Esd 9—10; Neh 13, 1-3. 23-27), at least in special circumstances. It is an appeal to a fuller appreciation of a past whose customs produced beautiful examples of virtue. The work must have pleased a good number of contemporaries. It is a fact that the prescriptions of Esdras and Nehemias encountered fierce opposition. Did they not arrive at the extremes that we read about in Deuteronomy (23, 4-7; cf. Neh 13, 1-3) concerning Ammonites and Moabites, and in Leviticus (18, 16; 20, 21) by prohibiting any union of brother-in-law and sister-in-law, without regard for the levirate law? And was it not somewhat difficult to reconcile the divorces demanded by Esdras (10, 1-11) and the strict interpretation of Malachias (2, 14-16) who preached fidelity to the first spouse?

By means of this reaction—and this is the essential point—one sees likewise the tendency to uproot the hatred that Judaism encouraged between Jews and pagans. Like the Book of Jonas, that of Ruth has

universalist tendencies. The God of Israel does not disdain the homage
of a foreigner. He places one in the ancestry of the Messias.

We can thus appreciate the importance of the Book of Ruth in the
historical context of postexilic Israel, and even perhaps use this context
to give the work a more precise date. In this regard, one can hardly go
amiss if he settles for the years which followed the weighty decisions
concerning mixed marriages.

§ 5. Historicity

The characters that dominate the narrative, the underlying intention of
the work, the circumstances and late date of the redaction—these are
so many arguments which put one on guard concerning the historicity
of the content of the work.

There could be no doubt that the Book of Ruth, like that of Esther,
is a work of art whose simplicity does not exclude a certain literary
arrangement. Certain contrasts are obviously contrived : Orpha, who
takes the easy way out (1, 14a), makes the steadfastness of Ruth stand
out (1, 14b-17); the near relative who forfeits his right because of self-
interest (4, 4-6) brings the generosity of Booz to the fore (4, 9-10). The
laments directed to Noemi (1, 19) are counterbalanced by the congratu-
lations given her (4, 12-17). These are features which, without presenting
an obstacle to historical truth, are evidence of a plan of presentation.

The symbolism of the names is somewhat more disturbing : Noemi,
my pleasantness; Mahalon, languor; Chelion, consumption; Orpha, she
who turns her back; Booz (Boaz=Baalaz : Baal is strong) : cf. Salambo=
sâlêm Baal. Does this not give the writing a certain symbolic value?

On the other hand, the presentation of the past contains certain
valid references. Furthermore, it was only by appealing to history that
the opposition to the legal prescriptions of the age of Esdras and Nehemias
could find an audience. And it cannot be excluded that when David
sought a refuge for his relatives in Moab (1 Sm 22, 3-4), he did it because
of his ancestry.

All things considered, it is wise not to reject the hypothesis of a
primitive tradition which the fame of David enhanced. The apparently
symbolic names are perhaps the product of popular fancy. The emphasis
given to the custom of goel would be the storyteller's own contribution.
He has passed on to us a pleasing account, nearer to what we call a short
story than to a midrash of the ponderous type we find in Paralipomenon.

CHAPTER V

LAMENTATIONS

Introductions, translations, commentaries, pp. 1 f. (L. DENNEFELD,
BPC*; A. GELIN, BJ*; T. PAFFRATH, HSAT*...).

G. RICIOTTI, Le Lamentazione di Geremia* (Turin, 1924).

A. CLAMER, "Lamentations," DTC, VIII, 2 (Paris, 1935), cols. 2526-
2537.

W. RUDOLPH, Die Klagelieder (Leipzig, 1939).

M. HALLER, "Die Klagelieder," Die fünf Megilloth (Tübingen, 1940).

A. GELIN, "Lamentations," SDB, V (Paris, 1950), cols. 237-251.

G. KNIGHT, Esther, Song of Songs and Lamentations (London : SCM,
1955).

N. K. GOTTWALD, Studies in the Book of Lamentations (London : SCM,
rev. ed. 1962).

B. ALBREKTSON, Studies in the Text and Theology of the Book of Lamentations (Lund, 1963).

This work is classified among the *Ketubim* in the Hebrew Bible, where
it is called *'eykâh* (how; cf. 1, 1; 2, 1; 4, 1) or *qînôth* (lament). In the
LXX, under the title Θρῆνοι, and in theVulgate, under that of *Lamen-
tationes*, it is placed immediately after the Prophet Jeremias. It belongs
to the group of the *megillot*. It was read each year on the 9th of Ab,
the day of fast commemorating the burning of Jerusalem in 586.

§ 1. Contents

The collection is composed of five poems, the common subject of which
is the destruction of Jerusalem and the Temple by Nabuchodonosor.

In the first poem the author recalls the fall of Jerusalem, the enslaved
queen sorrowing, weeping, abandoned, humiliated, deprived of leaders
and consolers (1, 1-11). The holy city, emotionally personified, implores
the compassion of men and the pardon of God (1, 12-22).

The second poem describes divine punishment's most terrible aspects. Yahweh has acted as an enemy : He has leveled the sanctuary and the altar. The Israelites who survived the sword succumb to famine (2, 1-12). Sion is being reminded why God treats her thus and how she is to take refuge in Him. The poet takes Yahweh as witness to the misery of His people (2, 13-22).

Although the calamities had in their variety and intensity reached the point of tragedy (3, 1-21), the poet nevertheless expresses in the third poem his confidence that God, although He has severely chastised His people, has not annihilated them. Their sins must have been many (3, 22-42). Would that the aid of God come to sweep away the enemy (3, 43-66)!

In the fourth poem the poet describes the miserable state of even the nobles and princes (4, 1-12). It is the sins of the priests and false prophets that are the cause of all the misfortune (4, 13-20). Let Edom rejoice; its turn will come (4, 21-23)!

The fifth poem, entitled the *Prayer of Jeremias the Prophet* in the Vulgate, is an ardent supplication which the author, in the name of his brethren, directs to the Lord who has punished the nation. The plea is expressed in heartrending terms (5, 1-6) : the sons are paying for their fathers, the worst of afflictions have been visited upon them, sadness holds sway over all flesh (5, 7-18). May God at last have mercy (5, 19-22)!

§ 2. Literary Genre

We are dealing with dirges, funeral wails. The Israelites, like all oriental peoples, were acquainted with funeral rites which involved either hired mourners (Jer 9, 17; cf. Am 5, 16-17), or relatives and friends of the deceased (2 Sm 1, 17; 3, 33), accompanied by musical instruments, especially the flute (Mt 9, 23). The chants proclaimed the profound change death had brought about. The opening exclamation, *'ey, 'eykâh*, underlined this metamorphosis—what a difference! It is true that in this way a person showed his personal sorrow, but he also thought that he was fulfilling a religious obligation toward the departed (cf. Ex 20, 12). The name of Yahweh, however, was not mentioned in these couplets. He was not the God of the dead, but of the living (Ps 113B [115]; Mt 22, 32).

The personification of groups induced poets to expand the genre of the dirge to apply it to individuals embodying the state or to nations considered as persons. Most frequently these dirges by extension take on the aspect of satiric compositions addressed to enemy princes or states (Na 3, 18-19; Is 14, 4-21; Ez 26, 15-18; 27, 3-36; 41, 10-18; 42, 17-18). But some are also motivated by the misfortunes which brought Israel to the brink of the grave : imminence of the exile (Jer 9, 7-22; cf. 10, 17. 18-19. 20); public calamity (Jer 14, 2-6); destruction (Am 5, 2); etc.

Some of these dirges are presented in the framework of a public gathering where the laments over the calamities are pronounced by the people or their representative and accompanied by ardent supplications (Ps 73 [74]; 78 [79]; 79 [80]; 88 [89]; Jer 14, 2-6; Is 63, 7—64, 11 : note 63, 19b—64, 1, a distraught appeal to the coming of God the Saviour). Others are more openly individual (Ps 3; 4; 5; 7; 21 [22]).

The Lamentations of Jeremias are related to these various forms; they are as a kind of synthesis of all of them. The 1st, 2nd, and 4th poems are, on the whole, public laments marked by vehement invocations of Yahweh, urgent appeals, and earnest confessions. The 5th lament is clearly a community prayer. As for the 3rd, it assumes a more individual character, like the confessions of Jeremias (Jer 11, 18—12, 6; 15, 10-21; 17, 12-18, 18-23; 20, 7-18) and the laments of Job (16, 8-17; 17, 6-9; 30, 1-23...), without ceasing to be evocative of the national catastrophe, and as such an echo of the common sadness of Israel. Could it be that this third lamentation, which in theme and imagery is close to the Book of Job, depends on it? In that case it would be more recent. It is also true that the dependence could be inverted. The question merits further study.

§ 3. Literary Evaluation

The metric and strophic pattern of Lamentations gives evidence of a conscious literary effort whose artificiality could have degenerated had the fundamental theme not been so tragic.

Each poem has as many strophes as there are letters in the Hebrew alphabet (22). All of them except the fifth are acrostic, that is, the initial letter of each verse follows the order of the normal alphabet (*pe* and *'ain* are inverted except in the first poem). The third is peculiar in that each of the three verses which compose its strophes begins with the same letter.

Added to these alphabetic arrangements are symmetrical repetitions of one or more words, a method of stressing the more important thoughts and making the structure of the strophe more evident.

The first four poems observe the rhythm of the *qînâ*. Dropping the
voice on a shorter second member gives the impression of sorrow, which
the author so obviously meant to express. In the fifth, the frequent
repetition of the same ending produces a sort of rhyme, even when the
ending does not always coincide with the end of a member.

The literary value of these poems has been universally acknowledged.
After so many centuries, the intense emotion that emerges from them
moves us still, just as we marvel at their wealth of imagery. The last
one in particular remains one of the most heartrending cries that ever
sprung from an anguished heart. Palestrina must have thought the
same; he made it the theme of one of his best compositions.

§ 4. Date and Author

Certain historical references verify the event indicated in the work, the
destruction of Jerusalem and the Temple. It suffices to recall 1, 1-4
(the deserted city, suspended cult); 1, 19 (famine during the siege);
2, 7 (invasion of the Temple and palace); 2, 9 (gates beaten down, king
and leaders in exile); 2, 15 (insults of passers-by); 4, 17 (defection of the
ally Egypt); 4, 19 (the captured fugitives; cf. Jer 39, 4-5). There is every
indication that the terror and anguish still hold sway. It is usually
admitted that Lamentations were composed sometime after 586, certainly
before the liberation (538). It should be observed that the 2nd and
and 4th poems seem to be the oldest. Rudolph goes even further and
dates the 3rd and 5th poems at the beginning of the invasion which
preceded the fall of Jerusalem, and the 1st on the morrow of the siege
of 597. In any case it is true that the spirit of these poetic pieces is shot
through with the literary thought of Jeremias (3), Ezechiel (2 and 4),
and anticipates in places (especially 1, 3, 5) the tone of Second-Isaias.

The influence of Jeremias is predominant throughout the work
(cf. 1, 15; 2, 13 : virgin, daughter of Sion, and Jer 8, 21. 22; 14, 17—;
Lam 1, 16; 2, 11. 18; 3, 48. 49 : fountain of tears, and Jer 9, 1. 18; 13, 17;
14, 17—; Lam 1, 14 : chained neck, and Jer 27, 2—; Lam 1, 14; 4, 13-15 :
sins of the priests and false prophets, and Jer 2, 8; 5, 32; 14, 13; 23,
10. 40, etc...). It was only natural that in the search for an author
the choice would settle upon this prophet, whom a text of Paralipomenon
(2 Par 35, 25) calls the author of lamentations. After all, was he not the
witness who was most closely and sadly related to the events? It is
evidently for that reason that the Jewish tradition, represented by
the LXX, the Targum and the Talmud, attributes the work to the prophet

of Anathoth. Origen (*In Ps*, 1), St. Hilary (*Prol. in Psalt.*, II, 15), St. Epiphanius (*Haer.*, VIII, 6), St. Jerome *(prol. Gal.)* seem to attest that in the beginning the work followed Jeremias in the Hebrew. The transferal could have been caused by liturgical use.

Still these arguments are not decisive. Internal criticism presents a number of difficulties which weaken the force of the alleged connections between the two books. Could Jeremias have subjected himself to such a complicated and artificial genre of poetry? How could he have celebrated the memory of Sedechias (4, 20; cf. Jer 22, 13-28; 37, 17-21), or have recalled the hope of aid from Egypt (4, 17; cf. Jer 37, 7-8), or have been a witness against the existence of prophetic revelation after the national catastrophe (2, 9; cf. Jer 42, 4-22), or still extol collective retribution (5, 7; cf. Jer 31, 29)? Furthermore, the reminiscences of Ezechiel and the Book of Consolation turn one's thought to a less unilateral hypothesis. And while it is true the title in the LXX is found likewise in Latin manuscripts and the Sixto-Clementine edition, it remains true that it is lacking in the Massoretic text and the Peshitta. This would seem to give greater importance to the correctness of the position the Book of Lamentations occupies in the Hebrew Bible, among the *Ketubim*.

Not only is it doubtful that Jeremias is the author of the work, but when the complexity of literary dependencies is examined, it would be reasonable to give some credit to the opinion of Eissfeldt and Haller (1940), who envision the plausibility of several authors. Even Rudolph (1939), who favors unity of origin, was constrained, by the date he placed on the first poem (597), to attribute it to a special author.

§ 5. Liturgical Use

The Catholic Church has introduced the Lamentations into the office of Holy Week. The Church sees in them, just as the Jews of the exilic and postexilic era did (cf. Za 7, 3; 8, 19), an expression of repentant sorrow, the fruit of faith in the irreversible salvific will of God, and a stimulant to confidence in His merciful pardon.

CHAPTER VI

ECCLESIASTES (QÔHELETH)

BIBLIOGRAPHY

Introductions, translations, commentaries, pp. 1 f. (D. BUZY, BPC*; R. PAUTREL, BJ*; A. ALLGEIER, HSAT*; G. A. BARTON, ICC...).

E. PODECHARD, L'Ecclésiaste* (Paris, 1912).

H. W. HERTZBERG, Der Prediger (Leipzig, 1932).

E. M. DE MANRESA, Ecclesiastes* (Barcelona, 1935).

M. HALLER, " Der Prediger, " Die fünf Megilloth (Tübingen, 1940).

R. GORDIS, The Wisdom of Ecclesiastes (New York, 1945).

J. J. WEBER, Job et l'Ecclésiaste* (Paris, 1947).

A. BEA, Liber Ecclesiastae qui ab Hebraeis dicitur Quohelet* (Rome, 1950).

H. L. GINSBERG, Studies in Koheleth (New York, 1950); " The Structure and Contents of the Book of Koheleth, " Suppl. VT, 5 (1955), pp. 138-149.

M. DANHOOD, " Canaanite-Phoenician Influence in Qoheleth, " Biblica, 33 (1952), pp. 191-221; " Qoheleth and Recent Discoveries, " Biblica, 39 (1958), pp. 302-318; " Qoheleth and Northwest Semitic Philology, " Biblica, 43 (1962), pp. 349-365.

G. R. DRIVER, " Problems and Solutions, " VT, 4 (1954), pp. 225-245.

R. GORDIS, Koheleth (New York, 1955).

R. MURPHY, " The ' Pensées ' of Coheleth, " CBQ, 17 (1955), pp. 304-314.

O. S. RANKIN, " The Book of Ecclesiastes, " IB (1956).

E. JONES, Proverbs and Ecclesiastes (London : SCM, 1962).

R. B. Y. SCOTT, Proverbs and Ecclesiastes (Garden City, N. Y. : Doubleday, 1965).

The term " Ecclesiastes, " a transcription of the Greek Ἐκκλησιαστής, corresponds to the Hebrew qôheleth, which comes from the root qhl whose sense in the qal form is to assemble. Qôheleth then as participle would signify either the assembler or the preacher of an assembly. The same meaning is arrived at if the word is derived from the substantive qâhâl which itself means assembly. In any case it is not necessary to identify the person thus designated with Wisdom, as might be suggested by the reference to Prv 8 and the feminine ending of qôheleth. On the one hand,

in the passages in the work where we meet this term (1, 2. 12; 12, 8. 9
and 7, 27; read here : *'âmar haqqôhelet*), the modifier is in the masculine,
On the other, it is known that nouns which signify a function or connote
a quality or title take the feminine ending (cf. Esd 2, 55 : *sôferet;* 57 :
pôkeret).

Taking these considerations into account, *qôheleth* would be the
outstanding preacher, the master of Wisdom, the head of a group of
sages. [1] To consider the assembly itself in reaction against the preacher
(Pautrel), is an interesting suggestion, but one difficult to prove.

§ 1. General View of the Work

The author of Ecclesiastes proposes to draw up the balance sheet of the
good and evil that constitute the lot of human life, and to investigate
whether this life is worth living (1, 3). The reader gathers immediately
(1, 2-21) the pejorative character which marks the enquiry.

The investigation is erratic. It is not presented under the form
of a dialogue, but rather a monologue or soliloquy. After having
investigated various opinions, the author discusses them, and passes on
to other forms of thought which present him the occasion to correct or
rectify the previous opinions. The developments are often partial,
fragmentary, controlled by narrow points of view.

Still it is possible to distinguish two series of reflections, the one
built into the other. The first is by far the more important, and develops
the book's main theme. It stands out for the critical and sharp turn the
inquiry takes, and this relates it to Job. The second is much briefer
and consists of small groups of opinions which counterbalance the preceding developments. And this relates it to Proverbs.

Tobac has shown how well this general conception, when applied
to the detail of the work, reveals immediately its composite character.
We here follow his analysis.

After the prologue (1, 1-11), which puts us in the ideological climate
of the whole work, three sections describe the disillusionment that
Wisdom and pleasures leave (1, 12—2, 26); human efforts ruled by events,
tyrannized by those in command, destined for death (3); the contradictions
found in the social order (4, 1—5, 8). In this context a double series
of maxims appears : the first group (4, 9-12) suggests, in reply to 4, 7-8
(an appeal for the solitary life), the advantages of the common life; the

---

[1] PODECHARD, *op. cit.*, p. 134; JOÜON, in *Bi* (1921), p. 53 ff.

second group (4, 17—5, 6), in a poorly chosen context, contains counsels relative to cult.

There follows a fourth section on the deceptions of riches (5, 9—6, 12). A third series of sayings (7, 1-12) opposes the stabilizing practice of moderating Wisdom to excesses in conduct (wantonness, mockery, anger). We read much the same in the fifth section : disillusionment caused by the contradiction in the lot of the just and the wicked (7, 13—9, 10). Two more series of advisory sayings aim to lessen the paradox; the one appeals to the universality of sin (7, 18-22), the other to submission to authority and the eventual judgment (8, 1-8).

The sixth and last section recalls the fickleness of fate, no matter what conduct, work, talent, or wisdom one employs to determine it (9, 11—11, 6). Just as previously, two more series of maxims intervene : the one praises Wisdom (9, 17—10, 4), the other, virtue and work (10, 10—11, 6). The allegory of old age (12, 1-8) is nothing more than a literary prolongation (we would call it a " sequence ") whose gloomy character cannot but accentuate and urge the precept on which it hangs : Be mindful of your Creator... (12, 1).

The epilogue contains a brief praise of Qôhelet and the words of the sages (12, 9-12). It resumes in closing the impressions which emerge from the book : fear God, obey Him, prepare for the judgment (12, 14).

§ 2. Doctrinal Content

A deeper examination reveals that the literary complexity of the work is not without relation to its doctrinal complexity. Ecclesiastes has many facets. It is peppered with ideological contrasts, but still replenished by a pure religious spring.

There can be no doubt that, against the melancholy background of this long " confession, " the dissonant elements are the first to stand out and clash. The author appears *disillusioned*. He sees only a reason for sadness in the perpetual movement of the universe (1, 4-10) and in the miserable state of mankind (1, 14. 18; 2, 1. 11. 16-23). So much so that death seems preferable to life (2, 17; 4, 2; 6, 3). Nevertheless, here and there, the reaction is to accuse this disillusioned man of epicurism. No matter how lamentable life is in his eyes, it still leaves open the possibility of enjoying *earthly pleasures*, especially those of the table (2, 24-25; 3, 12-13. 22; 5, 17-19; 8, 15; 9, 7-10; 11, 7. 8). Is this not the best that man can hope for, in effect, his final goal (2, 24; 3, 22; 5, 17c)? Naturally, such an attitude is conceivable only at the price of a certain rejection of the afterlife. And that is the point : Ecclesiastes seems to reject even that admittedly minimum of Revelation concerning the next life, which has filtered down. He is, in effect, so skeptical that he is not content to call into question the rightness of providential dispositions (3, 16; 6, 1-3; 8, 10. 14; 9, 5). The ever present incertitude which envelops the conditions of the future life seem to leave him with not only the unsolved problem of otherworldly retribution, but also even that of the immortality of the soul (3, 18-21).

But this pessimist, this epicurian, this skeptic, as he has been called, presents himself as a convinced Yahwist. For Ecclesiastes affirms his *faith in God*. He praises divine Wisdom (7, 12. 20; 9, 13-18) and convincingly professes the reality of Providence (3, 11. 14-15; 8, 17; 11, 5). It is God who gives and takes away life (5, 17; 8, 15; 9, 9; 12, 7), riches (5, 18; 6, 2), joy (2, 24; 3, 13; 5, 18-19); it is He who distributes good and bad fortune (7, 14). In addition, Qôheleth does not ignore the distinction between good and evil (3, 16; 4, 1; 5, 7; 7, 16; 8, 10. 14; 9, 2), and if he confesses ignorance about the nature of eternal retribution, at least he has no doubt about a future judgment (3, 17; 11, 9; 12, 13-14). Thus the notion of a moral act does not entirely escape him (2, 26; 7, 27; 8, 5. 13). So many positive convictions hold his skepticism in check.

Could not one say the same about his epicurism? Though Qôheleth understandbly does not rise to the height of Christian asceticism, he does hold that earthly pleasures are gifts of God (2, 24; 3, 13; 5, 18; 9, 7). He condemns their abuse (7, 26-27; 9, 3); he goes so far as to proclaim their vanity (2, 1-2; 11, 8-10). These convictions stand in contrast to hedonism.

While we cannot justify the paradoxical lesson of optimism that some ancients claimed to discover in the work, even the author's pessimism does not exclude opinions that reveal to us at least a friend of existence (11, 7), who has confidence in the foreknowledge of God (6, 10), his sovereign judge (12, 14) and the goal of man (12, 7). In a word, he is a realist.

The coexistence of such dissonant themes, together with the unusual structure of the book, poses a problem, that of its composition.

§ 3. Composition of the Work

The hypothesis of a primitive work which successive authors edited is unavoidable. So thought Siegfried and Podechard.

The present form of several sections partly substantiates this view. Attention centers especially on the epilogue (12, 9-14). There the title

Qôheleth is twice given to the author (12, 9. 10), while he attributes it to himself only once (1, 12). The author of the epilogue, then, must be distinct from Qôheleth. As a fervent disciple of the master, he probably also edited those passages in which the Sage is spoken of in the third person (1, 2; 7, 27; 12, 8).

The maxims inserted in the course of the work which are in metric form (4, 9-12; 4, 17—5, 6; 7, 1-12. 18. 22; 8, 1-4; nearly all of 10; 12, 2-6) betray a different hand. Do they not seem to mitigate the statements of Qôheleth?

This determination to correct is more evident in 12, 13-14; the author of the epilogue has recourse to a settling of accounts, while this perspective is more limited in the rest of the work. And would it be an exaggeration to say that other verses fit better in the same class as 12, 13-14 than in the general outlook of the work (cf. 2, 26ab; 3, 17; 7, 26b; 8, 2b. 5-8. 11. 13; 11, 7b; 12, 1a)?

Thus we are led to distinguish from Qôheleth, to whom belongs the substratum of the work, an epiloguist, a Sage *(hâkâm)*, a pious author *(hâsîd)*, and perhaps even more editors. Orthodoxy is not thereby offended, since Catholic circles admit that inspiration can use a number of writers to produce the work in its present form. But on the scientific plane this analysis remains problematic, except in the case of the epilogue. And Kuenen is probably right in saying that it is more difficult to deny the unity of the work than it is to demonstrate it.

§ 4. One Author

In effect, the coexistence of contrasting opinions can be explained in the case of a single author. Without refusing to admit, in such a fluctuating matter, the hypotheses which recur, more or less successfully, to stylistic criteria (presentation of diverse opinions, hints of a tortured soul, incomplete or interrupted editing), might not one simply see in the work the result of a critical reflection, which, while not arriving at a complete understanding, much less a solution, of the problems of the contingency of things created and of the retribution of good and evil, betrays the confused state of observations of unequal value? In reality, Qôheleth is a tortured Yahwist who meditates on the picture of disoriented human nature, and strives to describe its frustrations. Instead of situating the problem of the human condition above the accidental contingencies which give it such a divided appearance, he prefers to place it in the concrete context of experience in which, as a matter of fact, mankind is involved.

This does not prohibit him from sensing, or even affirming, the solutions that faith in Yahweh offers for the unrest and uncertainity of the human spirit. Not that he presents faith as an easy solution. One even gets the impression that he arrives at it only with effort. There is, however, no contradiction between those alternatives of doubt and conviction. Did not Paul too experience like agonies, and commend to the grace of God the task of realizing that unity to which the disconcerting duality that we are aspires? And will one not find in St. Augustine, Pascal, and many other troubled souls, the same answers that Ecclesiastes gave?

§ 5. Date of the Work

Such a state of soul, however, demands placing the work in a quite recent age. Now it is clear that the reference to Solomon (1, 1. 12) is no obstacle to a late date; the work's Aramaisms, and its appreciation of royal administration (1, 17; 4, 13; 5, 7; 10, 5-7. 20) are incompatible with Solomonic origin. Qôheleth is not the son of David. The author makes use of a literary fiction of his day. He introduces Solomon, the originator of Wisdom Literature, and, in the circumstances, he undoubtedly demonstrates understanding, because Solomon would not perhaps, in some respects, have refused to subscribe to this or that opinion of the work. That is the most one can say.

On the other hand, without going so far as to claim that the writing depends directly upon some Greek master or a Hellenist system of philosophy, it is certain that it fits well in the world of thought which characterized the Hellenistic epoch. The breaking of ideological ground at which the Sages worked could hardly have attained before this period the state of perfection which an analysis of Ecclesiastes supposes. In certain respects Qôheleth seems to be a contemporary of Job. Both write about similar problems : the enigma of life, suffering, evil, the uncertainty of the fate of man. Neither of them gives them a completely satisfying solution. They leave the ultimate explanation to be sought in God, in a still imprecise future life. Nevertheless, Ecclesiastes marks progress over Job. The latter considers earthly happiness an adequate satisfaction; Qôheleth goes so far as to join sorrow to the happiness one can experience here below. Job is astonished that the just is not overflowing with good things; Ecclesiastes maintains that even if he has his fill, he is still not happy. Earthly insatisfaction creates, more deeply in the Book of Qôheleth than in the Book of Job, the emptiness which Revelation will fill. Ecclesiastes is more recent than Job.

Besides, it is incontestible that the climate of the Ptolemaic domination (B.C. 300-170) provided an excellent occasion to present to the Jews questions about the insufficiency of earthly happiness. The world was then moving toward the ease, the comfort, and even the luxury of Greek civilization. Without being a moralist preacher, nor a philosopher who has worked out a thesis, nor a prophet who communicates a message, Qôheleth presents himself as one who recounts familiarly the results of his experience, in order to raise his compatriots to a more precise concept of earthly happiness : " If you want to be happy, enjoy the passing goods of existence, without forgetting that one day God will demand an account of your use of them. " If the Jews had accepted Greek culture with these wise reservations, the crisis they were about to face could have been avoided. Wisdom will propose to adapt Judaism to the Greeks; Ecclesiastes seems to have wanted to measure out to the Jews the satisfaction they could draw from Hellenism.

§ 6. Ecclesiastes in the Progress of Revelation

The reflections of Qôheleth are centered on the nothingness of earthly pleasures. They constitute one of the last steps in the path that will end in the discovery of sanctions beyond the grave. From then on the terrain is sufficiently prepared for the Spirit of God to sow with profit the seeds of the last doctrinal harvest of the Old Testament. The conception of collective retribution was already left far in the past. Insistence on the person, responsible for his acts, permitted the notion of individual retribution to emerge (Jer 31, 29-30; Ez 18, 33). But this still remained in the framework of earthly existence, and consequently exposed to the contradictions of life (Job). It was necessary to rise to the as yet unexplored heights of eternal sanctions. Such an effort supposed that, docile to both divine pedagogy and intellectual reflection, the sages would cease to consider temporal happiness as an unalloyed good, as a sovereign ultimate goal. It is to bring about this detachment that the author of Ecclesiastes dedicates himself with a rude frankness bordering on excess. While still looking with favor on earthly goods, he so forcefully affirms their vanity that imperceptibly he orients the mind of his disciples toward a certain " beyond the grave " preceded by the judgment of God (12, 13). The Book of Wisdom (2—5), in borrowing and developing the oracle of Daniel (12, 1-3), the faith of the seven martyred brothers and their mother (2 Mc 7, 9. 11. 14. 23. 29), as well as the conviction of Judas Machabeus and his historian (2 Mc 12, 43. 46), will open horizons on the destiny of mankind which Christ will illumine (Mt 5, 3-11; 25, 31-46; Lk 16, 19-31...).

§ 7. Canonicity

The Book of Ecclesiastes is protocanonical. It had a place in the Jewish canon in the 1st century of our era (4 Esd 14, 18-47; Josephus, *C. Ap.*, 1, 8); there are no indications that it was not included earlier. The doubts which were raised about its inspiration between 90 and 190 (despite the decision of the synod of Jamnia) were not successful in shaking Jewish belief. It is interesting to note that fragments of the book were found at Qumran. Theodore of Mopsuestia was the only Christian who minimized the inspired character of the work. The Second Council of Constantinople disapproved of his opinion in 553. [2]

---

[2] Cf. note 5, p. 439.

CHAPTER VII

ESTHER

BIBLIOGRAPHY

Introductions, translations, commentaries, pp. 1 f. (A. BARUCQ, *BJ**; L. SOUBIGOU, *BPC**; J. SCHILDENBERGER, *HSAT**; L. B. PATON, *ICC*...).

L. BIGOT, *Esther**, *DTC*, V, 1 (Paris, 1924), cols. 850-871.

M. HALLER, " Esther, " *Die fünf Megillôth* (Tübingen, 1940).

T. GASTER, *Purim and Hannukkah in Eastern and Western Traditions* (New York, 1950).

B. ANDERSON, " The Book of Esther, " *IB* (1954); " The Place of the Book of Esther in the Christian Bible, " *JR*, 30 (1950), pp. 32-43.

G. KNIGHT, *Esther, Song of Songs and Lamentations* (London : SCM, 1955).

The Book of Esther reads very differently in the Hebrew text and the LXX. The latter contains important passages which are not to be found in the Massoretic text. These fragments, which pose more than one problem, are besides arranged differently in the common Greek text than in the Lucian version, which seems to be a complete re-editing of the whole. Since these additions are listed among the deuterocanonical writings, we do not treat them here. The study of these Greek fragments will be treated in the next part. [1]

§ 1. Content of the Hebrew Work

A young Jewess named Esther, having been chosen queen by Assuerus after the repudiation of Vasthi, succeeds in saving her countrymen who were destined by a decree of the king to extermination. She is guided

---

[1] Cf. pp. 550 ff.

in her undertakings by her uncle Mardochai, who is exposed to the hatred of the first minister, Aman, whom the Jew, loyal to the king, has offended. Esther obtains Aman's condemnation, and Mardochai becomes first minister. The extermination decree is changed to an authorization for the Jews to defend their lives. Which is exactly what they did, massacring, on the day when they themselves were to have been slaughtered (13th Adar), 75,000 Persians, without counting those who died the following day. The feast of Purim recalls the event.

At first view the account leaves an unpleasant impression, that of exaltation of the hate which existed between the Jews and the pagans. In fact it is Aman who sets off the drama (3, 6), but is it not Mardochai who provokes the extreme reaction against the Jews by his arrogant behavior toward the minister (3, 2-5)? And does the defense of their life authorize the Jews to abandon themselves to the excess of a massacre which resembles bitter revenge (9, 1-10)? And what is to be said of Esther who requests a second day of slaughter (9, 11-15)! In addition, the name of God is not mentioned in the work. We could consider as an indication of disdain for this strange story the fact that neither Christ nor the authors of the New Testament cite it, especially since they were acquainted with the more religious Greek version.

Still, a more attentive reading of the book allows us to make a less severe judgment. God is not named, but He nonetheless directs the action. As in Racine's "Athalie," He is the principal actor. The characters, moreover, display by their actions their belief in Providence. Does not Mardochai appeal discretely to Providence when he suggests to Esther the meaning of her elevation to royalty (4, 13-14)? It would be reasonable to regard likewise as appeals for heavenly aid the penitential acts of Mardochai (4, 1), the invitation to fast addressed by the queen to all the Jews of Susan, and the example she and her servants give (4, 16). Mardochai and Esther, instructed about the mighty deeds of God in Israel, and convinced of the ascendency which Yahweh wanted to exercise in the midst of the pagans (Gn 45, 5-8; Dn 1, 9. 17), could not believe that in the end justice would succumb to iniquity. The faith of Abraham, so deeply anchored in the souls of his descendants, expected from the Almighty the revenge of good over evil. And it is the inevitability of such revenge that explains somewhat the massacre, undertaken, let it be remembered, in a tactic of legitimate defense (8, 10), since the decree of extermination of the Jews, untouchable like the sovereign decisions of the Achaemenids, could not be annulled.

The Greek fragments develop the import of the Hebrew work; they do not give it a new meaning.

§ 2. Historical Evaluation

The literary genre of the work will permit us to determine its historical value.

One would willingly enough incline to accept it as objective history, if he were content to take note of the exactness of certain details : distinction between the castle and the city (3, 15, suggested in 8, 14 and 9, 6. 11), between the royal residence and the harems (2, 13. 14); the impulsive and sensual character of the king (1, 11-12; 2, 1. 12; 3, 10; 6, 1-10; 7, 8-10; 8, 7-12; 9, 11-14) attested by history; the intolerance of Aman, who was not a Persian (3, 1); the administrative customs of the Achaemenids (1, 13-21); the irrevocability of the royal decrees (1, 19; 8, 8; cf. 11). But a fictional account can present traits of reality just as well as a work of history.

It is the contrary that cannot be verified. Now in the Book of Esther there are numerous unlikely facts. The impulsiveness of the king seems exaggerated : he surrounds himself with counselors before promulgating the deposition of Vasthi (1, 13-21), and authorizes without prior deliberation the massacre of his subjects (8, 11-12). The decree to exterminate the Jews contrasts with the benign tolerance of the princes toward the Israelites (cf. Esdras-Nehemias). And how imagine, on the plane of efficiency, the delay of eleven months (3, 12-15) or of nine months (8, 5. 13) granted the victims, so much so that the Jews would profit from them, but not the Persians! In addition, if Amestris was, at the time of the biblical account, the wife of Xerxes and the queen of Persia (cf. Herodotus, VII, 61; IX, 108-113), what likelihood is there of the investitures of Vasthi and Esther? One would also like to have an explanation of the king's prolonged ignorance of the origins of the heroine, whereas Mardochai, who is so solicitous for his niece, compromises the secret by his indiscretion (3, 4) and his comings and goings (2, 11). Besides, how old would Mardochai be in the reign of Assuerus (486-465) if he was deported to Babylonia by Nabuchodonosor in 597?

These indications against the historicity of the Book of Esther suggest an interpretation of the work in the framework of a literary genre more in accord with its appearance. The idea of intrigue, at first limited to the rivalry of two characters, Aman and Mardochai, then extended to the hostility of two peoples, Persian and Jew, reveal a concern in composition that smacks of the fictional. The characters follow well the author's plan : Aman and Mardochai, firmly set in an attitude of implacable opposition, cunning and crafty, wagering the highest stakes; Vasthi and Esther, the one a victim, the other exalted, the first foretelling in her humiliation the brilliant victory of her rival; Assuerus, a fanciful and puppet king who is manipulated from both sides with indecent facility. The handling of the action, wisely spiced with incidents which either slow or hasten the pace, interspersed with pleasant descriptions— this only heightens the impression that the author, who is obviously familiar with the methods of dialogue and protocol formulae, is, literarily speaking, more a dramatist than a historian.

Thus we are led to define better the nature of the work by comparing it to other writings which are related to it by quite evident characteristics.

There is a striking resemblance between the canonical book and the account left to us by Herodotus of the false Smerdis, whose imposture is denounced by Otanis with the aid of his daughter, a concubine of the king, and is punished by the massacre of the tribe of the Magians. The third Book of Machabees presents in a Jewish background an account that seems to copy Esther : Ptolemy Philopator, expelled from the Temple by the Jewish authorities, decrees that the Jews be thrown to elephants. His joyous banquets make him forget the order. He then recalls it, but it is the elephant drivers whom the elephants trample. Where upon the prince reverses the order. He praises the loyalty of the Jews and permits them to feast at his expense and to massacre the apostate brethren. It is remarkable that the accounts of Herodotus and the the third Book of Machabees both end, as does Esther, with the institution of a commemorative feast.

Even in the Bible, situations similar to the story of Esther are not lacking. It will suffice to recall the instance of Joseph, calumniated and imprisoned for his fidelity to virtue, then freed and made minister of the kingdom in which the sons of Jacob are to settle; of Judith, who saves the besieged people of Bethulia; of Daniel, Esdras and Nehemias, exemplary Jews, who for the good of their compatriots gain the favor of foreign princes.

In sum, the Book of Esther is another witness in favor of Providence, which insures the triumph of the Jews over the gentiles, a triumph which in their own way the Wisdom writers, especially that of Wisdom, have put in bold relief (cf. Wis 10—12).

So many indications permit the placing of Esther in the category of midrash of the haggadic type, [2] without denying its authentic historical ring, a quality in which it excels. [3]

---

[2] On *midrash* and *haggadah,* see pp. 173-175 (French ed.)

[3] Cf. A. ROBERT, *Guide to the Bible,* I (New York : Desclée, 1960), p. 308.

§ 3. Esther and the Feast of Purim

The Book of Esther ends in a passage that seems to attach the events described with the institution of the feast of Purim (9, 20-32; cf. 3, 7). What is to be made of this allusion?

It is certain that the Jews had a feast called Purim (lots) (Josephus, *Ant.*, XI, 6, 13). Its Babylonian name justifies considering it of Persian or Babylonian origin; beyond that, its origin is difficult to trace. [4] A close similarity has been noticed between Mardochai and Marduk, Esther and Ishtar. At the beginning of the year lots (purim) were cast and the victory of Marduk was celebrated. A number of Babylonian poems also celebrated the exaltation of Ishtar. Here is an instance of Jews and Babylonians joining their traditions against a common enemy. Keeping in mind the literary genre of the work, one does not have, however, the right to conclude solely upon Est 9, 20-32 and 3, 7 that the Jews in Persia instituted their feast in memory of their deliverance. The second Book of Machabees (15, 36) mentions a feast commemorating the liberation of the Jews from Persia, known in this period under the name " Day of Mardochai. " The passage which we read in Est 9, 20-32 seems to be a complicated addition (an overburdened text) destined to give meaning to the feast, whose quite vulgar and in any case clearly pagan attraction was displeasing, by relating it to the story of Esther which was read on the occasion. It was doubtless following this addition that the mention of " Purim " was added in 3, 7.

The matter can be thus summarized :

1) The Jews had a feast of pagan character, of Babylonian origin, analogous to the feasts which were celebrated nearly everywhere at the beginning of spring (Adar : end of February—beginning of March).

---

[4] The feast of *parwardîgân* comes to mind, *pordigan*, *phourdigân* in modern Persian; cf. the reading of Lucian : φρουραια. It is a feast of the dead, which occupied the last five days of the year (intercalary). Thus is explained the absence of the name of Yahweh in the Hebrew text of Esther. But would the Jews have accepted a feast in honor of the dead? Meissner appealed to the *Sacées*, a popular feast akin to the Bacchanalia and Saturnalia : during these feasts social conditions were over-turned with pleasure. Thus Aman and Vasthi would be dethroned by Mardochai and Esther, the first couple representing the gods of winter, and the second the gods of spring. But the *Sacées*, according to Strabo, were celebrated in the month of July, and it is improbable that the Jews were inspired by a mythological feast. Other historians have thought of the new year : Persian *(neurouz)* or Babylonian *(zagmuk)*. In the first hypothesis, the Purim would designate the gifts; in the second the lots. It seems that the origin of the Jewish feast is to be sought in the almost universal mentality which these various feasts reflect, but cannot be identified with any one of them. Cf. A. Bea, " De origine vocis pûr, " *Bi* (1940), pp. 198 f.

2) This feast was put in relation to the triumphal liberation of the Jews from Persia and was also called the day of Mardochai (2 Mc 15, 36).

3) Since it was the custom to read the Book of Esther on this day, it seemed good to justify the feast, which had lost none of its popular origin, under the name which had designated it from the beginning. The Book of Esther then received the appropriate additions.

4) Flavius Josephus is witness to the existence in the sacred calendar of Judaism of the feast of Purim which commemorates the deliverance of the Jews by Esther.

§ 4. Date and Author

The Hebrew text of the Book of Esther cannot be dated later than B.C. 114, when it was introduced into Egypt (cf. Greek Est 11, 3). Perhaps it existed before 160, because at that date, when the feast of Nicanor began to celebrated, the day of Mardochai was already known (2 Mc 15, 36). Nevertheless the commemorative feast could have preceded the editing of the work. The mentality revealed by the work, at once vengeful and triumphant, leads one to imagine an age in which the Jews, having come through a difficult period, allow themselves to hope for the reconquest of their national autonomy. Wherefore, the period which followed the crisis of the Machabean era would be quite apt. In our opinion, the end of the Persian period would be much less apt. It is nevertheless possible that the Book develops a traditional account, of popular origin, which dates back to the Persian period.

§ 5. Canonicity

The Hebrew book had a difficult time entering the Jewish canon. It has not yet been discovered at Qumran. The only allusion, and that indirect and disputable, made of it would be 2 Mc 15, 36. At the synod of Jamnia its admission was still in dispute. It was admitted only during the 2nd century. Probably the principal reason for this hesitation was that it was read on the profane feast of Purim.

The early Christians used the Greek Bible. They found the Book of Esther there and accepted it just as it was. Nevertheless, neither Christ nor the authors of the New Testament cited it. Moreover, Melito of Sardis (171) and St. Athanasius (370) would have excluded it from the canon, and Amphilocus (360) as well as St. Gregory Nazianzen (390) make reservations in the matter. It is also known that St. Jerome, who accepted it, rejected from his Latin translation the fragments which are read only in the Greek. Perhaps he thus wanted to underline the doubt which hangs over the Hebrew origin of these sections. He was unable to find them in any Hebrew manuscript or witness.

These hesitations and shadows notwithstanding, the canonicity of the work is well attested in Church documents well before the Council of Trent's definition (1546).

DANIEL

BIBLIOGRAPHY

Introductions, translations, commentaries, pp. 1 f. (P. J. DE MENASCE, BJ*; L. DENNEFELD, BPC*; J. GÖTTSBERGER, HSAT*; J. A. MONTGOMERY, ICC; S. DRIVER, CBSC...).

R. H. CHARLES, A Critical and Exegetical Commentary on the Book of Daniel (Oxford, 1929).

M. GRUENTHANER, " The Seventy Weeks, " CBQ, 1 (1939), pp. 44-54; " The Four Empires of Daniel, " CBQ, 8 (1946), pp. 72-82; " The Last King of Babylon, " CBQ, 11 (1949), pp. 406-427.

H. L. GINSBERG, Studies in Daniel (New York, 1948).

C. LATTEY, The Book of Daniel* (Dublin, 1948).

H. CAZELLES, " Daniel, " Catholicisme, III (Paris, 1950), pp. 447-453.

J. STEINMANN, Daniel* (Paris, 1951).

A. BENTZEN, Das Buch Daniel, 2 (Tübingen, 1952).

S. B. FROST, Old Testament Apocalyptic (London, 1952).

G. RINALDI, Daniele*³ (Turin, 1952).

E. W. HEATON, The Book of Daniel (London : SCM, 1955).

A. C. WELCH, Visions of the End : A Study in Daniel and Revelation (London, 1958).

H. H. ROWLEY, Darius the Mede and the Four World Empires in the Book of Daniel² (Cardiff : Univ. of Wales, 1959).

J. MUILENBURG, " The Son of Man in Daniel and the Ethiopic Apocalypse of Enoch, " JBL, 79 (1960), pp. 197-209.

N. PORTEOUS, Daniel, A Commentary (Philadelphia : Westminster, 1965).

D. S. RUSSELL, The Method and Message of Jewish Apocalyptic (Philadelphia : Westminster, 1965).

The Book of Daniel stands among the *Ketubim* in the Hebrew Bible, between Esther and Esdras-Nehemias. In the Greek Bible and in all the other versions it follows the three major Prophets, after Ezechiel. The versions have three sections which are not found in the Hebrew canon : the canticle of the three boys in the furnace (3, 24-90); the story of Susanna (13) and that of Bel and the dragon (14). These three deuterocanonical sections will be treated in the following part. [1] Here we will treat only the protocanonical writing, which is composed in two languages : 1, 1—2, 4a and 8—12 in Hebrew, and 2, 4b—7, 28 in Aramaic. This diversity of language has been attested again by the Qumran manuscripts which predate our era.

§ 1. The Biblical Account

The Book of Daniel has a composite literary structure, but the whole is marked by strong conceptual unity.

Literary diversity is very noticeable between the first six chapters, of a narrative character, and the last six, which pertain more to the prophetic genre. We will have occasion to go into greater detail concerning this diversity.

I. THE NARRATIVE SECTION

The author presents his hero, a Judean of noble birth, deported in 597 and introduced, with three other young Jews, into the court of Nabuchodonosor. There they all remain faithful to Yahweh (1).

The fame of Daniel grows in the measure that the young captive reveals a form of wisdom superior to that of the Chaldean Wise Men. The interpretation of a dream of Nabuchodonosor brings him high honors (2).

Meanwhile his companions are thrown into the fire for having refused to participate in an idolatrous act. Protected by Yahweh, they are heaped with favors by the king (3, 1-23. 91-97).

The superiority of the true God manifests itself again when Daniel interprets a second dream of Nabuchodonosor. The king will be reduced to the condition of an animal. And that is what happened (3, 98—4, 34).

Later the Prophet explains to Baltassar, during a banquet, the enigmatic words which the invasion of the Persians in Babylonia was, that very night, to verify (5).

Finally, Daniel is thrown into the lions' den, but encounters no harm there. Yahweh sustains him always.

II. THE PROPHETIC SECTION

Now it is Daniel who recounts his visions, which are four in number.

The first presents four great beasts who ascend from the sea : a winged lion, a devouring bear, a leopard with four heads and the wings

---

[1] Cf. pp. 552 f.

of a bird, and the fourth, undetermined, furnished with ten horns, to which is added an eleventh which uproots three of the horns and reveals the eyes of a man. An Ancient of days appears looking like a king. The fourth beast is put to death and the other three reduced to impotence. Some sort of son of man appears; to him the Ancient hands over eternal domination. At his request, Daniel receives the interpretation of the vision (7).

The second vision depicts a ram and a billy goat. The ram has two unequal horns and pushes successively toward the west, north, and south. The goat overthrows the ram, then grows, while his one horn is broken to make way for four horns of which one grows at the expense of the south, of the west, and of the glorious country (Palestine). It goes so far as to attack God, but after two thousand three hundred evenings and mornings the iniquity ends. The angel Gabriel explains to Daniel the meaning of the vision (8).

The third vision, that of the seventy weeks of years, is one of the most famous of the Old Testament. [2] It comprises, in a very tortuous system of computation, a whole series of epochs and events whose end, just as the beginning, has produced various interpretations. In any case, the oracle announces the coming of the kingdom of God (9).

There remains the fourth vision, whose clarity does not leave room to doubt that it views the age of the Seleucids and Ptolemies. Prepared by chapter 10, it projects an immense history film which begins with the undertakings of Xerxes I (486-465) against Greece, describes the conflicts after the death of Alexander the Great between the princes of the south (Egypt) and those of the north (Syria), and ends in the reign of Antiochus IV Epiphanes, the persecutor of the Jews who will, in the end, be persecuted by God (11).

In conclusion the Prophet has left us, without giving it perspective, a tableau in which are interwoven, by means of temporal liberation, eschatological assurances (12).

It is not difficult to reduce the two sections to unity. The whole Book is a solemn affirmation of the transcendence of the true God. A ruling idea emerges : Yahweh will always prevail. Persecutors pass away. The kingdom of God is coming. A message of hope, a source of consolation—such is the character which in the end marks and seals the apparently disparate elements of the writings, reducing them to unity.

[2] M. J. LAGRANGE, " Les Prophéties messianiques de Daniel, " *RB* (1930), pp. 179-198; *Le Judaïsme avant Jésus-Christ* (Paris, 1931), pp. 62 ff.

§ 2. Origin of the Work in its Present Form

I. DATA AND DISCUSSION

Until the end of the 19th century, Catholic exegetes generally held that the Book of Daniel was written by its hero who reveals himself a member of the Achaemenian household. At most they allowed certain reservations about some elements which they attributed to a more recent editor.

It seemed—and this was their principal argument—that Jewish tradition, both biblical and profane (1 Mc 2, 59-60; Mt 23, 15; Josephus, *Ant.*, XI, 78, 5), and Christian tradition as well, unanimous in their attestations, imposed this opinion. They attempted to confirm it by pointing out the many references in the work to the Chaldean milieu of the 6th century : the importance of magic, the education of young nobles in the palace, the solemnly dedicated, colossal statues of princes, punishment by fire and lions, the agreement of names (Baltassar, Sidrich, Misach, Abdenago : Dn 1, 7) and of certain descriptions (winged animals : 7, 4. 6; plane of Dura : 3, 1) with cuneiform documents. The bilinguism attested the adaptation the Hebrews made to Aramaic in their land of exile. The obvious unity of the work (parallelism of plan between 1—7 and 8—12), the progress and development of the visions and doctrines, the similarity of expression and style were alleged to establish the conclusion, and permitted some authors to include in the original work even the deuterocanonical parts. They were content to answer the objection of the language of the Greek fragments with the hypothesis of a translation.

Meanwhile the critical approach underlined the uneven probative value of these arguments. The place occupied by the Book of Daniel in the Jewish canon, among the *Ketubim* and not the *Nebiim*, proves that the latter collection was closed when the work was written. The postexilic books, especially Sirach in its enumeration of the glories of Israel (49), make no mention of Daniel. The Persian words call to mind an age later than the conquest of Cyrus, and the Greek words, a date later than the Hellenistic invasion of the Orient. [3] The Hebrew of the book by no means contradicts these conclusions, and the Aramaic is a western dialect, whereas one would expect an eastern dialect if the work had been composed in Babylonia in the 6th century, as Wilson has tried to

---

[3] See the lists drawn up by MONTGOMERY in his commentary, pp. 20-23, and cf. H. H. ROWLEY, *The Aramaic of the Old Testament*, pp. 152-156; SCHAEDER, *Iranische Beitrage* I studies many Persian words.

demonstrate. [4] Besides, the writer knew Babylonian history rather poorly : Baltassar (5, 2) is presented as the son of Nabuchodonosor, but he was the son of Nabonidus. This last would have been a better choice in the context of dreams : he was a diviner of dreams. The historical Gobryas is replaced by a certain Darius the Mede (6 and 9) who is completely ignored by history. [5] But the author is very informed about the Machabean period, about which he gives precise details. Finally, the doctrinal developments in the work—angelology, the resurrection of the body, the last judgment and eternal sanctions—relate too closely to the apocalyptic writings which multiplied starting in the 4th century to place the composition of the work in the 6th century.

II. CURRENT STATE OF THE QUESTION

The debate stimulated reflection which seems today to have reached maturity. It has been rightly observed that the traditional arguments, which are more " recitative " than " doctrinal, " have less to do with the author of the work, at least in its present form, than with the hero on stage or the title given the book. Similar references to Josue, Solomon and Job do not suffice to settle the controversies created by the origin of the books which bear their names. On the other hand, the hypothesis of a literary fiction does not in itself contradict the results of internal criticism; it is merely in conformity with the usage of the time. Contrarily, it is necessary to have recourse to somewhat absolete methods in order to explain away, in the hypothesis of ancient origin, the editorial peculiarities, the historical anomalies concerning Babylonian history, and the quite outstanding details of the Machabean period. Finally, the very doctrinal content of the work dissuades a date earlier than the age of apocalyptic writing. And if the unity of the work is incontestable, it is equally evident that it could just as well have been the work of a recent as an ancient author.

Hence the modifications of the older opinions, inherited from rabbinic Judaism, made by modern criticism. There are so many opinions and variations that it is impossible to give more than a brief summary of them here. Some authors decline to hold that Daniel wrote the whole book, but refuse to date the whole work in the Machabean age. J. A. Montgomery attributes the historical chapters (1—6) to an older author (Daniel or some unknown author), and the prophetic oracles

---

[4] " The Aramaic of Daniel " *Bibl. and Theol. Stud.* (1912), pp. 261-305.

[5] Cf. H. H. ROWLEY, *Darius the Mede and the Four World Empires in the Book of Daniel* (Cardiff, 1935); cf. *RB* (1936), p. 130.

(7—12) to a writer of the age of Antiochus-Epiphanes. Others (Baum-gartner, Hölscher, Haller) block together chapter 7 with the first six chapters and date this part of the work in the 3rd and 4th centuries. Still others (Riessler) make Daniel the author of the prophetic section, but judge the historical passages of a more recent date. Many (Nikel, Göttsberger, Lagrange) prefer not to determine the elements which an author of the 3rd or 2nd century used to compose the work as we know it now, or even (Junker) restrict the additions of the Machabean author to the visions of chapters 10—12. We leave unmentioned the hypotheses which, exploiting the diversity of language and content, chop the book into fragments, content to break the literary continuity from Aramaic to Hebrew and vice versa, without eliminating the internal anomalies (Lods).

In the end, the question is whether some critical principle does not authorize a conclusion which better appreciates the strong unity of the work. The principle is precisely this, that the incontestable unity demands one author. But Daniel cannot be the author of the whole work, as is proved by the sum of arguments presented in favor of a more recent origin; this conclusion especially emerges from the hypotheses which bring the date of more or less important passages down to the 2nd century. Logically then, the entire work in its present form should be attributed to a writer of the Machabean era. [6]

§ 3. Prior Sources

It would still be an exaggeration to conclude that the 2nd century author was not working with some antecedent material. The unity of the whole, which is ideological, does not extenuate the complexities, which are literary.

The passages of the narrative section could have existed separately before being collected. Their content retains traces of a primitive independance (anomalies of dialect between 1, 1-2. 4a, and 2, 4b—6, 29; of date between 1, 1-2 and 2, 1; the excessively changeable attitudes of Nabuchodonosor in 2, 47; 3, 13-19. 95-96; 4, 34; identity of themes of 2 and 4, and of 3 and 6; no mention of Daniel in 3, while his companions are mentioned in 2, 17. 40). In several cases the seams between the episodes are glaring (1, 21; 2, 1; 6, 1. 29); even their absence attests the prior isolation of the elements.

---

[6] Cf. H. H. Rowley, " The Unity of the Book of Daniel, " *The Servant of the Lord and Other Essays* (London, 1952).

The visions of the apocalyptic section stand out in a contextual background that is not always even (change from the third person : 7, 1; 10, 1 to the first person : 7, 28; 8, 2. 5. 27; 9, 2; 12, 3), indication of redactional contribution prolonging the narrative character of 1—6. The two languages likewise create a certain disparity between 7, where besides it is a question of a " dream, " as in 2 and 4, and 8—12 in which " visions " are recounted. Finally, the purely material juxtaposition of chapters 7—12 (lack of literary connection, bare chronological references to the reigns of Baltassar, Darius and Cyrus) heightens still more the impression of a heterogeneous block.

If one continues the analysis, traces of successive editings appear : 2, 43, in relation to 11, 7. 17, seems to be an addition to 2, 41-42 which is centered on the imagery of the dream; the prayers of 2 and 9 too give evidence, by the manner in which they are introduced, of a similar procedure. We could even suppose a stage in which oral traditions preceded written elaborations and the final editing of the book. This hypothesis has now received support from a Qumran manuscript [7] which contains a narration parallel to Daniel 4, but features not Nabuchodonosor but Nabonidus. The point of departure of the work in its present form, then, is to be placed further in the past : the author used a varied material provided by popular oriental traditions.

These views seem on the whole to agree with the works of Bentzen, Rinaldi, Ginsberg, and Cazelles. It is not impossible to conclude from it to a certain chronology of the composition of the work, though this point is still an object of serious discussion among scholars.

§ 4. Identity of the Hero

The identity of the hero is currently under discussion. Is he the same one mentioned by Ezechiel (14, 14. 20; 28, 5), or does the prophet of the Exile refer to a probably legendary character known from the documents of Ras Shamra? The argument drawn from the written form of the name, on which some have founded the distinction of the two characters, does not seem absolutely conclusive, since the name Dan-*i*-el, deprived of its *yod (mater lectionis)*, would be *dnil* in Ugaritic.

It is rather Ezechiel's grouping of Daniel with Noe and Job, two foreigners to the people of Israel, that leads some to believe that the Prophet of the Exile is not refering to a Judean deported to Babylonia.

---

[7] *RB* (1956), pp. 407-415.

In any hypothesis, it is evident that the characters of the canonical book are by no means incompatible with a really existing person. It should especially be noted that Jewish apocalyptic writings employ real personalities, sometimes very ancient ones. This is, alongside the concrete indications of the narration (1, 1. 2; 2, 1; 3, 16; 5, 1; 6, 29), an argument of some weight.

§ 5. Aim and Method of the Narration

Greater caution is called for in judging the historical references in the narrative section. It would seem that the second-century writer used in great measure the midrashic method and composed a haggada. His purpose was to draw up a spiritual commentary on the events of the Machabean period.

The young Jewish prince would occupy in Babylonia a role analogous to that which his descendants occupy during the Syrian persecution. Nabuchodonosor evokes Antiochus, both of whom profaned the Temple of Yahweh (4 Kgs 24, 13-15; 1 Mc 1, 22-24. 57-62). Babylon, just as Seleucid, set himself against Jerusalem, the city of the true God. It was a matter of using this insight and composing a model history, as was that of Achikar in the pagan world, or better yet, that of Tobias in Israel.

Daniel and his companions are scrupulously faithful to the dietary precepts of the Law (Dn 1, 8-16). The three companions of the Prophet refuse to adore the statue of Nabuchodonosor (Dn 3, 12-18). King Darius is not able to overcome the firm resistance of his subject when he decrees that prayers should be directed only to him (Dn 6, 11). Beautiful lessons for the Jews faced with the persecutory decrees of Antiochus!

And here we see that the resistance of the guests of Babylonia makes them capable of contributing by their Wisdom to the manifestation of Yahweh (Dn 1, 17; 2, 46-47; 4, 34; 5, 14-16). Yahweh works wonders to deliver them from the evils they willingly undergo for his Name (3, 49-50; 6, 22). Will this not happen when the persecution of Antiochus will have exhausted God's patience?

Considering the end to be accomplished, what importance does the change of names and situations have? Nabuchodonosor could be substituted for Nabodinus and Darius the Mede for Gobryas. The essential was to apply the ancient traditions in order to illumine, comfort and sustain the Jews persecuted by Antiochus Epiphanes. And that is the accomplishment of the haggadic section.

§ 6. Nature of the Visions

It is possible that even here the author owes a debt to ancient oracles. But he has impressed on these elements an original form in accord with the spirit of his age. The apocalyptic seed sown by the Prophet Ezechiel (Ez 25—32; 37—39) had blossomed. Several poems of the Book of Isaias (Is 13—14; 24—27; 34—35) mark an important step in this development. Certain parts of Enoch, of which fragments have recently been found at Qumran, are generally accepted as contemporary with the Machabean age : the apocalypse of the seventy weeks, the fall of the angels, and the assumption of the hero would be anterior to 165; the book of dreams, slightly posterior (about 161), projects a clear light on the Book of Daniel. It seems that it is in this line that the author of the canonical work should be placed. It was not alien to him to present history under the guise of prophecy, thus giving prophecy unaccustomed qualities, in order to move the reader's mind to eschatological events, of which the fall of the great empires was a preview. This is the purpose of chapters 7 to 12 of the work.

To this end the oracles of the haggadic section serve as a prelude. The interpretation of the dream of Nabuchodonosor is the leitmotiv which the accounts of the great empires develop. So it is that the visions of the four animals, of the ram and the goat, enlarge and specify the prognosis based upon this key oracle. The whole history of the Orient passes in review, summarized in the princes whom the animals symbolize. The symbols disappear in 10—11, to give way to designations whose anonymity is easily unmasked. But what impresses and at the same time guides the reader is the personality who closes the series, the persecutor par excellence, Antiochus Epiphanes. This eminently reveals the author's intention. After having proposed the example of Daniel and his companions to the persecuted Jews, after having emphasized the divine interventions in favor of the deportees, faithful under trial, he applies to the age in which his compatriots are living the examples he has drawn from another age. He places before their eyes the action of Providence which, through the catastrophes of empires, continues to work for the coming of the kingdom of God, protecting His people and assuring their survival. There is no doubt that the Jews of the Machabean era found consolation and comfort when they read these powerful pages. God's work is accomplished in the midst of trials, but its realization is guaranteed. The final vision (12), prophetic and therefore less precise, gives the work a conclusion which forcefully seals its unity.

As for the prophecy of the seventy weeks (9), that is a problem of its own. It is an example of *pesher*, that is, an " actualization " of the prophetic Scriptures according to the midrashic methods. The conclusions of Fr. Lagrange on the substance and purpose of this prophecy are sound [8] : " .... Let us first of all adhere to the meaning, and since it clearly calls for no calculation, let us cease to search for a mathematical indication of the year of the birth or death of Christ in a prophecy which forcefully announces the coming of the kingdom of God. *The events of the age of Antiochus and the Machabees* served as a *certain pledge of it.* " The Messianic interpretation, *in a typical sense,* is today generally accepted; the Jews themselves already interpreted this prophecy of the age of Antiochus. [9] The principal argument in favor of the literal Machabean interpretation is the " *Gesichtsfeld,* " the habitual field of vision of the prophetic section of the Book of Daniel. In all the visions the same general scheme is repeated, and the aim is always the age of Epiphanes. There is no reason to make an exception for chapter 9. A literal Messianic interpretation has nevertheless had some recent defenders. [10] It is to be noted that verse 24 is sometimes considered, even by the defenders of a typical Messianic sense, as Messianic in a literal sense. [11]

§ 7. Religious Meaning of the Work

I. A THEOLOGY OF HISTORY

The Book of Daniel, a haggadic commentary and apocalyptic representation of providential events, is a record whose meaning extends to all ages. Driver rightly noted (*Introd.*, p. 512) that it " traces a religious philosophy of history. " But this high purpose becomes incarnate in the decisive thrust which Messianism receives in these pages, vibrant with certain hope in the final triumph of God. In brief, the message of Daniel resumes and passes on the expectation of ages past and future. It is a point of arrival and of departure.

It is a point of arrival. The teaching of Daniel is situated at the end of a long tradition. By crystallizing the struggle between God and evil in the opposition of the empires to the Chosen People, it concentrates the long series of confrontations which history symbolized or described

---

[8] *RB* (1903), p. 198.

[9] F. CEUPPENS, *De Prophetiis messianicis* (Rome, 1935), pp. 490-521; G. RINALDI, *op. cit.* (Turin, 1947).

[10] R. P. CLOSEN, *VD* (1938), pp. 47-56, 115-125; J. LEVESQUE, *Rev. Apol.* I (1939), pp. 90-94; J. LINDER, *Commentarius in librium Danielis* (Paris, 1939).

[11] Cf. CEUPPENS, *op. cit., ad loc.*

from the beginning (the revolt of Adam, of mankind, of the builders of the tower of Babel) up to the resounding invasions of the potentates of Assyria (Teglath-pilessar III, Salmanasar V, Sennacherib) and of Babylonia (Nabopolassar, Nabuchodonosor). It reechoes the commentary of the Prophets : the pagan nations, even when God uses them to chastise his people, are destined to ruin (Is 10, 5-19. 27c-34; 14, 24-27; Jer 50—51; Is 13—14), while Israel is promised the triumph (Is 10, 20-27ab; 41, 8-20; Ez 36—37). Numerous ideas used by the *nabiim* come up again in the teaching of Daniel : Ezechiel (38, 15-18) and Joel (4, 2. 9-14) envision the last trials of the people of God; the idea of the judgment of God on the nations is common to all the great prophecies (Am 1—2; Is 14, 24-27; So 1—2; Jer 12, 14; 25, 15; Ez 25—32; Jl 4, 1-17); the resurrection of the dead had already been confusedly mentioned in the apocalypse of Isaias (26, 19) and Ezechiel (37, 11-14). Even Daniel's favorite symbols —the great felled tree, lions, leopards, rams, goats— are not without reference to more ancient books (cf. Os 13, 7-8; Is 15, 9; Jer 5, 6; 49, 19; 50, 17; Za 10, 3). And the stone that breaks up the mountain and shatters the statue (Dn 2, 44-45), might it not be that of Isaias (17, 10; 26, 4; 32, 2) and of Deuteronomy (32, 4-15), that is, Yahweh Himself? The author of Daniel collected all these contributions of the past, developed them and put them to use. The resulting synthesis is the work of a highly original writer. And such is the richness condensed in this body of prophetic history, in which the present situation is buttressed by so many former situations, that one does not hesitate to predict what the future holds.

II. MESSIANISM

Thus Messianism takes here a new beginning. For all ages the reading of Daniel suggests the substitution of the empires symbolized by the animals or designated by anonymous expressions by other empires or other forces, heirs of the monsters of chaos as were their predecessors, and who will oppose the kingdom of God and his Anointed One. The struggle between the City of God which is being built, and the City of the demon, which will experience successive dismantlement, will continue from age to age. The Apocalypse of St. John too, patterning its methods upon those of the author of Daniel, will apply the same rule to the conditions of his time. Enlarging even more the perspective, it will present in the framework of a changed symbolism, which is in many ways a debtor to the Book of Daniel, a vision of the trials of the primitive church, especially of the perescution of Nero and Domitian. The apologists of the future will be able in their turn, if not to adopt the method, at least to extract and apply the lesson.   Rather than search in the symbols which clothe past events for concrete images of future situations, they will use the triumphs of God over the powers of evil, in order to strengthen faith, stimulate hope, rekindle charity.   In the meantime they await the realization, after an uneven and tumultous history whose full sense will then be revealed, of the triumphal exaltation of God, the universal kingdom of Christ, the happiness of the elect.   Let us conclude with Fr. Lagrange : " Daniel was the first to envision world history... as the preparation for the reign of God, to join this splendid vision to the hopes of Israel, to carry the plan of God for men to the threshold of eternity. "[12]

Let us add to this general appreciation a very important point. With Daniel, the divine ambassador charged with bringing about the kingdom of God here below takes an entirely new aspect : he is not only the king, son of David; he is referred to under the mysterious title of Son of Man coming upon (or with) the clouds of heaven.   This transcendent Messianism directly prepares the way to the New Testament. A number of exegetes (Procksch, Eichrodt, Feuillet, Jacob) relate this new conception to Ezechiel's vision (chap. 1) by the River Kobar of the divine glory " as a figure of man."   Some bring into play the great developments of the Wisdom writers (Prv 8; Sir 24; Wis 6—9) on divine Wisdom personified.   The further development of the Son of Man tradition (Enoch, New Testament) seems to support this view. [13]

---

[12] *Le Judaïsme avant Jésus-Christ* (Paris, 1931), p. 72.

[13] A. FEUILLET, *Le fils de l'homme de Daniel et la tradition biblique, RB* (1953), pp. 170-202 and 321-346. Cf. in exactly the same sense P. J. DE MENASCE, *Daniel (BJ*, 2 ed.), pp. 21-22; R. LAURENTIN, *Structure et théologie de Luc I-II* (Paris, 1957), pp. 132-133

CHAPTER IX

ESDRAS AND NEHEMIAS

BIBLIOGRAPHY

Introductions, translations, commentaries, pp. 1 f. (A. GELIN, *BJ**;
P. MEDEBIELLE, *PBC**; M. REHM, *EBi**...).

C. C. TORREY, *Ezra Studies* (London, 1910).

A. C. WELCH, *Post-Exilic Judaism* (London, 1935).

A. S. KAPELRUD, *The Question of Authorship in the Ezra Narrative* (1944).

W. RUDOLPH, *Esra und Nehemia samt 3 Esra* (Tübingen, 1949).

H. H. ROWLEY, " The Chronological Order of Ezra and Nehemiah, "
The Servant of the Lord and Other Essays (London : Lutterworth, 1952),
pp. 131-159; " Nehemiah's Mission and Its Background, " *BJRL*, 37
(1954-1955), pp. 528-561; " Sanballat and the Samaritan Temple, "
BJRL, 38 (1955-1956), pp. 166-198.

R. A. BOWMAN, " The Books of Ezra and Nehemiah, " *IB* (1954).

K. GALLING, *Esra-Nehemia* (Göttingen, 1954).

E. BICKERMAN, *From Ezra to the Last of the Maccabees : Foundations of
Post-Biblical Judaism* (1962).

§ 1. The Book

I. DIVISION

In the beginning the Books of Esdras and Nehemias formed a single
unit with the Books of Paralipomenon whose account they continue
(cf. Esd 1, 1-4 and 2 Par 36, 22). In addition, Esdras and Nehemias,
like Paralipomenon, were not divided into two books until a later date.
The Alexandrian version at first respected the unity of the book (cf. Swete,
Rahlfs). It is not known when, nor under what influence, the division
took place. The inscription which opens the Book of Nehemias as we
have it could have been taken for the title of a distinct work. [1] Once the
division had been made, one finds in the Greek translation : Εσδρας α'
(the third Book of Esdras, apocryphal); Εσδρας β' (our first Book of

---

[1] Cf. L. GAUTIER, *Intr. à l'A.T.*, II, p. 380.

Esdras); Εσδρας γ' (our second Book of Esdras or Nehemias). But in most of the editions of the LXX, our two Books, Esdras and Nehemias, continue to form a single unit (Εσδρας β'). The division is in all Latin canons. The Vulgate canonized it, and the Hebrew Bible of Daniel Bomberg (1517) accepted it.

II. CONTENT OF THE BOOK

The general history (pp. 38-47) has already enabled us to date the work of the pioneers of the restoration. The present account, written in the course of the 3rd century, since it is the work of the Chronicler (see p. 503f.), centers on three principal themes : the reconstruction of the Temple (Esd 1—6 except 4, 6-23), the repair of the city (Esd 4, 6-23; Neh 1—13), the juridical establishement of Judaism (Esd 7—10).

After the edict of liberation, several parties of faithful Jews returned to Jerusalem. Leading the first group was Sassabasar, prince of Juda (Esd 1, 8), perhaps of royal blood (1 Par 3, 18, Greek), who had the rank of *peha* (governor, high commissioner : Esd 1—2). Nevertheless it falls to Zorobabel, of the Davidic line (Esd 3, 2. 8 : cf. Ag 2, 23) to restore the altar of sacrifice and to begin reconstruction of the Temple— which work was soon stopped by the Samaritans (Esd 3, 1-4; 5). [2]

After the reigns of Cyrus and Cambyses, given the favorable political situation, the rebuilders went back to work, encouraged by Aggeus (cf. Ag 1, 1-2. 10) and Zacharias (cf. Za 1, 16; 4, 8-10). The work, again hindered, this time by the Persian authorities, was at last completed after the authorities had permitted it. The repatriates celebrated the Passover in the rebuilt Temple in the 6th year of Darius (Esd 5, 1—6, 22).

Then the spiritual community begins to live again. Esdras, with a mandate from Artaxerxes in the 7th year of his reign, regulates cult and surpresses mixed marriages (Esd 7—10).

---

[2] We accept the distinction of Sassabasar and Zorobabel. Comparison of Esd 1, 8 (Sassabasar, prince of Juda) with Esd 3, 2. 8 (Zorobabel, son of Salatiel, therefore grandson of Joachin) is no obstacle to this distinction, considering 1 Par 3, 18 *Greek*, where Sassabasar is listed as *son* of Joachin. The comparison between Esd 1, 5-11 and Esd 2, 2 (cf. Neh 7, 7) would prove that Sassabasar is Zorobabel only if the caravan of 2, 1 ff., which is certainly prior to the reconstruction of the Temple (cf. 2, 70), must be identified with that of 1, 5 ff. Finally, the doubt which rests on the authenticity of the name of Zorobabel in 3, 2. 8 prohibits a valid comparison of these texts with Esd 5, 16 in order to prove the identification of the two persons. The text of Za 4, 9 is not in itself definitive, because Zorobabel certainly assumed the function of builder very early. All things considered, the distinction of names corresponds to that of the persons, and the attempts to impose them on one and the same subject lose all practical interest.

In the 20th year of Artaxerxes, Nehemias arrives in Jerusalem. He oversees the reconstruction of the walls, impeded until then by Samaritan intrigues (Esd 4, 6-23), works to bring about social peace, decrees security measures, and prepares the way for peaceful coexistence (Neh 1, 1—7, 73a).

We then find Esdras, assisted by Nehemias (cf. Neh 8, 9), proceeding to the reading of the Law, to the feast of Tabernacles and an expiatory ceremony which seals community participation (Neh 7, 73b—10, 40).

Then coexistence is put into effect, followed by the dedication of the wall, and various lists (Neh 11, 1—12, 47).

The *peha*, who had returned to Babylonia in the 32nd year of Artaxerxes, comes back to Judea with imperial authorization and an edict against crying abuses (Neh 13).

§ 2. Chronological Reconstruction

The biblical account presents striking anomalies. A more satisfactory chronological order can be conjectured by a critical examination of the sources and their use. [3]

I. SOURCES

The memoirs of Esdras and Nehemias form the main outline of the work.

The memoir of Esdras is easy to recognize in the obviously related chronological indications : Esd 7, 9 (1st day of 1st month), 8, 31 (12th day of same month), 7, 8-9 (1st day of 5th month), Neh 7, 73b—8, 18 (the first 8 days of 7th month), Esd 10, 9 (20th day of 9th month), 10, 16-17 (from 1st day of 10th month to 1st day of 1st month). Afterwards Esdras remains in Jerusalem about a year. The substance of his report to the Persian authorities can be drawn from Esd 7, 1—10, 44 and Neh 7, 73b—9, 37.

The memoir of Nehemias comprises the first seven chapters of the book, except for two documents inserted there : the one contemporary (3, 1-32) which preserves, perhaps in fictional dress, the names of the rebuilders; the other (7, 6-73a), more ancient, enumerates the first repatriates. To this unit must be added Neh 13, 1-31, the account of the *peha*'s second term, and undoubtedly 10, the last verses of which (31-40) are connected with 13 : Nehemias figures at the head of the signers

---

[3] Cf. A. GELIN, *Esdras-Néhémie*, pp. 13-22 and 49-50.

of the community pact. Some fragments at the end of the book also belong to it (Neh 11, 1-2. 20. 25a; 12, 27a. 30-32. 37-40. 43), whereas others (Neh 11, 21-24. 25b-35; 12, 1-9. 10-11. 12-26) must have been added later.

The Aramaic source is also very obvious. It provides the account of the Samaritan opposition to the reconstruction of the wall (Esd 4, 6-23) and of the Temple (Esd 5, 1—6, 18). Within this document are inserted fragments of official Persian documents (Esd 4, 9-10. 11b-16. 17b-22; 5, 7b-17; 6, 2b-12).

A Hebrew source for the first chapters of Esdras (Esd 1, 1-4; 5) could perhaps be admitted. Certain details (Esd 1, 2-4. 8-11) seem to require it.

II. Use of documents

The Chronicler dismembered the memoir of Esdras by inserting the section which should follow Esd 8, 36 (reading of the Law, feast of Tabernacles, confession of sins) in the framework of the Book of Nehemias (Neh 7, 73b—9, 37). He is generally unobtrusive in his presentation, except perhaps in rearranging the text when the account is in the third person. He probably composed the prologue (Esd 7, 1-11). It is less certain whether he wrote the very biblical-sounding decree of Artaxerxes.

If one keeps in mind that it contains variously dated documents, it results that the memoir of Nehemias has not undergone major editorial retouches. The intense emotional accent that distinguishes it militates against any suspicion of falsification. If the hand of the Chronicler is apparent in 12, 33-36. 41-42, it is precisely because these verses clash with the whole of the account.

The Aramaic source was obviously reproduced after the events. Opposition against the reconstruction of the walls (Esd 4, 6-23) is evidently subsequent to the reconstruction of the Temple : the names of the kings cited sufficiently demonstrate it. There is also a certain clumsiness in the seam between Esd 4, 23 and 5, 1 : verse 24 of chapter 4 is redactional.

As for the Hebrew source, it is best to say that if it existed, the Chronicler has absorbed it in his account. There will always be some difficulty in interpreting correctly Esd 3, 2-8 and 4, 1-3 : it seems that Zorobabel was substituted for Sassabasar, and the irritation of the Samaritans is expressed prematurely (compare 3, 8 with 5, 2 on the one hand, and 4, 1-3 with 5, 3 on the other). Was not his intention perhaps to excuse the inertia of the repatriates which Aggeus quite harshly reproves (Ag 1, 14-15)?

III. CHRONOLOGICAL ORDER

The problem

After the various documents have been identified, a chronological reconstruction of the events would be relatively easy, if there were no doubt about the relative dating of the activities of Esdras and Nehemias.

The problem has generally been reduced to these two postulates : Nehemias supposes Esdras *or* Esdras supposes Nehemias. If Esdras preceded Nehemias, the first stay of the scribe at Jerusalem would have to be dated in the 7th year of Artaxerxes I (464-424) and therefore in 458, and the first stay of Nehemias in the 20th year of the same Artaxerxes, that is, in 445. If Nehemias preceded Esdras, the latter could have come to Jerusalem only in the 7th year of Artaxerxes II (405-359), that is in 398. [4]

The older commentators held the first opinion, and it is still held by many today, notably Eissfeldt, Höpfl-Miller, de Vaux, [5] Fernandez. The second opinion gathers around Van Hoonacker the majority of modern exegetes, among others Touzard, Mowinckel, Rowley, [6] Snaith, [7] Cazelles. There are worthwhile arguments on both sides : appeals to the necessary priority of the legal and cultic restoration of Esdras, or to the necessary priority of the political and social activity of Nehemias; insistence upon certain chronological details favorable to one or the other position. [8]

---

[4] We pass over the abandoned hypotheses of KAULEN, HOBERG and LAGRANGE (1894). This last adopted the positions of VAN HOONACKER, which were treated at length in *RB* (1890), 151 ff., 317 ff.; (1923), 481 ff.; (1924), 23 ff.

[5] Art. *Israël* in *SDB*, IV, cols. 764-769.

[6] *The Chronological Order of Esdras and Nehemias*. Cf. *The Servant of the Lord* (London, 1952), pp. 131-159.

[7] " The Date of Ezra's Arrival in Jerusalem, " *ZAW* (1951), pp. 53-65.

[8] In favor of the Esdras-Nehemias hypothesis are : the present order in the Bible; the existence at the time of Nehemias of cultic material, product of the mission of Esdras (Esd 7, 14-22); the shock of the Scribe in encountering mixed marriages (9—10), difficult to explain if he had already collaborated with Nehemias to root out this blight (Neh 10, 31); and especially the preparatory character of the spiritual work of Esdras with respect to the more politico-social activity of Nehemias.

In favor of the Nehemias-Esdras sequence are : the contemporaneity of Esdras and Johanan, high priest in 411-408 (Elephantine Doc., Pap. Cowley, 30) and son (Esd 10, 6) or rather grandson (Neh 12, 10-12) of Eliasib, himself high priest and contemporary of Nehemias (Neh 3, 1; 13, 4); the allusion of Esdras to the work of Nehemias (Esd 9, 9), while the memoir of Nehemias makes no mention of Esdras; the rather tolerant attitude of the *peha* toward mixed marriages, hardly conceivable if Esdras had already taken his draconian measures (compare Esd 9—10 and Neh 6, 18; 10, 31; 13, 23-27); the situation at Jerusalem when Esdras arrived (Esd 8, 29; 10, 5), a consequence of the coexistence policy of Nehemias (Neh 11, 1—2); the

A compromise hypothesis

We cannot enter into the maze of the controversy. Faced with the difficulty of making a positive choice, we lean toward the Esdras-Nehemias hypothesis, observing that the Nehemias-Esdras sequence involves two Artaxerxes, while Paralipomenon seems to warrant only one.

But we are also tempted to accept a compromise solution which, despite the objections that it can arouse, has at least the advantage of breaking the dilemma : Nehemias supposes Esdras *or* Esdras supposes Nehemias. It is sufficient to place the mission of Esdras between the two missions of Nehemias. We would then read the 27th year (Wellhausen, Procksch) or the 37th year (Bertholet, Albright, Gelin, Rudolph) of King Artaxerxes I in Esd 7, 8, that is, either 438 or 428. The choice of the 27th year would have the advantage of explaining the presence of Esdras alongside Nehemias at the time of the solemn promulgation of the Law (Neh 7, 73b—8, 18; cf. 8, 9), and why the report of Esdras was dislocated, since the activity of the scribe was combined with that of the *peha*. Thus we would answer the double demand : Esdras *and* Nehemias suppose one another.

In this hypothesis, the order of events would be the following :

Between 538 and 520 several caravans of repatriates arrived in Jerusalem, first of all those led by Sassabasar. He sets up the altar of holocaust and lays the foundations of the Temple (Esd 1, 1—3, 13).

From 520 to 515 the work of reconstruction, encouraged by Aggeus and Zacharias (Esd 5, 1; cf. Ag 1—2; Za 2, 5-17), is brought to conclusion by Zorobabel. The Temple is consecrated and the Passover is celebrated in it (Esd 5, 1—6, 22).

Between 515 and 445 the effective Samaritan opposition to the restoration of the walls took place (under Xerxes I, 486-465, and Artaxerxes I, 464-424 : Esd 4, 6-23).

In the 20th year of Artaxerxes (445), Nehemias begins his first mission. The walls are rebuilt, arrangements for coexistence are made, the work finished, and the dedication of the walls celebrated (Neh 1, 1—4, 17; 6, 1—7, 73a; 11, 1-20. 25a; 12, 27-32. 37-40. 43). The material order is reestablished.

In the 27th year of Artaxerxes (438), Esdras organizes the spiritual leadership of the community (Esd 7, 1—8, 36). He lectures on the Law

absence of all the families which returned with Esdras (Esd 8, 1-20) from the list of Neh 3; the almost withdrawn role of Esdras under Nehemias' rule, hardly reconciliable with the high offices he would already have filled (cf. Neh 8, 2. 4; 12, 35). Cf. V. PAVLOVSKY, " Die Chronologie der Tätigkeit Esdras. Versuch einer neuen Lösung, " *Bi* (1957), pp. 257-305; 428-456.

(Neh 7, 73b—8, 12), presides over the feast of Tabernacles (Neh 8, 13-18), decides to stamp out mixed marriages (Esd 9—10), and stirs his compatriots to just repentance (Neh 9, 1-2).

In the 32nd year of Artaxerxes (433), Nehemias returns to Susa after twelve years of rule (Neh 5, 14). He nevertheless fulfills a second mission in Judea before the death of Artaxerxes (424). In the course of his second stay, the *peha* has to take measures against abuses, in the tradition of Esdras, in order to defend the legal and cultic code of the community (Neh 13, 4-31). It is in this situation that he submits the document of renewal of the covenant to the leaders, levites, and priests for ratification (Neh 10).

Let it be clearly understood that we are only presenting a hypothesis. One of the other solutions proposed by authorities in the field, equally hypothetical, might be preferred. If the most common is chosen (Nehemias-Esdras), it will be easy to arrange the events accordingly and put in more striking relief the mission of Esdras, who came to Judea in 398, in the 7th year of Artaxerxes II. [9]

§ 3. Historicity

It is difficult to underestimate the historical value of these books. The Chronicler's sources are certainly trustworthy, and his handling of them does not affect the substance of their content. Besides, his explicit or implicit references to Oriental history leave the best of impressions. The conciliatory measures of the Achaemenids in favor of the Jerusalem community conform to their customary dispositions for their subject provinces. [10] And it is only right to point out the exactness of many details of the work : the administrative system of the Persian Stat eis correctly outlined, with precise notations on the relations of governors among themselves and with the great King (Esd 4, 7-23; 5, 3-17; 6, 1-13). The Samaritan opposition is completely in conformity with the ingrained anti-Judean mentality of the Northern Kingdom, aggravated by syncretism caused by the contributions of the Mesopotamean deportees (4 Kgs 17, 24), which hardens and becomes the schismatic Judaism of Garizim. And the restoration conforms to past prophecies, at the same time that it agrees remarkably with the contemporary ones (Ag 1—2; Za 1—8 and also Mal 1, 6-10; 2, 1-24). The grand historico-legislative digest, undoubtedly composed in Babylonia, does not more than orches-

---

[9] Cf. CAZELLES, " La mission d'Esdras, " *VT* (1954), pp. 113-140.

[10] R. DE VAUX, " Les décrets de Cyrus et de Darius sur la reconstruction du Temple, " *RB* (1937), pp. 29-57.

trate the statements of the Chronicler. How else explain the reaction of the Hasidim and the Machabean revolt, if the repatriates, spiritual sons of Ezechiel, had not put into practice the burning impulse of the Prophet of the Exile?

Still it is right to observe that the Chronicler reveals some of his favorite themes, especially his attachment to the Davidic monarchy, which is apparent in his mention of *Judean* and *Benjaminite* repatriates (Esd 1, 5; 4, 1; Neh 11, 4), and the importance he attaches to " Davidic " institutions : cultic rites, role of the priests, function of the levites (Neh 12, 44-47).

§ 4. Religious Meaning

The restoration appears as a resumption of the salvific will of God. It is a new step in progress toward Christ, after those of the promise, the alliance, the Babylonian captivity. But this stage has particular characteristics which must be discussed.

The almost exclusively religious aspect of the community stands out. One could have believed in a restoration of the terrestrial kingdom of David, the coming of the Messianic prince, the establishment of the universal reign of Yahweh (Ag 2, 4-9; Za 6, 10-17; cf. Is 60—62). It was soon necessary to dispel all illusion. Neither Zorobabel, though a descendant of David (Esd 3, 2) and acclaimed by Aggeus (Ag 2, 23), nor even less Nehemias, not of the Davidic line, will reestablish the royalty. Both fervent Yahwists devoted to the great work of restoration give an example of perfect loyalty to Persian authorities. These latter, in spite of some liberal measures (Esd 1, 7-10; 6, 4b-5. 8-10; 7, 13-26; Neh 2, 4-9), gave evidence of a certain harshness in their administration (Esd 4, 6-23; 5, 3-5), especially in the matter of taxes (Neh 5, 4. 15). Political autonomy could no longer be hoped for. So the repatriates retreat into themselves, around the Temple, in the shadow of the walls. The Law, enriched, meditated and deepened, and recognized besides by Babylon as the law of the land, became the object of their contemplation. Little by little it weaves a net of observances around them. The Jewish community becomes more oriented toward its specific excellence, Yahwism, than toward the reconquest of civil independence.

A marked isolationist tendency results. " Judaism, " the product of restoration, is on the road to juridicism. It became a protective barrier, but at the same time a wall of separation from the Gentiles. And in this way did it not perhaps descend to the esoteric, rather than opening the door that leads to the kingdom of God?

Not at all. The prophets sustain Messianic hope. In their eyes it appears with ever greater radiance. Undoubtedly the reign of God appears to them centered on the holy city, colored by Judaism. Still they celebrate the conversion of the pagans (Is 56, 1-8). Religious universalism is constantly affirmed (Is 66, 18-21; 24, 18-23; 25, 6-10; Mal 1, 10-14; Jl 3, 1-4). It inspires the songs which celebrate the nations streaming to the holy rites (Ps 95 [96], 7-8; 97 [98], 4-6). In truth, a missionary spirit animates the best sons of Israel.

But is it not precisely from the hardening of their religious institutions, from their zeal for the Law and their interest in deepening it by making it interior, that the subjects of Zorobabel, of Nehemias [11] and Esdras draw the strength to respond, despite contradictions of the time, to the urging of the *nabiim?* No doubt mediocre souls will shut themselves up in egoism and will blame their harsh situation on God (Mal 2, 17). Some preexilic disorders will reappear : especially social inequalities with the excesses that follow from either side (Neh 5; Za 7, 8-12; 8, 16-17). The wound of mixed marriages will not soon be closed (Mal 2, 10-16), and cultic frauds will be favored by the poverty of the numerous offerers (Mal 1, 8. 12-14). Nevertheless, some noble Israelites refine their knowledge of the divine. In the measure that it becomes more spiritual, their souls come nearer to God. The Anawim Psalms ring with touching pleas, which reveal their authors' familiarity with Yahweh (Ps 114-115 [116], 119 [120], 122 [123], 123 [124], 129 [130], 130 [131], etc...). Others exalt God, the benefactor of His People, faithful to His covenant, accepting the thankful homage of the residents of Jerusalem (Ps 110 [111], 111 [112], 134 [135], 135 [136]).

When seen in relation with this comforting evidence, the institutions which were born during the Exile grew firm : synagogues in which the Law and the Prophets are read, a corps of scribes faithful to the traditions of Ezechiel and Esdras, the council of the Sanhedrin, which was to assume later an imposing juridical form. [12]

We can at least suppose that it is in this spiritual ascent that the elite of the community progressed, until the terrible crisis that shook it to its foundations, the crisis of Hellenism after Alexander the Great's conquest of the Orient. The Book of Nehemias closes rather abruptly : perhaps it had a sequel which has not come down to us.

---

[11] J. Coste, " Portrait de Néhémie, " *Bible et Vie chrétienne* (1953), pp. 44-56.

[12] J. Touzard, " L'âme juive au temps des Perses, " *RB* (1916), pp. 299-341; (1917), pp. 54-137 and 451-488; (1918), pp. 336-402; (1919), pp. 5-88; (1920), pp. 5-42; (1923), pp. 59-79.

THE BOOKS OF PARALIPOMENON OR THE CHRONICLES

BIBLIOGRAPHY

Introductions, translations, commentaries, p. 1 f. (L. MARCHAL, BPC*; H. CAZELLES, BJ*; J. GÖTTSBERGER, HSAT*...).

G. VON RAD, Das Geschichtsbild des chronistischen Werkes (Stuttgart, 1930).

A. C. WELCH, The Work of the Chronicler, its Purpose and Date (Oxford, 1939).

A. NOORTZIJ, " Les intentions du chroniste, " RB (1940), pp. 161-168.

A. BEA, " Neuere Arbeiten zum Problem der Chronikbücher, Bi (1941), pp. 46-58.

A. M. BRUNET, " Le Chroniste et ses sources, " RB (1953), pp. 481-508; (1954), pp. 349-386.

W. A. L. ELMSIE, " The First and Second Books of Chronicles, " IB (1954).

K. GALLING, Die Bücher der Chronik (Göttingen, 1954).

W. RUDOLPH, " Problems of the Books of Chronicles, " VT, 4 (1954), pp. 401-405; Chronikbücher (Tübingen, 1955).

D. N. FREEDMAN, " The Chronicler's Purpose, " CBQ, 23 (1961), pp. 436-442.

W. F. ALBRIGHT, " The Date and Personality of the Chronicler, " JBL, 82 (1963), pp. 369-381.

The Books called Chronicles are presented in the Hebrew Bible under the title " Dibrey hayyamim, " that is, the events or acts of the days (journal), or perhaps of the years (annals). In fact their content is no way measured by days or years. Hence, the name " Chronicon totius divinae historiae " given them by St. Jerome, fits better this collection of accounts, if not its literary tendency.

The title " Chronicles " was for a long time overshadowed by that of παραλειπόμενων (LXX), Paralipomenon, usually used by the Fathers in the sense of " things left out " (by the earlier historical books), rather than in the sense of " things handed down, " defended by some modern authors.

In the beginning our Books of Chronicles composed one volume. The division dates from the Alexandrian translation. Later versions propagated it. Since 1448, this division has been in use in Hebrew manuscripts. The Bible of Bomberg canonized it (1517).

It is moreover certain that the Books of Esdras and Nehemias are a sequel to the Chronicles. To recognize this it is sufficient to compare 2 Par 36 and Esd 1, 1-4. Similiarities of vocabulary, style, and mentality likewise indicate unity of authorship.

§ 1. General View of the Work

Taking this last remark into consideration, the work of the Chronicler seems to be the most important part of a history, which, beginning with the " Origins, " took the reader to the end of, or perhaps beyond, the Persian age. Reduced to the dimensions of the two books of Chronicles this history covers the time from Creation to the beginning of the Exile. Nevertheless, the long period from Adam to David is represented principally by genealogies (1 Par 1—9), whereas that from David to the Exile contains more or less important facts about the Davidic kings (1 Par 10—29 : David; 2 Par 1—9 : Solomon; 10—36 : kings of Juda).

The very presence of genealogies at the beginning of the book is significant. It is well known that Israelite mentality, in conformity with primitive Semitic law, attributed a fundamental value to the group (family, clan, tribe). Responsibility, considered them as collective, obliged the group to keep the genealogical record up to date. And if it is true that the Chronicler is sympathetic to the universalist current, it is just as important to remember that the reform of Esdras and Nehemias had accidentally favored an isolationist tendency. Judaism took on this aspect for a time; it felt it necessary to exhibit Israelite ascendancy.

§ 2. The Chronicler's Sources

I. HISTORICAL SOURCES

The work is basically a repetition, in an anthological form, of ancient writings augmented by oral traditions.

The author uses first of all older writings, of which he often reproduces the text, with or without appreciable modifications. Thus it is possible to indicate among the sources he had before him :

1) *Inspired writings*. In the section 1 Par 1—9, the genealogies are taken from *Genesis, Numbers, Exodus, Josue, Ruth....* From 1, 10 to the end, entire passages come from *Samuel* and *Kings* (1 Sm 31— 4 Kgs 24). We have here an extensive reuse of past material, which corresponds well to the method of the age (cf. the relations between *Deuteronomy* and the *Book of the Covenant;* the first prophecies of Jeremias and Osee), and especially to its underlying mentality (the cult of Scripture —living meditation of the Scripture sustained itself and provided a principle for interpreting events). Consequently, the Chronicler did not need to cite sources; his readers could not fail to recognize them.

2) *Profane sources*. Here, on the contrary, the references [1] are explicit. They are inserted sometimes in the body, but more frequently at the end, of the passages.

Some of those sources belong to a collection of *historical writings :* the Book of the Kings of Israel and Juda (2 Par 27, 7; 35, 27; 36, 8 etc.); the Book of the Kings of Juda and Israel (2 Par 16, 11; 25, 26; 32, 32 etc.); the Book of the Kings of Israel (1 Par 9, 1; 2 Par 20, 34); Acts of the Kings of Israel (2 Par 33, 18); midrash on the Book of Kings (2 Par 24, 27). The first four titles are probably the same book. And the midrash is possibly not a distinct work; the literary genre is similar throughout. Thus the Chronicler would have had before him a vast compilation of diverse documents, which scarcely formed a unit. Besides, it is impossible to determine whether these documents are parallel to, or identical with, those used by the Books of Kings, or whether they have been reworked after the pattern of the latter, and whether, and in what measure, the Chronicler depends more or less directly on the sources of the Books of Kings or on the Books themselves.

II. OTHER SOURCES

Other non-canonical sources are attributed to known persons : Samuel the Seer (1 Par 29, 29); Nathan the Prophet (*ibid.* and 2 Par 9, 29); Gad the Seer (1 Par 29, 29); Iddo the Seer (2 Par 9, 29; 12, 15); Semeias the Prophet (2 Par 12, 15); Jehu the son of Hanani (2 Par 20, 34); Hozai (perhaps *hôzim*, the seers, or *hôzayw, his* seers [of Manasses] : 2 Par 33, 19); midrash of Iddo the Prophet (2 Par 13, 22); the Vision of Isaias (2 Par 32, 32); Ahias the Silonite (2 Par 9, 29); the relation of the Acts of Ozias written by the Prophet Isaias (2 Par 26, 22).

---

[1] E. PODECHARD, " Les références du Chroniqueur, " *RB* (1915), pp. 236-247.

By reason of the quality of the personages cited, these sources are called *prophetic*. It will be noted that they cover periods of history more or less remote (10th to 8th centuries). It is possible that these writings at one time made up a single collection, an anthology of prophetic relations (cf. the reading *hôzim*, suggested by the LXX in 2 Par 33, 19). Were not the first historical books supposedly written by *nabiim?* Still the possibility is far from being a proven fact; the texts cited are not unquestionably favorable to this hypothesis. But the contrary opinion lacks proof as well. Some outstanding critics think, moreover, that these writings of Samuel, Iddo, etc. are presented under names which, according to the custom of the age, are no more than literary fictions. We would in this case be faced with documents of a recent date, much like the Apocalypses and the Apocrypha. Witness what, much later, one finds in the non-canonical literature of the archives of the Qumran sect : the struggle of the children of light, a midrash on Habacuc! So the very character of the sources which the inspired Chronicler used leads us to think that his work is the product of similar methods.

He had, finally, to collect oral traditions : recollections preserved in Judea, passed down by the repatriates after the return from exile, and sometimes associated to more recent events. No doubt these traditions were inserted into the plan of the work with some uncertainty. They were floating elements which the Chronicler fixed according to their frame of reference, and perhaps also according to their relation to the purpose he had in mind.

§ 3. Purpose and Literary Genre of Chronicles

The Chronicler followed a set plan. To judge by the results of a comparison of his account with his known sources (especially the Books of Samuel and Kings), it is impossible to avoid the conclusion that our author proposed not only to write history, but deliberately set out to put a religious doctrine in plain relief. It is not so much the material likeness of his account to his sources that sustains this conviction, but rather the formal comparison of the two series of writings. A constant tendency is discernible : to justify by history the solutions given to complex problems in the postexilic community, and especially to refer the fundamental elements of the Jewish community to David, without neglecting, however, the Mosaic origin even of the Davidic institutions.

Now such methods are characteristic of a literary genre much used in that age : the midrash.

I. MIDRASH [2]

The midrash, following the religious sense of the verb *dâraš* (to consult the divinity), is a writing that tries to investigate and use ancient texts in order to explain the present. This research, however, does not heed demands imposed by our western mentality. Our exegesis aims to give the text the meaning required by the objective reconstruction of time and place. Thus we discover the literary genres of the Bible including the midrash. Midrashic research aimed, rather than to discern the precise meaning, to draw from the text numerous and diverse ideas that resulted in maxims of justification and edification. The word of God in putting on the clothing of human language should not lose any of its universal meaning. It remains charged with a volume of knowledge and contains the universality of wisdom. It is to be approached with our own reason, but also it is to be treated with our imagination. Thus the authors of the midrashim proceeded. The midrashim assumed an historical, philosophical, juridical, mystical character. The midrash is then at the same time a form of intellectual speculation and of imaginative development founded on Scripture and in the sense of tradition. [3]

Midrashim assumed multiple aspects. [4] They found their way into all sorts of books. In the Wisdom writings legal ordinances are the occasion for certain language changes; thus in certain proverbs that constitute a type of updating of the Law destined to spread Yahwism. Also ancient accounts give rise to imaginative developments : in this sense compare Wis 10, 15—12, 27 (a recollection of the Exodus) and 16, 1—19, 22 (plagues of Egypt) to the accounts of the Pentateuch. The midrash in this instance in some way amplifies history. In the prophetic genre history is given a meaning, while the future is colored according to the mentality of the age of the nabiim (cf. Ez 16; 40—45; Is 40 f.; Dn 1—6). In the legalist works the ancient historico-juridical texts proliferate with details and moral applications. Just compare the priestly code with the more ancient passages (J, E, D). Finally, in the historical books canonical and non-canonical sources are used or simply recopied with the fixed purpose of adapting them, even embellishing them, to support a thesis according to the common exegesis of an age. Tobias, Judith, Esther furnish classical examples of midrashic literature. [5]

---

[2] See pp. 481 f.
[3] Cf. R. BLOCH, art. " Midrash, " *SDB*, V, cols. 1263 ff.
[4] See pp. 173-177 (French ed.).
[5] Cf. A. ROBERT, *RB* (1935), pp. 345-350.

The Books of Chronicles are to be interpreted in the light of this literary genre. The Chronicler uses certain objective facts, and in this way he is an historian. But he sometimes arranges them to serve his thesis, and in this way he is a midrashic author. His objectivity is influenced by his interpretation. [6]

II. CRITICAL OPINIONS

Two exaggerated positions are to be avoided : the first is that of J. Wellhausen. He maintained that midrash is essentially an idealization of the past. The midrashic authors teach us only about the historical and doctrinal ideas of their time. The authors record past centuries exclusively from these ideas. Thus the Chronicler judaized, in the light of the priestly code, the history of ancient Israel. [7] In general the disciples of Wellhausen were less radical than their master. They held that a certain number of documents used by the Chronicler have objective value. They did not consider the facts of the work as *a priori* unacceptable. Nevertheless the essential positions remained inflexible with Torrey (1909-1910), Curtis (1930), Pfeiffer (1941). With J. W. Rothstein (1923) the theory leaned towards granting that the Chronicles have an historical value. The existence of serious sources contemporary to Samuel and the Kings, and partially identical with them, was admitted. A first redaction would have arranged these memoirs according to the model of P. A second redaction arranged them according to the Hexateuch. Von Rad [8] (1930) held for these two strata, but accentuated the influence of the Hexateuch and strongly stressed that of D. According to A. C. Welch (1939), the second stratum was the outcome of a compromise in which P prevailed over D, which in effect had principally inspired the first editor. In short, the Wellhausian movement assumed a certain form according to which the influence of P, associated not strictly with that of D, but with the Hexateuch as a whole, would have influenced the Chronicler. This would all the same depend on trustworthy sources of history.

The second position, by way of reaction to minimizing the historical sense of Chronicles, set about explaining the least discrepancies without

---

[6] Cf. LAGRANGE, *RB* (1916), pp. 501-504; *Le judaïsme avant Jésus-Christ*, pp. XV-XX; L. DENNEFELD, *Le judaïsme biblique* (Paris, 1932), pp. 38-56; J. BONSIRVEN, *Exégèse rabbinique, exégèse paulinienne*, pp. 250-259 and *passim; SDB*, IV, cols. 565-567.

[7] *PROLEGOMENA* VI, 1905, 165-223.

[8] G. VON RAD, *Das Geschithtsbild des Chron. Werkes* (Stuttgart, 1930).

taking into account the literary genre of the work. This method would easily create in the reader the opposite impression it set out to produce.

Now Catholic exegetes follow a path which, without accepting the extreme opinions of the radical critique, endeavors to take notice of literary method of the age in order to appreciate the exact objective value of the Chronicler's account.

Thus we do not consider all the details added to the Books of Samuel and Kings as purely imaginative. The different sources of these works to which the Chronicler refers are not necessarily unreliable. The very documents used in Samuel-Kings could have contained information not used in these works but which a later historian could have taken up. Moreover, the religion of Israel was rooted in history. The Chronicler then, no matter what his intentions were, could not boldly disregard objectivity without the risk of weakening his thesis by deliberately ignoring the evidence of facts.

The exegete must find the right starting point. In general a number of data proper to Chronicles are held to be exact : cities fortified by Roboam (2 Par 11, 5-12a) and by Ozias (26, 6-15); construction work by Joathan (27, 3b-4); details concerning the burial of Asa (16, 14) and Ezechias (32, 33); details about the death of Ochozias, killed by Jehu (22, 7-9); circumstances of the death of Josias at Megiddo (35, 20-25).... Extra-biblical documents have sometime confirmed facts presented by our author : the inscription of Karnak concerning the invasion by Sesac (2 Par 12, 2-11); inscriptions of Assarhaddon and Assurbanipal concerning Manasses (33, 11-13). The reign of Joatham is rightly presented as an era of prosperity and military success (27, 3-6; cf. Is 2, 7-16). The details furnished by Chronicles about the underground aquaduct of Ezechias (32, 30) are more complete than the brief reference in the Book of Kings (4 Kgs 20, 20).

The author does, however, present views that sometimes do not correspond with those of his predecessors. Sometimes he perpetrates important omissions, modifies expressions, inverts the order of events, adds personal glosses, and explains facts in the light of tradition.

Examples of this genre have become classic : David's adultery and homicide are passed over in silence. There is no mention of the bloody drama of the King's old age. If there is a question of the census and the plague, it is because these events are connected with the choice of the Temple site. And David was to prepare for its construction. However, it is not God but Satan who inspires the King with a desire to take the census (1 Par 21, 1; cf. 2 Sm 24, 1).

Solomon is idealized even more boldly. There is no question of competition with Adonias nor of decline at the end of his life. If he offered sacrifice at Gabaon, it was certainly not to conform to the usage of his time (cf. 3 Kgs 3, 2-3), but because there was in that high place " the tabernacle of the covenant of the Lord " which Moses had made in the wilderness (2 Par 1, 3), and here verse 4 justifies David who offered sacrifices in Jerusalem.

Besides, one has the impression that the process of earthly reward is a bit exaggerated. The good kings—those who are in the line of Deuteronomy or the priestly code, destroying the high places, protecting the levites—are showered with blessings (2 Par 14—15 : Asa; 17—20 : Josaphat; 29—32 : Ezechias; 34—35 : Josias). Nevertheless the eye of God is on their least infidelity (2 Par 16, 1-12; 20, 35-37; 32, 31; 35, 20-22). One can imagine what is in store for unfaithful kings. Joram of Juda not only loses control over Moab (4 Kgs 3, 4-27) and Edom (8, 20-22); he is subjected to an invasion by the Philistines and Arabians, devoured by a stomach disorder and excluded from his father's grave (2 Par 21, 11-21; cf. 4 Kgs 8, 24). Achaz, already castigated by the author of the Book of Kings (4 Kgs 16, 1-20), receives a double measure of affliction in the Chronicles (2 Par 28, 5-8). In brief, the Chronicler has a way of seeing or not seeing things that is often enough in contrast with the facts presented in Samuel-Kings, the only historical work with which we can compare his. The differences (cf. Vannutelli's synopsis) are sometimes difficult to reconcile (compare 2 Kgs 21, 19 and 1 Par 20, 5; 2 Kgs 8, 18 and 1 Par 18, 17; 2 Kgs 24, 24 and 1 Par 21, 10; 3 Kgs 9, 10 and 2 Par 8, 8....). It becomes evident that the author sacrificed the role of historian to that of the panegyrist, the apologist or the theologian.

§ 4. Religious Value of the Work

We are thus led to define the intentions and objective proper to the Chronicler. His main objective is to present a panoramic view of the kingdom of God in the framework of the Davidic monarchy, past but not destroyed.

The genealogies already betray this plan : the lines of schismatic tribes are not given beyond the Davidic era; those of Benjamin and the Levites, who remained faithful to the dynasty, are continued until the Exile; the genealogy of the holy King's descendants is continued to the age of Esdras and Nehemias (5th century).

In the Chronicles the kings of Israel are only mentioned in their relation to the sons of David. *David himself is the center* and the culmination of the account; it is he who is the principal artisan of the kingdom of God!

Just as Moses was the mediator of the alliance between Yahweh and
the Israelitic community of Sinai (the *'edah* of the priestly redaction), thus
David was put in charge of the alliance (2 Par 13, 5) which was to associate
God and the community *(qâhâl)* destined to live in Chanaan. This
covenant, whose effects extended to Davidic kings, truly inaugurated
the universal reign of Yahweh. Even after the northern tribes' schism,
the frontiers of Juda and Benjamin were opened to different descendant
clans of Jacob : people of Ephraim, Manasses, Simeon, Aser, Issachar,
Zabulon (cf. 2 Par 15, 8-15; 30, 1-22). Even foreign tribes, including
Egyptian representatives, were not excluded. David was made the head
of a universal kingdom.

One can understand that the entire historical vision of the Chronicler
must adjust to this basic fact whose Messianic coloring is obvious. And
so the oracle of Nathan is seen in a new light (compare 2 Kgs 7, 14. 16
and 1 Par 17, 13. 14) : it goes beyond the horizon of Solomon. The
Temple, the dwelling place of Yahweh, appears as the center of an enriched
cult. Does not all the liturgy organized there stem from David? The
son of Jesse not only moved the ark from Obededom's house to Sion,
he not only prepared for the construction of Yahweh's house, he also
arranged the services of the Dwelling. Here we have the levites joining
the priests (1 Par 23). The sacerdotal law and the Deuteronomical
tradition limited their roles (Nm 1, 50-54; 3, 7. 8; 4, 15; 7, 9; Dt 10, 8;
18, 1-8), but the Davidic liturgy qualified them to function in the sanctuary
until they could assume their office definitely in the Temple. In short,
David instituted the levites as Moses had instituted the priests. It is
he who determined the types and details of both, and provided for the
organization of the sacred music. He laid the ground for all the Temple
functions (24—26).

This Temple, as it should, had already known a brilliant fame.
The entire life of Israel was centered on it. The moral and religious life,
the sanctification of souls, took place there through ritual acts, purifica-
tions, sacrifices, especially thanksgiving sacrifices and participation in
sacred feasts. It is there that one sought and found God, because the
Covenant must be renewed after apostasies and become more profound
in the measure that revelation is extended. The Chronicler delights in
recalling the solemn feasts celebrated with the singing of the psalms and
the sound of harps, citterns, trumpets and cymbals (2 Par 5, 11-14;
6, 6; 29, 25-30; 30, 21).

Thus the Chronicler views the religious community in the kingdom
of God over which ruled David and his successors, the anointed of Yahweh,
the predecessors of the Messias. Should not at least the prestige of the

house of David be restored at a time when the restoration of the historical monarchy was impossible? To do this, should not the merits of the dynasty be stressed, against the objections to it, thus maintaining faith and hope in a second David? This faith and hope ran through the oracles of the nabiim and the ardent pleas of the psalmists (cf. Ps 88 [89]).

The fervent religious conviction of the Chronicler is manifested in his historical accounts expanded to benefit the theology of the Kingdom. The work of Ezechiel and the priestly law profoundly influence the spirit of the book and the description of the sacred rites. The legislation of Deuteronomy accentuates, more strongly than in the Books of Kings, the judgment of the kings, and inspires reforms and developments that are at work in the Kingdom (Asa, Josaphat, Ezechias, Josias). The transcendence of Yahweh, more and more acknowledged, maintains in souls a respect for the monotheistic ideal. This ideal is more clearly affirmed and purified in the measure that the spirituality and holiness of the Divine Being are better perceived (the Angel of Yahweh). Yet His love is a cause of joy and happiness. Already the King of peace takes the place of the warlike God. The Davidic kingdom is a kingdom of peace, defended by Yahweh for the faithful, or paternally chastised by the jealous God for those who reject his love.

§ 5. Date of the Work

The content, language of a later age, influence of the priestly law on the concepts and terminology of the author make it clearly impossible to place the redaction of the Chronicles before the Exile. If one considers the numerous genealogical lists which contain descendants beyond the return from the captivity, and especially the Davidic genealogies continued until the end of the 5th century, then the date cannot be before the year 400. This conclusion must be drawn if the primitive union of Chronicles and Esdras-Nehemias is considered, as well as the influence of Esdras and the Torah on the mentality of the author. The choice of Albright to use this as a *terminus a quo* and put the redaction at the beginning of the 4th century is understandable. If, however, the one author theory is accepted (contrary to Galling who holds for two Chroniclers), it seems that the work belongs to a more recent era. The mention of the high priest Jeddoa (Neh 12, 22) in a list of Nehemias would indicate a date after 330, since his pontificate was contemporaneous with Alexander the Great, if Josephus is reliable. True, this pericope could have been added to the primitive text, but there is also a question of the daric [Persian gold coin] in the historical Davidic context (1 Par 29, 7). Such a monetary designation would suppose that the connection with Darius had been lost in reference to this exchange. Now the last king with this name was Darius III Codoman who died after the battle of Hecatompylos in 330. Moreover, the appearance of the work fits well with a later date in the course of the 3rd century. The author seems to want to concentrate on the Temple. This would indicate that his work was composed at a time when Judean Yahwism risked being wrecked by the combined efforts of the *Samaritan schism* that developed beginning in 350 and was completed by the construction of the Garizim temple, the collusion of high priest successors of Simon I the Just with the Tobiades (sister of Onias II, married to a son of Tobias around 240) and the financial support of Ptolemy III Evergete (Joseph's administration about 220). This puts us in the second half of the 3rd century. At least it is known that in 157 Eupolem used a Greek translation of the Book of Chronicles. It is equally probable that Ecclesiasticus referred to it in his portrait of David (Sir 47, 2-11) about 180.

§ 6. Canonicity and Liturgical Use

If the work appeared in such a climate, one would think that it could not please discordant elements, the Sadducean priests, while it did please fervent Jews, the Assideans and later the Pharisees. This opposition delayed its acceptance into the Jewish Canon : it was given the last place, cut off from Esdras and Nehemias which had already been admitted. Undoubtedly it was at the Synod of Jamnia (about A.D. 95) that its canonicity was officially recognized. By that time the Sadducees had lost all authority after the destruction of the Temple (70), and the view of the Pharisees held sway.

Christians, except perhaps in the Syriac Church, accepted the canonicity of Chronicles without difficulty. Moreover, the spirit of the work was easily in accord with that of the first communities founded by the apostles. The authors of the New Testament refer more or less overtly to the text of the Chronicles (cf. Mt 23, 35 and 2 Par 24, 21 and the context Heb 9, 11-12 and 1 Par 16, 1-2; Heb 11, 13 and 1 Par 29, 15). The liturgy uses it sometimes, especially in the canticle of Lauds for the *feria secunda* (1 Par 29, 10-13), in a number of antiphons and responses of the Vesperal and the Diurnal (Christmas, the feasts of the Trinity, Sacred Heart, Holy Angels), and the offertory of the common of the dedication of a church (1 Par 29, 17-18).

PART V

THE DEUTEROCANONICAL BOOKS

by A. Lefèvre

See the general commentaries, p. 1 f..

E. KAUTZSCH, *Die Apokryphen und Pseudepigraphen des Alten Testaments*, I. *Die Apokryphen* (Tübingen, 1900).

L. E. TONY ANDRÉ, *Apocryphes de l'Ancien Testament* (Florence, 1903).

R. H. CHARLES, *The Apocrypha and Pseudepigrapha of the Old Testament*, I. *Apocrypha* (Oxford, 1913), *APOT*.

W. O. E. OESTERLEY, *An Introduction to the Books of the Apocrypha* (London, 1935).

E. J. GOODSPEED, *The Story of the Apocrypha* (1939).

R. H. PFEIFFER, *History of New Testament Times* (New York : Harper, 1949).

S. ZEITLIN ET AL. (eds.), *Jewish Apocryphal Literature* (New York, 1950).

BRUCE M. METZGER, *An Introduction to the Apocrypha* (New York-Oxford, 1957).

L. H. BROCKINGTON, *A Critical Introduction to the Apocrypha* (1961).

M. S. ENSLIN (ed.), *The Apocrypha*[2] (1962).

B. M. METZGER, *The Oxford Annotated Apocrypha* (New York : Oxford, 1965).

The books we call deuterocanonical are inspired in the same way as the protocanonical books. But collectively they express a more advanced stage of revelation. Even the deuterocanonical fragments of books found in the Palestinian canon (Daniel and Esther) disclose a different style and mentality. In many respects the deuterocanonical books seem to be a prolongation of the Hagiographa. Consequently we prefer to treat them separately, after the latter. We will recall that the Protestants call them " Apocrypha. "

These seven books do not form a homogeneous whole. The variety of literary genres found in the Hagiographa appears here also. It includes edifying accounts, meditations and teachings from the sapiential school, and histories of different tendencies. Yet some characteristics are common to all of them. All were composed at a later date, when the age of spontaneity had died out. They are a reflective type of literature, fruits of a period of maturity, and as such they give us something that is precious. For this reflection on the history and literature of the past advances the tradition of Israel right up to the threshold of the New Testament.

For most of the deuterocanonical works we have only the Greek text in the manuscripts and editions of the LXX.

CHAPTER I

BARUCH

BIBLIOGRAPHY

Introductions, translations, commentaries, pp. 1 f. and 506 (A. GELIN, BJ*; L. DENNEFELD, BPC*; V. HAMP, EB*; B. P. SAYDON, CCHS*...).

HARWELL, *The Principal Versions of Baruch* (New Haven : Yale, 1915).

P. HEINISCH, " Zur entstehung des Buches Baruch, " *Theol. und Glaube*, 20 (1928), pp. 696-710.

A. GELIN, " Tables, " *DTC* (Paris, 1953), pp. 379 f.

A. PENNA, *Baruch** (Turin-Rome, 1953).

Following the Book of Jeremias, the MSS of the LXX place Baruch, Lamentations and the Letter of Jeremias, generally in that order. We find the same grouping in the lists of the books declared canonical by the Greek Fathers (Athanasius, Cyril of Jerusalem) and by the Council of Laodicea. Baruch is also considered an appendix to Jeremias, and is cited by that name; so it is in the most ancient citations known (Athenagoras, Irenaeus).

Our Vulgate adds the letter of Jeremias to Baruch as chapter six. But this is not too significant since the long title shows well enough that it is a distinct work. On the other hand, the good MSS of the Vulgate completely omit Baruch, as did St. Jerome, haunted by *hebraica veritas*. It is an earlier version which is included in the Latin Bible.

§ 1. Composition

After the prologue (1, 1-14), we can clearly distinguish three sections : a psalm of penitence (1, 15—3, 8), a praise of Wisdom as identified with the Law (3, 9—4, 4), and a discourse of exhortation and consolation (4, 5—5, 9). These sections belong to three different literary genres, the psalm-prayer, the sapiential poem, and the prophetic discourse. Keeping in mind that the Greek, full of Semitisms in the first part, becomes purer in the last section (which explains the hypothesis of a Hebraic original in part), and that the final discourse supposes the imminent return to Jerusalem, while the prologue puts us at the beginning of the Exile, we can understand why the unity of authorship is hotly contested. But opinions on authorship and the dating of different parts differ considerably. Some Catholics maintain that the psalm is by Baruch but, following Heinisch, they attribute the final discourse to a disciple of Second Isaias, and they put the sapiential poem at some undetermined date after the Exile. Others opt for dates ranging from the 3rd century B.C. to the 2nd century A.D. In other words, the internal criticism is hard to handle.

Actually, if Baruch did write the book, it is hard to explain why the Jewish tradition neglected the original. We know, however, that pseudepigrapha were admissible, even on the part of inspired authors (Eccl, Ct, Wis of pseudo-Solomon). We can rightly inquire whether the same literary fiction comes into play here. This would not be too surprising since the pseudonym Baruch is often found in apocryphal literature. An examination of the work will allow us to form an opinion on the matter.

§ 2. Contents

According to the prologue, the prayer was read in Babylon on the anniversary of the destruction of Jerusalem, on the fifth of the month of Ab, during the assembly in which the Law was read. Pilgrims setting out for Jerusalem to celebrate the Feast of Tabernacles brought the prayer to have it recited in the Lord's house during the feast and the ferial days following, since they offered sacrifices there. This all fits in well with Jewish custom in the Diaspora from the time of Esdras until St. Paul. We have two prayers analogous to Esdras, composed in similar circumstances (Esd 8; Neh 9). But the prologue adds a certain number of facts, dates, proper names, historical settings, all of which contribute more difficulty than useful information. We don't know the year for the date of the tenth of Siwan (1, 8); by contrast the year 5, the seventh of the month (1, 2) is all the more surprising, as the date seems to be taken from 4 Kgs 25, 8 with the substitution of "year" for "month." At any rate, it is hard to envision the exiles grouping about Jechonias in the fifth year after the sack of Jerusalem (cf. 4 Kgs 25, 27), and Nabuchodonosor rebuilding the ruins of the Temple. The idea of praying for Nabuchodonosor and his son Baltassar (? cf. Dn 5, 2) far exceeds the precepts of Jer 29, and is inspired by the practice held in honor since the Persian epoch (Esd 6, 10; 7, 23). And last but not least, the supposition that there was a regular cult at Jerusalem at that time, with a possibility of offering holocausts, is at variance with history; nothing like this takes place until the return of the high priest Josue (Esd 3). It makes more sense to call this prologue an artificial construction, at least from a modern standpoint. In its own era, it is edifying history. The dates and names insert into the great religious history of Israel the ordinary occurrence of the annual pilgrimage, which evoked the great dates of return from exile, while looking forward to the definitive restoration. This process reveals a late epoch, far removed from the time of Baruch.

The " Prayer of the Exiles " (1, 15—3, 8) rests its argument on a humble confession of sins to appeal to divine mercy. This literary genre, a psalm of collective penitence, is found in all the books of the Old Testament (3 Kgs 8, 46-53; Ps 79; Sir 36, 1-19; Dn 3, 26-45). The idea comes from the prophets, Osee (14, 3-4) and especially Jeremias (3, 22-25; 10, 19-25; 14, 19-22; etc.); the most polished example is Is 63, 11—64, 11. The psalm is closely related to the prayers of Esdras (Esd 9, 6-15; Neh 9, 6-37), and still more to the almost identical formularies of Neh 1, 5-11 and Dn 9, 4-19.

Within such a fixed literary genre, and in the easily recognizable words of Jeremias, seeking his inspiration in the Law of Moses (esp. Dt 28—30) as expressly cited, our author has nevertheless succeeded in creating an original little masterpiece which aroused, as we know, the enthusiasm of good La Fontaine. He knew how to make the prayer progress in successive waves which somewhat overlap and push at one another. A very profound religious sense finds, in the sense of shame for sin, an assurance of being pardoned and of singing God's praises.

To date this prayer, some put it alongside Dn 9 which Baruch imitated. But it is difficult to determine in what sense this influence comes to bear, or if the two prayers don't depend on an ordinary prayer. Besides, the doctrine of Baruch on the last ends, less advanced than in Daniel, indicates an earlier date. It might fit in the beginning of the 2nd century, with Ben Sira, who also provides a good means of comparison (Sir 36).

The section in the sapiential style (3, 9—4, 4) is an exhortation, as the formulae of introduction (3, 9-14) and conclusion (4, 2-4) indicate. The meat of the section is the " Hymn to Wisdom " (3, 15—4, 1). It is beyond all human research. The rich and powerful of the earth, the people of the East who were considered the most wise, did not know it, nor did the renowned giants of the days of old, and that is why they all perished. It is futile to climb up to the heavens to seek it, or to cross the sea to buy it with money; He who has created the world and rules it, He alone knows it, and He has given it to Jacob His servant. This Wisdom has appeared among men : it is the divine and eternal Law, which gives life.

Our author imitates here the hymn to Wisdom of Jb 28, but he continues to draw his religious inspiration from Dt 30 (cf. Dt 4, 1-8). Ben Sira also offers some points for comparison (Sir 1, 1-20; 24, 1-32). We can therefore conclude that this composition also dates from around 200.

The discourse of consolation which ends the book (4, 5—5, 9) is symmetrical to the psalm of penitence in the beginning. In his speech to the children of Israel (4, 5-9), the poet recalls that their woes arise from having offended the eternal God, their Author who has nursed them, and Jerusalem, the mother who reared them. The speech thus passes into the mouth of Jerusalem who recalls the pain she has endured because of her heedless children and the pleas she has directed to the Eternal One for their own good. These cries are heard, and she announces to her children their speedy return (4, 9-39). The Eternal One answers by the mouth of the prophet that the mourning of Jerusalem is over and her children will be brought back (4, 30—5, 9).

The author continues to draw his inspiration from Dt (esp. 32). The picture of Jerusalem sighing her complaint and then consoling her children is borrowed from Lamentations and from Second Isaias (Is 40, 1-11; 49, 14-26; etc.); the elements in the consolation by which God answers her come from Is 60—62 especially. Once again the author's merit lies in his skilful composition. We progress in successive waves from the sense of sin to the joy of salvation. By giving Jerusalem the central place between the scolding of the prophet and the granting of salvation by the Eternal One, the author carefully sets in relief the role of mediator of the city-mother which prefigures the Church.

The last verses of this discourse (4, 36—5, 9) are found almost word for word in one of the apocryphal psalms of Solomon (Ps Sol 11). These psalms may date from the 1st century B.C. and must be later than Baruch, since they speak a more developed doctrine concerning the last things. Aside from more precise data, the connection between this discourse and the preceding chapters leads us to place it also in the first decades of the 2nd century.

There actually is a connection between the various parts of the book. If the consolation at the end is a response to the prayer at the beginning, it is the Law that intervenes to reinstate Israel in her privileges. The formulae of exhortation which permeate the hymn to Law-Wisdom (3, 9-14; 4, 2-4) bring out this connection. The prologue recalls the Festival with octave (1, 14), that is, Tabernacles, the feast of the renewal of the Covenant by the recalling of the Law. This reference can be taken seriously. The ceremonies of the time of Esdras offer a good point of comparison (Esd 9—10; Neh 8—9). Though not a liturgical text as such, Baruch hands down quite well the feelings of a Jew of the Diaspora who unites himself to the feasts of Jerusalem.

§ 3. Doctrine

The teaching of the Book of Baruch forms a drama of sin, conversion, and salvation. Law-Wisdom, a gift of God and source of life, plays the most important role. Revelation, the sheer grace of God, saves man from sin. As for the last things, Baruch has the current doctrine of the Old Testament up to the 2nd century. Since he wrote from a collective standpoint, the problem of the world beyond does not pose an acute problem. On the other hand, he has a quite original title for God, calling Him the Eternal One. He is the only one in the Bible to use this expression; elsewhere we find scores of times " the eternal God, " but never the adjective alone. This preoccupation with eternity haunted the author from the start. The psalm of penitence aspired to an eternal Covenant (2, 35), but it rested on the sad thought that we disappear without returning, while God abides forever (3, 3). The remedy was then given in the Law, which likewise endures forever (4, 1), but which leads men to eternal peace (3, 13). Salvation comes finally from the eternal God (4, 8) who has been offended but who reveals His glory first of all in chastising, then in saving the sinner. The Eternal One pervades the couplets of the consolation discourse (4, 10. 14. 21. 22. 24. 35; 5, 2) which announces eternal joy (4, 23. 29; 5, 1. 4). This opposition between changing, ephemeral man and the eternity of God, ever the same, faithful to accomplish His word, is a customary theme in prophetic literature, but the insistence of Baruch gives it new force.

The adjective " eternal " has no equivalent in Hebrew that permits the substantive use, and in fact it is found alone only in works written directly in Greek (2 and 3 Mc). Everything points to the fact that the last part of Baruch was also written in Greek, which confirms the late date assigned to it.

The Fathers of the Church willingly concede a Messianic sense to 3, 37 : " Then she was revealed on the earth and she conversed among men. " The author clearly says that he is dealing with Mosaic law, identified

THE DEUTEROCANONICAL BOOKS

with Wisdom; he is not thinking of the Messias. The Messianic application is still correct after the revelation of the New Testament : the Word of God, His Wisdom, is the Son of God who became man (Jn 1; Heb 1; etc.).

§ 4. Appendix : The Letter of Jeremias[1]

All the modern commentaries agree with St. Jerome in admitting that this letter is pseudepigraphic. But that in no way conflicts with its canonicity which is, as is true with Baruch, better attested than that of some deuterocanonical books, since it is admitted in the lists of Athanasius, Cyril of Jerusalem and the Council of Laodicea.

It is admitted today that the Greek text we have is translated from a Hebrew original. The errors by the translator leave no room for doubt. The clearest error, in v. 71, clothes the idols " in purple and marble, " while this is a well known formula taken from the parable of the evil rich man " clothed in purple and byssus " (Lk 16, 19); the Hebrew *shesh* can mean precious white cloth (Prv 31, 22) or costly white stone (Ct 5, 15).

The *date* is more difficult to establish. The letter is certainly later than the definitive version of Jeremias, and this puts it in the postexilic period. A rather low date must be assigned in this period, to the time when pseudepigraphy was in vogue, starting with the 3rd century. This plea against idols could well take place within the period of Greek domination. Alexander had rebuilt the Esagil destroyed by Xerxes, and gave new life to the cult of the Babylonian gods. The Seleucids imitated him in this work of restoration, and it is from the ritual of this period that we have become acquainted with the feast of the Babylonian new year. This renewal of idolatrous cult is the reason for the letter.

This letter is really a long *satire* against the idols. A short introduction aims the message at the Israelites living in Babylon, inviting them to remain faithful to the true God. A short exhortation recurs at the end of each couplet to break the monotony of the indictment. The writer's art is reduced to that as he accumulates, with little order and some repetition, all the traits which show the powerlessness of the idols. But if he lacks the art of composition, he can be cutting and he chooses traits that are meaningful.

As the other writings of this era, this one is inspired by the ancient works. Its models are Second Isaias (esp. Is 44, 9-20), and above all

---

[1] A. ROBERT, " Jérémie (letter of), " *SDB*, IV (1949), cols. 849-857.

Jer 10, 1-16, which is already a supplement to the authentic works of Jeremias. But its inspiration is not solely bookish; its description of Babylonian customs shows that it knows how to open its eyes. Archeology and secular documents confirm its documentary value.

From a doctrinal standpoint, the letter adds nothing to the prophetic sources cited above. It is, at greater length, what the psalms sing (Ps 115, 4-8; Ps 135, 15-18). The subject will be treated again later in Wisdom in greater depth (Wis 13—15).

CHAPTER II

TOBIAS

BIBLIOGRAPHY

Introductions, translations, commentaries, pp. 1 f. and 506 (R. PAUTREL, *BJ**; A. CLAMER, *BPC**; A. MILLER, *HSAT**; F. STUMMER, *EB**; F. DE VINE, *CCHS**...).

C. C. TORREY, " ' Nineveh ' in the Book of Tobit, " *JBL*, 41 (1922), pp. 237-245.

H. BEVENOT, " The Primitive Book of Tobit, " *Bibliotheca Sacra**, 83 (1926), pp. 55-84.

A. CLAMER, " Tobie (Livre de), " *DTC*, IV (1946), cols. 1153-1176.

R. PAUTREL, " Trois textes de Tobie sur Raphaël, " *RSR*, XXXIX (1951-1952), pp. 115-124.

G. PRIERO, *Tobia** (Turin-Rome, 1953).

§ 1. Texts

In the Greek manuscripts, Tobias forms a group with Judith and Esther. The place of this group varies. It comes right after the great historical books in the Sinaiticus, after the sapiential books in the Vaticanus, and after the Prophets in the Alexandrinus. The text differs a great deal from one manuscript to another. The accepted text (Vat., Alex., miniscules) has been somewhat altered, and what the story gains in edification, it loses in picturesque detail. The Sinaiticus reflects best the primitive text, and it contains a vivid and colorful narrative. It was the basis for the ancient Latin versions. The three main texts, Vat., Sin., and Lat., have been published in full in the great critical edition of the LXX at Cambridge (1940).

All known versions depend on one or another of the Greek recension, even the Hebrew and Aramaic texts of the Middle Ages. But it is generally agreed today that the Greek itself is a translation from a Semitic original. Although placed outside the regular canon of the Scriptures, Tobias always was popular with the Jews. Thus St. Jerome procured an Aramaic text, in light of the translation given in the Vulgate. He did not begin this work wholeheartedly, since he did not believe that what he was translating was canonical. But he did not wish to avoid the entreaties of Bishops Chromatius and Heliodorus : " I have satisfied your wishes, not my tastes, and I did the best I could, " he wrote them. Aramaic was not at all familiar to him, and he translated with the aid of an interpreter. A Jew read to him in Hebrew the text written in Aramaic, and St. Jerome dictated immediately to his copyist the Latin translation. The work took only a day (*PL* 29, 23-26).

Can this ancient Aramaic text be found? Surely the Vulgate does not allow for its reconstruction, for it is too influenced by older Latin versions, as well as by the ascetical notions of Jerome. An Aramaic Tobias, found and published in 1875 by Neubauer, cannot be the original; it betrays the influence of the Greek versions. Until further findings, the Sinaiticus represents the form closest to the original. Recently the manuscripts found around Qumran have yielded Hebrew and Aramaic fragments of Tobias, [1] which can be dated around the beginning of the Christian era. Their publication will perhaps require a revision of our point of view. The Book of Tobias must have been written in the 3rd or 2nd century B.C.

§ 2. Contents

In spite of differences of detail, all the recensions are in accord with the overall story. As a kind of introduction, old Tobias recounts the fortune and woes of his life up to the time of the story. An Israelite of the tribe of Nephtali, he was, already in the time of the ancients the only one to practice the Law faithfully. Deported to Ninive with his wife Anna and his son Tobias, he remained faithful there despite all his trials, up to the time when his scruples of righteousness brought down on him the almost blasphemous reproaches of his wife. Ruined, blind, abandoned by all, he turns to God and begs him, in a humble and penitent prayer, to take him out of this wicked world where he has nothing to hope for (1, 3—3, 6).

Now at the same hour, continues the narrator, at Ecbatana, Sara, daughter of Raguel, is suffering abuse from a servant girl who derides her misfortune. She had seen all seven of her husbands die successively as they attempted to espouse her. A jealous demon, Asmodeus, killed them before they could approach her. She also sends forth a cry of anguish to God, asking the Lord to put an end to her days and to her humiliation (3, 7-15).

Both prayers are heard, and God sends His angel Raphael who will direct the play (3, 16-17).

---

[1] *RB* (1953), p. 86; (1956), p. 60.

The main actor will be the young Tobias. His father gives him some lengthy advice, which makes of chap. 4 a small collection of proverbs on good works; next he sends him to recover an important sum of money left in deposit with a certain Gabael, in the heart of Media (5, 1-3). It is then that Raphael, under the name of Azarias, offers to lead the young man (5, 4-22). The angel is not only a guide; he teaches the young Tobias what to do in the face of danger, he teaches him the remedies for the blindness of his father and against the wicked works of the demons, he brags about the charms of his cousin Sara, and invites him to ask for her hand in marriage (chap. 6). When he arrives at Ecbatana, Tobias insistently asks for the hand of his cousin, and to the great astonishment of the parents, the first night passes without incident. Fourteen days of rejoicing are none too much to fete the happy couple. In the meantime Azarias himself goes to recover the money and bring back Gabael (7—9). Meanwhile, at Ninive, Anna and Tobias are anxious about not seeing their son return; hence young Tobias is urging his departure, and begins the return journey with his wife, always under the guidance of the angel. The joy of the homecoming reaches its peak when Tobias returns sight to his father, through the cure pointed out by Raphael. Once again there is lengthy rejoicing to fete the young couple (10—11).

Nothing remains but to take leave of the actors. Raphael reveals his identity before disappearing, but not before he gives, in certain proverbs, a new teaching on good works. Finally he invites his hearers to give thanks to Providence (chap. 12). Tobias is eager to fulfill this duty in a hymn which enlarges on the prophetic views concerning the future glory of Jerusalem (chap. 13). The old man's death is like that of the patriarchs. Upon his deathbed he unveils the future to his son, and once again recommends filial piety to him, as well as the practice of good works and the fear of God (14, 1-11). Young Tobias, after rendering his final duty to his father, and then to his mother, moves to Ecbatana to perform the same duties in the declining days of his wife's parents. He dies at a ripe age, after having had the consolation of seeing the realization of the prophecies of his dying father (14, 12-15).

§ 3. Literary Genre

The Book of Tobias, within its minor genre, is one of the literary jewels of the Bible. Its charm emerges best in the recension of Sinaiticus, or in one of the good translations recently made, such as in the Jerusalem Bible. The liveliness of narration and dialogue, the picturesque observations, the simple but evocative words, the supple and varied composition which joins continuity with suspense, the finely described characters, and especially the beautiful soul, vibrant yet serene, of the inspired and humanistic scribe, all contribute to the irresistible charm of this book which lifts up our hearts with the joy of doing well under the surveillance of God.

In composing this story, the author naturally looked for his inspiration in the tales of Genesis. The story of Joseph and especially the mission of Eliezer (Gn 24) furnished him models of narration as well as themes to exploit. Like the old book of the Patriarchs, Tobias is a book of " benedictions. " The benedictions exchanged for greeting or taking leave call down the blessing of God and return it to Him in thanksgiving (9, 6; 11, 17); the prayers permeating the book, cries for help (3, 11; 8, 5-7) or songs of thanks (8, 15-17; 11, 14-15; 12, 6; 13, 1-19), happily begin with the beautiful formula of benediction which appears generally in Jewish prayer even in our own day. The book closes with such a formula, and the author hopes that all nations will some day join their voices to that of Jerusalem to bless the Lord (14, 7).

The benediction is the happiness which comes from God, and praise returns this happiness to its source. The fundamental theme of the book is the *way of happiness*. This way, which is the sapiential teaching, is concretized here in a real journey; but this journey is above all a symbol. Fear of God in the observance of His commandments, a fear consisting of love and confidence, piety full of respect and attentiveness toward father and mother, scrupulous justice and honesty in social relationships, effective concern for all the brethren in need, such is the way of happiness. This will not prevent evil from touching the just man. But this evil will be welcomed as a merited and purifying trial, as a promise of the happiness which God gives without fail to those who allow themselves to be formed in wisdom by Him. Moreover this benediction is awaited on earth, the benediction promised to Abraham, a progeny which possesses the earth (4, 12), and a long life to see this happy prosperity. The question of a reward in the afterlife is not even posed.

§ 4. Doctrine

The book has added new light on another point, or at least more precision about a traditional doctrine : the role of angels, good or bad, is here put in special relief. The names Raphael and Asmodeus are meaningful : the one kills, the other cures. The fumigations that chase out Asmodeus depend on a medicine not compatible with magic recipes, but the main result seems to show that the exterminator only has power against the transgressors of the Law. Sara, as heiress, was reserved for a man within her relationship (Nm 27, 9-11; 36, 1-12), and God punishes with death those who violate the *laws of marriage* (cf. Lv 20); Asmodeus is only the instrument of divine justice. Raphael attends to the servants of God. He trains them through salutary trials, but he upholds them in their troubles and offers their good works and prayers to God (12, 12-14 and *passim*). The teaching couched in these images is already that of the New Testament.

The whole teaching of the book bears the mark of the sapiential books, teaching which is practical as well as profoundly religious. We are not surprised to find there recipes for medicine (cf. Sir 31, 19-21; 38, 1-15), nor to find the wise man occupying important positions near kings (cf. Sir 38, 33; 39, 4). Two collections of proverbs well underline the *didactic end* of the author (4, 3-19; 12, 6-10; 14, 8); we find parallels in Ben Sira, who gives a teaching akin to that of Tobias. The literary genre of Tobias is clear enough and parallel to the sapiential genre. The search for beauty, both literary and esthetic, is an aim of this genre, as is the transmission of moral and religious teaching. In these conditions the question of historicity loses much of its interest. Today no one recognizes strict historicity here. Naturally the occurrence of real events is at the basis of the story, but these events are masked in intentional disguises, under literary embellishments which make them unrecognizable to us. Moreover, we lose nothing thereby, since the intention of the author was not to satisfy the curiosity of historians.

§ 5. Tobias and Ahiqar

For a long time Tobias has been compared with Ahiqar. The wisdom of Ahiqar has been very successful in the realm of letters : it passed into our language under the guise of the Life of Aesop, the first of La Fontaine's Fables, after having proliferated into all the literatures of the East. It is readily admitted today that the story of Ahiqar comes from Babylon. Its pagan origin did not prevent it from being relished by the Jews of Elephantine, who have given us the most ancient copy in Aramaic, unfortunately in very bad condition (papyrus of the 5th century). The wisdom of Ahiqar is presented in the form of a narrative lined with a collection of proverbs; the fusion of the two elements is not as well done as in Tobias. In favor at the court of Sennacherib, then of Assarhaddon, Ahiqar was reviled by Nadan, his adopted son, who was quite anxious to take his place. Though condemned to death, he was saved by the executors who held him in concealment. But when the king expresses sorrow at the loss of such a counselor, Ahiqar is brought in alive. He saves Assarhaddon from great embarrassment, while Nadan dies of vexation about this. The author of Tobias has well summed up the moral of this story (14, 10-11, where Nadan has become Nadab); he makes Ahiqar a nephew of Tobias (1, 21-22; 2, 10; 11, 18).

This all seems to rank Tobias and Ahiqar in the same literary genre. Assyriologists think they have found the historical prototype of Ahiqar; perhaps Tobias will have the same luck some day, but that will not change the teaching of the inspired book. A strange variation in the title of Ahiqar is instructive. The Syriac recension, well within the Christian era, entitles it " Proverbs or History of Ahiqar, " while the old title of the Aramaic papyrus simply said " Proverbs of Ahiqar. " The old authors did not have about the historical value of this literary genre the illusions that the more recent copyists had.

Tobias is already cited in the letter of St. Polycarp to the Philippians (10, 12). The Fathers did not make commentaries on the book, but the personage of Tobias is freely used in examples (as the *De Tobia* of St. Ambrose, *PL* 14, 759-794). The Roman liturgy only uses it in the recent office of the Archangel Raphael and in the readings for September with corresponding responses; but it is sometimes inspired by its formulae, as in the Introit of the Trinity (cf. Tb 12, 6).

CHAPTER III

JUDITH

BIBLIOGRAPHY

Introductions, translations, commentaries, pp. 1 f. and 506 (A. BARUCQ, *BJ**; L. SOUBIGOU, *BPC**; A. MILLER, *HSAT**; J. STUMMER, *EB**; A. E. COWLEY, *APOT*...).

F. ZIMMERMAN, " Aids for the Recovery of the Hebrew Original of Judith, " *JBL*, 57 (1938), pp. 67-74.

A. LEFÈVRE, " Judith, " *SDB*, IV (Paris, 1949), cols. 1315-1321.

P. SKEHAN, " Why Leave Out *Judith?* " *CBQ*, 24 (1962), pp. 147-154; " The Hand of Judith, " *CBQ*, 25 (1963), pp. 94-110.

§ 1. Texts

The Book of Judith, written in Hebrew or Aramaic, exists only in the *Greek translation.* The text has not undergone as serious changes as has Tobias, although one can discover several recensions. The more recent versions (Latin, Syriac, etc.) all stem from the Greek. The Vulgate gives quite a shorter text which is the fruit of St. Jerome's revision according to the Aramaic text. This Aramaic text is lost without a trace, and we cannot trust the Vulgate to form an idea of it, for St. Jerome tells us himself that his work on this was done rather hastily and without real care (*PL* 29, 37-40). He did not admit the canonicity of the book, although he had heard about a decree of the Council of Nicea on the subject. The Book of Judith was nevertheless used by the Fathers since the 1st century. St. Clement of Rome (1 Cor 55) already cites Judith with Esther as an example of self-sacrifice for the common good.

§ 2. Literary Genre

The genre of this book does not fit in with the historical genre of Kings, or even of Paralipomenon. The reign of Nabuchodonosor, called king of the great city of Ninive, is put a little after the return from captivity; the Temple has already been rebuilt. We know that Ninive was destroyed in 612, that the Assyrian Empire perished in 610, that Nabuchodonosor reigned in Babylon from 604 to 562, and that he destroyed Jerusalem and the Temple. We also know that Cyrus crushed the power of Nabuchodonosor's successors and ended the captivity in 538, but that the Temple was only rebuilt under Darius in 515. Could the author have committed the gross error of making Nabuchodonosor responsible for such disparate events? Not at all. Even though modern research had great difficulty in discovering the above dates, no Jew was ignorant of the respective roles of Assur, Nabuchodonosor and the Persians in the destiny of Jerusalem. Only two hypotheses remain possible. Either the account of real events is veiled under pseudonyms, or the author writes historical fiction for a didactic purpose, borrowing elements from quite diverse epochs. In either case, the procedure hides the intention of the author.

If we are concerned with a real event, it should be possible to determine either the place or the epoch. Every date before Darius is excluded, since the Temple was rebuilt. This brings us to the Persian era, unless we must seek an even later date. Many details fit the Persian era. Holophernes and Bagoas are Persian names possessed by well-known persons. Holophernes turns up as head of the armies of Artaxerxes III Ochos in an expedition against Egypt, where a counselor of the king bears the name Bagoas (Diod. Sic. XVI, 47; XXXI, 19). Certain details are typically Persian (" preparing the earth and water, " 2, 7; " the god of the heavens, " 5, 8, etc.). Moreover the final chant designates the Persians as the invaders (16, 10). Thus it is that a place for Judith has been sought in the history of this era. The Chronicle of Eusebius, in Jerome's version, mentions the reign of Cambyses, and St. Augustine accepts this date. Sulpicius Severus (*ca.* 420) seems better informed in placing this episode under Artaxerxes Ochos, who according to the Chronicle of Eusebius deported the Jews to Hyrcania, probably on the occasion of his Egyptian campaigns. But the Holophernes, of whom Diodorus speaks, by no means perished miserably. He returns to the satrapy of Cappadocia laden with honors, with the expectation that his descendants will have there a kingly title. If the history of Judith has a historical basis in this epoch, it can only be a very minimal episode. The army which went down towards Egypt had to protect its flanks. A detachment in front of the mountain passes must have known the event described in Judith. But their obscure chief gained renown and his forces have consequently been enlarged.

According to this hypothesis, the book must have looked back on the event a long time after its happening. It might well be dated in the 3rd century. Certain traits come from Greek usages (crowns, 3, 7; 15, 13), or late Jewish usages (presabbath, 8, 6). On the other hand, Nabuchodonosor and Holophernes are not persecutors who wish evil

upon Jewish religious institutions, in the manner of the Seleucids who
force the introduction of Hellenic customs to Jerusalem. The pretensions
of the pagan king to divinity (3, 8; 6, 2) by no means exceed the swagger
of the kings of Assur in the Book of Isaias (Is 14, 4-21; 37, 22-29). We
find ourselves, therefore, before the Machabean persecutions; certain
chapters of Daniel (Dn 1—6) and the Book of Ecclesiasticus seem to
reflect the same milieu as Judith.

The author is not writing a historical work. His Nabuchodonosor
is a type of the enemies of Jerusalem, or rather a type of the pagan
whose pride must be put to shame. If he has taken a real episode as a
point of departure, our author is not interested in it for its own sake,
but for its symbolic value. He has little interest in the exact description
of places, persons, and events; so it would be a waste of time to seek to
reconstruct the historical event by which he was inspired. Aside from
this, it would be vain curiosity, since the narrator does not wish to
teach us a particular fact in the history of Israel, but the general sense
of this history. This narrator is an artist who knows how to draw out
his effects. Judith does not appear until chap. 8; the action has much
time to develop. The first seven chapters present the setting of the
drama. First there is a description of the distant background, and then
the schema begins to center our view upon the exact place where the
tragedy is enacted. At the same time that the geographical location
narrows, the forces of evil are converging to close in on the tiny people of
God. One would have to overlook the too well known denouement,
in order to feel the agony from this closing of the vise.

§ 3. Contents

In the background of the canvas looms a colossal Nabuchodonosor
(chap. 1). Arphaxad, a rival of his stature, builds before him a city
with walls of fantastic thickness. Against such an adversary, Nabuchodonosor calls upon the forces of the entire world, from Elam and Persia
to the ends of Egypt and Ethiopia. The entire West scorns this appeal.
With only his eastern troops, Nabuchodonosor overthrows Ecbatana
as if it were a house of cards. The victory was celebrated on the spot
with 120 days of merrymaking; but the western peoples, among whom
Jerusalem and Samaria occupied a rather modest position, had nothing
but bread.

The action develops slowly. Nabuchodonosor remains thereafter
in solemn isolation befitting a god (3, 8). Holophernes assumes the
task of waging vengeance upon the rebels (2, 1-3). Near Ninive, a huge

army is assembled and armed and advances forcefully to the West. In one strike it reaches the western sea and the boundaries of Japhet, the coasts of Ionia. Suddenly deciding to march to the south it lays waste to Syria and Damascus and forces the entire coast, from Tyre to Gaza, to submit. The army then heads for Egypt. Already in the plain of Esdrelon, it must reach the coastal route by passing over the hills that join the mountains of Samaria to Mount Carmel. The reassembly in the plain takes a whole month (3, 9-10).

The time for action has arrived. The invading force is at the foot of the mountains which defend the access to Jerusalem. The narrator gives us a month of respite in order to allow us to fathom the tragedy of the situation. Against a great conquering army, Israel is a poor little people that has just escaped the bonds of captivity (4, 3). The chief-priest sends an order to the frontiers to bar the passes, especially at Bethulia; meanwhile solemn prayer and fasting are ordered, to beg the Lord not to deliver the house of Israel into the hands of the impious (4, 4-15).

This resistance throws Holophernes into a fury. But the astute narrator does not hasten the attack. Holophernes has called together the local chieftains in order to be informed on the local situation. An Ammonite, Achior, relates at length what it is that makes Israel a people different from all others; their history proves that they are invincible as long as they are faithful to their God. The whole council laughs at him scornfully. "There is no god but Nabuchodonosor, says Holophernes" (6, 2). Achior is sent up to the front; let him go and share the lot of this invincible people. In the city, Achior reveals the plans and the pride of Holophernes. For those besieged, as for the reader, the mission of Achior was not without its function. The issue of the battle is clarified: God and Nabuchodonosor are present as well as the two armies. Some see in this an apocalyptic trace as in Ez 38—39 or in the "War of the children of light and of darkness," found at Qumran.

Finally Holophernes launches his attack (7, 1-3). The people of Bethulia are shut up within the walls (7, 4-5). On the advice of the Ammonite and Moabite allies who know the country, the impetuous general defers the final attack. He has control of the water supply at the foot of the city, and those under siege can only surrender or die of thirst. Within the city, the leaders are ready to hold out. But the populace would have said with Quohelet that a living dog is better than a dead lion. They prefer to live in slavery rather than die of hunger and thirst, along with their children. The head of the city obtains a delay of five

days, through great effort. Who knows if the Lord will show His power
here in favor of His people? Nabuchodonosor had taken five years to
overcome Ecbatana; God has five days to beat the mighty and victorious
army.

It is at this point that the heroine enters the scene. Judith has been
a widow for several years. Although wealthy, she lives a life of prayer
and fasting. As in the case of Daniel and his companions, this strictness
in religious observances only makes her beauty shine more brilliantly
(8, 1-8). She calls together the elders of the city and reproaches them
for treating God like a man, in imposing upon him an ultimatum. He
deserves an unlimited confidence, whether He chooses to chastise us or to
save us. Their duty is to sacrifice themselves in defense of the frontier
and of the holy city. Ozias replies that in five days God has an opportunity to send rain and to fill the cisterns. It is useless to wait for a
miracle, answers Judith. Let me go out of the city with my handmaid,
and before the five days are up, you will see what God can do through
the hand of a woman (8, 9-36).

The *hand of God* must accomplish everything; Judith therefore
addresses an ardent prayer to the God of her father Simeon, before going
into action (chap. 9). On these mountains where the patriarch beat
down the seducers of his sister, a seducer of the children of Israel is acting
sacrilegiously; may God help His handmaid to seduce the seducer and to
beat him down. Then, unhurriedly, she can launch into action. She
observes the rites of feminine seduction as well as those of the Law
(10, 1-5). Thus she proceeds before the enemy. From the outposts to
the tent of the general, her beauty opens the way for her (10, 6-23).

Placed in the presence of the seducer of her brothers, she leads him
astray as much by the charm of her conversation as by her beauty
(chap. 11). But amidst the pagans, she stays faithful to God. Each
night she goes to the stream outside camp; after the ritual ablutions, she
sends up a pure prayer to God. During the day, she does not touch the
food of the pagans, but eats provisions which she has brought along
with her, prepared by her handmaid. Three days of waiting pass in this
way (12, 1-9). Finally on the fourth day the bait is taken; the general
is ashamed of the respect which this Jewess has imposed upon him
(12, 10-12). He invites her to a banquet. She shows up, calm as ever.
She is left alone with this drunken ruffian. With one last prayer to ask
strength of the God of Israel, she cuts off the head of Holophernes with the
sword which hangs from the bed-post. As usual, she is allowed to leave
the camp; she goes straight to Bethulia with Holophernes's head in the
sack used for the provisions of her handmaid (13, 1-10).

The night ends in *thanksgiving*. Ozias blesses this wise, brave woman, and the God who has guided her action. Achior, overcome at the sight of Holophernes' head, confesses his faith in the God of Israel, and has himself circumcised on the battlefield. When the fifth day comes, it is to make known the triumph of Israel. The enemy is in retreat; Israel comes from everywhere to gather the spoils. From Jerusalem the chief-priest himself arrives with the council in order to congratulate Judith : *Tu gloria Jerusalem*. The new Debora intones the song of victory, which is also a hymn of thanksgiving; then the procession makes its way to Jerusalem to make an offering in the Temple of the spoils of the enemy (16, 18-20).

Judith will live a long life, rich and honored, but refusing to all who offer themselves to break her widowhood. Israel rejoices peacefully until her death, and for long after (16, 21-25).

§ 4. Theology and Morality

Some moralists have condemned the action of Judith who, to achieve a good end, the liberation of her people, uses bad means, deception and seduction. This condemnation overlooks the fact that the book is not a case of conscience nor a book of an edifying nature, but a page of theology. To his enemies as to his servants, God applies the law of talion. Judith is an instrument of justice in His hands. He who wished to seduce Israel into the ways of idolatry must himself be seduced and led astray. The key of the book is the prayer of Judith (chap. 9). Inversely, those who are faithful to God can count on His faithfulness. Judith acts in the role of a prophet; it is God who has put the words into her mouth. She is a model of observance of the Law and of confidence in God. Those who imitate her can count on the *protection of God*. On the other extreme, that pride which reaches even up to God, leads the imitators of Holophernes into the most abject vice and degradation where they will find the miserable end they deserve. Lightening from heaven does not carry out the *just judgments of God*, but they are shown in the normal consequences of human actions. Through the example of Achior the author even carefully shows that no one is excluded from the salvation that comes from Israel.

Cleverness added to courage, prudence in counsel, and calmness and strength in execution, these qualities embellished with a beauty which shines as much in conversation as in appearance, make of Judith a fine example of the ideal Jewish humanist. The Christians did not cease to admire her all the more, since her chastity in widowhood seemed to them a foretaste of Christian virginity. The liturgy only applies the texts of Judith to Mary in recent offices; but these applications are not devoid of all basis. She who cut off the head of the enemy of God and of His people is well in line with her who is to crush the head of the serpent. The beauty of Judith remains, however, quite pale alongside her who is full of grace.

CHAPTER IV

THE BOOKS OF MACHABEES

BIBLIOGRAPHY

Introductions, translations, commentaries, pp. 1 f. and 506 (F. M. ABEL, BJ*; M. GRANDCLAUDON, BPC*; D. D. SCHÖTZ, EBi*; W. O. E. OESTERLEY, APOT...).

E. BICKERMANN, "Makkabäerbücher" in PAULY-WISSOWA, Realenc. des Alt, XIV (Stuttgart, 1928), pp. 779-800; Die Makkabäer (Berlin, 1935); Der Gott der Makkabäer (Berlin, 1937).

E. BICKERMAN, The Maccabees (New York, 1947).

F. M. ABEL, " Les livres des Maccabées, " EB (Paris, 1949).

S. ZEITLIN—S. TEDESCHE, The First Book of Maccabees (New York, 1950); The Second Book of Maccabees (New York, 1954).

R. NORTH, " Maccabean Sabbath Years, " Biblica, 34 (1953), pp. 501-515.

A. LEFÈVRE, "Maccabées (Livres 1 and 2), SDB, V (Paris, 1953), cols. 597-612.

A. PENNA, Libri dei Maccabei* (Turin-Rome, 1953).

J. C. DANCY, A Commentary on 1 Maccabees (Oxford, 1954).

W. H. BROWNLEE, " Maccabees, Books of, " IDB, III, pp. 201-215.

W. FARMER, Maccabees, Zealots and Josephus (1956).

T. W. MANSON, "Martyrs and Martyrdom, " BJRL, 39 (1956-1957), pp. 463-484.

§ 1. Title and Texts

The Books of Machabees owe their title to the surname of Judas, the main hero of the story. The meaning of the name is a matter for discussion. It may derive from *maqqaba*, "hammer" (cf. the surname Charles Martel). It well becomes the man who smashed the horn of iniquity (1 Mc 2, 48; cf. Za 2, 1-4). This surname had become as the proper name of Judas (1 Mc 5, 34; 2 Mc *passim*). The giving of this name to the two books broadens its meaning, for the Church thereby designates the seven martyred brothers (2 Mc 7), the only saints of the Old Testament of whom the Latin rite still makes mention. This imprecise usage entails some risk of misunderstanding. The Latin translator of the *Onomasticon* (ed. Klostermann, p. 133; PL 23, 911) is already surprised that the relics of the seven martyred Machabee brothers are venerated in Antioch, since the family tomb (Judas) is in a well-known place at Modin in Palestine (1 Mc 9, 19; 13, 25).

In the Greek MSS of the Bible, the Books of Machabees are quite diversely represented. [1] While the Alexandrinus (5th c.) has four books of Machabees and the Sinaiticus (4th c.) only has the first and fourth, the Vaticanus (4th c.) doesn't have any. The ancient Latin versions contain only the first two books, those which the Church retains as canonical. [2] The Vulgate follows this version, which St. Jerome did not wish to alter; yet the Vulgate is hardly a fair testimony of the Latin text. The best testimonies have been edited by Dom De Bruyne who studied the question for a long time.

§ 2. Book 1

I. CONTENTS

Mc 1 covers a forty-year period, 175-135, from the accession of Antiochus IV to the throne of Syria to the death of Simon, the last of the Machabee brothers. This is the history of the first Asmonean generation, unfolding in chronological order. After an introduction describing the situation at the offset (1—2), it relates the successive leadership of the Jewish resistance by Judas (3, 1—9, 22), Jonathan (9, 23—12, 54), and Simon (13—16).

The historian knows the art of composition. His introduction is a diptych recounting the progress of impiety (chap. 1) and the growing resistance (chap. 2). On one side is Hellenism, personified in Alexander, sending forth a shoot that grows until it sets the abomination on the altar of Jerusalem; the wrath has come on Israel. On the other side, Judaism is incarnated in Mattathias, the chief of the Asmonean dynasty. He calls for resistance, organizes it, and in dying leaves as his will an impassioned plea to his sons to fight to the death for the people and for the Law. The faithful Jews are going to halt the unbridling of wrath.

The sons of Mattathias fell one by one into the breach, but each one led the fight with his particular temperament and his own method. *Judas* is the hero of the battles. He fires his troops with an irresistible force by the religious flame burning brightly in his exhortations as well as in his prayers before battle (3, 18-22. 58-59; 4, 8-11. 30-33;

---

[1] W. KAPLER, *Maccabaeorum liber I* (Septuagint) (Göttingen, 1936).

[2] D. DE BRUYNE, *Les anciennes traductions latines des Machabées** (Analecta Maredsolana IV) (Maredsous, 1932); *RB* (1921), pp. 405-409; (1922), pp. 31-54; (1930), pp. 503-519; (cf. 1933), pp. 263-265.

7, 41-42). Having beaten the Syrian army, he returns as a conqueror to Jerusalem, where he purifies the Temple (3—4). Thence he shines forth to the farthest boundaries of the territory, everywhere present to help his persecuted compatriots (chap. 5). Epiphones dies miserably on a distant mission (6, 1-16); against his successors, Eupator (6, 16-23) and Demetrius (7), Judas pursues the fight until his brilliant victory over Nicanor. The two feasts of the Dedication and of the day of Nicanor (4, 59 and 7, 49) will preserve for posterity the memory of his exploits. The narrator inserts documents concerning the diplomatic activity of Judas (chap. 8), and then relates his glorious death in a desperate combat (9, 1-22).

Jonathan does not have the heroic grandeur of his brother. He is more adapted to rugged guerrilla warfare than to open battle, and he is a very shrewd politician. Because of these qualities he " judges " Israel in peace for about seven years (9, 23-73). When the Seleucid throne is disputed between Demetrius and Alexander Balas, the wary Jonathan plays the role of arbiter so well that both attribute to him all the honors of the sovereign pontificate in Jerusalem, even as far as the title of chamberlain of the king. Demetrius capitulates; Jonathan obtains from Alexander the purple robe with the titles of strategus and partaker of his dominion (10, 1-66). After a reign of five years, Alexander is supplanted by his cousin Demetrius II; for fifteen years the throne of Antioch will be in dispute among two or even three pretenders. This embroilment is just the thing for the diplomacy of Jonathan, who succeeds in maintaining his privileges, and has his brother Simon appointed strategus of the coastal province. It is an irony of history that the brothers of Judas, having been made officers of the king, control all of the territory of Palestine for the benefit of the successors of Epiphanes. The shrewd diplomat renewed old relations with Sparta. The two brothers enforced the Jewish position by filling the country with strongholds (10, 66—12, 38). How could the clever old warrior allow himself to fall for the trick of Tryphon? Once captured, he will soon be put to death (12, 39-54; 13, 23).

Simon did not await the death of Jonathan to regain control of the situation. Fighting and negotiating at the same time, he does not succeed in saving his brother, but he chases Trypho from the territory and resumes friendly relations with Demetrius II, who recognizes him as head of the Jewish nation (13, 1-42). This marks the beginning of a new era, the era of liberation : " Letters and contracts came to be dated from the first year of Simon " (the year 170 of the Greeks = B.C. 142 : 13, 42). Valorous and shrewd like his brothers, Simon knows also how to deal with clemency; thus he obtains with the least output the surrender of the last isles of resistance, in particular that of the famous Acre at Jerusalem (13, 43-53). In order to eulogize such a savior of the country, the author has no qualms about using characteristics which were employed in speaking of the Messianic hope (14, 1-15). Sparta, Rome and Antioch recognize the sovereignty of Simon, ethnarch of the Jews (14, 16—15, 24). A passing quarrel with Antiochus VII, who reigned during the captivity of his brother Demetrius II, gives the sons of Simon a chance to show their valor (16, 1-10). The renowned old man dies during a banquet from the blow of a mediocre rival. But the book closes with the name of his son John, who was to be the father of the Asmonean kings.

The conclusion of the book imitates the formula which ends each reign in the Book of Kings. This supposes that the author is writing after the death of John Hyrcanus, which took place in 104 after a pontificate of over thirty years. His sons Aristobulus I (104-103) and Alexander Janneus (103-76) assumed the kingly title. This book must have been written under the reign of Janneus to glorify the ancestors of the dynasty.

St. Jerome had seen the original Hebrew text. Origen has given us the early title in a barely readable transcription, σαρβηθ σαρβαναιελ. The Greek version of the LXX is the source for all existing translations : the ancient Latin version preserved good readings throughout, permitting a better reading of the actual Greek MSS.

II. LITERARY GENRE

Living in Palestine and writing in the sacred language, the author imitated the literary forms of the ancient historical books (Judges, Samuel, Kings). But the Hellenistic influence taught him how to compose with a supple style. His accounts are sober, with a dash of enthusiasm. Especially the prayers, songs of thanksgiving, speeches of the leaders, and eulogy of heroes are emotional and all strive for the manner of expression found in the ancient biblical poems.

We must take into account this traditional style in estimating the value of the author's statements : " Not one of them escaped " (7, 46), " Not one perished " (5, 54). Such expressions, as well as large numbers, are not the formulae of a modern statistician, but are the very appropriate testimony of one living close to the facts. This testimony has much value. Numerous official documents are reproduced (10 in chaps. 11—15 alone); they are considered to be of highest quality by specialists of antiquity. Even if the form has suffered in the process of a double translation, we can have confidence in the author when he says he is transcribing a letter or giving a summary of it.

The sacred author emphasizes the religious meaning of events, but he only ties them in according to chronological order. This lack of historical reflection on causal sequence has saved him from the mistakes which Josephus made in trying to do the work of a historian. The chronology is given according to the Greek era of the Seleucids which begins in the autumn of 312.

III. TEACHING

The *religious views* of the author are those of the ancient historians, imbued with the theology of Deuteronomy : " Observe the Law and you will possess the earth. " The Law is at the center of everything; it is the Law which divides men into two camps. The struggle is not between the Seleucids and the Asmoneans, nor even between the pagan kingdoms and the Jewish state; it is between the observers of the Law and their enemies. The sons of Mattathias have no scruples in dealing with pagan powers as long as this can serve to insure the observance of the Law. But even though they count on the promises of the Covenant, they do not rest in a quietistic fatalism. The author has no praise for those who let themselves be slaughtered so as not to violate the repose of the Sabbath. It is better to fight in order to make possible the observance of the Law. They even go further to the extent of forcefully imposing respect for the religious prescriptions (2, 39-48). The greatest glory is to die, weapon in hand, in defense of the Law (2, 64). This history thus extols human values at the same time as it extols supernatural values : faith gives rise to heroism, and the service of the country is merged with service of God.

Some rather precise political aims are hinted at in this book. When John Hyrcanus and his sons ran into opposition from the strict observers of the Law, the Pharisees, it became useful to recall that the Asmonean dynasty owed its rise to power to its zeal for the Law. The Asmonean prejudice, felt everywhere, is sometimes emphasized without false timidity (5, 62). On the other hand, the Assideans, the spiritual ancestors of the Pharisees, do not always show common sense in their lofty fidelity to the Law (7, 8-18). These allusions discreetly recall to the Pharisees the fact that their rallying to the Asmoneans would perhaps be the best way to serve the interests of the Law.

Nevertheless, this history leaves the Christian unsatisfied. It appears somewhat excessive to us that deep religious sentiment can go so far as to avoid pronouncing the name of God. But the predominance of the Law and the silence of the prophets are not without danger. The possession of the earth bears the risk of limiting the ambitions of hope; the eulogy of Simon, in Messianic terms, manifests this idea. In fact, even with the Chosen People, the union of the political and the religious does not come about without risk of confusion. Mattathias would never have thought that his sons would have to worry about the favor of pagan kings in order to obtain dignities and functions in their state, even less the function of chief priest. This deviation became more accentuated later, when the sons of John Hyrcanus had taken on the title of king. We know that this dynasty succeeded in putting on the throne of Jerusalem the Idumean Herod : a strange result from an uprising so pure in its origins.

§ 3. Book 2

Although it recounts in part the same history, the second book is very different from the first in many respects. First of all, it was written in Greek. Since the text is lacking in the most ancient MSS (Vat., Sin.), the old Latin version is a valuable witness here. The author, probably an Alexandrian Jew, tells us he is summarizing a work of five books by Jason of Cyrene. We know nothing of this Jason and his work. The summary which our inspired author gives us recounts the persecution from its remote beginnings in 175, and then the struggles of Judas Machabee up to his victory over Nicanor in 160.

I. Contents

As a sort of introduction (1, 1—2, 18), two letters from the Jews of Jerusalem are transcribed. They invite their brethren from Egypt to come and celebrate with them the feast of the Dedication on 25 Casleu. The letter is dated 124, the fortieth anniversary of the purification of the Temple by Judas. The second letter is more ancient; after recalling the death of Antiochus the persecutor, it gives a long account of the marvelous deeds which mark the first restoration of the Temple under Nehemias, so as to heighten the importance of the actual feast. These documents, originating from Jerusalem, are translated from the Hebrew.

Then the proper work of the author begins in a preface where he explains his intentions and his method (2, 19-32). He has laboriously deciphered the massive work of Jason, full of numbers; he makes himself derive from it a readable story for the use of cultured people. In order to do so, he had to take liberty with the sources; and yet he is not writing a history in the technical sense of the term. This is a unique case in the Bible; the inspired author himself defines for us what literary genre he will use.

The work develops in five episodes, where the Temple always occupies the center of perspective.

Under the care of a pious high priest such as Onias, the holiness of the Temple is inviolable; Heliodorus learns this at his own expense (chap. 3).

When the office of chief priest becomes the prey of intriguers in favor of Hellenization, such as Jason and Menelaus, the wrath of God weighs heavy on Israel, the Temple is looted and profaned by impure victims. The sacrifice which faithful Jews make of their life is an expiation which will stop the wrath of the All-Powerful (4—7).

" The wrath of the Lord having changed into mercy, " Judas overthrows the pagans. Antiochus dies with the realization that the hand of God has stricken him. Judas purifies the Temple (8, 1—10, 9).

Under the administration of Lysias, who rules for Eupator, Judas wages war on all fronts, against the royal troops, against the Hellenized cities, and against the surrounding pagan peoples. Thus he obtains recognition of freedom of worship; Lysias even has sacrifices offered in the Temple, and asks the neighboring cities not to trouble the Jews (10, 10—13, 26). The intriguer Menelaus is put to death.

Under Demetrius, who has killed Lysias and Eupator, a new pretender, Alcimus, wishes to become chief priest with the support of the king. Nicanor, leader of the royal army, blasphemes against the Temple. He is defeated and slain by Judas. His head is exposed in front of the Temple, and they sing : " Blessed is he who has kept his dwelling free from all defilement. " A feast will recall this victory each year (14, 1—15, 37).

Finally, in fine rhetorical style, the writer takes his leave from the reader, praising his work for its modesty of expression (15, 38-39).

II. Literary genre

Each of these episodes is composed in the *oratorical manner* : this is a discourse to move and to persuade. With Onias we have a taste of the peace in the regular service of the Temple; then we share his anguish when the holy place is threatened; lastly we share the joy of triumph when the chastised Heliodorus becomes aware of the holiness of God who dwells there. In the second discourse, impiety and the anger of God progress from Jason to Menelaus and from the plundering of the Temple to its profanation; by contrast the death of the martyrs, which is supposed to put a halt to the wrath of God, leaves the reader with an impression of hope. In the last three discourses, Judas is exalted while his enemies are beaten down, Epiphanes, Lysias and Eupator, and finally Nicanor. Each proclaims in its own fashion the glory of the All-Powerful who

manifests Himself in the Temple. Everything works together for the
glory of God who has set His dwelling place in Jerusalem (3, 38; 7, 37;
10, 7; 13, 23; 15, 34).

The author pleads his case like a lawyer. He artfully selects and
highlights emotional episodes. Resounding epithets, biting remarks,
and a broad but not bombastic style, all this is the work of an orator.
We find ourselves here in a genre widespread in Hellenistic literature,
a genre rightly called *pathetic history*.

With this in mind we are able to size up the statements of the author.
He is concerned with clarifying the meaning and religious import of the
events related; but he neglects details which a careful historian would
demand. Chronological order yields to the demands of oratorical composition. Within the narrative the orator rightfully may choose and
magnify outstanding traits. The " help from heaven " (1 Mc 16, 3) here
assumes the form of heavenly signs (2 Mc 3, 24-26; 10, 29-30; 11, 8;
cf. 12, 22; 15, 11-16). These " epiphanies, " apparitions of the gods
coming to help combatants, were common in the Hellenistic genre of
pathetic history which Jason of Cyrene imitates. The Jewish author
has transposed the process so as to make it conform with his faith in
Providence which governs the world through the angels. The inspired
author has borrowed these tales from Jason.

In spite of oratorical liberties, 2 Mc remains a *historical* work. His
plea derives its historical value from the historicity of facts which were
not at all remote. Actually a comparison with the first book allows
us to verify the exactness of its documentation (cf. *below* the table of
concordance with the two books). The documents proper to the second
book (letters and decrees : 2 Mc 9, 17-27; 11, 16-38) are presented with the
same guarantee of authenticity as those of the first. The festal letter
at the beginning (1, 1-9) is just what we might expect from the scribes
of Jerusalem. The long reminder that goes with it (1, 10—2, 18) has many
characteristics of a haggadic construction. Our author had no illusions,
and he took care to give a more exact account of the death of Antiochus
(chap. 9, cf. 1, 13-17). On two important points 2 Mc happily completes
the ideas, brief as they are, of 1 Mc : the part taken by the chief priests
in the attempts at Hellenization (2 Mc 4) better explains the origins
of the conflict, and the arrangements made with Lysias (2 Mc 11) replace
the purification of the Temple in a more realistic historical context.

III. Doctrine

It is especially from the religious point of view that the second book
surpasses the first. The cult of the Law is no longer linked with political

aims. The struggle is between Judaism (the word appears here for the first time : 2, 21; 8, 1; 14, 38) and Hellenism (4, 13). They are diametrically opposed. Compromise can only lead to disaster (4, 7-17), and there is no question of accepting the office of chief priest through the nod of a pagan king (11, 2-3).

This uncompromising trait of religion stems from its *holiness*. The sacred Law could not be broken (6, 23. 28), even if it were a case of legitimate self-defense (5, 25; 6, 6; 15, 3). The holy Lord of all holiness (14, 36) can allow no stain upon the holy land, in the holy city, in His holy dwelling, and among His holy people. The sword of Judas is holy too, inasmuch as it comes from God (15, 16), and it is no surprise to find the heavenly armies taking part in the fighting.

The stakes of the battle are really beyond this earth. We could even say that Judas is striving for the coming of the kingdom of the saints, which Daniel mentions. Faith in a resurrection transfers to another world the enjoyment of the good things promised (7; 14, 16). But while awaiting this outcome, all the saints strive steadily for the coming of the kingdom. Prayer, ritual sacrifice, and voluntary sacrifice of one's own life have effects which are not limited merely to the present generation (15, 11-16; 12, 39-45; 7, 32-38). Such Judaism does not undergo the risk of being sidetracked into a political movement, since it transcends earthly values.

If there is one distinguishing mark to show the difference between the two books, it is their view of the *martyrs*. In the first book, their death is only a result of the wrath which has come upon Israel (1 Mc 1, 64); it is armed resistance that will turn aside this wrath, and the sword of Judas will effect this (3, 8). In the second book, the pain suffered is indeed a chastisement, but its voluntary acceptance is itself an expiation that stems the wrath of God; if Judas comes off victoriously, it is because his sacrifice has been acceptable (2 Mc 7, 36; 8, 5).

IV. INFLUENCE

2 Mc must have been composed shortly after the reception of the letter from Jerusalem on the Dedication. This puts it before 1 Mc, about 120. The book of Jason, a few years previous to this, is therefore close to the events. In the Jewish milieu, Philo seems to have been familiar with 2 Mc; 4 Mc, a little later, forms a long treatise on the martyrs which derives its inspiration from 2 Mc. But Josephus, who uses 1 Mc frequently, does not seem to have known 2 Mc. In the NT, Heb 11, 35 must refer back to the martyrs of 2 Mc 6—7. Among the Fathers of the Church,

the citations begin in the 3rd century. The cult of the seven martyred brothers must have begun in Antioch in the 4th century, for St. John Chrysostom gave two discourses in their honor. [3] Aside from the Scripture readings in the breviary for the month of October, the Roman liturgy does not use the first book; readings from the second are used in the Mass of the Dead, at the Mass for Peace, and on Ember Saturday during Lent.

§ 4. Concordance of the Two Books

This table gives corresponding sections of 1 and 2 Mc; it serves to show the liberties which 2 Mc takes with the chronological order.

Accession of Antiochus IV Epiphanes
(September 175)

Hellenism at Jerusalem	1, 10-15	4
Plundering of the Temple (169)	16-28	5, 1-20
Misdeeds of the governors	29-32	21,26
The Acre, stronghold of Hellenism	33-40	
Enforced Hellenization	41-55	6, 1-9
The abomination on the altar	54, 59	
Massacre of the faithful	56-63	10-11
Divine wrath	64	12-17
Eleazar. The seven brother martyrs		18-7, 42
Mattathias and his sons resist	2, 1-28	cf. 5, 27
Slaughter of observers of the Sabbath	29-38	cf. 5, 25; 6, 11
Organized resistance	39-48	
Last will and death of Mattathias	49-70	
Judas begins his campaign	3, 1-26	8, 1-7
Epiphanes in the East, Lysias regent	27-37	cf. 10, 10-13
Judas defeats Nicanor and Gorgias at Emmaus	3, 38—4, 25	8, 8-29, 34-36
Résumé of the other campaigns		30-33
First campaign of Lysias	4, 26-35	11, 1-12
Negotiations, tolerance		13-21, 27-38
Cleansing of the Temple, Dedication	36-61	10, 1-8
Struggles against neighboring peoples	5, 1-67	10, 14-23; 12, 1-45
Timothy killed at Gazara		10, 24-38
Death of Epiphanes (*ca.* December 164)	6, 1-16	9, cf. 1, 13-17
Decree of pacification by Eupator		11, 22-26
Lysias remains regent	17	10, 9-11
Attempts of Judas against Acre	18-27	
Second campaign of Lysias	28-54	13, 1-22
Peace obtained, Lysias retires	55-63	23-26
Demetrius acquires the throne	7, 1-4	14, 1-2
(*ca.* November 162)		
Intrigues of Alcimus, Bacchides	5-25	3-4
New offensive of Alcimus, Nicanor	26-32	5-30
Nicanor blasphemes against the Temple	33-38	31-36
Heroism of Razis		37-46
The day of Nicanor	39-49	15

Only dates (B.C.) verifiable from secular sources are given. The events proper to 2 Mc, put in italics, are outside the series, impossible to date.

---

[3] *PG*, 50, 617-626 : cf. H. DELEHAYE, *Origine du culte des martyrs* [2*] (Brussels, 1933), pp. 201-202.

CHAPTER V

WISDOM

BIBLIOGRAPHY

Introductions, translations, commentaries, pp. 1 f. and 506 (J. J. WEBER, *BPC**; E. OSTY, *BJ**; J. FISCHER, *EBi**; C. LATTEY, *CCHS**; S. HOLMES, *APOT* . . .).

P. HEINISCH, *Das Buch der Weisheit** (Münster, 1912).

C. E. PURINTON, " Translation Greek in the Wisdom of Solomon, " *JBL*, 47 (1928), pp. 276-304.

MACDONALD, *The Hebrew Philosophical Genius* (1936).

J. FICHTNER, *Weisheit Salomos* (Tübingen, 1938).

L. BIGOT, " Sagesse (Le livre de la), " *DTC*, XIV (Paris, 1939), cols. 703-744.

H. DUESBERG, *Les scribes inspirés**, II (Paris, 1939), pp. 441-592.

A. M. DUBARLE, *Les sages d'Israël** (Paris, 1946), pp. 187-235.

P. SKEHAN, " Isaias and the Teaching of the Book of Wisdom, " *CBQ*, 10 (1948), pp. 384-397; " Borrowings from the Psalms in the Book of Wisdom, " *CBQ*, 3 (1941); *The Literary Relationship Between the Book of Wisdom and the Protocanonical Books of the Old Testament* (1938).

J. HENNING, " The Book of Wisdom in the Liturgy, " *CBQ*, 14 (1952), pp. 233-236.

J. REIDER, *The Book of Wisdom* (New York, 1957).

R. MURPHY, " To Know Your Might is the Root of Immortality (Wis xv : 3), " *CBQ*, 25 (1963), pp. 88-93.

A. WRIGHT, " The Structure of Wisdom 11-19, " *CBQ*, 27 (1964), pp. 28-34.

§ 1. The Book

I. TITLE

This book is called Wisdom of Solomon by the Greek MSS of the Bible, which place it just before the Wisdom of the Son of Sira in the group of sapiential books. The Vulgate simply calls it the Book of Wisdom, in order to emphasize its superior quality within the sapiential genre. It is actually the most interesting as far as doctrine is concerned, the closest to the New Testament, and also the most well composed. It was written in Greek by an author who possessed a facility in this language. Already St. Jerome noted this, and for this reason left it out of the canon, in which he only admitted Hebrew books. Nevertheless, as W.O.E. Oesterley puts it (*Introduction*, p. 196), " this book was certainly regarded in the early Church as one of the most important, perhaps the most important, of the books which we list as apocryphal. " It is frequently cited or used by the Fathers, and the canon of Muratori (2nd c.) ranks it among the books of the New Testament written by the " friends of Solomon. "

II. Author

The attribution to Solomon is obviously fictitious; St. Augustine knows this as well as St. Jerome and Origen do. In placing his teaching on the lips of Solomon, to whom he attributes an audience of kings, the author heightens the glory of his work according to the custom of the time; by so doing he also gives it a place within the traditional development of Israelite wisdom. The author is unknown, but his emphasis on everything in relation to Egypt leads us to believe that he is writing in Alexandria, or at some important center of Jewish culture. The attribution of the book to Philo, already pointed out by St. Jerome, has found some partisans in our times; but the doctrine, the exegetical methods, the style and the language are too different for one to hold this opinion. The assimilation of Greek culture is much more superficial than that of the Jewish philosopher. The tone of the book would fit in well in the first half of the 1st century B.C., when the Jews of Egypt were exposed to the vagaries of Ptolemy VIII.

§ 2. Composition

The present work exhibits a unity of composition to which we are not accustomed in the Hebrew sapiential books. Still we would not expect to find here the logic of a modern philosophical treatise. The style undergoes quite obvious variations from one part to another; but this is not necessarily evidence of more than one author. It suffices to say that the book was not all written in one stroke, and that the author was under the literary influence of the sources in which he sought his inspiration. The first chapters (1—5) rely mainly on the Prophets, and their style is quite Hebraic; chapters 6—9, which, just as the Proverbs, use bits and pieces from Greek philosophy, are already marked by a lesser degree of biblical style; the last chapters (10—19), where the history of Israel is quite distant from the canonical sources, have a style entirely independent of the OT.

The divisions which we have just indicated leave us with three main parts of the work : the way of Wisdom, opposed to the way of the impious (1—5); Wisdom itself (6-9); and the works of Wisdom in the unfolding of history (10—19).

I. WISDOM AND THE IMPIOUS

The substance of the introduction is a hortatory discourse (1, 1-15). " Seek God, instead of running after death. Love justice, which is immortal. " *Wisdom is presented as a spirit which comes from God, but which becomes more interior to man than himself.* It is offered in order to guide him along the path which leads to God; as an interior witness of the most secret thoughts, Wisdom brings upon those who despise her an inexorable judgment. To reject her is to deliver oneself up to death. Appearances may be deceiving at times, but reality will appear when the justice of God is revealed.

The following chapters describe this judgment. They unfold in the form of a *trial*. We hear first the impious, who find themselves called friends of death (1, 16). Death is really the only absolute for them, and they judge everything by this criterion. The road appears very short to them, but the certainty of death incites them to take unlimited pleasure in life (2, 1-9). They have only revilement and hatred towards the words of the Just One whose conduct is a reproach to them. May his death make them right (2, 10-20)!

The just do not plead their own cause, but the wise man will explain the true doctrine in a series of images opposed to one another. These madmen are ignorant of the fact that life is a mystery hidden in God (2, 21-24); the death of the just is only apparent (3, 1-4). The *judgment of God* will make the glory of the just appear (3, 5-9), as well as the unmitigated misery of the wicked who have been chastised even into their descendants (3, 10-12). In what does a fruitful life consist? Even there appearances are deceiving. The barrenness of the just (3, 13-15) is blessed, while the offspring of adulterers is destined for evil (3, 16-19); barrenness joined with virtue produces lasting fruit (4, 1-2), while the abundant offspring of the impious perishes into nothingness (4, 3-6). What is a long life? It is the life of the just, suddenly snatched away, but redeemed at the judgment (4, 7-15), whereas the wicked will be struck down due to a long life of sin (4, 16-20).

The judgment also reveals the *true values*. The just man presents himself with assurance, though always silent (5, 1); the wicked come with trembling, forced to admit their mistake when it is too late (5, 2-14).

The long confession (5, 3-13) is just the opposite of the insolent speech
at the beginning, but does not make up for it (2, 1-20). The just will
reign eternally with the Lord (5, 15-16), while the divine spirit becomes
a storm which overthrows the wicked (5, 17-23). The warnings in the
beginning come true on the last day.

II. TRUE WISDOM

Wisdom has led the just to true royalty; an easy transition leads Solomon
into his exposition on *kingly Wisdom* (6—9). He begins by warning the
kings to think of the strict judgment awaiting them (6, 1-11). Then he
arouses a desire for wisdom in his noble listeners by picturing it in the
brightest light possible (6, 12-25). Wisdom goes before those who seek
her and brings them to the very throne of God to reign eternally. In
his generosity, Solomon finds no greater joy than that of sharing the
treasure which he has received as a grace; in order to make known the
blessings of Wisdom, he will describe his own experience.

Solomon begins by recalling that he is a man like all other men
(7, 1-6). It is only through a gift of God, the answer to his prayers, that
he has become wise (7, 7). He esteemed Wisdom above all (7, 8-10),
and he was not deceived, for it brought him all good things (7, 11-14).
In his discourse he elaborates upon the qualities which give Wisdom
such great value : it teaches everything about creation (7, 15-21), for it is
the all-pervading harmony at the heart of all existence (7, 22-24); more
precisely, *it is the emanation of the beauty and power of God unto all creation*,
thus rendering lovable to the Creator the beings in whom He finds Himself,
especially in the human soul (7, 25—8, 1). So it is that Solomon sought
for and loved this Wisdom, the only object of divine love (8, 2-3), inasmuch
as she procures all good things, wealth and virtue, wit and knowledge,
and everlasting renown (8, 4-13). Wisdom assists the king in governing
men and is with him in his moments of leisure to relax him (8, 14-16).
With this in mind Solomon still knows that this Wisdom is beyond all
his deserving, in spite of his natural talent. He can obtain it only by
prayer (8, 17-21). The prayer of Solomon (chap. 9) is the highpoint of the
entire treatise on Wisdom (6—8), in which he summarizes the essential
characteristics of it. This is also the spiritual highpoint of the book.

III. THE WORKS OF WISDOM

The last word of the prayer evoked the saving role of Wisdom (9, 18);
the remainder of the book will show Wisdom at work in this role. It has
saved the patriarchs from Adam to Joseph from all dangers of body and
soul; but those who stray from her, such as Cain and Sodom, have brought

catastrophe upon the earth (10, 1-14). Wisdom also saved the Chosen People through her servant Moses, whereas she has made her enemies perish (10, 15-21). This entire history, retold without a proper name, is quite clear to one who has read Genesis and Exodus.

The salvation of the people is then resumed and expanded in detail, A series of seven episodes contrast the manner in which God forms His children by salutary trials, to the manner in which He brings the wicked to their ruin with the same means. Seven plagues come into play, thirst (11, 2-14), famine (16, 1-4), animal bites (16, 5-14), hailstorm instead of manna (16, 15-29), darkness (17, 1—18, 4), wretched death, (18, 5-25), and the abyss (19, 1-12).

God's course of action could thus seem to be lacking in goodness or in justice. A twofold digression, inserted between the two first episodes, answers the objection. God has shown His mercy even to pagan people (11, 15—12, 27). Idolaters are alone responsible for their ruin : in making creatures their gods, they have made all creation their enemy (11, 15-16). The lengthy diatribe against idolatry brings to the fore the responsibility of pagans led astray by vanity (13—15). It is through their folly that they have lost the blessing that God had set upon all creatures (15, 19).

The conclusion of the book takes up the same idea under a different form (19, 13-22). The elements of creation form a harmony which operates to the disadvantage of those who oppose the divine order, while it is the joy and glory of the people of God.

§ 3. The Book of Wisdom and Hellenism

In itself, the Book of Wisdom has achieved the harmony of an entirely new genre by uniting *qualities of the Hebraic mentality to those of the Greek spirit*. In spite of some borrowings from Greek logic, such as the outline of a sorite (6, 17-20), the author remains faithful to the parallelism, mainly antithetic, which is dear to the Hebraic style; chaps. 1—5 and 10—19 are entirely built on this model. But the Alexandrian Jew has acquired the Greek art of transition. He passes painlessly from one development to another. The link between chapters 10 and 11 is the masterpiece of the genre. In the seven examples of men saved in chap. 10, Wisdom has been at work (10, 1. 3. 5. 6. 10. 13. 15). In the seven episodes of chaps. 11 to 19 God is at work, and a form of prayer develops which addresses itself to God in the second person, as in the psalms of thanksgiving. The first invocation to the Lord is neatly linked to the end of the eulogy to Wisdom (10, 20), while at the beginning of the psalm of thanksgiving a statement in the third person does not specify whether it refers to Wisdom or to God (11, 1). The artifice is a little too obvious, and a person familiar with the Dialogues of Plato would find our author somewhat crude; however, the veneer of Greek culture gives us a more ready access to him than do the old masterpieces of Hebraic Wisdom, such as Job or Proverbs 1—9.

Greek philosophy has not exercised a very profound influence. Some terms are borrowed from the eclectic philosophy of the age, in which Stoicism was dominant. In general they serve to translate various ideas long admitted into the religious thoughts of the Israelites (πρόνοια 14, 3; διοικεῖν 8, 1; 12, 18; 15, 1; στοιχεῖα 7, 17; 19, 18; συνέχον 1, 7; etc.). The assimilation remains superficial and incomplete. Thus we find that the soul is at times in opposition to the body as in Platonic thought (9, 15), and sometimes it is parallel with it, as in Hebraic usage where either soul or body can be used to designate a living person (1, 4). Likewise justice is sometimes the cardinal virtue of the philosophers (8, 7 end), and sometimes the free gift by which God makes man conformable to divine law (8, 7 beginning), a peculiarly Hebrew concept.

§ 4. Doctrine

The doctrine is indeed that of the OT. It has a Hellenized facade in order to meet the demands of the readers, the Jews of the Diaspora, and through them the demands of the more or less sympathetic pagans. During the Machabean era, Israel had taken on a clearer consciousness of retribution in the afterlife. Daniel and 2 Mc on this matter spoke of resurrection (Dn 12, 2-3; 2 Mc 7); Wisdom avoids this notion which offended the Greeks (cf. Acts 17, 32), and speaks of immortality, a Greek word without an equivalent in the OT. But we are not concerned here with the immortality of the soul which the philosophers demonstrate, although it is presupposed; the immortality which Wisdom gives is the blessed immortality, a sharing in the eternity of God (2, 23; 5, 15; 6, 19). The wealth of revealed truth, of which the prophets give us a glimpse in often obscure images, finds a clear and precise expression in its contact with Greek thought.

A new synthesis, the teaching of the Book of Wisdom is deeply traditional. There would be no difficulty in finding its elements scattered throughout the prophets and the sapiential books. But this presentation answered to the needs of the age and constituted the final preparation of the human spirit for Christian revelation.

There were at that time many doctrines of salvation. Salvation was sought in the mysteries, in philosophy, and in Gnosticism. Wisdom answers this need. The mystique which provides entrance into divine mysteries is Wisdom (8, 4); it is she who teaches all knowledge, including that of nature, of man, and that of pleasing God (7, 21. 27; 8, 5-18). The philosophy of good fortune is too transitory; Wisdom teaches the justice which leads to immortality (1—5). But this justice and this wisdom are not qualities that man can acquire through his own resources, a fact which both Jews and Greeks have a hard time admitting : *encrateia* is a grace one must ask of God (8, 19-21). The road to salvation is justice, but it is a justice that first of all must be a gift of God in order to become a virtue of man.

What then is Wisdom? Nothing less than God Himself in communication with spiritual creation. Already in Wisdom God gives to His creatures a reflection of His beauty (7, 22—8, 1), the internal cohesion making all things subsist (1, 7); but *to man God communicates in a more intimate manner* which assumes an acceptance by a free creature; thus man enters into participation with the divine nature, and with His immortality (1-15; 2, 23). Wisdom enters the soul which is open to her and makes it lovable in the eyes of God (9, 10-12; 10, 16); she leads it along the paths of the service of God to the life close to God, the eternal life (6, 9-21; 10).

We are on the threshold of the NT. St. Paul and St. John use the same formulae in speaking about the spirit which God sends into the heart of His faithful to make them acceptable in His eyes, and to make charity grow in them along with all virtues. The glory of the Word is described likewise in terms borrowed from Wisdom (Col 1, 15; Heb 1, 3; etc.). We must not ask more of our author than what he knows. The Trinity has not been revealed to him. But he has advanced as far as possible the preparation of the human spirit to receive this revelation.

CHAPTER VI

ECCLESIASTICUS (SIRACH)

BIBLIOGRAPHY

Introductions, translations, commentaries, pp. 1 f. and 506 (C. SPICQ, *BPC**; H. DUESBERG—P. AUVRAY, *BJ**; V. HAMP, *EBi**; G. H. BOX—W. O. E. OESTERLEY, *APOT*...).

N. PETERS, *Das Buch Jesus-Sirach oder Ecclesiasticus** (Münster, 1913).

J. MARCUS, *The Newly Discovered Hebrew of Ben Sira* (Philadelphia, 1931).

G. R. DRIVER, " Hebrew Notes on the ' Wisdom of Jesus ben Sirach ', " *JBL*, 53 (1934), pp. 273-290.

H. DUESBERG, *Les scribes inspirés**, II (Paris, 1939), pp. 232-440.

A. M. DUBARLE, *Les Sages d'Israël** (Paris, 1946), pp. 147-185.

L. ROTH, " Ecclesiasticus in the Synagogue Service, " *JBL*, 71 (1952), pp. 171-178.

R. SIEBENECK, " May Their Bones Return to Life! — Sirach's Praise of the Fathers, " *CBQ*, 21 (1959), pp. 411-428.

L. HARTMANN, "Sirach in Hebrew and Greek, " *CBQ*, 23 (1961), pp. 443-451.

A. DiLELLA, " Qumran and the Geniza Fragments of Sirach, " *CBQ*, 24 (1962), pp. 245-267.

Ecclesiasticus has in Greek the title " Wisdom of the Son of Sirach. " The author mentions himself near the end of the book (50, 27), adding that he is from Jerusalem. The Latin name, Ecclesiasticus, has not yet been fully explained, but it is in use by the time of Cyprian.

§ 1. Text

Jesus, the son, or rather descendant, of Sirach, wrote in Hebrew. His grandson put the work into Greek for the use of the Jews of Alexandria, among whom he lived during the 38th year of Ptolemy Euergetes. He tells us this in the prologue that he places at the beginning of his translation. Of the two Ptolemy Euergetes, only the second, Ptolemy VII, has a reign of over 38 years (170-116); thus the grandson must have translated the work after 132. We can reasonably suppose that Ben Sirach himself wrote about fifty years earlier, about 180. In his youth he may have seen the chief priest Simon II, whose majesty had overwhelmed him (50, 1-21).

St. Jerome had seen the Hebrew text which Jewish authors cite up to the 10th century; then it falls into oblivion until our own time. In 1896 some pages bought by chance in the East produced several fragments of it. Subsequent inquiry showed that these pages had originated in Cairo from the geniza of an old synagogue. The source was carefully explored, the scattered pages were reassembled, and the libraries of Europe and America now possess about 2/3 of the Hebrew text of the recovered book. The fragments come from five different copies, dating from the 11th or 12th century. [1]

These discoveries gave new impetus to textual study. The textual tradition of Sir is one of the most complicated. The Greek is longer than the Hebrew, and the Latin (unrevised by St. Jerome) is longer still. Yet the Latin is on the whole the translation of a Greek text, and the Greek comes from a Hebrew original. Certain additions are of Latin and Greek origin, but some even stem from a Hebrew text that is already glossed. Even the specialists have had a hard time unraveling this confusion, but one thing is certain : the successive editors of the text, whether Hebrew, Greek, or Latin, all had the tendency to add explanations of their own.

To heighten the confusion, the Greek exemplar from which all the MSS derive had reversed the order of two sections (30, 25—33, 13a changed places with 33, 13b—36, 16a). Through this displacement and the abundance of superscripts there resulted a variation in the numbering of chapters and verses among the various editions, a fact which tries the patience of researchers.

§ 2. Contents

The work of Ben Sirach, by its very nature, could expect such disturbances. It is a collection of sentences without order on the most disparate topics. The Greek has interspersed the book with titles (2, 1; 18, 30; 20, 27; 23, 7; 24, 1; 30, 1. 14. 16; 32, 1; 33, 25; 44, 1; 51, 1); but these titles often concern only short passages and do not constitute a division of the

---

[1] I. Levi, *The Hebrew Text of the Book of Ecclesiasticus* (Leyden, 1951); J. Touzard, " L'original hébreu de l'Ecclésiastique, " *RB* (1897), pp. 547-573; (1898), pp. 33-58; id., " Nouveaux fragments hébreux de l'Ecclésiastique, " *RB* (1900), pp. 45-62, 525-563.

work. Only the title of 44, 1, " The Eulogy of the Fathers, " is already in the Hebrew text, and it is at the head of an important section (44—50). Neater divisions are marked by two little epilogues (24, 28-32 and 33, 16-18) analogous to the final epilogue (50, 27-29; 51, 13-30); we can evince from this that the early book was gradually increased by successive appendages.

Within the body of the work a certain number of *poems to the glory of Wisdom or of God the Creator* serve at the same time to divide it up and to link the partial collections to one another. A hymn to Wisdom begins the series (1, 1-10); it is prolonged by a group of statements about wisdom and the fear of God (1, 11-30). Then come the first rudiments of formation in wisdom. A courage made of wisdom and confidence is necessary in order to begin the journey (chap. 2). The first steps are filial piety (3, 1-16), respect for all that exceeds the capacity of a beginner (3, 17-27), and the works of mercy which make the beginning wise man ready, and render him beloved to God and man (3, 28—4, 10). This ends with a eulogy to Wisdom who trains her children for glory, making them pass through instructive trials (4, 11-19).

In the following collection, the disciple learns to *discern true values*, good and bad shame, confidence and presumption, and the advantages and dangers of friendship (4, 20—6, 17). A new invitation to enroll in the school of those wise in the fear of the Lord (6, 18-37), to enter it with both courage and modesty, begins a collection of sayings which usher the disciple into the great task of life in society (7, 1—14, 19). All elements of human society pass in review, the professional and family settings, priests and the poor, the aged and the dead, the hot-tempered, the sot, all temperaments, women, friends, the powerful, the princely. The teacher profits from this in teaching his disciple the just mean, so difficult to maintain in regard to material goods, for death takes away honor and riches alike. Beyond the thought of death, it is the fear of God that sums up this teaching. The eulogy of the wise man who fears God (14, 20—15, 10) and a series of thoughts on man before God (15, 11—16, 21) end with a hymn to the Creator (16, 22—18, 13).

Within the easy-going collection that follows we can see a twofold warning against the excesses of the tongue and against lustful involvements (18, 14—23, 27). After a prayer to obtain the grace of self-mastery (23, 1-6), the series ends with advice on the use of speech (23, 7-15) and on adultery (23, 16-27). The collection ends with a poem in which Wisdom sings her own praises (24, 1-27), in imitation of Prv 1—9 where the eulogy to Wisdom follows the admonition against adultery (Prv 7 and 8).

In the *epilogue* (24, 28-32) the teacher encourages his pupil to drink at the fountain of Wisdom as he did. Thus the handbook of the apprentice wise man ends. Amid its apparent disorder we can follow the progressive initiation into the study and practice of wisdom.

The *first supplement* (25, 1—33, 18) closes with an epilogue analogous to the preceding one but more brief (33, 16-18). The fear of God is the main preoccupation; certain themes recur constantly : women (25, 1. 12-25; 26, 1-18), conversations (27, 4-24) and disputes (28, 8-26), service done to one's neighbor (29, 1-20), peace in the family, in moderation (29, 21—32, 14).

The *last supplement* is like the last will of the teacher. The thought of death forms the framework for it (33, 19-23 and 41, 1-13) and is touched upon several times. The inheritance which the wise man leaves is his long experience which even extends beyond the boundaries of his people (34, 9—36, 19); he has learned much from his dealings with people (36, 20—37, 26), ever maintaining that moderation so conducive to good health (37, 27—38, 23). All occupations are honorable since they serve society, but the role of wise man is higher than any other (38, 24—39, 11). This thought uplifts the old teacher (39, 12-15) and he sings a hymn to the Lord whose works reveal His Wisdom (39, 15-35). From this we naturally pass on to the praise of God in creation (42, 15—43, 33), and then to the eulogy of those who carry on the work of God through the wisdom which He has granted them (44—50). We find in this work, so poorly composed from our point of view, a continuous movement, in successive waves; thereby the reader, or rather the pupil, goes from the practice of wisdom to the contemplation of God as seen through his well-ordered creation, the world and man.

§ 3. Literary Genre

Sirach uses classical literary forms of the sapiential genre. The *mashal* remains the framework, taking on various enlargements and elaborations in the manner of Prv 1—9 or 25—27. One series of sayings is linked together by the repetition of one expression, " the fear of God " (1, 11-30); the *mashal* with number sequence arranges the sayings in a progressive order (25, 7-11). Sirach combines these two forms and obtains, so to speak, a *mashal* of the second degree (40, 18-27). The wise man did not form his pupils in thinking without at the same time teaching them how to express themselves; all the subtle or elegant usages of the *mashal* find their models here. Sirach knows how to paint a character portrait (38, 24—39, 11), although he has not acquired a mastery of the classics

(Prv 5—7, cf. Wis 23, 16—27). His eulogies to Wisdom do not, however, achieve the perfection of his models (Jb 28; Prv 8, cf. Wis 1, 1-10; 24, 1-27). On the other hand, he has his own lovely series of historical portraits (44—50). Even more so than the impersonal sayings of the old proverbs (Prv 10—22), it is the exhortation which is predominant in Wis, as in Prv 1—9. Sirach puts his own personality into it (24, 28-32; 33, 16-18; 39, 12-14; 51, 13-30) with the lyrical tenor of the sapiential psalms (cf. Ps 34, 37, etc.), mixing prayers of supplication and thanksgiving with his exhortations (22, 25—23, 6; 36, 1-19; 51, 1-12). This is also the case with his hymns to the Creator (42, 15—43, 33) or his meditations upon the human condition (16, 22—18, 13; 39, 15-35); these recall the poetry of the psalms. The poetry of Ben Sira belongs to an old genre in which the forms and themes have become cliches; at least it is a valuable witness to the activity of the scribes in the working out of the later selections of the Psalter.

§ 4. Teaching

Wisdom is an especially valuable document of the *morality* and *doctrine* of Judaism shortly before the heroic age of the Machabees. This book, and the teaching which it reflects, knew how to form characters opposed to the pressure of triumphant Hellenism. The fear of God is at the basis of everything; this fear consists of respect and obedience, as well as absolute confidence in the God of the Covenant. Sirach is careful to warn his disciples that they will not escape trials; they are indispensable in forming character. Looseness, insincerity and carelessness in morality and education are enemies against which one must ever be on his guard. Forceful yet discreet, he knows how to use the means at his disposal, and he knows how to deal with every sort of person. His *forcefulness* may seem impolite to us, and his *prudence* borders on mistrust, but these were hard times. Sirach is, at any rate, healthy in mind and body, full of good humor; although he stands for forceful methods in education, he has no admiration for old prattlers and grumblers. He does not look down on good food, and music is a pleasure to him. This honorable man of Judaism is in general quite congenial, and it is always profitable and enjoyable to converse with him.

The *religion* of Sirach is as sturdy as his humanism, from which it is inseparable. Everything rests on faith in the God of the Covenant. This faith must show itself in works, works of worship certainly, but above all in the practice of justice and mercy towards one's neighbor. This picture of Palestinian Judaism in the 2nd century, just before the rifts which divided the Sadducees and Pharisees, gives us an idea of the soul of the pious Jew, aside from sectarian groups, up to the time of Jesus. [2] Not everything here reaches the heights of the Sermon on the Mount, but we find various traits already present. We learn how to pray to God as a father (23, 1. 4), and we already know that this father will only pardon us if we ourselves know how to pardon (28, 1-7).

§ 5. Limitations and Influence

On one point the theology of this book seems rather restricted : the destiny of man and of humanity receives no illumination from above. The pious man awaits his reward on this earth, in his own person or through his children. Israel hopes for salvation on this earth. The thought of death often recurs in this book as an obsession, but the answer will not be fully elucidated except through the death of the Machabean martyrs.

Must we also reproach Sirach for too narrow a view in his identification of Wisdom with the Law of Moses? Perhaps less than it seems at first glance. In continuity with Dt 4, 5-8, the Prophets (eg., Is 2, 3; 51, 4) and the Psalms (19, 119, etc.) find within the Law a manifestation of the word of God which harmoniously orders the world as well as the conduct of men. [3] There is certainly a risk of declining into slavishness to the letter, but this is also a continuity in development of revelation which culminates in the theology of the Logos in St. John.

The liturgy of the synagogue must have used the Wisdom of Sirach for a long time. We know that even in the 10th century there were copies of it provided with the reading signs ordinarily reserved for the Bible. [4] Christian liturgy makes frequent use of it as does the teaching of the Fathers. Clement of Alexandria cites it so abundantly that he serves as a textual witness on a par with biblical MSS. Christians will always profit from a visit in the school of this wise man. This even-tempered, serious and good-humored teacher knows how to inculcate the practice of solid virtue. He wonderfully unites in his teaching the depth of revealed religion with a sane, down to earth *humanism*.

---

[2] J. TRINQUET, " Les liens ' sadocites ' de l'écrit de Damas, des manuscrits de la Mer Morte et de l'Ecclésiastique*, " *VT*, I (1951), pp. 287-292.

[3] Cf. A. ROBERT, " Le sens du mot Loi dans le Ps 119, " *RB* (1937), pp. 182-206.

[4] C. ROTH, " Ecclesiasticus in the Synagogue Service, " *JBL*, LXXI (1952), pp. 171-178.

CHAPTER VII

SUPPLEMENTS TO THE
BOOKS OF ESTHER AND DANIEL

BIBLIOGRAPHY

See the Books of Esther (p. 466) and of Daniel (p. 473).

§ 1. Supplements to Esther

The Book of Esther is accepted by the Church in two different forms. The Hebrew narrative, admitted by the Vulgate (1, 1—10, 3) and by the Peshitto, is shorter. Before St. Jerome, in Latin as in Greek, a longer narrative was used. When St. Jerome had translated the Hebrew narrative, he added as supplementary the principal elements of the narrative admitted up to that time which were not included in his version. Thus separated from their context, these " supplements " (10, 4—16, 24) became difficult to use. We find them in place in the edition of the LXX; but the editors have not adopted a uniform system of reference. We present below the series of supplements, with the mode of reference, 1) of the Vulgate, 2) of Swete, followed by the large edition of the LXX of Cambridge, and 3) the mode of Rahlfs, followed by the Bible of Jerusalem.

	Vulgate	Swete	Rahlfs
1. Dream of Mardocheus	11, 2-12	A, 1-11	1, 1a-b
2. Conspiracy against Assuerus	12, 1-6	A, 12-17	1, 1m-r
3. Edict for the extermination of the Jews	13, 1-7	B, 1-7	3, 13a-g
4. Prayer of Mardocheus	13, 8-18	C, 1-11	4, 17a-i
5. Prayer of Esther	14, 1-19	C, 12-30	4, 17k-z
6. The appeal of Mardocheus to Esther	15, 1-3	4, 8	4, 8
7. Reception of Esther by Assuerus	15, 4-19	D, 1-16	5, 1a-2b
8. Edict in favor of the Jews	16, 1-24	E, 1-24	8, 12a-x
9. Meaning of the initial dream	10, 4-13	F, 1-10	10, 3a-k
10. Acknowledgment of a letter	11, 1	F, 11	10, 3l

If we pose question of the origin of these appendices, one thing is certain : they were not produced for the Hebrew text. Thus 12, 1-6 already appears in 2, 21-23 with irreconcilable variations; the decrees are duplications of the résumés (3, 13 and 8, 11-12), and the gist of the second (16, 1-24) does not correspond to its résumé (8, 11-12). These are not, properly speaking, actual supplements, but we are dealing with two different editions of Esther.

What connection is there between the two editions? Many Catholic scholars have long admitted that the lengthier edition, originally in Hebrew or in Aramaic, was the original edition of which we only have the Greek translation; the Hebrew Massoretic text would then be an abridgment, purged of all allusion to religion because of the profane character of the feast of Purim. Inversely, St. Robert Bellarmine thinks that the Massoretic Hebrew represents the original edition, and that another author started with it to write a *longer account* which is the basis of the Greek text. This hypothesis is more in line with the midrash development, well known in later Jewish literature.

We also tend to admit more and more that the Greek of the appendices is not a translation Greek : the decrees were certainly composed in Greek, and they are an essential part of the long edition. The question is complicated by the fact that the Greek text is handed down to us in three quite different states. The common text, represented by the large uncials and already used by Josephus, seems to be a compromise between the original Greek text and the Hebrew; this may be the work of a certain Lysimachus (11, 1), who was brought to Egypt in the fourth year of Ptolemy and Cleopatra (B.C. 112 or 47). The Lucianic text, represented by four minuscules, is a much later revision. But the text which the old Latin witnesses, notable both for its coherence and its important omissions (12, 1-6; 9, 1-2. 5-19; 11, 1), seems to be the most ancient. Schildenberger finds here proof of a Greek account at the start; this solution, although it does not solve all the difficulties, seems to be the most probable. The value of the old Latin as proof of the oldest Greek text has good parallels in the Books of Tobias and Machabees.

The *literary genre* of the " supplements, " or rather of the Greek edition, is the same as that of the original Hebrew, a story freely treated in order to teach. The new developments introduced by our Jewish Hellenist are well summed up by St. Jerome : " He has improvised, as one does in a school exercise, to underline the sentiments of one undergoing an injustice or inflicting it upon someone else " (*PL* 28, 1433).

Thus the author pursued a precise end, for he offered to the Jews of the Diaspora something more readable in the Hellenized milieu, more genteel thanks to the suppression of characteristics too inimical to pagans (9, 5-19), more religious also, and more demonstrative of the action of Providence and the efficaciousness of prayer. The doctrinal contribution of deuterocanonical developments does not seem very great.

§ 2. Supplements to Daniel

The Greek appendices in the Book of Daniel form two distinct groups. Within chap. 3 (the three Hebrews in the furnace), the *prayer of Azarias* and the *canticle of Azarias* and his companions are inserted; a few narrative verses link these to the context (Vulgate : 3, 24-90). At the end of the book have been added two tales about Daniel, the *judgment of Susanna* and the old men (at the beginning of the book in Theodotion; after chap. 12 in the LXX; Vulgate : 13), and the episodes of *Bel and of the Dragon* (at the end of the book in the two Greek versions; Vulgate : 14). These appendices come from Semitic originals, either Hebrew or Aramaic; but they may have been reassembled and rearranged only in the Greek version.

I. SUPPLEMENTS TO CHAPTER III

The pieces inserted in chap. 3 must have been written in Hebrew. The prayer of Azarias (Vulgate : 3, 26-45) is like the one in Daniel (9, 4-19); it is the people's confession of sin to obtain the mercy of God, that is, deliverance from present calamities. See above, p. 509, about this genre as regards Bar 1, 15—3, 8. Here we find a reflection of the condition of the Machabean martyrs; the prayer develops the same themes as does the discourse of the martyrs (2 Mc 7, 32-38) : we suffer because we are sinners, but our sacrifice will appease the wrath of God, and we will be glorified while our persecutors will be chastised. As always, it is the just man who utters this confession in the name of the guilty people from whom he would not think of dissociating himself; such is the way with Jeremias (14, 7-19), Esdras (9, 6-15), Nehemias (1, 5-11), Daniel (9, 4-19) and the martyrs (2 Mc 7, 32). This prayer, composed of common cliches in a form widespread throughout the Psalms and elsewhere, derives its originality from the situation which it reflects. The offering of oneself as an expiatory sacrifice (3, 39-40, used in the Offertory of the Roman Mass) takes on a particular emphasis when compared to the one of the young martyr (2 Mc 7, 37-38). By inserting this prayer here, the inspired author makes of these three young persons of the ancient account a type of the martyrs of his era.

The canticle of the three Hebrews in the furnace consists of two parts. The first (3, 52-55) is in the style of blessings popular in Jewish prayer : *baruk atta...* (rare in the Hebrew Bible : Ps 119, 12 and 1 Par 29, 10; more often we find : *baruk adonay*). The second part adds to the hymn of praise of all creation (3, 56-87) a hymn of thanksgiving on the part of the Hebrews delivered from danger (3, 88-90). These hymns, less energetic in their makeup than the psalms that served as their models (esp. Ps 148), are well adapted to common recitation; the Christian liturgies of the East and West have always made use of them.

The introductory verses (25 and 51) serve as titles. The account of verses 46-50 borrows its elements from the Aramaic text; on the one hand, the gist of verses 22-23 is resumed and somewhat emphasized, and on the other hand, we are prepared for the mention of the angel in verses 92 (25) and 95 (28). Since Rothstein, [1] many see in these verses a vestige of the early Aramaic account, which would fill in the gap between verses 23 and 24 (91). It remains to be seen whether the abrupt transition, without psychological preparation, enables the reader to share more fully in the surprise of the king. It is a matter of taste, says Montgomery, [2] who sees in verses 46-50 an awkward filling-in of the compiler. Everything seems to indicate that he is right. In any case, the actual state of the Aramaic text is attested to near the beginning of the Christian era by a fragment found in grotto I of Qumran.

II. CHAPTERS 13—14

The accounts of chaps. 13—14 belong to the cycle of Daniel, from which Dn 1—6 also borrows; they likewise belong in the category of edifying tales (*fabulae*, according to St. Jerome), but they are far superior in literary worth. The story of Susanna is one of the lovely tales of the Bible. The Babylonian context is artificial. The teaching is that of the later sapiential literature, saturated with the piety of the psalms : calumniated innocence obtains divine help through prayer, and wisdom is not the privilege of old people but of the virtuous (cf. Ps 119, 22-23. 100). Primitive Christian art has pictured Susanna as a lamb among wolves; this image is already suggested by Ps 119, 176.

The stories of Bel and the Dragon are full of satirical spirit which contrasts with the tone of Dn 6. These tales illustrate the struggle which the Letter of Jeremias preached (cf. p. 512), in reaction to the pagan renewal of the 3rd century. The story of Susanna can also be dated from this period. Origen (*PG* 2, 41-86) already defended the existence of a Hebrew or Aramaic original. This is also the general opinion today.

These picturesque stories have had great success in Christian iconography since the first centuries. [3] They furnish lessons for the Masses in Lent.

---

[1] In KAUTZSCH, *Apokryphen* (1900), p. 175.

[2] *Daniel*, *ICC* (1927), p. 9.

[3] Cf. Dom LECLERCQ, " Cappella greca, " " Daniel, " " Suzanne, " *Dict. d'archéol. chrétienne et de liturgie.*

CONCLUSION

THE FORMATION OF THE OLD TESTAMENT

by P. Grelot

BIBLIOGRAPHY

P. HEINISCH, *History of the Old Testament** (Collegeville : Liturgical Press, 1952).

H. H. ROWLEY, *The Growth of the Old Testament* (London, 1950).

While the present volume is not concerned with a doctrinal examination of the Old Testament (see the following pages), the following are some of the important books treating of this aspect of Old Testament study.

W. EICHRODT, *Theology of the Old Testament*, I (Philadelphia : Westminster, 1961).

P. HEINISCH, *Theology of the Old Testament** (Collegeville : Liturgical Press, 1952).

O. PROCKSCH, *Theologie des Alten Testaments* (Gütersloh, 1950).

P. VAN IMSCHOOT, *Theology of the Old Testament*. Vol. I : *God* (New York : Desclee, 1965).

E. JACOB, *Theology of the Old Testament* (New York : Harper, 1958).

G. VON RAD, *Old Testament Theology*, I (New York : Harper, 1962).

T. C. VRIEZEN, *An Outline of Old Testament Theology* (Oxford, 1958).

PRELIMINARY REMARKS

§ 1. The Genesis of the Bible

The various parts of the Old Testament have been studied in the preceding chapters. After having traced as a whole the history of Israel from the patriarchal period to the threshold of the New Testament, each of the biblical books was analyzed in the framework of the broader category in which it is now present : Torah, prophets, hagiographers and deuterocanonical books. It will be profitable now to take up again from a new angle the results of these analyses, in order to present as a whole the development of the Old Testament from an essentially *literary* point of view. It is not as though this were the principal aspect of the Bible; its doctrinal value is infinitely more important. But in order to realize what was, in its concrete reality, the progress of divine revelation linked to the spiritual education of Israel, it is necessary to follow first of all step by step the genesis of the collection of books, which, in each period, testify to it. The historical framework of its formation henceforth is known and each book or book fragment has been the object of a critical and doctrinal exposition; it is fitting to show groupings, linkings, influences, and subordinations which could not be the object of the preceding studies since they separated for practical reasons works deriving from the same time or the same milieu. If, in this perspective, it sometimes happens that a side-glance is cast upon some works foreign to the Bible, it does not follow that they are being put on the same footing as the Bible. What we are trying to retrace here is not a history of Hebraic and Jewish literature, but only the gradual formation of the inspired books.

Thus conceived, the literary history of the Old Testament affords a solid point of departure for biblical theology, in order for the latter to be something else than a repertory of themes, presented independently from the historical development which, from the faith of Abraham, leads to the Judaism contemporaneous with Christ. That is to say that this development itself will constantly be sketched on the background of our study. We will avoid, however, attempting on the sole plan of the Old Testament a doctrinal synthesis which could seem desirable to more than one reader. It is because, first of all, the Christian study of the Bible cannot separate the two Covenants; the theological meaning of the Old Testament, which we must uphold, reveals itself only in light of the New Testament. The first constitutes an ascent toward Christ; but it still carries with it, on the level of institutions as well as of ideas, provisional materials which must either be surpassed or rethought. Christ, in His person, His acts and His words, clarifies, in retrospect, all that precedes Him; He is, by that very fact, a principle of interpretation and a criterion for choice. We will therefore reserve the synthesis of biblical theology for the time when the New Testament will allow us to define the meaning of the Old Testament, since in its original novelty, it will be a fulfilment of the Sacred Scriptures.

Furthermore, it seems useful to us not to confuse two aspects of the Old Testament which despite the fact that they are closely united, are yet quite distinct : the books where biblical revelation was crystallized and the complex of institutions where these books were born. God, by various means, spoke to a people whom He was calling to the faith. The people not only preserved His Word in the form of a written collection which grew with time, but also in its living tradition, much more elusive, even though the writings which it left us find their roots in it. In order to be complete, a history of revelation should evoke this living tradition which is the echo of the Divine Word in the history of a human community. One would then have to go beyond the framework of the Bible and give a place, for instance, to the literary productions of Judaism during the last centuries before Christ and during the time of the New Testament : is it not in relation to this concrete milieu, broader than the canon of the Scriptures shows it to be, that Jesus preached and lived, that the Gospel was announced, and the Church founded, in short that the New Covenant relieved the Old? So be it; but our present intention is more restricted; we are studying the Sacred Scriptures and them alone; we are trying to realize how their collection was made. This undoubtedly requires close attention to the life of the Chosen People, in all the meanderings of a complicated history, but only as a term of reference without which the genesis of the Bible could not at all be understood.

§ 2. Limits and Divisions of this Sketch

Useful as a genetic study of the Bible is, it nonetheless entails a measure of uncertainty. Not only because our information on Israelite and Jewish literature is sparse : it is understood that we are limiting our study only to the preserved works which appear in the canon. But, even for these, how many precise details are lacking! The localities, the authors and even the periods cause problems. Next to assured critical conclusions, there are times when we can only count upon probable or possible solutions. A tableau like the one we are undertaking here can only be presented therefore as a provisional plan. If it allows a better view of the organic unity of the Bible, it is certain that the future will bring corrections, and more precise and perfect details to it. It is important to understand it with this reservation of principle, which from the outset establishes its limitations.

As to the great literary periods of the Old Testament, they coincide in a way with that of the history of Israel. The period of preparation which precedes the reign of David is very important from the historical and religious point of view, since it sees revelation born with Abraham, become more precise with Moses, and implanted in Chanaan after the conquest and at the time of the Judges. But on the literary level, it is much more difficult to capture because, in a certain measure, its productions were incorporated into vaster syntheses, done during the royal period. With David and Solomon, Israelite literature soars under its written form, when Jerusalem becomes an important cultural center (10th-9th centuries). After the schism, this literature develops in a parallel fashion in the two kingdoms of Juda and of Israel; but primarily, the two traditions meet when the " remnant " of Israel takes refuge in Juda after the ruin of Samaria (9th-8th centuries). The humiliation of Juda during the apogee of Assyria coincides with an apparently slack literary period; then, during the last fifty years of the Judean State, there is a renewal which continues at the time of the Babylonian captivity, while the theocratic organization of Judaism little by little replaces the former political institutions of the royal period (7th-6th centuries). The Persian period sees Judaism becoming established; at the same time, collections of the ancient books become a body and new literary currents are developed (6th-4th centuries). Finally, the conquests of Alexander place Judaism opposite the Hellenistic civilization, and its literature suffers the shocks of this confrontation (4th-1st centuries). We will thus distinguish six successive periods, while recognizing that such a schema comprises its share of artificiality.

CHAPTER I

AT THE ORIGINS OF THE BIBLE : MOSES

§ 1. From the Age of the Oral Tradition to the Written Civilization

If revelation occurs at a time when the Near East has for a long time already reached a written civilization, the human community which receives it accedes to it only little by little. The fact is elucidated by the Bible itself. The Hebrew patriarchs which Genesis describes to us still belong to the nomadic or semi-nomadic age where oral traditions reign. Subsequently, Exodus evokes the use of writing at the time of Moses (Ex 17, 14; 34, 28). But one must surely not exaggerate its extension for if at the time of the Judges, the art of writing seems spread even to the common people, it is only with precise and defined ends of an altogether practical order (Jgs 8, 14). Finally, one enters fully into the domain of the written civilization when Israel becomes master of the urban centers and especially when David establishes his monarchy in Jerusalem.

It is therefore normal to place oneself first of all in the perspective of this historical framework when one wants to study the birth of sacred literature in the people of God, and from that point of view, to cast a glance on the preceding centuries to draw a balance sheet on them, without trying to trace their literary history in detail. The point of view of the royal scribes is then seen; these latter were interested in collecting all the inheritance of the past and transmitted it to us in their books.

It must also be noted that the oral tradition did not end at the moment when written literature was in full sway. It was born first and had served as a cradle for the archaic works established before the royal period. It then continued subsequently to feed literature from century to century, thanks to its partially autonomous development. For example, with respect to the Pentateuch, the priestly narrators drew materials that had been previously unexploited. Likewise, one must not represent the oral tradition and written literature as two domains foreign to one another from the point of view of the means of expression used. Solomon's contemporaries must not have seen any appreciable difference between the narratives spread orally (as had been the immemorial custom) and the narrations put into form by the court scribes, for the art of the latter proceeded from that of the ancient story-tellers and the transition from the one to the other was effected rather imperceptibly. However, an important turn of events took place at the moment when there was fixed in writing what up to then had been entrusted to the living memory of men.

§ 2. The Traditions of Israel [1]

Israelite traditions, at the time of the monarchy, appear under extremely varied aspects as to their origin, their aim, their form and their atmosphere. The internal unity of the nation is already an established fact, but from social groups which, though conscious of a certain original relationship, yet have had various historical experiences. Each of these groups (clans, tribes and groups of tribes) has its own traditions. Thus, Gn 38 is peculiar to Juda, while the wars of Josue apparently refer to the battles of the Benjaminites and in Gn 4 a Kenite origin is discerned. [2] Other traditions are bound up with places : burial places or battlegrounds, former tribal resting places (such as Cades) or venerated shrines (such as Sichem). [3] Each institution, finally, has its own traditions, especilaly the shrine of the Ark of the Covenant, which since Exodus has a whole history, and the Aaronite clergy, guardian of a tradition of worship formed at Cades. [4]

It would be a mistake to look in these traditions only for memories of history. Their aims differ profoundly according to each case. Often, it is actually a question of preserving the memory of ancestors and of their accomplishments : military leaders, such as the Judges and most recently Saul; religious leaders, such as Samuel; Moses, founder of the nation and its legislator; the fathers of the race, Abraham, Isaac, Jacob whose tradition subsists in the places where they have lived. But it happens also that the adventures of the groups are hidden behind the exploits of eponymous heroes (Gn 34) or that the religious causality is brought out in preference to secondary details (as in the Exodus from Egypt). Furthermore, with the help of hindsight, history has become schematized. The most important elements still emerge next to a large number that are forgotten; they center around a few very living figures which animate an anonymous mass : it is thus that popular memory can narrate the

---

[1] Cf. p. 130 ff.
[2] Cf. pp. 131, 140 and 182.
[3] Cf. p. 175.
[4] Cf. p. 156.

past. However, many traditions have a purpose of an entirely different order : they explain the how and the why of present customs (cf. the rite of the paschal lamb), names of places (Jgs 2, 1-5), the state of the tribes (Gn 49); they tell the origin of groups, institutions and tribes, frequently resorting to the procedure of eponyms, organizing them into genealogies, which is a popular way of explaining with simplicity the origin of things. [5] It also happens that these traditions tend to give rules of conduct, either by conveying juridical or ritual material which is imposed to be practiced by the Israelites (Gn 32, 33; Ex 12, 21-22), or by introducing moral or religious lessons about the history of former heroes (the story of Joseph) : this is a feature of popular wisdom known in all countries. It is constantly this Jewish conception of God, of the world, of man and of history which is thus concretely expressed in order to be transmitted from one age to the next. The traditions contain practically all the baggage of national culture before the creation of a written literature.

As to the forms in which they are presented, some are already fixed (we will come back to them later), but most are still fluctuating. They are canvasses in prose, more or less precise in their details. Their genres [6] vary, from the very short etiological narrative to the more developed episode which tends to be transformed into a " short story. " On this point, it is difficult to distinguish what belongs properly to the traditional sources used by the chroniclers of the royal period and what was actually done by them. It is possible, however, to hold as probable that as a whole they respected the manner of the materials they had at hand.

Let us add that the atmosphere of the narratives differs considerably from one to the other. The story is realistic and down to earth in the miserable adventure of Abimelek; but the story is treated as a religious epic in the exodus from Egypt. The harsh enthusiasm of the war of conquest contrasts with the rustic calm brought about by the memory of Abraham and Isaac. The pilgrimage to Sinai is very closely linked to notions of worship, while the stories of Joseph and Samson, each in its way, serve to inculcate a lesson of wisdom. There is no doubt that these variations already existed in the ancient traditions when they were still being transmitted orally. It would be wrong therefore to consider the traditions as formless, pre-literary or infra-literary materials. At the time when they are going to be collected, they already constitute a true literature whose genres are a prelude to those of written literature.

---

[5] Cf. art. " Généalogies, "* *Catholicisme,* IV (Paris, 1956) 1811 ff.

[6] Cf. pp. 132, 136 (French ed.).

It is even likely that, from the time of the Judges, they tended to group themselves into *cycles*. Either according to their historical origin : cycles of conquest and of Judges, cycle of Saul... Or, according to their geographical roots : cycles of Bersabee, of Sichem, of Cades, of Bethel (of shrines, most of the time). Or finally according to the institutions that preserve them : traditions of the Aaronite clergy, traditions around the Ark of the Covenant, tribal traditions... Better still, as national unity becomes a reality, not only in fact but in the consciousness of men, particular groups of memories and customs also tended to become interpenetrated to become the common good of all Israel. Thus, the state in which the royal scribes find them is the result of a more or less long, more or less complicated evolution. On the whole, they make up a rich treasure, both cultural and religious.

§ 3. The Most Ancient Written Texts : Moses

In the framework of the oral traditions, Israel also possesses the first elements of a written tradition. In fact, the specimens of archaic texts that the Bible has preserved are perhaps only the remnants of a much more extensive literary production, for the poetic texts allow us to see, starting with the 12th century, the existence of an art which far surpasses its first stammerings. In this regard a remarkable difference is observed between the refrains of the nomadic times, brief and short-winded, and the war-chants of the conquest, like those of Josue (fragmentary) and of Debora : Israel had quickly assimilated the culture of the conquered lands. Let us notice again, in the order of worship, the refrains of the Ark; in the prophetic " genre, " the oracles of Jacob, Balaam and Moses; with the sapiential literature, there are the apology of Jotham and the parable of Nathan; finally, the two elegies of David, prior to his reign in Jerusalem. We even know the title of two collections of works of this type used by Hebrew historians : the book of *Jashar* and that of " The Wars of Yahweh "; [7] but it is difficult to say if they are ancient or if the initiative is that of the Solomonian scribes. These first manifestations of the Israelite literary genius make it rather probable that certain traditions had been put into written prose relatively early, although on this point the texts do not bear up under scrutiny. It is known, however, that several pages attributed by critics to the Elohist or to the Yahwist traditions contain a very definite archaic flavor; moreover, it is likely that certain prayer formulae in more recent recensions existed before in some way in the Israelite shrines from the time of the Judges.

---

[7] Cf. p. 133.

But it is especially in the matter of law that the existence of ancient written texts is solidly attested by the Bible. Moses' activity in this field is too strongly affirmed by Hebrew tradition for us to deny him any literary activity, even if it is difficult to circumscribe it. There is agreement on the earliness of the Book of the Covenant (Ex 20,22— 23, 33), despite the trace of certain refinements, and of the ethical *Decalogue* (Ex 20 and Dt 5), probably enlarged by its later revisors, and there is no stringent reason which could oblige us to deny to Moses what remains the core of the Mosaic Law. But one would unduly restrict Moses' part in the Torah, if one attributed to him only these few writings : around them is centered the common law which largely overflows its limits and which is Mosaic just as they are. Finally, one can say that with Moses the Bible, as an *inspired book*, was born at the same time as the people of Israel was itself born by contracting a covenant with Yahweh. At the time when Hebrew literature begins to develop in a more tangible way, thanks to a concurrence of providential circumstances, the personality of the founder of the nation already dominates it, not only by the texts which derive from him, but by his religious message which will entirely impregnate it.

CHAPTER II

JERUSALEM, CULTURAL CENTER

§ 1. Hebrew Culture at the Beginning of the Monarchy

Saul's monarchy prolonged in many ways the period of the Judges; David's finally transformed the nation. It created the Israelite State by superimposing upon the former framework of the tribes, a specifically Chanaanite institution : centralized urban kingship. At the same time that Israel is peacefully absorbing independent populations, it takes on structures that are mostly inspired from contemporary monarchies : those of Phenicia and even, all things being equal, of Egypt. In keeping with this social and political development, the religion of Israel finds a new balance. Victoriously overcoming the crisis of the time of the Judges, it finally incorporates what could be assimilated from the Chanaanite cults in matters of rite, concepts and phraseology.

Two facts mark this change. First of all, kingship is henceforth part and parcel of the religious charter of the nation : the monarch, the anointed of Yahweh, becomes a part of theocracy and the promises of the Covenant are personally renewed to him, for himself and for his race (2 Sm 7). In the second place, with the transfer of the Ark to Jerusalem, the old confederational shrine of the tribes, formerly located in Sichem and Silo, is now located in the royal capital, which becomes the holy place par excellence, the one where " Yahweh makes His name dwell. " In the preceding ages, a first form of hope had developed; that of living happily in a land " flowing with milk and honey, " and of ruling over the peoples " who do not know Yahweh. " To these fundamental elements are added henceforth those that have been introduced by a most recent history; the king and the holy city and soon the Temple enrich the tableau of the marvelous future which Israel expects from its God. Let us add that in Jerusalem there is realized a sort of synthesis between two currents of cults which both issued from Hebrew origins : that of the North, linked to the shrine of the Ark, which thus reflects in a very direct way the tradition of Moses and of Josue; and that of the South, coming also from the tradition of Cades, which had already been able to open to independent worship elements by assimilating them. This duality is found, it seems, in the two priests attached to the person of David : Ebiathar, a descendant of Eli, who will be dismissed under Solomon; Sadoq, whose genealogy ties him to the lineage of Aaron and who finally will prevail alone.

Such is the framework in which Israelite culture is affirmed. Once the urban kingship is created, a whole people of scribes tends to the affairs of the palace : it is charged with keeping the annals of the reign, preserving the archives, writing the correspondence, administering the goods of the royal house, collecting the taxes.[1] Schools furnish the training for this personnel; along with the sons of functionaries, the royal princes and the members of the aristocratic families receive there a more perfect education; naturally the clergy of the royal shrine profit from this movement. These institutions take on unequaled scope under Solomon;[2] thus, everything is ready for the flourishing of a literature of learned men, still rooted in popular tradition, but wearing the stamp of the literate caste whence it emanates.

To create this cultural foyer, the Hebrew state does not start from scratch. On the one hand, the preceding periods (Moses and the Judges) have left to it institutions where the first elements of the national culture have already been developed in an embryonic manner. On the other hand, while absorbing Jerusalem and the other Chanaanite cities, David incorporated into his state and transferred to the religion of Yahweh the indigenous institutions of a much more ancient origin : scribes, cantors, etc.... Finally, as the political and economic horizon of Israel becomes wider, especially under the reign of Solomon, the country is introduced into an international traffic of ideas and of artistic tastes which is favorable to the flourishing of letters. It is not astonishing in these conditions to see Hebrew literature reach its classical period in the 10th century, without always being able to distinguish the origin, national or foreign, of the elements which are narrowly fused in it.

§ 2. The Vestiges of an Administration

The archives and the administrative and juridical documents do not properly speaking belong to literature; however, they constitute for historians a source of information of the first order. The Books of Samuel and of Kings have preserved a certain number of them which come either from the royal chancery or from the archives of the Temple. This is sufficient to allow us to see an essential aspect of the activity of the royal scribes.

---

[1] Cf. p. 215.

[2] Cf. pp. 226 ff.

Given the profound evolution of the institutions which marks this period, one would expect to find also in the texts the trace of a juridical activity directed toward a legislative reformulation. But on this point investigations prove to be rather disappointing. The Book of the Covenant [3] presupposes a more archaic economic and social state, and the Yahwist Decalogue (Ex 34) deals essentially with worship. It seems therefore that, in the time of David and Solomon, royal law is exercised only in the framework of ancient customs, partially codified, without yet attaining a reformulation of Mosaic law. The adaptation to new circumstances of the texts and customs of yesteryear is thus left to the appreciation of those who fill the positions of judges, and this flexibility guarantees a living law always dominated by the authority of Moses.

§ 3. Around the Worship

We would like to know in detail the transformation and the development of the rituals, which took place after the removal of the Ark to Jerusalem and especially after the building of the Temple of Solomon. The state of the evidence does not allow us to satisfy our curiosity : this is because the rites and religious customs are much more easily transmitted from one generation to the next by the simple operation of the existing institutions than by dead documents. Texts such as Ex 13, 3-10 and 34, 10-26 (except for Deuteronomist additions) can preserve in a succinct form old Yahwist rituals brought from Cades by the Aaronite clergy. But to these archaic rites, the Yahwist Decalogue (Ex 34) adds others which are more easily understood as adaptations to Yahwism of agrarian rites long since implanted in Chanaan (especially the three agricultural feasts of the annual cycle). One could therefore think here of a composition during the royal period, which would also have left traces in some places in the Book of the Covenant (Ex 22, 28-29; 23, 14-19). Finally, one must look for the collections of customs done during the periods of David and Solomon in the late priestly compilations made in " Sadoqite " milieus. The conservative spirit of the religious centers assures us that these texts substantially reflect the ancient tradition; but one should not overlook the part played by more recent adaptations : ritual conservatism is not necessarily fixed. From the point of view in which we place ourselves here, these compilations are therefore utilizable only with some difficulty.

In Chanaanite and Aramean centers, prophetism was linked with

---

[3] Cf. p. 132.

worship, [4] such as, it seems, Hebrew prophetism at the time of the Judges. Thus, in David's service one finds two accredited seers, Gad and Nathan, and the texts give us some idea of the oracles performed by these religious counselors of the king in the exercise of their official capacities. Furthermore, their personality already breaks through the framework of professional prophetism, both by the authentic inspiration which is manifested in them and by their freedom of speech with regard to the king : they thus announce the grand-style prophets of the following centuries. The oracle of Nathan [5] preserved in 2 Sm 7 (with Deuteronomist glosses) is of first-rate importance : it is at the origin of dynastic Messianism. The question of the two " royal psalms " is more difficult : these are Ps 2 and 110 which contain prophetic oracles. [6] The first apparently alludes to 2 Sm 7; but some authors see in it rather a late literary imitation. [7] On the other hand, the archaic origin of Ps 110 is often retained, because there are rather strong arguments in favor of it. [8] Some even see here a Hebrew adaptation of a royal enthronement psalm of Jebusean origin; whence would come the mention of royal priesthood, actually exercised by David (2 Sm 6, 17-18) and by Solomon (3 Kgs 3, 15) and of Melchisedech, king-priest of Salem, whose inheritance would have been received by David. The hypothesis cannot be considered as demonstrated.

These two texts introduce the problem of the psalms. [9] One should not be surprised that a large number of them are attributed to David. He was a poet and musician himself as is shown in his two elegies on the death of Saul and of Abner. The king surely must have played an important role in the development of worship lyricism. The genre existed before him, both with the Hebrews and with the Chanaanites, and especially in the city of Jerusalem whose personnel he incorporated into his service. The transfer of the Ark could have given him the opportunity of organizing a guild of cantors which must have become increasingly important after the building of the Temple. It is hardly doubtful that originally Chanaanite hymns were then adapted to the liturgy of Yahweh; in any case, the style of the native poetry did not fail to influence the new compositions. Unfortunately, in the present

---

[4] Cf. p. 254.

[5] Cf. p. 208.

[6] Cf. pp. 388 f.

[7] Cf. A. ROBERT, " Considérations sur le messianisme du Ps. 2 "*, *Mélanges Jules Lebreton, I* (RSR, April-October, 1951), pp. 88-98.

[8] E. PODECHARD, *Le Psautier*, II (1954), pp. 168-183.

[9] Cf. p. 369 ff.

state of the problem, it is difficult to say what part of the psalter dates from this period. For example, the following are generally placed among the ancient psalms : 18 (royal *Te Deum*), 20 and 21 (prayers for the king), 24, 7-10 (processional of the Ark), 29 (with heavy Chanaanite coloring), 72 (retouched later on)... But in fact there are as many questions as there are psalms. One can admit that from the very beginning of the royal period, most of the genres and literary canons now present in the psalter [10] were already fixed and their place in the liturgy was determined by usage. However, a literary current such as that one is bound to be developed normally with time; there should be no hurry in wanting to reconstitute a whole " royal liturgy " on the basis of the internal criticism of the psalter and the analogies offered by the other Semitic religions. There are certainly relations, but they are not easy to pinpoint and in particular the existence in Israel of a " New Year's day " similar to that of neighboring religions remains problematic.

§ 4. Wisdom Literature

With the schools for scribes Wisdom literature [11] also takes hold in Israel. The Bible honors Solomon with it, and attributes to him considerable literary activity (3 Kgs 5, 9-14). One must take hyperbole into consideration, but there is no reason for doubting this testimony. In fact, Wisdom is at that time an international fact, and traces of it are found from Egypt to Mesopotamia; if the Chanaanite documents are lacking on this point, the fact is probably accidental (cf. 3 Kgs 5, 11; Ez 27, 8-9 and 28, 3-4).

Wisdom is first of all the concern of the king : the art of governing well and of succeeding in temporal matters. But this art concerns also many people in the royal administration : every scribe must be a wise man; that is why the education he receives strives to impart this knowledge to him. Doubtless a practical wisdom; but from the knowledge of man and of the world, full of refined psychology, is easily developed a reflection which, altogether empirical at its origins, rapidly tends toward speculation, especially when it blends in the data of religious thought. With respect to this, one can say, for example, that the ancient oriental myths [12] which were vivid expressions of a conception of the human world in its relations to the gods, bordered on the sapiential genre.

---

[10] Cf. p. 379 ff.
[11] Cf. p. 410 f.
[12] Cf. pp. 127-129 (French ed.).

In Israel, this literary current crosses immediately on its way a religious tradition solidly anchored in the minds. Surely it is first of all receptive to maxims of all kinds, similar to those collected in the Book of Proverbs (10, 1—22, 16; 25—29). A large portion of these, especially those which appear to be the " mirror of the king's people " (Duesberg), can date back to Solomon, but the later development of the genre must be reckoned with. [13] But from the very outset, wisdom, knowledge, and discernment are considered as a privilege of Yahweh who alone can give them to men (2 Sm 14, 17 and 20; 3 Kgs 3, 9; cf. Gn 3). Thereby, all the moral ideal of Yahwism, its conception of the world and of man seem to be one of the areas of the sapiential field; there is no frontier between it and religious reflection. We will not be astonished to find trace of the sapiential current in a good number of writings which theoretically depend on altogether different literary genres.

§ 5. Memorialists and Historians [14]

Such are the intellectual components of the milieu in which a very important historiography is going to develop by leaps and bounds; in Jerusalem from the reign of David and especially from that of Solomon, a well-organized clergy, a caste of scribes and an already ancient prophetism are so side-by-side that their fields overlap. Born at their crossroads historiography will reflect in variable proportions their respective preoccupations. The work of the annalists precedes historiography properly speaking and opens the way for it. We no longer have the official chronicles of the kings; but in their dryness, certain indications give us some idea of them (2 Sm 8). As to the work of the memorialists and the historians, this directly outclasses all that oriental antiquity has left us in this genre. In Assyria, the royal annals are dithyrambs in praise of the monarch; in Egypt one particular event of the reign is recounted, but without yet creating a continuous historiography; with the Hittites, religious causality in history is not ignored, but one does not rise to broad views embracing whole reigns or even longer periods. It is difficult to say in what measure the knowledge of the former stimulates the genius of Israelite scribes; they nonetheless draw from their faith a concept of man and of history which allows them to catch a broader glimpse of the events. With them, all the actors of history, even the greatest, remain subject to a divine law which surpasses them, judges them, commands their destinies because, consciously or not, they

---

[13] Cf. p. 413 f.
[14] Cf. p. 202 ff.

are the artisans of Yahweh's design. Whence come both breadth of outlook and remarkable impartiality.

From the reign of David, it seems that a long narrative retraces already the origins of the Israelite monarchy, from the anointing of Saul to the capture of Jerusalem (that is, during the whole duration of the wars of independence). A history of the Ark of the Covenant perhaps has to date from the same period; it traces its history from its capture by the Philistines to its transferral into the royal city. The masterpiece of this genre, probably written under Solomon, is the history of David's succession (2 Sm 10—20 and 3 Kgs 1—2). Then there is a history of Solomon (where the author of Kings drew the matter of 3 Kgs 3—11); without counting the remarks devoted to particular episodes or to the exploits of David's paladins (2 Sm 21—24), but their date is more doubtful. All these pieces treat of contemporary events, whose actors or witnesses are often still living. Recourse to oral tradition is discernible in some places (David's youth); and this is normal for the matter treated. As for the style, it prolongs and brings to its perfection the art of ancient storytellers : all the popular vim and vigor passed into these productions of literate men.

§ 6. A Synthesis of Sacred History [15]

But the traditions of Israel allow us to go much further back into the past; by drawing abundantly from this trove, the Israelite scribes are going to achieve a large work of religious history. These traditions, as has been seen, were already becoming interpenetrated and were beginning to take form from the time of the Judges. Now, after the establishment of the monarchy and the foundation of the empire, their total meaning becomes more evident, in a broader perspective. The Israelite historians discover the profound unity, underlying both their expansion and their diversity : the unity of a *sacred history* directed by God; of a history whose point of departure is the promise made to Abraham, whose heart is the Covenant and whose justification and purpose is the glory of Yahweh present in His Temple and triumphant by the victories of the Anointed One. This is not merely a simple human reconstruction, but a view of faith which becomes explicit under divine inspiration.

Since all the traditions preserved in the various parts of the nation are thus convergent, it is the duty of historians to stress the link which

---

[15] Cf. p. 133 ff.

united them around memories of the Exodus and of Sinai, which are as it were their center of gravity. On the other hand, they underline, from the earliest centuries, the cohesion of all the Hebrew groups called to live in fateful solidarity inside the people of Yahweh : these groups are members of the same family. Whence the importance of the genealogies around which will be centered the sacred history; more than extracts of civil-status, they will be a concrete translation of the profound idea which polarizes all of history : that of the divine choice which singled out men called to make up the people of God.

That is why, contrary to the ancient traditions of India for example, which dealt essentially with worship and were independent of time, those of Israel are fixed in the framework of a history. It is a real history but told with the help of the most diverse of materials; it is a very human history, but its religious significance is much more important than the precision of the details. It is this history which drains all the other components of the national tradition (law, customs, worship, folklore) and establishes them in the perspective where they derive their profound meaning. Furthermore, this history will go back beyond the patriarchal period, beyond even the oriental empires and the faraway neolithic age, the rather imprecise memory of which hovers in chapters 4—11 of Genesis. It will even incorporate sacred cosmogony which Israelite monotheism contrasts to the pagan myths, whose images it does not fear to use again for its own doctrine. Moreover, creation is the point of departure of the divine design which was little by little revealed with the call of the patriarchs, the deliverance from Egypt, the Covenant at Sinai, the gift of the " promised land, " the installation of the monarchy, the promises made to David and the choice of the Temple at Jerusalem as the residence of Yahweh among men... And if Yahweh had thus painfully and gradually to form this people called to serve Him and to procure His glory from a barbarian human mass by giving to it little by little the rules of conduct capable of making of it a wise people, is it not because at the beginning, at the origins, a mysterious catastrophe had disturbed the order of a world that had issued from His hands in perfect condition? By explaining on the one hand the present condition of man and on the other the meaning of the historical work of God, the inspired book thus introduces into the picture of the origins the fact of human sin which right from this period interferes with divine will and from century to century continues to place obstacles before the unfolding of Yahweh's design.

Such is the grandiose plan of this work which, for lack of knowing exactly its author or authors, we call the holy Yahwist history (J).

It is of little importance if it was realized in one stroke or by one author; if it contained or not in a continuous story all of past history up to the period of David and of Solomon; if it used, next to pieces drawn from the oral tradition, certain bits of more ancient writings (J[1] or L of the critics); if certain pieces, where theology is more closely allied, were added after the event to the primitive collection. It is sufficient to notice that it existed at least virtually in a whole collection of accounts related by doctrine and by the editorial procedures used. Just as diverse as the materials that serve as its base, it sometimes borders on religious lyricism (the flight from Egypt), sometimes on sapiential teaching (Gn 3; the story of Joseph); sometimes on historiography (the story of Gideon) and sometimes on juridical teaching (Mosaic Torah and certain etiological accounts). On the whole, it is a literary monument without parallel in the history of religions, because it condenses in it what is specific and irreducible in Yahwism : a theology of history based on the theology of the Promise. As to its composition, it is difficult to suggest precise dates : we would ascribe the whole work to the reign of Solomon; but, for many authors, the work would have spread itself over the following century in the cultured centers of the court and of the Temple. There is no doubt that it then played a role in the training of the elite just as did in Egypt sapiential literature or with the priests of Mesopotamia the Sumero-Akkadian myths; but what a difference in intellectual and religious climate!

Thus, at the cultural and political climax which marks the first century of the Israelite monarchy, in a certain sense the Bible can be said to have a literary structure. Around this nucleus of sacred texts dating back to the Mosaic period, the traditions of God's people were crystallized in written form. They nonetheless continued to be transmitted orally; so, other crystallizations will subsequently appear analogous to the first. But the fundamental ideas of the Yahwist writer—or school—first synthesis of a revelation started long ago, will continue to assert itself to similar syntheses attempted in slightly different perspectives. The New Testament itself, by fulfilling the revelation of the secrets of the mysterious plan of God, will show in Christ the crowning and the completion of this age-long work, the first outlines of which were being shown by the Yahwist.

CHAPTER III

THE PARALLEL KINGDOMS

§ 1. The Tradition of Israel and that of Juda

From this schism which follows the reign of Solomon on, the kingdoms of Juda and of Israel find themselves in rather different situations. [1] In Jerusalem, the continuity of the Davidic dynasty assures a certain internal stability; but, on the religious level, the kingdom experiences alternately rises of Chanaanite paganism and Yahwist renewal, according to the attitudes of its kings. Nonetheless, the Temple remains a stronghold for the religious traditions of the nation; it is the place where " Yahweh roars " (Am 1, 2), and from this place will be prepared the revolution that will overthrow Athalia; Isaias also receives his vocation here. In its shadow, the literature inaugurated during the reigns of David and of Solomon continues to develop (worship lyricism, rituals, common law, wisdom, religious historiography, archives and annals); it is not possible to follow this development closely. The permanent armor of this intellectual activity is made up of three fundamental institutions : scribes (or wise men), priests and prophets (Jer 18, 18; cf. 2, 8).

In Israel on the contrary, if the secession is upheld by the country populations tired of tributes that are too heavy, by the clergy of the provincial shrines, whom Jerusalem risks offending, and by the prophetic bodies hostile to innovations in the name of ancient tradition, it is virtually the merchant class and the landowners who take the gain of it to their profit. Thus the monarchy leaning on this class will withdraw from primitive Yahwism more than the Judean monarchy. Following the schism and especially after the founding of Samaria, a second center of culture, emulator and rival of Jerusalem, grows in the court of the kings of Israel; its light falls on rich classes, on the clergy of royal sanctuaries created in order to compete with Solomon's Temple, on the caste of the officials. But the kingdom of the North is too open to foreign influences, especially those of Tyre, causing the nation's religious tradition to suffer. One may notice it in particular when Omri marries his son Achab to the Tyrenian Jezabel : the political fortune of the " house of

---

[1] Cf. pp. 19 and 220.

Omri " and the relative cultural expansion which accompanies it then are tied to the renewal of Chanaanite paganism. The cult of a national God, in the measure to which it subsists, tends to be no longer anything but a syncretized Yahwism; from the reign of Jeroboam I, the sign of the golden calf was an unequivocal indication of this falling away. Thus it is not surprising that the literary productions of the time left only a few traces in the Bible : the fervent Yahwists to whom we owe the holy books had no choice but to let them fall into oblivion. The happy exception of Psalm 45, if one were to interpret it as a royal epithalamium, would be due to an allegorical re-interpretation which would define its biblical sense. However, the archeological documentation hints at a certain administrative (ostraca) and artistic (the ivories of Samaria) activity, which was fairly intense during the 9th and the 8th centuries.

In Israel during the 9th century, the attachment to authentic Yahwist tradition is, with exceptions, true more of strangers to the cultural movement : the " sons of prophets " who gravitate around Elias and Eliseus give no evidence of preoccupations of a cultural nature, not considering the Rekabites or an old soldier like Jehu. The literary consequence : the speeches of Elias and Eliseus have not come down to us in original MS, though the oracle of Micheas, son of Yimla, (3 Kgs 22, 1-28) is an exception to this. The religious consequence : the Yahwism of the North, reacting against a syncretism which seems tied to modern institutions, remains more archaic, and closer to what it had been at the time of the Judges in the shrines of the country. The Mosaic tradition is present there, it would seem, though less well developed than at Jerusalem, or rather, it develops along another line, more conservative regarding the ideas and the rites of Chanaan, and in more direct relation with the form it had assumed in the ancient shrine of the Ark. It is symptomatic to see Elias pilgrimaging to Horeb to renew his faith or to rebuild the altar of Carmel in the ancient manner (cf. Ex 20, 24-25). It is true that at the same time local shrines of the same kind also exist in the Judean countryside; but the Temple of Jerusalem already initiates a centralization which is soon realized.

§ 2. The Prophetic Influence in Israel

The revolution of Jehu (841), however, allows the prophetic influence to gain ground in cultivated circles; even kings seek the counsel of Eliseus. Thus one may glimpse the formation of fervent circles whose members also belong to state institutions : priestly colleges and scribes of the administration. United by a common attachment to the spirit of Elias and Eliseus, they end the current of reform in literary works, quite similar in their form to those which appeared in Jerusalem in the 10th century when the same spirit of religious fervor moved the scribes of the court and the Temple. There is first of all the collating and the fixing in writing of traditions relative to Elias and Eliseus. The cycle of Elias may have been edited toward the end of the 9th century; that of Eliseus at present mixed with a history of Aramean wars, around 750. Next to popular tales which bear the mark of their origins, one may find beautiful pages worthy of the best historians, such as the story of the revolution of Jehu (4 Kgs 9, 1—10, 27).

There is much evidence supporting a relation of the Elohist material of the Pentateuch (E) to the same milieu, as well as several narratives found in the " early prophets, " from the wars of Josue to the history of Saul. This recension of ancient traditions is comparable to Yahwist sacred history, to which it is often related in matter and sometimes even in literary expression. It may have included written documents edited much earlier : probably certain tales waxing an archaic flavor (E[1] of the critics); certainly the Decalogue of Ex 20 and the Book of the Covenant. But on the whole, one would surmise rather the shaping of an oral tradition which was still alive, with the added influence of the work edited in Yahwist circles. But whereas for the historians of Jerusalem sacred history culminated in the establishment of the Davidic monarchy and the Solomonian Temple, those of Israel show a greater reserve with regard to modern institutions. Their more conservative point of view, which is explained as a reaction against the abuses of the time, prolong the tradition of the shrine of the Ark into the time of the Judges. The Yahwism which they dream of seeing revived is less that of the Davidic epoch than that of the Exodus, of the desert, of the conquest : here is their ideal. With them this is not an archaism of poor quality but rather a desire to remain faithful to the most essential values of the national religion. Besides, they feel the needs of their time; proof is that in retracing past history they bring it up to date to find in it rules of conduct to be used by their contemporaries. Hence an emphasis on the " prophetic " side of the great ancestors (Abraham, Joseph, Moses, or Samuel); from this also come certain polemical jabs against the worship of the golden calf (Ex 32) or of the Chanaanite Baal (Jgs 6, 25-32) and against the institution of monarchy itself (1 Sm 8 and 12).

Certain of these traits may be more easily understood if one admits that the Elohist collection was made in the course of the 8th century, under the brilliant and prosperous rule of Jeroboam II, as a salutary reaction against the social and religious disorders which were only too apparent. In fact, a similar spirit, sometimes even identical themes, are found in the preaching of Amos and especially of Osee. The first of these two " writer prophets " (a very poor expression) has no ties with the fervent circles of the North : he is a Judean, whose hard and vigorous poetry bursts directly from popular sap. Putting these oracles into writing seems to have been in part his personal work (cf. 7, 1-4; 8, 1; 9, 1), in part that of disciples spontaneously grouped about him; but it is with the Judeans, Isaias and Micheas, that one will afterwards have to look to find the trace of his influence. On the other hand, the work of Osee, deeply rooted in the religious tradition of the North, noticeably enriches the current of thought in which it buries itself. Though it takes certain characteristic themes from it (moral decalogue, attachment to the Covenant and to the ideal time in the desert, memories of the ancestor Jacob, the preponderance of Ephraim, and the hostility to the golden calf and even to the institution of royalty), it introduces into it other themes which reappear later (love of Yahweh for His people, affective religion, comparison of the Covenant to an espousal, announcement of a new Covenant after the purification of guilty Israel). With Osee, the sacred history, from now on prolonged until new times yet to come, assumes the appearance of a drama of love in which Yahweh and Israel are partners : an original interpretation which is a direct prelude to the revelation of the love of God in the New Testament.

In the atmosphere of the prophetic movement, a juridic reform is preparing itself, parallel to the historico-religious work of which we have just spoken. When Osee alludes to " articles of law " (8, 2), he is thinking, undoubtedly, of the ancient legislative compilations (Moral Decalogue and Book of the Covenant). But in the 8th century, this written law no longer corresponds exactly to the practical needs of an evolved society : its rule is surpassed by the facts. It must be adapted to the circumstances, completed, and on certain points, remade, so that it may present an effective barrier to the abuses of power of the royal administration, to the extortions of the rich, the venality of the judges, the moral and religious laxity, which, from Elias to Osee, were unceasingly denounced by the prophets. Such a work presupposes first an evolution of customary law before becoming crystallized into a code. The prophetic preaching, completely in the service of the authentic tradition, indicates in what sense the reform must be directed. Now fervent circles influenced by this reform include levite-priests, guardians of customs and laws, called on more than once to practice law in trials (Dt 17, 18-20). Such is the jurisprudence which, by completing existing texts, prepares the constitution of a new code. This will come in its time, probably after the ruin of Samaria, when the rooting of a foreign aristocracy in the country makes spiritual resistance an urgency if one wishes to save the threatened tradition. Further, the fall of the kingdom of the North will then invite reflection : it will show the necessity of the reform to which the prophets have been vainly exhorting the nation for a century and a half. But on what basis could it be wrought except on the Mosaic Torah itself, enriched by a recent prophetic contribution and readapted to the needs of the time? This is, it would seem, the state of mind which will preside over the edition of the Deuteronomist Code (Dt 12, 2— 26, 15), which we would prefer to relate to the tradition of the North rather than to Judean circles, though it may have been written down in the South (see *below*).

§ 3. The Prophetic Influence in Juda

While this work is being done in original priestly circles of Israel, the kingdom of Juda is won over, in turn, by the influence of prophetism. Amos, the Judean, preached in the North in about 750; his preoccupations and several of his themes reappear in the following decades in Isaias and Micheas, although one cannot clearly define the relation of the latter with the group of disciples which preserved the oracles of the shepherd of Teqoa. The connection is probably closer with Micheas, a man of the country, apparently without culture. But we know that at the time of Ezechias, this preacher, in his crude syntax, deeply impressed minds and hastened the religious reform of the country (Jer 26, 17-19).

The personality of Isaias is more typical of the tradition of Jerusalem. No doubt his supernatural inspiration and his native genius enjoy a profound originality. But he does not stand out in his century as an erratic fragment; rather his work can be situated at the juncture of various literary and doctrinal currents which we have noted in the Judean capital. He is connected with the Sadoqite ministry by his knowledge of its technical vocabulary and by his echoing of certain aspects of its theology : the glory of Yahweh, the holy God in His royal majesty; the essential role of the Temple, His abode. On the other hand, some of his major ideas recover themes dear to " Yahwist " historians : the doctrine of the " remnant, " directly related to the Yahwist interpretation of the Deluge; attachment to the Davidic dynasty, which is supported by the oracle of Nathan. Finally, the prophet did not misuse a literate education : he practices the *mashal*, a sapiential genre *par excellence*, and when he denounces a false wisdom impregnated with pride, it is to contrast it to a true wisdom, pierced by a religious spirit, a gift of the

divine Spirit. Although a messenger of punishment, as were Amos and
Osee, Isaias is no less attached to the national hope; but, like Osee,
he carries it forward to a " second time. " The comparison of this
eschatology with that of Osee is instructive, however. The latter sought
the golden age of Israel at the time of Exodus and the desert; Isaias
finds it in the Davidic and Solomonian epoch, the purified image of which
he projects into the future in order to evoke the reign of the future " son
of David. " On both sides, the concept of the end of the world takes
on the air of a Paradise regained, but the historical experience associated
with this wondrous evocation does not exactly cover the same period :
for Osee tied himself again to the tradition of the North, which reappears
also in Deuteronomy, whereas Isaias endorses the doctrinal development
peculiar to the sanctuary of Jerusalem. The fundamental dualism of the
nation will thus be found even in the prophetic milieu; but it would be
useless, however, to oppose two complementary currents each attentive
to different aspects of the divine work : the unique revelation progresses
on both sides, along lines which will, in the end, be united.

There is yet another point on which the Book of Isaias gives us a
valuable piece of information. It shows us the prophet surrounded by
a circle of disciples. In their " hearts, " that is, in their living memories,
he " binds his testimony and seals his teaching " (8, 16). Thus the
prophet appears with the unexpected traits of a master of wisdom who
concentrates his care on the formation of a restricted group. One grasps
in the raw the existence of one of those faithful groups which gather
the words of every inspired man and prolong his activity. Such is the
distant origin of pietist groups called to play such a great role in the
formation of Judaism. The Isaian circle preserves the oracles of the
master, which have already been set down in writing under his dictation;
it also preserves the memory of a few important facts of his life
(cf. 7; 36—39). One will be indebted to it for the making of his collection,
a compilation which through the care of new inspired men allied with
the same school, will increase in time.

§ 4. After the Fall of Samaria

After the fall of Samaria, the remaining devout Israelites in a country
decimated by deportation, seek support in the South. At the same time,
Jerusalem is reforming itself. From this a double literary activity results.
On the one hand, Ezechias tries to gather the cultural and moral if not
the political heritage of the North, in order to rebuild around Jerusalem
a sort of national unity. His scribes make a collation of Solomonian

proverbs (Prv 25, 1). Above all, they revise and complete the collections
of ancient traditions formed during the course of preceding centuries in
the Judean capital (a Yahwist collection) with the help of materials
which Israelite refugees have brought with them (Elohist collection).
Such at least is the hypothesis which, in the actual state of our knowledge, would best explain the origin of the J-E compilation (sometimes
called Jehovist compilation) used in the Pentateuch. [2] The Book of
Judges could have received in the same manner its almost definitive form
(except for additions due to later revisions). [3] It is interesting to thus
see the traditions of the North and South converge once again, as at the
time of the conquest and at the beginning of the monarchy, to form a
wholly Israelite *Tradition :* the people of the Covenant remains attached
to its internal unity in the midst of historical troubles in which it is
steeped despite itself.

An autonomous survival of Elohist traditions in circles of Israelite
origin, in refuge in Jerusalem, must not however be excluded : the
Deuteronomist literature will constitute its direct prolonging. It is
exactly in these circles that the Deuteronomist code seems to us to have
been edited, probably during the very reign of Ezechias, on the basis
of ancient material of which we have spoken. [4] If finally the levite-
priests, to whom it is due, deposit it in the Temple at Jerusalem, where
it will be rediscovered a century later, it is because the Ark of the
Covenant is located there. Behind the royal Temple, they see the ancient
federal shrine of the tribes, the same one which an ancient tradition,
mentioned in Deuteronomy and the Book of Josue placed at Sichem
and at Garizim (Dt 11, 29-30; 27, 4-8 and 11-26; Jos 8, 30-35; 24, 1
and 25-26). In order to cut short the liturgical deviations of the high
places, they dream of making it the only legitimate sanctuary of Yahweh
in Israel. But for the time being, Sichem is occupied by the semi-pagan
Samaritans and the Ark is in Jerusalem; because of this fact, it is
Jerusalem which will finally inherit the traditions of the North. One
more century will have to pass before the code which synthesizes its
religious and social requirements will receive official sanction and will
start to become a reality.

In fact, the reign of Ezechias was only the beginning of a reforming
movement which does not survive his death. The campaigns of
Sennacherib spell the end of the political fall of Juda. Under Manasses,

[2] Cf. p. 153.
[3] Cf. pp. 191 ff.
[4] Cf. G. Ricciotti, *Histoire d'Israël*, I, 485 and 513.

the double influence of ancient Chanaanite paganism (the eternal temptation of Israel) and of Assyrian forms of worship provoke the gradual
degradation of official Yahwism, which has become more and more
syncretized (4 Kgs 21, 1-9).   The resistance to national apostasy remains
the work of fervent circles resulting on the one hand from milieus where
Deuteronomy was born, and on the other hand from the disciples of
Isaias.   These groupings which are without a defined status, and are
the distant ancestors of Jewish pietism, struggle against the meddlings
of the powers, but we cannot exactly determine the extent of their
influence.   However, in order to feed their religious faithfulness, they
preserve as a treasure the books willed to them by previous centuries
and use them as spiritual sustenance.   The Mosaic Torah, written and
oral, is their rule of life; sacred history is the object of their meditations;
the oracles of the prophets teach them at the same time the fear of
Yahweh, the need for a conversion of the heart and for an unfailing
hope.   Divine revelation which is the basis for their faith is thus present
to them under the form of books which they become used to considering
as sacred because they find in them the Word of God.

CHAPTER IV

THE ORIGINS OF JUDAISM

§ 1. The Deuteronomist Movement

The weakness of Assyria allows the kingdom of Juda to enjoy a certain amount of glory from the time Josias takes over the reins of power (*ca.* 630). From that time the progressive elimination of Assyrian cults, the first manifestation of nationalism, prepares from afar a much deeper reform. This was provoked in 622 by the discovery in the Temple of the Deuteronomic Code, which had been left there 100 years before. Converging witnesses showed that a profound renovation was about to take place. For Josias, in order to restore his kingdom on the basis of the Covenant and of the Mosaic Torah, immediately applied the Law at the cost of radical measures (4 Kgs 22—23).

This religious policy marks a date in literary history. In fact, with the recognition of Deuteronomy as the law of the state, the northern tradition is fully sown in Jerusalem. At the same time, the work of synthesis undertaken by the scribes of Ezechias is resumed and completed, resulting in a theological and historical literature of great depth. On the one hand, the code that was adopted during the renewal of the Covenant (cf. 4 Kgs 23, 1-3) is completed by parenetic discourses which structure it and sharpen its impact; the doctrine and the spirituality of the pietist circles of the North flourished there in long periods charged with religious emotion. On the other hand, all the historical material accumulated during the preceding centuries is methodically assembled and organized at the cost of glosses and revisions which are easily recognizable by their style. On the whole, the work covers our canonical books, from Genesis to Kings, but not in their present state because the passages of priestly origin are added later. The Deuteronomist additions are rare in Genesis, Exodus, and Numbers; whereas the end of Moses' story (E) is linked up with Deuteronomy; the Book of Josue is given rather important amplifications, while the Book of Judges takes on its profound meaning by the addition of chapter 2 which clarifies its general thesis; finally the Books of Samuel and Kings, composed of various materials, retrace all the events from the Philistine wars to the renewal of the Covenant by Josias. The method of Deuteron omis historians has already been explained. Usually, in their works, the sources are juxtaposed rather than blended, and they are respected not only in their essential meaning but also to the letter; thus, they are still discernible through analysis. This manner of compiling documents did not prevent great theological theses from underlying these books of religious history : the doctrine of the Covenant is verified in all its facts. The teaching which comes from it is related to that of the parenetic discourses of Deuteronomy; it is like a concrete teaching which seeks to awaken in hearts the desire to love Yahweh, to keep His Covenant, and to obey His law in order to live in peace in His holy land. There is something else to note. In adapting itself to Jerusalem, the Deuteronomist tradition becomes enriched. Its concept of national hope, surpassing what it had been in the 8th century with Osee, entails from then on a profound attachment to the Davidic dynasty (cf. 2 Sm 7) and to the Solomonian Temple (3 Kgs 8).

Unfortunately, the reforming activity of Josias ended with his tragic death. Though the code sanctioned by him still kept its official value, its application left much to be desired. The Deuteronomist movement subsisted, nevertheless, in the circles which had previously supported it. As keepers of its writings, they perpetuated its spirit; and much more, they completed them and brought them to light to make of them, in the midst of the national disaster culminated by the destruction of Jerusalem, the charter for future restorations. Thus Deuteronomy and the Book of Kings were enriched in their new editions, with pieces which assumed the death of Josias, Jerusalem destroyed and the people dispersed. It is generally estimated that a work of this kind was carried out during the restoration of the 6th century. In the meantime, the legislation of Josias, which had remained the official law in the country conquered by the Babylonians and connected by them to the province of Samaria, was introduced under this title even to the Samaritans, for whom Jerusalem had become the only possible place for the worship of Yahweh since Josias had destroyed the high places in the North. This situation was to have important consequences later on : God leads history through unexpected detours.

§ 2. Rebirth of Prophetism

It would be impossible to affirm with certitude that the prophetic spirit ever completely ceased to be manifest, even under the reign of Manasses; but it was at least dormant. When it reappeared in full bloom under Josias it reestablished ties with the two pietist currents noted above :

the one grouped around the disciples of Isaias, ends with Sophonias; the other, which depends on the tradition of Osee and the North, reappears in Jeremias. It is not known to which of the two should be related Nahum, the announcer of the ruin of Ninive (shortly before 612), and Habacuc who, toward the end of the 6th century, sketched on an evocation of the Chaldean invasion his sorrowful reflections, his curses on the aggressor, his song of faith. The two works have some affinity to liturgical poetry; but this does not suffice to make of their authors " cultic prophets, " a corporate body which Jeremias has shown us in a very poor light; no doubt they imitated its literary genre as Jeremias himself does on occasion.

The long ministry of Jeremias was concerned not only in having us relive in spirit the last decades of Judean history. It informs us rather fully on the religious personality of the prophet himself. Not only do we see him struggling against a crowd of enemies who have vowed to destroy him : nationalist politicians, priests and official prophets; but we also know what echoes the events of his painful mission awakened in his soul. The same affective spirituality, which in his discourses caused him to present Yahweh as a father and a spouse, colors the passages in which he reveals the dark rooms of his soul : this is the intimacy of an incessant dialogue with Him who called him and who continues to give him an extraordinary strength of soul during a ministry full of disappointments.

Although a diffident man, Jeremias maintained a surprising prestige among his diverse listeners; but he hardly had disciples. A faithful friend remained close to him : Baruch, who seemed to belong to Deuteronomist circles, if one can judge by his style, was his secretary; he collected his sayings and read them publicly at the risk of his life. When after the destruction of Jerusalem and the murder of Godolias the governor, the old prophet was dragged to Egypt by fanatic Jews, Baruch followed him there. After his death he gathered the scattered pieces of his work and added biographical chapters which are the apology of a persecuted man of God : had not Jeremias been right in the face of everyone, as evidenced by the recent catastrophe? But Jeremias also left a message of hope to his dispersed compatriots. He explained it in terms which recall somewhat the Messianism of Isaias (23, 5-6) but, in a stronger way, that of Osee. Like the Deuteronomist scribes, he constantly had in mind the thought of the Covenant at Sinai and the entry into the holy land. Through Israel's fault, this plan of divine love sketched in the past ended in failure. But after purifying His people, Yahweh will begin again; this will then be a new Covenant inscribed in all hearts (31, 31-34) and a return to the holy land under the guidance of the Shepherd of Israel (23, 1-4; 31, 1-22). By this updating of ancient history, Jeremias managed to stress its religious significance, which had been exploited in another manner, more moralizing, by Deuteronomist historians : without Israel's knowing it, the events through which it had lived since the Exodus bore prophetic weight.

Probably framed in Egypt, Jeremias' collection must have been brought to Palestine fairly early during the Exile (after 570). It was apparently edited there in Deuteronomist circles. When it was communicated to the Eastern Diaspora, it was enriched by new additions (notably chaps. 50—51), so that toward 520 it had taken the shape it was to preserve in the Hebrew Bible; still the Greek Bible has it in a slightly different form. Isolated and misunderstood during his lifetime, the prophet thus exercised a profound influence in Judea as well as in Babylonia after his death.

§ 3. The Priestly Tradition

The name " priestly " is given to the tradition which is proper to the clergy of Jerusalem. This expression consecrated by the use of exegetes is useful but a little ambiguous, for the Deuteronomist code is also probably of priestly origin; but it is our opinion that it comes from the shrines in the North. We have already seen how, after the royal period, this tradition of the Temple of Jerusalem is linked also to the very origins of Israel in many ways. [1]

The introduction of the Deuteronomist tradition in Jerusalem as the law of the Temple was not accomplished without provoking some struggles. Certainly the exclusive privilege recognized in the sanctuary, whose task it is theirs to guard satisfied the Sadoqite priests; but they intended to maintain their privileges. That is why 4 Kgs 23, 9 remarks that Dt 18, 7 remained a dead issue. The levitical priests of the provinces did not receive the right to officiate in the national shrine. However, the event also provoked, as a counter-stroke, an original development of priestly customs and doctrine. The result of this work was crystallized in a little collection which, however recent its writing, no less expressed very ancient concepts : the " code of holiness " (Lev 17—26, with the exception of later additions). [2] Undoubtedly all the critics do not agree in assigning this date to the work in question; however, it seems to us to be situated between Deuteronomy and Ezechiel. Throughout this booklet there appears a sensitively different spirituality from that of

---

[1] Cf. p. 568.
[2] Cf. p. 156 f.

Deuteronomy, all centered around divine greatness and sanctity. What is most profound in the liturgical service, the spirit of religion, appears in it as the supreme motive of all human action. All obedience to the Law of Yahweh is assimilated to a sort of liturgical service : in all circumstances the " holy " people works to the glory of its God just as the priests do in the Temple. Such is the core of the doctrine of the milieu out of which, towards the same period, issues forth a very original prophetic figure : Ezechiel. [3]

Even once seized by the prophetic spirit, Ezechiel remained profoundly affected by his original association with the priesthood of Jerusalem. There is discussion as to when he was deported to Babylon : 597 or 586; the question is of secondary importance. It is more important to notice his dependence on the code of holiness, his contact with Osee, the Deuteronomist and perhaps Jeremias; this shows what his readings were. For Ezechiel is clearly a " man of the book. " When he first saw his vocation, the Word of God was present to him not in the form of an oral message (cf. Is 6, 6-7; Jer 1, 9) but of a written volume (Ez 2, 9—3, 2). It is a sign of the times. Furthermore, his work shows him to be erudite : he is not ignorant either of the data of Phoenician mythology (Ez 28), nor of certain characteristics of Mesopotamian art (Ez 1); especially he displays a deep knowledge of the laws and rituals used in the Temple.

His message of conversion, prior to the ruin of Jerusalem, no doubt echoes the preoccupations of the Deuteronomist circles, but he reinterprets them in a way in keeping with the Sadoqite theology. The doctrine of individual retribution is affirmed in it, but as a datum rather badly coordinated to the whole of the system; this could be a development of the doctrine of the " remnant " (cf. 9, 1-4) which recalls the message of Isaias. As for the plans for the future which the prophet draws up after 586, by mixing eschatological evocations and practical data, once again we can trace there the priestly tradition : the purification of hearts in the new Israel has a ritual aspect about it (36, 16 ff.); the holy city and the Temple, the priests, sons of Sadoq, to whom are joined the other levitical priests, and the fulfilment of the ceremonies according to the prescribed calendar occupy stage-front; on the contrary the prince of Israel *(naśi)* is reduced to a subordinate position, subordinate to the priesthood. Ezechiel thus sketches the picture of a new theocracy which introduces in its own manner the state-like organization of the royal period. In fact, the Judaism which will issue from the test of Israel will resemble this picture rather closely, with the exception that

[3] Cf. p. 317 ff.

no prince will be able to maintain himself next to the high priests, who
have become the undisputed leaders of the nation.

The manner in which the Book of Ezechiel at present appears, allows
us somewhat to see extensive editorial reworking produced after the
death of the prophet, in the schools of priestly scribes which had inherited
his written work and his spirit. [4] These schools must be looked for in
the Eastern Diaspora, and it is this same milieu and in this same
atmosphere that the priestly traditions give birth to a vast historico-
judaic *corpus* where Mosaic legislation is readopted in a more specifically
ritualistic manner. The circumstances of the priests exiled far from their
Temple obliged them to accurately collate the customaries and the rituals,
with an eye toward the day when they will return home; furthermore,
they must outline for the deported Jews rules of conduct to protect
them against the contagion of paganism. The fundamental writing called
the Priestly Code [5] seems to answer this double purpose. But, as always
in Israel, the Torah thus edited on the basis of the ancestral tradition
is presented in a living manner in the framework of a holy history.
Taking up again the plan of the Yahwist and systematizing it even more,
the priestly scribes show how the plan of the Covenant of Yahweh was
realized during the course of the ages in four stages : creation, the
covenant with Noah, the patriarchal covenant and the Mosaic Covenant.
In each stage, God gave His laws to men until He founded, through
Moses, the Israelite theocracy centered around the liturgical service to
Yahweh in the Sanctuary of the Ark. At the top of the hierarchy of
the holy people thus set apart from the other nations, Yahweh placed
at the same time Aaron, Moses' brother, the ancestor to the line of high
priests. This is not profane history written with the preoccupations of
modern critics; it is a theology of the Chosen People presented in an
elaborate doctrinal synthesis. In the concrete framework of the sojourn
in the desert, the authors draw up the ideal prototype of the institutions
about which they dream. Archaic in certain respects, their work
assimilates everything acquired during the previous centuries to present
a program for the future. It thus prolongs the sketch of Ezechiel and
gives to Judaism its charter.

§ 4. The Consolation of the Exiles

Thus once the institutions created by the Davidic monarchy are ruined,
the people of God finds the means to survive in a form that is both very

---

[4] Cf. pp. 320-322.
[5] Cf. p. 157 ff.

new and very old : after the royal period it reestablishes ties with the sacral community born on Sinai. However, it preserves an important inheritance from the royal period. First of all there are the sacred books : the Mosaic Torah represented by several collections, from the Book of the Covenant to the Sacerdotal Code, to say nothing of a customary law which will not be late in becoming established; history books re-edited several times : at the beginning of the monarchy, under Ezechias, under Josias, and since the destruction of Jerusalem; psalms, the number of which is impossible to judge; and finally the wisdom maxims preserved by the royal scribes. This collection of works gives witness to a revelation profoundly united in its essential principles, but varied, however, in its expression as much as in the currents which are manifested therein. Israel not only possesses a religious wisdom which sets it apart from its neighboring peoples; the national hope which arose from the Sinaitic Covenant took on at this time an unequaled breadth thanks to the contribution of prophetic eschatology. The dispersed people draws from it a reason for living in the midst of difficult conditions imposed upon it. The whole experience of its past is now projected into the future and it thus continues to feed its hopes.

During the Exile, the Jews regroup in local communities and thus escape assimilation. Each community has its natural functionaries : the heads of families and the elders, the levitic and priestly caste which is hereditary, and finally the literate laymen, former civil servants who will find new markets for their talents as scribes. Schools are little by little founded, as the Jews become adjusted to their new ways of life and find the means to improve their material condition. The heirs to the former pietist groups, disciples of the prophets, members of the Deuteronomist or priestly circles, are the soul of this nascent Judaism. If Judaism finds in its natural functionaries a support to *last*, it is thanks to its most fervent members that God causes it to become conscious of itself. In the " remnant of the just " which escaped the disaster, the people finds spiritual guides capable of orienting it in a manner consonant with the wishes of Yahweh.

In Palestine there remains a restricted worship, for which the Temple of Jerusalem continues to be the center despite its shabby condition; it is likely that the Lamentations were composed in this framework, on the occasion of a solemn mourning celebrated on the anniversary of the ruin of the Temple. [6] It is probable that some psalms were also born in similar circumstances. In Babylonia and in other lands of exile,

---

[6] Cf. p. 453 ff.

the religious practices must be adapted to the new living circumstances. Certain exterior rites take on then an increased importance : the Sabbath, prohibitions, circumcision, and fasts on the traditional dates. Furthermore, the local communities habitually meet on determined days to pray together : this is a distant origin of synagogal worship. From the ancient worship of the shrines, all possible elements were preserved : recitations or readings of the Torah and of sacred history (written or only confided to traditional schemata), exhortation, prayer and the signing of hymns and the blessing of the assembly.

These meetings undoubtedly play an important role in the constitution of the sacred books. Already established texts are used—and thus is explained in part the preservation of ancient works. In second place, the synagogal liturgy can be considered as the *Sitz im Leben* of a certain number of new works. For example, the same meditation on Exodus, which allows one to suppose a previous reading, is found again in the penitential liturgy of Is 63, 7—64, 11, the exhortations to confidence of Is 43, 16-21, the meditation of Ps 78, 105 or 106. In the second case would not this look like a sermon for Easter time, in which the past would have been updated in order to draw from it the hope of a new deliverance? It is in this manner that *midrash* was born, [7] from a reflection on the Scriptures which are now the consolation of Israel in its time of trial. Naturally the schools of priests, of cantors or of scribes are narrowly linked to the communities of the exile as to their places of worship meetings. The ancient books are collected there, copied, edited and enriched with glosses which complete them and apply them to the needs of the times. The young scribes learn there their trade at the same time as their hearts and minds are trained. Therefore, in the works which flow from their pens, there are multiple allusions to and a systematic re-use of expressions consecrated by usage (what is called the anthological style).

Such is the milieu in which can be best explained, in our opinion, the composition of the great prophetic work which reached us through the Book of Isaias. In a circle where is perpetuated the tradition of the disciples of the prophet, an author who has remained anonymous addresses to the exiles between 547 (the first victory of Cyrus) and 538 (decree of emancipation of the Jews), a message of consolation [8] wherein can be distinguished, despite the very pronounced literary personality of the author, numerous references to the preexilian books : Isaias,

---

[7] Cf. p. 498.
[8] Cf. p. 332 ff.

Nahum (cf. Is 52, 7-10), Sophonias (Is 49, 13), Jeremias, Deuteronomy, the ancient traditions of Israel and certain aspects of the priestly tradition, without considering a certain affinity with the style of the Wisdom writings. The author is truly literate, as well as a very capable poet; his message especially constitutes one of the peaks of the Old Testament. Not only the eschatology with which his book is completely impregnated is purified of its political elements in order to be centered on the reign of Yahweh in Jerusalem, His holy city, in a perspective of complete universalism; not only the people of this kingdom, beneficiaries of eschatological salvation, is represented in the image of the *'anawim :* a people seeking justice, which has the Law of Yahweh in its heart; but to the royal Messias, either peaceful or warlike, is substituted the high figure of the Servant, mediator of a new covenant and spiritual saviour of the multitudes by his suffering, which is a new sacrifice of expiation. This *Gospel* surpasses by far the doctrinal import of several anonymous works almost contemporary to it such as Is 13—14 or Jer 50—51. [9]

Did the prophet of the captivity come back from the exile with the first repatriates and did he then pursue his ministry, so that the last poems of the Servant would take place in the bitter context of the year following 538? There is discussion on this point. In any case, his collection, composed through his own care or that of his disciples, exercised a profound influence in Jerusalem in the first quarter of the 6th century, in a parallel manner to the Deuteronomist, to the books of Jeremias and, perhaps to a lesser degree, of Ezechiel. But with this quarter century there begins the period of the second Temple. Once the shrine is rebuilt, Judaism refinds its center. In the midst of new political difficulties, it will acquire its definitive equilibrium.

---

[9] Cf. pp. 287 and 308.

CHAPTER V

JUDAISM DURING THE PERSIAN PERIOD

§ 1. Prophetism at the Time of the Second Temple

During the Persian period, it becomes more difficult to follow the chronological order of the formation of the collection of sacred books. On the one hand, data to retrace the history of Judaism are lacking more than once, especially between the years 515 and 445 and from 398 to Alexander. On the other hand, the biblical works themselves do not date themselves very easily, witness to the diversity of opinions shared by the exegetes. However what appears more clearly is the development of the different currents which give expression to the Revelation. They will therefore serve as guidelines.

Around the reconstruction of the Temple, we notice first of all a certain prophetic activity. [1] But while Aggeus, Isaias 34—35 and 56—66 (whose unity of authorship is problematic) extend especially the line of the message of consolation, the visions of Zacharias 1—8 follow rather the footsteps of Ezechiel by their recourses to all sorts of complicated symbols. In a general way, the prophetic genre moreover manifests a tendency to evolve. It is less spontaneous, closer to the written style than to the spoken word. The new authors have attended the schools for scribes; they are aware of the works of their predecessors and sometimes point them out (cf. Is 35). The various preoccupations of an lill-known period conflict in juxtaposed pages whose exact historica framework is often unknown to us (especially for Is 56—66); whence, next to one another, there appear fires of religious nationalism (Is 63, 1-6) and proclamations of universalism (Is 56, 1-8). The repatriates are re-established in their country at the cost of a thousand difficulties; the South is invaded by the Edomites, upon whom the Jews call down the divine wrath (Is 34; 63, 1-6; Abd). [2] Their hope is exalted however at the sight of their reconstructed city (Is 60—62).

As time goes on, a sort of disassociation of prophetism takes place. On the one hand, the role of the prophet as preacher and guide to consciences is being assumed by the wisdom master; on the other hand,

---

[1] Cf. p. 344 ff.
[2] Cf. pp. 348 ff. and 360 f.

eschatological oracles undergo an autonomous development, often at the hands of anonymous authors, in a style where conventional clichés and obscure expressions abound. We cannot, for example, exclude the fact that Ez 38—39 was added to the book of the prophets at about this time in the circles where it was being preserved. [3] According to other critics, Is 24—27 would be ascribed the date of 485 at the time when Babylon was laid to ruin by the armies of Xerxes. But these are only hypotheses, for the works of this type are difficult to date. If the collection of Malachias [4] (only slightly affected by this development of prophetism) can be placed rather accurately around the time when Nehemias came to Juda (middle of the 5th century), Joel escapes the grasp of the historians. [5] Finally, the second part of Zacharias (9—14), [6] contemporaneous with the conquests of Alexander, presents an enigmatic aspect despite the frequent re-use of images drawn from the ancient prophetic works. It is a work for the initiated rather than the echo of a public action. Furthermore, the book foresees the extinction of a decried prophetism (Za 13, 2-6). Soon the combination of the former eschatological oracle and of the prophetic vision (already frequent in Ezechiel and Zacharias) will give birth to a new genre : the apocalypse, a revelation of the divine secrets manifested in dreams or in symbolic visions. The anguishes of fervent souls, who desire to understand the meaning of a deceitful present, and to be enlightened on the future realization of the plan of God, will all pass into this strange literary form, which during the next period will undergo a growing development.

§ 2. The Development of the Wisdom Current

The Wisdom current does not date from the Persian period. We have seen it take root in Israel at the time of Solomon. Imbued even at this time by the Yahwist ferment which, in the biblical framework, already gave a peculiar twist to the wisdom of nations, it developed all during the royal period in the circles of the scribes, ending in collections of maxims and exercising its influence on certain other sectors of literature, such as historiography. With the captivity its former literary creations took their place in the treasure of national traditions. As for the scribe, he will no longer be only a functionary who edits acts or annals, but

---

[3] Cf. p. 628.
[4] Cf. p. 354.
[5] Cf. p. 358.
[6] Cf. p. 361.

rather a pious man who will enrich the sacred books by meditating upon the ancient texts.

Henceforth, the Wisdom current will experience a great development, at the same time as the religious influence of Yahwism presents itself in a clearer and more direct fashion. It overflows even into the prophetic collections (Is 40, 12-26) as it did in some of the most recent Deuteronomic chapters. But, in general, it preserves the same exterior appearance, affecting a language accessible to every upright man; however, in this apparently neutral expression, it systematically transposes the data of Mosaic and prophetic revelation. Its very method allows it to do its deed with everything, retaining the assimilable elements which foreign literatures can offer (these include Edomite, Phoenician, Egyptian and Assyrian literatures); but, in the final analysis, its essential sources show up : the sacred books, with which the anonymous scribes nourish their thought to the point that they impregnate their vocabulary with the expressions that they find in them. Under this sapiential form, the doctrine of the Covenant takes on a less specifically national character, and this effort at adjustment corresponds to one of the tendencies which, from the Exile onwards, are manifested inside Judaism : next to a strict nationalism, a current affirms itself, one that is more universalistic and more missionary. Wisdom literature will be for it an instrument of penetration even in the pagan circles where it will recruit proselytes, for, in its framework, there is elaborated a doctrine on human life parallel to that reflection which in Greece towards the same period gives birth to philosophy.

At the chronological point of departure of this literature there is the collection of Proverbs. [7] Comprising several ancient collections, it is furnished with a substantial introduction by its editor (Prv 1—9) whose theological scope is much larger. The dates assigned to the work by critics vary from the beginning of the 5th century to the end of the 4th; the time around 480 can be held if we admit that the work precedes Job (Robert). Treating the problems of the righteous and happy life and of divine retribution, the Proverbs serenely repeat a resolutely optimistic traditional thesis : the way of justice is that of life, that of sin leads to death. To this thesis the poet of Job (*ca.* 450 : Dhorme) offers a contrary factual argument. The suffering of the just is a painful problem! Mesopotamian thought had not ignored this problem and we can admit at least an indirect literary influence on Job from the works that this literature had produced on the subject. But finally it is by virtue of

---

[7] Cf. p. 407 ff.

specifically Yahwist data that the dialogue of Job and of his friends is elaborated; if it ends with no firm conclusion on the level of theoretical reflection, it is at least noticeable that biblical revelation does not grow in a rectilinear fashion, but through a process of *sic et non :* divine light will not be manifested to man except at the end of a painful experiment where he will have fathomed the mystery of his condition. The timeliness of the problems treated by Proverbs and Job appears even more when we relate these books to a certain number of apparently contemporary psalms, which treat the same problems.

§ 3. The Development of Religious Lyricism

It is known that the problem of the psalter is resolved by critics in radically different ways, whatever be their sectarian allegiances. Some tend to appeal to the royal period for almost all the psalms; others place a large number of them (if not the majority) after the Exile. In fact it would be very strange if the religious lyricism of the preexilian period left only a few traces in the Bible, when it is known what care the scribes used to collect the other literary works prior to the destruction of Jerusalem. However, account must be taken of two facts : the readaptation of ancient psalms to new perspectives of Jewish life and thought, when they are reconsidered after the Exile, and the natural development of genres from the past in the corporations of cantors created around the second Temple. The result is that the solution of the problem of the psalms can only be complex. If it is evident that some are ancient (those who clearly speak of the king or come from the Israel of the North), it is possible to hesitate for a number of others. Practically speaking it is their literary and doctrinal situation with respect to the prophetic texts which, very often, constitutes the principal element for their dates.

Critics gladly relate to the postexilian period several categories of works whose dependence upon the prophets seems assured : wisdom psalms such as Pss 1, 34, 37, or legalistic psalms, such as Pss 19, 8 ff and 119; the suffering psalms, born in the circle of the " poor " [8] which prolong certain themes of Jeremias, even though the genre of individual or collective lamentation is ancient; the psalms of the kingdom of Yahweh, at least when after Second-Isaias they present the kingdom in an eschatological perspective; the " historical " psalms; and the psalms into which pass the spiritual deceptions which are accumulated in the

---

[8] A. GELIN, *Les Pauvres de Yahvé* (Paris, 1953), p. 41 f.

Jewish soul during the Persian period. These general indications leave intact the question raised by each individual psalm; they want only to show how the study of the psalter allows us to penetrate further into the interior drama lived by Judaism after the great dream of the returning years (538-515) is dissipated. At the same time, it is possible to discover how the Scriptures are then for the believers the only reliable source of hope; their prayers feed on them so much so that the theology of the Prophets, of Deuteronomy or of the priestly current passes entirely into its inspired expression.

The Canticle of Canticles can be linked to religious lyricism, and a good number of interpreters give the end of the Persian period as its date. But this is as far as their agreement goes. We have read [9] that some see in it a collection of human love songs with the marriaeg ceremonies being their framework *(Sitz im Leben);* others consider them as symbolic poems, more or less allegorized, which would sing the spiritual marriage of Yahweh and Israel. Perhaps these theses are not as removed as they first appear, if one realizes that the introduction of the Canticle among the sacred books read publicly in the synagogal liturgy could not have been done without this book being jointly interpreted in relation to the prophetic texts where the Covenant was compared to a marriage (Osee, Jeremias, Ezechiel and 2nd and 3rd Isaias). It could be an allegorical reinterpretation of ancient marriage poems or a lyrical composition hiding a secret meaning behind the sumptuous images of a refined art : in either case, the Canticle testifies to the ingeniousness of the Jewish scribes, skilled at exploiting the prophetic writings and at using an apparently hermetic language to translate the revealed doctrine.

§ 4. From History to Midrash

Ancient Israel was not unaware of the historical genre under, however, extremely varied forms. Nonetheless, it has been seen that the literary form of *narrative* was not always used for the purpose of historical teaching, even without taking into account the diversity which could affect it in itself (epic narrative, etiological narrative, popular tradition, historiographical narration, etc...). All sorts of teachings could be translated in them in a concrete manner : juridical, moral or theological. Generally reflection on the historical traditions of Israel or the texts which testify to the past led even to a higher plane than history : that of doctrine and spirituality as in the works of the Deuteronomist school.

[9] Cf. p. 436 ff.

In the priestly current, the genre tended to become even more stylized; it did not fear to reconstruct the past in a systematic manner by inextricably mixing the data of tradition and the theological concepts of the narrators. This method of developing history with an essentially didactic purpose, with a view to seeking in it a religious significance capable of teaching and edifying souls, is nothing other than one of the forms of midrash. The priestly holy history already obeys the fundamental laws of the genre. After the Exile, it will experience a greater and greater development, without sacrificing a parallel persistence of historiography.

For example, the sources used by the Chronicler in the Books of Esdras-Nehemias [10] are clearly situated on the historical side of the narrative genre : memories of the return, anti-Samaritan dossier, and remembrances of both Nehemias and Esdras. On the other hand, it is the essentially didactic narrative which is developed in the Book of Jonas, [11] and the delightful " novella " of Ruth, even if in fact this latter rests on a valid historical tradition (the genealogy of David).

Midrash, however, does not always take on a narrative form. Thus, the so-called " historical " psalms (78, 105, 106) are also *midrashim*, which flourish in meditation and prayer instead of only ending in stylized narratives of the past. So also, when later eschatological texts, which are generally anonymous, repeat, while developing them, themes and expressions drawn from the prophetic writings, this systematic reinterpretation of ancient material is still in a way midrash : the texts were carefully studied and their meaning was clarified in the light of other passages; finally their explanation gives birth to a new Scripture. Since the discoveries of Qumran, the name *pesher* is given to the exegesis of prophetic texts which tend to bring them up to date in order to clarify the meaning of present events and of " what will happen later on. " The Jewish tradition itself has called *halakha* the exploitation of the Scriptures to find in them rules of conduct and *haggada* the free development grafted upon the Scriptures with a view only to edification, especially when it includes narrative materials drawn from the popular tradition or from the imagination of the interpreters. It would be wrong to see in these, literary genres foreign to the Bible : they are the natural result of its reading by the Jewish people. We believe that the first traces of those genres can already be found in the inspired books of the Persian period.

---

[10] Pp. 485 ff.
[11] Cf. p. 356 ff.

§ 5. The Fixing of the Torah

The center of Jewish thought is neither the Wisdom current nor religious lyricism, or even the prophetic teaching : it is the Torah. In the Persian period, it is fixed in its definitive form. It has been seen how, as early as the Mosaic period, it was the charter of the Covenant; then, in the royal period, it tended to become crystallized into two parallel currents : that of the North, represented by the moral Decalogue and by the Book of the Covenant; and that of the South, attested especially by the cultic Decalogue (Ex 34). At the end, these two currents, while intercrossing several times, experienced their own development, the first giving rise to Deuteronomy, the second to the code of holiness, to the Torah of Ezechiel and to the fundamental writing of the priestly code. Next to these written recensions there remained furthermore a customary law and rituals whose transmission could be accomplished orally without injuring their faithful preservation. During the captivity, it seems that the spirit of the Deuteronomist current dominated the intellectual and religious center that Judaism preserved in Palestine, while that of the priestly current was perpetuated in the Babylonian schools imbued with the influence of Ezechiel. Upon their return from the exile, the Sadoqite priests who came back with Josue brought back with them not only oral traditions, but written works which, for them, enjoyed an authority equal to the books already legally sanctioned in the prior period : ancient juridical compilations and Deuteronomy. Furthermore, from the return onwards, the ancient customaries of the Temple are put back into force, now that the worship service is started anew. It seems that it is in these circumstances that several codes drawn at this time from the Pentateuch are edited, on the basis of preexilian traditions readapted to the needs of the times : code of sacrifices, code of purity, various tariffs. [12]

Whatever be the solution to these very controverted problems, when Nehemias accomplishes in Judea his mission so important for the future of Judaism, the situation of the Torah is complicated. On the one hand, a certain number of texts are probably already recognized by the Persian authorities as the *law of the state* in Israel : these are the archaic codes and Deuteronomy. Undoubtedly there must be added local customs, but it is impossible to say what is their official status. It is rather likely that the priestly compilations are an object of dispute between the repatriated Jews from Babylonia and the " people of the country, " especially the Samaritans. In fact, these latter also claim the worship of the " God of heaven " and Jerusalem became their center of worship

---

[12] Cf. pp. 161 ff.

since the time when Josias had destroyed all the high places of the former Northern Kingdom. It seems that it was to avoid this opposition of two groups that the Persian authorities undertook at this time to fix once and for all their laws and their status. Such seems to have been the mission of Esdras, which could preferably be placed in 398 (some propose the 5th century). [13] To prepare the unification of Jewish laws into a *corpus* officially sanctioned by the state, jurists, belonging to the " priestly " schools (of Babylon such as Edras himself, or of Palestine) would then have added to the prior texts supplementary articles destined to make them harmonious among themselves and to adapt them to the needs of the times. Finally the historico-juridical entirety of the Pentateuch seems to have come from this work, by blending the two great currents which inherit all the Israelite past : the Deuteronomist and the priestly. [14]

In the present state of our knowledge, this presentation of things seems the most satisfactory *salvo meliore judicio*. On the one hand, it assigns to the fixation of the Torah a set of circumstances which allow us to understand its motive and its importance; on the other hand, it shows how the work accomplished at the time of Esdras did not have as its object to create anew nor to sanction the result of a juridical evolution completely ordered by factors external to the religion of Israel, but on the contrary to collect in a reasoned compilation the proliferation of texts issued from Israelite tradition, such as it had been developed throughout the ages.

Even if there enters into the hypothesis a share of disputable conjectures, it is certain that, well before the Persian period, the Torah is fixed. Samaritans and Jews will preserve it under the same form after their separation (which is preferably placed toward the beginning of the Greek period, even if the prodromes date back to preceding decades). Inside Judaism, the divergences will henceforth bear only on its practical interpretation : harmonization of apparently contradictory passages, proper value of the non-written customs, and of the solutions proposed by the private doctors. On this point, the various tendencies will continue to be confronted, opposing especially the priestly circles with the lay doctors; but this no longer concerns the formation of the holy books.

---

[13] Cf. p. 491.
[14] Cf. p. 162 f.

CHAPTER VI

JUDAISM IN THE HELLENISTIC PERIOD

§ 1. The Development of Genres in Palestinian Judaism

Documents are almost completely lacking to retrace the history of Judaism during the 4th and 3rd centuries. However, it is at this time that the Jewish institutions find their definitive equilibrium after the fixing of the Torah. Fixed through the cares of the priestly legists, the Torah is confided first of all to the clergy, divided into 24 classes followed by the levitical orders, among which the cantors have henceforth taken their place. In order to interpret it, the priests intend to hold only to the letter; on the contrary, the literate laymen, the Wise Men, who attribute in their study and in their teaching a large place to other ancient writings, give equal attention to the written Torah and to customs (called " oral Torah "). The gap between the two tendencies will widen with time to end in the sects of the Asmonean period.

With the conquests of Alexander, the Hellenist civilization invades the East, but Judaism does not immediately conflict with it. The most noticeable repercussion of the political changes which took place around 330 seems to be, for Palestinian Judaism, the definitive schism of the Samaritan community which was already virtually realized during the preceding decades but was consummated only with the construction of the temple of Garizim (at an uncertain date). Various institutions compete at this time for the preservation and explanation of the ancient books, as well as for the composition of new ones : priestly circles of the temple and the corporation of cantors, schools for scribes, and the synagogal liturgy. The communities of the Diaspora also have their schools and their synagogues, but we have very little information on their operation and on their real influence in the constitution of the biblical collection. We can only suspect the Eastern origin of the traditions which are at the basis of Daniel, of Tobias and of Esther; but the transmission of these materials until their actual writing remains out of reach.

The fixing of the Torah leads as a counterstroke to that of the prophetic collections. But here, it becomes difficult to assign dates. The last pages of the Book of Isaias seem to be chapters 24—27; certain critics place them around 485, while others place them around the Greek period. The content and the order of Jeremias are considerably different in the Hebrew and the Greek : it is possible to see in this a rather late final draft. For Ezechiel, a certain affinity to the supplementary laws of the Pentateuch is noticed in some passages; while also the date of chapters 38—39 remains under discussion, certain critics place them during the Greek period. In the group of the *Prophetae priores* the priestly rewritings seem more numerous for Josue than for the other books; but it may not be necessary to suppose an editorial work later than the fixing of the Torah. Finally, in the collection of the twelve minor prophets only one characteristic ensemble brings us back to the Greek period, toward the last quarter of the 4th century : Za 9—14. But even these chapters are added as a supplement to the already formed book, just as Is 24—27 is added to the Book of Isaias; it is possible to envisage in these two cases an insertion later than the formation of these collections, as though these were enlarged editions. All this allows one to see a rather large work of collating and editing, realized in these schools for scribes in the 5th and 4th centuries. The collection of the Ketubim then includes several important works : the Proverbs and Job, the most ancient of the Megillot (Lamentations, Ruth, and the Canticle of Canticles which can be brought into this period), but the canonical grouping of the five books does not as yet appear achieved. As for the psalter, it is not known to exactly what date its cloture is to be assigned. Perhaps we must go as late as the beginning of the Hellenistic period, but the existence of Machabean psalms is very problematical.

It is in this group of Ketubim that we must look for the few works composed after Alexander. The great work of the Chronicler (1 and 2 Par, Esd and Neh), seems to have as its framework the reaction of orthodox Judaism to the schismatic Samaritans; in this perspective, it would be easy to explain its insistence upon the legitimacy of the unique sanctuary of Jerusalem and of the unique Davidic dynasty, from which will come the Messias. Using ancient materials, the book (at present divided into four volumes) could well have been born towards the end of the 4th century or during the 3rd). As it has for its purpose to justify through history a theological thesis, it resorts more often to midrash techniques than, for example, to works of history resulting from the Deuteronomist current; but already, on this point, the priestly sacred history has already opened the way. With the Book of Esther whose date is unfortunately not clear, we are fully into haggadic midrash, even if the story told has its point of departure in facts. Linked to the feast of the *Purim*, the work has, furthermore, an orientation to worship.

In the category of the Wisdom writings, Ecclesiastes[1] manifests a certain knowledge of Greek thought, but this contact is without depth; his literary activity can be placed in the 3rd century. Tobias[2] (toward the same time) could rather be tied to Eastern origins (especially in what concerns its angelology), but the place of its composition is a subject of discussion. In any case, this book is distinguished by the way in which it narrowly unites wisdom teaching, the narrative techniques of the *haggada* and the recourse to lyricism : in the lower Jewish literature, the ancient literary currents are thus readily joined. The same mixture reappears in the collection of Baruch,[3] whose most ancient sections could go back to the 3rd century and be of Palestinian origin. Finally, toward the beginning of the 2nd century, Ecclesiasticus (Ben Sira),[4] master of a school at Jerusalem, in his composite collection makes the inventory of Wisdom in his time : the data from the Torah, from the prophetic teachings and from the more ancient wisdom writings appear in it as closely united. Less creative than in the past, Judaism thus feeds upon what it has acquired, waiting for the Day when the prophetic oracles will be realized, when Yahweh will reign and where the Messias will be at the head of His people.

§ 2. The Confrontation between Judaism and Hellenism

The first contacts between Judaism and Hellenism, at the time of the domination of the Ptolemies over Palestine, did not lead to any crisis. On the contrary, the creation of a large Jewish community in Alexandria led little by little to the translation of the essentials of Jewish ideas into the Greek language; during the course of the 3rd century, the Torah was translated, then other sacred books, at dates more difficult to establish.

The conflict breaks out in Palestinian Judaism, under Antiochus Epiphanes. The Machabean crisis is located at the outset of a rather abundant non-canonical literature, which we cannot deal with here. It is necessary to note only the development at this time of the apocalyptic genre; the oldest sections of the Book of Enoch could be assigned a date around 170. These are the circumstances when the traditions of Daniel perhaps already edited in part, start to take shape, serving as a framework for the only apocalypse properly so-called which

---

[1] Cf. p. 458 ff.
[2] Cf. p. 514 ff.
[3] Cf. p. 507 ff.
[4] Cf. p. 544 ff.

appears in the canon of the Old Testament. [5] The book seems to reflect the thought of the *hasidim*, who had been rallied to Judas Machabee toward the beginning of the holy war. A similar spirit, although more nationalistic, is found again in the *haggada* of Judith, [6] which seems to echo the climate of the Machabean wars. Under the Asmonean dynasty the history of the war of independence finds a good narrator (I Machabees) [7] whose work intimately joins to the traditional techniques of Hebrew historiography a recourse to those of Greek historiography. As for the work of Jason the Cyrene, who related the same events, we only have a Greek summary of it, composed in Alexandria; [8] there again, Hebrew historiography readily mingled with *haggada* evolves toward the genre of pathetic history, similar to the one practiced by contemporary Hellenism.

Finally, it is in the framework of Alexandrine Judaism that the confrontation of Judaism and Hellenism is resolved, not by a conflict or an absorption of the first by the second, but by a victory of biblical Revelation, which had become capable of assimilating certain elements of Hellenism. The fact is not yet very felt in the recent parts of the Book of Baruch; chapters 4, 5—5, 9 which give the appearance of a sermon delivered in a synagogue and which perhaps were written in Greek, only echo the prophetic Scriptures. [9] The " Letter of Jeremias " is a diatribe against idolatry, which gives us some idea of Jewish apologetics. [10] The deuterocanonical additions to Esther and Daniel contain nothing specifically Greek. [11] We must wait for the Wisdom of Solomon (during the 1st century) [12] to see the inspired literature express itself in a Greek terminology. Still we must remark that this terminology is put into the service of a perfectly traditional doctrine. We know that since the 5th century, the Wisdom current agitated the problem of individual retribution. At the time of Antiochus' persecution, the Book of Daniel had, in our opinion, shed light on this problem in revealing the resurrection of the just, called to share the kingdom of God at the end of time. This is this participation of the just in beatific immortality that the Wisdom book explicitly teaches, transposing an essential datum of Jewish apocalyptic into sapiential language.

---

[5] Cf. p. 473 ff.
[6] Cf. p. 520 ff.
[7] Cf. p. 527 ff.
[8] Cf. p. 532 ff.
[9] Cf. p. 510 ff.
[10] Cf. p. 512 ff.
[11] Cf. p. 550 ff.
[12] Cf. p. 537 ff.

Judaism continues therefore to enrich its inspired literature at a time when its non-canonical productions start to become more and more numerous. But very often these productions represent less the great traditional current than the spirit of the sects which, as early as the Machabean period, are more and more opposed to one another. Without talking about the Samaritans, three principal sects are distinguished at the end of the 2nd century : the Sadducees, who support the Asmonean dynasty; the Pharisees, who refuse to recognize the legitimacy of the non-Davidic royalty; and the " Sadoqites, " whose exact origin remains still a problem and who lead to Essenism. This tableau of a divided Judaism is instructive. It shows how difficult it is at this time to define Jewish orthodoxy on the sole basis of Scripture and oral tradition. On both sides, there are currents and tendencies whose definitive synthesis has not been made. Even in the Torah, the harmonizing of the different lines of development, represented by pieces more juxtaposed than blended, give rise to discussion. The concept of individual retribution, and of Messianism is not the same in the sects we have just mentioned, no more than is the list of books considered as sacred. Finally, the recourse to Scripture cannot always be sufficient to resolve the controversies, since they crystallize divine revelation in its successive stages : whence there are apparent contradictions between equally inspired passages, but born at different periods and in different places, answering very different needs and resolving them in a more or less complete manner. The reason for this state of fact only appears in the light of the New Testament. In fact, Judaism is only a provisory and preparatory economy which tends towards a " fulfilment. " Christ, in His person, His work and His teaching, " will fulfill the Scriptures, " finally making explicit their meaning and their import, by reason of the divine plan which, from the very beginning, led toward it.

Thus, we will finish this rapid synthesis. The reader will not forget that in sketching it, we have incorporated into it more than one hypothetical element, when critical problems were raised that have not been definitively solved. Not that the value of the Bible as historical document would thereby be questioned. But today it is not sufficient to affirm this value as a whole without going into detail in order to determine the exact dates of the events, the dates of the inspired books and their places of origin. It is from this point of view that questions are still being asked. To make a choice in these debates, to propose probable points of view founded on serious arguments, was the only possible attitude in matters where research is not complete. It is then legitimate to hope that after these approximations there will come firmer certitudes and that our knowledge of the Old Testament will grow in accuracy even in its minute details. Discussions of this nature moreover leave intact the properly doctrinal value of the Sacred Books : whoever be their human authors and whatever be their dates, God speaks to us through them, and what is essential is to grasp His message. But if, furthermore, it is possible to reconstitute in a sure way the steps of divine pedagogy which led our Fathers in the faith (cf. Gal 3, 24) to Christ, then the relation of the Old Testament to Christ only becomes clearer, and faith finds in this an additional benefit. This is why the critical study of the Old Testament is worthwhile attempting : far from leading to skepticism, its only aim is to penetrate further into the knowledge of Revelation.

INDEX OF AUTHORS

INDEX OF SUBJECTS

NY.35. — Printed in Belgium by Desclée & Co, Éditeurs, S. A., Tournai — 10.943
D — 1968 — 0002 — 49

MAPS

The Near East in Ancient Times

Palestine of the Old Testament

Egypt, the Sinai Peninsula and Palestine at the Exodus

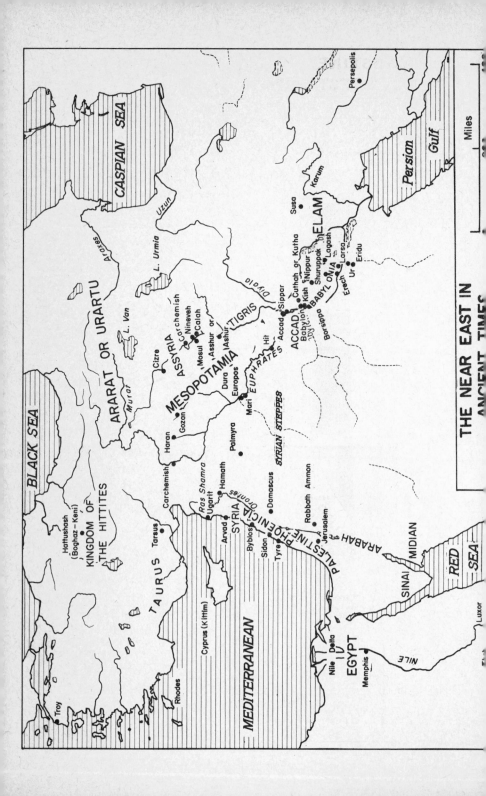

THE NEAR EAST IN
ANCIENT TIMES

PALESTINE
OF THE OLD TESTAMENT

0   10   20   30 mls.

Isohyet 200 ○○○○○○○○○ Limit of barley cultivation

Isohyet 500 ------- Limit of mediterranean cultivation

THE GREAT

SEA

Spot heights are given in metres

m.	ft.
900	2953
600	1968
400	1312
100	328
0	0
-300	-984

M. Celle

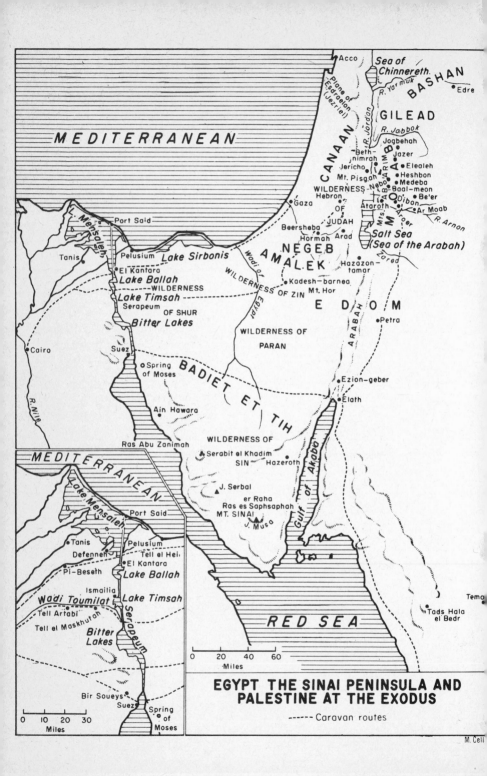

EGYPT THE SINAI PENINSULA AND PALESTINE AT THE EXODUS

----- Caravan routes

M. Cell